Java™ 2:
The Complete Reference,
Fifth Edition

About the Author

Herbert Schildt is the world's leading programming author. He is an authority on the C, C++, Java, and C# languages, and is a master Windows programmer. His programming books have sold more that 3 million copies worldwide and have been translated into all major foreign languages. He is the author of numerous bestsellers, including *Java 2: The Complete Reference*, *Java 2: A Beginner's Guide*, *Java 2 Programmers Reference*, *C++: The Complete Reference*, *C: The Complete Reference*, and *C#: The Complete Reference*. Schildt holds a master's degree in computer science from the University of Illinois. He can be reached at his consulting office at (217) 586-4683.

Java™ 2:
The Complete Reference,
Fifth Edition

Herbert Schildt

Tata McGraw Hill Education Private Limited
NEW DELHI

McGraw-Hill Offices

New Delhi New York St Louis San Francisco Auckland Bogotá Caracas
Kuala Lumpur Lisbon London Madrid Mexico City Milan Montreal
San Juan Santiago Singapore Sidney Tokyo Toronto

Tata McGraw-Hill

Java™ 2: The Complete Reference, Fifth Edition

48th reprint 2010
DZZYCDRZDDRRA

Reprinted in India by arrangement with The McGraw-Hill Companies,
Inc., New York

Sales territories: India, Pakistan, Nepal, Bangladesh, Sri Lanka and Bhutan

ISBN-13: 978-0-07-049543-2
ISBN-10: 0-07-049543-2

Published by the Tata McGraw Hill Education Private Limited,
7 West Patel Nagar, New Delhi 110 008, and printed at
Pashupati Printers Pvt. Ltd., Delhi 110 095

The McGraw·Hill Companies

Contents at a Glance

Struts pgming, architecture, configuring executing

Java 2 Unleashed
9, 10 15, 18, 19, 24, 25, 26, 30, 31, 32,
33, 37, 38, 39, 43, 44, 45

Contents

Part I
The Java Language

Part II

The Java Library

Part IV

Applying Java

Preface

The past few years document the following fact: The Web has irrevocably recast the face of computing and programmers unwilling to master its environment will be left behind.

The preceding is a strong statement. It is also true. More and more, applications must interface to the Web. It no longer matters much what the application is, near universal Web access is dragging, pushing, and coaxing programmers to program for the online world, and Java is the language that many will use to do it. Frankly, fluency in Java is no longer an option for the professional programmer, it is a requirement. This book will help you acquire it.

Aside from being the preeminent language of the Internet, Java is important for another reason: it has altered the course of computer language development. Many of the features first mainstreamed by Java are now finding their way into other languages. For example, the new C# language is strongly influenced by Java. Knowledge of Java opens the door to the latest innovations in programming. Put directly, Java is one of the world's most important computer languages.

A Book for All Programmers

To use this book does not require any previous programming experience. However, if you come from a C/C++ background, then you will be able to advance a bit more rapidly. As most readers will know, Java is similar, in form and spirit, to C/C++. Thus, knowledge of those langauges helps, but is not necessary. Even if you have never programmed before, you can learn to program in Java using this book.

What's Inside

This book covers all aspects of the Java programming language. Part 1 presents an in-depth tutorial of the Java language. It begins with the basics, including such things as data types, control statements, and classes. Part 1 also discusses Java's exception-handling mechanism, multithreading subsystem, packages, and interfaces.

Part 2 examines the standard Java library. As you will learn, much of Java's power is found in its library. Topics include strings, I/O, networking, the standard utilities, the Collections Framework, applets, GUI-based controls, and imaging.

Part 3 looks at some issues relating to the Java development environment, including an overview of Java Beans, Servlets, and Swing.

Part 4 presents a number of high-powered Java applets that serve as extended examples of the way Java can be applied. The final applet, called Scrabblet, is a complete, multiuser networked game. It shows how to handle some of the toughest issues involved in Web-based programming.

What's New in the Fifth Edition

The differences between this and the previous editions of this book mostly involve those features added by Java 2, version 1.4. Of the many new features found in version 1.4, perhaps the most important are the **assert** keyword, the channel-based I/O subsystem, chained exceptions, and networking enhancements. This fifth edition has been fully updated to reflect those and other additions. New features are clearly noted in the text, as are features added by previous releases.

This fifth edition also updates and restores the Sevlets chapter. Previously this chapter relied upon the now out-dated JSDK (Java Servlets Developers Kit) to develop and test servlets. It now uses Apache Tomcat, which is the currently recommended tool.

Don't Forget: Code on the Web

Remember, the source code for all of the examples and projects in this book is available free-of-charge on the Web at **www.osborne.com**.

Special Thanks

Special thanks to Patrick Naughton. Patrick was one of the creators of the Java language. He also helped write the first edition of this book. For example, much of the material in chapters 17, 18, 23, 29, 30, 31, and 32 was initially provided by Patrick. His insights, expertise, and energy contributed greatly to the success of this book.

Thanks also go to Joe O'Neil for providing the initial drafts for chapters 24, 25, 26, and 27. Joe has helped on several of my books and, as always, his efforts are appreciated.

HERBERT SCHILDT
May 25, 2002
Mahomet, Illinois

For Further Study

Java 2: The Complete Reference is your gateway to the Herb Schildt series of programming books. Here are some others that you will find of interest:

To learn more about Java programming, we recommend the following:

>*Java 2: A Beginner's Guide*

>*Java 2 Programmer's Reference*

To learn about C++, you will find these books especially helpful:

>*C++: The Complete Reference*

>*C++: A Beginner's Guide*

>*Teach Yourself C++*

>*C++ From the Ground Up*

>*STL Programming From the Ground Up*

To learn about C#, we suggest the following Schildt books:

>*C#: A Beginner's Guide*

>*C#: The Complete Reference*

If you want to learn more about the C language, the foundation of all modern programming, then the following titles will be of interest:

>*C: The Complete Reference*

>*Teach Yourself C*

When you need solid answers, fast, turn to Herbert Schildt, the recognized authority on programming.

The
Complete
Reference

Part I

The Java Language

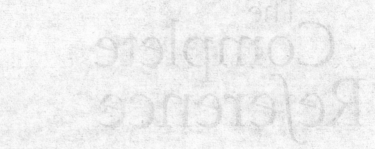

The
Complete
Reference

Chapter 1

The Genesis of Java

When the chronicle of computer languages is written, the following will be said: B led to C, C evolved into C++, and C++ set the stage for Java. To understand Java is to understand the reasons that drove its creation, the forces that shaped it, and the legacy that it inherits. Like the successful computer languages that came before, Java is a blend of the best elements of its rich heritage combined with the innovative concepts required by its unique environment. While the remaining chapters of this book describe the practical aspects of Java—including its syntax, libraries, and applications—in this chapter, you will learn how and why Java came about, and what makes it so important.

Although Java has become inseparably linked with the online environment of the Internet, it is important to remember that Java is first and foremost a programming language. Computer language innovation and development occurs for two fundamental reasons:

- To adapt to changing environments and uses
- To implement refinements and improvements in the art of programming

As you will see, the creation of Java was driven by both elements in nearly equal measure.

Java's Lineage

Java is related to C++, which is a direct descendent of C. Much of the character of Java is inherited from these two languages. From C, Java derives its syntax. Many of Java's object-oriented features were influenced by C++. In fact, several of Java's defining characteristics come from—or are responses to—its predecessors. Moreover, the creation of Java was deeply rooted in the process of refinement and adaptation that has been occurring in computer programming languages for the past three decades. For these reasons, this section reviews the sequence of events and forces that led up to Java. As you will see, each innovation in language design was driven by the need to solve a fundamental problem that the preceding languages could not solve. Java is no exception.

The Birth of Modern Programming: C

The C language shook the computer world. Its impact should not be underestimated, because it fundamentally changed the way programming was approached and thought about. The creation of C was a direct result of the need for a structured, efficient, high-level language that could replace assembly code when creating systems programs. As you probably know, when a computer language is designed, trade-offs are often made, such as the following:

- Ease-of-use versus power
- Safety versus efficiency
- Rigidity versus extensibility

Prior to C, programmers usually had to choose between languages that optimized one set of traits or the other. For example, although FORTRAN could be used to write fairly efficient programs for scientific applications, it was not very good for systems code. And while BASIC was easy to learn, it wasn't very powerful, and its lack of structure made its usefulness questionable for large programs. Assembly language can be used to produce highly efficient programs, but it is not easy to learn or use effectively. Further, debugging assembly code can be quite difficult.

Another compounding problem was that early computer languages such as BASIC, COBOL, and FORTRAN were not designed around structured principles. Instead, they relied upon the GOTO as a primary means of program control. As a result, programs written using these languages tended to produce "spaghetti code"—a mass of tangled jumps and conditional branches that make a program virtually impossible to understand. While languages like Pascal are structured, they were not designed for efficiency, and failed to include certain features necessary to make them applicable to a wide range of programs. (Specifically, given the standard dialects of Pascal available at the time, it was not practical to consider using Pascal for systems-level code.)

So, just prior to the invention of C, no one language had reconciled the conflicting attributes that had dogged earlier efforts. Yet the need for such a language was pressing. By the early 1970s, the computer revolution was beginning to take hold, and the demand for software was rapidly outpacing programmers' ability to produce it. A great deal of effort was being expended in academic circles in an attempt to create a better computer language. But, and perhaps most importantly, a secondary force was beginning to be felt. Computer hardware was finally becoming common enough that a critical mass was being reached. No longer were computers kept behind locked doors. For the first time, programmers were gaining virtually unlimited access to their machines. This allowed the freedom to experiment. It also allowed programmers to begin to create their own tools. On the eve of C's creation, the stage was set for a quantum leap forward in computer languages.

Invented and first implemented by Dennis Ritchie on a DEC PDP-11 running the UNIX operating system, C was the result of a development process that started with an older language called BCPL, developed by Martin Richards. BCPL influenced a language called B, invented by Ken Thompson, which led to the development of C in the 1970s. For many years, the de facto standard for C was the one supplied with the UNIX operating system and described in *The C Programming Language* by Brian Kernighan and Dennis Ritchie (Prentice-Hall, 1978). C was formally standardized in December 1989, when the American National Standards Institute (ANSI) standard for C was adopted.

The creation of C is considered by many to have marked the beginning of the modern age of computer languages. It successfully synthesized the conflicting attributes that had so troubled earlier languages. The result was a powerful, efficient, structured language that was relatively easy to learn. It also included one other, nearly intangible aspect: it was a *programmer's* language. Prior to the invention of C, computer languages were generally designed either as academic exercises or by bureaucratic committees. C is different. It was designed, implemented, and developed by real, working programmers, reflecting the way that they approached the job of programming. Its features were honed, tested, thought about, and rethought by the people who actually used the language. The result was a language that programmers liked to use. Indeed, C quickly attracted many followers who had a near-religious zeal for it. As such, it found wide and rapid acceptance in the programmer community. In short, C is a language designed by and for programmers. As you will see, Java has inherited this legacy.

The Need for C++

During the late 1970s and early 1980s, C became the dominant computer programming language, and it is still widely used today. Since C is a successful and useful language, you might ask why a need for something else existed. The answer is *complexity*. Throughout the history of programming, the increasing complexity of programs has driven the need for better ways to manage that complexity. C++ is a response to that need. To better understand why managing program complexity is fundamental to the creation of C++, consider the following.

Approaches to programming have changed dramatically since the invention of the computer. For example, when computers were first invented, programming was done by manually toggling in the binary machine instructions by use of the front panel. As long as programs were just a few hundred instructions long, this approach worked. As programs grew, assembly language was invented so that a programmer could deal with larger, increasingly complex programs by using symbolic representations of the machine instructions. As programs continued to grow, high-level languages were introduced that gave the programmer more tools with which to handle complexity.

The first widespread language was, of course, FORTRAN. While FORTRAN was an impressive first step, it is hardly a language that encourages clear and easy-to-understand programs. The 1960s gave birth to *structured programming*. This is the method of programming championed by languages such as C. The use of structured languages enabled programmers to write, for the first time, moderately complex programs fairly easily. However, even with structured programming methods, once a project reaches a certain size, its complexity exceeds what a programmer can manage. By the early 1980s, many projects were pushing the structured approach past its limits. To solve this problem, a new way to program was invented, called *object-oriented programming* (*OOP*). Object-oriented programming is discussed in detail later in this book, but here is a brief definition: OOP is a programming methodology that helps organize complex programs through the use of inheritance, encapsulation, and polymorphism.

In the final analysis, although C is one of the world's great programming languages, there is a limit to its ability to handle complexity. Once a program exceeds somewhere between 25,000 and 100,000 lines of code, it becomes so complex that it is difficult to grasp as a totality. C++ allows this barrier to be broken, and helps the programmer comprehend and manage larger programs.

C++ was invented by Bjarne Stroustrup in 1979, while he was working at Bell Laboratories in Murray Hill, New Jersey. Stroustrup initially called the new language "C with Classes." However, in 1983, the name was changed to C++. C++ extends C by adding object-oriented features. Because C++ is built upon the foundation of C, it includes all of C's features, attributes, and benefits. This is a crucial reason for the success of C++ as a language. The invention of C++ was not an attempt to create a completely new programming language. Instead, it was an enhancement to an already highly successful one.

The Stage Is Set for Java

By the end of the 1980s and the early 1990s, object-oriented programming using C++ took hold. Indeed, for a brief moment it seemed as if programmers had finally found the perfect language. Because C++ blended the high efficiency and stylistic elements of C with the object-oriented paradigm, it was a language that could be used to create a wide range of programs. However, just as in the past, forces were brewing that would, once again, drive computer language evolution forward. Within a few years, the World Wide Web and the Internet would reach critical mass. This event would precipitate another revolution in programming.

The Creation of Java

Java was conceived by James Gosling, Patrick Naughton, Chris Warth, Ed Frank, and Mike Sheridan at Sun Microsystems, Inc. in 1991. It took 18 months to develop the first working version. This language was initially called "Oak" but was renamed "Java" in 1995. Between the initial implementation of Oak in the fall of 1992 and the public announcement of Java in the spring of 1995, many more people contributed to the design and evolution of the language. Bill Joy, Arthur van Hoff, Jonathan Payne, Frank Yellin, and Tim Lindholm were key contributors to the maturing of the original prototype.

Somewhat surprisingly, the original impetus for Java was not the Internet! Instead, the primary motivation was the need for a platform-independent (that is, architecture-neutral) language that could be used to create software to be embedded in various consumer electronic devices, such as microwave ovens and remote controls. As you can probably guess, many different types of CPUs are used as controllers. The trouble with C and C++ (and most other languages) is that they are designed to be compiled for a specific target. Although it is possible to compile a C++ program for just about any type of CPU, to do so requires a full C++ compiler targeted for that CPU. The problem is that compilers are expensive and time-consuming to create. An easier— and more cost-efficient—solution was needed. In an attempt to find such a solution, Gosling and others began work on a portable, platform-independent language that could be used to produce code that would run on a variety of CPUs under differing environments. This effort ultimately led to the creation of Java.

About the time that the details of Java were being worked out, a second, and ultimately more important, factor was emerging that would play a crucial role in the future of Java. This second force was, of course, the World Wide Web. Had the Web not taken shape at about the same time that Java was being implemented, Java might have remained a useful but obscure language for programming consumer electronics. However, with the emergence of the World Wide Web, Java was propelled to the forefront of computer language design, because the Web, too, demanded portable programs.

Most programmers learn early in their careers that portable programs are as elusive as they are desirable. While the quest for a way to create efficient, portable (platform-independent) programs is nearly as old as the discipline of programming itself, it had taken a back seat to other, more pressing problems. Further, because much of the computer world had divided itself into the three competing camps of Intel, Macintosh, and UNIX, most programmers stayed within their fortified boundaries, and the urgent need for portable code was reduced. However, with the advent of the Internet and the Web, the old problem of portability returned with a vengeance. After all, the Internet consists of a diverse, distributed universe populated with many types of computers, operating systems, and CPUs. Even though many types of platforms are attached to the Internet, users would like them all to be able to run the same program. What was once an irritating but low-priority problem had become a high-profile necessity.

By 1993, it became obvious to members of the Java design team that the problems of portability frequently encountered when creating code for embedded controllers are also found when attempting to create code for the Internet. In fact, the same problem that Java was initially designed to solve on a small scale could also be applied to the Internet on a large scale. This realization caused the focus of Java to switch from consumer electronics to Internet programming. So, while the desire for an architecture-neutral programming language provided the initial spark, the Internet ultimately led to Java's large-scale success.

As mentioned earlier, Java derives much of its character from C and C++. This is by intent. The Java designers knew that using the familiar syntax of C and echoing the object-oriented features of C++ would make their language appealing to the legions of experienced C/C++ programmers. In addition to the surface similarities, Java shares some of the other attributes that helped make C and C++ successful. First, Java was designed, tested, and refined by real, working programmers. It is a language grounded in the needs and experiences of the people who devised it. Thus, Java is also a programmer's language. Second, Java is cohesive and logically consistent. Third, except for those constraints imposed by the Internet environment, Java gives you, the programmer, full control. If you program well, your programs reflect it. If you program poorly, your programs reflect that, too. Put differently, Java is not a language with training wheels. It is a language for professional programmers.

Because of the similarities between Java and C++, it is tempting to think of Java as simply the "Internet version of C++." However, to do so would be a large mistake. Java has significant practical and philosophical differences. While it is true that Java was influenced by C++, it is not an enhanced version of C++. For example, Java is neither upwardly nor downwardly compatible with C++. Of course, the similarities with C++ are significant, and if you are a C++ programmer, then you will feel right at home with Java. One other point: Java was not designed to replace C++. Java was designed to solve a certain set of problems. C++ was designed to solve a different set of problems. Both will coexist for many years to come.

As mentioned at the start of this chapter, computer languages evolve for two reasons: to adapt to changes in environment and to implement advances in the art of programming. The environmental change that prompted Java was the need for platform-independent programs destined for distribution on the Internet. However, Java also embodies changes in the way that people approach the writing of programs. Specifically, Java enhances and refines the object-oriented paradigm used by C++. Thus, Java is not a language that exists in isolation. Rather, it is part of an ongoing process begun many years ago. This fact alone is enough to ensure Java a place in computer language history. Java is to Internet programming what C was to systems programming: a revolutionary force that changed the world.

The C# Connection

The reach and power of Java continues to be felt in the world of computer language development. Many of its innovative features, constructs, and concepts have become part of the baseline for any new language. The success of Java is simply too important to ignore.

Perhaps the most important example of Java's influence is C#. Recently created by Microsoft to support the .NET Framework, C# is closely related to Java. For example, both share the same general C++-style syntax, support distributed programming, and utilize the same object model. There are, of course, differences between Java and C#, but the overall "look and feel" of these languages is very similar. This "cross-pollination" from Java to C# is the strongest testimonial to date that Java redefined the way we think about and use a computer language.

Why Java Is Important to the Internet

The Internet helped catapult Java to the forefront of programming, and Java, in turn, has had a profound effect on the Internet. The reason for this is quite simple: Java expands the universe of objects that can move about freely in cyberspace. In a network, two very broad categories of objects are transmitted between the server and your personal computer: passive information and dynamic, active programs. For example, when you read your e-mail, you are viewing passive data. Even when you download a program, the program's code is still only passive data until you execute it. However, a second type of object can be transmitted to your computer: a dynamic, self-executing program. Such a program is an active agent on the client computer, yet is initiated by the server. For example, a program might be provided by the server to display properly the data that the server is sending.

As desirable as dynamic, networked programs are, they also present serious problems in the areas of security and portability. Prior to Java, cyberspace was effectively closed to half the entities that now live there. As you will see, Java addresses those concerns and, by doing so, has opened the door to an exciting new form of program: the applet.

Java Applets and Applications

Java can be used to create two types of programs: applications and applets. An *application* is a program that runs on your computer, under the operating system of that computer. That is, an application created by Java is more or less like one created using C or C++. When used to create applications, Java is not much different from any other computer language. Rather, it is Java's ability to create applets that makes it important. An *applet* is an application designed to be transmitted over the Internet and executed by a Java-compatible Web browser. An applet is actually a tiny Java program, dynamically downloaded across the network, just like an image, sound file, or video clip. The important difference is that an applet is an *intelligent program*, not just an animation or media file. In other words, an applet is a program that can react to user input and dynamically change—not just run the same animation or sound over and over.

As exciting as applets are, they would be nothing more than wishful thinking if Java were not able to address the two fundamental problems associated with them: security and portability. Before continuing, let's define what these two terms mean relative to the Internet.

Security

As you are likely aware, every time that you download a "normal" program, you are risking a viral infection. Prior to Java, most users did not download executable programs frequently, and those who did scanned them for viruses prior to execution. Even so, most users still worried about the possibility of infecting their systems with a virus. In addition to viruses, another type of malicious program exists that must be guarded against. This type of program can gather private information, such as credit card numbers, bank account balances, and passwords, by searching the contents of your computer's local file system. Java answers both of these concerns by providing a "firewall" between a networked application and your computer.

When you use a Java-compatible Web browser, you can safely download Java applets without fear of viral infection or malicious intent. Java achieves this protection by confining a Java program to the Java execution environment and not allowing it access to other parts of the computer. (You will see how this is accomplished shortly.) The ability to download applets with confidence that no harm will be done and that no security will be breached is considered by many to be the single most important aspect of Java.

Portability

As discussed earlier, many types of computers and operating systems are in use throughout the world—and many are connected to the Internet. For programs to be dynamically downloaded to all the various types of platforms connected to the Internet, some means of generating portable executable code is needed. As you will soon see, the same mechanism that helps ensure security also helps create portability. Indeed, Java's solution to these two problems is both elegant and efficient.

Java's Magic: The Bytecode

The key that allows Java to solve both the security and the portability problems just described is that the output of a Java compiler is not executable code. Rather, it is bytecode. *Bytecode* is a highly optimized set of instructions designed to be executed by the Java run-time system, which is called the *Java Virtual Machine* (JVM). That is, in its standard form, the JVM is an *interpreter for bytecode*. This may come as a bit of a surprise. As you know, C++ is compiled to executable code. In fact, most modern languages are designed to be compiled, not interpreted—mostly because of performance concerns. However, the fact that a Java program is executed by the JVM helps solve the major problems associated with downloading programs over the Internet. Here is why.

Translating a Java program into bytecode helps makes it much easier to run a program in a wide variety of environments. The reason is straightforward: only the JVM needs to be implemented for each platform. Once the run-time package exists for a given system, any Java program can run on it. Remember, although the details of the JVM will differ from platform to platform, all interpret the same Java bytecode. If a Java program were compiled to native code, then different versions of the same program would have to exist for each type of CPU connected to the Internet. This is, of course, not a feasible solution. Thus, the interpretation of bytecode is the easiest way to create truly portable programs.

The fact that a Java program is interpreted also helps to make it secure. Because the execution of every Java program is under the control of the JVM, the JVM can contain the program and prevent it from generating side effects outside of the system. As you will see, safety is also enhanced by certain restrictions that exist in the Java language.

When a program is interpreted, it generally runs substantially slower than it would run if compiled to executable code. However, with Java, the differential between the two is not so great. The use of bytecode enables the Java run-time system to execute programs much faster than you might expect.

Although Java was designed for interpretation, there is technically nothing about Java that prevents on-the-fly compilation of bytecode into native code. Along these lines, Sun supplies its Just In Time (JIT) compiler for bytecode, which is included in the Java 2 release. When the JIT compiler is part of the JVM, it compiles bytecode into executable code in real time, on a piece-by-piece, demand basis. It is important to understand that it is not possible to compile an entire Java program into executable code all at once, because Java performs various run-time checks that can be done only at run time. Instead, the JIT compiles code as it is needed, during execution. However, the just-in-time approach still yields a significant performance boost. Even when dynamic compilation is applied to bytecode, the portability and safety features still apply, because the run-time system (which performs the compilation) still is in charge of the execution environment. Whether your Java program is actually interpreted in the traditional way or compiled on-the-fly, its functionality is the same.

The Java Buzzwords

No discussion of the genesis of Java is complete without a look at the Java buzzwords. Although the fundamental forces that necessitated the invention of Java are portability and security, other factors also played an important role in molding the final form of the language. The key considerations were summed up by the Java team in the following list of buzzwords:

- Simple
- Secure
- Portable
- Object-oriented
- Robust
- Multithreaded
- Architecture-neutral
- Interpreted
- High performance
- Distributed
- Dynamic

Two of these buzzwords have already been discussed: secure and portable. Let's examine what each of the others implies.

Simple

Java was designed to be easy for the professional programmer to learn and use effectively. Assuming that you have some programming experience, you will not find Java hard to master. If you already understand the basic concepts of object-oriented programming, learning Java will be even easier. Best of all, if you are an experienced C++ programmer, moving to Java will require very little effort. Because Java inherits the C/C++ syntax and many of the object-oriented features of C++, most programmers have little trouble learning Java. Also, some of the more confusing concepts from C++ are either left out of Java or implemented in a cleaner, more approachable manner.

Beyond its similarities with C/C++, Java has another attribute that makes it easy to learn: it makes an effort not to have *surprising* features. In Java, there are a small number of clearly defined ways to accomplish a given task.

Object-Oriented

Although influenced by its predecessors, Java was not designed to be source-code compatible with any other language. This allowed the Java team the freedom to design with a blank slate. One outcome of this was a clean, usable, pragmatic approach to objects. Borrowing liberally from many seminal object-software environments of the last few decades, Java manages to strike a balance between the purist's "everything is an object" paradigm and the pragmatist's "stay out of my way" model. The object model in Java is simple and easy to extend, while simple types, such as integers, are kept as high-performance nonobjects.

Robust

The multiplatformed environment of the Web places extraordinary demands on a program, because the program must execute reliably in a variety of systems. Thus, the ability to create robust programs was given a high priority in the design of Java. To gain reliability, Java restricts you in a few key areas, to force you to find your mistakes early in program development. At the same time, Java frees you from having to worry about many of the most common causes of programming errors. Because Java is a strictly typed language, it checks your code at compile time. However, it also checks your code at run time. In fact, many hard-to-track-down bugs that often turn up in hard-to-reproduce run-time situations are simply impossible to create in Java. Knowing that what you have written will behave in a predictable way under diverse conditions is a key feature of Java.

To better understand how Java is robust, consider two of the main reasons for program failure: memory management mistakes and mishandled exceptional conditions (that is, run-time errors). Memory management can be a difficult, tedious task in traditional programming environments. For example, in C/C++, the programmer must manually allocate and free all dynamic memory. This sometimes leads to problems, because programmers will either forget to free memory that has been previously allocated or, worse, try to free some memory that another part of their code is still using. Java virtually eliminates these problems by managing memory allocation and deallocation for you. (In fact, deallocation is completely automatic, because Java provides garbage collection for unused objects.) Exceptional conditions in traditional environments often arise in situations such as division by zero or "file not found," and they must be managed with clumsy and hard-to-read constructs. Java helps in this area by providing object-oriented exception handling. In a well-written Java program, all run-time errors can—and should—be managed by your program.

Multithreaded

Java was designed to meet the real-world requirement of creating interactive, networked programs. To accomplish this, Java supports multithreaded programming, which allows you to write programs that do many things simultaneously. The Java run-time system comes with an elegant yet sophisticated solution for multiprocess synchronization that enables you to construct smoothly running interactive systems. Java's easy-to-use approach to multithreading allows you to think about the specific behavior of your program, not the multitasking subsystem.

Architecture-Neutral

A central issue for the Java designers was that of code longevity and portability. One of the main problems facing programmers is that no guarantee exists that if you write a program today, it will run tomorrow—even on the same machine. Operating system upgrades, processor upgrades, and changes in core system resources can all combine to make a program malfunction. The Java designers made several hard decisions in the Java language and the Java Virtual Machine in an attempt to alter this situation. Their goal was "write once; run anywhere, any time, forever." To a great extent, this goal was accomplished.

Interpreted and High Performance

As described earlier, Java enables the creation of cross-platform programs by compiling into an intermediate representation called Java bytecode. This code can be interpreted on any system that provides a Java Virtual Machine. Most previous attempts at cross-platform solutions have done so at the expense of performance. Other interpreted systems, such as BASIC, Tcl, and PERL, suffer from almost insurmountable performance deficits. Java, however, was designed to perform well on very low-power CPUs. As explained earlier, while it is true that Java was engineered for interpretation, the Java bytecode was carefully designed so that it would be easy to translate directly into native machine code for very high performance by using a just-in-time compiler. Java run-time systems that provide this feature lose none of the benefits of the platform-independent code. "High-performance cross-platform" is no longer an oxymoron.

Distributed

Java is designed for the distributed environment of the Internet, because it handles TCP/IP protocols. In fact, accessing a resource using a URL is not much different from accessing a file. The original version of Java (Oak) included features for intra-address-space messaging. This allowed objects on two different computers to execute procedures remotely. Java revived these interfaces in a package called *Remote Method Invocation* (*RMI*). This feature brings an unparalleled level of abstraction to client/server programming.

Dynamic

Java programs carry with them substantial amounts of run-time type information that is used to verify and resolve accesses to objects at run time. This makes it possible to dynamically link code in a safe and expedient manner. This is crucial to the robustness of the applet environment, in which small fragments of bytecode may be dynamically updated on a running system.

The Continuing Revolution

The initial release of Java was nothing short of revolutionary, but it did not mark the end of Java's era of rapid innovation. Unlike most other software systems that usually settle into a pattern of small, incremental improvements, Java continued to evolve at an explosive pace. Soon after the release of Java 1.0, the designers of Java had already created Java 1.1. The features added by Java 1.1 were more significant and substantial than the increase in the minor revision number would have you think. Java 1.1 added many new library elements, redefined the way events are handled by applets, and reconfigured many features of the 1.0 library. It also deprecated (rendered obsolete) several features originally defined by Java 1.0. Thus, Java 1.1 both added and subtracted attributes from its original specification.

The next major release of Java was Java 2. Java 2 was a watershed event, marking the beginning of the "modern age" of this rapidly evolving language! The first release of Java 2 carried the version number 1.2. It may seem odd that the first release of Java 2 used the 1.2 version number. The reason is that it originally referred to the version of the Java libraries, but it was generalized to refer to the entire release, itself. Java 2 added support for a number of new features, such as Swing and the Collections framework, and it enhanced the Java Virtual Machine and various programming tools. Java 2 also contained a few deprecations. The most important affected the **Thread** class in which the methods **suspend( )**, **resume( )**, and **stop( )** were deprecated.

The next release of Java was Java 2, version 1.3. This version of Java was the first major upgrade to the original Java 2 release. For the most part it added to existing functionality and "tightened up" the development environment. In general, programs written for version 1.2 and those written for version 1.3 are source-code compatible. Although version 1.3 contained a smaller set of changes than the preceding three major releases, it was nevertheless important.

The current release of Java is Java 2, version 1.4. This release contains several important upgrades, enhancements, and additions. For example, it adds the new keyword **assert**, chained exceptions, and a channel-based I/O subsystem. It also makes changes to the Collections Framework and the networking classes. In addition, numerous small changes are made throughout. Despite the significant number of new features, version 1.4 maintains nearly 100 percent source-code compatibility with prior versions.

This book covers all versions of Java 2. Of course, most of the material applies to earlier versions of Java, too. Throughout this book, when a feature applies to a specific version of Java, it will be so noted. Otherwise, you can simply assume that it applies to Java, in general. Also, when referring to those features common to all versions of Java 2, this book will simply use the term *Java 2*, without a reference to a version number.

The
Complete
Reference

Java™ 2

Chapter 2

An Overview of Java

Like all other computer languages, the elements of Java do not exist in isolation. Rather, they work together to form the language as a whole. However, this interrelatedness can make it difficult to describe one aspect of Java without involving several others. Often a discussion of one feature implies prior knowledge of another. For this reason, this chapter presents a quick overview of several key features of Java. The material described here will give you a foothold that will allow you to write and understand simple programs. Most of the topics discussed will be examined in greater detail in the remaining chapters of Part 1.

Object-Oriented Programming

Object-oriented programming is at the core of Java. In fact, all Java programs are object-oriented—this isn't an option the way that it is in C++, for example. OOP is so integral to Java that you must understand its basic principles before you can write even simple Java programs. Therefore, this chapter begins with a discussion of the theoretical aspects of OOP.

Two Paradigms

As you know, all computer programs consist of two elements: code and data. Furthermore, a program can be conceptually organized around its code or around its data. That is, some programs are written around "what is happening" and others are written around "who is being affected." These are the two paradigms that govern how a program is constructed. The first way is called the *process-oriented model*. This approach characterizes a program as a series of linear steps (that is, code). The process-oriented model can be thought of as *code acting on data*. Procedural languages such as C employ this model to considerable success. However, as mentioned in Chapter 1, problems with this approach appear as programs grow larger and more complex.

To manage increasing complexity, the second approach, called *object-oriented programming*, was conceived. Object-oriented programming organizes a program around its data (that is, objects) and a set of well-defined interfaces to that data. An object-oriented program can be characterized as *data controlling access to code*. As you will see, by switching the controlling entity to data, you can achieve several organizational benefits.

Abstraction

An essential element of object-oriented programming is *abstraction*. Humans manage complexity through abstraction. For example, people do not think of a car as a set of tens of thousands of individual parts. They think of it as a well-defined object with its own unique behavior. This abstraction allows people to use a car to drive to the grocery store without being overwhelmed by the complexity of the parts that form the car. They can ignore the details of how the engine, transmission, and braking systems work. Instead they are free to utilize the object as a whole.

A powerful way to manage abstraction is through the use of hierarchical classifications. This allows you to layer the semantics of complex systems, breaking them into more manageable pieces. From the outside, the car is a single object. Once inside, you see that the car consists of several subsystems: steering, brakes, sound system, seat belts, heating, cellular phone, and so on. In turn, each of these subsystems is made up of more specialized units. For instance, the sound system consists of a radio, a CD player, and/or a tape player. The point is that you manage the complexity of the car (or any other complex system) through the use of hierarchical abstractions.

Hierarchical abstractions of complex systems can also be applied to computer programs. The data from a traditional process-oriented program can be transformed by abstraction into its component objects. A sequence of process steps can become a collection of messages between these objects. Thus, each of these objects describes its own unique behavior. You can treat these objects as concrete entities that respond to messages telling them to *do something*. This is the essence of object-oriented programming.

Object-oriented concepts form the heart of Java just as they form the basis for human understanding. It is important that you understand how these concepts translate into programs. As you will see, object-oriented programming is a powerful and natural paradigm for creating programs that survive the inevitable changes accompanying the life cycle of any major software project, including conception, growth, and aging. For example, once you have well-defined objects and clean, reliable interfaces to those objects, you can gracefully decommission or replace parts of an older system without fear.

The Three OOP Principles

All object-oriented programming languages provide mechanisms that help you implement the object-oriented model. They are encapsulation, inheritance, and polymorphism. Let's take a look at these concepts now.

Encapsulation

Encapsulation is the mechanism that binds together code and the data it manipulates, and keeps both safe from outside interference and misuse. One way to think about encapsulation is as a protective wrapper that prevents the code and data from being arbitrarily accessed by other code defined outside the wrapper. Access to the code and data inside the wrapper is tightly controlled through a well-defined interface. To relate this to the real world, consider the automatic transmission on an automobile. It encapsulates hundreds of bits of information about your engine, such as how much you are accelerating, the pitch of the surface you are on, and the position of the shift lever. You, as the user, have only one method of affecting this complex encapsulation: by moving the gear-shift lever. You can't affect the transmission by using the turn signal or windshield wipers, for example. Thus, the gear-shift lever is a well-defined (indeed, unique) interface to the transmission. Further, what occurs inside the transmission does not affect objects outside the transmission. For example, shifting gears does not turn on the headlights! Because an automatic transmission is encapsulated, dozens of car manufacturers can implement one in any way they please. However, from the driver's point of view, they all work the same. This same idea can be applied to programming. The power of encapsulated code is that everyone knows how to access it and thus can use it regardless of the implementation details—and without fear of unexpected side effects.

In Java the basis of encapsulation is the class. Although the class will be examined in great detail later in this book, the following brief discussion will be helpful now. A *class* defines the structure and behavior (data and code) that will be shared by a set of objects. Each object of a given class contains the structure and behavior defined by the class, as if it were stamped out by a mold in the shape of the class. For this reason, objects are sometimes referred to as *instances of a class.* Thus, a class is a logical construct; an object has physical reality.

When you create a class, you will specify the code and data that constitute that class. Collectively, these elements are called *members* of the class. Specifically, the data defined by the class are referred to as *member variables* or *instance variables.* The code that operates on that data is referred to as *member methods* or just *methods.* (If you are familiar with C/C++, it may help to know that what a Java programmer calls a *method,* a C/C++ programmer calls a *function.*) In properly written Java programs, the methods define how the member variables can be used. This means that the behavior and interface of a class are defined by the methods that operate on its instance data.

Since the purpose of a class is to encapsulate complexity, there are mechanisms for hiding the complexity of the implementation inside the class. Each method or variable in a class may be marked private or public. The *public* interface of a class represents everything that external users of the class need to know, or may know. The *private* methods and data can only be accessed by code that is a member of the class. Therefore, any other code that is not a member of the class cannot access a private method or variable. Since the private members of a class may only be accessed by other parts of your program through the class' public methods, you can ensure that no improper actions take place. Of course, this means that the public interface should be carefully designed not to expose too much of the inner workings of a class (see Figure 2-1).

Inheritance

Inheritance is the process by which one object acquires the properties of another object. This is important because it supports the concept of hierarchical classification. As mentioned earlier, most knowledge is made manageable by hierarchical (that is, top-down) classifications. For example, a Golden Retriever is part of the classification *dog,* which in turn is part of the *mammal* class, which is under the larger class *animal.* Without the use of hierarchies, each object would need to define all of its characteristics explicitly. However, by use of inheritance, an object need only define those qualities that make it unique within its class. It can inherit its general attributes from its parent. Thus, it is the inheritance mechanism that makes it possible for one object to be a specific instance of a more general case. Let's take a closer look at this process.

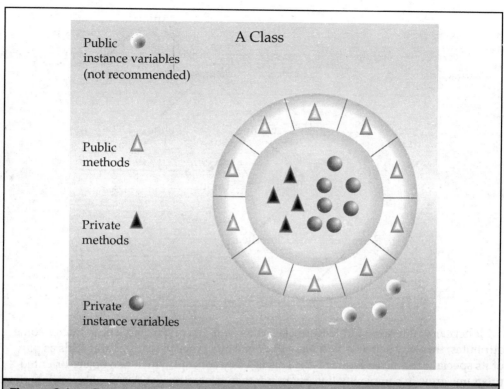

Public instance variables (not recommended)

Public methods

Private methods

Private instance variables

A Class

Figure 2-1.   *Encapsulation: public methods can be used to protect private data*

Most people naturally view the world as made up of objects that are related to each other in a hierarchical way, such as animals, mammals, and dogs. If you wanted to describe animals in an abstract way, you would say they have some attributes, such as size, intelligence, and type of skeletal system. Animals also have certain behavioral aspects; they eat, breathe, and sleep. This description of attributes and behavior is the *class* definition for animals.

If you wanted to describe a more specific class of animals, such as mammals, they would have more specific attributes, such as type of teeth, and mammary glands. This is known as a *subclass* of animals, where animals are referred to as mammals' *superclass*.

Since mammals are simply more precisely specified animals, they *inherit* all of the attributes from animals. A deeply inherited subclass inherits all of the attributes from each of its ancestors in the *class hierarchy*.

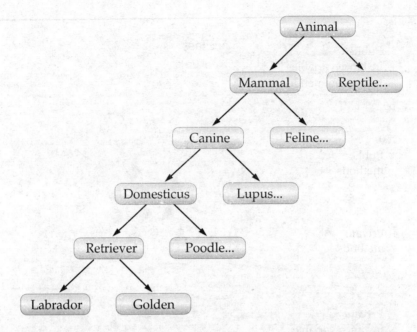

Inheritance interacts with encapsulation as well. If a given class encapsulates some attributes, then any subclass will have the same attributes *plus* any that it adds as part of its specialization (see Figure 2-2). This is a key concept which lets object-oriented programs grow in complexity linearly rather than geometrically. A new subclass inherits all of the attributes of all of its ancestors. It does not have unpredictable interactions with the majority of the rest of the code in the system.

Polymorphism

Polymorphism (from the Greek, meaning "many forms") is a feature that allows one interface to be used for a general class of actions. The specific action is determined by the exact nature of the situation. Consider a stack (which is a last-in, first-out list). You might have a program that requires three types of stacks. One stack is used for integer values, one for floating-point values, and one for characters. The algorithm that implements each stack is the same, even though the data being stored differs. In a non–object-oriented language, you would be required to create three different sets of stack routines, with each set using different names. However, because of polymorphism, in Java you can specify a general set of stack routines that all share the same names.

More generally, the concept of polymorphism is often expressed by the phrase "one interface, multiple methods." This means that it is possible to design a generic interface to a group of related activities. This helps reduce complexity by allowing the same interface to be used to specify a *general class of action*. It is the compiler's job to select the *specific action* (that is, method) as it applies to each situation. You, the programmer, do not need to make this selection manually. You need only remember and utilize the general interface.

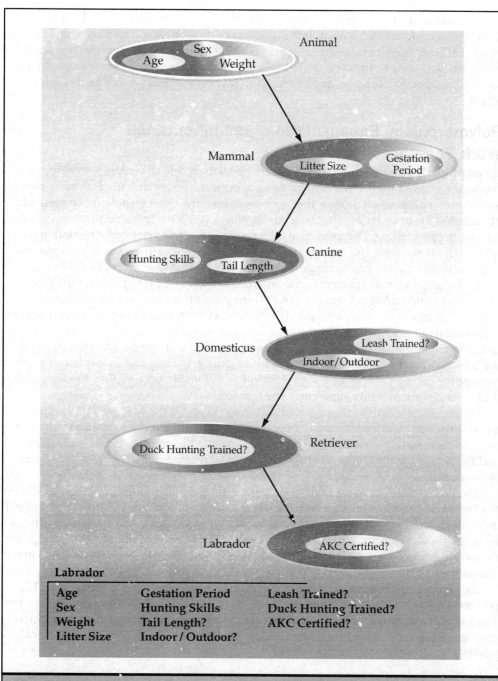

Figure 2-2. *Labrador inherits the encapsulation of all of its superclasses*

Extending the dog analogy, a dog's sense of smell is polymorphic. If the dog smells a cat, it will bark and run after it. If the dog smells its food, it will salivate and run to its bowl. The same sense of smell is at work in both situations. The difference is what is being smelled, that is, the type of data being operated upon by the dog's nose! This same general concept can be implemented in Java as it applies to methods within a Java program.

Polymorphism, Encapsulation, and Inheritance Work Together

When properly applied, polymorphism, encapsulation, and inheritance combine to produce a programming environment that supports the development of far more robust and scaleable programs than does the process-oriented model. A well-designed hierarchy of classes is the basis for reusing the code in which you have invested time and effort developing and testing. Encapsulation allows you to migrate your implementations over time without breaking the code that depends on the public interface of your classes. Polymorphism allows you to create clean, sensible, readable, and resilient code.

Of the two real-world examples, the automobile more completely illustrates the power of object-oriented design. Dogs are fun to think about from an inheritance standpoint, but cars are more like programs. All drivers rely on inheritance to drive different types (subclasses) of vehicles. Whether the vehicle is a school bus, a Mercedes sedan, a Porsche, or the family minivan, drivers can all more or less find and operate the steering wheel, the brakes, and the accelerator. After a bit of gear grinding, most people can even manage the difference between a stick shift and an automatic, because they fundamentally understand their common superclass, the transmission.

People interface with encapsulated features on cars all the time. The brake and gas pedals hide an incredible array of complexity with an interface so simple you can operate them with your feet! The implementation of the engine, the style of brakes, and the size of the tires have no effect on how you interface with the class definition of the pedals.

The final attribute, polymorphism, is clearly reflected in the ability of car manufacturers to offer a wide array of options on basically the same vehicle. For example, you can get an antilock braking system or traditional brakes, power or rack-and-pinion steering, 4-, 6-, or 8-cylinder engines. Either way, you will still press the break pedal to stop, turn the steering wheel to change direction, and press the accelerator when you want to move. The same interface can be used to control a number of different implementations.

As you can see, it is through the application of encapsulation, inheritance, and polymorphism that the individual parts are transformed into the object known as a car. The same is also true of computer programs. By the application of object-oriented principles, the various parts of a complex program can be brought together to form a cohesive, robust, maintainable whole.

As mentioned at the start of this section, every Java program is object-oriented. Or, put more precisely, every Java program involves encapsulation, inheritance, and polymorphism. Although the short example programs shown in the rest of this chapter and in the next few chapters may not seem to exhibit all of these features, they are nevertheless present. As you will see, many of the features supplied by Java are part of its built-in class libraries, which do make extensive use of encapsulation, inheritance, and polymorphism.

A First Simple Program

Now that the basic object-oriented underpinning of Java has been discussed, let's look at some actual Java programs. Let's start by compiling and running the short sample program shown here. As you will see, this involves a little more work than you might imagine.

```
/*
   This is a simple Java program.
   Call this file "Example.java".
*/
class Example {
  // Your program begins with a call to main().
  public static void main(String args[]) {
    System.out.println("This is a simple Java program.");
  }
}
```

Note   *The descriptions that follow use the standard Java 2 SDK (Software Development Kit), which is available from Sun Microsystems. If you are using a different Java development environment, then you may need to follow a different procedure for compiling and executing Java programs. In this case, consult your compiler's documentation for details.*

Entering the Program

For most computer languages, the name of the file that holds the source code to a program is arbitrary. However, this is not the case with Java. The first thing that you must learn about Java is that the name you give to a source file is very important. For this example, the name of the source file should be **Example.java**. Let's see why.

In Java, a source file is officially called a *compilation unit*. It is a text file that contains one or more class definitions. The Java compiler requires that a source file use the **.java** filename extension. Notice that the file extension is four characters long. As you might guess, your operating system must be capable of supporting long filenames. This means that DOS and Windows 3.1 are not capable of supporting Java. However, Windows 95/98 and Windows NT/2000/XP work just fine.

As you can see by looking at the program, the name of the class defined by the program is also **Example**. This is not a coincidence. In Java, all code must reside inside a class. By convention, the name of that class should match the name of the file that holds the program. You should also make sure that the capitalization of the filename matches the class name. The reason for this is that Java is case-sensitive. At this point, the convention that filenames correspond to class names may seem arbitrary. However, this convention makes it easier to maintain and organize your programs.

Compiling the Program

To compile the **Example** program, execute the compiler, **javac**, specifying the name of the source file on the command line, as shown here:

```
C:\>javac Example.java
```

The **javac** compiler creates a file called **Example.class** that contains the bytecode version of the program. As discussed earlier, the Java bytecode is the intermediate representation of your program that contains instructions the Java interpreter will execute. Thus, the output of **javac** is not code that can be directly executed.

To actually run the program, you must use the Java interpreter, called **java**. To do so, pass the class name **Example** as a command-line argument, as shown here:

```
C:\>java Example
```

When the program is run, the following output is displayed:

```
This is a simple Java program.
```

When Java source code is compiled, each individual class is put into its own output file named after the class and using the **.class** extension. This is why it is a good idea to give your Java source files the same name as the class they contain—the name of the source file will match the name of the **.class** file. When you execute the Java interpreter as just shown, you are actually specifying the name of the class that you want the interpreter to execute. It will automatically search for a file by that name that has the **.class** extension. If it finds the file, it will execute the code contained in the specified class.

A Closer Look at the First Sample Program

Although **Example.java** is quite short, it includes several key features which are common to all Java programs. Let's closely examine each part of the program. The program begins with the following lines:

```
/*
   This is a simple Java program.
   Call this file "Example.java".
*/
```

This is a *comment*. Like most other programming languages, Java lets you enter a remark into a program's source file. The contents of a comment are ignored by the compiler. Instead, a comment describes or explains the operation of the program to anyone who is reading its source code. In this case, the comment describes the program and reminds you that the source file should be called **Example.java**. Of course, in real applications, comments generally explain how some part of the program works or what a specific feature does.

Java supports three styles of comments. The one shown at the top of the program is called a *multiline comment*. This type of comment must begin with /* and end with */. Anything between these two comment symbols is ignored by the compiler. As the name suggests, a multiline comment may be several lines long.

The next line of code in the program is shown here:

```
class Example {
```

This line uses the keyword **class** to declare that a new class is being defined. **Example** is an *identifier* that is the name of the class. The entire class definition, including all of its members, will be between the opening curly brace ({) and the closing curly brace (}). The use of the curly braces in Java is identical to the way they are used in C, C++, and C#. For the moment, don't worry too much about the details of a class except to note that in Java, all program activity occurs within one. This is one reason why all Java programs are (at least a little bit) object-oriented.

The next line in the program is the *single-line comment*, shown here:

```
// Your program begins with a call to main().
```

This is the second type of comment supported by Java. A *single-line comment* begins with a // and ends at the end of the line. As a general rule, programmers use multiline comments for longer remarks and single-line comments for brief, line-by-line descriptions.

The next line of code is shown here:

```
public static void main(String args[]) {
```

This line begins the **main( )** method. As the comment preceding it suggests, this is the line at which the program will begin executing. All Java applications begin execution by calling **main( )**. (This is just like C/C++.) The exact meaning of each part of this line cannot be given now, since it involves a detailed understanding of Java's approach to encapsulation. However, since most of the examples in the first part of this book will use this line of code, let's take a brief look at each part now.

The **public** keyword is an *access specifier*, which allows the programmer to control the visibility of class members. When a class member is preceded by **public**, then that member may be accessed by code outside the class in which it is declared. (The opposite of **public** is **private**, which prevents a member from being used by code defined outside of its class.) In this case, **main( )** must be declared as **public**, since it must be called by code outside of its class when the program is started. The keyword **static** allows **main( )** to be called without having to instantiate a particular instance of the class. This is necessary since **main( )** is called by the Java interpreter before any objects are made. The keyword **void** simply tells the compiler that **main( )** does not return a value. As you will see, methods may also return values. If all this seems a bit confusing, don't worry. All of these concepts will be discussed in detail in subsequent chapters.

As stated, **main( )** is the method called when a Java application begins. Keep in mind that Java is case-sensitive. Thus, **Main** is different from **main**. It is important to understand that the Java compiler will compile classes that do not contain a **main( )** method. But the Java interpreter has no way to run these classes. So, if you had typed **Main** instead of **main**, the compiler would still compile your program. However, the Java interpreter would report an error because it would be unable to find the **main( )** method.

Any information that you need to pass to a method is received by variables specified within the set of parentheses that follow the name of the method. These variables are called *parameters*. If there are no parameters required for a given method, you still need to include the empty parentheses. In **main( )**, there is only one parameter, albeit a complicated one. **String args[ ]** declares a parameter named **args**, which is an array of instances of the class **String**. (*Arrays* are collections of similar objects.) Objects of type **String** store character strings. In this case, **args** receives any command-line arguments present when the program is executed. This program does not make use of this information, but other programs shown later in this book will.

The last character on the line is the **{**. This signals the start of **main( )**'s body. All of the code that comprises a method will occur between the method's opening curly brace and its closing curly brace.

One other point: **main( )** is simply a starting place for your program. A complex program will have dozens of classes, only one of which will need to have a **main( )** method to get things started. When you begin creating applets—Java programs that are embedded in Web browsers—you won't use **main( )** at all, since the Web browser uses a different means of starting the execution of applets.

The next line of code is shown here. Notice that it occurs inside **main( )**.

```
System.out.println("This is a simple Java program.");
```

This line outputs the string "This is a simple Java program." followed by a new line on the screen. Output is actually accomplished by the built-in **println( )** method. In this case, **println( )** displays the string which is passed to it. As you will see, **println( )** can be used to display other types of information, too. The line begins with **System.out**. While too complicated to explain in detail at this time, briefly, **System** is a predefined class that provides access to the system, and **out** is the output stream that is connected to the console.

As you have probably guessed, console output (and input) is not used frequently in real Java programs and applets. Since most modern computing environments are windowed and graphical in nature, console I/O is used mostly for simple, utility programs and for demonstration programs. Later in this book, you will learn other ways to generate output using Java. But for now, we will continue to use the console I/O methods.

Notice that the **println( )** statement ends with a semicolon. All statements in Java end with a semicolon. The reason that the other lines in the program do not end in a semicolon is that they are not, technically, statements.

The first } in the program ends **main( )**, and the last } ends the **Example** class definition.

A Second Short Program

Perhaps no other concept is more fundamental to a programming language than that of a variable. As you probably know, a *variable* is a named memory location that may be assigned a value by your program. The value of a variable may be changed during the execution of the program. The next program shows how a variable is declared and how it is assigned a value. In addition, the program also illustrates some new aspects of console output. As the comments at the top of the program state, you should call this file **Example2.java**.

```
/*
   Here is another short example.
   Call this file "Example2.java".
*/
```

```
class Example2 {
  public static void main(String args[]) {
    int num; // this declares a variable called num

    num = 100; // this assigns num the value 100

    System.out.println("This is num: " + num);

    num = num * 2;

    System.out.print("The value of num * 2 is ");
    System.out.println(num);
  }
}
```

When you run this program, you will see the following output:

```
This is num: 100
The value of num * 2 is 200
```

Let's take a close look at why this output is generated. The first new line in the program is shown here:

```
int num; // this declares a variable called num
```

This line declares an integer variable called **num**. Java (like most other languages) requires that variables be declared before they are used.

Following is the general form of a variable declaration:

type var-name;

Here, *type* specifies the type of variable being declared, and *var-name* is the name of the variable. If you want to declare more than one variable of the specified type, you may use a comma-separated list of variable names. Java defines several data types, including integer, character, and floating-point. The keyword **int** specifies an integer type.

In the program, the line

```
num = 100; // this assigns num the value 100
```

assigns to **num** the value 100. In Java, the assignment operator is a single equal sign. The next line of code outputs the value of **num** preceded by the string "This is num:".

```
System.out.println("This is num: " + num);
```

In this statement, the plus sign causes the value of **num** to be appended to the string that precedes it, and then the resulting string is output. (Actually, **num** is first converted from an integer into its string equivalent and then concatenated with the string that precedes it. This process is described in detail later in this book.) This approach can be generalized. Using the **+** operator, you can string together as many items as you want within a single **println( )** statement.

The next line of code assigns **num** the value of **num** times 2. Like most other languages, Java uses the ***** operator to indicate multiplication. After this line executes, **num** will contain the value 200.

Here are the next two lines in the program:

```
System.out.print("The value of num * 2 is ");
System.out.println(num);
```

Several new things are occurring here. First, the built-in method **print( )** is used to display the string "The value of num * 2 is ". This string is *not* followed by a newline. This means that when the next output is generated, it will start on the same line. The **print( )** method is just like **println( )**, except that it does not output a newline character after each call. Now look at the call to **println( )**. Notice that **num** is used by itself. Both **print( )** and **println( )** can be used to output values of any of Java's built-in types.

Two Control Statements

Although Chapter 5 will look closely at control statements, two are briefly introduced here so that they can be used in example programs in Chapters 3 and 4. They will also help illustrate an important aspect of Java: blocks of code.

The if Statement

The Java **if** statement works much like the IF statement in any other language. Further, it is syntactically identical to the **if** statements in C, C++, and C#. Its simplest form is shown here:

if(*condition*) *statement*;

Here, *condition* is a Boolean expression. If *condition* is true, then the statement is executed. If *condition* is false, then the statement is bypassed. Here is an example:

```
if(num < 100) println("num is less than 100");
```

In this case, if **num** contains a value that is less than 100, the conditional expression is true, and **println( )** will execute. If **num** contains a value greater than or equal to 100, then the **println( )** method is bypassed.

As you will see in Chapter 4, Java defines a full complement of relational operators which may be used in a conditional expression. Here are a few:

Operator	Meaning
<	Less than
>	Greater than
==	Equal to

Notice that the test for equality is the double equal sign.

Here is a program that illustrates the **if** statement:

```
/*
  Demonstrate the if.

  Call this file "IfSample.java".
*/
class IfSample {
  public static void main(String args[]) {
    int x, y;

    x = 10;
    y = 20;

    if(x < y) System.out.println("x is less than y");

    x = x * 2;
    if(x == y) System.out.println("x now equal to y");

    x = x * 2;
    if(x > y) System.out.println("x now greater than y");
```

```
  // this won't display anything
  if(x == y) System.out.println("you won't see this");
  }
}
```

The output generated by this program is shown here:

```
x is less than y
x now equal to y
x now greater than y
```

Notice one other thing in this program. The line

```
int x, y;
```

declares two variables, **x** and **y**, by use of a comma-separated list.

The for Loop

As you may know from your previous programming experience, loop statements are an important part of nearly any programming language. Java is no exception. In fact, as you will see in Chapter 5, Java supplies a powerful assortment of loop constructs. Perhaps the most versatile is the **for** loop. If you are familiar with C, C++, or C#, then you will be pleased to know that the **for** loop in Java works the same way it does in those languages. If you don't know C/C++/C#, the **for** loop is still easy to use. The simplest form of the **for** loop is shown here:

for(*initialization; condition; iteration*) *statement;*

In its most common form, the *initialization* portion of the loop sets a loop control variable to an initial value. The *condition* is a Boolean expression that tests the loop control variable. If the outcome of that test is true, the **for** loop continues to iterate. If it is false, the loop terminates. The *iteration* expression determines how the loop control variable is changed each time the loop iterates. Here is a short program that illustrates the **for** loop:

```
/*
  Demonstrate the for loop.

  Call this file "ForTest.java".
```

```
*/
class ForTest {
  public static void main(String args[]) {
    int x;

    for(x = 0; x<10; x = x+1)
      System.out.println("This is x: " + x);

  }
}
```

This program generates the following output:

```
This is x: 0
This is x: 1
This is x: 2
This is x: 3
This is x: 4
This is x: 5
This is x: 6
This is x: 7
This is x: 8
This is x: 9
```

In this example, **x** is the loop control variable. It is initialized to zero in the initialization portion of the **for**. At the start of each iteration (including the first one), the conditional test **x < 10** is performed. If the outcome of this test is true, the **println( )** statement is executed, and then the iteration portion of the loop is executed. This process continues until the conditional test is false.

As a point of interest, in professionally written Java programs you will almost never see the iteration portion of the loop written as shown in the preceding program. That is, you will seldom see statements like this:

```
x = x + 1;
```

The reason is that Java includes a special increment operator which performs this operation more efficiently. The increment operator is **++**. (That is, two plus signs back to back.) The increment operator increases its operand by one. By use of the increment operator, the preceding statement can be written like this:

```
x++;
```

Thus, the **for** in the preceding program will usually be written like this:

```
for(x = 0; x<10; x++)
```

You might want to try this. As you will see, the loop still runs exactly the same as it did before.

Java also provides a decrement operator, which is specified as – –. This operator decreases its operand by one.

Using Blocks of Code

Java allows two or more statements to be grouped into *blocks of code,* also called *code blocks.* This is done by enclosing the statements between opening and closing curly braces. Once a block of code has been created, it becomes a logical unit that can be used any place that a single statement can. For example, a block can be a target for Java's **if** and **for** statements. Consider this **if** statement:

```
if(x < y) { // begin a block
    x = y;
    y = 0;
} // end of block
```

Here, if **x** is less than **y**, then both statements inside the block will be executed. Thus, the two statements inside the block form a logical unit, and one statement cannot execute without the other also executing. The key point here is that whenever you need to logically link two or more statements, you do so by creating a block.

Let's look at another example. The following program uses a block of code as the target of a **for** loop.

```
/*
   Demonstrate a block of code.

   Call this file "BlockTest.java"
*/
class BlockTest {
```

```
public static void main(String args[]) {
  int x, y;

  y = 20;

  // the target of this loop is a block
  for(x = 0; x<10; x++) {
    System.out.println("This is x: " + x);
    System.out.println("This is y: " + y);
    y = y - 2;
  }
}
```

The output generated by this program is shown here:

```
This is x: 0
This is y: 20
This is x: 1
This is y: 18
This is x: 2
This is y: 16
This is x: 3
This is y: 14
This is x: 4
This is y: 12
This is x: 5
This is y: 10
This is x: 6
This is y: 8
This is x: 7
This is y: 6
This is x: 8
This is y: 4
This is x: 9
This is y: 2
```

In this case, the target of the **for** loop is a block of code and not just a single statement. Thus, each time the loop iterates, the three statements inside the block will be executed. This fact is, of course, evidenced by the output generated by the program.

As you will see later in this book, blocks of code have additional properties and uses. However, the main reason for their existence is to create logically inseparable units of code.

Lexical Issues

Now that you have seen several short Java programs, it is time to more formally describe the atomic elements of Java. Java programs are a collection of whitespace, identifiers, comments, literals, operators, separators, and keywords. The operators are described in the next chapter. The others are described next.

Whitespace

Java is a free-form language. This means that you do not need to follow any special indentation rules. For example, the **Example** program could have been written all on one line or in any other strange way you felt like typing it, as long as there was at least one whitespace character between each token that was not already delineated by an operator or separator. In Java, whitespace is a space, tab, or newline.

Identifiers

Identifiers are used for class names, method names, and variable names. An identifier may be any descriptive sequence of uppercase and lowercase letters, numbers, or the underscore and dollar-sign characters. They must not begin with a number, lest they be confused with a numeric literal. Again, Java is case-sensitive, so **VALUE** is a different identifier than **Value**. Some examples of valid identifiers are:

AvgTemp   count   a4 $test   this_is_ok

Invalid variable names include:

2count   high-temp   Not/ok

Literals

A constant value in Java is created by using a *literal* representation of it. For example, here are some literals:

100   98.6   'X'   "This is a test"

Left to right, the first literal specifies an integer, the next is a floating-point value, the third is a character constant, and the last is a string. A literal can be used anywhere a value of its type is allowed.

Comments

As mentioned, there are three types of comments defined by Java. You have already seen two: single-line and multiline. The third type is called a *documentation comment*. This type of comment is used to produce an HTML file that documents your program. The documentation comment begins with a /** and ends with a */. Documentation comments are explained in Appendix A.

Separators

In Java, there are a few characters that are used as separators. The most commonly used separator in Java is the semicolon. As you have seen, it is used to terminate statements. The separators are shown in the following table:

Symbol	Name	Purpose
( )	Parentheses	Used to contain lists of parameters in method definition and invocation. Also used for defining precedence in expressions, containing expressions in control statements, and surrounding cast types.
{ }	Braces	Used to contain the values of automatically initialized arrays. Also used to define a block of code, for classes, methods, and local scopes.
[ ]	Brackets	Used to declare array types. Also used when dereferencing array values.
;	Semicolon	Terminates statements.
,	Comma	Separates consecutive identifiers in a variable declaration. Also used to chain statements together inside a **for** statement.
.	Period	Used to separate package names from subpackages and classes. Also used to separate a variable or method from a reference variable.

The Java Keywords

There are 49 reserved keywords currently defined in the Java language (see Table 2-1). These keywords, combined with the syntax of the operators and separators, form the definition of the Java language. These keywords cannot be used as names for a variable, class, or method.

abstract	continue	goto	package	synchronized
assert	default	if	private	this
boolean	do	implements	protected	throw
break	double	import	public	throws
byte	else	instanceof	return	transient
case	extends	int	short	try
catch	final	interface	static	void
char	finally	long	strictfp	volatile
class	float	native	super	while
const	for	new	switch	

Table 2-1.   *Java Reserved Keywords*

The keywords **const** and **goto** are reserved but not used. In the early days of Java, several other keywords were reserved for possible future use. However, the current specification for Java only defines the keywords shown in Table 2-1. The **assert** keyword was added by Java 2, version 1.4

In addition to the keywords, Java reserves the following: **true**, **false**, and **null**. These are values defined by Java. You may not use these words for the names of variables, classes, and so on.

The Java Class Libraries

The sample programs shown in this chapter make use of two of Java's built-in methods: **println( )** and **print( )**. As mentioned, these methods are members of the **System** class, which is a class predefined by Java that is automatically included in your programs. In the larger view, the Java environment relies on several built-in class libraries that contain many built-in methods that provide support for such things as I/O, string handling, networking, and graphics. The standard classes also provide support for windowed output. Thus, Java as a totality is a combination of the Java language itself, plus its standard classes. As you will see, the class libraries provide much of the functionality that comes with Java. Indeed, part of becoming a Java programmer is learning to use the standard Java classes. Throughout Part I of this book, various elements of the standard library classes and methods are described as needed. In Part II, the class libraries are described in detail.

Chapter 3

Data Types, Variables, and Arrays

This chapter examines three of Java's most fundamental elements: data types, variables, and arrays. As with all modern programming languages, Java supports several types of data. You may use these types to declare variables and to create arrays. As you will see, Java's approach to these items is clean, efficient, and cohesive.

Java Is a Strongly Typed Language

It is important to state at the outset that Java is a strongly typed language. Indeed, part of Java's safety and robustness comes from this fact. Let's see what this means. First, every variable has a type, every expression has a type, and every type is strictly defined. Second, all assignments, whether explicit or via parameter passing in method calls, are checked for type compatibility. There are no automatic coercions or conversions of conflicting types as in some languages. The Java compiler checks all expressions and parameters to ensure that the types are compatible. Any type mismatches are errors that must be corrected before the compiler will finish compiling the class.

Note   *If you come from a C or C++ background, keep in mind that Java is more strictly typed than either language. For example, in C/C++ you can assign a floating-point value to an integer. In Java, you cannot. Also, in C there is not necessarily strong type-checking between a parameter and an argument. In Java, there is. You might find Java's strong type-checking a bit tedious at first. But remember, in the long run it will help reduce the possibility of errors in your code.*

The Simple Types

Java defines eight simple (or elemental) types of data: **byte**, **short**, **int**, **long**, **char**, **float**, **double**, and **boolean**. These can be put in four groups:

- Integers   This group includes **byte**, **short**, **int**, and **long**, which are for whole-valued signed numbers.

- Floating-point numbers   This group includes **float** and **double**, which represent numbers with fractional precision.

- Characters   This group includes **char**, which represents symbols in a character set, like letters and numbers.

- Boolean   This group includes **boolean**, which is a special type for representing true/false values.

You can use these types as-is, or to construct arrays or your own class types. Thus, they form the basis for all other types of data that you can create.

The simple types represent single values—not complex objects. Although Java is otherwise completely object-oriented, the simple types are not. They are analogous to the simple types found in most other non–object-oriented languages. The reason for this is efficiency. Making the simple types into objects would have degraded performance too much.

The simple types are defined to have an explicit range and mathematical behavior. Languages such as C and C++ allow the size of an integer to vary based upon the dictates of the execution environment. However, Java is different. Because of Java's portability requirement, all data types have a strictly defined range. For example, an **int** is always 32 bits, regardless of the particular platform. This allows programs to be written that are guaranteed to run *without porting* on any machine architecture. While strictly specifying the size of an integer may cause a small loss of performance in some environments, it is necessary in order to achieve portability.

Let's look at each type of data in turn.

Integers

Java defines four integer types: **byte**, **short**, **int**, and **long**. All of these are signed, positive and negative values. Java does not support unsigned, positive-only integers. Many other computer languages, including C/C++, support both signed and unsigned integers. However, Java's designers felt that unsigned integers were unnecessary. Specifically, they felt that the concept of *unsigned* was used mostly to specify the behavior of the *high-order bit*, which defined the *sign* of an **int** when expressed as a number. As you will see in Chapter 4, Java manages the meaning of the high-order bit differently, by adding a special "unsigned right shift" operator. Thus, the need for an unsigned integer type was eliminated.

The *width* of an integer type should not be thought of as the amount of storage it consumes, but rather as the *behavior* it defines for variables and expressions of that type. The Java run-time environment is free to use whatever size it wants, as long as the types behave as you declared them. In fact, at least one implementation stores **byte**s and **short**s as 32-bit (rather than 8- and 16-bit) values to improve performance, because that is the word size of most computers currently in use.

The width and ranges of these integer types vary widely, as shown in this table:

Name	Width	Range
long	64	–9,223,372,036,854,775,808 to 9,223,372,036,854,775,807
int	32	–2,147,483,648 to 2,147,483,647
short	16	–32,768 to 32,767
byte	8	–128 to 127

Let's look at each type of integer.

byte

The smallest integer type is **byte**. This is a signed 8-bit type that has a range from –128 to 127. Variables of type **byte** are especially useful when you're working with a stream of data from a network or file. They are also useful when you're working with raw binary data that may not be directly compatible with Java's other built-in types.

Byte variables are declared by use of the **byte** keyword. For example, the following declares two **byte** variables called **b** and **c**:

```
byte b, c;
```

short

short is a signed 16-bit type. It has a range from –32,768 to 32,767. It is probably the least-used Java type, since it is defined as having its high byte first (called *big-endian* format). This type is mostly applicable to 16-bit computers, which are becoming increasingly scarce.

Here are some examples of **short** variable declarations:

```
short s;
short t;
```

*"Endianness" describes how multibyte data types, such as **short**, **int**, and **long**, are stored in memory. If it takes 2 bytes to represent a **short**, then which one comes first, the most significant or the least significant? To say that a machine is big-endian, means that the most significant byte is first, followed by the least significant one. Machines such as the SPARC and PowerPC are big-endian, while the Intel x86 series is little-endian.*

int

The most commonly used integer type is **int**. It is a signed 32-bit type that has a range from –2,147,483,648 to 2,147,483,647. In addition to other uses, variables of type **int** are commonly employed to control loops and to index arrays. Any time you have an integer expression involving **byte**s, **short**s, **int**s, and literal numbers, the entire expression is *promoted* to **int** before the calculation is done.

The **int** type is the most versatile and efficient type, and it should be used most of the time when you want to create a number for counting or indexing arrays or doing integer math. It may seem that using **short** or **byte** will save space, but there is no guarantee that Java won't promote those types to **int** internally anyway. Remember, type determines behavior, not size. (The only exception is arrays, where **byte** is guaranteed to use only one byte per array element, **short** will use two bytes, and **int** will use four.)

long

long is a signed 64-bit type and is useful for those occasions where an **int** type is not large enough to hold the desired value. The range of a **long** is quite large. This makes it useful when big, whole numbers are needed. For example, here is a program that computes the number of miles that light will travel in a specified number of days.

```java
// Compute distance light travels using long variables.
class Light {
  public static void main(String args[]) {
    int lightspeed;
    long days;
    long seconds;
    long distance;

    // approximate speed of light in miles per second
    lightspeed = 186000;

    days = 1000; // specify number of days here

    seconds = days * 24 * 60 * 60; // convert to seconds

    distance = lightspeed * seconds; // compute distance

    System.out.print("In " + days);
    System.out.print(" days light will travel about ");
    System.out.println(distance + " miles.");
  }
}
```

This program generates the following output:

```
In 1000 days light will travel about 16070400000000 miles.
```

Clearly, the result could not have been held in an **int** variable.

Floating-Point Types

Floating-point numbers, also known as *real* numbers, are used when evaluating expressions that require fractional precision. For example, calculations such as square root, or transcendentals such as sine and cosine, result in a value whose precision requires a floating-point type. Java implements the standard (IEEE–754) set of floating-point types and operators. There are two kinds of floating-point types, **float** and **double**, which represent single- and double-precision numbers, respectively. Their width and ranges are shown here:

Name	Width in Bits	Approximate Range
double	64	4.9e–324 to 1.8e+308
float	32	1.4e–045 to 3.4e+038

Each of these floating-point types is examined next.

float

The type **float** specifies a *single-precision* value that uses 32 bits of storage. Single precision is faster on some processors and takes half as much space as double precision, but will become imprecise when the values are either very large or very small. Variables of type **float** are useful when you need a fractional component, but don't require a large degree of precision. For example, **float** can be useful when representing dollars and cents.

Here are some example **float** variable declarations:

```
float hightemp, lowtemp;
```

double

Double precision, as denoted by the **double** keyword, uses 64 bits to store a value. Double precision is actually faster than single precision on some modern processors that have been optimized for high-speed mathematical calculations. All transcendental math functions, such as **sin( )**, **cos( )**, and **sqrt( )**, return **double** values. When you need to maintain accuracy over many iterative calculations, or are manipulating large-valued numbers, **double** is the best choice.

Here is a short program that uses **double** variables to compute the area of a circle:

```
// Compute the area of a circle.
class Area {
  public static void main(String args[]) {
    double pi, r, a;

    r = 10.8; // radius of circle
    pi = 3.1416; // pi, approximately
    a = pi * r * r; // compute area
```

```
   System.out.println("Area of circle is " + a);
 }
}
```

Characters

In Java, the data type used to store characters is **char**. However, C/C++ programmers beware: **char** in Java is not the same as **char** in C or C++. In C/C++, **char** is an integer type that is 8 bits wide. This is *not* the case in Java. Instead, Java uses Unicode to represent characters. *Unicode* defines a fully international character set that can represent all of the characters found in all human languages. It is a unification of dozens of character sets, such as Latin, Greek, Arabic, Cyrillic, Hebrew, Katakana, Hangul, and many more. For this purpose, it requires 16 bits. Thus, in Java **char** is a 16-bit type. The range of a **char** is 0 to 65,536. There are no negative **char**s. The standard set of characters known as ASCII still ranges from 0 to 127 as always, and the extended 8-bit character set, ISO-Latin-1, ranges from 0 to 255. Since Java is designed to allow applets to be written for worldwide use, it makes sense that it would use Unicode to represent characters. Of course, the use of Unicode is somewhat inefficient for languages such as English, German, Spanish, or French, whose characters can easily be contained within 8 bits. But such is the price that must be paid for global portability.

Note   *More information about Unicode can be found at* http://www.unicode.org.

Here is a program that demonstrates **char** variables:

```
// Demonstrate char data type.
class CharDemo {
  public static void main(String args[]) {
    char ch1, ch2;

    ch1 = 88; // code for X
    ch2 = 'Y';

    System.out.print("ch1 and ch2: ");
    System.out.println(ch1 + " " + ch2);
  }
}
```

This program displays the following output:

```
ch1 and ch2: X Y
```

Notice that **ch1** is assigned the value 88, which is the ASCII (and Unicode) value that corresponds to the letter *X*. As mentioned, the ASCII character set occupies the first 127 values in the Unicode character set. For this reason, all the "old tricks" that you have used with characters in the past will work in Java, too.

Even though **char**s are not integers, in many cases you can operate on them as if they were integers. This allows you to add two characters together, or to increment the value of a character variable. For example, consider the following program:

```java
// char variables behave like integers.
class CharDemo2 {
  public static void main(String args[]) {
    char ch1;

    ch1 = 'X';
    System.out.println("ch1 contains " + ch1);

    ch1++; // increment ch1
    System.out.println("ch1 is now " + ch1);
  }
}
```

The output generated by this program is shown here:

```
ch1 contains X
ch1 is now Y
```

In the program, **ch1** is first given the value *X*. Next, **ch1** is incremented. This results in **ch1** containing *Y*, the next character in the ASCII (and Unicode) sequence.

Booleans

Java has a simple type, called **boolean**, for logical values. It can have only one of two possible values, **true** or **false**. This is the type returned by all relational operators, such as **a < b**. **boolean** is also the type *required* by the conditional expressions that govern the control statements such as **if** and **for**.

Here is a program that demonstrates the **boolean** type:

```
// Demonstrate boolean values.
class BoolTest {
  public static void main(String args[]) {
    boolean b;

    b = false;
    System.out.println("b is " + b);
    b = true;
    System.out.println("b is " + b);

    // a boolean value can control the if statement
    if(b) System.out.println("This is executed.");

    b = false;
    if(b) System.out.println("This is not executed.");

    // outcome of a relational operator is a boolean value
    System.out.println("10 > 9 is " + (10 > 9));
  }
}
```

The output generated by this program is shown here:

```
b is false
b is true
This is executed.
10 > 9 is true
```

There are three interesting things to notice about this program. First, as you can see, when a **boolean** value is output by **println( )**, "true" or "false" is displayed. Second, the value of a **boolean** variable is sufficient, by itself, to control the **if** statement. There is no need to write an **if** statement like this:

```
if(b == true) ...
```

Third, the outcome of a relational operator, such as **<**, is a **boolean** value. This is why the expression **10 > 9** displays the value "true." Further, the extra set of parentheses around **10 > 9** is necessary because the **+** operator has a higher precedence than the **>**.

A Closer Look at Literals

Literals were mentioned briefly in Chapter 2. Now that the built-in types have been formally described, let's take a closer look at them.

Integer Literals

Integers are probably the most commonly used type in the typical program. Any whole number value is an integer literal. Examples are 1, 2, 3, and 42. These are all decimal values, meaning they are describing a base 10 number. There are two other bases which can be used in integer literals, *octal* (base eight) and *hexadecimal* (base 16). Octal values are denoted in Java by a leading zero. Normal decimal numbers cannot have a leading zero. Thus, the seemingly valid value 09 will produce an error from the compiler, since 9 is outside of octal's 0 to 7 range. A more common base for numbers used by programmers is hexadecimal, which matches cleanly with modulo 8 word sizes, such as 8, 16, 32, and 64 bits. You signify a hexadecimal constant with a leading zero-x, (**0x** or **0X**). The range of a hexadecimal digit is 0 to 15, so A through F (or *a* through *f*) are substituted for 10 through 15.

Integer literals create an **int** value, which in Java is a 32-bit integer value. Since Java is strongly typed, you might be wondering how it is possible to assign an integer literal to one of Java's other integer types, such as **byte** or **long**, without causing a type mismatch error. Fortunately, such situations are easily handled. When a literal value is assigned to a **byte** or **short** variable, no error is generated if the literal value is within the range of the target type. Also, an integer literal can always be assigned to a **long** variable. However, to specify a **long** literal, you will need to explicitly tell the compiler that the literal value is of type **long**. You do this by appending an upper- or lowercase *L* to the literal. For example, 0x7ffffffffffffffffL or 9223372036854775807L is the largest **long**.

Floating-Point Literals

Floating-point numbers represent decimal values with a fractional component. They can be expressed in either standard or scientific notation. *Standard notation* consists of a whole number component followed by a decimal point followed by a fractional component. For example, 2.0, 3.14159, and 0.6667 represent valid standard-notation floating-point numbers. *Scientific notation* uses a standard-notation, floating-point number plus a suffix that specifies a power of 10 by which the number is to be multiplied. The exponent is indicated by an *E* or *e* followed by a decimal number, which can be positive or negative. Examples include 6.022E23, 314159E–05, and 2e+100.

Floating-point literals in Java default to **double** precision. To specify a **float** literal, you must append an *F* or *f* to the constant. You can also explicitly specify a **double** literal by appending a *D* or *d*. Doing so is, of course, redundant. The default **double** type consumes 64 bits of storage, while the less-accurate **float** type requires only 32 bits.

Boolean Literals

Boolean literals are simple. There are only two logical values that a **boolean** value can have, **true** and **false**. The values of **true** and **false** do not convert into any numerical representation. The **true** literal in Java does not equal 1, nor does the **false** literal equal 0. In Java, they can only be assigned to variables declared as **boolean**, or used in expressions with Boolean operators.

Character Literals

Characters in Java are indices into the Unicode character set. They are 16-bit values that can be converted into integers and manipulated with the integer operators, such as the addition and subtraction operators. A literal character is represented inside a pair of single quotes. All of the visible ASCII characters can be directly entered inside the quotes, such as *'a'*, *'z'*, and *'@'*. For characters that are impossible to enter directly, there are several escape sequences, which allow you to enter the character you need, such as '\'' for the single-quote character itself, and **'\n'** for the newline character. There is also a mechanism for directly entering the value of a character in octal or hexadecimal. For octal notation use the backslash followed by the three-digit number. For example, *'\141'* is the letter *'a'*. For hexadecimal, you enter a backslash-u (**\u**), then exactly four hexadecimal digits. For example, *'\u0061'* is the ISO-Latin-1 *'a'* because the top byte is zero. *'\ua432'* is a Japanese Katakana character. Table 3-1 shows the character escape sequences.

Escape Sequence	Description
\ddd	Octal character (ddd)
\uxxxx	Hexadecimal UNICODE character (xxxx)
\'	Single quote
\"	Double quote
\\	Backslash
\r	Carriage return
\n	New line (also known as line feed)
\f	Form feed
\t	Tab
\b	Backspace

Table 3-1.   *Character Escape Sequences*

String Literals

String literals in Java are specified like they are in most other languages—by enclosing a sequence of characters between a pair of double quotes. Examples of string literals are

"Hello World"
"two\nlines"
"\"This is in quotes\""

The escape sequences and octal/hexadecimal notations that were defined for character literals work the same way inside of string literals. One important thing to note about Java strings is that they must begin and end on the same line. There is no line-continuation escape sequence as there is in other languages.

As you may know, in some other languages, including C/C++, strings are implemented as arrays of characters. However, this is not the case in Java. Strings are actually object types. As you will see later in this book, because Java implements strings as objects, Java includes extensive string-handling capabilities that are both powerful and easy to use.

Variables

The variable is the basic unit of storage in a Java program. A variable is defined by the combination of an identifier, a type, and an optional initializer. In addition, all variables have a scope, which defines their visibility, and a lifetime. These elements are examined next.

Declaring a Variable

In Java, all variables must be declared before they can be used. The basic form of a variable declaration is shown here:

type identifier [= *value*][, *identifier* [= *value*] ...] ;

The *type* is one of Java's atomic types, or the name of a class or interface. (Class and interface types are discussed later in Part I of this book.) The *identifier* is the name of the variable. You can initialize the variable by specifying an equal sign and a value. Keep in mind that the initialization expression must result in a value of the same (or compatible) type as that specified for the variable. To declare more than one variable of the specified type, use a comma-separated list.

Here are several examples of variable declarations of various types. Note that some include an initialization.

```
int a, b, c;           // declares three ints, a, b, and c.
int d = 3, e, f = 5;   // declares three more ints, initializing
                       // d and f.
byte z = 22;           // initializes z.
double pi = 3.14159;   // declares an approximation of pi.
char x = 'x';          // the variable x has the value 'x'.
```

The identifiers that you choose have nothing intrinsic in their names that indicates their type. Many readers will remember when FORTRAN predefined all identifiers from **I** through **N** to be of type **INTEGER** while all other identifiers were **REAL**. Java allows any properly formed identifier to have any declared type.

Dynamic Initialization

Although the preceding examples have used only constants as initializers, Java allows variables to be initialized dynamically, using any expression valid at the time the variable is declared.

For example, here is a short program that computes the length of the hypotenuse of a right triangle given the lengths of its two opposing sides:

```
// Demonstrate dynamic initialization.
class DynInit {
    public static void main(String args[]) {
        double a = 3.0, b = 4.0;

        // c is dynamically initialized
        double c = Math.sqrt(a * a + b * b);

        System.out.println("Hypotenuse is " + c);
    }
}
```

Here, three local variables—**a**, **b**,and **c**—are declared. The first two, **a** and **b**, are initialized by constants. However, **c** is initialized dynamically to the length of the hypotenuse (using the Pythagorean theorem). The program uses another of Java's built-in methods, **sqrt( )**, which is a member of the **Math** class, to compute the square root of its argument. The key point here is that the initialization expression may use any element valid at the time of the initialization, including calls to methods, other variables, or literals.

The Scope and Lifetime of Variables

So far, all of the variables used have been declared at the start of the **main( )** method. However, Java allows variables to be declared within any block. As explained in Chapter 2, a block is begun with an opening curly brace and ended by a closing curly brace. A block defines a *scope*. Thus, each time you start a new block, you are creating a new scope. As you probably know from your previous programming experience, a scope determines what objects are visible to other parts of your program. It also determines the lifetime of those objects.

Most other computer languages define two general categories of scopes: global and local. However, these traditional scopes do not fit well with Java's strict, object-oriented model. While it is possible to create what amounts to being a global scope, it is by far the exception, not the rule. In Java, the two major scopes are those defined by a class and those defined by a method. Even this distinction is somewhat artificial. However, since the class scope has several unique properties and attributes that do not apply to the scope defined by a method, this distinction makes some sense. Because of the differences, a discussion of class scope (and variables declared within it) is deferred until Chapter 6, when classes are described. For now, we will only examine the scopes defined by or within a method.

The scope defined by a method begins with its opening curly brace. However, if that method has parameters, they too are included within the method's scope. Although this book will look more closely at parameters in Chapter 5, for the sake of this discussion, they work the same as any other method variable.

As a general rule, variables declared inside a scope are not visible (that is, accessible) to code that is defined outside that scope. Thus, when you declare a variable within a scope, you are localizing that variable and protecting it from unauthorized access and/or modification. Indeed, the scope rules provide the foundation for encapsulation.

Scopes can be nested. For example, each time you create a block of code, you are creating a new, nested scope. When this occurs, the outer scope encloses the inner scope. This means that objects declared in the outer scope will be visible to code within the inner scope. However, the reverse is not true. Objects declared within the inner scope will not be visible outside it.

To understand the effect of nested scopes, consider the following program:

```
// Demonstrate block scope.
class Scope {
  public static void main(String args[]) {
    int x; // known to all code within main

    x = 10;
    if(x == 10) { // start new scope
```

```
    int y = 20; // known only to this block

    // x and y both known here.
    System.out.println("x and y: " + x + " " + y);
    x = y * 2;
  }
  // y = 100; // Error! y not known here

  // x is still known here.
  System.out.println("x is " + x);
  }
}
```

As the comments indicate, the variable **x** is declared at the start of **main( )**'s scope and is accessible to all subsequent code within **main( )**. Within the **if** block, **y** is declared. Since a block defines a scope, **y** is only visible to other code within its block. This is why outside of its block, the line **y = 100;** is commented out. If you remove the leading comment symbol, a compile-time error will occur, because **y** is not visible outside of its block. Within the **if** block, **x** can be used because code within a block (that is, a nested scope) has access to variables declared by an enclosing scope.

Within a block, variables can be declared at any point, but are valid only after they are declared. Thus, if you define a variable at the start of a method, it is available to all of the code within that method. Conversely, if you declare a variable at the end of a block, it is effectively useless, because no code will have access to it. For example, this fragment is invalid because **count** cannot be used prior to its declaration:

```
// This fragment is wrong!
count = 100; // oops!  cannot use count before it is declared!
int count;
```

Here is another important point to remember: variables are created when their scope is entered, and destroyed when their scope is left. This means that a variable will not hold its value once it has gone out of scope. Therefore, variables declared within a method will not hold their values between calls to that method. Also, a variable declared within a block will lose its value when the block is left. Thus, the lifetime of a variable is confined to its scope.

If a variable declaration includes an initializer, then that variable will be reinitialized each time the block in which it is declared is entered. For example, consider the next program.

```
// Demonstrate lifetime of a variable.
class LifeTime {
  public static void main(String args[]) {
    int x;

    for(x = 0; x < 3; x++) {
      int y = -1; // y is initialized each time block is entered
      System.out.println("y is: " + y); // this always prints -1
      y = 100;
      System.out.println("y is now: " + y);
    }
  }
}
```

The output generated by this program is shown here:

```
y is: -1
y is now: 100
y is: -1
y is now: 100
y is: -1
y is now: 100
```

As you can see, **y** is always reinitialized to –1 each time the inner **for** loop is entered. Even though it is subsequently assigned the value 100, this value is lost.

One last point: Although blocks can be nested, you cannot declare a variable to have the same name as one in an outer scope. In this regard, Java differs from C and C++. Here is an example that tries to declare two separate variables with the same name. In Java, this is illegal. In C/C++, it would be legal and the two **bar**s would be separate.

```
// This program will not compile
class ScopeErr {
  public static void main(String args[]) {
    int bar = 1;
    {                     // creates a new scope
      int bar = 2; // Compile-time error - bar already defined!
    }
  }
}
```

Type Conversion and Casting

If you have previous programming experience, then you already know that it is fairly common to assign a value of one type to a variable of another type. If the two types are compatible, then Java will perform the conversion automatically. For example, it is always possible to assign an **int** value to a **long** variable. However, not all types are compatible, and thus, not all type conversions are implicitly allowed. For instance, there is no conversion defined from **double** to **byte**. Fortunately, it is still possible to obtain a conversion between incompatible types. To do so, you must use a *cast*, which performs an explicit conversion between incompatible types. Let's look at both automatic type conversions and casting.

Java's Automatic Conversions

When one type of data is assigned to another type of variable, an *automatic type conversion* will take place if the following two conditions are met:

- The two types are compatible.
- The destination type is larger than the source type.

When these two conditions are met, a *widening conversion* takes place. For example, the **int** type is always large enough to hold all valid **byte** values, so no explicit cast statement is required.

For widening conversions, the numeric types, including integer and floating-point types, are compatible with each other. However, the numeric types are not compatible with **char** or **boolean**. Also, **char** and **boolean** are not compatible with each other.

As mentioned earlier, Java also performs an automatic type conversion when storing a literal integer constant into variables of type **byte**, **short**, or **long**.

Casting Incompatible Types

Although the automatic type conversions are helpful, they will not fulfill all needs. For example, what if you want to assign an **int** value to a **byte** variable? This conversion will not be performed automatically, because a **byte** is smaller than an **int**. This kind of conversion is sometimes called a *narrowing conversion*, since you are explicitly making the value narrower so that it will fit into the target type.

To create a conversion between two incompatible types, you must use a cast. A *cast* is simply an explicit type conversion. It has this general form:

(target-type) value

Here, *target-type* specifies the desired type to convert the specified value to. For example, the following fragment casts an **int** to a **byte**. If the integer's value is larger than the range of a **byte**, it will be reduced modulo (the remainder of an integer division by the) **byte**'s range.

```
int a;
byte b;
// ...
b = (byte) a;
```

A different type of conversion will occur when a floating-point value is assigned to an integer type: *truncation*. As you know, integers do not have fractional components. Thus, when a floating-point value is assigned to an integer type, the fractional component is lost. For example, if the value 1.23 is assigned to an integer, the resulting value will simply be 1. The 0.23 will have been truncated. Of course, if the size of the whole number component is too large to fit into the target integer type, then that value will be reduced modulo the target type's range.

The following program demonstrates some type conversions that require casts:

```
// Demonstrate casts.
class Conversion {
  public static void main(String args[]) {
    byte b;
    int i = 257;
    double d = 323.142;

    System.out.println("\nConversion of int to byte.");
    b = (byte) i;
    System.out.println("i and b " + i + " " + b);

    System.out.println("\nConversion of double to int.");
    i = (int) d;
    System.out.println("d and i " + d + " " + i);

    System.out.println("\nConversion of double to byte.");
    b = (byte) d;
    System.out.println("d and b " + d + " " + b);
  }
}
```

This program generates the following output:

```
Conversion of int to byte.
i and b 257 1

Conversion of double to int.
d and i 323.142 323

Conversion of double to byte.
d and b 323.142 67
```

Let's look at each conversion. When the value 257 is cast into a **byte** variable, the result is the remainder of the division of 257 by 256 (the range of a **byte**), which is 1 in this case. When the **d** is converted to an **int**, its fractional component is lost. When **d** is converted to a **byte**, its fractional component is lost, *and* the value is reduced modulo 256, which in this case is 67.

Automatic Type Promotion in Expressions

In addition to assignments, there is another place where certain type conversions may occur: in expressions. To see why, consider the following. In an expression, the precision required of an intermediate value will sometimes exceed the range of either operand. For example, examine the following expression:

```
byte a = 40;
byte b = 50;
byte c = 100;
int d = a * b / c;
```

The result of the intermediate term **a** * **b** easily exceeds the range of either of its **byte** operands. To handle this kind of problem, Java automatically promotes each **byte** or **short** operand to **int** when evaluating an expression. This means that the subexpression **a** * **b** is performed using integers—not bytes. Thus, 2,000, the result of the intermediate expression, **50** * **40**, is legal even though **a** and **b** are both specified as type **byte**.

As useful as the automatic promotions are, they can cause confusing compile-time errors. For example, this seemingly correct code causes a problem:

```
byte b = 50;
b = b * 2; // Error! Cannot assign an int to a byte!
```

The code is attempting to store 50 * 2, a perfectly valid **byte** value, back into a **byte** variable. However, because the operands were automatically promoted to **int** when the expression was evaluated, the result has also been promoted to **int**. Thus, the result of the expression is now of type **int**, which cannot be assigned to a **byte** without the use of a cast. This is true even if, as in this particular case, the value being assigned would still fit in the target type.

In cases where you understand the consequences of overflow, you should use an explicit cast, such as

```
byte b = 50;
b = (byte)(b * 2);
```

which yields the correct value of 100.

The Type Promotion Rules

In addition to the elevation of **byte**s and **short**s to **int**, Java defines several *type promotion rules* that apply to expressions. They are as follows. First, all **byte** and **short** values are promoted to **int**, as just described. Then, if one operand is a **long**, the whole expression is promoted to **long**. If one operand is a **float**, the entire expression is promoted to **float**. If any of the operands is **double**, the result is **double**.

The following program demonstrates how each value in the expression gets promoted to match the second argument to each binary operator:

```
class Promote {
  public static void main(String args[]) {
    byte b = 42;
    char c = 'a';
    short s = 1024;
    int i = 50000;
    float f = 5.67f;
    double d = .1234;
    double result = (f * b) + (i / c) - (d * s);
    System.out.println((f * b) + " + " + (i / c) + " - " + (d * s));
    System.out.println("result = " + result);
  }
}
```

Let's look closely at the type promotions that occur in this line from the program:

```
double result = (f * b) + (i / c) - (d * s);
```

In the first subexpression, **f** * **b**, **b** is promoted to a **float** and the result of the subexpression is **float**. Next, in the subexpression **i** / **c**, **c** is promoted to **int**, and the result is of type **int**. Then, in **d** * **s**, the value of **s** is promoted to **double**, and the type of the subexpression is **double**. Finally, these three intermediate values, **float**, **int**, and **double**, are considered. The outcome of **float** plus an **int** is a **float**. Then the resultant **float** minus the last **double** is promoted to **double**, which is the type for the final result of the expression.

Arrays

An *array* is a group of like-typed variables that are referred to by a common name. Arrays of any type can be created and may have one or more dimensions. A specific element in an array is accessed by its index. Arrays offer a convenient means of grouping related information.

If you are familiar with C/C++, be careful. Arrays in Java work differently than they do in those languages.

One-Dimensional Arrays

A *one-dimensional array* is, essentially, a list of like-typed variables. To create an array, you first must create an array variable of the desired type. The general form of a one-dimensional array declaration is

> *type var-name*[ ];

Here, *type* declares the base type of the array. The base type determines the data type of each element that comprises the array. Thus, the base type for the array determines what type of data the array will hold. For example, the following declares an array named **month_days** with the type "array of int":

```
int month_days[];
```

Although this declaration establishes the fact that **month_days** is an array variable, no array actually exists. In fact, the value of **month_days** is set to **null**, which represents an array with no value. To link **month_days** with an actual, physical array of integers, you must allocate one using **new** and assign it to **month_days**. **new** is a special operator that allocates memory.

You will look more closely at **new** in a later chapter, but you need to use it now to allocate memory for arrays. The general form of **new** as it applies to one-dimensional arrays appears as follows:

> *array-var* = new *type*[*size*];

Here, *type* specifies the type of data being allocated, *size* specifies the number of elements in the array, and *array-var* is the array variable that is linked to the array. That is, to use **new** to allocate an array, you must specify the type and number of elements to allocate. The elements in the array allocated by **new** will automatically be initialized to zero. This example allocates a 12-element array of integers and links them to **month_days**.

```
month_days = new int[12];
```

After this statement executes, **month_days** will refer to an array of 12 integers. Further, all elements in the array will be initialized to zero.

Let's review: Obtaining an array is a two-step process. First, you must declare a variable of the desired array type. Second, you must allocate the memory that will hold the array, using **new**, and assign it to the array variable. Thus, in Java all arrays are dynamically allocated. If the concept of dynamic allocation is unfamiliar to you, don't worry. It will be described at length later in this book.

Once you have allocated an array, you can access a specific element in the array by specifying its index within square brackets. All array indexes start at zero. For example, this statement assigns the value 28 to the second element of **month_days**.

```
month_days[1] = 28;
```

The next line displays the value stored at index 3.

```
System.out.println(month_days[3]);
```

Putting together all the pieces, here is a program that creates an array of the number of days in each month.

```
// Demonstrate a one-dimensional array.
class Array {
```

```
public static void main(String args[]) {
  int month_days[];
  month_days = new int[12];
  month_days[0] = 31;
  month_days[1] = 28;
  month_days[2] = 31;
  month_days[3] = 30;
  month_days[4] = 31;
  month_days[5] = 30;
  month_days[6] = 31;
  month_days[7] = 31;
  month_days[8] = 30;
  month_days[9] = 31;
  month_days[10] = 30;
  month_days[11] = 31;
  System.out.println("April has " + month_days[3] + " days.");
  }
}
```

When you run this program, it prints the number of days in April. As mentioned, Java array indexes start with zero, so the number of days in April is **month_days[3]** or 30.

It is possible to combine the declaration of the array variable with the allocation of the array itself, as shown here:

```
int month_days[] = new int[12];
```

This is the way that you will normally see it done in professionally written Java programs.

Arrays can be initialized when they are declared. The process is much the same as that used to initialize the simple types. An *array initializer* is a list of comma-separated expressions surrounded by curly braces. The commas separate the values of the array elements. The array will automatically be created large enough to hold the number of elements you specify in the array initializer. There is no need to use **new**. For example, to store the number of days in each month, the following code creates an initialized array of integers:

```
// An improved version of the previous program.
class AutoArray {
  public static void main(String args[]) {
```

```
        int month_days[] = { 31, 28, 31, 30, 31, 30, 31, 31, 30, 31,
                             30, 31 };
        System.out.println("April has " + month_days[3] + " days.");
    }
}
```

When you run this program, you see the same output as that generated by the previous version.

Java strictly checks to make sure you do not accidentally try to store or reference values outside of the range of the array. The Java run-time system will check to be sure that all array indexes are in the correct range. (In this regard, Java is fundamentally different from C/C++, which provide no run-time boundary checks.) For example, the run-time system will check the value of each index into **month_days** to make sure that it is between 0 and 11 inclusive. If you try to access elements outside the range of the array (negative numbers or numbers greater than the length of the array), you will cause a run-time error.

Here is one more example that uses a one-dimensional array. It finds the average of a set of numbers.

```
// Average an array of values.
class Average {
    public static void main(String args[]) {
        double nums[] = {10.1, 11.2, 12.3, 13.4, 14.5};
        double result = 0;
        int i;

        for(i=0; i<5; i++)
            result = result + nums[i];

        System.out.println("Average is " + result / 5);
    }
}
```

Multidimensional Arrays

In Java, *multidimensional arrays* are actually arrays of arrays. These, as you might expect, look and act like regular multidimensional arrays. However, as you will see, there are a couple of subtle differences. To declare a multidimensional array variable, specify each additional index using another set of square brackets. For example, the following declares a two-dimensional array variable called **twoD**.

```
int twoD[][] = new int[4][5];
```

This allocates a 4 by 5 array and assigns it to **twoD**. Internally this matrix is implemented as an *array* of *arrays* of **int**. Conceptually, this array will look like the one shown in Figure 3-1.

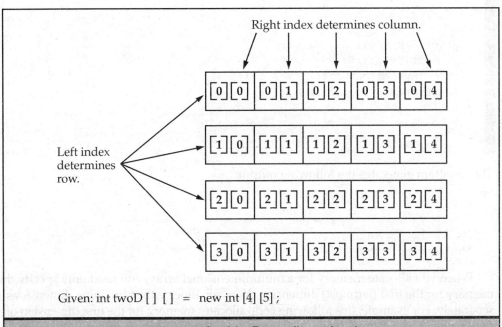

Figure 3-1. *A conceptual view of a 4 by 5, two-dimensional array*

The following program numbers each element in the array from left to right, top to bottom, and then displays these values:

```java
// Demonstrate a two-dimensional array.
class TwoDArray {
  public static void main(String args[]) {
    int twoD[][]= new int[4][5];
    int i, j, k = 0;

    for(i=0; i<4; i++)
      for(j=0; j<5; j++) {
        twoD[i][j] = k;
        k++;

    }

    for(i=0; i<4; i++) {
      for(j=0; j<5; j++)
        System.out.print(twoD[i][j] + " ");
      System.out.println();
    }
  }
}
```

This program generates the following output:

```
0  1  2  3  4
5  6  7  8  9
10 11 12 13 14
15 16 17 18 19
```

When you allocate memory for a multidimensional array, you need only specify the memory for the first (leftmost) dimension. You can allocate the remaining dimensions separately. For example, this following code allocates memory for the first dimension of **twoD** when it is declared. It allocates the second dimension manually.

```java
int twoD[][] = new int[4][];
twoD[0] = new int[5];
twoD[1] = new int[5];
twoD[2] = new int[5];
twoD[3] = new int[5];
```

While there is no advantage to individually allocating the second dimension arrays in this situation, there may be in others. For example, when you allocate dimensions manually, you do not need to allocate the same number of elements for each dimension. As stated earlier, since multidimensional arrays are actually arrays of arrays, the length of each array is under your control. For example, the following program creates a two-dimensional array in which the sizes of the second dimension are unequal.

```java
// Manually allocate differing size second dimensions.
class TwoDAgain {
  public static void main(String args[]) {
    int twoD[][] = new int[4][];
    twoD[0] = new int[1];
    twoD[1] = new int[2];
    twoD[2] = new int[3];
    twoD[3] = new int[4];

    int i, j, k = 0;

    for(i=0; i<4; i++)
      for(j=0; j<i+1; j++) {
        twoD[i][j] = k;
        k++;
      }

    for(i=0; i<4; i++) {
      for(j=0; j<i+1; j++)
        System.out.print(twoD[i][j] + " ");
      System.out.println();
    }
  }
}
```

This program generates the following output:

```
0
1 2
3 4 5
6 7 8 9
```

The array created by this program looks like this:

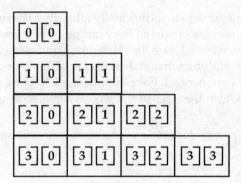

The use of uneven (or, irregular) multidimensional arrays is not recommended for most applications, because it runs contrary to what people expect to find when a multidimensional array is encountered. However, it can be used effectively in some situations. For example, if you need a very large two-dimensional array that is sparsely populated (that is, one in which not all of the elements will be used), then an irregular array might be a perfect solution.

It is possible to initialize multidimensional arrays. To do so, simply enclose each dimension's initializer within its own set of curly braces. The following program creates a matrix where each element contains the product of the row and column indexes. Also notice that you can use expressions as well as literal values inside of array initializers.

```java
// Initialize a two-dimensional array.
class Matrix {
  public static void main(String args[]) {
    double m[][] = {
      { 0*0, 1*0, 2*0, 3*0 },
      { 0*1, 1*1, 2*1, 3*1 },
      { 0*2, 1*2, 2*2, 3*2 },
      { 0*3, 1*3, 2*3, 3*3 }
    };
    int i, j;

    for(i=0; i<4; i++) {
      for(j=0; j<4; j++)
        System.out.print(m[i][j] + " ");
      System.out.println();
    }
  }
}
```

When you run this program, you will get the following output:

```
0.0  0.0  0.0  0.0
0.0  1.0  2.0  3.0
0.0  2.0  4.0  6.0
0.0  3.0  6.0  9.0
```

As you can see, each row in the array is initialized as specified in the initialization lists.

Let's look at one more example that uses a multidimensional array. The following program creates a 3 by 4 by 5, three-dimensional array. It then loads each element with the product of its indexes. Finally, it displays these products.

```java
// Demonstrate a three-dimensional array.
class threeDMatrix {
  public static void main(String args[]) {
    int threeD[][][] = new int[3][4][5];
    int i, j, k;

    for(i=0; i<3; i++)
      for(j=0; j<4; j++)
        for(k=0; k<5; k++)
          threeD[i][j][k] = i * j * k;

    for(i=0; i<3; i++) {
      for(j=0; j<4; j++) {
        for(k=0; k<5; k++)
          System.out.print(threeD[i][j][k] + " ");
        System.out.println();
      }
      System.out.println();
    }
  }
}
```

This program generates the following output:

```
0 0 0 0 0
0 0 0 0 0
0 0 0 0 0
0 0 0 0 0
```

```
0  0  0  0  0
0  1  2  3  4
0  2  4  6  8
0  3  6  9  12

0  0  0  0  0
0  2  4  6  8
0  4  8  12  16
0  6  12  18  24
```

Alternative Array Declaration Syntax

There is a second form that may be used to declare an array:

type[ ] *var-name;*

Here, the square brackets follow the type specifier, and not the name of the array variable. For example, the following two declarations are equivalent:

```
int al[] = new int[3];
int[] a2 = new int[3];
```

The following declarations are also equivalent:

```
char twod1[][] = new char[3][4];
char[][] twod2 = new char[3][4];
```

This alternative declaration form is included as a convenience, and is also useful when specifying an array as a return type for a method.

A Few Words About Strings

As you may have noticed, in the preceding discussion of data types and arrays there has been no mention of strings or a string data type. This is not because Java does not support such a type—it does. It is just that Java's string type, called **String**, is not a simple type. Nor is it simply an array of characters (as are strings in C/C++). Rather, **String** defines an object, and a full description of it requires an understanding of several object-related features. As such, it will be covered later in this book, after objects are described. However, so that you can use simple strings in example programs, the following brief introduction is in order.

The **String** type is used to declare string variables. You can also declare arrays of strings. A quoted string constant can be assigned to a **String** variable. A variable of type **String** can be assigned to another variable of type **String**. You can use an object of type **String** as an argument to **println( )**. For example, consider the following fragment:

```
String str = "this is a test";
System.out.println(str);
```

Here, **str** is an object of type **String**. It is assigned the string "this is a test". This string is displayed by the **println( )** statement.

As you will see later, **String** objects have many special features and attributes that make them quite powerful and easy to use. However, for the next few chapters, you will be using them only in their simplest form.

A Note to C/C++ Programmers About Pointers

If you are an experienced C/C++ programmer, then you know that these languages provide support for pointers. However, no mention of pointers has been made in this chapter. The reason for this is simple: Java does not support or allow pointers. (Or more properly, Java does not support pointers that can be accessed and/or modified by the programmer.) Java cannot allow pointers, because doing so would allow Java applets to breach the firewall between the Java execution environment and the host computer. (Remember, a pointer can be given any address in memory—even addresses that might be outside the Java run-time system.) Since C/C++ make extensive use of pointers, you might be thinking that their loss is a significant disadvantage to Java. However, this is not true. Java is designed in such a way that as long as you stay within the confines of the execution environment, you will never need to use a pointer, nor would there be any benefit in using one. For tips on converting C/C++ code to Java, including pointers, see Chapter 29.

A Note to C/C++ Programmers About Pointers

The
Complete
Reference

Java™ 2

Chapter 4

Operators

Java provides a rich operator environment. Most of its operators can be divided into the following four groups: arithmetic, bitwise, relational, and logical. Java also defines some additional operators that handle certain special situations. This chapter describes all of Java's operators except for the type comparison operator **instanceof**, which is examined in Chapter 12.

If you are familiar with C/C++/C#, then you will be pleased to know that most operators in Java work just like they do in those languages. However, there are some subtle differences, so a careful reading is advised.

Arithmetic Operators

Arithmetic operators are used in mathematical expressions in the same way that they are used in algebra. The following table lists the arithmetic operators:

Operator	Result
+	Addition
–	Subtraction (also unary minus)
*	Multiplication
/	Division
%	Modulus
++	Increment
+=	Addition assignment
–=	Subtraction assignment
*=	Multiplication assignment
/=	Division assignment
%=	Modulus assignment
– –	Decrement

The operands of the arithmetic operators must be of a numeric type. You cannot use them on **boolean** types, but you can use them on **char** types, since the **char** type in Java is, essentially, a subset of **int**.

The Basic Arithmetic Operators

The basic arithmetic operations—addition, subtraction, multiplication, and division—all behave as you would expect for all numeric types. The minus operator also has a unary form which negates its single operand. Remember that when the division operator is applied to an integer type, there will be no fractional component attached to the result.

The following simple example program demonstrates the arithmetic operators. It also illustrates the difference between floating-point division and integer division.

```
// Demonstrate the basic arithmetic operators.
class BasicMath {
  public static void main(String args[]) {
    // arithmetic using integers
    System.out.println("Integer Arithmetic");
    int a = 1 + 1;
    int b = a * 3;
    int c = b / 4;
    int d = c - a;
    int e = -d;
    System.out.println("a = " + a);
    System.out.println("b = " + b);
    System.out.println("c = " + c);
    System.out.println("d = " + d);
    System.out.println("e = " + e);

    // arithmetic using doubles
    System.out.println("\nFloating Point Arithmetic");
    double da = 1 + 1;
    double db = da * 3;
    double dc = db / 4;
    double dd = dc - a;
    double de = -dd;
    System.out.println("da = " + da);
    System.out.println("db = " + db);
    System.out.println("dc = " + dc);
    System.out.println("dd = " + dd);
    System.out.println("de = " + de);
  }
}
```

When you run this program, you will see the following output:

```
Integer Arithmetic
a = 2
b = 6
c = 1
```

```
d = -1
e = 1

Floating Point Arithmetic
da = 2.0
db = 6.0
dc = 1.5
dd = -0.5
de = 0.5
```

The Modulus Operator

The modulus operator, %, returns the remainder of a division operation. It can be applied to floating-point types as well as integer types. (This differs from C/C++, in which the % can only be applied to integer types.) The following example program demonstrates the %:

```
// Demonstrate the % operator.
class Modulus {
  public static void main(String args[]) {
    int x = 42;
    double y = 42.25;

    System.out.println("x mod 10 = " + x % 10);
    System.out.println("y mod 10 = " + y % 10);
  }
}
```

When you run this program you will get the following output:

```
x mod 10 = 2
y mod 10 = 2.25
```

Arithmetic Assignment Operators

Java provides special operators that can be used to combine an arithmetic operation with an assignment. As you probably know, statements like the following are quite common in programming:

```
a = a + 4;
```

In Java, you can rewrite this statement as shown here:

```
a += 4;
```

This version uses the **+=** assignment operator. Both statements perform the same action: they increase the value of **a** by 4.

Here is another example,

```
a = a % 2;
```

which can be expressed as

```
a %= 2;
```

In this case, the **%=** obtains the remainder of **a**/2 and puts that result back into **a**.

There are assignment operators for all of the arithmetic, binary operators. Thus, any statement of the form

   var = var op expression;

can be rewritten as

   var op= expression;

The assignment operators provide two benefits. First, they save you a bit of typing, because they are "shorthand" for their equivalent long forms. Second, they are implemented more efficiently by the Java run-time system than are their equivalent long forms. For these reasons, you will often see the assignment operators used in professionally written Java programs.

Here is a sample program that shows several *op=* operator assignments in action:

```
// Demonstrate several assignment operators.
class OpEquals {
  public static void main(String args[]) {
    int a = 1;
    int b = 2;
    int c = 3;

    a += 5;
    b *= 4;
```

```
    c += a * b;
    c %= 6;
    System.out.println("a = " + a);
    System.out.println("b = " + b);
    System.out.println("c = " + c);
  }
}
```

The output of this program is shown here:

```
a = 6
b = 8
c = 3
```

Increment and Decrement

The ++ and the – – are Java's increment and decrement operators. They were introduced in Chapter 2. Here they will be discussed in detail. As you will see, they have some special properties that make them quite interesting. Let's begin by reviewing precisely what the increment and decrement operators do.

The increment operator increases its operand by one. The decrement operator decreases its operand by one. For example, this statement:

```
x = x + 1;
```

can be rewritten like this by use of the increment operator:

```
x++;
```

Similarly, this statement:

```
x = x - 1;
```

is equivalent to

```
x--;
```

These operators are unique in that they can appear both in *postfix* form, where they follow the operand as just shown, and *prefix* form, where they precede the operand. In the foregoing examples, there is no difference between the prefix and postfix forms. However, when the increment and/or decrement operators are part of a larger expression, then a subtle, yet powerful, difference between these two forms appears. In the prefix form, the operand is incremented or decremented before the value is obtained for use in the expression. In postfix form, the previous value is obtained for use in the expression, and then the operand is modified. For example:

```
x = 42;
y = ++x;
```

In this case, **y** is set to 43 as you would expect, because the increment occurs *before* **x** is assigned to **y**. Thus, the line **y = ++x;** is the equivalent of these two statements:

```
x = x + 1;
y = x;
```

However, when written like this,

```
x = 42;
y = x++;
```

the value of **x** is obtained before the increment operator is executed, so the value of **y** is 42. Of course, in both cases **x** is set to 43. Here, the line **y = x++;** is the equivalent of these two statements:

```
y = x;
x = x + 1;
```

The following program demonstrates the increment operator.

```
// Demonstrate ++.
class IncDec {
  public static void main(String args[]) {
    int a = 1;
    int b = 2;
    int c;
```

```
      int d;
      c = ++b;
      d = a++;
      c++;
      System.out.println("a = " + a);
      System.out.println("b = " + b);
      System.out.println("c = " + c);
      System.out.println("d = " + d);
    }
}
```

The output of this program follows:

```
a = 2
b = 3
c = 4
d = 1
```

The Bitwise Operators

Java defines several *bitwise operators* which can be applied to the integer types, **long**, **int**, **short**, **char**, and **byte**. These operators act upon the individual bits of their operands. They are summarized in the following table:

Operator	Result
~	Bitwise unary NOT
&	Bitwise AND
|	Bitwise OR
^	Bitwise exclusive OR
>>	Shift right
>>>	Shift right zero fill
<<	Shift left
&=	Bitwise AND assignment
|=	Bitwise OR assignment

Operator	Result
^=	Bitwise exclusive OR assignment
>>=	Shift right assignment
>>>=	Shift right zero fill assignment
<<=	Shift left assignment

Since the bitwise operators manipulate the bits within an integer, it is important to understand what effects such manipulations may have on a value. Specifically, it is useful to know how Java stores integer values and how it represents negative numbers. So, before continuing, let's briefly review these two topics.

All of the integer types are represented by binary numbers of varying bit widths. For example, the **byte** value for 42 in binary is 00101010, where each position represents a power of two, starting with 2^0 at the rightmost bit. The next bit position to the left would be 2^1, or 2, continuing toward the left with 2^2, or 4, then 8, 16, 32, and so on. So 42 has 1 bits set at positions 1, 3, and 5 (counting from 0 at the right); thus 42 is the sum of $2^1 + 2^3 + 2^5$, which is 2 + 8 + 32.

All of the integer types (except **char**) are signed integers. This means that they can represent negative values as well as positive ones. Java uses an encoding known as *two's complement,* which means that negative numbers are represented by inverting (changing 1's to 0's and vice versa) all of the bits in a value, then adding 1 to the result. For example, –42 is represented by inverting all of the bits in 42, or 00101010, which yields 11010101, then adding 1, which results in 11010110, or –42. To decode a negative number, first invert all of the bits, then add 1. –42, or 11010110 inverted yields 00101001, or 41, so when you add 1 you get 42.

The reason Java (and most other computer languages) uses two's complement is easy to see when you consider the issue of *zero crossing*. Assuming a **byte** value, zero is represented by 00000000. In one's complement, simply inverting all of the bits creates 11111111, which creates negative zero. The trouble is that negative zero is invalid in integer math. This problem is solved by using two's complement to represent negative values. When using two's complement, 1 is added to the complement, producing 100000000. This produces a 1 bit too far to the left to fit back into the **byte** value, resulting in the desired behavior, where –0 is the same as 0, and 11111111 is the encoding for –1. Although we used a **byte** value in the preceding example, the same basic principle applies to all of Java's integer types.

Because Java uses two's complement to store negative numbers—and because all integers are signed values in Java—applying the bitwise operators can easily produce unexpected results. For example, turning on the high-order bit will cause the resulting value to be interpreted as a negative number, whether this is what you intended or not. To avoid unpleasant surprises, just remember that the high-order bit determines the sign of an integer no matter how that high-order bit gets set.

The Bitwise Logical Operators

The bitwise logical operators are &, |, ^, and ~. The following table shows the outcome of each operation. In the discussion that follows, keep in mind that the bitwise operators are applied to each individual bit within each operand.

A	B	A | B	A & B	A ^ B	~A
0	0	0	0	0	1
1	0	1	0	1	0
0	1	1	0	1	1
1	1	1	1	0	0

The Bitwise NOT

Also called the *bitwise complement,* the unary NOT operator, ~, inverts all of the bits of its operand. For example, the number 42, which has the following bit pattern:

    00101010

becomes

    11010101

after the NOT operator is applied.

The Bitwise AND

The AND operator, &, produces a 1 bit if both operands are also 1. A zero is produced in all other cases. Here is an example:

```
  00101010    42
&00001111    15
-------------
  00001010    10
```

The Bitwise OR

The OR operator, |, combines bits such that if either of the bits in the operands is a 1, then the resultant bit is a 1, as shown here:

```
  00101010    42
| 00001111    15
-------------
  00101111    47
```

The Bitwise XOR

The XOR operator, ^, combines bits such that if exactly one operand is 1, then the result is 1. Otherwise, the result is zero. The following example shows the effect of the ^. This example also demonstrates a useful attribute of the XOR operation. Notice how the bit pattern of 42 is inverted wherever the second operand has a 1 bit. Wherever the second operand has a 0 bit, the first operand is unchanged. You will find this property useful when performing some types of bit manipulations.

```
  00101010    42
^ 00001111    15
-------------
  00100101    37
```

Using the Bitwise Logical Operators

The following program demonstrates the bitwise logical operators:

```java
// Demonstrate the bitwise logical operators.
class BitLogic {
  public static void main(String args[]) {
    String binary[] = {
      "0000", "0001", "0010", "0011", "0100", "0101", "0110", "0111",
      "1000", "1001", "1010", "1011", "1100", "1101", "1110", "1111"
    };
    int a = 3; // 0 + 2 + 1 or 0011 in binary
    int b = 6; // 4 + 2 + 0 or 0110 in binary
    int c = a | b;
    int d = a & b;
    int e = a ^ b;
    int f = (~a & b) | (a & ~b);
    int g = ~a & 0x0f;

    System.out.println("        a = " + binary[a]);
    System.out.println("        b = " + binary[b]);
    System.out.println("      a|b = " + binary[c]);
    System.out.println("      a&b = " + binary[d]);
    System.out.println("      a^b = " + binary[e]);
    System.out.println("~a&b|a&~b = " + binary[f]);
    System.out.println("       ~a = " + binary[g]);
  }
}
```

In this example, **a** and **b** have bit patterns which present all four possibilities for two binary digits: 0-0, 0-1, 1-0, and 1-1. You can see how the | and & operate on each bit by the results in **c** and **d**. The values assigned to **e** and **f** are the same and illustrate how the ^ works. The string array named **binary** holds the human-readable, binary representation of the numbers 0 through 15. In this example, the array is indexed to show the binary representation of each result. The array is constructed such that the correct string representation of a binary value **n** is stored in **binary[n]**. The value of **~a** is ANDed with **0x0f** (0000 1111 in binary) in order to reduce its value to less than 16, so it can be printed by use of the **binary** array. Here is the output from this program:

```
        a = 0011
        b = 0110
      a|b = 0111
      a&b = 0010
      a^b = 0101
~a&b|a&~b = 0101
       ~a = 1100
```

The Left Shift

The left shift operator, <<, shifts all of the bits in a value to the left a specified number of times. It has this general form:

value << num

Here, *num* specifies the number of positions to left-shift the value in *value*. That is, the << moves all of the bits in the specified value to the left by the number of bit positions specified by *num*. For each shift left, the high-order bit is shifted out (and lost), and a zero is brought in on the right. This means that when a left shift is applied to an **int** operand, bits are lost once they are shifted past bit position 31. If the operand is a **long**, then bits are lost after bit position 63.

Java's automatic type promotions produce unexpected results when you are shifting **byte** and **short** values. As you know, **byte** and **short** values are promoted to **int** when an expression is evaluated. Furthermore, the result of such an expression is also an **int**. This means that the outcome of a left shift on a **byte** or **short** value will be an **int**, and the bits shifted left will not be lost until they shift past bit position 31. Furthermore, a negative **byte** or **short** value will be sign-extended when it is promoted to **int**. Thus, the high-order bits will be filled with 1's. For these reasons, to perform a left shift on a **byte** or **short** implies that you must discard the high-order bytes of the **int** result. For example, if you left-shift a **byte** value, that value will first be promoted to **int** and then shifted. This means that you must discard the top three bytes of the result if what you want is the result of a shifted **byte** value. The easiest way to do this is to simply cast the result back into a **byte**. The following program demonstrates this concept:

```
// Left shifting a byte value.
class ByteShift {
  public static void main(String args[]) {
    byte a = 64, b;
    int i;

    i = a << 2;
    b = (byte) (a << 2);

    System.out.println("Original value of a: " + a);
    System.out.println("i and b: " + i + " " + b);
  }
}
```

The output generated by this program is shown here:

```
Original value of a: 64
i and b: 256 0
```

Since **a** is promoted to **int** for the purposes of evaluation, left-shifting the value 64 (0100 0000) twice results in **i** containing the value 256 (1 0000 0000). However, the value in **b** contains 0 because after the shift, the low-order byte is now zero. Its only 1 bit has been shifted out.

Since each left shift has the effect of doubling the original value, programmers frequently use this fact as an efficient alternative to multiplying by 2. But you need to watch out. If you shift a 1 bit into the high-order position (bit 31 or 63), the value will become negative. The following program illustrates this point:

```
// Left shifting as a quick way to multiply by 2.
class MultByTwo {
  public static void main(String args[]) {
    int i;
    int num = 0xFFFFFFE;

    for(i=0; i<4; i++) {
      num = num << 1;
      System.out.println(num);
    }
  }
}
```

The program generates the following output:

```
536870908
1073741816
2147483632
-32
```

The starting value was carefully chosen so that after being shifted left 4 bit positions, it would produce –32. As you can see, when a 1 bit is shifted into bit 31, the number is interpreted as negative.

The Right Shift

The right shift operator, >>, shifts all of the bits in a value to the right a specified number of times. Its general form is shown here:

value >> *num*

Here, *num* specifies the number of positions to right-shift the value in *value*. That is, the >> moves all of the bits in the specified value to the right the number of bit positions specified by *num*.

The following code fragment shifts the value 32 to the right by two positions, resulting in **a** being set to 8:

```
int a = 32;
a = a >> 2; // a now contains 8
```

When a value has bits that are "shifted off," those bits are lost. For example, the next code fragment shifts the value 35 to the right two positions, which causes the two low-order bits to be lost, resulting again in **a** being set to 8.

```
int a = 35;
a = a >> 2; // a still contains 8
```

Looking at the same operation in binary shows more clearly how this happens:

```
00100011    35
>> 2
00001000     8
```

Each time you shift a value to the right, it divides that value by two—and discards any remainder. You can take advantage of this for high-performance integer division by 2. Of course, you must be sure that you are not shifting any bits off the right end.

When you are shifting right, the top (leftmost) bits exposed by the right shift are filled in with the previous contents of the top bit. This is called *sign extension* and serves to preserve the sign of negative numbers when you shift them right. For example, –8 >> 1 is –4, which, in binary, is

```
11111000    -8
>>1
11111100    -4
```

It is interesting to note that if you shift –1 right, the result always remains –1, since sign extension keeps bringing in more ones in the high-order bits.

Sometimes it is not desirable to sign-extend values when you are shifting them to the right. For example, the following program converts a **byte** value to its hexadecimal string representation. Notice that the shifted value is masked by ANDing it with **0x0f** to discard any sign-extended bits so that the value can be used as an index into the array of hexadecimal characters.

```
// Masking sign extension.
class HexByte {
  static public void main(String args[]) {
    char hex[] = {
      '0', '1', '2', '3', '4', '5', '6', '7',
      '8', '9', 'a', 'b', 'c', 'd', 'e', 'f'
    };
    byte b = (byte) 0xf1;

    System.out.println("b = 0x" + hex[(b >> 4) & 0x0f] + hex[b & 0x0f]);
  }
}
```

Here is the output of this program:

```
b = 0xf1
```

The Unsigned Right Shift

As you have just seen, the >> operator automatically fills the high-order bit with its previous contents each time a shift occurs. This preserves the sign of the value. However, sometimes this is undesirable. For example, if you are shifting something that does not represent a numeric value, you may not want sign extension to take place. This situation is common when you are working with pixel-based values and graphics. In these cases you will generally want to shift a zero into the high-order bit no matter what its initial value was. This is known as an *unsigned shift*. To accomplish this, you will use Java's unsigned, shift-right operator, >>>, which always shifts zeros into the high-order bit.

The following code fragment demonstrates the >>>. Here, **a** is set to –1, which sets all 32 bits to 1 in binary. This value is then shifted right 24 bits, filling the top 24 bits with zeros, ignoring normal sign extension. This sets **a** to 255.

```
int a = -1;
a = a >>> 24;
```

Here is the same operation in binary form to further illustrate what is happening:

```
11111111 11111111 11111111 11111111    –1  in binary as an int
>>>24
00000000 00000000 00000000 11111111    255  in binary as an int
```

The >>> operator is often not as useful as you might like, since it is only meaningful for 32- and 64-bit values. Remember, smaller values are automatically promoted to **int** in expressions. This means that sign-extension occurs and that the shift will take place on a 32-bit rather than on an 8- or 16-bit value. That is, one might expect an unsigned right shift on a **byte** value to zero-fill beginning at bit 7. But this is not the case, since it is a 32-bit value that is actually being shifted. The following program demonstrates this effect:

```
// Unsigned shifting a byte value.
class ByteUShift {
  static public void main(String args[]) {
    char hex[] = {
       '0', '1', '2', '3', '4', '5', '6', '7',
       '8', '9', 'a', 'b', 'c', 'd', 'e', 'f'
    };
    byte b = (byte) 0xf1;
    byte c = (byte) (b >> 4);
    byte d = (byte) (b >>> 4);
    byte e = (byte) ((b & 0xff) >> 4);
```

```
        System.out.println("                b = 0x"
          + hex[(b >> 4) & 0x0f] + hex[b & 0x0f]);
        System.out.println("            b >> 4 = 0x"
          + hex[(c >> 4) & 0x0f] + hex[c & 0x0f]);
        System.out.println("           b >>> 4 = 0x"
          + hex[(d >> 4) & 0x0f] + hex[d & 0x0f]);
        System.out.println("(b & 0xff) >> 4 = 0x"
          + hex[(e >> 4) & 0x0f] + hex[e & 0x0f]);
    }
}
```

The following output of this program shows how the **>>>** operator appears to do nothing when dealing with bytes. The variable **b** is set to an arbitrary negative **byte** value for this demonstration. Then **c** is assigned the **byte** value of **b** shifted right by four, which is 0xff because of the expected sign extension. Then **d** is assigned the **byte** value of **b** unsigned shifted right by four, which you might have expected to be 0x0f, but is actually 0xff because of the sign extension that happened when **b** was promoted to **int** before the shift. The last expression sets **e** to the **byte** value of **b** masked to 8 bits using the AND operator, then shifted right by four, which produces the expected value of 0x0f. Notice that the unsigned shift right operator was not used for **d**, since the state of the sign bit after the AND was known.

```
                b = 0xf1
           b >> 4 = 0xff
          b >>> 4 = 0xff
   (b & 0xff) >> 4 = 0x0f
```

Bitwise Operator Assignments

All of the binary bitwise operators have a shorthand form similar to that of the algebraic operators, which combines the assignment with the bitwise operation. For example, the following two statements, which shift the value in **a** right by four bits, are equivalent:

```
a = a >> 4;
a >>= 4;
```

Likewise, the following two statements, which result in **a** being assigned the bitwise expression **a** OR **b**, are equivalent:

```
a = a | b;
a |= b;
```

The following program creates a few integer variables and then uses the shorthand form of bitwise operator assignments to manipulate the variables:

```
class OpBitEquals {
  public static void main(String args[]) {
    int a = 1;
    int b = 2;
    int c = 3;

    a |= 4;
    b >>= 1;
    c <<= 1;
    a ^= c;
    System.out.println("a = " + a);
    System.out.println("b = " + b);
    System.out.println("c = " + c);
  }
}
```

The output of this program is shown here:

```
a = 3
b = 1
c = 6
```

Relational Operators

The *relational operators* determine the relationship that one operand has to the other. Specifically, they determine equality and ordering. The relational operators are shown here:

Operator	Result
==	Equal to
!=	Not equal to
>	Greater thar

Operator	Result
<	Less than
>=	Greater than or equal to
<=	Less than or equal to

The outcome of these operations is a **boolean** value. The relational operators are most frequently used in the expressions that control the **if** statement and the various loop statements.

Any type in Java, including integers, floating-point numbers, characters, and Booleans can be compared using the equality test, **==**, and the inequality test, **!=**. Notice that in Java (as in C/C++/C#) equality is denoted with two equal signs, not one. (Remember: a single equal sign is the assignment operator.) Only numeric types can be compared using the ordering operators. That is, only integer, floating-point, and character operands may be compared to see which is greater or less than the other.

As stated, the result produced by a relational operator is a **boolean** value. For example, the following code fragment is perfectly valid:

```
int a = 4;
int b = 1;
boolean c = a < b;
```

In this case, the result of **a<b** (which is **false**) is stored in **c**.

If you are coming from a C/C++ background, please note the following. In C/C++, these types of statements are very common:

```
int done;
// ...
if(!done) ... // Valid in C/C++
if(done) ...   // but not in Java.
```

In Java, these statements must be written like this:

```
if(done == 0)) ... // This is Java-style.
if(done != 0) ...
```

The reason is that Java does not define true and false in the same way as C/C++. In C/C++, true is any nonzero value and false is zero. In Java, **true** and **false** are nonnumeric values which do not relate to zero or nonzero. Therefore, to test for zero or nonzero, you must explicitly employ one or more of the relational operators.

Boolean Logical Operators

The Boolean logical operators shown here operate only on **boolean** operands. All of the binary logical operators combine two **boolean** values to form a resultant **boolean** value.

Operator	Result
&	Logical AND
|	Logical OR
^	Logical XOR (exclusive OR)
||	Short-circuit OR
&&	Short-circuit AND
!	Logical unary NOT
&=	AND assignment
|=	OR assignment
^=	XOR assignment
==	Equal to
!=	Not equal to
?:	Ternary if-then-else

The logical Boolean operators, &, |, and ^, operate on **boolean** values in the same way that they operate on the bits of an integer. The logical ! operator inverts the Boolean state: **!true == false** and **!false == true**. The following table shows the effect of each logical operation:

A	B	A | B	A & B	A ^ B	!A
False	False	False	False	False	True
True	False	True	False	True	False
False	True	True	False	True	True
True	True	True	True	False	False

Here is a program that is almost the same as the **BitLogic** example shown earlier, but it operates on **boolean** logical values instead of binary bits:

```
// Demonstrate the boolean logical operators.
class BoolLogic {
  public static void main(String args[]) {
    boolean a = true;
    boolean b = false;
    boolean c = a | b;
    boolean d = a & b;
    boolean e = a ^ b;
    boolean f = (!a & b) | (a & !b);
    boolean g = !a;
    System.out.println("        a = " + a);
    System.out.println("        b = " + b);
    System.out.println("      a|b = " + c);
    System.out.println("      a&b = " + d);
    System.out.println("      a^b = " + e);
    System.out.println("!a&b|a&!b = " + f);
    System.out.println("       !a = " + g);
  }
}
```

After running this program, you will see that the same logical rules apply to
boolean values as they did to bits. As you can see from the following output, the
string representation of a Java **boolean** value is one of the literal values **true** or **false**:

```
        a = true
        b = false
      a|b = true
      a&b = false
      a^b = true
a&b|a&!b = true
       !a = false
```

Short-Circuit Logical Operators

Java provides two interesting Boolean operators not found in many other computer
languages. These are secondary versions of the Boolean AND and OR operators, and
are known as *short-circuit* logical operators. As you can see from the preceding table,
the OR operator results in **true** when **A** is **true**, no matter what **B** is. Similarly, the AND

operator results in **false** when **A** is **false**, no matter what **B** is. If you use the | | and && forms, rather than the | and & forms of these operators, Java will not bother to evaluate the right-hand operand when the outcome of the expression can be determined by the left operand alone. This is very useful when the right-hand operand depends on the left one being **true** or **false** in order to function properly. For example, the following code fragment shows how you can take advantage of short-circuit logical evaluation to be sure that a division operation will be valid before evaluating it:

```
if (denom != 0 && num / denom > 10)
```

Since the short-circuit form of AND (**&&**) is used, there is no risk of causing a run-time exception when **denom** is zero. If this line of code were written using the single & version of AND, both sides would have to be evaluated, causing a run-time exception when **denom** is zero.

It is standard practice to use the short-circuit forms of AND and OR in cases involving Boolean logic, leaving the single-character versions exclusively for bitwise operations. However, there are exceptions to this rule. For example, consider the following statement:

```
if(c==1 & e++ < 100) d = 100;
```

Here, using a single & ensures that the increment operation will be applied to **e** whether **c** is equal to 1 or not.

The Assignment Operator

You have been using the assignment operator since Chapter 2. Now it is time to take a formal look at it. The *assignment operator* is the single equal sign, **=**. The assignment operator works in Java much as it does in any other computer language. It has this general form:

var = expression;

Here, the type of *var* must be compatible with the type of *expression*.

The assignment operator does have one interesting attribute that you may not be familiar with: it allows you to create a chain of assignments. For example, consider this fragment:

```
int x, y, z;

x = y = z = 100; // set x, y, and z to 100
```

This fragment sets the variables **x**, **y**, and **z** to 100 using a single statement. This works because the = is an operator that yields the value of the right-hand expression. Thus, the value of **z = 100** is 100, which is then assigned to **y**, which in turn is assigned to **x**. Using a "chain of assignment" is an easy way to set a group of variables to a common value.

The ? Operator

Java includes a special *ternary* (three-way) *operator* that can replace certain types of if-then-else statements. This operator is the **?**, and it works in Java much like it does in C, C++, and C#. It can seem somewhat confusing at first, but the **?** can be used very effectively once mastered. The **?** has this general form:

expression1 **?** *expression2* : *expression3*

Here, *expression1* can be any expression that evaluates to a **boolean** value. If *expression1* is **true**, then *expression2* is evaluated; otherwise, *expression3* is evaluated. The result of the **?** operation is that of the expression evaluated. Both *expression2* and *expression3* are required to return the same type, which can't be **void**.

Here is an example of the way that the **?** is employed:

```
ratio = denom == 0 ? 0 : num / denom;
```

When Java evaluates this assignment expression, it first looks at the expression to the *left* of the question mark. If **denom** equals zero, then the expression *between* the question mark and the colon is evaluated and used as the value of the entire **?** expression. If **denom** does not equal zero, then the expression *after* the colon is evaluated and used for the value of the entire **?** expression. The result produced by the **?** operator is then assigned to **ratio**.

Here is a program that demonstrates the **?** operator. It uses it to obtain the absolute value of a variable.

```
// Demonstrate ?.
class Ternary {
  public static void main(String args[]) {
```

```
    int i, k;

    i = 10;
    k = i < 0 ? -i : i; // get absolute value of i
    System.out.print("Absolute value of ");
    System.out.println(i + " is " + k);

    i = -10;
    k = i < 0 ? -i : i; // get absolute value of i
    System.out.print("Absolute value of ");
    System.out.println(i + " is " + k);
  }
}
```

The output generated by the program is shown here:

```
Absolute value of 10 is 10
Absolute value of -10 is 10
```

Operator Precedence

Table 4-1 shows the order of precedence for Java operators, from highest to lowest. Notice that the first row shows items that you may not normally think of as operators: parentheses, square brackets, and the dot operator. Parentheses are used to alter the precedence of an operation. As you know from the previous chapter, the square brackets provide array indexing. The dot operator is used to dereference objects and will be discussed later in this book.

Using Parentheses

Parentheses raise the precedence of the operations that are inside them. This is often necessary to obtain the result you desire. For example, consider the following expression:

```
a >> b + 3
```

THE JAVA LANGUAGE

Highest			
( )	[ ]	.	
++	– –	~	!
*	/	%	
+	–		
>>	>>>	<<	
>	>=	<	<=
==	!=		
&			
^			
|			
&&			
||			
?:			
=	op=		
Lowest			

Table 4-1.   *The Precedence of the Java Operators*

This expression first adds 3 to **b** and then shifts **a** right by that result. That is, this expression can be rewritten using redundant parentheses like this:

```
a >> (b + 3)
```

However, if you want to first shift **a** right by **b** positions and then add 3 to that result, you will need to parenthesize the expression like this:

```
(a >> b) + 3
```

In addition to altering the normal precedence of an operator, parentheses can sometimes be used to help clarify the meaning of an expression. For anyone reading your code, a complicated expression can be difficult to understand. Adding redundant but clarifying parentheses to complex expressions can help prevent confusion later. For example, which of the following expressions is easier to read?

```
a | 4 + c >> b & 7
(a | (((4 + c) >> b) & 7))
```

One other point: parentheses (redundant or not) do not degrade the performance of your program. Therefore, adding parentheses to reduce ambiguity does not negatively affect your program.

Chapter 5

Control Statements

programming language uses *control* statements to cause the flow of execution to advance and branch based on changes to the state of a program. Java's program control statements can be put into the following categories: selection, iteration, and jump. *Selection* statements allow your program to choose different paths of execution based upon the outcome of an expression or the state of a variable. *Iteration* statements enable program execution to repeat one or more statements (that is, iteration statements form loops). *Jump* statements allow your program to execute in a nonlinear fashion. All of Java's control statements are examined here.

Note   *If you know C/C++/C#, then Java's control statements will be familiar territory. In fact, Java's control statements are nearly identical to those in those languages. However, there are a few differences—especially in the **break** and **continue** statements.*

Java's Selection Statements

Java supports two selection statements: **if** and **switch**. These statements allow you to control the flow of your program's execution based upon conditions known only during run time. You will be pleasantly surprised by the power and flexibility contained in these two statements.

The **if** statement was introduced in Chapter 2. It is examined in detail here. The **if** statement is Java's conditional branch statement. It can be used to route program execution through two different paths. Here is the general form of the **if** statement:

if (*condition*) *statement1*;
else *statement2*;

Here, each *statement* may be a single statement or a compound statement enclosed in curly braces (that is, a *block*). The *condition* is any expression that returns a **boolean** value. The **else** clause is optional.

The **if** works like this: If the *condition* is true, then *statement1* is executed. Otherwise, *statement2* (if it exists) is executed. In no case will both statements be executed. For example, consider the following:

```
int a, b;
// ...
if(a < b) a = 0;
else b = 0;
```

Here, if **a** is less than **b**, then **a** is set to zero. Otherwise, **b** is set to zero. In no case are they both set to zero.

Most often, the expression used to control the **if** will involve the relational operators. However, this is not technically necessary. It is possible to control the **if** using a single **boolean** variable, as shown in this code fragment:

```
boolean dataAvailable;
// ...
if (dataAvailable)
  ProcessData();
else
  waitForMoreData();
```

Remember, only one statement can appear directly after the **if** or the **else**. If you want to include more statements, you'll need to create a block, as in this fragment:

```
int bytesAvailable;
// ...
if (bytesAvailable > 0) {
  ProcessData();
  bytesAvailable -= n;
} else
  waitForMoreData();
```

Here, both statements within the **if** block will execute if **bytesAvailable** is greater than zero.

Some programmers find it convenient to include the curly braces when using the **if**, even when there is only one statement in each clause. This makes it easy to add another statement at a later date, and you don't have to worry about forgetting the braces. In fact, forgetting to define a block when one is needed is a common cause of errors. For example, consider the following code fragment:

```
int bytesAvailable;
// ...
if (bytesAvailable > 0) {
  ProcessData();
  bytesAvailable -= n;
} else
  waitForMoreData();
  bytesAvailable = n;
```

It seems clear that the statement **bytesAvailable = n;** was intended to be executed inside the **else** clause, because of the indentation level. However, as you recall, whitespace is insignificant to Java, and there is no way for the compiler to know what was intended. This code will compile without complaint, but it will behave incorrectly when run. The preceding example is fixed in the code that follows:

```
int bytesAvailable;
// ...
if (bytesAvailable > 0) {
  ProcessData();
  bytesAvailable -= n;
} else {
  waitForMoreData();
  bytesAvailable = n;
}
```

Nested ifs

A *nested* **if** is an **if** statement that is the target of another **if** or **else**. Nested **ifs** are very common in programming. When you nest **ifs**, the main thing to remember is that an **else** statement always refers to the nearest **if** statement that is within the same block as the **else** and that is not already associated with an **else**. Here is an example:

```
if(i == 10) {
  if(j < 20) a = b;
  if(k > 100) c = d; // this if is
  else a = c;        // associated with this else
}
else a = d;          // this else refers to if(i == 10)
```

As the comments indicate, the final **else** is not associated with **if(j<20)**, because it is not in the same block (even though it is the nearest **if** without an **else**). Rather, the final **else** is associated with **if(i==10)**. The inner **else** refers to **if(k>100)**, because it is the closest **if** within the same block.

The if-else-if Ladder

A common programming construct that is based upon a sequence of nested **ifs** is the *if-else-if ladder*. It looks like this:

if(condition)
  statement;
else if(condition)

```
  statement;
else if(condition)
  statement;
    .
    .
    .
else
  statement;
```

The **if** statements are executed from the top down. As soon as one of the conditions controlling the **if** is **true**, the statement associated with that **if** is executed, and the rest of the ladder is bypassed. If none of the conditions is true, then the final **else** statement will be executed. The final **else** acts as a default condition; that is, if all other conditional tests fail, then the last **else** statement is performed. If there is no final **else** and all other conditions are **false**, then no action will take place.

Here is a program that uses an **if-else-if** ladder to determine which season a particular month is in.

```java
// Demonstrate if-else-if statements.
class IfElse {
  public static void main(String args[]) {
    int month = 4; // April
    String season;

    if(month == 12 || month == 1 || month == 2)
      season = "Winter";
    else if(month == 3 || month == 4 || month == 5)
      season = "Spring";
    else if(month == 6 || month == 7 || month == 8)
      season = "Summer";
    else if(month == 9 || month == 10 || month == 11)
      season = "Autumn";
    else
      season = "Bogus Month";

    System.out.println("April is in the " + season + ".");
  }
}
```

Here is the output produced by the program:

```
April is in the Spring.
```

You might want to experiment with this program before moving on. As you will find, no matter what value you give **month**, one and only one assignment statement within the ladder will be executed.

switch

The **switch** statement is Java's multiway branch statement. It provides an easy way to dispatch execution to different parts of your code based on the value of an expression. As such, it often provides a better alternative than a large series of **if-else-if** statements. Here is the general form of a **switch** statement:

```
switch (expression) {
  case value1:
    // statement sequence
    break;
  case value2:
    // statement sequence
    break;
    .
    .
    .
  case valueN:
    // statement sequence
    break;
  default:
    // default statement sequence
}
```

The *expression* must be of type **byte**, **short**, **int**, or **char**; each of the *values* specified in the **case** statements must be of a type compatible with the expression. Each **case** value must be a unique literal (that is, it must be a constant, not a variable). Duplicate **case** values are not allowed.

The **switch** statement works like this: The value of the expression is compared with each of the literal values in the **case** statements. If a match is found, the code sequence following that **case** statement is executed. If none of the constants matches the value of the expression, then the **default** statement is executed. However, the **default** statement is optional. If no **case** matches and no **default** is present, then no further action is taken.

The **break** statement is used inside the **switch** to terminate a statement sequence. When a **break** statement is encountered, execution branches to the first line of code that follows the entire **switch** statement. This has the effect of "jumping out" of the **switch**.

Here is a simple example that uses a **switch** statement:

```
// A simple example of the switch.
class SampleSwitch {
  public static void main(String args[]) {
    for(int i=0; i<6; i++)
      switch(i) {
        case 0:
          System.out.println("i is zero.");
          break;
        case 1:
          System.out.println("i is one.");
          break;
        case 2:
          System.out.println("i is two.");
          break;
        case 3:
          System.out.println("i is three.");
          break;
        default:
          System.out.println("i is greater than 3.");
      }
  }
}
```

The output produced by this program is shown here:

```
i is zero.
i is one.
i is two.
i is three.
i is greater than 3.
i is greater than 3.
```

As you can see, each time through the loop, the statements associated with the **case** constant that matches **i** are executed. All others are bypassed. After **i** is greater than 3, no **case** statements match, so the **default** statement is executed.

The **break** statement is optional. If you omit the **break**, execution will continue on into the next **case**. It is sometimes desirable to have multiple **cases** without **break** statements between them. For example, consider the following program:

```
// In a switch, break statements are optional.
class MissingBreak {
```

```java
public static void main(String args[]) {
  for(int i=0; i<12; i++)
    switch(i) {
      case 0:
      case 1:
      case 2:
      case 3:
      case 4:
        System.out.println("i is less than 5");
        break;
      case 5:
      case 6:
      case 7:
      case 8:
      case 9:
        System.out.println("i is less than 10");
        break;
      default:
        System.out.println("i is 10 or more");
    }
  }
}
```

This program generates the following output:

```
i is less than 5
i is less than 5
i is less than 5
i is less than 5
i is less than 5
i is less than 10
i is less than 10
i is less than 10
i is less than 10
i is less than 10
i is 10 or more
i is 10 or more
```

As you can see, execution falls through each **case** until a **break** statement (or the end of the **switch**) is reached.

While the preceding example is, of course, contrived for the sake of illustration, omitting the **break** statement has many practical applications in real programs. To sample its more realistic usage, consider the following rewrite of the season example shown earlier. This version uses a **switch** to provide a more efficient implementation.

```java
// An improved version of the season program.
class Switch {
    public static void main(String args[]) {
        int month = 4;
        String season;
        switch (month) {
          case 12:
          case 1:
          case 2:
            season = "Winter";
            break;
          case 3:
          case 4:
          case 5:
            season = "Spring";
            break;
          case 6:
          case 7:
          case 8:
            season = "Summer";
            break;
          case 9:
          case 10:
          case 11:
            season = "Autumn";
            break;
          default:
            season = "Bogus Month";
        }
        System.out.println("April is in the " + season + ".");
    }
}
```

Nested switch Statements

You can use a **switch** as part of the statement sequence of an outer **switch**. This is called a *nested* **switch**. Since a **switch** statement defines its own block, no conflicts arise between the **case** constants in the inner **switch** and those in the outer **switch**. For example, the following fragment is perfectly valid:

```
switch(count) {
  case 1:
    switch(target) { // nested switch
      case 0:
        System.out.println("target is zero");
        break;
      case 1: // no conflicts with outer switch
        System.out.println("target is one");
        break;
    }
    break;
  case 2: // ...
```

Here, the **case 1:** statement in the inner switch does not conflict with the **case 1:** statement in the outer switch. The **count** variable is only compared with the list of cases at the outer level. If **count** is 1, then **target** is compared with the inner list cases.

In summary, there are three important features of the **switch** statement to note:

- The **switch** differs from the **if** in that **switch** can only test for equality, whereas **if** can evaluate any type of Boolean expression. That is, the **switch** looks only for a match between the value of the expression and one of its **case** constants.

- No two **case** constants in the same **switch** can have identical values. Of course, a **switch** statement enclosed by an outer **switch** can have **case** constants in common.

- A **switch** statement is usually more efficient than a set of nested **if**s.

The last point is particularly interesting because it gives insight into how the Java compiler works. When it compiles a **switch** statement, the Java compiler will inspect each of the **case** constants and create a "jump table" that it will use for selecting the path of execution depending on the value of the expression. Therefore, if you need to select among a large group of values, a **switch** statement will run much faster than the equivalent logic coded using a sequence of **if-else**s. The compiler can do this because it knows that the **case** constants are all the same type and simply must be compared for equality with the **switch** expression. The compiler has no such knowledge of a long list of **if** expressions.

Iteration Statements

Java's iteration statements are **for**, **while**, and **do-while**. These statements create what we commonly call *loops*. As you probably know, a loop repeatedly executes the same set of instructions until a termination condition is met. As you will see, Java has a loop to fit any programming need.

while

The **while** loop is Java's most fundamental looping statement. It repeats a statement or block while its controlling expression is true. Here is its general form:

```
while(condition) {
    // body of loop
}
```

The *condition* can be any Boolean expression. The body of the loop will be executed as long as the conditional expression is true. When *condition* becomes false, control passes to the next line of code immediately following the loop. The curly braces are unnecessary if only a single statement is being repeated.

Here is a **while** loop that counts down from 10, printing exactly ten lines of "tick":

```
// Demonstrate the while loop.
class While {
  public static void main(String args[]) {
    int n = 10;

    while(n > 0) {
      System.out.println("tick " + n);
      n--;
    }
  }
}
```

When you run this program, it will "tick" ten times:

```
tick 10
tick 9
tick 8
tick 7
tick 6
tick 5
tick 4
```

```
tick 3
tick 2
tick 1
```

Since the **while** loop evaluates its conditional expression at the top of the loop, the body of the loop will not execute even once if the condition is false to begin with. For example, in the following fragment, the call to **println( )** is never executed:

```
int a = 10, b = 20;

while(a > b)
  System.out.println("This will not be displayed");
```

The body of the **while** (or any other of Java's loops) can be empty. This is because a *null statement* (one that consists only of a semicolon) is syntactically valid in Java. For example, consider the following program:

```
// The target of a loop can be empty.
class NoBody {
  public static void main(String args[]) {
    int i, j;

    i = 100;
    j = 200;

    // find midpoint between i and j
    while(++i < --j) ; // no body in this loop

    System.out.println("Midpoint is " + i);
  }
}
```

This program finds the midpoint between **i** and **j**. It generates the following output:

```
Midpoint is 150
```

Here is how the **while** loop works. The value of **i** is incremented, and the value of **j** is decremented. These values are then compared with one another. If the new value of **i** is still less than the new value of **j**, then the loop repeats. If **i** is equal to or greater than **j**, the loop stops. Upon exit from the loop, **i** will hold a value that is midway between the original values of **i** and **j**. (Of course, this procedure only works when **i** is less than **j** to begin with.) As you can see, there is no need for a loop body; all of the action occurs within the conditional expression, itself. In professionally written Java code, short loops are frequently coded without bodies when the controlling expression can handle all of the details itself.

do-while

As you just saw, if the conditional expression controlling a **while** loop is initially false, then the body of the loop will not be executed at all. However, sometimes it is desirable to execute the body of a **while** loop at least once, even if the conditional expression is false to begin with. In other words, there are times when you would like to test the termination expression at the end of the loop rather than at the beginning. Fortunately, Java supplies a loop that does just that: the **do-while**. The **do-while** loop always executes its body at least once, because its conditional expression is at the bottom of the loop. Its general form is

```
do {
  // body of loop
} while (condition);
```

Each iteration of the **do-while** loop first executes the body of the loop and then evaluates the conditional expression. If this expression is true, the loop will repeat. Otherwise, the loop terminates. As with all of Java's loops, *condition* must be a Boolean expression.

Here is a reworked version of the "tick" program that demonstrates the **do-while** loop. It generates the same output as before.

```
// Demonstrate the do-while loop.
class DoWhile {
  public static void main(String args[]) {
    int n = 10;

    do {
      System.out.println("tick " + n);
      n--;
    } while(n > 0);
  }
}
```

The loop in the preceding program, while technically correct, can be written more efficiently as follows:

```
do {
  System.out.println("tick " + n);
} while(--n > 0);
```

In this example, the expression **(– –n > 0)** combines the decrement of **n** and the test for zero into one expression. Here is how it works. First, the – –n statement executes, decrementing **n** and returning the new value of **n**. This value is then compared with zero. If it is greater than zero, the loop continues; otherwise it terminates.

The **do-while** loop is especially useful when you process a menu selection, because you will usually want the body of a menu loop to execute at least once. Consider the following program which implements a very simple help system for Java's selection and iteration statements:

```java
// Using a do-while to process a menu selection
class Menu {
  public static void main(String args[])
    throws java.io.IOException {
    char choice;

    do {
      System.out.println("Help on:");
      System.out.println("  1. if");
      System.out.println("  2. switch");
      System.out.println("  3. while");
      System.out.println("  4. do-while");
      System.out.println("  5. for\n");
      System.out.println("Choose one:");
      choice = (char) System.in.read();
    } while( choice < '1' || choice > '5');

    System.out.println("\n");

    switch(choice) {
      case '1':
        System.out.println("The if:\n");
        System.out.println("if(condition) statement;");
        System.out.println("else statement;");
        break;
      case '2':
```

```
      System.out.println("The switch:\n");
      System.out.println("switch(expression) {");
      System.out.println("  case constant:");
      System.out.println("    statement sequence");
      System.out.println("  break;");
      System.out.println("  // ...");
      System.out.println("}");
      break;
    case '3':
      System.out.println("The while:\n");
      System.out.println("while(condition) statement;");
      break;
    case '4':
      System.out.println("The do-while:\n");
      System.out.println("do {");
      System.out.println("  statement;");
      System.out.println("} while (condition);");
      break;
    case '5':
      System.out.println("The for:\n");
      System.out.print("for(init; condition; iteration)");
      System.out.println(" statement;");
      break;
    }
  }
}
```

Here is a sample run produced by this program:

```
Help on:
  1. if
  2. switch
  3. while
  4. do-while
  5. for
Choose one:
4
The do-while:
do {
  statement;
} while (condition);
```

In the program, the **do-while** loop is used to verify that the user has entered a valid choice. If not, then the user is reprompted. Since the menu must be displayed at least once, the **do-while** is the perfect loop to accomplish this.

A few other points about this example: Notice that characters are read from the keyboard by calling **System.in.read( )**. This is one of Java's console input functions. Although Java's console I/O methods won't be discussed in detail until Chapter 12, **System.in.read( )** is used here to obtain the user's choice. It reads characters from standard input (returned as integers, which is why the return value was cast to **char**). By default, standard input is line buffered, so you must press ENTER before any characters that you type will be sent to your program.

Java's console input is quite limited and awkward to work with. Further, most real-world Java programs and applets will be graphical and window-based. For these reasons, not much use of console input has been made in this book. However, it is useful in this context. One other point: Because **System.in.read( )** is being used, the program must specify the **throws java.io.IOException** clause. This line is necessary to handle input errors. It is part of Java's exception handling features, which are discussed in Chapter 10.

for

You were introduced to a simple form of the **for** loop in Chapter 2. As you will see, it is a powerful and versatile construct. Here is the general form of the **for** statement:

```
for(initialization; condition; iteration) {
  // body
}
```

If only one statement is being repeated, there is no need for the curly braces.

The **for** loop operates as follows. When the loop first starts, the *initialization* portion of the loop is executed. Generally, this is an expression that sets the value of the *loop control variable*, which acts as a counter that controls the loop. It is important to understand that the initialization expression is only executed once. Next, *condition* is evaluated. This must be a Boolean expression. It usually tests the loop control variable against a target value. If this expression is true, then the body of the loop is executed. If it is false, the loop terminates. Next, the *iteration* portion of the loop is executed. This is usually an expression that increments or decrements the loop control variable. The loop then iterates, first evaluating the conditional expression, then executing the body of the loop, and then executing the iteration expression with each pass. This process repeats until the controlling expression is false.

Here is a version of the "tick" program that uses a **for** loop:

```
// Demonstrate the for loop.
class ForTick {
  public static void main(String args[]) {
    int n;

    for(n=10; n>0; n--)
      System.out.println("tick " + n);
  }
}
```

Declaring Loop Control Variables Inside the for Loop

Often the variable that controls a **for** loop is only needed for the purposes of the loop and is not used elsewhere. When this is the case, it is possible to declare the variable inside the initialization portion of the **for**. For example, here is the preceding program recoded so that the loop control variable **n** is declared as an **int** inside the **for**:

```
// Declare a loop control variable inside the for.
class ForTick {
  public static void main(String args[]) {

    // here, n is declared inside of the for loop
    for(int n=10; n>0; n--)
      System.out.println("tick " + n);
  }
}
```

When you declare a variable inside a **for** loop, there is one important point to remember: the scope of that variable ends when the **for** statement does. (That is, the scope of the variable is limited to the **for** loop.) Outside the **for** loop, the variable will cease to exist. If you need to use the loop control variable elsewhere in your program, you will not be able to declare it inside the **for** loop.

When the loop control variable will not be needed elsewhere, most Java programmers declare it inside the **for**. For example, here is a simple program that tests for prime numbers. Notice that the loop control variable, **i**, is declared inside the **for** since it is not needed elsewhere.

```
// Test for primes.
class FindPrime {
```

```
public static void main(String args[]) {
  int num;
  boolean isPrime = true;

  num = 14;
  for(int i=2; i <= num/2; i++) {
    if((num % i) == 0) {
      isPrime = false;
      break;
    }
  }
  if(isPrime) System.out.println("Prime");
  else System.out.println("Not Prime");
  }
}
```

Using the Comma

There will be times when you will want to include more than one statement in the
initialization and iteration portions of the **for** loop. For example, consider the loop
in the following program:

```
class Sample {
  public static void main(String args[]) {
    int a, b;

    b = 4;
    for(a=1; a<b; a++) {
      System.out.println("a = " + a);
      System.out.println("b = " + b);
      b--;
    }
  }
}
```

As you can see, the loop is controlled by the interaction of two variables. Since the loop
is governed by two variables, it would be useful if both could be included in the **for**
statement, itself, instead of **b** being handled manually. Fortunately, Java provides a way
to accomplish this. To allow two or more variables to control a **for** loop, Java permits
you to include multiple statements in both the initialization and iteration portions of
the **for**. Each statement is separated from the next by a comma.

Using the comma, the preceding **for** loop can be more efficiently coded as shown here:

```
// Using the comma.
class Comma {
  public static void main(String args[]) {
    int a, b;

    for(a=1, b=4; a<b; a++, b--) {
      System.out.println("a = " + a);
      System.out.println("b = " + b);
    }
  }
}
```

In this example, the initialization portion sets the values of both **a** and **b**. The two comma-separated statements in the iteration portion are executed each time the loop repeats. The program generates the following output:

```
a = 1
b = 4
a = 2
b = 3
```

*If you are familiar with C/C++, then you know that in those languages the comma is an operator that can be used in any valid expression. However, this is not the case with Java. In Java, the comma is a separator that applies only to the **for** loop.*

Some for Loop Variations

The **for** loop supports a number of variations that increase its power and applicability. The reason it is so flexible is that its three parts, the initialization, the conditional test, and the iteration, do not need to be used for only those purposes. In fact, the three sections of the **for** can be used for any purpose you desire. Let's look at some examples.

One of the most common variations involves the conditional expression. Specifically, this expression does not need to test the loop control variable against some target value. In fact, the condition controlling the **for** can be any Boolean expression. For example, consider the following fragment:

```
boolean done = false;

for(int i=1; !done; i++) {
```

```
  // ...
  if(interrupted()) done = true;
}
```

In this example, the **for** loop continues to run until the **boolean** variable **done** is set to **true**. It does not test the value of **i**.

Here is another interesting **for** loop variation. Either the initialization or the iteration expression or both may be absent, as in this next program:

```
// Parts of the for loop can be empty.
class ForVar {
  public static void main(String args[]) {
    int i;
    boolean done = false;

    i = 0;
    for( ; !done; ) {
      System.out.println("i is " + i);
      if(i == 10) done = true;
      i++;
    }
  }
}
```

Here, the initialization and iteration expressions have been moved out of the **for**. Thus, parts of the **for** are empty. While this is of no value in this simple example—indeed, it would be considered quite poor style—there can be times when this type of approach makes sense. For example, if the initial condition is set through a complex expression elsewhere in the program or if the loop control variable changes in a nonsequential manner determined by actions that occur within the body of the loop, it may be appropriate to leave these parts of the **for** empty.

Here is one more **for** loop variation. You can intentionally create an infinite loop (a loop that never terminates) if you leave all three parts of the **for** empty. For example:

```
for( ; ; ) {
  // ...
}
```

This loop will run forever, because there is no condition under which it will terminate. Although there are some programs, such as operating system command processors, that require an infinite loop, most "infinite loops" are really just loops with special termination requirements. As you will soon see, there is a way to terminate a loop— even an infinite loop like the one shown—that does not make use of the normal loop conditional expression.

Nested Loops

Like all other programming languages, Java allows loops to be nested. That is, one loop may be inside another. For example, here is a program that nests **for** loops:

```
// Loops may be nested.
class Nested {
  public static void main(String args[]) {
    int i, j;

    for(i=0; i<10; i++) {
      for(j=i; j<10; j++)
        System.out.print(".");
      System.out.println();
    }
  }
}
```

The output produced by this program is shown here:

```
. . . . . . . . . .
. . . . . . . . .
. . . . . . . .
. . . . . . .
. . . . . .
. . . . .
. . . .
. . .
. .
.
```

Jump Statements

Java supports three jump statements: **break**, **continue**, and **return**. These statements transfer control to another part of your program. Each is examined here.

Note	In addition to the jump statements discussed here, Java supports one other way that you can change your program's flow of execution: through exception handling. Exception handling provides a structured method by which run-time errors can be trapped and handled by your program. It is supported by the keywords **try**, **catch**, **throw**, **throws**, and **finally**. In essence, the exception handling mechanism allows your program to perform a nonlocal branch. Since exception handling is a large topic, it is discussed in its own chapter, Chapter 10.

Using break

In Java, the **break** statement has three uses. First, as you have seen, it terminates a statement sequence in a **switch** statement. Second, it can be used to exit a loop. Third, it can be used as a "civilized" form of goto. The last two uses are explained here.

Using break to Exit a Loop

By using **break**, you can force immediate termination of a loop, bypassing the conditional expression and any remaining code in the body of the loop. When a **break** statement is encountered inside a loop, the loop is terminated and program control resumes at the next statement following the loop. Here is a simple example:

```
// Using break to exit a loop.
class BreakLoop {
  public static void main(String args[]) {
    for(int i=0; i<100; i++) {
      if(i == 10) break; // terminate loop if i is 10
      System.out.println("i: " + i);
    }
    System.out.println("Loop complete.");
  }
}
```

This program generates the following output:

```
i:  0
i:  1
i:  2
i:  3
i:  4
i:  5
i:  6
i:  7
i:  8
```

```
i: 9
Loop complete.
```

As you can see, although the **for** loop is designed to run from 0 to 99, the **break** statement causes it to terminate early, when **i** equals 10.

The **break** statement can be used with any of Java's loops, including intentionally infinite loops. For example, here is the preceding program coded by use of a **while** loop. The output from this program is the same as just shown.

```java
// Using break to exit a while loop.
class BreakLoop2 {
  public static void main(String args[]) {
    int i = 0;

    while(i < 100) {
      if(i == 10) break; // terminate loop if i is 10
      System.out.println("i: " + i);
      i++;
    }
    System.out.println("Loop complete.");
  }
}
```

When used inside a set of nested loops, the **break** statement will only break out of the innermost loop. For example:

```java
// Using break with nested loops.
class BreakLoop3 {
  public static void main(String args[]) {
    for(int i=0; i<3; i++) {
      System.out.print("Pass " + i + ": ");
      for(int j=0; j<100; j++) {
        if(j == 10) break; // terminate loop if j is 10
        System.out.print(j + " ");
      }
      System.out.println();
    }
    System.out.println("Loops complete.");
  }
}
```

This program generates the following output:

```
Pass 0: 0 1 2 3 4 5 6 7 8 9
Pass 1: 0 1 2 3 4 5 6 7 8 9
Pass 2: 0 1 2 3 4 5 6 7 8 9
Loops complete.
```

As you can see, the **break** statement in the inner loop only causes termination of that loop. The outer loop is unaffected.

Here are two other points to remember about **break**. First, more than one **break** statement may appear in a loop. However, be careful. Too many **break** statements have the tendency to destructure your code. Second, the **break** that terminates a **switch** statement affects only that **switch** statement and not any enclosing loops.

 *break was not designed to provide the normal means by which a loop is terminated. The loop's conditional expression serves this purpose. The **break** statement should be used to cancel a loop only when some sort of special situation occurs.*

Using break as a Form of Goto

In addition to its uses with the **switch** statement and loops, the **break** statement can also be employed by itself to provide a "civilized" form of the goto statement. Java does not have a goto statement, because it provides a way to branch in an arbitrary and unstructured manner. This usually makes goto-ridden code hard to understand and hard to maintain. It also prohibits certain compiler optimizations. There are, however, a few places where the goto is a valuable and legitimate construct for flow control. For example, the goto can be useful when you are exiting from a deeply nested set of loops. To handle such situations, Java defines an expanded form of the **break** statement. By using this form of **break**, you can break out of one or more blocks of code. These blocks need not be part of a loop or a **switch**. They can be any block. Further, you can specify precisely where execution will resume, because this form of **break** works with a label. As you will see, **break** gives you the benefits of a goto without its problems.

The general form of the labeled **break** statement is shown here:

break *label*;

Here, *label* is the name of a label that identifies a block of code. When this form of **break** executes, control is transferred out of the named block of code. The labeled block of code must enclose the **break** statement, but it does not need to be the immediately enclosing block. This means that you can use a labeled **break** statement to exit from a set of nested blocks. But you cannot use **break** to transfer control to a block of code that does not enclose the **break** statement.

To name a block, put a label at the start of it. A *label* is any valid Java identifier followed by a colon. Once you have labeled a block, you can then use this label as the target of a **break** statement. Doing so causes execution to resume at the *end* of the labeled block. For example, the following program shows three nested blocks, each with its own label. The **break** statement causes execution to jump forward, past the end of the block labeled **second**, skipping the two **println( )** statements.

```java
// Using break as a civilized form of goto.
class Break {
  public static void main(String args[]) {
    boolean t = true;

    first: {
      second: {
        third: {
          System.out.println("Before the break.");
          if(t) break second; // break out of second block
          System.out.println("This won't execute");
        }
        System.out.println("This won't execute");
      }
      System.out.println("This is after second block.");
    }
  }
}
```

Running this program generates the following output:

```
Before the break.
This is after second block.
```

One of the most common uses for a labeled **break** statement is to exit from nested loops. For example, in the following program, the outer loop executes only once:

```java
// Using break to exit from nested loops
class BreakLoop4 {
  public static void main(String args[]) {
    outer: for(int i=0; i<3; i++) {
      System.out.print("Pass " + i + ": ");
      for(int j=0; j<100; j++) {
        if(j == 10) break outer; // exit both loops
        System.out.print(j + " ");
```

```
        }
        System.out.println("This will not print");
      }
      System.out.println("Loops complete.");
    }
  }
```

This program generates the following output:

```
Pass 0:  0 1 2 3 4 5 6 7 8 9 Loops complete.
```

As you can see, when the inner loop breaks to the outer loop, both loops have been terminated.

Keep in mind that you cannot break to any label which is not defined for an enclosing block. For example, the following program is invalid and will not compile:

```
// This program contains an error.
class BreakErr {
  public static void main(String args[]) {

    one: for(int i=0; i<3; i++) {
      System.out.print("Pass " + i + ": ");
    }

    for(int j=0; j<100; j++) {
      if(j == 10) break one; // WRONG
      System.out.print(j + " ");
    }
  }
}
```

Since the loop labeled **one** does not enclose the **break** statement, it is not possible to transfer control to that block.

Using continue

Sometimes it is useful to force an early iteration of a loop. That is, you might want to continue running the loop, but stop processing the remainder of the code in its body for this particular iteration. This is, in effect, a goto just past the body of the loop, to the loop's end. The **continue** statement performs such an action. In **while** and **do-while** loops, a **continue** statement causes control to be transferred directly to the conditional expression that controls the loop. In a **for** loop, control goes first to the iteration portion of the **for** statement and then to the conditional expression. For all three loops, any intermediate code is bypassed.

Here is an example program that uses **continue** to cause two numbers to be printed on each line:

```
// Demonstrate continue.
class Continue {
  public static void main(String args[]) {
    for(int i=0; i<10; i++) {
      System.out.print(i + " ");
      if (i%2 == 0) continue;
      System.out.println("");
    }
  }
}
```

This code uses the % operator to check if **i** is even. If it is, the loop continues without printing a newline. Here is the output from this program:

```
0 1
2 3
4 5
6 7
8 9
```

As with the **break** statement, **continue** may specify a label to describe which enclosing loop to continue. Here is an example program that uses **continue** to print a triangular multiplication table for 0 through 9.

```
// Using continue with a label.
class ContinueLabel {
  public static void main(String args[]) {
outer: for (int i=0; i<10; i++) {
        for(int j=0; j<10; j++) {
          if(j > i) {
            System.out.println();
            continue outer;
          }
          System.out.print(" " + (i * j));
        }
      }
      System.out.println();
    }
  }
}
```

The **continue** statement in this example terminates the loop counting **j** and continues with the next iteration of the loop counting **i**. Here is the output of this program:

```
0
0 1
0 2 4
0 3 6 9
0 4 8 12 16
0 5 10 15 20 25
0 6 12 18 24 30 36
0 7 14 21 28 35 42 49
0 8 16 24 32 40 48 56 64
0 9 18 27 36 45 54 63 72 81
```

Good uses of **continue** are rare. One reason is that Java provides a rich set of loop statements which fit most applications. However, for those special circumstances in which early iteration is needed, the **continue** statement provides a structured way to accomplish it.

return

The last control statement is **return**. The **return** statement is used to explicitly return from a method. That is, it causes program control to transfer back to the caller of the method. As such, it is categorized as a jump statement. Although a full discussion of **return** must wait until methods are discussed in Chapter 7, a brief look at **return** is presented here.

At any time in a method the **return** statement can be used to cause execution to branch back to the caller of the method. Thus, the **return** statement immediately terminates the method in which it is executed. The following example illustrates this point. Here, **return** causes execution to return to the Java run-time system, since it is the run-time system that calls **main( )**.

```java
// Demonstrate return.
class Return {
  public static void main(String args[]) {
    boolean t = true;
```

```
    System.out.println("Before the return.");

    if(t) return; // return to caller

    System.out.println("This won't execute.");
  }
}
```

The output from this program is shown here:

```
Before the return.
```

As you can see, the final **println( )** statement is not executed. As soon as **return** is executed, control passes back to the caller.

One last point: In the preceding program, the **if(t)** statement is necessary. Without it, the Java compiler would flag an "unreachable code" error, because the compiler would know that the last **println( )** statement would never be executed. To prevent this error, the **if** statement is used here to trick the compiler for the sake of this demonstration.

The
Complete
Reference

Java™ 2

Chapter 6

Introducing Classes

The class is at the core of Java. It is the logical construct upon which the entire Java language is built because it defines the shape and nature of an object. As such, the class forms the basis for object-oriented programming in Java. Any concept you wish to implement in a Java program must be encapsulated within a class.

Because the class is so fundamental to Java, this and the next few chapters will be devoted to it. Here, you will be introduced to the basic elements of a class and learn how a class can be used to create objects. You will also learn about methods, constructors, and the **this** keyword.

Class Fundamentals

Classes have been used since the beginning of this book. However, until now, only the most rudimentary form of a class has been used. The classes created in the preceding chapters primarily exist simply to encapsulate the **main( )** method, which has been used to demonstrate the basics of the Java syntax. As you will see, classes are substantially more powerful than the limited ones presented so far.

Perhaps the most important thing to understand about a class is that it defines a new data type. Once defined, this new type can be used to create objects of that type. Thus, a class is a *template* for an object, and an object is an *instance* of a class. Because an object is an instance of a class, you will often see the two words *object* and *instance* used interchangeably.

The General Form of a Class

When you define a class, you declare its exact form and nature. You do this by specifying the data that it contains and the code that operates on that data. While very simple classes may contain only code or only data, most real-world classes contain both. As you will see, a class' code defines the interface to its data.

A class is declared by use of the **class** keyword. The classes that have been used up to this point are actually very limited examples of its complete form. Classes can (and usually do) get much more complex. The general form of a **class** definition is shown here:

```
class classname {
  type instance-variable1;
  type instance-variable2;
  // ...
  type instance-variableN;

  type methodname1(parameter-list) {
       // body of method
  }
  type methodname2(parameter-list) {
       // body of method
```

```
   }
     // ...
   type methodnameN(parameter-list) {
       // body of method
   }
 }
```

The data, or variables, defined within a **class** are called *instance variables*. The code is contained within *methods*. Collectively, the methods and variables defined within a class are called *members* of the class. In most classes, the instance variables are acted upon and accessed by the methods defined for that class. Thus, it is the methods that determine how a class' data can be used.

Variables defined within a class are called instance variables because each instance of the class (that is, each object of the class) contains its own copy of these variables. Thus, the data for one object is separate and unique from the data for another. We will come back to this point shortly, but it is an important concept to learn early.

All methods have the same general form as **main( )**, which we have been using thus far. However, most methods will not be specified as **static** or **public**. Notice that the general form of a class does not specify a **main( )** method. Java classes do not need to have a **main( )** method. You only specify one if that class is the starting point for your program. Further, applets don't require a **main( )** method at all.

Note *C++ programmers will notice that the class declaration and the implementation of the methods are stored in the same place and not defined separately. This sometimes makes for very large .java files, since any class must be entirely defined in a single source file. This design feature was built into Java because it was felt that in the long run, having specification, declaration, and implementation all in one place makes for code that is easier to maintain.*

A Simple Class

Let's begin our study of the class with a simple example. Here is a class called **Box** that defines three instance variables: **width**, **height**, and **depth**. Currently, **Box** does not contain any methods (but some will be added soon).

```
class Box {
  double width;
  double height;
  double depth;
}
```

As stated, a class defines a new type of data. In this case, the new data type is called **Box**. You will use this name to declare objects of type **Box**. It is important to remember that a **class** declaration only creates a template; it does not create an actual object. Thus, the preceding code does not cause any objects of type **Box** to come into existence.

To actually create a **Box** object, you will use a statement like the following:

```
Box mybox = new Box(); // create a Box object called mybox
```

After this statement executes, **mybox** will be an instance of **Box**. Thus, it will have "physical" reality. For the moment, don't worry about the details of this statement.

Again, each time you create an instance of a class, you are creating an object that contains its own copy of each instance variable defined by the class. Thus, every **Box** object will contain its own copies of the instance variables **width**, **height**, and **depth**. To access these variables, you will use the *dot* (.) operator. The dot operator links the name of the object with the name of an instance variable. For example, to assign the **width** variable of **mybox** the value 100, you would use the following statement:

```
mybox.width = 100;
```

This statement tells the compiler to assign the copy of **width** that is contained within the **mybox** object the value of 100. In general, you use the dot operator to access both the instance variables and the methods within an object.

Here is a complete program that uses the **Box** class:

```
/* A program that uses the Box class.

   Call this file BoxDemo.java
*/
class Box {
  double width;
  double height;
  double depth;
}

// This class declares an object of type Box.
class BoxDemo {
  public static void main(String args[]) {
    Box mybox = new Box();
    double vol;

    // assign values to mybox's instance variables
    mybox.width = 10;
```

```
      mybox.height = 20;
      mybox.depth = 15;

      // compute volume of box
      vol = mybox.width * mybox.height * mybox.depth;

      System.out.println("Volume is " + vol);
   }
}
```

You should call the file that contains this program **BoxDemo.java**, because the **main( )** method is in the class called **BoxDemo**, not the class called **Box**. When you compile this program, you will find that two **.class** files have been created, one for **Box** and one for **BoxDemo**. The Java compiler automatically puts each class into its own **.class** file. It is not necessary for both the **Box** and the **BoxDemo** class to actually be in the same source file. You could put each class in its own file, called **Box.java** and **BoxDemo.java**, respectively.

To run this program, you must execute **BoxDemo.class**. When you do, you will see the following output:

```
Volume is 3000.0
```

As stated earlier, each object has its own copies of the instance variables. This means that if you have two **Box** objects, each has its own copy of **depth**, **width**, and **height**. It is important to understand that changes to the instance variables of one object have no effect on the instance variables of another. For example, the following program declares two **Box** objects:

```
// This program declares two Box objects.

class Box {
   double width;
   double height;
   double depth;
}

class BoxDemo2 {
   public static void main(String args[]) {
      Box mybox1 = new Box();
      Box mybox2 = new Box();
```

```
    double vol;

    // assign values to mybox1's instance variables
    mybox1.width = 10;
    mybox1.height = 20;
    mybox1.depth = 15;

    /* assign different values to mybox2's
       instance variables */
    mybox2.width = 3;
    mybox2.height = 6;
    mybox2.depth = 9;

    // compute volume of first box
    vol = mybox1.width * mybox1.height * mybox1.depth;
    System.out.println("Volume is " + vol);

    // compute volume of second box
    vol = mybox2.width * mybox2.height * mybox2.depth;
    System.out.println("Volume is " + vol);
  }
}
```

The output produced by this program is shown here:

```
Volume is 3000.0
Volume is 162.0
```

As you can see, **mybox1**'s data is completely separate from the data contained in **mybox2**.

Declaring Objects

As just explained, when you create a class, you are creating a new data type. You can use this type to declare objects of that type. However, obtaining objects of a class is a two-step process. First, you must declare a variable of the class type. This variable does not define an object. Instead, it is simply a variable that can *refer* to an object. Second, you must acquire an actual, physical copy of the object and assign it to that variable. You can do this using the **new** operator. The **new** operator dynamically allocates (that is, allocates at run time) memory for an object and returns a reference to it. This reference is, more or less, the address in memory of the object allocated by **new**.

This reference is then stored in the variable. Thus, in Java, all class objects must be dynamically allocated. Let's look at the details of this procedure.

In the preceding sample programs, a line similar to the following is used to declare an object of type **Box**:

```
Box mybox = new Box();
```

This statement combines the two steps just described. It can be rewritten like this to show each step more clearly:

```
Box mybox; // declare reference to object
mybox = new Box(); // allocate a Box object
```

The first line declares **mybox** as a reference to an object of type **Box**. After this line executes, **mybox** contains the value **null**, which indicates that it does not yet point to an actual object. Any attempt to use **mybox** at this point will result in a compile-time error. The next line allocates an actual object and assigns a reference to it to **mybox**. After the second line executes, you can use **mybox** as if it were a **Box** object. But in reality, **mybox** simply holds the memory address of the actual **Box** object. The effect of these two lines of code is depicted in Figure 6-1.

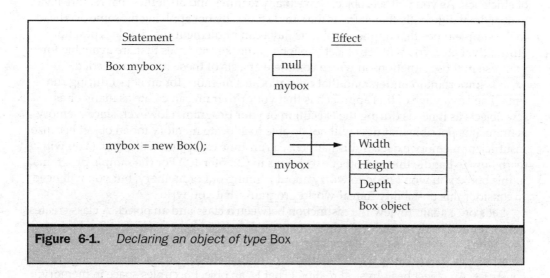

Figure 6-1.   *Declaring an object of type* Box

Those readers familiar with C/C++ have probably noticed that object references appear to be similar to pointers. This suspicion is, essentially, correct. An object reference is similar to a memory pointer. The main difference—and the key to Java's safety—is that you cannot manipulate references as you can actual pointers. Thus, you cannot cause an object reference to point to an arbitrary memory location or manipulate it like an integer.

A Closer Look at new

As just explained, the **new** operator dynamically allocates memory for an object. It has this general form:

> *class-var* = new *classname*( );

Here, *class-var* is a variable of the class type being created. The *classname* is the name of the class that is being instantiated. The class name followed by parentheses specifies the *constructor* for the class. A constructor defines what occurs when an object of a class is created. Constructors are an important part of all classes and have many significant attributes. Most real-world classes explicitly define their own constructors within their class definition. However, if no explicit constructor is specified, then Java will automatically supply a default constructor. This is the case with **Box**. For now, we will use the default constructor. Soon, you will see how to define your own constructors.

At this point, you might be wondering why you do not need to use **new** for such things as integers or characters. The answer is that Java's simple types are not implemented as objects. Rather, they are implemented as "normal" variables. This is done in the interest of efficiency. As you will see, objects have many features and attributes that require Java to treat them differently than it treats the simple types. By not applying the same overhead to the simple types that applies to objects, Java can implement the simple types more efficiently. Later, you will see object versions of the simple types that are available for your use in those situations in which complete objects of these types are needed.

It is important to understand that **new** allocates memory for an object during run time. The advantage of this approach is that your program can create as many or as few objects as it needs during the execution of your program. However, since memory is finite, it is possible that **new** will not be able to allocate memory for an object because insufficient memory exists. If this happens, a run-time exception will occur. (You will learn how to handle this and other exceptions in Chapter 10.) For the sample programs in this book, you won't need to worry about running out of memory, but you will need to consider this possibility in real-world programs that you write.

Let's once again review the distinction between a class and an object. A class creates a new data type that can be used to create objects. That is, a class creates a logical framework that defines the relationship between its members. When you declare an object of a class, you are creating an instance of that class. Thus, a class is a logical construct. An object has physical reality. (That is, an object occupies space in memory.) It is important to keep this distinction clearly in mind.

Assigning Object Reference Variables

Object reference variables act differently than you might expect when an assignment takes place. For example, what do you think the following fragment does?

```
Box b1 = new Box();
Box b2 = b1;
```

You might think that **b2** is being assigned a reference to a copy of the object referred to by **b1**. That is, you might think that **b1** and **b2** refer to separate and distinct objects. However, this would be wrong. Instead, after this fragment executes, **b1** and **b2** will both refer to the *same* object. The assignment of **b1** to **b2** did not allocate any memory or copy any part of the original object. It simply makes **b2** refer to the same object as does **b1**. Thus, any changes made to the object through **b2** will affect the object to which **b1** is referring, since they are the same object.

This situation is depicted here:

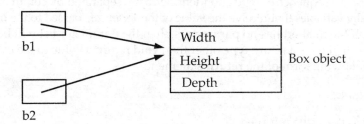

Although **b1** and **b2** both refer to the same object, they are not linked in any other way. For example, a subsequent assignment to **b1** will simply *unhook* **b1** from the original object without affecting the object or affecting **b2**. For example:

```
Box b1 = new Box();
Box b2 = b1;
// ...
b1 = null;
```

Here, **b1** has been set to **null**, but **b2** still points to the original object.

When you assign one object reference variable to another object reference variable, you are not creating a copy of the object, you are only making a copy of the reference.

Introducing Methods

As mentioned at the beginning of this chapter, classes usually consist of two things: instance variables and methods. The topic of methods is a large one because Java gives them so much power and flexibility. In fact, much of the next chapter is devoted to methods. However, there are some fundamentals that you need to learn now so that you can begin to add methods to your classes.

This is the general form of a method:

```
type name(parameter-list) {
    // body of method
}
```

Here, *type* specifies the type of data returned by the method. This can be any valid type, including class types that you create. If the method does not return a value, its return type must be **void**. The name of the method is specified by *name*. This can be any legal identifier other than those already used by other items within the current scope. The *parameter-list* is a sequence of type and identifier pairs separated by commas. Parameters are essentially variables that receive the value of the *arguments* passed to the method when it is called. If the method has no parameters, then the parameter list will be empty.

Methods that have a return type other than **void** return a value to the calling routine using the following form of the **return** statement:

```
return value;
```

Here, *value* is the value returned.

In the next few sections, you will see how to create various types of methods, including those that take parameters and those that return values.

Adding a Method to the Box Class

Although it is perfectly fine to create a class that contains only data, it rarely happens. Most of the time you will use methods to access the instance variables defined by the class. In fact, methods define the interface to most classes. This allows the class implementor to hide the specific layout of internal data structures behind cleaner method abstractions. In addition to defining methods that provide access to data, you can also define methods that are used internally by the class itself.

Let's begin by adding a method to the **Box** class. It may have occurred to you while looking at the preceding programs that the computation of a box's volume was something that was best handled by the **Box** class rather than the **BoxDemo** class. After all, since the volume of a box is dependent upon the size of the box, it makes sense to have the **Box** class compute it. To do this, you must add a method to **Box**, as shown here:

```
// This program includes a method inside the box class.

class Box {
  double width;
  double height;
  double depth;

  // display volume of a box
  void volume() {
    System.out.print("Volume is ");
    System.out.println(width * height * depth);
  }
}

class BoxDemo3 {
  public static void main(String args[]) {
    Box mybox1 = new Box();
    Box mybox2 = new Box();

    // assign values to mybox1's instance variables
    mybox1.width = 10;
    mybox1.height = 20;
    mybox1.depth = 15;

    /* assign different values to mybox2's
       instance variables */
    mybox2.width = 3;
    mybox2.height = 6;
    mybox2.depth = 9;

    // display volume of first box
    mybox1.volume();

    // display volume of second box
    mybox2.volume();
  }
}
```

This program generates the following output, which is the same as the previous version.

```
Volume is 3000.0
Volume is 162.0
```

Look closely at the following two lines of code:

```
mybox1.volume();
mybox2.volume();
```

The first line here invokes the **volume( )** method on **mybox1**. That is, it calls **volume( )** relative to the **mybox1** object, using the object's name followed by the dot operator. Thus, the call to **mybox1.volume( )** displays the volume of the box defined by **mybox1**, and the call to **mybox2.volume( )** displays the volume of the box defined by **mybox2**. Each time **volume( )** is invoked, it displays the volume for the specified box.

If you are unfamiliar with the concept of calling a method, the following discussion will help clear things up. When **mybox1.volume( )** is executed, the Java run-time system transfers control to the code defined inside **volume( )**. After the statements inside **volume( )** have executed, control is returned to the calling routine, and execution resumes with the line of code following the call. In the most general sense, a method is Java's way of implementing subroutines.

There is something very important to notice inside the **volume( )** method: the instance variables **width**, **height**, and **depth** are referred to directly, without preceding them with an object name or the dot operator. When a method uses an instance variable that is defined by its class, it does so directly, without explicit reference to an object and without use of the dot operator. This is easy to understand if you think about it. A method is always invoked relative to some object of its class. Once this invocation has occurred, the object is known. Thus, within a method, there is no need to specify the object a second time. This means that **width**, **height**, and **depth** inside **volume( )** implicitly refer to the copies of those variables found in the object that invokes **volume( )**.

Let's review: When an instance variable is accessed by code that is not part of the class in which that instance variable is defined, it must be done through an object, by use of the dot operator. However, when an instance variable is accessed by code that is part of the same class as the instance variable, that variable can be referred to directly. The same thing applies to methods.

Returning a Value

While the implementation of **volume( )** does move the computation of a box's volume inside the **Box** class where it belongs, it is not the best way to do it. For example, what if another part of your program wanted to know the volume of a box, but not display its value? A better way to implement **volume( )** is to have it compute the volume of the box and return the result to the caller. The following example, an improved version of the preceding program, does just that:

```
// Now, volume() returns the volume of a box.

class Box {
  double width;
  double height;
  double depth;

  // compute and return volume
  double volume() {
    return width * height * depth;
  }
}

class BoxDemo4 {
  public static void main(String args[]) {
    Box mybox1 = new Box();
    Box mybox2 = new Box();
    double vol;

    // assign values to mybox1's instance variables
    mybox1.width = 10;
    mybox1.height = 20;
    mybox1.depth = 15;

    /* assign different values to mybox2's
       instance variables */
    mybox2.width = 3;
    mybox2.height = 6;
    mybox2.depth = 9;

    // get volume of first box
    vol = mybox1.volume();
    System.out.println("Volume is " + vol);

    // get volume of second box
    vol = mybox2.volume();
    System.out.println("Volume is " + vol);
  }
}
```

As you can see, when **volume( )** is called, it is put on the right side of an assignment statement. On the left is a variable, in this case **vol**, that will receive the value returned by **volume( )**. Thus, after

```
vol = mybox1.volume();
```

executes, the value of **mybox1.volume( )** is 3,000 and this value then is stored in **vol**. There are two important things to understand about returning values:

■ The type of data returned by a method must be compatible with the return type specified by the method. For example, if the return type of some method is **boolean**, you could not return an integer.

■ The variable receiving the value returned by a method (such as **vol**, in this case) must also be compatible with the return type specified for the method.

One more point: The preceding program can be written a bit more efficiently because there is actually no need for the **vol** variable. The call to **volume( )** could have been used in the **println( )** statement directly, as shown here:

```
System.out.println("Volume is " + mybox1.volume());
```

In this case, when **println( )** is executed, **mybox1.volume( )** will be called automatically and its value will be passed to **println( )**.

Adding a Method That Takes Parameters

While some methods don't need parameters, most do. Parameters allow a method to be generalized. That is, a parameterized method can operate on a variety of data and/or be used in a number of slightly different situations. To illustrate this point, let's use a very simple example. Here is a method that returns the square of the number 10:

```
int square()
{
  return 10 * 10;
}
```

While this method does, indeed, return the value of 10 squared, its use is very limited. However, if you modify the method so that it takes a parameter, as shown next, then you can make **square( )** much more useful.

```
int square(int i)
{
   return i * i;
}
```

Now, **square( )** will return the square of whatever value it is called with. That is, **square( )** is now a general-purpose method that can compute the square of any integer value, rather than just 10.

Here is an example:

```
int x, y;
x = square(5); // x equals 25
x = square(9); // x equals 81
y = 2;
x = square(y); // x equals 4
```

In the first call to **square( )**, the value 5 will be passed into parameter **i**. In the second call, **i** will receive the value 9. The third invocation passes the value of **y**, which is 2 in this example. As these examples show, **square( )** is able to return the square of whatever data it is passed.

It is important to keep the two terms *parameter* and *argument* straight. A *parameter* is a variable defined by a method that receives a value when the method is called. For example, in **square( )**, **i** is a parameter. An *argument* is a value that is passed to a method when it is invoked. For example, **square(100)** passes 100 as an argument. Inside **square( )**, the parameter **i** receives that value.

You can use a parameterized method to improve the **Box** class. In the preceding examples, the dimensions of each box had to be set separately by use of a sequence of statements, such as:

```
mybox1.width = 10;
mybox1.height = 20;
mybox1.depth = 15;
```

While this code works, it is troubling for two reasons. First, it is clumsy and error prone. For example, it would be easy to forget to set a dimension. Second, in well-designed Java programs, instance variables should be accessed only through methods defined by their class. In the future, you can change the behavior of a method, but you can't change the behavior of an exposed instance variable.

Thus, a better approach to setting the dimensions of a box is to create a method that takes the dimension of a box in its parameters and sets each instance variable appropriately. This concept is implemented by the following program:

```
// This program uses a parameterized method.

class Box {
  double width;
  double height;
  double depth;

  // compute and return volume
  double volume() {
    return width * height * depth;
  }

  // sets dimensions of box
  void setDim(double w, double h, double d) {
    width = w;
    height = h;
    depth = d;
  }
}

class BoxDemo5 {
  public static void main(String args[]) {
    Box mybox1 = new Box();
    Box mybox2 = new Box();
    double vol;

    // initialize each box
    mybox1.setDim(10, 20, 15);
    mybox2.setDim(3, 6, 9);

    // get volume of first box
    vol = mybox1.volume();
    System.out.println("Volume is " + vol);

    // get volume of second box
    vol = mybox2.volume();
    System.out.println("Volume is " + vol);
  }
}
```

As you can see, the **setDim( )** method is used to set the dimensions of each box. For example, when

```
mybox1.setDim(10, 20, 15);
```

is executed, 10 is copied into parameter **w**, 20 is copied into **h**, and 15 is copied into **d**. Inside **setDim( )** the values of **w**, **h**, and **d** are then assigned to **width**, **height**, and **depth**, respectively.

For many readers, the concepts presented in the preceding sections will be familiar. However, if such things as method calls, arguments, and parameters are new to you, then you might want to take some time to experiment before moving on. The concepts of the method invocation, parameters, and return values are fundamental to Java programming.

Constructors

It can be tedious to initialize all of the variables in a class each time an instance is created. Even when you add convenience functions like **setDim( )**, it would be simpler and more concise to have all of the setup done at the time the object is first created. Because the requirement for initialization is so common, Java allows objects to initialize themselves when they are created. This automatic initialization is performed through the use of a constructor.

A *constructor* initializes an object immediately upon creation. It has the same name as the class in which it resides and is syntactically similar to a method. Once defined, the constructor is automatically called immediately after the object is created, before the **new** operator completes. Constructors look a little strange because they have no return type, not even **void**. This is because the implicit return type of a class' constructor is the class type itself. It is the constructor's job to initialize the internal state of an object so that the code creating an instance will have a fully initialized, usable object immediately.

You can rework the **Box** example so that the dimensions of a box are automatically initialized when an object is constructed. To do so, replace **setDim( )** with a constructor. Let's begin by defining a simple constructor that simply sets the dimensions of each box to the same values. This version is shown here:

```
/* Here, Box uses a constructor to initialize the
   dimensions of a box.
*/
class Box {
  double width;
  double height;
```

```
    double depth;

    // This is the constructor for Box.
    Box() {
      System.out.println("Constructing Box");
      width = 10;
      height = 10;
      depth = 10;
    }

    // compute and return volume
    double volume() {
      return width * height * depth;
    }
}

class BoxDemo6 {
  public static void main(String args[]) {
    // declare, allocate, and initialize Box objects
    Box mybox1 = new Box();
    Box mybox2 = new Box();

    double vol;

    // get volume of first box
    vol = mybox1.volume();
    System.out.println("Volume is " + vol);

    // get volume of second box
    vol = mybox2.volume();
    System.out.println("Volume is " + vol);
  }
}
```

When this program is run, it generates the following results:

```
Constructing Box
Constructing Box
Volume is 1000.0
Volume is 1000.0
```

As you can see, both **mybox1** and **mybox2** were initialized by the **Box( )** constructor when they were created. Since the constructor gives all boxes the same dimensions, 10 by 10 by 10, both **mybox1** and **mybox2** will have the same volume. The **println( )** statement inside **Box( )** is for the sake of illustration only. Most constructors will not display anything. They will simply initialize an object.

Before moving on, let's reexamine the **new** operator. As you know, when you allocate an object, you use the following general form:

class-var = new *classname*( );

Now you can understand why the parentheses are needed after the class name. What is actually happening is that the constructor for the class is being called. Thus, in the line

```
Box mybox1 = new Box();
```

new Box( ) is calling the **Box( )** constructor. When you do not explicitly define a constructor for a class, then Java creates a default constructor for the class. This is why the preceding line of code worked in earlier versions of **Box** that did not define a constructor. The default constructor automatically initializes all instance variables to zero. The default constructor is often sufficient for simple classes, but it usually won't do for more sophisticated ones. Once you define your own constructor, the default constructor is no longer used.

Parameterized Constructors

While the **Box( )** constructor in the preceding example does initialize a **Box** object, it is not very useful—all boxes have the same dimensions. What is needed is a way to construct **Box** objects of various dimensions. The easy solution is to add parameters to the constructor. As you can probably guess, this makes them much more useful. For example, the following version of **Box** defines a parameterized constructor which sets the dimensions of a box as specified by those parameters. Pay special attention to how **Box** objects are created.

```
/* Here, Box uses a parameterized constructor to
   initialize the dimensions of a box.
*/
class Box {
  double width;
  double height;
  double depth;
```

```
// This is the constructor for Box.
Box(double w, double h, double d) {
  width = w;
  height = h;
  depth = d;
}

// compute and return volume
double volume() {
  return width * height * depth;
}
}

class BoxDemo7 {
  public static void main(String args[]) {
    // declare, allocate, and initialize Box objects
    Box mybox1 = new Box(10, 20, 15);
    Box mybox2 = new Box(3, 6, 9);

    double vol;

    // get volume of first box
    vol = mybox1.volume();
    System.out.println("Volume is " + vol);

    // get volume of second box
    vol = mybox2.volume();
    System.out.println("Volume is " + vol);
  }
}
```

The output from this program is shown here:

```
Volume is 3000.0
Volume is 162.0
```

As you can see, each object is initialized as specified in the parameters to its constructor. For example, in the following line,

```
Box mybox1 = new Box(10, 20, 15);
```

the values 10, 20, and 15 are passed to the **Box( )** constructor when **new** creates the object. Thus, **mybox1**'s copy of **width**, **height**, and **depth** will contain the values 10, 20, and 15, respectively.

The this Keyword

Sometimes a method will need to refer to the object that invoked it. To allow this, Java defines the **this** keyword. **this** can be used inside any method to refer to the *current* object. That is, **this** is always a reference to the object on which the method was invoked. You can use **this** anywhere a reference to an object of the current class' type is permitted.

To better understand what **this** refers to, consider the following version of **Box( )**:

```
// A redundant use of this.
Box(double w, double h, double d) {
   this.width = w;
   this.height = h;
   this.depth = d;
}
```

This version of **Box( )** operates exactly like the earlier version. The use of **this** is redundant, but perfectly correct. Inside **Box( )**, **this** will always refer to the invoking object. While it is redundant in this case, **this** is useful in other contexts, one of which is explained in the next section.

Instance Variable Hiding

As you know, it is illegal in Java to declare two local variables with the same name inside the same or enclosing scopes. Interestingly, you can have local variables, including formal parameters to methods, which overlap with the names of the class' instance variables. However, when a local variable has the same name as an instance variable, the local variable *hides* the instance variable. This is why **width**, **height**, and **depth** were not used as the names of the parameters to the **Box( )** constructor inside the **Box** class. If they had been, then **width** would have referred to the formal parameter, hiding the instance variable **width**. While it is usually easier to simply use different names, there is another way around this situation. Because **this** lets you refer directly to the object, you can use it to resolve any name space collisions that might occur between instance variables and local variables. For example, here is another version of

Box( ), which uses **width**, **height**, and **depth** for parameter names and then uses **this** to access the instance variables by the same name:

```
// Use this to resolve name-space collisions.
Box(double width, double height, double depth) {
  this.width = width;
  this.height = height;
  this.depth = depth;
}
```

A word of caution: The use of **this** in such a context can sometimes be confusing, and some programmers are careful not to use local variables and formal parameter names that hide instance variables. Of course, other programmers believe the contrary—that it is a good convention to use the same names for clarity, and use **this** to overcome the instance variable hiding. It is a matter of taste which approach you adopt.

Although **this** is of no significant value in the examples just shown, it is very useful in certain situations.

Garbage Collection

Since objects are dynamically allocated by using the **new** operator, you might be wondering how such objects are destroyed and their memory released for later reallocation. In some languages, such as C++, dynamically allocated objects must be manually released by use of a **delete** operator. Java takes a different approach; it handles deallocation for you automatically. The technique that accomplishes this is called *garbage collection*. It works like this: when no references to an object exist, that object is assumed to be no longer needed, and the memory occupied by the object can be reclaimed. There is no explicit need to destroy objects as in C++. Garbage collection only occurs sporadically (if at all) during the execution of your program. It will not occur simply because one or more objects exist that are no longer used. Furthermore, different Java run-time implementations will take varying approaches to garbage collection, but for the most part, you should not have to think about it while writing your programs.

The finalize( ) Method

Sometimes an object will need to perform some action when it is destroyed. For example, if an object is holding some non-Java resource such as a file handle or window character font, then you might want to make sure these resources are freed before an object is destroyed. To handle such situations, Java provides a mechanism called *finalization*. By using finalization, you can define specific actions that will occur when an object is just about to be reclaimed by the garbage collector.

To add a finalizer to a class, you simply define the **finalize( )** method. The Java run time calls that method whenever it is about to recycle an object of that class. Inside the **finalize( )** method you will specify those actions that must be performed before an object is destroyed. The garbage collector runs periodically, checking for objects that are no longer referenced by any running state or indirectly through other referenced objects. Right before an asset is freed, the Java run time calls the **finalize( )** method on the object.

The **finalize( )** method has this general form:

```
protected void finalize( )
{
// finalization code here
}
```

Here, the keyword **protected** is a specifier that prevents access to **finalize( )** by code defined outside its class. This and the other access specifiers are explained in Chapter 7.

It is important to understand that **finalize( )** is only called just prior to garbage collection. It is not called when an object goes out-of-scope, for example. This means that you cannot know when—or even if—**finalize( )** will be executed. Therefore, your program should provide other means of releasing system resources, etc., used by the object. It must not rely on **finalize( )** for normal program operation.

Note *If you are familiar with C++, then you know that C++ allows you to define a destructor for a class, which is called when an object goes out-of-scope. Java does not support this idea or provide for destructors. The* **finalize( )** *method only approximates the function of a destructor. As you get more experienced with Java, you will see that the need for destructor functions is minimal because of Java's garbage collection subsystem.*

A Stack Class

While the **Box** class is useful to illustrate the essential elements of a class, it is of little practical value. To show the real power of classes, this chapter will conclude with a more sophisticated example. As you recall from the discussion of object-oriented programming (OOP) presented in Chapter 2, one of OOP's most important benefits is the encapsulation of data and the code that manipulates that data. As you have seen, the class is the mechanism by which encapsulation is achieved in Java. By creating a class, you are creating a new data type that defines both the nature of the data being manipulated and the routines used to manipulate it. Further, the methods define a consistent and controlled interface to the class' data. Thus, you can use the class through its methods without having to worry about the details of its implementation or how the data is actually managed within the class. In a sense, a class is like a "data engine." No knowledge of what goes on inside the engine is required to use the engine through its controls. In fact, since the details are hidden, its inner workings can be changed as needed. As long as your code uses the class through its methods, internal details can change without causing side effects outside the class.

To see a practical application of the preceding discussion, let's develop one of the archetypal examples of encapsulation: the stack. A *stack* stores data using first-in, last-out ordering. That is, a stack is like a stack of plates on a table—the first plate put down on the table is the last plate to be used. Stacks are controlled through two operations traditionally called *push* and *pop*. To put an item on top of the stack, you will use push. To take an item off the stack, you will use pop. As you will see, it is easy to encapsulate the entire stack mechanism.

Here is a class called **Stack** that implements a stack for integers:

```java
// This class defines an integer stack that can hold 10 values.
class Stack {
  int stck[] = new int[10];
  int tos;

  // Initialize top-of-stack
  Stack() {
    tos = -1;
  }

  // Push an item onto the stack
  void push(int item) {
    if(tos==9)
      System.out.println("Stack is full.");
    else
      stck[++tos] = item;
  }

  // Pop an item from the stack
  int pop() {
    if(tos < 0) {
      System.out.println("Stack underflow.");
      return 0;
    }
    else
      return stck[tos--];
  }
}
```

As you can see, the **Stack** class defines two data items and three methods. The stack of integers is held by the array **stck**. This array is indexed by the variable **tos**, which always contains the index of the top of the stack. The **Stack( )** constructor initializes **tos** to –1, which indicates an empty stack. The method **push( )** puts an item on the stack. To retrieve an item, call **pop( )**. Since access to the stack is through **push( )** and **pop( )**, the fact that the stack is held in an array is actually not relevant to using the stack. For example, the stack could be held in a more complicated data structure, such as a linked list, yet the interface defined by **push( )** and **pop( )** would remain the same.

The class **TestStack**, shown here, demonstrates the **Stack** class. It creates two integer stacks, pushes some values onto each, and then pops them off.

```
class TestStack {
  public static void main(String args[]) {
    Stack mystack1 = new Stack();
    Stack mystack2 = new Stack();

    // push some numbers onto the stack
    for(int i=0; i<10; i++) mystack1.push(i);
    for(int i=10; i<20; i++) mystack2.push(i);

    // pop those numbers off the stack
    System.out.println("Stack in mystack1:");
    for(int i=0; i<10; i++)
      System.out.println(mystack1.pop());

    System.out.println("Stack in mystack2:");
    for(int i=0; i<10; i++)
      System.out.println(mystack2.pop());
  }
}
```

This program generates the following output:

```
Stack in mystack1:
9
8
7
6
5
4
3
2
```

```
1
0
Stack in mystack2:
19
18
17
16
15
14
13
12
11
10
```

As you can see, the contents of each stack are separate.

One last point about the **Stack** class. As it is currently implemented, it is possible for the array that holds the stack, **stck**, to be altered by code outside of the **Stack** class. This leaves **Stack** open to misuse or mischief. In the next chapter, you will see how to remedy this situation.

The
Complete
Reference

Chapter 7

A Closer Look at
Methods and Classes

T his chapter continues the discussion of methods and classes begun in the preceding chapter. It examines several topics relating to methods, including overloading, parameter passing, and recursion. The chapter then returns to the class, discussing access control, the use of the keyword **static**, and one of Java's most important built-in classes: **String**.

Overloading Methods

In Java it is possible to define two or more methods within the same class that share the same name, as long as their parameter declarations are different. When this is the case, the methods are said to be *overloaded*, and the process is referred to as *method overloading*. Method overloading is one of the ways that Java implements polymorphism. If you have never used a language that allows the overloading of methods, then the concept may seem strange at first. But as you will see, method overloading is one of Java's most exciting and useful features.

When an overloaded method is invoked, Java uses the type and/or number of arguments as its guide to determine which version of the overloaded method to actually call. Thus, overloaded methods must differ in the type and/or number of their parameters. While overloaded methods may have different return types, the return type alone is insufficient to distinguish two versions of a method. When Java encounters a call to an overloaded method, it simply executes the version of the method whose parameters match the arguments used in the call.

Here is a simple example that illustrates method overloading:

```java
// Demonstrate method overloading.
class OverloadDemo {
  void test() {
    System.out.println("No parameters");
  }

  // Overload test for one integer parameter.
  void test(int a) {
    System.out.println("a: " + a);
  }

  // Overload test for two integer parameters.
  void test(int a, int b) {
    System.out.println("a and b: " + a + " " + b);
  }

  // overload test for a double parameter
  double test(double a) {
```

```
      System.out.println("double a: " + a);
      return a*a;
   }
}

class Overload {
  public static void main(String args[]) {
    OverloadDemo ob = new OverloadDemo();
    double result;

    // call all versions of test()
    ob.test();
    ob.test(10);
    ob.test(10, 20);
    result = ob.test(123.25);
    System.out.println("Result of ob.test(123.25): " + result);
  }
}
```

This program generates the following output:

```
No parameters
a: 10
a and b: 10 20
double a: 123.25
Result of ob.test(123.25): 15190.5625
```

As you can see, **test( )** is overloaded four times. The first version takes no parameters, the second takes one integer parameter, the third takes two integer parameters, and the fourth takes one **double** parameter. The fact that the fourth version of **test( )** also returns a value is of no consequence relative to overloading, since return types do not play a role in overload resolution.

When an overloaded method is called, Java looks for a match between the arguments used to call the method and the method's parameters. However, this match need not always be exact. In some cases Java's automatic type conversions can play a role in overload resolution. For example, consider the following program:

```
// Automatic type conversions apply to overloading.
class OverloadDemo {
  void test() {
```

```
      System.out.println("No parameters");
  }

  // Overload test for two integer parameters.
  void test(int a, int b) {
    System.out.println("a and b: " + a + " " + b);
  }

  // overload test for a double parameter
  void test(double a) {
    System.out.println("Inside test(double) a: " + a);
  }
}

class Overload {
  public static void main(String args[]) {
    OverloadDemo ob = new OverloadDemo();
    int i = 88;

    ob.test();
    ob.test(10, 20);

    ob.test(i); // this will invoke test(double)
    ob.test(123.2); // this will invoke test(double)
  }
}
```

This program generates the following output:

```
No parameters
a and b: 10 20
Inside test(double) a: 88
Inside test(double) a: 123.2
```

As you can see, this version of **OverloadDemo** does not define **test(int)**. Therefore, when **test( )** is called with an integer argument inside **Overload**, no matching method is found. However, Java can automatically convert an integer into a **double**, and this conversion can be used to resolve the call. Therefore, after **test(int)** is not found, Java elevates **i** to **double** and then calls **test(double)**. Of course, if **test(int)** had been defined, it would have been called instead. Java will employ its automatic type conversions only if no exact match is found.

Method overloading supports polymorphism because it is one way that Java implements the "one interface, multiple methods" paradigm. To understand how, consider the following. In languages that do not support method overloading, each method must be given a unique name. However, frequently you will want to implement essentially the same method for different types of data. Consider the absolute value function. In languages that do not support overloading, there are usually three or more versions of this function, each with a slightly different name. For instance, in C, the function **abs( )** returns the absolute value of an integer, **labs( )** returns the absolute value of a long integer, and **fabs( )** returns the absolute value of a floating-point value. Since C does not support overloading, each function has to have its own name, even though all three functions do essentially the same thing. This makes the situation more complex, conceptually, than it actually is. Although the underlying concept of each function is the same, you still have three names to remember. This situation does not occur in Java, because each absolute value method can use the same name. Indeed, Java's standard class library includes an absolute value method, called **abs( )**. This method is overloaded by Java's **Math** class to handle all numeric types. Java determines which version of **abs( )** to call based upon the type of argument.

The value of overloading is that it allows related methods to be accessed by use of a common name. Thus, the name **abs** represents the *general action* which is being performed. It is left to the compiler to choose the right *specific* version for a particular circumstance. You, the programmer, need only remember the general operation being performed. Through the application of polymorphism, several names have been reduced to one. Although this example is fairly simple, if you expand the concept, you can see how overloading can help you manage greater complexity.

When you overload a method, each version of that method can perform any activity you desire. There is no rule stating that overloaded methods must relate to one another. However, from a stylistic point of view, method overloading implies a relationship. Thus, while you can use the same name to overload unrelated methods, you should not. For example, you could use the name **sqr** to create methods that return the *square* of an integer and the *square root* of a floating-point value. But these two operations are fundamentally different. Applying method overloading in this manner defeats its original purpose. In practice, you should only overload closely related operations.

Overloading Constructors

In addition to overloading normal methods, you can also overload constructor methods. In fact, for most real-world classes that you create, overloaded constructors will be the norm, not the exception. To understand why, let's return to the **Box** class developed in the preceding chapter. Following is the latest version of **Box**:

```
class Box {
  double width;
  double height;
  double depth;

  // This is the constructor for Box.
  Box(double w, double h, double d) {
    width = w;
    height = h;
    depth = d;
  }

  // compute and return volume
  double volume() {
    return width * height * depth;
  }
}
```

As you can see, the **Box( )** constructor requires three parameters. This means that all declarations of **Box** objects must pass three arguments to the **Box( )** constructor. For example, the following statement is currently invalid:

```
Box ob = new Box();
```

Since **Box( )** requires three arguments, it's an error to call it without them. This raises some important questions. What if you simply wanted a box and did not care (or know) what its initial dimensions were? Or, what if you want to be able to initialize a cube by specifying only one value that would be used for all three dimensions? As the **Box** class is currently written, these other options are not available to you.

Fortunately, the solution to these problems is quite easy: simply overload the **Box** constructor so that it handles the situations just described. Here is a program that contains an improved version of **Box** that does just that:

```
/* Here, Box defines three constructors to initialize
   the dimensions of a box various ways.
*/
class Box {
  double width;
  double height;
  double depth;
```

```java
    // constructor used when all dimensions specified
    Box(double w, double h, double d) {
      width = w;
      height = h;
      depth = d;
    }

    // constructor used when no dimensions specified
    Box() {
      width = -1;  // use -1 to indicate
      height = -1; // an uninitialized
      depth = -1;  // box
    }

    // constructor used when cube is created
    Box(double len) {
      width = height = depth = len;
    }

    // compute and return volume
    double volume() {
      return width * height * depth;
    }
}

class OverloadCons {
  public static void main(String args[]) {
    // create boxes using the various constructors
    Box mybox1 = new Box(10, 20, 15);
    Box mybox2 = new Box();
    Box mycube = new Box(7);

    double vol;

    // get volume of first box
    vol = mybox1.volume();
    System.out.println("Volume of mybox1 is " + vol);

    // get volume of second box
    vol = mybox2.volume();
    System.out.println("Volume of mybox2 is " + vol);
```

```
    // get volume of cube
    vol = mycube.volume();
    System.out.println("Volume of mycube is " + vol);
  }
}
```

The output produced by this program is shown here:

```
Volume of mybox1 is 3000.0
Volume of mybox2 is -1.0
Volume of mycube is 343.0
```

As you can see, the proper overloaded constructor is called based upon the parameters specified when **new** is executed.

Using Objects as Parameters

So far we have only been using simple types as parameters to methods. However, it is both correct and common to pass objects to methods. For example, consider the following short program:

```
// Objects may be passed to methods.
class Test {
  int a, b;

  Test(int i, int j) {
    a = i;
    b = j;
  }

  // return true if o is equal to the invoking object
  boolean equals(Test o) {
    if(o.a == a && o.b == b) return true;
    else return false;
  }
}

class PassOb {
  public static void main(String args[]) {
```

```
    Test ob1 = new Test(100, 22);
    Test ob2 = new Test(100, 22);
    Test ob3 = new Test(-1, -1);

    System.out.println("ob1 == ob2: " + ob1.equals(ob2));

    System.out.println("ob1 == ob3: " + ob1.equals(ob3));
  }
}
```

This program generates the following output:

```
ob1 == ob2: true
ob1 == ob3: false
```

As you can see, the **equals( )** method inside **Test** compares two objects for equality and returns the result. That is, it compares the invoking object with the one that it is passed. If they contain the same values, then the method returns **true**. Otherwise, it returns **false**. Notice that the parameter **o** in **equals( )** specifies **Test** as its type. Although **Test** is a class type created by the program, it is used in just the same way as Java's built-in types.

One of the most common uses of object parameters involves constructors. Frequently you will want to construct a new object so that it is initially the same as some existing object. To do this, you must define a constructor that takes an object of its class as a parameter. For example, the following version of **Box** allows one object to initialize another:

```
// Here, Box allows one object to initialize another.

class Box {
  double width;
  double height;
  double depth;

  // construct clone of an object
  Box(Box ob) { // pass object to constructor
    width = ob.width;
    height = ob.height;
    depth = ob.depth;
  }
```

```java
    // constructor used when all dimensions specified
    Box(double w, double h, double d) {
      width = w;
      height = h;
      depth = d;
    }

    // constructor used when no dimensions specified
    Box() {
      width = -1;  // use -1 to indicate
      height = -1; // an uninitialized
      depth = -1;  // box
    }

    // constructor used when cube is created
    Box(double len) {
      width = height = depth = len;
    }

    // compute and return volume
    double volume() {
      return width * height * depth;
    }
}

class OverloadCons2 {
  public static void main(String args[]) {
    // create boxes using the various constructors
    Box mybox1 = new Box(10, 20, 15);
    Box mybox2 = new Box();
    Box mycube = new Box(7);

    Box myclone = new Box(mybox1);

    double vol;

    // get volume of first box
    vol = mybox1.volume();
    System.out.println("Volume of mybox1 is " + vol);
```

```
    // get volume of second box
    vol = mybox2.volume();
    System.out.println("Volume of mybox2 is " + vol);

    // get volume of cube
    vol = mycube.volume();
    System.out.println("Volume of cube is " + vol);

    // get volume of clone
    vol = myclone.volume();
    System.out.println("Volume of clone is " + vol);
  }
}
```

As you will see when you begin to create your own classes, providing many forms of constructor methods is usually required to allow objects to be constructed in a convenient and efficient manner.

A Closer Look at Argument Passing

In general, there are two ways that a computer language can pass an argument to a subroutine. The first way is *call-by-value*. This method copies the *value* of an argument into the formal parameter of the subroutine. Therefore, changes made to the parameter of the subroutine have no effect on the argument. The second way an argument can be passed is *call-by-reference*. In this method, a reference to an argument (not the value of the argument) is passed to the parameter. Inside the subroutine, this reference is used to access the actual argument specified in the call. This means that changes made to the parameter will affect the argument used to call the subroutine. As you will see, Java uses both approaches, depending upon what is passed.

In Java, when you pass a simple type to a method, it is passed by value. Thus, what occurs to the parameter that receives the argument has no effect outside the method. For example, consider the following program:

```
// Simple types are passed by value.
class Test {
  void meth(int i, int j) {
    i *= 2;
    j /= 2;
  }
}
```

```
class CallByValue {
  public static void main(String args[]) {
    Test ob = new Test();

    int a = 15, b = 20;

    System.out.println("a and b before call: " +
                         a + " " + b);

    ob.meth(a, b);

    System.out.println("a and b after call: " +
                         a + " " + b);
  }
}
```

The output from this program is shown here:

```
a and b before call: 15 20
a and b after call: 15 20
```

As you can see, the operations that occur inside **meth( )** have no effect on the values of **a** and **b** used in the call; their values here did not change to 30 and 10.

When you pass an object to a method, the situation changes dramatically, because objects are passed by reference. Keep in mind that when you create a variable of a class type, you are only creating a reference to an object. Thus, when you pass this reference to a method, the parameter that receives it will refer to the same object as that referred to by the argument. This effectively means that objects are passed to methods by use of call-by-reference. Changes to the object inside the method *do* affect the object used as an argument. For example, consider the following program:

```
// Objects are passed by reference.

class Test {
  int a, b;

  Test(int i, int j) {
    a = i;
    b = j;
  }
```

```
// pass an object
void meth(Test o) {
  o.a *= 2;

  o.b /= 2;
}
}

class CallByRef {
  public static void main(String args[]) {
    Test ob = new Test(15, 20);

    System.out.println("ob.a and ob.b before call: " +
                    ob.a + " " + ob.b);

    ob.meth(ob);

    System.out.println("ob.a and ob.b after call: " +
                    ob.a + " " + ob.b);
  }
}
```

This program generates the following output:

```
ob.a and ob.b before call: 15 20
ob.a and ob.b after call: 30 10
```

As you can see, in this case, the actions inside **meth( )** have affected the object used as an argument.

As a point of interest, when an object reference is passed to a method, the reference itself is passed by use of call-by-value. However, since the value being passed refers to an object, the copy of that value will still refer to the same object that its corresponding argument does.

 When a simple type is passed to a method, it is done by use of call-by-value. Objects are passed by use of call-by-reference.

Returning Objects

A method can return any type of data, including class types that you create. For example, in the following program, the **incrByTen( )** method returns an object in which the value of **a** is ten greater than it is in the invoking object.

```
// Returning an object.
class Test {
  int a;

  Test(int i) {
    a = i;
  }

  Test incrByTen() {
    Test temp = new Test(a+10);
    return temp;
  }
}

class RetOb {
  public static void main(String args[]) {
    Test ob1 = new Test(2);
    Test ob2;

    ob2 = ob1.incrByTen();
    System.out.println("ob1.a: " + ob1.a);
    System.out.println("ob2.a: " + ob2.a);

    ob2 = ob2.incrByTen();
    System.out.println("ob2.a after second increase: "
                       + ob2.a);
  }
}
```

The output generated by this program is shown here:

```
ob1.a: 2
ob2.a: 12
ob2.a after second increase: 22
```

As you can see, each time **incrByTen( )** is invoked, a new object is created, and a reference to it is returned to the calling routine.

The preceding program makes another important point: Since all objects are dynamically allocated using **new**, you don't need to worry about an object going out-of-scope because the method in which it was created terminates. The object will continue to exist as long as there is a reference to it somewhere in your program. When there are no references to it, the object will be reclaimed the next time garbage collection takes place.

Recursion

Java supports *recursion*. Recursion is the process of defining something in terms of itself. As it relates to Java programming, recursion is the attribute that allows a method to call itself. A method that calls itself is said to be *recursive*.

The classic example of recursion is the computation of the factorial of a number. The factorial of a number N is the product of all the whole numbers between 1 and N. For example, 3 factorial is $1 \times 2 \times 3$, or 6. Here is how a factorial can be computed by use of a recursive method:

```java
// A simple example of recursion.
class Factorial {
  // this is a recursive function
  int fact(int n) {
    int result;

    if(n==1) return 1;
    result = fact(n-1) * n;
    return result;
  }
}

class Recursion {
  public static void main(String args[]) {
    Factorial f = new Factorial();

    System.out.println("Factorial of 3 is " + f.fact(3));
    System.out.println("Factorial of 4 is " + f.fact(4));
    System.out.println("Factorial of 5 is " + f.fact(5));
  }
}
```

The output from this program is shown here:

```
Factorial of 3 is 6
Factorial of 4 is 24
Factorial of 5 is 120
```

If you are unfamiliar with recursive methods, then the operation of **fact( )** may seem a bit confusing. Here is how it works. When **fact( )** is called with an argument of 1, the function returns 1; otherwise it returns the product of **fact(n–1)*n**. To evaluate this expression, **fact( )** is called with **n–1**. This process repeats until **n** equals 1 and the calls to the method begin returning.

To better understand how the **fact( )** method works, let's go through a short example. When you compute the factorial of 3, the first call to **fact( )** will cause a second call to be made with an argument of 2. This invocation will cause **fact( )** to be called a third time with an argument of 1. This call will return 1, which is then multiplied by 2 (the value of **n** in the second invocation). This result (which is 2) is then returned to the original invocation of **fact( )** and multiplied by 3 (the original value of **n**). This yields the answer, 6. You might find it interesting to insert **println( )** statements into **fact( )** which will show at what level each call is and what the intermediate answers are.

When a method calls itself, new local variables and parameters are allocated storage on the stack, and the method code is executed with these new variables from the start. A recursive call does not make a new copy of the method. Only the arguments are new. As each recursive call returns, the old local variables and parameters are removed from the stack, and execution resumes at the point of the call inside the method. Recursive methods could be said to "telescope" out and back.

Recursive versions of many routines may execute a bit more slowly than the iterative equivalent because of the added overhead of the additional function calls. Many recursive calls to a method could cause a stack overrun. Because storage for parameters and local variables is on the stack and each new call creates a new copy of these variables, it is possible that the stack could be exhausted. If this occurs, the Java run-time system will cause an exception. However, you probably will not have to worry about this unless a recursive routine runs wild.

The main advantage to recursive methods is that they can be used to create clearer and simpler versions of several algorithms than can their iterative relatives. For example, the QuickSort sorting algorithm is quite difficult to implement in an iterative way. Some problems, especially AI-related ones, seem to lend themselves to recursive solutions. Finally, some people seem to think recursively more easily than iteratively.

When writing recursive methods, you must have an **if** statement somewhere to force the method to return without the recursive call being executed. If you don't do this, once you call the method, it will never return. This is a very common error in working with recursion. Use **println( )** statements liberally during development so that you can watch what is going on and abort execution if you see that you have made a mistake.

Here is one more example of recursion. The recursive method **printArray( )** prints the first **i** elements in the array **values**.

```
// Another example that uses recursion.

class RecTest {
  int values[];

  RecTest(int i) {
    values = new int[i];
  }

  // display array -- recursively
  void printArray(int i) {
    if(i==0) return;
    else printArray(i-1);
    System.out.println("[" + (i-1) + "] " + values[i-1]);
  }
}

class Recursion2 {
  public static void main(String args[]) {
    RecTest ob = new RecTest(10);
    int i;

    for(i=0; i<10; i++) ob.values[i] = i;

    ob.printArray(10);
  }
}
```

This program generates the following output:

```
[0] 0
[1] 1
[2] 2
[3] 3
[4] 4
[5] 5
[6] 6
```

```
[7]  7
[8]  8
[9]  9
```

Introducing Access Control

As you know, encapsulation links data with the code that manipulates it. However, encapsulation provides another important attribute: *access control.* Through encapsulation, you can control what parts of a program can access the members of a class. By controlling access, you can prevent misuse. For example, allowing access to data only through a well-defined set of methods, you can prevent the misuse of that data. Thus, when correctly implemented, a class creates a "black box" which may be used, but the inner workings of which are not open to tampering. However, the classes that were presented earlier do not completely meet this goal. For example, consider the **Stack** class shown at the end of Chapter 6. While it is true that the methods **push( )** and **pop( )** do provide a controlled interface to the stack, this interface is not enforced. That is, it is possible for another part of the program to bypass these methods and access the stack directly. Of course, in the wrong hands, this could lead to trouble. In this section you will be introduced to the mechanism by which you can precisely control access to the various members of a class.

How a member can be accessed is determined by the *access specifier* that modifies its declaration. Java supplies a rich set of access specifiers. Some aspects of access control are related mostly to inheritance or packages. (A *package* is, essentially, a grouping of classes.) These parts of Java's access control mechanism will be discussed later. Here, let's begin by examining access control as it applies to a single class. Once you understand the fundamentals of access control, the rest will be easy.

Java's access specifiers are **public**, **private**, and **protected**. Java also defines a default access level. **protected** applies only when inheritance is involved. The other access specifiers are described next.

Let's begin by defining **public** and **private**. When a member of a class is modified by the **public** specifier, then that member can be accessed by any other code. When a member of a class is specified as **private**, then that member can only be accessed by other members of its class. Now you can understand why **main( )** has always been preceded by the **public** specifier. It is called by code that is outside the program—that is, by the Java run-time system. When no access specifier is used, then by default the member of a class is public within its own package, but cannot be accessed outside of its package. (Packages are discussed in the following chapter.)

In the classes developed so far, all members of a class have used the default access mode, which is essentially public. However, this is not what you will typically want to be the case. Usually, you will want to restrict access to the data members of a class—allowing access only through methods. Also, there will be times when you will want to define methods which are private to a class.

An access specifier precedes the rest of a member's type specification. That is, it must begin a member's declaration statement. Here is an example:

```
public int i;
private double j;

private int myMethod(int a, char b) { // ...
```

To understand the effects of public and private access, consider the following program:

```
/* This program demonstrates the difference between
   public and private.
*/
class Test {
  int a; // default access
  public int b; // public access
  private int c; // private access

  // methods to access c
  void setc(int i) { // set c's value
    c = i;
  }
  int getc() { // get c's value
    return c;
  }
}

class AccessTest {
  public static void main(String args[]) {
    Test ob = new Test();

    // These are OK, a and b may be accessed directly
    ob.a = 10;
    ob.b = 20;

    // This is not OK and will cause an error
//  ob.c = 100; // Error!

    // You must access c through its methods
    ob.setc(100); // OK
```

```
System.out.println("a, b, and c: " + ob.a + " " +
                   ob.b + " " + ob.getc());
  }
}
```

As you can see, inside the **Test** class, **a** uses default access, which for this example is the same as specifying **public**. **b** is explicitly specified as **public**. Member **c** is given private access. This means that it cannot be accessed by code outside of its class. So, inside the **AccessTest** class, **c** cannot be used directly. It must be accessed through its public methods: **setc( )** and **getc( )**. If you were to remove the comment symbol from the beginning of the following line,

```
//  ob.c = 100; // Error!
```

then you would not be able to compile this program because of the access violation.

To see how access control can be applied to a more practical example, consider the following improved version of the **Stack** class shown at the end of Chapter 6.

```
// This class defines an integer stack that can hold 10 values.
class Stack {
  /* Now, both stck and tos are private.  This means
     that they cannot be accidentally or maliciously
     altered in a way that would be harmful to the stack.
  */
  private int stck[] = new int[10];
  private int tos;

  // Initialize top-of-stack
  Stack() {
    tos = -1;
  }

  // Push an item onto the stack
  void push(int item) {
    if(tos==9)
      System.out.println("Stack is full.");
    else
      stck[++tos] = item;
  }
```

```
// Pop an item from the stack
int pop() {
  if(tos < 0) {
    System.out.println("Stack underflow.");
    return 0;
  }
  else
    return stck[tos--];
}
}
```

As you can see, now both **stck**, which holds the stack, and **tos**, which is the index of the top of the stack, are specified as **private**. This means that they cannot be accessed or altered except through **push( )** and **pop( )**. Making **tos** private, for example, prevents other parts of your program from inadvertently setting it to a value that is beyond the end of the **stck** array.

The following program demonstrates the improved **Stack** class. Try removing the commented-out lines to prove to yourself that the **stck** and **tos** members are, indeed, inaccessible.

```
class TestStack {
  public static void main(String args[]) {
    Stack mystack1 = new Stack();
    Stack mystack2 = new Stack();

    // push some numbers onto the stack
    for(int i=0; i<10; i++) mystack1.push(i);
    for(int i=10; i<20; i++) mystack2.push(i);

    // pop those numbers off the stack
    System.out.println("Stack in mystack1:");
    for(int i=0; i<10; i++)
      System.out.println(mystack1.pop());

    System.out.println("Stack in mystack2:");
    for(int i=0; i<10; i++)
      System.out.println(mystack2.pop());

    // these statements are not legal
    // mystack1.tos = -2;
    // mystack2.stck[3] = 100;
```

```
      }
   }
```

Although methods will usually provide access to the data defined by a class, this does not always have to be the case. It is perfectly proper to allow an instance variable to be public when there is good reason to do so. For example, most of the simple classes in this book were created with little concern about controlling access to instance variables for the sake of simplicity. However, in most real-world classes, you will need to allow operations on data only through methods. The next chapter will return to the topic of access control. As you will see, it is particularly important when inheritance is involved.

Understanding static

There will be times when you will want to define a class member that will be used independently of any object of that class. Normally a class member must be accessed only in conjunction with an object of its class. However, it is possible to create a member that can be used by itself, without reference to a specific instance. To create such a member, precede its declaration with the keyword **static**. When a member is declared **static**, it can be accessed before any objects of its class are created, and without reference to any object. You can declare both methods and variables to be **static**. The most common example of a **static** member is **main( )**. **main( )** is declared as **static** because it must be called before any objects exist.

Instance variables declared as **static** are, essentially, global variables. When objects of its class are declared, no copy of a **static** variable is made. Instead, all instances of the class share the same **static** variable.

Methods declared as **static** have several restrictions:

■ They can only call other **static** methods.

■ They must only access **static** data.

■ They cannot refer to **this** or **super** in any way. (The keyword **super** relates to inheritance and is described in the next chapter.)

If you need to do computation in order to initialize your **static** variables, you can declare a **static** block which gets executed exactly once, when the class is first loaded. The following example shows a class that has a **static** method, some **static** variables, and a **static** initialization block:

```
// Demonstrate static variables, methods, and blocks.
class UseStatic {
```

```
static int a = 3;
static int b;

static void meth(int x) {
  System.out.println("x = " + x);
  System.out.println("a = " + a);
  System.out.println("b = " + b);
}

static {
  System.out.println("Static block initialized.");
  b = a * 4;
}

public static void main(String args[]) {
  meth(42);
}
}
```

As soon as the **UseStatic** class is loaded, all of the **static** statements are run. First, **a** is set to **3**, then the **static** block executes (printing a message), and finally, **b** is initialized to **a * 4** or **12**. Then **main( )** is called, which calls **meth( )**, passing **42** to **x**. The three **println( )** statements refer to the two **static** variables **a** and **b**, as well as to the local variable **x**.

Remember *It is illegal to refer to any instance variables inside of a **static** method.*

Here is the output of the program:

```
Static block initialized.
x = 42
a = 3
b = 12
```

Outside of the class in which they are defined, **static** methods and variables can be used independently of any object. To do so, you need only specify the name of their class followed by the dot operator. For example, if you wish to call a **static** method from outside its class, you can do so using the following general form:

classname.method( )

Here, *classname* is the name of the class in which the **static** method is declared. As you can see, this format is similar to that used to call non-**static** methods through object- reference variables. A **static** variable can be accessed in the same way—by use of the dot operator on the name of the class. This is how Java implements a controlled version of global methods and global variables.

Here is an example. Inside **main( )**, the **static** method **callme( )** and the **static** variable **b** are accessed outside of their class.

```
class StaticDemo {
  static int a = 42;
  static int b = 99;
  static void callme() {
    System.out.println("a = " + a);
  }
}

class StaticByName {
  public static void main(String args[]) {
    StaticDemo.callme();
    System.out.println("b = " + StaticDemo.b);
  }
}
```

Here is the output of this program:

```
a = 42
b = 99
```

Introducing final

A variable can be declared as **final**. Doing so prevents its contents from being modified. This means that you must initialize a **final** variable when it is declared. (In this usage, **final** is similar to **const** in C/C++/C#.) For example:

```
final int FILE_NEW = 1;
final int FILE_OPEN = 2;
final int FILE_SAVE = 3;
final int FILE_SAVEAS = 4;
final int FILE_QUIT = 5;
```

Subsequent parts of your program can now use **FILE_OPEN**, etc., as if they were constants, without fear that a value has been changed.

It is a common coding convention to choose all uppercase identifiers for **final** variables. Variables declared as **final** do not occupy memory on a per-instance basis. Thus, a **final** variable is essentially a constant.

The keyword **final** can also be applied to methods, but its meaning is substantially different than when it is applied to variables. This second usage of **final** is described in the next chapter, when inheritance is described.

Arrays Revisited

Arrays were introduced earlier in this book, before classes had been discussed. Now that you know about classes, an important point can be made about arrays: they are implemented as objects. Because of this, there is a special array attribute that you will want to take advantage of. Specifically, the size of an array—that is, the number of elements that an array can hold—is found in its **length** instance variable. All arrays have this variable, and it will always hold the size of the array. Here is a program that demonstrates this property:

```
// This program demonstrates the length array member.
class Length {
  public static void main(String args[]) {
    int a1[] = new int[10];
    int a2[] = {3, 5, 7, 1, 8, 99, 44, -10};
    int a3[] = {4, 3, 2, 1};

    System.out.println("length of a1 is " + a1.length);
    System.out.println("length of a2 is " + a2.length);
    System.out.println("length of a3 is " + a3.length);
  }
}
```

This program displays the following output:

```
length of a1 is 10
length of a2 is 8
length of a3 is 4
```

As you can see, the size of each array is displayed. Keep in mind that the value of **length** has nothing to do with the number of elements that are actually in use. It only reflects the number of elements that the array is designed to hold.

You can put the **length** member to good use in many situations. For example, here is an improved version of the **Stack** class. As you might recall, the earlier versions of this class always created a ten-element stack. The following version lets you create stacks of any size. The value of **stck.length** is used to prevent the stack from overflowing.

```java
// Improved Stack class that uses the length array member.
class Stack {
  private int stck[];
  private int tos;

  // allocate and initialize stack
  Stack(int size) {
    stck = new int[size];
    tos = -1;
  }

  // Push an item onto the stack
  void push(int item) {
    if(tos==stck.length-1) // use length member
      System.out.println("Stack is full.");
    else
      stck[++tos] = item;
  }

  // Pop an item from the stack
  int pop() {
    if(tos < 0) {
      System.out.println("Stack underflow.");
      return 0;
    }
    else
      return stck[tos--];
  }
}

class TestStack2 {
  public static void main(String args[]) {
    Stack mystack1 = new Stack(5);
    Stack mystack2 = new Stack(8);
```

```
      // push some numbers onto the stack
      for(int i=0; i<5; i++) mystack1.push(i);
      for(int i=0; i<8; i++) mystack2.push(i);

      // pop those numbers off the stack
      System.out.println("Stack in mystack1:");
      for(int i=0; i<5; i++)
        System.out.println(mystack1.pop());

      System.out.println("Stack in mystack2:");
      for(int i=0; i<8; i++)
        System.out.println(mystack2.pop());
  }
}
```

Notice that the program creates two stacks: one five elements deep and the other eight elements deep. As you can see, the fact that arrays maintain their own length information makes it easy to create stacks of any size.

Introducing Nested and Inner Classes

It is possible to define a class within another class; such classes are known as *nested classes*. The scope of a nested class is bounded by the scope of its enclosing class. Thus, if class B is defined within class A, then B is known to A, but not outside of A. A nested class has access to the members, including private members, of the class in which it is nested. However, the enclosing class does not have access to the members of the nested class.

There are two types of nested classes: *static* and *non-static*. A static nested class is one which has the **static** modifier applied. Because it is static, it must access the members of its enclosing class through an object. That is, it cannot refer to members of its enclosing class directly. Because of this restriction, static nested classes are seldom used.

The most important type of nested class is the *inner* class. An inner class is a non-static nested class. It has access to all of the variables and methods of its outer class and may refer to them directly in the same way that other non-static members of the outer class do. Thus, an inner class is fully within the scope of its enclosing class.

The following program illustrates how to define and use an inner class. The class named **Outer** has one instance variable named **outer_x**, one instance method named **test( )**, and defines one inner class called **Inner**.

```
// Demonstrate an inner class.
class Outer {
  int outer_x = 100;
```

```
  void test() {
    Inner inner = new Inner();
    inner.display();
  }

  // this is an inner class
  class Inner {
    void display() {
      System.out.println("display: outer_x = " + outer_x);
    }
  }
}

class InnerClassDemo {
  public static void main(String args[]) {
    Outer outer = new Outer();
    outer.test();
  }
}
```

Output from this application is shown here:

```
display: outer_x = 100
```

In the program, an inner class named **Inner** is defined within the scope of class
Outer. Therefore, any code in class **Inner** can directly access the variable **outer_x**. An
instance method named **display( )** is defined inside **Inner**. This method displays
outer_x on the standard output stream. The **main( )** method of **InnerClassDemo**
creates an instance of class **Outer** and invokes its **test( )** method. That method creates
an instance of class **Inner** and the **display( )** method is called.

It is important to realize that class **Inner** is known only within the scope of class
Outer. The Java compiler generates an error message if any code outside of class **Outer**
attempts to instantiate class **Inner**. Generalizing, a nested class is no different than any
other program element: it is known only within its enclosing scope.

As explained, an inner class has access to all of the members of its enclosing class,
but the reverse is not true. Members of the inner class are known only within the scope
of the inner class and may not be used by the outer class. For example,

```
// This program will not compile.
class Outer {
  int outer_x = 100;

  void test() {
    Inner inner = new Inner();
    inner.display();
  }

  // this is an inner class
  class Inner {
    int y = 10; // y is local to Inner
    void display() {
      System.out.println("display: outer_x = " + outer_x);
    }
  }

  void showy() {
    System.out.println(y); // error, y not known here!
  }
}

class InnerClassDemo {
  public static void main(String args[]) {
    Outer outer = new Outer();
    outer.test();
  }
}
```

Here, **y** is declared as an instance variable of **Inner**. Thus it is not known outside of that class and it cannot be used by **showy( )**.

Although we have been focusing on nested classes declared within an outer class scope, it is possible to define inner classes within any block scope. For example, you can define a nested class within the block defined by a method or even within the body of a **for** loop, as this next program shows.

```
// Define an inner class within a for loop.
class Outer {
  int outer_x = 100;
```

```
void test() {
  for(int i=0; i<10; i++) {
    class Inner {
      void display() {
        System.out.println("display: outer_x = " + outer_x);
      }
    }
    Inner inner = new Inner();
    inner.display();
  }
}
}

class InnerClassDemo {
  public static void main(String args[]) {
    Outer outer = new Outer();
    outer.test();
  }
}
```

The output from this version of the program is shown here.

```
display: outer_x = 100
display: outer_x = 100
display: outer_x = 100
display: outer_x = 100
display: outer_x = 100
display: outer_x = 100
display: outer_x = 100
display: outer_x = 100
display: outer_x = 100
display: outer_x = 100
```

While nested classes are not used in most day-to-day programming, they are particularly helpful when handling events in an applet. We will return to the topic of nested classes in Chapter 20. There you will see how inner classes can be used to simplify the code needed to handle certain types of events. You will also learn about *anonymous inner classes*, which are inner classes that don't have a name.

One final point: Nested classes were not allowed by the original 1.0 specification for Java. They were added by Java 1.1.

Exploring the String Class

Although the **String** class will be examined in depth in Part II of this book, a short exploration of it is warranted now, because we will be using strings in some of the example programs shown toward the end of Part I. **String** is probably the most commonly used class in Java's class library. The obvious reason for this is that strings are a very important part of programming.

The first thing to understand about strings is that every string you create is actually an object of type **String**. Even string constants are actually **String** objects. For example, in the statement

```
System.out.println("This is a String, too");
```

the string "This is a String, too" is a **String** constant. Fortunately, Java handles **String** constants in the same way that other computer languages handle "normal" strings, so you don't have to worry about this.

The second thing to understand about strings is that objects of type **String** are immutable; once a **String** object is created, its contents cannot be altered. While this may seem like a serious restriction, it is not, for two reasons:

- ■ If you need to change a string, you can always create a new one that contains the modifications.

- ■ Java defines a peer class of **String**, called **StringBuffer**, which allows strings to be altered, so all of the normal string manipulations are still available in Java. (**StringBuffer** is described in Part II of this book.)

Strings can be constructed a variety of ways. The easiest is to use a statement like this:

```
String myString = "this is a test";
```

Once you have created a **String** object, you can use it anywhere that a string is allowed. For example, this statement displays **myString**:

```
System.out.println(myString);
```

Java defines one operator for **String** objects: **+**. It is used to concatenate two strings. For example, this statement

```
String myString = "I" + " like " + "Java.";
```

results in **myString** containing "I like Java."

The following program demonstrates the preceding concepts:

```
// Demonstrating Strings.
class StringDemo {
  public static void main(String args[]) {
    String strOb1 = "First String";
    String strOb2 = "Second String";
    String strOb3 = strOb1 + " and " + strOb2;

    System.out.println(strOb1);
    System.out.println(strOb2);
    System.out.println(strOb3);
  }
}
```

The output produced by this program is shown here:

```
First String
Second String
First String and Second String
```

The **String** class contains several methods that you can use. Here are a few. You can test two strings for equality by using **equals( )**. You can obtain the length of a string by calling the **length( )** method. You can obtain the character at a specified index within a string by calling **charAt( )**. The general forms of these three methods are shown here:

boolean equals(String *object*)
int length( )
char charAt(int *index*)

Here is a program that demonstrates these methods:

```
// Demonstrating some String methods.
class StringDemo2 {
  public static void main(String args[]) {
    String strOb1 = "First String";
    String strOb2 = "Second String";
    String strOb3 = strOb1;

    System.out.println("Length of strOb1: " +
                  strOb1.length());

    System.out.println("Char at index 3 in strOb1: " +
                  strOb1.charAt(3));
```

```
    if(strOb1.equals(strOb2))
      System.out.println("strOb1 == strOb2");
    else
      System.out.println("strOb1 != strOb2");

    if(strOb1.equals(strOb3))
      System.out.println("strOb1 == strOb3");
    else
      System.out.println("strOb1 != strOb3");
  }
}
```

This program generates the following output:

```
Length of strOb1: 12
Char at index 3 in strOb1: s
strOb1 != strOb2
strOb1 == strOb3
```

Of course, you can have arrays of strings, just like you can have arrays of any other type of object. For example:

```
// Demonstrate String arrays.
class StringDemo3 {
  public static void main(String args[]) {
    String str[] = { "one", "two", "three" };

    for(int i=0; i<str.length; i++)
      System.out.println("str[" + i + "]: " +
                         str[i]);
  }
}
```

Here is the output from this program:

```
str[0]: one
str[1]: two
str[2]: three
```

As you will see in the following section, string arrays play an important part in many Java programs.

Using Command-Line Arguments

Sometimes you will want to pass information into a program when you run it. This is accomplished by passing *command-line arguments* to **main( )**. A command-line argument is the information that directly follows the program's name on the command line when it is executed. To access the command-line arguments inside a Java program is quite easy—they are stored as strings in the **String** array passed to **main( )**. For example, the following program displays all of the command-line arguments that it is called with:

```
// Display all command-line arguments.
class CommandLine {
  public static void main(String args[]) {
    for(int i=0; i<args.length; i++)
      System.out.println("args[" + i + "]: " +
                         args[i]);
  }
}
```

Try executing this program, as shown here:

```
java CommandLine this is a test 100 -1
```

When you do, you will see the following output:

```
args[0]: this
args[1]: is
args[2]: a
args[3]: test
args[4]: 100
args[5]: -1
```

All command-line arguments are passed as strings. You must convert numeric values to their internal forms manually, as explained in Chapter 14.

The
Complete
Reference

Java™ 2

Chapter 8

Inheritance

Inheritance is one of the cornerstones of object-oriented programming because it allows the creation of hierarchical classifications. Using inheritance, you can create a general class that defines traits common to a set of related items. This class can then be inherited by other, more specific classes, each adding those things that are unique to it. In the terminology of Java, a class that is inherited is called a *superclass.* The class that does the inheriting is called a *subclass.* Therefore, a subclass is a specialized version of a superclass. It inherits all of the instance variables and methods defined by the superclass and adds its own, unique elements.

Inheritance Basics

To inherit a class, you simply incorporate the definition of one class into another by using the **extends** keyword. To see how, let's begin with a short example. The following program creates a superclass called **A** and a subclass called **B**. Notice how the keyword **extends** is used to create a subclass of **A**.

```
// A simple example of inheritance.

// Create a superclass.
class A {
  int i, j;

  void showij() {
    System.out.println("i and j: " + i + " " + j);
  }
}

// Create a subclass by extending class A.
class B extends A {
  int k;

  void showk() {
    System.out.println("k: " + k);
  }
  void sum() {
    System.out.println("i+j+k: " + (i+j+k));
  }
}

class SimpleInheritance {
  public static void main(String args[]) {
    A superOb = new A();
```

```
    B subOb = new B();

    // The superclass may be used by itself.
    superOb.i = 10;
    superOb.j = 20;
    System.out.println("Contents of superOb: ");
    superOb.showij();
    System.out.println();

    /* The subclass has access to all public members of
       its superclass. */
    subOb.i = 7;
    subOb.j = 8;
    subOb.k = 9;
    System.out.println("Contents of subOb: ");
    subOb.showij();
    subOb.showk();
    System.out.println();

    System.out.println("Sum of i, j and k in subOb:");
    subOb.sum();
  }
}
```

The output from this program is shown here:

```
Contents of superOb:
i and j: 10 20

Contents of subOb:
i and j: 7 8
k: 9

Sum of i, j and k in subOb:
i+j+k: 24
```

As you can see, the subclass **B** includes all of the members of its superclass, **A**. This is why **subOb** can access **i** and **j** and call **showij( )**. Also, inside **sum( )**, **i** and **j** can be referred to directly, as if they were part of **B**.

Even though **A** is a superclass for **B**, it is also a completely independent, stand-alone class. Being a superclass for a subclass does not mean that the superclass cannot be used by itself. Further, a subclass can be a superclass for another subclass. The general form of a **class** declaration that inherits a superclass is shown here:

```
class subclass-name extends superclass-name {
  // body of class
}
```

You can only specify one superclass for any subclass that you create. Java does not support the inheritance of multiple superclasses into a single subclass. (This differs from C++, in which you can inherit multiple base classes.) You can, as stated, create a hierarchy of inheritance in which a subclass becomes a superclass of another subclass. However, no class can be a superclass of itself.

Member Access and Inheritance

Although a subclass includes all of the members of its superclass, it cannot access those members of the superclass that have been declared as **private**. For example, consider the following simple class hierarchy:

```
/* In a class hierarchy, private members remain
   private to their class.

   This program contains an error and will not
   compile.
*/

// Create a superclass.
class A {
  int i; // public by default
  private int j; // private to A

  void setij(int x, int y) {
    i = x;
    j = y;
  }
}

// A's j is not accessible here.
class B extends A {
  int total;
```

THE JAVA LANGUAGE

```
  void sum() {
    total = i + j; // ERROR, j is not accessible here
  }
}

class Access {
  public static void main(String args[]) {
    B subOb = new B();

    subOb.setij(10, 12);

    subOb.sum();
    System.out.println("Total is " + subOb.total);
  }
}
```

This program will not compile because the reference to **j** inside the **sum( )** method of **B** causes an access violation. Since **j** is declared as **private**, it is only accessible by other members of its own class. Subclasses have no access to it.

 A class member that has been declared as private will remain private to its class. It is not accessible by any code outside its class, including subclasses.

A More Practical Example

Let's look at a more practical example that will help illustrate the power of inheritance. Here, the final version of the **Box** class developed in the preceding chapter will be extended to include a fourth component called **weight**. Thus, the new class will contain a box's width, height, depth, and weight.

```
// This program uses inheritance to extend Box.
class Box {
  double width;
  double height;
  double depth;

  // construct clone of an object
  Box(Box ob) { // pass object to constructor
    width = ob.width;
    height = ob.height;
```

```java
    depth = ob.depth;
  }

  // constructor used when all dimensions specified
  Box(double w, double h, double d) {
    width = w;
    height = h;
    depth = d;
  }

  // constructor used when no dimensions specified
  Box() {
    width = -1;   // use -1 to indicate
    height = -1; // an uninitialized
    depth = -1;   // box
  }

  // constructor used when cube is created
  Box(double len) {
    width = height = depth = len;
  }

  // compute and return volume
  double volume() {
    return width * height * depth;
  }
}

// Here, Box is extended to include weight.
class BoxWeight extends Box {
  double weight; // weight of box

  // constructor for BoxWeight
  BoxWeight(double w, double h, double d, double m) {
    width = w;
    height = h;
    depth = d;
    weight = m;
  }
}
```

```
class DemoBoxWeight {
  public static void main(String args[]) {
    BoxWeight mybox1 = new BoxWeight(10, 20, 15, 34.3);
    BoxWeight mybox2 = new BoxWeight(2, 3, 4, 0.076);
    double vol;

    vol = mybox1.volume();
    System.out.println("Volume of mybox1 is " + vol);
    System.out.println("Weight of mybox1 is " + mybox1.weight);
    System.out.println();

    vol = mybox2.volume();
    System.out.println("Volume of mybox2 is " + vol);
    System.out.println("Weight of mybox2 is " + mybox2.weight);
  }
}
```

The output from this program is shown here:

```
Volume of mybox1 is 3000.0
Weight of mybox1 is 34.3

Volume of mybox2 is 24.0
Weight of mybox2 is 0.076
```

BoxWeight inherits all of the characteristics of **Box** and adds to them the **weight** component. It is not necessary for **BoxWeight** to re-create all of the features found in **Box**. It can simply extend **Box** to meet its own purposes.

A major advantage of inheritance is that once you have created a superclass that defines the attributes common to a set of objects, it can be used to create any number of more specific subclasses. Each subclass can precisely tailor its own classification. For example, the following class inherits **Box** and adds a color attribute:

```
// Here, Box is extended to include color.
class ColorBox extends Box {
  int color; // color of box

  ColorBox(double w, double h, double d, int c) {
    width = w;
```

```
    height = h;
    depth = d;
    color = c;
  }
}
```

Remember, once you have created a superclass that defines the general aspects of an object, that superclass can be inherited to form specialized classes. Each subclass simply adds its own, unique attributes. This is the essence of inheritance.

A Superclass Variable Can Reference a Subclass Object

A reference variable of a superclass can be assigned a reference to any subclass derived from that superclass. You will find this aspect of inheritance quite useful in a variety of situations. For example, consider the following:

```
class RefDemo {
  public static void main(String args[]) {
    BoxWeight weightbox = new BoxWeight(3, 5, 7, 8.37);
    Box plainbox = new Box();
    double vol;

    vol = weightbox.volume();
    System.out.println("Volume of weightbox is " + vol);
    System.out.println("Weight of weightbox is " +
                        weightbox.weight);
    System.out.println();

    // assign BoxWeight reference to Box reference
    plainbox = weightbox;

    vol = plainbox.volume(); // OK, volume() defined in Box
    System.out.println("Volume of plainbox is " + vol);

    /* The following statement is invalid because plainbox
       does not define a weight member. */
//  System.out.println("Weight of plainbox is " + plainbox.weight);
  }
}
```

Here, **weightbox** is a reference to **BoxWeight** objects, and **plainbox** is a reference to **Box** objects. Since **BoxWeight** is a subclass of **Box**, it is permissible to assign **plainbox** a reference to the **weightbox** object.

It is important to understand that it is the type of the reference variable—not the type of the object that it refers to—that determines what members can be accessed. That is, when a reference to a subclass object is assigned to a superclass reference variable, you will have access only to those parts of the object defined by the superclass. This is why **plainbox** can't access **weight** even when it refers to a **BoxWeight** object. If you think about it, this makes sense, because the superclass has no knowledge of what a subclass adds to it. This is why the last line of code in the preceding fragment is commented out. It is not possible for a **Box** reference to access the **weight** field, because it does not define one.

Although the preceding may seem a bit esoteric, it has some important practical applications—two of which are discussed later in this chapter.

Using super

In the preceding examples, classes derived from **Box** were not implemented as efficiently or as robustly as they could have been. For example, the constructor for **BoxWeight** explicitly initializes the **width**, **height**, and **depth** fields of **Box( )**. Not only does this duplicate code found in its superclass, which is inefficient, but it implies that a subclass must be granted access to these members. However, there will be times when you will want to create a superclass that keeps the details of its implementation to itself (that is, that keeps its data members private). In this case, there would be no way for a subclass to directly access or initialize these variables on its own. Since encapsulation is a primary attribute of OOP, it is not surprising that Java provides a solution to this problem. Whenever a subclass needs to refer to its immediate superclass, it can do so by use of the keyword **super**.

super has two general forms. The first calls the superclass' constructor. The second is used to access a member of the superclass that has been hidden by a member of a subclass. Each use is examined here.

Using super to Call Superclass Constructors

A subclass can call a constructor method defined by its superclass by use of the following form of **super**:

super(*parameter-list*);

Here, *parameter-list* specifies any parameters needed by the constructor in the superclass. **super( )** must always be the first statement executed inside a subclass' constructor.

To see how **super( )** is used, consider this improved version of the **BoxWeight( )** class:

```
// BoxWeight now uses super to initialize its Box attributes.
class BoxWeight extends Box {
  double weight; // weight of box

  // initialize width, height, and depth using super()
  BoxWeight(double w, double h, double d, double m) {
    super(w, h, d); // call superclass constructor
    weight = m;
  }
}
```

Here, **BoxWeight( )** calls **super( )** with the parameters **w**, **h**, and **d**. This causes the **Box( )** constructor to be called, which initializes **width**, **height**, and **depth** using these values. **BoxWeight** no longer initializes these values itself. It only needs to initialize the value unique to it: **weight**. This leaves **Box** free to make these values **private** if desired.

In the preceding example, **super( )** was called with three arguments. Since constructors can be overloaded, **super( )** can be called using any form defined by the superclass. The constructor executed will be the one that matches the arguments. For example, here is a complete implementation of **BoxWeight** that provides constructors for the various ways that a box can be constructed. In each case, **super( )** is called using the appropriate arguments. Notice that **width**, **height**, and **depth** have been made private within **Box**.

```
// A complete implementation of BoxWeight.
class Box {
  private double width;
  private double height;
  private double depth;

  // construct clone of an object
  Box(Box ob) { // pass object to constructor
    width = ob.width;
    height = ob.height;
    depth = ob.depth;
  }
```

```
  // constructor used when all dimensions specified
  Box(double w, double h, double d) {
    width = w;
    height = h;
    depth = d;
  }

  // constructor used when no dimensions specified
  Box() {
    width = -1;  // use -1 to indicate
    height = -1; // an uninitialized
    depth = -1;  // box
  }

  // constructor used when cube is created
  Box(double len) {
    width = height = depth = len;
  }

  // compute and return volume
  double volume() {
    return width * height * depth;
  }
}

// BoxWeight now fully implements all constructors.
class BoxWeight extends Box {
  double weight; // weight of box

  // construct clone of an object
  BoxWeight(BoxWeight ob) { // pass object to constructor
    super(ob);
    weight = ob.weight;
  }

  // constructor when all parameters are specified
  BoxWeight(double w, double h, double d, double m) {
    super(w, h, d); // call superclass constructor
    weight = m;
  }
```

```
  // default constructor
  BoxWeight() {
    super();
    weight = -1;
  }

  // constructor used when cube is created
  BoxWeight(double len, double m) {
    super(len);
    weight = m;
  }
}

class DemoSuper {
  public static void main(String args[]) {
    BoxWeight mybox1 = new BoxWeight(10, 20, 15, 34.3);
    BoxWeight mybox2 = new BoxWeight(2, 3, 4, 0.076);
    BoxWeight mybox3 = new BoxWeight(); // default
    BoxWeight mycube = new BoxWeight(3, 2);
    BoxWeight myclone = new BoxWeight(mybox1);
    double vol;

    vol = mybox1.volume();
    System.out.println("Volume of mybox1 is " + vol);
    System.out.println("Weight of mybox1 is " + mybox1.weight);
    System.out.println();

    vol = mybox2.volume();
    System.out.println("Volume of mybox2 is " + vol);
    System.out.println("Weight of mybox2 is " + mybox2.weight);
    System.out.println();

    vol = mybox3.volume();
    System.out.println("Volume of mybox3 is " + vol);
    System.out.println("Weight of mybox3 is " + mybox3.weight);
    System.out.println();

    vol = myclone.volume();
    System.out.println("Volume of myclone is " + vol);
    System.out.println("Weight of myclone is " + myclone.weight);
    System.out.println();
```

```
    vol = mycube.volume();
    System.out.println("Volume of mycube is " + vol);
    System.out.println("Weight of mycube is " + mycube.weight);
    System.out.println();
  }
}
```

This program generates the following output:

```
Volume of mybox1 is 3000.0
Weight of mybox1 is 34.3

Volume of mybox2 is 24.0
Weight of mybox2 is 0.076

Volume of mybox3 is -1.0
Weight of mybox3 is -1.0

Volume of myclone is 3000.0
Weight of myclone is 34.3

Volume of mycube is 27.0
Weight of mycube is 2.0
```

Pay special attention to this constructor in **BoxWeight( )**:

```
// construct clone of an object
BoxWeight(BoxWeight ob) { // pass object to constructor
  super(ob);
  weight = ob.weight;
}
```

Notice that **super( )** is called with an object of type **BoxWeight**—not of type **Box**. This still invokes the constructor **Box(Box ob)**. As mentioned earlier, a superclass variable can be used to reference any object derived from that class. Thus, we are able to pass a **BoxWeight** object to the **Box** constructor. Of course, **Box** only has knowledge of its own members.

Let's review the key concepts behind **super( )**. When a subclass calls **super( )**, it is calling the constructor of its immediate superclass. Thus, **super( )** always refers to the superclass immediately above the calling class. This is true even in a multileveled hierarchy. Also, **super( )** must always be the first statement executed inside a subclass constructor.

A Second Use for super

The second form of **super** acts somewhat like **this**, except that it always refers to the superclass of the subclass in which it is used. This usage has the following general form:

super.*member*

Here, *member* can be either a method or an instance variable.

This second form of **super** is most applicable to situations in which member names of a subclass hide members by the same name in the superclass. Consider this simple class hierarchy:

```java
// Using super to overcome name hiding.
class A {
  int i;
}

// Create a subclass by extending class A.
class B extends A {
  int i; // this i hides the i in A

  B(int a, int b) {
    super.i = a; // i in A
    i = b; // i in B
  }

  void show() {
    System.out.println("i in superclass: " + super.i);
    System.out.println("i in subclass: " + i);
  }
}

class UseSuper {
  public static void main(String args[]) {
    B subOb = new B(1, 2);

    subOb.show();
  }
}
```

This program displays the following:

```
i in superclass: 1
i in subclass: 2
```

Although the instance variable **i** in **B** hides the **i** in **A**, **super** allows access to the **i** defined in the superclass. As you will see, **super** can also be used to call methods that are hidden by a subclass.

Creating a Multilevel Hierarchy

Up to this point, we have been using simple class hierarchies that consist of only a superclass and a subclass. However, you can build hierarchies that contain as many layers of inheritance as you like. As mentioned, it is perfectly acceptable to use a subclass as a superclass of another. For example, given three classes called **A**, **B**, and **C**, **C** can be a subclass of **B**, which is a subclass of **A**. When this type of situation occurs, each subclass inherits all of the traits found in all of its superclasses. In this case, **C** inherits all aspects of **B** and **A**. To see how a multilevel hierarchy can be useful, consider the following program. In it, the subclass **BoxWeight** is used as a superclass to create the subclass called **Shipment**. **Shipment** inherits all of the traits of **BoxWeight** and **Box**, and adds a field called **cost**, which holds the cost of shipping such a parcel.

```java
// Extend BoxWeight to include shipping costs.

// Start with Box.
class Box {
  private double width;
  private double height;
  private double depth;

  // construct clone of an object
  Box(Box ob) { // pass object to constructor
    width = ob.width;
    height = ob.height;
    depth = ob.depth;
  }

  // constructor used when all dimensions specified
  Box(double w, double h, double d) {
    width = w;
    height = h;
```

```
    depth = d;
  }

  // constructor used when no dimensions specified
  Box() {
    width = -1;  // use -1 to indicate
    height = -1; // an uninitialized
    depth = -1;  // box
  }

  // constructor used when cube is created
  Box(double len) {
    width = height = depth = len;
  }

  // compute and return volume
  double volume() {
    return width * height * depth;
  }
}

// Add weight.
class BoxWeight extends Box {
  double weight; // weight of box

  // construct clone of an object
  BoxWeight(BoxWeight ob) { // pass object to constructor
    super(ob);
    weight = ob.weight;
  }
  // constructor when all parameters are specified
  BoxWeight(double w, double h, double d, double m) {
    super(w, h, d); // call superclass constructor
    weight = m;
  }

  // default constructor
  BoxWeight() {
    super();
    weight = -1;
  }
```

```java
  // constructor used when cube is created
  BoxWeight(double len, double m) {
    super(len);
    weight = m;
  }
}

// Add shipping costs
class Shipment extends BoxWeight {
  double cost;

  // construct clone of an object
  Shipment(Shipment ob) { // pass object to constructor
    super(ob);
    cost = ob.cost;
  }

  // constructor when all parameters are specified
  Shipment(double w, double h, double d,
           double m, double c) {
    super(w, h, d, m); // call superclass constructor
    cost = c;
  }

  // default constructor
  Shipment() {
    super();
    cost = -1;
  }

  // constructor used when cube is created
  Shipment(double len, double m, double c) {
    super(len, m);
    cost = c;
  }
}

class DemoShipment {
  public static void main(String args[]) {
    Shipment shipment1 =
```

```
                       new Shipment(10, 20, 15, 10, 3.41);
        Shipment shipment2 =
                       new Shipment(2, 3, 4, 0.76, 1.28);

        double vol;

        vol = shipment1.volume();
        System.out.println("Volume of shipment1 is " + vol);
        System.out.println("Weight of shipment1 is "
                            + shipment1.weight);
        System.out.println("Shipping cost: $" + shipment1.cost);
        System.out.println();

        vol = shipment2.volume();
        System.out.println("Volume of shipment2 is " + vol);
        System.out.println("Weight of shipment2 is "
                            + shipment2.weight);
        System.out.println("Shipping cost: $" + shipment2.cost);
    }
}
```

The output of this program is shown here:

```
Volume of shipment1 is 3000.0
Weight of shipment1 is 10.0
Shipping cost: $3.41

Volume of shipment2 is 24.0
Weight of shipment2 is 0.76
Shipping cost: $1.28
```

Because of inheritance, **Shipment** can make use of the previously defined classes of **Box** and **BoxWeight**, adding only the extra information it needs for its own, specific application. This is part of the value of inheritance; it allows the reuse of code.

This example illustrates one other important point: **super( )** always refers to the constructor in the closest superclass. The **super( )** in **Shipment** calls the constructor in **BoxWeight**. The **super( )** in **BoxWeight** calls the constructor in **Box**. In a class hierarchy, if a superclass constructor requires parameters, then all subclasses must pass those parameters "up the line." This is true whether or not a subclass needs parameters of its own.

> | **Note** | *In the preceding program, the entire class hierarchy, including **Box**, **BoxWeight**, and **Shipment**, is shown all in one file. This is for your convenience only. In Java, all three classes could have been placed into their own files and compiled separately. In fact, using separate files is the norm, not the exception, in creating class hierarchies.*

When Constructors Are Called

When a class hierarchy is created, in what order are the constructors for the classes that make up the hierarchy called? For example, given a subclass called **B** and a superclass called **A**, is **A**'s constructor called before **B**'s, or vice versa? The answer is that in a class hierarchy, constructors are called in order of derivation, from superclass to subclass. Further, since **super( )** must be the first statement executed in a subclass' constructor, this order is the same whether or not **super( )** is used. If **super( )** is not used, then the default or parameterless constructor of each superclass will be executed. The following program illustrates when constructors are executed:

```java
// Demonstrate when constructors are called.

// Create a super class.
class A {
  A() {
    System.out.println("Inside A's constructor.");
  }
}

// Create a subclass by extending class A.
class B extends A {
  B() {
    System.out.println("Inside B's constructor.");
  }
}

// Create another subclass by extending B.
class C extends B {
  C() {
    System.out.println("Inside C's constructor.");
  }
}

class CallingCons {
  public static void main(String args[]) {
```

```
    C c = new C();
  }
}
```

The output from this program is shown here:

```
Inside A's constructor
Inside B's constructor
Inside C's constructor
```

As you can see, the constructors are called in order of derivation.

If you think about it, it makes sense that constructors are executed in order of derivation. Because a superclass has no knowledge of any subclass, any initialization it needs to perform is separate from and possibly prerequisite to any initialization performed by the subclass. Therefore, it must be executed first.

Method Overriding

In a class hierarchy, when a method in a subclass has the same name and type signature as a method in its superclass, then the method in the subclass is said to *override* the method in the superclass. When an overridden method is called from within a subclass, it will always refer to the version of that method defined by the subclass. The version of the method defined by the superclass will be hidden. Consider the following:

```
// Method overriding.
class A {
  int i, j;
  A(int a, int b) {
    i = a;
    j = b;
  }

  // display i and j
  void show() {
    System.out.println("i and j: " + i + " " + j);
  }
}

class B extends A {
```

```
    int k;

  B(int a, int b, int c) {
    super(a, b);
    k = c;
  }

  // display k - this overrides show() in A
  void show() {
    System.out.println("k: " + k);
  }
}

class Override {
  public static void main(String args[]) {
    B subOb = new B(1, 2, 3);

    subOb.show(); // this calls show() in B
  }
}
```

The output produced by this program is shown here:

```
k: 3
```

When **show( )** is invoked on an object of type **B**, the version of **show( )** defined within **B** is used. That is, the version of **show( )** inside **B** overrides the version declared in **A**.

If you wish to access the superclass version of an overridden function, you can do so by using **super**. For example, in this version of **B**, the superclass version of **show( )** is invoked within the subclass' version. This allows all instance variables to be displayed.

```
class B extends A {
  int k;

  B(int a, int b, int c) {
    super(a, b);
    k = c;
  }
```

```
void show() {
  super.show(); // this calls A's show()
  System.out.println("k: " + k);
}
}
```

If you substitute this version of **A** into the previous program, you will see the following output:

```
i and j: 1 2
k: 3
```

Here, **super.show( )** calls the superclass version of **show( )**.

Method overriding occurs *only* when the names and the type signatures of the two methods are identical. If they are not, then the two methods are simply overloaded. For example, consider this modified version of the preceding example:

```
// Methods with differing type signatures are overloaded - not
// overridden.
class A {
  int i, j;

  A(int a, int b) {
    i = a;
    j = b;
  }

  // display i and j
  void show() {
    System.out.println("i and j: " + i + " " + j);
  }
}

// Create a subclass by extending class A.
class B extends A {
  int k;

  B(int a, int b, int c) {
    super(a, b);
    k = c;
```

```
  }

  // overload show()
  void show(String msg) {
    System.out.println(msg + k);
  }
}

class Override {
  public static void main(String args[]) {
    B subOb = new B(1, 2, 3);

    subOb.show("This is k: "); // this calls show() in B
    subOb.show(); // this calls show() in A
  }
}
```

The output produced by this program is shown here:

```
This is k: 3
i and j: 1 2
```

The version of **show( )** in **B** takes a string parameter. This makes its type signature different from the one in **A**, which takes no parameters. Therefore, no overriding (or name hiding) takes place.

Dynamic Method Dispatch

While the examples in the preceding section demonstrate the mechanics of method overriding, they do not show its power. Indeed, if there were nothing more to method overriding than a name space convention, then it would be, at best, an interesting curiosity, but of little real value. However, this is not the case. Method overriding forms the basis for one of Java's most powerful concepts: *dynamic method dispatch*. Dynamic method dispatch is the mechanism by which a call to an overridden method is resolved at run time, rather than compile time. Dynamic method dispatch is important because this is how Java implements run-time polymorphism.

Let's begin by restating an important principle: a superclass reference variable can refer to a subclass object. Java uses this fact to resolve calls to overridden methods at run time. Here is how. When an overridden method is called through a superclass reference, Java determines which version of that method to execute based upon the type of the object being referred to at the time the call occurs. Thus, this determination is made at run time. When different types of objects are referred to, different versions of an overridden method will be called. In other words, *it is the type of the object being referred to* (not the type of the reference variable) that determines which version of an overridden method will be executed. Therefore, if a superclass contains a method that is overridden by a subclass, then when different types of objects are referred to through a superclass reference variable, different versions of the method are executed.

Here is an example that illustrates dynamic method dispatch:

```java
// Dynamic Method Dispatch
class A {
  void callme() {
    System.out.println("Inside A's callme method");
  }
}

class B extends A {
  // override callme()
  void callme() {
    System.out.println("Inside B's callme method");
  }
}

class C extends A {
  // override callme()
  void callme() {
    System.out.println("Inside C's callme method");
  }
}

class Dispatch {
  public static void main(String args[]) {
    A a = new A(); // object of type A
    B b = new B(); // object of type B
    C c = new C(); // object of type C
    A r; // obtain a reference of type A

    r = a; // r refers to an A object
    r.callme(); // calls A's version of callme

    r = b; // r refers to a B object
    r.callme(); // calls B's version of callme
```

```
    r = c; // r refers to a C object
    r.callme(); // calls C's version of callme
  }
}
```

The output from the program is shown here:

```
Inside A's callme method
Inside B's callme method
Inside C's callme method
```

This program creates one superclass called **A** and two subclasses of it, called **B** and **C**. Subclasses **B** and **C** override **callme( )** declared in **A**. Inside the **main( )** method, objects of type **A**, **B**, and **C** are declared. Also, a reference of type **A**, called **r**, is declared. The program then assigns a reference to each type of object to **r** and uses that reference to invoke **callme( )**. As the output shows, the version of **callme( )** executed is determined by the type of object being referred to at the time of the call. Had it been determined by the type of the reference variable, **r**, you would see three calls to **A**'s **callme( )** method.

> **Note**   *Readers familiar with C++ or C# will recognize that overridden methods in Java are similar to virtual functions in those languages.*

Why Overridden Methods?

As stated earlier, overridden methods allow Java to support run-time polymorphism. Polymorphism is essential to object-oriented programming for one reason: it allows a general class to specify methods that will be common to all of its derivatives, while allowing subclasses to define the specific implementation of some or all of those methods. Overridden methods are another way that Java implements the "one interface, multiple methods" aspect of polymorphism.

Part of the key to successfully applying polymorphism is understanding that the superclasses and subclasses form a hierarchy which moves from lesser to greater specialization. Used correctly, the superclass provides all elements that a subclass can use directly. It also defines those methods that the derived class must implement on its own. This allows the subclass the flexibility to define its own methods, yet still enforces a consistent interface. Thus, by combining inheritance with overridden methods, a superclass can define the general form of the methods that will be used by all of its subclasses.

Dynamic, run-time polymorphism is one of the most powerful mechanisms that object-oriented design brings to bear on code reuse and robustness. The ability of existing code libraries to call methods on instances of new classes without recompiling while maintaining a clean abstract interface is a profoundly powerful tool.

Applying Method Overriding

Let's look at a more practical example that uses method overriding. The following program creates a superclass called **Figure** that stores the dimensions of various two-dimensional objects. It also defines a method called **area( )** that computes the area of an object. The program derives two subclasses from **Figure**. The first is **Rectangle** and the second is **Triangle**. Each of these subclasses overrides **area( )** so that it returns the area of a rectangle and a triangle, respectively.

```
// Using run-time polymorphism.
class Figure {
  double dim1;
  double dim2;

  Figure(double a, double b) {
    dim1 = a;
    dim2 = b;
  }

  double area() {
    System.out.println("Area for Figure is undefined.");
    return 0;
  }
}

class Rectangle extends Figure {
  Rectangle(double a, double b) {
    super(a, b);
  }

  // override area for rectangle
  double area() {
    System.out.println("Inside Area for Rectangle.");
    return dim1 * dim2;
  }
}

class Triangle extends Figure {
```

```
  Triangle(double a, double b) {
    super(a, b);
  }

  // override area for right triangle
  double area() {
    System.out.println("Inside Area for Triangle.");
    return dim1 * dim2 / 2;
  }
}

class FindAreas {
  public static void main(String args[]) {
    Figure f = new Figure(10, 10);
    Rectangle r = new Rectangle(9, 5);
    Triangle t = new Triangle(10, 8);

    Figure figref;

    figref = r;
    System.out.println("Area is " + figref.area());

    figref = t;
    System.out.println("Area is " + figref.area());

    figref = f;
    System.out.println("Area is " + figref.area());
  }
}
```

The output from the program is shown here:

```
Inside Area for Rectangle.
Area is 45
Inside Area for Triangle.
Area is 40
Area for Figure is undefined.
Area is 0
```

Through the dual mechanisms of inheritance and run-time polymorphism, it is possible to define one consistent interface that is used by several different, yet related, types of objects. In this case, if an object is derived from **Figure**, then its area can be obtained by calling **area( )**. The interface to this operation is the same no matter what type of figure is being used.

Using Abstract Classes

There are situations in which you will want to define a superclass that declares the structure of a given abstraction without providing a complete implementation of every method. That is, sometimes you will want to create a superclass that only defines a generalized form that will be shared by all of its subclasses, leaving it to each subclass to fill in the details. Such a class determines the nature of the methods that the subclasses must implement. One way this situation can occur is when a superclass is unable to create a meaningful implementation for a method. This is the case with the class **Figure** used in the preceding example. The definition of **area( )** is simply a placeholder. It will not compute and display the area of any type of object.

As you will see as you create your own class libraries, it is not uncommon for a method to have no meaningful definition in the context of its superclass. You can handle this situation two ways. One way, as shown in the previous example, is to simply have it report a warning message. While this approach can be useful in certain situations—such as debugging—it is not usually appropriate. You may have methods which must be overridden by the subclass in order for the subclass to have any meaning. Consider the class **Triangle**. It has no meaning if **area( )** is not defined. In this case, you want some way to ensure that a subclass does, indeed, override all necessary methods. Java's solution to this problem is the *abstract method*.

You can require that certain methods be overridden by subclasses by specifying the **abstract** type modifier. These methods are sometimes referred to as *subclasser responsibility* because they have no implementation specified in the superclass. Thus, a subclass must override them—it cannot simply use the version defined in the superclass. To declare an abstract method, use this general form:

abstract *type name(parameter-list)*;

As you can see, no method body is present.

Any class that contains one or more abstract methods must also be declared abstract. To declare a class abstract, you simply use the **abstract** keyword in front of the **class** keyword at the beginning of the class declaration. There can be no objects of an abstract class. That is, an abstract class cannot be directly instantiated with the **new** operator. Such objects would be useless, because an abstract class is not fully defined. Also, you cannot declare abstract constructors, or abstract static methods. Any subclass of an abstract class must either implement all of the abstract methods in the superclass, or be itself declared **abstract**.

Here is a simple example of a class with an abstract method, followed by a class which implements that method:

```
// A Simple demonstration of abstract.
abstract class A {
  abstract void callme();

  // concrete methods are still allowed in abstract classes
  void callmetoo() {
    System.out.println("This is a concrete method.");
  }
}

class B extends A {
  void callme() {
    System.out.println("B's implementation of callme.");
  }
}

class AbstractDemo {
  public static void main(String args[]) {
    B b = new B();

    b.callme();
    b.callmetoo();
  }
}
```

Notice that no objects of class **A** are declared in the program. As mentioned, it is not possible to instantiate an abstract class. One other point: class **A** implements a concrete method called **callmetoo( )**. This is perfectly acceptable. Abstract classes can include as much implementation as they see fit.

Although abstract classes cannot be used to instantiate objects, they can be used to create object references, because Java's approach to run-time polymorphism is implemented through the use of superclass references. Thus, it must be possible to create a reference to an abstract class so that it can be used to point to a subclass object. You will see this feature put to use in the next example.

Using an abstract class, you can improve the **Figure** class shown earlier. Since there is no meaningful concept of area for an undefined two-dimensional figure, the following version of the program declares **area( )** as abstract inside **Figure**. This, of course, means that all classes derived from **Figure** must override **area( )**.

```
// Using abstract methods and classes.
abstract class Figure {
```

```
    double dim1;
    double dim2;

  Figure(double a, double b) {
    dim1 = a;
    dim2 = b;
  }

  // area is now an abstract method
  abstract double area();
}

class Rectangle extends Figure {
  Rectangle(double a, double b) {
    super(a, b);
  }

  // override area for rectangle
  double area() {
    System.out.println("Inside Area for Rectangle.");
    return dim1 * dim2;
  }
}

class Triangle extends Figure {
  Triangle(double a, double b) {
    super(a, b);
  }

  // override area for right triangle
  double area() {
    System.out.println("Inside Area for Triangle.");
    return dim1 * dim2 / 2;
  }
}

class AbstractAreas {
  public static void main(String args[]) {
  // Figure f = new Figure(10, 10); // illegal now
    Rectangle r = new Rectangle(9, 5);
    Triangle t = new Triangle(10, 8);
```

```
Figure figref; // this is OK, no object is created

figref = r;
System.out.println("Area is " + figref.area());

figref = t;
System.out.println("Area is " + figref.area());
}
}
```

As the comment inside **main( )** indicates, it is no longer possible to declare objects of type **Figure**, since it is now abstract. And, all subclasses of **Figure** must override **area( )**. To prove this to yourself, try creating a subclass that does not override **area( )**. You will receive a compile-time error.

Although it is not possible to create an object of type **Figure**, you can create a reference variable of type **Figure**. The variable **figref** is declared as a reference to **Figure**, which means that it can be used to refer to an object of any class derived from **Figure**. As explained, it is through superclass reference variables that overridden methods are resolved at run time.

Using final with Inheritance

The keyword **final** has three uses. First, it can be used to create the equivalent of a named constant. This use was described in the preceding chapter. The other two uses of **final** apply to inheritance. Both are examined here.

Using final to Prevent Overriding

While method overriding is one of Java's most powerful features, there will be times when you will want to prevent it from occurring. To disallow a method from being overridden, specify **final** as a modifier at the start of its declaration. Methods declared as **final** cannot be overridden. The following fragment illustrates **final**:

```
class A {
  final void meth() {
    System.out.println("This is a final method.");
  }
}

class B extends A {
  void meth() { // ERROR! Can't override.
```

```
        System.out.println("Illegal!");
    }
}
```

Because **meth( )** is declared as **final**, it cannot be overridden in **B**. If you attempt to do so, a compile-time error will result.

Methods declared as **final** can sometimes provide a performance enhancement: The compiler is free to *inline* calls to them because it "knows" they will not be overridden by a subclass. When a small **final** method is called, often the Java compiler can copy the bytecode for the subroutine directly inline with the compiled code of the calling method, thus eliminating the costly overhead associated with a method call. Inlining is only an option with **final** methods. Normally, Java resolves calls to methods dynamically, at run time. This is called *late binding*. However, since **final** methods cannot be overridden, a call to one can be resolved at compile time. This is called *early binding*.

Using final to Prevent Inheritance

Sometimes you will want to prevent a class from being inherited. To do this, precede the class declaration with **final**. Declaring a class as **final** implicitly declares all of its methods as **final**, too. As you might expect, it is illegal to declare a class as both **abstract** and **final** since an abstract class is incomplete by itself and relies upon its subclasses to provide complete implementations.

Here is an example of a **final** class:

```
final class A {
    // ...
}

// The following class is illegal.
class B extends A { // ERROR! Can't subclass A
    // ...
}
```

As the comments imply, it is illegal for **B** to inherit **A** since **A** is declared as **final**.

The Object Class

There is one special class, **Object**, defined by Java. All other classes are subclasses of **Object**. That is, **Object** is a superclass of all other classes. This means that a reference variable of type **Object** can refer to an object of any other class. Also, since arrays are implemented as classes, a variable of type **Object** can also refer to any array.

Object defines the following methods, which means that they are available in every object.

Method	Purpose
Object clone( )	Creates a new object that is the same as the object being cloned.
boolean equals(Object *object*)	Determines whether one object is equal to another.
void finalize( )	Called before an unused object is recycled.
Class getClass( )	Obtains the class of an object at run time.
int hashCode( )	Returns the hash code associated with the invoking object.
void notify( )	Resumes execution of a thread waiting on the invoking object.
void notifyAll( )	Resumes execution of all threads waiting on the invoking object.
String toString( )	Returns a string that describes the object.
void wait( ) void wait(long *milliseconds*) void wait(long *milliseconds*, int *nanoseconds*)	Waits on another thread of execution.

The methods **getClass( )**, **notify( )**, **notifyAll( )**, and **wait( )** are declared as **final**. You may override the others. These methods are described elsewhere in this book. However, notice two methods now: **equals( )** and **toString( )**. The **equals( )** method compares the contents of two objects. It returns **true** if the objects are equivalent, and **false** otherwise. The **toString( )** method returns a string that contains a description of the object on which it is called. Also, this method is automatically called when an object is output using **println( )**. Many classes override this method. Doing so allows them to tailor a description specifically for the types of objects that they create. See Chapter 13 for more information on **toString( )**.

The
Complete
Reference

Java™ 2

Chapter 9

Packages and
Interfaces

This chapter examines two of Java's most innovative features: packages and interfaces. *Packages* are containers for classes that are used to keep the class name space compartmentalized. For example, a package allows you to create a class named **List**, which you can store in your own package without concern that it will collide with some other class named **List** stored elsewhere. Packages are stored in a hierarchical manner and are explicitly imported into new class definitions.

In previous chapters you have seen how methods define the interface to the data in a class. Through the use of the **interface** keyword, Java allows you to fully abstract the interface from its implementation. Using **interface**, you can specify a set of methods which can be implemented by one or more classes. The **interface**, itself, does not actually define any implementation. Although they are similar to abstract classes, **interfaces** have an additional capability: A class can implement more than one interface. By contrast, a class can only inherit a single superclass (abstract or otherwise).

Packages and interfaces are two of the basic components of a Java program. In general, a Java source file can contain any (or all) of the following four internal parts:

- A single package statement (optional)
- Any number of import statements (optional)
- A single public class declaration (required)
- Any number of classes private to the package (optional)

Only one of these—the single public class declaration—has been used in the examples so far. This chapter will explore the remaining parts.

Packages

In the preceding chapters, the name of each example class was taken from the same name space. This means that a unique name had to be used for each class to avoid name collisions. After a while, without some way to manage the name space, you could run out of convenient, descriptive names for individual classes. You also need some way to be assured that the name you choose for a class will be reasonably unique and not collide with class names chosen by other programmers. (Imagine a small group of programmers fighting over who gets to use the name "Foobar" as a class name. Or, imagine the entire Internet community arguing over who first named a class "Espresso.") Thankfully, Java provides a mechanism for partitioning the class name space into more manageable chunks. This mechanism is the package. The package is both a naming and a visibility control mechanism. You can define classes inside a package that are not accessible by code outside that package. You can also define class members that are only exposed to other members of the same package. This allows your classes to have intimate knowledge of each other, but not expose that knowledge to the rest of the world.

Defining a Package

To create a package is quite easy: simply include a **package** command as the first statement in a Java source file. Any classes declared within that file will belong to the specified package. The **package** statement defines a name space in which classes are stored. If you omit the **package** statement, the class names are put into the default package, which has no name. (This is why you haven't had to worry about packages before now.) While the default package is fine for short, sample programs, it is inadequate for real applications. Most of the time, you will define a package for your code.

This is the general form of the **package** statement:

package *pkg*;

Here, *pkg* is the name of the package. For example, the following statement creates a package called **MyPackage**.

```
package MyPackage;
```

Java uses file system directories to store packages. For example, the **.class** files for any classes you declare to be part of **MyPackage** must be stored in a directory called **MyPackage**. Remember that case is significant, and the directory name must match the package name exactly.

More than one file can include the same **package** statement. The **package** statement simply specifies to which package the classes defined in a file belong. It does not exclude other classes in other files from being part of that same package. Most real-world packages are spread across many files.

You can create a hierarchy of packages. To do so, simply separate each package name from the one above it by use of a period. The general form of a multileveled package statement is shown here:

package *pkg1*[.*pkg2*[.*pkg3*]];

A package hierarchy must be reflected in the file system of your Java development system. For example, a package declared as

```
package java.awt.image;
```

needs to be stored in **java/awt/image**, **java\awt\image**, or **java:awt:image** on your UNIX, Windows, or Macintosh file system, respectively. Be sure to choose your package names carefully. You cannot rename a package without renaming the directory in which the classes are stored.

Finding Packages and CLASSPATH

As just explained, packages are mirrored by directories. This raises an important question: How does the Java run-time system know where to look for packages that you create? The answer has two parts. First, by default, the Java run-time system uses the current working directory as its starting point. Thus, if your package is in the current directory, or a subdirectory of the current directory, it will be found. Second, you can specify a directory path or paths by setting the **CLASSPATH** environmental variable.

For example, consider the following package specification.

```
package MyPack;
```

In order for a program to find **MyPack**, one of two things must be true. Either the program is executed from a directory immediately above **MyPack**, or **CLASSPATH** must be set to include the path to **MyPack**. The first alternative is the easiest (and doesn't require a change to **CLASSPATH**), but the second alternative lets your program find **MyPack** no matter what directory the program is in. Ultimately, the choice is yours.

The easiest way to try the examples shown in this book is to simply create the package directories below your current development directory, put the **.class** files into the appropriate directories and then execute the programs from the development directory. This is the approach assumed by the examples.

A Short Package Example

Keeping the preceding discussion in mind, you can try this simple package:

```
// A simple package
package MyPack;

class Balance {
  String name;
  double bal;

  Balance(String n, double b) {
    name = n;
    bal = b;
  }

  void show() {
    if(bal<0)
      System.out.print("--> ");
```

```
      System.out.println(name + ": $" + bal);
   }
}

class AccountBalance {
  public static void main(String args[]) {
    Balance current[] = new Balance[3];

    current[0] = new Balance("K. J. Fielding", 123.23);
    current[1] = new Balance("Will Tell", 157.02);
    current[2] = new Balance("Tom Jackson", -12.33);

    for(int i=0; i<3; i++) current[i].show();
  }
}
```

Call this file **AccountBalance.java**, and put it in a directory called **MyPack**.

Next, compile the file. Make sure that the resulting **.class** file is also in the **MyPack** directory. Then try executing the **AccountBalance** class, using the following command line:

```
java MyPack.AccountBalance
```

Remember, you will need to be in the directory above **MyPack** when you execute this command, or to have your **CLASSPATH** environmental variable set appropriately.

As explained, **AccountBalance** is now part of the package **MyPack**. This means that it cannot be executed by itself. That is, you cannot use this command line:

```
java AccountBalance
```

AccountBalance must be qualified with its package name.

Access Protection

In the preceding chapters, you learned about various aspects of Java's access control mechanism and its access specifiers. For example, you already know that access to a **private** member of a class is granted only to other members of that class. Packages add another dimension to access control. As you will see, Java provides many levels of protection to allow fine-grained control over the visibility of variables and methods within classes, subclasses, and packages.

Classes and packages are both means of encapsulating and containing the name space and scope of variables and methods. Packages act as containers for classes and other subordinate packages. Classes act as containers for data and code. The class is Java's smallest unit of abstraction. Because of the interplay between classes and packages, Java addresses four categories of visibility for class members:

- Subclasses in the same package
- Non-subclasses in the same package
- Subclasses in different packages
- Classes that are neither in the same package nor subclasses

The three access specifiers, **private**, **public**, and **protected**, provide a variety of ways to produce the many levels of access required by these categories. Table 9-1 sums up the interactions.

While Java's access control mechanism may seem complicated, we can simplify it as follows. Anything declared **public** can be accessed from anywhere. Anything declared **private** cannot be seen outside of its class. When a member does not have an explicit access specification, it is visible to subclasses as well as to other classes in the same package. This is the default access. If you want to allow an element to be seen outside your current package, but only to classes that subclass your class directly, then declare that element **protected**.

Table 9-1 applies only to members of classes. A class has only two possible access levels: default and public. When a class is declared as **public**, it is accessible by any other code. If a class has default access, then it can only be accessed by other code within its same package.

	Private	No modifier	Protected	Public
Same class	Yes	Yes	Yes	Yes
Same package subclass	No	Yes	Yes	Yes
Same package non-subclass	No	Yes	Yes	Yes
Different package subclass	No	No	Yes	Yes
Different package non-subclass	No	No	No	Yes

Table 9-1. *Class Member Access*

An Access Example

The following example shows all combinations of the access control modifiers. This example has two packages and five classes. Remember that the classes for the two different packages need to be stored in directories named after their respective packages—in this case, **p1** and **p2**.

The source for the first package defines three classes: **Protection**, **Derived**, and **SamePackage**. The first class defines four **int** variables in each of the legal protection modes. The variable **n** is declared with the default protection, **n_pri** is **private**, **n_pro** is **protected**, and **n_pub** is **public**.

Each subsequent class in this example will try to access the variables in an instance of this class. The lines that will not compile due to access restrictions are commented out by use of the single-line comment //. Before each of these lines is a comment listing the places from which this level of protection would allow access.

The second class, **Derived**, is a subclass of **Protection** in the same package, **p1**. This grants **Derived** access to every variable in **Protection** except for **n_pri**, the **private** one. The third class, **SamePackage**, is not a subclass of **Protection**, but is in the same package and also has access to all but **n_pri**.

This is file **Protection.java**:

```
package p1;

public class Protection {
  int n = 1;
  private int n_pri = 2;
  protected int n_pro = 3;
  public int n_pub = 4;

  public Protection() {
    System.out.println("base constructor");
    System.out.println("n = " + n);
    System.out.println("n_pri = " + n_pri);
    System.out.println("n_pro = " + n_pro);
    System.out.println("n_pub = " + n_pub);
  }
}
```

This is file **Derived.java**:

```
package p1;

class Derived extends Protection {
  Derived() {
```

```
      System.out.println("derived constructor");
      System.out.println("n = " + n);

//    class only
//    System.out.println("n_pri = " + n_pri);

      System.out.println("n_pro = " + n_pro);
      System.out.println("n_pub = " + n_pub);
  }
}
```

This is file **SamePackage.java**:

```
package p1;

class SamePackage {
  SamePackage() {

    Protection p = new Protection();
    System.out.println("same package constructor");
    System.out.println("n = " + p.n);

//  class only
//    System.out.println("n_pri = " + p.n_pri);
    System.out.println("n_pro = " + p.n_pro);
    System.out.println("n_pub = " + p.n_pub);
  }
}
```

Following is the source code for the other package, **p2**. The two classes defined in **p2** cover the other two conditions which are affected by access control. The first class, **Protection2**, is a subclass of **p1.Protection**. This grants access to all of **p1.Protection**'s variables except for **n_pri** (because it is **private**) and **n**, the variable declared with the default protection. Remember, the default only allows access from within the class or the package, not extra-package subclasses. Finally, the class **OtherPackage** has access to only one variable, **n_pub**, which was declared **public**.

This is file **Protection2.java**:

```
package p2;

class Protection2 extends p1.Protection {
```

```
   Protection2() {
     System.out.println("derived other package constructor");

//   class or package only
//   System.out.println("n = " + n);

//   class only
//   System.out.println("n_pri = " + n_pri);

     System.out.println("n_pro = " + n_pro);
     System.out.println("n_pub = " + n_pub);
   }
}
```

This is file **OtherPackage.java**:

```
package p2;

class OtherPackage {
  OtherPackage() {
    p1.Protection p = new p1.Protection();
    System.out.println("other package constructor");

//   class or package only
//   System.out.println("n = " + p.n);

//   class only
//   System.out.println("n_pri = " + p.n_pri);

//   class, subclass or package only
//   System.out.println("n_pro = " + p.n_pro);

     System.out.println("n_pub = " + p.n_pub);
   }
}
```

If you wish to try these two packages, here are two test files you can use. The one for package **p1** is shown here:

```
// Demo package p1.
package p1;
```

```
// Instantiate the various classes in p1.
public class Demo {
  public static void main(String args[]) {
    Protection ob1 = new Protection();
    Derived ob2 = new Derived();
    SamePackage ob3 = new SamePackage();
  }
}
```

The test file for **p2** is shown next:

```
// Demo package p2.
package p2;

// Instantiate the various classes in p2.
public class Demo {
  public static void main(String args[]) {
    Protection2 ob1 = new Protection2();
    OtherPackage ob2 = new OtherPackage();
  }
}
```

Importing Packages

Given that packages exist and are a good mechanism for compartmentalizing diverse classes from each other, it is easy to see why all of the built-in Java classes are stored in packages. There are no core Java classes in the unnamed default package; all of the standard classes are stored in some named package. Since classes within packages must be fully qualified with their package name or names, it could become tedious to type in the long dot-separated package path name for every class you want to use. For this reason, Java includes the **import** statement to bring certain classes, or entire packages, into visibility. Once imported, a class can be referred to directly, using only its name. The **import** statement is a convenience to the programmer and is not technically needed to write a complete Java program. If you are going to refer to a few dozen classes in your application, however, the **import** statement will save a lot of typing.

In a Java source file, **import** statements occur immediately following the **package** statement (if it exists) and before any class definitions. This is the general form of the **import** statement:

import *pkg1*[*.pkg2*].(*classname* | *);

Here, *pkg1* is the name of a top-level package, and *pkg2* is the name of a subordinate package inside the outer package separated by a dot (.). There is no practical limit on the depth of a package hierarchy, except that imposed by the file system. Finally, you specify either an explicit *classname* or a star (*), which indicates that the Java compiler should import the entire package. This code fragment shows both forms in use:

```
import java.util.Date;
import java.io.*;
```

The star form may increase compilation time—especially if you import several large packages. For this reason it is a good idea to explicitly name the classes that you want to use rather than importing whole packages. However, the star form has absolutely no effect on the run-time performance or size of your classes.

All of the standard Java classes included with Java are stored in a package called **java**. The basic language functions are stored in a package inside of the **java** package called **java.lang**. Normally, you have to import every package or class that you want to use, but since Java is useless without much of the functionality in **java.lang**, it is implicitly imported by the compiler for all programs. This is equivalent to the following line being at the top of all of your programs:

```
import java.lang.*;
```

If a class with the same name exists in two different packages that you import using the star form, the compiler will remain silent, unless you try to use one of the classes. In that case, you will get a compile-time error and have to explicitly name the class specifying its package.

Any place you use a class name, you can use its fully qualified name, which includes its full package hierarchy. For example, this fragment uses an import statement:

```
import java.util.*;
class MyDate extends Date {
}
```

The same example without the **import** statement looks like this:

```
class MyDate extends java.util.Date {
}
```

As shown in Table 9-1, when a package is imported, only those items within the package declared as **public** will be available to non-subclasses in the importing code. For example, if you want the **Balance** class of the package **MyPack** shown earlier to be available as a stand-alone class for general use outside of **MyPack**, then you will need to declare it as **public** and put it into its own file, as shown here:

```
package MyPack;

/* Now, the Balance class, its constructor, and its
   show() method are public.  This means that they can
   be used by non-subclass code outside their package.
*/
public class Balance {
  String name;
  double bal;

  public Balance(String n, double b) {
    name = n;
    bal = b;
  }

  public void show() {
    if(bal<0)
      System.out.print("--> ");
    System.out.println(name + ": $" + bal);
  }
}
```

As you can see, the **Balance** class is now **public**. Also, its constructor and its **show( )** method are **public**, too. This means that they can be accessed by any type of code outside the **MyPack** package. For example, here **TestBalance** imports **MyPack** and is then able to make use of the **Balance** class:

```
import MyPack.*;

class TestBalance {
  public static void main(String args[]) {

    /* Because Balance is public, you may use Balance
       class and call its constructor. */
    Balance test = new Balance("J. J. Jaspers", 99.88);
```

```
    test.show(); // you may also call show()
  }
}
```

As an experiment, remove the **public** specifier from the **Balance** class and then try compiling **TestBalance**. As explained, errors will result.

Interfaces

Using the keyword **interface**, you can fully abstract a class' interface from its implementation. That is, using **interface**, you can specify what a class must do, but not how it does it. Interfaces are syntactically similar to classes, but they lack instance variables, and their methods are declared without any body. In practice, this means that you can define interfaces which don't make assumptions about how they are implemented. Once it is defined, any number of classes can implement an **interface**. Also, one class can implement any number of interfaces.

To implement an interface, a class must create the complete set of methods defined by the interface. However, each class is free to determine the details of its own implementation. By providing the **interface** keyword, Java allows you to fully utilize the "one interface, multiple methods" aspect of polymorphism.

Interfaces are designed to support dynamic method resolution at run time. Normally, in order for a method to be called from one class to another, both classes need to be present at compile time so the Java compiler can check to ensure that the method signatures are compatible. This requirement by itself makes for a static and nonextensible classing environment. Inevitably in a system like this, functionality gets pushed up higher and higher in the class hierarchy so that the mechanisms will be available to more and more subclasses. Interfaces are designed to avoid this problem. They disconnect the definition of a method or set of methods from the inheritance hierarchy. Since interfaces are in a different hierarchy from classes, it is possible for classes that are unrelated in terms of the class hierarchy to implement the same interface. This is where the real power of interfaces is realized.

Interfaces add most of the functionality that is required for many applications which would normally resort to using multiple inheritance in a language such as C++.

Defining an Interface

An interface is defined much like a class. This is the general form of an interface:

access interface *name* {
    return-type method-name1(parameter-list);
    return-type method-name2(parameter-list);
    type final-varname1 = value;

```
        type final-varname2 = value;
        // ...
        return-type method-nameN(parameter-list);
        type final-varnameN = value;
    }
```

Here, *access* is either **public** or not used. When no access specifier is included, then default access results, and the interface is only available to other members of the package in which it is declared. When it is declared as **public**, the interface can be used by any other code. *name* is the name of the interface, and can be any valid identifier. Notice that the methods which are declared have no bodies. They end with a semicolon after the parameter list. They are, essentially, abstract methods; there can be no default implementation of any method specified within an interface. Each class that includes an interface must implement all of the methods.

Variables can be declared inside of interface declarations. They are implicitly **final** and **static**, meaning they cannot be changed by the implementing class. They must also be initialized with a constant value. All methods and variables are implicitly **public** if the interface, itself, is declared as **public**.

Here is an example of an interface definition. It declares a simple interface which contains one method called **callback( )** that takes a single integer parameter.

```
interface Callback {
  void callback(int param);
}
```

Implementing Interfaces

Once an **interface** has been defined, one or more classes can implement that interface. To implement an interface, include the **implements** clause in a class definition, and then create the methods defined by the interface. The general form of a class that includes the **implements** clause looks like this:

```
access class classname [extends superclass]
            [implements interface [,interface...]] {
    // class-body
}
```

Here, *access* is either **public** or not used. If a class implements more than one interface, the interfaces are separated with a comma. If a class implements two interfaces that declare the same method, then the same method will be used by clients of either interface. The methods that implement an interface must be declared **public**. Also, the type signature of the implementing method must match exactly the type signature specified in the **interface** definition.

Here is a small example class that implements the **Callback** interface shown earlier.

```
class Client implements Callback {
  // Implement Callback's interface
  public void callback(int p) {

    System.out.println("callback called with " + p);
  }
}
```

Notice that **callback( )** is declared using the **public** access specifier.

 *When you implement an interface method, it must be declared as **public**.*

It is both permissible and common for classes that implement interfaces to define additional members of their own. For example, the following version of **Client** implements **callback( )** and adds the method **nonIfaceMeth( )**:

```
class Client implements Callback {
  // Implement Callback's interface
  public void callback(int p) {
    System.out.println("callback called with " + p);
  }

  void nonIfaceMeth() {
    System.out.println("Classes that implement interfaces " +
                       "may also define other members, too.");
  }
}
```

Accessing Implementations Through Interface References

You can declare variables as object references that use an interface rather than a class type. Any instance of any class that implements the declared interface can be referred to by such a variable. When you call a method through one of these references, the correct version will be called based on the actual instance of the interface being referred to. This is one of the key features of interfaces. The method to be executed is looked up dynamically at run time, allowing classes to be created later than the code which calls methods on them. The calling code can dispatch through an interface without having to know anything about the "callee." This process is similar to using a superclass reference to access a subclass object, as described in Chapter 8.

Because dynamic lookup of a method at run time incurs a significant overhead when compared with the normal method invocation in Java, you should be careful not to use interfaces casually in performance-critical code.

The following example calls the **callback( )** method via an interface reference variable:

```
class TestIface {
  public static void main(String args[]) {
    Callback c = new Client();
    c.callback(42);
  }
}
```

The output of this program is shown here:

```
callback called with 42
```

Notice that variable **c** is declared to be of the interface type **Callback**, yet it was assigned an instance of **Client**. Although **c** can be used to access the **callback( )** method, it cannot access any other members of the **Client** class. An interface reference variable only has knowledge of the methods declared by its **interface** declaration. Thus, **c** could not be used to access **nonIfaceMeth( )** since it is defined by **Client** but not **Callback**.

While the preceding example shows, mechanically, how an interface reference variable can access an implementation object, it does not demonstrate the polymorphic power of such a reference. To sample this usage, first create the second implementation of **Callback**, shown here:

```
// Another implementation of Callback.
class AnotherClient implements Callback {
  // Implement Callback's interface
  public void callback(int p) {
    System.out.println("Another version of callback");
    System.out.println("p squared is " + (p*p));
  }
}
```

Now, try the following class:

```
class TestIface2 {
  public static void main(String args[]) {
    Callback c = new Client();
```

```
    AnotherClient ob = new AnotherClient();

    c.callback(42);

    c = ob; // c now refers to AnotherClient object
    c.callback(42);
  }
}
```

The output from this program is shown here:

```
callback called with 42
Another version of callback
p squared is 1764
```

As you can see, the version of **callback( )** that is called is determined by the type of object that **c** refers to at run time. While this is a very simple example, you will see another, more practical one shortly.

Partial Implementations

If a class includes an interface but does not fully implement the methods defined by that interface, then that class must be declared as **abstract**. For example:

```
abstract class Incomplete implements Callback {
  int a, b;
  void show() {
    System.out.println(a + " " + b);
  }
  // ...
}
```

Here, the class **Incomplete** does not implement **callback( )** and must be declared as abstract. Any class that inherits **Incomplete** must implement **callback( )** or be declared **abstract** itself.

Applying Interfaces

To understand the power of interfaces, let's look at a more practical example. In earlier chapters you developed a class called **Stack** that implemented a simple fixed-size stack. However, there are many ways to implement a stack. For example, the stack can be of a fixed size or it can be "growable." The stack can also be held in an array, a linked list, a binary tree, and so on. No matter how the stack is implemented, the interface to the stack remains the same. That is, the methods **push( )** and **pop( )** define the interface to the stack independently of the details of the implementation. Because the interface to a stack is separate from its implementation, it is easy to define a stack interface, leaving it to each implementation to define the specifics. Let's look at two examples.

First, here is the interface that defines an integer stack. Put this in a file called **IntStack.java**. This interface will be used by both stack implementations.

```
// Define an integer stack interface.
interface IntStack {
  void push(int item); // store an item
  int pop(); // retrieve an item
}
```

The following program creates a class called **FixedStack** that implements a fixed-length version of an integer stack:

```
// An implementation of IntStack that uses fixed storage.
class FixedStack implements IntStack {
  private int stck[];
  private int tos;

  // allocate and initialize stack
  FixedStack(int size) {
    stck = new int[size];
    tos = -1;
  }

  // Push an item onto the stack
  public void push(int item) {
    if(tos==stck.length-1) // use length member
      System.out.println("Stack is full.");
    else
      stck[++tos] = item;
  }

  // Pop an item from the stack
  public int pop() {
    if(tos < 0) {
      System.out.println("Stack underflow.");
      return 0;
    }
    else
      return stck[tos--];
  }
}
```

```
class IFTest {
  public static void main(String args[]) {
    FixedStack mystack1 = new FixedStack(5);
    FixedStack mystack2 = new FixedStack(8);

    // push some numbers onto the stack
    for(int i=0; i<5; i++) mystack1.push(i);
    for(int i=0; i<8; i++) mystack2.push(i);

    // pop those numbers off the stack
    System.out.println("Stack in mystack1:");
    for(int i=0; i<5; i++)
       System.out.println(mystack1.pop());

    System.out.println("Stack in mystack2:");
    for(int i=0; i<8; i++)
       System.out.println(mystack2.pop());
  }
}
```

Following is another implementation of **IntStack** that creates a dynamic stack by use of the same **interface** definition. In this implementation, each stack is constructed with an initial length. If this initial length is exceeded, then the stack is increased in size. Each time more room is needed, the size of the stack is doubled.

```
// Implement a "growable" stack.
class DynStack implements IntStack {
  private int stck[];
  private int tos;

  // allocate and initialize stack
  DynStack(int size) {
    stck = new int[size];
    tos = -1;
  }

  // Push an item onto the stack
  public void push(int item) {
    // if stack is full, allocate a larger stack
    if(tos==stck.length-1) {
      int temp[] = new int[stck.length * 2]; // double size
      for(int i=0; i<stck.length; i++) temp[i] = stck[i];
```

```
        stck = temp;
        stck[++tos] = item;
      }
      else
        stck[++tos] = item;
   }

   // Pop an item from the stack
   public int pop() {
     if(tos < 0) {
       System.out.println("Stack underflow.");
       return 0;
     }
     else
       return stck[tos--];
   }
}

class IFTest2 {
   public static void main(String args[]) {
     DynStack mystack1 = new DynStack(5);
     DynStack mystack2 = new DynStack(8);

     // these loops cause each stack to grow
     for(int i=0; i<12; i++) mystack1.push(i);
     for(int i=0; i<20; i++) mystack2.push(i);

     System.out.println("Stack in mystack1:");
     for(int i=0; i<12; i++)
       System.out.println(mystack1.pop());

     System.out.println("Stack in mystack2:");
     for(int i=0; i<20; i++)
       System.out.println(mystack2.pop());
   }
}
```

The following class uses both the **FixedStack** and **DynStack** implementations.
It does so through an interface reference. This means that calls to **push( )** and **pop( )**
are resolved at run time rather than at compile time.

```
/* Create an interface variable and
   access stacks through it.
*/
class IFTest3 {
  public static void main(String args[]) {
    IntStack mystack; // create an interface reference variable
    DynStack ds = new DynStack(5);
    FixedStack fs = new FixedStack(8);

    mystack = ds; // load dynamic stack
    // push some numbers onto the stack
    for(int i=0; i<12; i++) mystack.push(i);

    mystack = fs; // load fixed stack
    for(int i=0; i<8; i++) mystack.push(i);


    mystack = ds;
    System.out.println("Values in dynamic stack:");
    for(int i=0; i<12; i++)
      System.out.println(mystack.pop());

    mystack = fs;
    System.out.println("Values in fixed stack:");
    for(int i=0; i<8; i++)
      System.out.println(mystack.pop());
  }
}
```

In this program, **mystack** is a reference to the **IntStack** interface. Thus, when it refers to **ds**, it uses the versions of **push( )** and **pop( )** defined by the **DynStack** implementation. When it refers to **fs**, it uses the versions of **push( )** and **pop( )** defined by **FixedStack**. As explained, these determinations are made at run time. Accessing multiple implementations of an interface through an interface reference variable is the most powerful way that Java achieves run-time polymorphism.

Variables in Interfaces

You can use interfaces to import shared constants into multiple classes by simply declaring an interface that contains variables which are initialized to the desired values. When you include that interface in a class (that is, when you "implement" the interface), all of those variable names will be in scope as constants. This is similar to using a header file in C/C++ to create a large number of **#defined** constants or **const** declarations. If an interface contains no methods, then any class that includes such an interface doesn't actually implement anything. It is as if that class were importing the constant variables into the class name space as **final** variables. The next example uses this technique to implement an automated "decision maker":

```java
import java.util.Random;

interface SharedConstants {
  int NO = 0;
  int YES = 1;
  int MAYBE = 2;
  int LATER = 3;
  int SOON = 4;
  int NEVER = 5;
}

class Question implements SharedConstants {
  Random rand = new Random();
  int ask() {
    int prob = (int) (100 * rand.nextDouble());
    if (prob < 30)
      return NO;          // 30%
    else if (prob < 60)
      return YES;         // 30%
    else if (prob < 75)
      return LATER;       // 15%
    else if (prob < 98)
      return SOON;        // 13%

    else
      return NEVER;       // 2%
  }
}

class AskMe implements SharedConstants {
  static void answer(int result) {
    switch(result) {
      case NO:
        System.out.println("No");
        break;
      case YES:
        System.out.println("Yes");
```

```
      break;
    case MAYBE:
      System.out.println("Maybe");
      break;
    case LATER:
      System.out.println("Later");
      break;
    case SOON:
      System.out.println("Soon");
      break;
    case NEVER:
      System.out.println("Never");
      break;
  }
}

public static void main(String args[]) {
  Question q = new Question();
  answer(q.ask());
  answer(q.ask());
  answer(q.ask());
  answer(q.ask());
}
}
```

Notice that this program makes use of one of Java's standard classes: **Random**. This class provides pseudorandom numbers. It contains several methods which allow you to obtain random numbers in the form required by your program. In this example, the method **nextDouble( )** is used. It returns random numbers in the range 0.0 to 1.0.

In this sample program, the two classes, **Question** and **AskMe**, both implement the **SharedConstants** interface where **NO, YES, MAYBE, SOON, LATER**, and **NEVER** are defined. Inside each class, the code refers to these constants as if each class had defined or inherited them directly. Here is the output of a sample run of this program. Note that the results are different each time it is run.

```
Later
Soon
No
Yes
```

Interfaces Can Be Extended

One interface can inherit another by use of the keyword **extends**. The syntax is the same as for inheriting classes. When a class implements an interface that inherits another interface, it must provide implementations for all methods defined within the interface inheritance chain. Following is an example:

```
// One interface can extend another.
interface A {
  void meth1();
  void meth2();
}

// B now includes meth1() and meth2() -- it adds meth3().
interface B extends A {
  void meth3();
}

// This class must implement all of A and B
class MyClass implements B {
  public void meth1() {
    System.out.println("Implement meth1().");
  }

  public void meth2() {
    System.out.println("Implement meth2().");
  }

  public void meth3() {
    System.out.println("Implement meth3().");
  }

}

class IFExtend {
  public static void main(String arg[]) {
    MyClass ob = new MyClass();
```

```
    ob.meth1();
    ob.meth2();
    ob.meth3();
  }
}
```

As an experiment you might want to try removing the implementation for **meth1( )** in **MyClass**. This will cause a compile-time error. As stated earlier, any class that implements an interface must implement all methods defined by that interface, including any that are inherited from other interfaces.

Although the examples we've included in this book do not make frequent use of packages or interfaces, both of these tools are an important part of the Java programming environment. Virtually all real programs and applets that you write in Java will be contained within packages. A number will probably implement interfaces as well. It is important, therefore, that you be comfortable with their usage.

The Complete Reference

Java™ 2

Chapter 10

Exception Handling

This chapter examines Java's exception-handling mechanism. An *exception* is an abnormal condition that arises in a code sequence at run time. In other words, an exception is a run-time error. In computer languages that do not support exception handling, errors must be checked and handled manually—typically through the use of error codes, and so on. This approach is as cumbersome as it is troublesome. Java's exception handling avoids these problems and, in the process, brings run-time error management into the object-oriented world.

For the most part, exception handling has not changed since the original version of Java. However, Java 2, version 1.4 has added a new subsystem called the *chained exception facility*. This feature is described near the end of this chapter.

Exception-Handling Fundamentals

A Java exception is an object that describes an exceptional (that is, error) condition that has occurred in a piece of code. When an exceptional condition arises, an object representing that exception is created and *thrown* in the method that caused the error. That method may choose to handle the exception itself, or pass it on. Either way, at some point, the exception is *caught* and processed. Exceptions can be generated by the Java run-time system, or they can be manually generated by your code. Exceptions thrown by Java relate to fundamental errors that violate the rules of the Java language or the constraints of the Java execution environment. Manually generated exceptions are typically used to report some error condition to the caller of a method.

Java exception handling is managed via five keywords: **try**, **catch**, **throw**, **throws**, and **finally**. Briefly, here is how they work. Program statements that you want to monitor for exceptions are contained within a **try** block. If an exception occurs within the **try** block, it is thrown. Your code can catch this exception (using **catch**) and handle it in some rational manner. System-generated exceptions are automatically thrown by the Java run-time system. To manually throw an exception, use the keyword **throw**. Any exception that is thrown out of a method must be specified as such by a **throws** clause. Any code that absolutely must be executed before a method returns is put in a **finally** block.

This is the general form of an exception-handling block:

```
try {
  // block of code to monitor for errors
}

catch (ExceptionType1 exOb) {
    // exception handler for ExceptionType1
}
catch (ExceptionType2 exOb) {
    // exception handler for ExceptionType2
}
// ...
```

```
        finally {
            // block of code to be executed before try block ends
        }
```

Here, *ExceptionType* is the type of exception that has occurred. The remainder of this chapter describes how to apply this framework.

Exception Types

All exception types are subclasses of the built-in class **Throwable**. Thus, **Throwable** is at the top of the exception class hierarchy. Immediately below **Throwable** are two subclasses that partition exceptions into two distinct branches. One branch is headed by **Exception**. This class is used for exceptional conditions that user programs should catch. This is also the class that you will subclass to create your own custom exception types. There is an important subclass of **Exception**, called **RuntimeException**. Exceptions of this type are automatically defined for the programs that you write and include things such as division by zero and invalid array indexing.

The other branch is topped by **Error**, which defines exceptions that are not expected to be caught under normal circumstances by your program. Exceptions of type **Error** are used by the Java run-time system to indicate errors having to do with the run-time environment, itself. Stack overflow is an example of such an error. This chapter will not be dealing with exceptions of type **Error**, because these are typically created in response to catastrophic failures that cannot usually be handled by your program.

Uncaught Exceptions

Before you learn how to handle exceptions in your program, it is useful to see what happens when you don't handle them. This small program includes an expression that intentionally causes a divide-by-zero error.

```
class Exc0 {
    public static void main(String args[]) {
        int d = 0;
        int a = 42 / d;
    }
}
```

When the Java run-time system detects the attempt to divide by zero, it constructs a new exception object and then *throws* this exception. This causes the execution of **Exc0** to stop, because once an exception has been thrown, it must be *caught* by an exception handler and dealt with immediately. In this example, we haven't supplied any exception handlers of our own, so the exception is caught by the default handler provided by the

Java run-time system. Any exception that is not caught by your program will ultimately be processed by the default handler. The default handler displays a string describing the exception, prints a stack trace from the point at which the exception occurred, and terminates the program.

Here is the output generated when this example is executed.

```
java.lang.ArithmeticException: / by zero
        at Exc0.main(Exc0.java:4)
```

Notice how the class name, **Exc0**; the method name, **main**; the filename, **Exc0.java**; and the line number, **4**, are all included in the simple stack trace. Also, notice that the type of the exception thrown is a subclass of **Exception** called **ArithmeticException**, which more specifically describes what type of error happened. As discussed later in this chapter, Java supplies several built-in exception types that match the various sorts of run-time errors that can be generated.

The stack trace will always show the sequence of method invocations that led up to the error. For example, here is another version of the preceding program that introduces the same error but in a method separate from **main( )**:

```
class Exc1 {
  static void subroutine() {
    int d = 0;
    int a = 10 / d;
  }
  public static void main(String args[]) {
    Exc1.subroutine();
  }
}
```

The resulting stack trace from the default exception handler shows how the entire call stack is displayed:

```
java.lang.ArithmeticException: / by zero
    at Exc1.subroutine(Exc1.java:4)
    at Exc1.main(Exc1.java:7)
```

As you can see, the bottom of the stack is **main**'s line 7, which is the call to **subroutine( )**, which caused the exception at line 4. The call stack is quite useful for debugging, because it pinpoints the precise sequence of steps that led to the error.

Using try and catch

Although the default exception handler provided by the Java run-time system is useful for debugging, you will usually want to handle an exception yourself. Doing so provides two benefits. First, it allows you to fix the error. Second, it prevents the program from automatically terminating. Most users would be confused (to say the least) if your program stopped running and printed a stack trace whenever an error occurred! Fortunately, it is quite easy to prevent this.

To guard against and handle a run-time error, simply enclose the code that you want to monitor inside a **try** block. Immediately following the **try** block, include a **catch** clause that specifies the exception type that you wish to catch. To illustrate how easily this can be done, the following program includes a **try** block and a **catch** clause which processes the **ArithmeticException** generated by the division-by-zero error:

```
class Exc2 {
  public static void main(String args[]) {
    int d, a;
    try { // monitor a block of code.
       d = 0;
       a = 42 / d;
       System.out.println("This will not be printed.");
    } catch (ArithmeticException e) { // catch divide-by-zero error
       System.out.println("Division by zero.");
    }
    System.out.println("After catch statement.");
  }
}
```

This program generates the following output:

```
Division by zero.
After catch statement.
```

Notice that the call to **println( )** inside the **try** block is never executed. Once an exception is thrown, program control transfers out of the **try** block into the **catch** block. Put differently, **catch** is not "called," so execution never "returns" to the **try** block from a **catch**. Thus, the line "This will not be printed." is not displayed. Once the **catch** statement has executed, program control continues with the next line in the program following the entire **try**/**catch** mechanism.

A **try** and its **catch** statement form a unit. The scope of the **catch** clause is restricted to those statements specified by the immediately preceding **try** statement. A **catch** statement cannot catch an exception thrown by another **try** statement (except in the case of nested **try** statements, described shortly). The statements that are protected by **try** must be surrounded by curly braces. (That is, they must be within a block.) You cannot use **try** on a single statement.

The goal of most well-constructed **catch** clauses should be to resolve the exceptional condition and then continue on as if the error had never happened. For example, in the next program each iteration of the **for** loop obtains two random integers. Those two integers are divided by each other, and the result is used to divide the value 12345. The final result is put into **a**. If either division operation causes a divide-by-zero error, it is caught, the value of **a** is set to zero, and the program continues.

```java
// Handle an exception and move on.
import java.util.Random;

class HandleError {
  public static void main(String args[]) {
    int a=0, b=0, c=0;
    Random r = new Random();

    for(int i=0; i<32000; i++) {
      try {
        b = r.nextInt();
        c = r.nextInt();
        a = 12345 / (b/c);
      } catch (ArithmeticException e) {
        System.out.println("Division by zero.");
        a = 0; // set a to zero and continue
      }
      System.out.println("a: " + a);
    }
  }
}
```

Displaying a Description of an Exception

Throwable overrides the **toString( )** method (defined by **Object**) so that it returns a string containing a description of the exception. You can display this description in a **println( )** statement by simply passing the exception as an argument. For example, the **catch** block in the preceding program can be rewritten like this:

```
catch (ArithmeticException e) {
  System.out.println("Exception: " + e);
  a = 0; // set a to zero and continue
}
```

When this version is substituted in the program, and the program is run, each divide-by-zero error displays the following message:

```
Exception: java.lang.ArithmeticException: / by zero
```

While it is of no particular value in this context, the ability to display a description of an exception is valuable in other circumstances—particularly when you are experimenting with exceptions or when you are debugging.

Multiple catch Clauses

In some cases, more than one exception could be raised by a single piece of code. To handle this type of situation, you can specify two or more **catch** clauses, each catching a different type of exception. When an exception is thrown, each **catch** statement is inspected in order, and the first one whose type matches that of the exception is executed. After one **catch** statement executes, the others are bypassed, and execution continues after the **try/catch** block. The following example traps two different exception types:

```
// Demonstrate multiple catch statements.
class MultiCatch {
  public static void main(String args[]) {
    try {
      int a = args.length;
      System.out.println("a = " + a);
      int b = 42 / a;
      int c[] = { 1 };
      c[42] = 99;
    } catch(ArithmeticException e) {
      System.out.println("Divide by 0: " + e);
    } catch(ArrayIndexOutOfBoundsException e) {
      System.out.println("Array index oob: " + e);
    }
    System.out.println("After try/catch blocks.");
  }
}
```

This program will cause a division-by-zero exception if it is started with no command-line parameters, since **a** will equal zero. It will survive the division if you provide a command-line argument, setting **a** to something larger than zero. But it will cause an **ArrayIndexOutOfBoundsException**, since the **int** array **c** has a length of 1, yet the program attempts to assign a value to **c[42]**.

Here is the output generated by running it both ways:

```
C:\>java MultiCatch
a = 0
Divide by 0: java.lang.ArithmeticException: / by zero
After try/catch blocks.

C:\>java MultiCatch TestArg
a = 1
Array index oob: java.lang.ArrayIndexOutOfBoundsException
After try/catch blocks.
```

When you use multiple **catch** statements, it is important to remember that exception subclasses must come before any of their superclasses. This is because a **catch** statement that uses a superclass will catch exceptions of that type plus any of its subclasses. Thus, a subclass would never be reached if it came after its superclass. Further, in Java, unreachable code is an error. For example, consider the following program:

```
/* This program contains an error.

   A subclass must come before its superclass in
   a series of catch statements. If not,
   unreachable code will be created and a
   compile-time error will result.
*/
class SuperSubCatch {
  public static void main(String args[]) {
    try {
      int a = 0;
      int b = 42 / a;
    } catch(Exception e) {
      System.out.println("Generic Exception catch.");
    }
    /* This catch is never reached because
       ArithmeticException is a subclass of Exception. */
    catch(ArithmeticException e) { // ERROR - unreachable
      System.out.println("This is never reached.");
```

```
      }
    }
  }
```

If you try to compile this program, you will receive an error message stating that the second **catch** statement is unreachable because the exception has already been caught. Since **ArithmeticException** is a subclass of **Exception**, the first **catch** statement will handle all **Exception**-based errors, including **ArithmeticException**. This means that the second **catch** statement will never execute. To fix the problem, reverse the order of the **catch** statements.

Nested try Statements

The **try** statement can be nested. That is, a **try** statement can be inside the block of another **try**. Each time a **try** statement is entered, the context of that exception is pushed on the stack. If an inner **try** statement does not have a **catch** handler for a particular exception, the stack is unwound and the next **try** statement's **catch** handlers are inspected for a match. This continues until one of the **catch** statements succeeds, or until all of the nested **try** statements are exhausted. If no **catch** statement matches, then the Java run-time system will handle the exception. Here is an example that uses nested **try** statements:

```
// An example of nested try statements.
class NestTry {
  public static void main(String args[]) {
    try {
      int a = args.length;

      /* If no command-line args are present,
         the following statement will generate
         a divide-by-zero exception. */
      int b = 42 / a;

      System.out.println("a = " + a);

      try { // nested try block
        /* If one command-line arg is used,
           then a divide-by-zero exception
           will be generated by the following code. */
        if(a==1) a = a/(a-a); // division by zero
```

```
        /* If two command-line args are used,
           then generate an out-of-bounds exception. */
        if(a==2) {
          int c[] = { 1 };
          c[42] = 99; // generate an out-of-bounds exception
        }
      } catch(ArrayIndexOutOfBoundsException e) {
        System.out.println("Array index out-of-bounds: " + e);
      }

    } catch(ArithmeticException e) {
      System.out.println("Divide by 0: " + e);
    }
  }
}
```

As you can see, this program nests one **try** block within another. The program works as follows. When you execute the program with no command-line arguments, a divide-by-zero exception is generated by the outer **try** block. Execution of the program by one command-line argument generates a divide-by-zero exception from within the nested **try** block. Since the inner block does not catch this exception, it is passed on to the outer **try** block, where it is handled. If you execute the program with two command-line arguments, an array boundary exception is generated from within the inner **try** block. Here are sample runs that illustrate each case:

```
C:\>java NestTry
Divide by 0: java.lang.ArithmeticException: / by zero

C:\>java NestTry One
a = 1
Divide by 0: java.lang.ArithmeticException: / by zero

C:\>java NestTry One Two
a = 2
Array index out-of-bounds:
   java.lang.ArrayIndexOutOfBoundsException
```

Nesting of **try** statements can occur in less obvious ways when method calls are involved. For example, you can enclose a call to a method within a **try** block. Inside that method is another **try** statement. In this case, the **try** within the method is still nested inside the outer **try** block, which calls the method. Here is the previous program recoded so that the nested **try** block is moved inside the method **nesttry( )**:

```
/* Try statements can be implicitly nested via
   calls to methods. */
class MethNestTry {
  static void nesttry(int a) {
    try { // nested try block
      /* If one command-line arg is used,
         then a divide-by-zero exception
         will be generated by the following code. */
      if(a==1) a = a/(a-a); // division by zero

      /* If two command-line args are used,
         then generate an out-of-bounds exception. */
      if(a==2) {
        int c[] = { 1 };
        c[42] = 99; // generate an out-of-bounds exception
      }
    } catch(ArrayIndexOutOfBoundsException e) {
      System.out.println("Array index out-of-bounds: " + e);
    }
  }

  public static void main(String args[]) {
    try {
      int a = args.length;

      /* If no command-line args are present,
         the following statement will generate
         a divide-by-zero exception. */
      int b = 42 / a;
      System.out.println("a = " + a);

      nesttry(a);
    } catch(ArithmeticException e) {
      System.out.println("Divide by 0: " + e);
    }
  }
}
```

The output of this program is identical to that of the preceding example.

throw

So far, you have only been catching exceptions that are thrown by the Java run-time system. However, it is possible for your program to throw an exception explicitly, using the **throw** statement. The general form of **throw** is shown here:

throw *ThrowableInstance*;

Here, *ThrowableInstance* must be an object of type **Throwable** or a subclass of **Throwable**. Simple types, such as **int** or **char**, as well as non-**Throwable** classes, such as **String** and **Object**, cannot be used as exceptions. There are two ways you can obtain a **Throwable** object: using a parameter into a **catch** clause, or creating one with the **new** operator.

The flow of execution stops immediately after the **throw** statement; any subsequent statements are not executed. The nearest enclosing **try** block is inspected to see if it has a **catch** statement that matches the type of the exception. If it does find a match, control is transferred to that statement. If not, then the next enclosing **try** statement is inspected, and so on. If no matching **catch** is found, then the default exception handler halts the program and prints the stack trace.

Here is a sample program that creates and throws an exception. The handler that catches the exception rethrows it to the outer handler.

```
// Demonstrate throw.
class ThrowDemo {
  static void demoproc() {
    try {
      throw new NullPointerException("demo");
    } catch(NullPointerException e) {
      System.out.println("Caught inside demoproc.");
      throw e; // rethrow the exception
    }
  }

  public static void main(String args[]) {
    try {
      demoproc();
    } catch(NullPointerException e) {
      System.out.println("Recaught: " + e);
    }
  }
}
```

This program gets two chances to deal with the same error. First, **main( )** sets up an exception context and then calls **demoproc( )**. The **demoproc( )** method then sets up another exception-handling context and immediately throws a new instance of **NullPointerException,** which is caught on the next line. The exception is then rethrown. Here is the resulting output:

```
Caught inside demoproc.
Recaught: java.lang.NullPointerException: demo
```

The program also illustrates how to create one of Java's standard exception objects. Pay close attention to this line:

```
throw new NullPointerException("demo");
```

Here, **new** is used to construct an instance of **NullPointerException**. All of Java's built-in run-time exceptions have at least two constructors: one with no parameter and one that takes a string parameter. When the second form is used, the argument specifies a string that describes the exception. This string is displayed when the object is used as an argument to **print( )** or **println( )**. It can also be obtained by a call to **getMessage( )**, which is defined by **Throwable**.

throws

If a method is capable of causing an exception that it does not handle, it must specify this behavior so that callers of the method can guard themselves against that exception. You do this by including a **throws** clause in the method's declaration. A **throws** clause lists the types of exceptions that a method might throw. This is necessary for all exceptions, except those of type **Error** or **RuntimeException**, or any of their subclasses. All other exceptions that a method can throw must be declared in the **throws** clause. If they are not, a compile-time error will result.

This is the general form of a method declaration that includes a **throws** clause:

type method-name(parameter-list) throws *exception-list*
{
  // body of method
}

Here, *exception-list* is a comma-separated list of the exceptions that a method can throw.

Following is an example of an incorrect program that tries to throw an exception that it does not catch. Because the program does not specify a **throws** clause to declare this fact, the program will not compile.

```
// This program contains an error and will not compile.
class ThrowsDemo {
  static void throwOne() {
    System.out.println("Inside throwOne.");
    throw new IllegalAccessException("demo");
  }
  public static void main(String args[]) {
    throwOne();
  }
}
```

To make this example compile, you need to make two changes. First, you need to declare that **throwOne( )** throws **IllegalAccessException**. Second, **main( )** must define a **try/catch** statement that catches this exception.

The corrected example is shown here:

```
// This is now correct.
class ThrowsDemo {
  static void throwOne() throws IllegalAccessException {
    System.out.println("Inside throwOne.");
    throw new IllegalAccessException("demo");
  }
  public static void main(String args[]) {
    try {
      throwOne();
    } catch (IllegalAccessException e) {
      System.out.println("Caught " + e);
    }
  }
}
```

Here is the output generated by running this example program:

```
inside throwOne
caught java.lang.IllegalAccessException: demo
```

finally

When exceptions are thrown, execution in a method takes a rather abrupt, nonlinear path that alters the normal flow through the method. Depending upon how the method is coded, it is even possible for an exception to cause the method to return prematurely. This could be a problem in some methods. For example, if a method opens a file upon entry and closes it upon exit, then you will not want the code that closes the file to be bypassed by the exception-handling mechanism. The **finally** keyword is designed to address this contingency.

finally creates a block of code that will be executed after a **try/catch** block has completed and before the code following the **try/catch** block. The **finally** block will execute whether or not an exception is thrown. If an exception is thrown, the **finally** block will execute even if no **catch** statement matches the exception. Any time a method is about to return to the caller from inside a **try/catch** block, via an uncaught exception or an explicit return statement, the **finally** clause is also executed just before the method returns. This can be useful for closing file handles and freeing up any other resources that might have been allocated at the beginning of a method with the intent of disposing of them before returning. The **finally** clause is optional. However, each **try** statement requires at least one **catch** or a **finally** clause.

Here is an example program that shows three methods that exit in various ways, none without executing their **finally** clauses:

```
// Demonstrate finally.
class FinallyDemo {
  // Through an exception out of the method.
  static void procA() {
    try {
      System.out.println("inside procA");
      throw new RuntimeException("demo");
    } finally {
      System.out.println("procA's finally");
    }
  }

  // Return from within a try block.
  static void procB() {
    try {
      System.out.println("inside procB");
      return;
    } finally {
```

```
      System.out.println("procB's finally");
   }
}
// Execute a try block normally.
static void procC() {
   try {
      System.out.println("inside procC");
   } finally {
      System.out.println("procC's finally");
   }
}

public static void main(String args[]) {
   try {
      procA();
   } catch (Exception e) {
      System.out.println("Exception caught");
   }
   procB();
   procC();
}
}
```

In this example, **procA( )** prematurely breaks out of the **try** by throwing an exception. The **finally** clause is executed on the way out. **procB( )**'s **try** statement is exited via a **return** statement. The **finally** clause is executed before **procB( )** returns. In **procC( )**, the **try** statement executes normally, without error. However, the **finally** block is still executed.

 *If a **finally** block is associated with a **try**, the **finally** block will be executed upon conclusion of the **try**.*

Here is the output generated by the preceding program:

```
inside procA
procA's finally
Exception caught
inside procB
procB's finally
inside procC
procC's finally
```

Java's Built-in Exceptions

Inside the standard package **java.lang**, Java defines several exception classes. A few have been used by the preceding examples. The most general of these exceptions are subclasses of the standard type **RuntimeException**. Since **java.lang** is implicitly imported into all Java programs, most exceptions derived from **RuntimeException** are automatically available. Furthermore, they need not be included in any method's **throws** list. In the language of Java, these are called *unchecked exceptions* because the compiler does not check to see if a method handles or throws these exceptions. The unchecked exceptions defined in **java.lang** are listed in Table 10-1. Table 10-2 lists those exceptions defined by **java.lang** that must be included in a method's **throws** list if that method can generate one of these exceptions and does not handle it itself. These are called *checked exceptions*. Java defines several other types of exceptions that relate to its various class libraries.

Exception	Meaning
ArithmeticException	Arithmetic error, such as divide-by-zero.
ArrayIndexOutOfBoundsException	Array index is out-of-bounds.
ArrayStoreException	Assignment to an array element of an incompatible type.
ClassCastException	Invalid cast.
IllegalArgumentException	Illegal argument used to invoke a method.
IllegalMonitorStateException	Illegal monitor operation, such as waiting on an unlocked thread.
IllegalStateException	Environment or application is in incorrect state.
IllegalThreadStateException	Requested operation not compatible with current thread state.
IndexOutOfBoundsException	Some type of index is out-of-bounds.
NegativeArraySizeException	Array created with a negative size.

Table 10-1. *Java's Unchecked* RuntimeException *Subclasses*

Exception	Meaning
NullPointerException	Invalid use of a null reference.
NumberFormatException	Invalid conversion of a string to a numeric format.
SecurityException	Attempt to violate security.
StringIndexOutOfBounds	Attempt to index outside the bounds of a string.
UnsupportedOperationException	An unsupported operation was encountered.

Table 10-1. *Java's Unchecked* RuntimeException *Subclasses* (continued)

Exception	Meaning
ClassNotFoundException	Class not found.
CloneNotSupportedException	Attempt to clone an object that does not implement the **Cloneable** interface.
IllegalAccessException	Access to a class is denied.
InstantiationException	Attempt to create an object of an abstract class or interface.
InterruptedException	One thread has been interrupted by another thread.
NoSuchFieldException	A requested field does not exist.
NoSuchMethodException	A requested method does not exist.

Table 10-2. *Java's Checked Exceptions Defined in* java.lang

Creating Your Own Exception Subclasses

Although Java's built-in exceptions handle most common errors, you will probably want to create your own exception types to handle situations specific to your applications. This is quite easy to do: just define a subclass of **Exception** (which is, of course, a subclass of **Throwable**). Your subclasses don't need to actually implement anything—it is their existence in the type system that allows you to use them as exceptions.

The **Exception** class does not define any methods of its own. It does, of course, inherit those methods provided by **Throwable**. Thus, all exceptions, including those that you create, have the methods defined by **Throwable** available to them. They are shown in Table 10-3. Notice that several methods were added by Java 2, version 1.4. You may also wish to override one or more of these methods in exception classes that you create.

Method	Description
Throwable fillInStackTrace( )	Returns a **Throwable** object that contains a completed stack trace. This object can be rethrown.
Throwable getCause( )	Returns the exception that underlies the current exception. If there is no underlying exception, **null** is returned. Added by Java 2, version 1.4.
String getLocalizedMessage( )	Returns a localized description of the exception.
String getMessage( )	Returns a description of the exception.
StackTraceElement[ ] getStackTrace( )	Returns an array that contains the stack trace, one element at a time as an array of **StackTraceElement**. The method at the top of the stack is the last method called before the exception was thrown. This method is found in the first element of the array. The **StackTraceElement** class gives your program access to information about each element in the trace, such as its method name. Added by Java 2, version 1.4
Throwable initCause(Throwable *causeExc*)	Associates *causeExc* with the invoking exception as a cause of the invoking exception. Returns a reference to the exception. Added by Java 2, version 1.4

Table 10-3. *The Methods Defined by* Throwable

Method	Description
void printStackTrace( )	Displays the stack trace.
void printStackTrace(PrintStream *stream*)	Sends the stack trace to the specified stream.
void printStackTrace(PrintWriter *stream*)	Sends the stack trace to the specified stream.
void setStackTrace(StackTraceElement *elements*[ ])	Sets the stack trace to the elements passed in *elements*. This method is for specialized applications, not normal use. Added by Java 2, version 1.4
String toString( )	Returns a **String** object containing a description of the exception. This method is called by **println( )** when outputting a **Throwable** object.

Table 10-3. *The Methods Defined by* Throwable *(continued)*

The following example declares a new subclass of **Exception** and then uses that subclass to signal an error condition in a method. It overrides the **toString( )** method, allowing the description of the exception to be displayed using **println( )**.

```
// This program creates a custom exception type.
class MyException extends Exception {
  private int detail;

  MyException(int a) {
    detail = a;
  }

  public String toString() {
    return "MyException[" + detail + "]";
  }
}

class ExceptionDemo {
  static void compute(int a) throws MyException {
    System.out.println("Called compute(" + a + ")");
```

```
    if(a > 10)
      throw new MyException(a);
    System.out.println("Normal exit");
  }

  public static void main(String args[]) {
    try {
      compute(1);
      compute(20);
    } catch (MyException e) {
      System.out.println("Caught " + e);
    }
  }
}
```

This example defines a subclass of **Exception** called **MyException**. This subclass is quite simple: it has only a constructor plus an overloaded **toString( )** method that displays the value of the exception. The **ExceptionDemo** class defines a method named **compute( )** that throws a **MyException** object. The exception is thrown when **compute( )**'s integer parameter is greater than 10. The **main( )** method sets up an exception handler for **MyException**, then calls **compute( )** with a legal value (less than 10) and an illegal one to show both paths through the code. Here is the result:

```
Called compute(1)
Normal exit
Called compute(20)
Caught MyException[20]
```

Chained Exceptions

Java 2, version 1.4 added a new feature to the exception subsystem: *chained exceptions*. The chained exception feature allows you to associate another exception with an exception. This second exception describes the cause of the first exception. For example, imagine a situation in which a method throws an **ArithmeticException** because of an attempt to divide by zero. However, the actual cause of the problem was that an I/O error occurred, which caused the divisor to be set improperly. Although the method must certainly throw an **ArithmeticException**, since that is the error that occurred, you might also want to let the calling code know that the underlying cause was an I/O error. Chained exceptions let you handle this, and any other situation in which layers of exceptions exist.

To allow chained exceptions, Java 2, version 1.4 added two constructors and two methods to **Throwable**. The constructors are shown here.

Throwable(Throwable *causeExc*)
Throwable(String *msg*, Throwable *causeExc*)

In the first form, *causeExc* is the exception that causes the current exception. That is, *causeExc* is the underlying reason that an exception occurred. The second form allows you to specify a description at the same time that you specify a cause exception. These two constructors have also been added to the **Error**, **Exception**, and **RuntimeException** classes.

The chained exception methods added to **Throwable** are **getCause( )** and **initCause( )**. These methods are shown in Table 10-3, and are repeated here for the sake of discussion.

Throwable getCause( )
Throwable initCause(Throwable *causeExc*)

The **getCause( )** method returns the exception that underlies the current exception. If there is no underlying exception, **null** is returned. The **initCause( )** method associates *causeExc* with the invoking exception and returns a reference to the exception. Thus, you can associate a cause with an exception after the exception has been created. However, the cause exception can be set only once. Thus, you can call **initCause( )** only once for each exception object. Furthermore, if the cause exception was set by a constructor, then you can't set it again using **initCause( )**.

In general, **initCause( )** is used to set a cause for legacy exception classes which don't support the two additional constructors described earlier. At the time of this writing, most of Java's built-in exceptions, such as **ArithmeticException**, do not define the additional constructors. Thus, you will use **initCause( )** if you need to add an exception chain to these exceptions. When creating your own exception classes you will want to add the two chained-exception constructors if you will be using your exceptions in situations in which layered exceptions are possible.

Here is an example that illustrates the mechanics of handling chained exceptions.

```java
// Demonstrate exception chaining.
class ChainExcDemo {
  static void demoproc() {
    // create an exception
    NullPointerException e =
      new NullPointerException("top layer");

    // add a cause
    e.initCause(new ArithmeticException("cause"));

    throw e;
  }

  public static void main(String args[]) {
    try {
      demoproc();
```

```
    } catch(NullPointerException e) {
        // display top level exception
        System.out.println("Caught: " + e);

        // display cause exception
        System.out.println("Original cause: " +
                            e.getCause());
    }
  }
}
```

The output from the program is shown here.

```
Caught: java.lang.NullPointerException: top layer
Original cause: java.lang.ArithmeticException: cause
```

In this example, the top-level exception is **NullPointerException**. To it is added a cause exception, **ArithmeticException**. When the exception is thrown out of **demoproc( )**, it is caught by **main( )**. There, the top-level exception is displayed, followed by the underlying exception, which is obtained by calling **getCause( )**.

Chained exceptions can be carried on to whatever depth is necessary. Thus, the cause exception can, itself, have a cause. Be aware that overly long chains of exceptions may indicate poor design.

Chained exceptions are not something that every program will need. However, in cases in which knowledge of an underlying cause is useful, they offer an elegant solution.

Using Exceptions

Exception handling provides a powerful mechanism for controlling complex programs that have many dynamic run-time characteristics. It is important to think of **try**, **throw**, and **catch** as clean ways to handle errors and unusual boundary conditions in your program's logic. If you are like most programmers, then you probably are used to returning an error code when a method fails. When you are programming in Java, you should break this habit. When a method can fail, have it throw an exception. This is a cleaner way to handle failure modes.

One last point: Java's exception-handling statements should not be considered a general mechanism for nonlocal branching. If you do so, it will only confuse your code and make it hard to maintain.

The Complete Reference

Java™ 2

Chapter 11

Multithreaded Programming

Unlike most other computer languages, Java provides built-in support for *multithreaded programming*. A multithreaded program contains two or more parts that can run concurrently. Each part of such a program is called a *thread*, and each thread defines a separate path of execution. Thus, multithreading is a specialized form of multitasking.

You are almost certainly acquainted with multitasking, because it is supported by virtually all modern operating systems. However, there are two distinct types of multitasking: process-based and thread-based. It is important to understand the difference between the two. For most readers, process-based multitasking is the more familiar form. A *process* is, in essence, a program that is executing. Thus, *process-based* multitasking is the feature that allows your computer to run two or more programs concurrently. For example, process-based multitasking enables you to run the Java compiler at the same time that you are using a text editor. In process-based multitasking, a program is the smallest unit of code that can be dispatched by the scheduler.

In a *thread-based* multitasking environment, the thread is the smallest unit of dispatchable code. This means that a single program can perform two or more tasks simultaneously. For instance, a text editor can format text at the same time that it is printing, as long as these two actions are being performed by two separate threads. Thus, process-based multitasking deals with the "big picture," and thread-based multitasking handles the details.

Multitasking threads require less overhead than multitasking processes. Processes are heavyweight tasks that require their own separate address spaces. Interprocess communication is expensive and limited. Context switching from one process to another is also costly. Threads, on the other hand, are lightweight. They share the same address space and cooperatively share the same heavyweight process. Interthread communication is inexpensive, and context switching from one thread to the next is low cost. While Java programs make use of process-based multitasking environments, process-based multitasking is not under the control of Java. However, multithreaded multitasking is.

Multithreading enables you to write very efficient programs that make maximum use of the CPU, because idle time can be kept to a minimum. This is especially important for the interactive, networked environment in which Java operates, because idle time is common. For example, the transmission rate of data over a network is much slower than the rate at which the computer can process it. Even local file system resources are read and written at a much slower pace than they can be processed by the CPU. And, of course, user input is much slower than the computer. In a traditional, single-threaded environment, your program has to wait for each of these tasks to finish before it can proceed to the next one—even though the CPU is sitting idle most of the time. Multithreading lets you gain access to this idle time and put it to good use.

If you have programmed for operating systems such as Windows 98 or Windows 2000, then you are already familiar with multithreaded programming. However, the fact that Java manages threads makes multithreading especially convenient, because many of the details are handled for you.

The Java Thread Model

The Java run-time system depends on threads for many things, and all the class libraries are designed with multithreading in mind. In fact, Java uses threads to enable the entire environment to be asynchronous. This helps reduce inefficiency by preventing the waste of CPU cycles.

The value of a multithreaded environment is best understood in contrast to its counterpart. Single-threaded systems use an approach called an *event loop* with *polling*. In this model, a single thread of control runs in an infinite loop, polling a single event queue to decide what to do next. Once this polling mechanism returns with, say, a signal that a network file is ready to be read, then the event loop dispatches control to the appropriate event handler. Until this event handler returns, nothing else can happen in the system. This wastes CPU time. It can also result in one part of a program dominating the system and preventing any other events from being processed. In general, in a singled-threaded environment, when a thread *blocks* (that is, suspends execution) because it is waiting for some resource, the entire program stops running.

The benefit of Java's multithreading is that the main loop/polling mechanism is eliminated. One thread can pause without stopping other parts of your program. For example, the idle time created when a thread reads data from a network or waits for user input can be utilized elsewhere. Multithreading allows animation loops to sleep for a second between each frame without causing the whole system to pause. When a thread blocks in a Java program, only the single thread that is blocked pauses. All other threads continue to run.

Threads exist in several states. A thread can be *running*. It can be *ready to run* as soon as it gets CPU time. A running thread can be *suspended*, which temporarily suspends its activity. A suspended thread can then be *resumed*, allowing it to pick up where it left off. A thread can be *blocked* when waiting for a resource. At any time, a thread can be terminated, which halts its execution immediately. Once terminated, a thread cannot be resumed.

Thread Priorities

Java assigns to each thread a priority that determines how that thread should be treated with respect to the others. Thread priorities are integers that specify the relative priority of one thread to another. As an absolute value, a priority is meaningless; a higher-priority thread doesn't run any faster than a lower-priority thread if it is the only thread running. Instead, a thread's priority is used to decide when to switch from one running thread to the next. This is called a *context switch*. The rules that determine when a context switch takes place are simple:

- ■ *A thread can voluntarily relinquish control.* This is done by explicitly yielding, sleeping, or blocking on pending I/O. In this scenario, all other threads are examined, and the highest-priority thread that is ready to run is given the CPU.

■ *A thread can be preempted by a higher-priority thread.* In this case, a lower-priority thread that does not yield the processor is simply preempted—no matter what it is doing—by a higher-priority thread. Basically, as soon as a higher-priority thread wants to run, it does. This is called *preemptive multitasking*.

In cases where two threads with the same priority are competing for CPU cycles, the situation is a bit complicated. For operating systems such as Windows 98, threads of equal priority are time-sliced automatically in round-robin fashion. For other types of operating systems, threads of equal priority must voluntarily yield control to their peers. If they don't, the other threads will not run.

 Problems can arise from the differences in the way that operating systems context-switch threads of equal priority.

Synchronization

Because multithreading introduces an asynchronous behavior to your programs, there must be a way for you to enforce synchronicity when you need it. For example, if you want two threads to communicate and share a complicated data structure, such as a linked list, you need some way to ensure that they don't conflict with each other. That is, you must prevent one thread from writing data while another thread is in the middle of reading it. For this purpose, Java implements an elegant twist on an age-old model of interprocess synchronization: the *monitor*. The monitor is a control mechanism first defined by C.A.R. Hoare. You can think of a monitor as a very small box that can hold only one thread. Once a thread enters a monitor, all other threads must wait until that thread exits the monitor. In this way, a monitor can be used to protect a shared asset from being manipulated by more than one thread at a time.

Most multithreaded systems expose monitors as objects that your program must explicitly acquire and manipulate. Java provides a cleaner solution. There is no class "Monitor"; instead, each object has its own implicit monitor that is automatically entered when one of the object's synchronized methods is called. Once a thread is inside a synchronized method, no other thread can call any other synchronized method on the same object. This enables you to write very clear and concise multithreaded code, because synchronization support is built in to the language.

Messaging

After you divide your program into separate threads, you need to define how they will communicate with each other. When programming with most other languages, you must depend on the operating system to establish communication between threads. This, of course, adds overhead. By contrast, Java provides a clean, low-cost way for two or more threads to talk to each other, via calls to predefined methods that all objects have. Java's messaging system allows a thread to enter a synchronized method on an object, and then wait there until some other thread explicitly notifies it to come out.

The Thread Class and the Runnable Interface

Java's multithreading system is built upon the **Thread** class, its methods, and its companion interface, **Runnable**. **Thread** encapsulates a thread of execution. Since you can't directly refer to the ethereal state of a running thread, you will deal with it through its proxy, the **Thread** instance that spawned it. To create a new thread, your program will either extend **Thread** or implement the **Runnable** interface.

The **Thread** class defines several methods that help manage threads. The ones that will be used in this chapter are shown here:

Method	Meaning
getName	Obtain a thread's name.
getPriority	Obtain a thread's priority.
isAlive	Determine if a thread is still running.
join	Wait for a thread to terminate.
run	Entry point for the thread.
sleep	Suspend a thread for a period of time.
start	Start a thread by calling its run method.

Thus far, all the examples in this book have used a single thread of execution. The remainder of this chapter explains how to use **Thread** and **Runnable** to create and manage threads, beginning with the one thread that all Java programs have: the main thread.

The Main Thread

When a Java program starts up, one thread begins running immediately. This is usually called the *main thread* of your program, because it is the one that is executed when your program begins. The main thread is important for two reasons:

- It is the thread from which other "child" threads will be spawned.
- Often it must be the last thread to finish execution because it performs various shutdown actions.

Although the main thread is created automatically when your program is started, it can be controlled through a **Thread** object. To do so, you must obtain a reference to it by calling the method **currentThread( )**, which is a **public static** member of **Thread**. Its general form is shown here:

static Thread currentThread( )

This method returns a reference to the thread in which it is called. Once you have a reference to the main thread, you can control it just like any other thread.

Let's begin by reviewing the following example:

```
// Controlling the main Thread.
class CurrentThreadDemo {
  public static void main(String args[]) {
    Thread t = Thread.currentThread();

    System.out.println("Current thread: " + t);

    // change the name of the thread
    t.setName("My Thread");
    System.out.println("After name change: " + t);

    try {
      for(int n = 5; n > 0; n--) {
        System.out.println(n);
        Thread.sleep(1000);
      }
    } catch (InterruptedException e) {
      System.out.println("Main thread interrupted");
    }
  }
}
```

In this program, a reference to the current thread (the main thread, in this case) is obtained by calling **currentThread( )**, and this reference is stored in the local variable **t**. Next, the program displays information about the thread. The program then calls **setName( )** to change the internal name of the thread. Information about the thread is then redisplayed. Next, a loop counts down from five, pausing one second between each line. The pause is accomplished by the **sleep( )** method. The argument to **sleep( )** specifies the delay period in milliseconds. Notice the **try/catch** block around this loop. The **sleep( )** method in **Thread** might throw an **InterruptedException**. This would happen if some other thread wanted to interrupt this sleeping one. This example just prints a message if it gets interrupted. In a real program, you would need to handle this differently. Here is the output generated by this program:

```
Current thread: Thread[main,5,main]
After name change: Thread[My Thread,5,main]
5
4
3
2
1
```

Notice the output produced when **t** is used as an argument to **println( )**. This displays, in order: the name of the thread, its priority, and the name of its group. By default, the name of the main thread is **main**. Its priority is 5, which is the default value, and **main** is also the name of the group of threads to which this thread belongs. A *thread group* is a data structure that controls the state of a collection of threads as a whole. This process is managed by the particular run-time environment and is not discussed in detail here. After the name of the thread is changed, **t** is again output. This time, the new name of the thread is displayed.

Let's look more closely at the methods defined by **Thread** that are used in the program. The **sleep( )** method causes the thread from which it is called to suspend execution for the specified period of milliseconds. Its general form is shown here:

static void sleep(long *milliseconds*) throws InterruptedException

The number of milliseconds to suspend is specified in *milliseconds*. This method may throw an **InterruptedException**.

The **sleep( )** method has a second form, shown next, which allows you to specify the period in terms of milliseconds and nanoseconds:

static void sleep(long *milliseconds*, int *nanoseconds*) throws InterruptedException

This second form is useful only in environments that allow timing periods as short as nanoseconds.

As the preceding program shows, you can set the name of a thread by using **setName( )**. You can obtain the name of a thread by calling **getName( )** (but note that this procedure is not shown in the program). These methods are members of the **Thread** class and are declared like this:

final void setName(String *threadName*)

final String getName( )

Here, *threadName* specifies the name of the thread.

Creating a Thread

In the most general sense, you create a thread by instantiating an object of type **Thread**. Java defines two ways in which this can be accomplished:

- You can implement the **Runnable** interface.
- You can extend the **Thread** class, itself.

The following two sections look at each method, in turn.

Implementing Runnable

The easiest way to create a thread is to create a class that implements the **Runnable** interface. **Runnable** abstracts a unit of executable code. You can construct a thread on any object that implements **Runnable**. To implement **Runnable**, a class need only implement a single method called **run( )**, which is declared like this:

public void run( )

Inside **run( )**, you will define the code that constitutes the new thread. It is important to understand that **run( )** can call other methods, use other classes, and declare variables, just like the main thread can. The only difference is that **run( )** establishes the entry point for another, concurrent thread of execution within your program. This thread will end when **run( )** returns.

After you create a class that implements **Runnable**, you will instantiate an object of type **Thread** from within that class. **Thread** defines several constructors. The one that we will use is shown here:

Thread(Runnable *threadOb*, String *threadName*)

In this constructor, *threadOb* is an instance of a class that implements the **Runnable** interface. This defines where execution of the thread will begin. The name of the new thread is specified by *threadName*.

After the new thread is created, it will not start running until you call its **start( )** method, which is declared within **Thread**. In essence, **start( )** executes a call to **run( )**. The **start( )** method is shown here:

void start( )

Here is an example that creates a new thread and starts it running:

```java
// Create a second thread.
class NewThread implements Runnable {
  Thread t;

  NewThread() {
    // Create a new, second thread
    t = new Thread(this, "Demo Thread");
    System.out.println("Child thread: " + t);
    t.start(); // Start the thread
  }

  // This is the entry point for the second thread.
  public void run() {
    try {
      for(int i = 5; i > 0; i--) {
        System.out.println("Child Thread: " + i);
        Thread.sleep(500);
      }
    } catch (InterruptedException e) {
      System.out.println("Child interrupted.");
    }
    System.out.println("Exiting child thread.");
  }
}

class ThreadDemo {
  public static void main(String args[]) {
    new NewThread(); // create a new thread

    try {
      for(int i = 5; i > 0; i--) {
        System.out.println("Main Thread: " + i);
        Thread.sleep(1000);
      }
    } catch (InterruptedException e) {
      System.out.println("Main thread interrupted.");
    }
    System.out.println("Main thread exiting.");
  }
}
```

Inside **NewThread**'s constructor, a new **Thread** object is created by the following statement:

```
t = new Thread(this, "Demo Thread");
```

Passing **this** as the first argument indicates that you want the new thread to call the **run( )** method on **this** object. Next, **start( )** is called, which starts the thread of execution beginning at the **run( )** method. This causes the child thread's **for** loop to begin. After calling **start( )**, **NewThread**'s constructor returns to **main( )**. When the main thread resumes, it enters its **for** loop. Both threads continue running, sharing the CPU, until their loops finish. The output produced by this program is as follows:

```
Child thread: Thread[Demo Thread,5,main]
Main Thread: 5
Child Thread: 5
Child Thread: 4
Main Thread: 4
Child Thread: 3
Child Thread: 2
Main Thread: 3
Child Thread: 1
Exiting child thread.
Main Thread: 2
Main Thread: 1
Main thread exiting.
```

As mentioned earlier, in a multithreaded program, often the main thread must be the last thread to finish running. In fact, for some older JVMs, if the main thread finishes before a child thread has completed, then the Java run-time system may "hang." The preceding program ensures that the main thread finishes last, because the main thread sleeps for 1,000 milliseconds between iterations, but the child thread sleeps for only 500 milliseconds. This causes the child thread to terminate earlier than the main thread. Shortly, you will see a better way to wait for a thread to finish.

Extending Thread

The second way to create a thread is to create a new class that extends **Thread**, and then to create an instance of that class. The extending class must override the **run( )** method, which is the entry point for the new thread. It must also call **start( )** to begin execution of the new thread. Here is the preceding program rewritten to extend **Thread**:

```java
// Create a second thread by extending Thread
class NewThread extends Thread {

  NewThread() {
    // Create a new, second thread
    super("Demo Thread");
    System.out.println("Child thread: " + this);
    start(); // Start the thread
  }

  // This is the entry point for the second thread.
  public void run() {
    try {
      for(int i = 5; i > 0; i--) {
        System.out.println("Child Thread: " + i);
        Thread.sleep(500);
      }
    } catch (InterruptedException e) {
      System.out.println("Child interrupted.");
    }
    System.out.println("Exiting child thread.");
  }
}

class ExtendThread {
  public static void main(String args[]) {
    new NewThread(); // create a new thread

    try {
      for(int i = 5; i > 0; i--) {
        System.out.println("Main Thread: " + i);
        Thread.sleep(1000);
      }
    } catch (InterruptedException e) {
      System.out.println("Main thread interrupted.");
    }
    System.out.println("Main thread exiting.");
  }
}
```

This program generates the same output as the preceding version. As you can see, the child thread is created by instantiating an object of **NewThread**, which is derived from **Thread**.

Notice the call to **super( )** inside **NewThread**. This invokes the following form of the **Thread** constructor:

    public Thread(String *threadName*)

Here, *threadName* specifies the name of the thread.

Choosing an Approach

At this point, you might be wondering why Java has two ways to create child threads, and which approach is better. The answers to these questions turn on the same point. The **Thread** class defines several methods that can be overridden by a derived class. Of these methods, the only one that *must* be overridden is **run( )**. This is, of course, the same method required when you implement **Runnable**. Many Java programmers feel that classes should be extended only when they are being enhanced or modified in some way. So, if you will not be overriding any of **Thread**'s other methods, it is probably best simply to implement **Runnable**. This is up to you, of course. However, throughout the rest of this chapter, we will create threads by using classes that implement **Runnable**.

Creating Multiple Threads

So far, you have been using only two threads: the main thread and one child thread. However, your program can spawn as many threads as it needs. For example, the following program creates three child threads:

```
// Create multiple threads.
class NewThread implements Runnable {
  String name; // name of thread
  Thread t;

  NewThread(String threadname) {
    name = threadname;
    t = new Thread(this, name);
    System.out.println("New thread: " + t);
    t.start(); // Start the thread
  }

  // This is the entry point for thread.
  public void run() {
```

```
    try {
      for(int i = 5; i > 0; i--) {
        System.out.println(name + ": " + i);
        Thread.sleep(1000);
      }
    } catch (InterruptedException e) {
      System.out.println(name + "Interrupted");
    }
    System.out.println(name + " exiting.");
  }
}

class MultiThreadDemo {
  public static void main(String args[]) {
    new NewThread("One"); // start threads
    new NewThread("Two");
    new NewThread("Three");

    try {
      // wait for other threads to end
      Thread.sleep(10000);
    } catch (InterruptedException e) {
      System.out.println("Main thread Interrupted");
    }

    System.out.println("Main thread exiting.");
  }
}
```

The output from this program is shown here:

```
New thread: Thread[One,5,main]
New thread: Thread[Two,5,main]
New thread: Thread[Three,5,main]
One: 5
Two: 5
Three: 5
One: 4
Two: 4
Three: 4
One: 3
Three: 3
Two: 3
```

```
One: 2
Three: 2
Two: 2
One: 1
Three: 1
Two: 1
One exiting.
Two exiting.
Three exiting.
Main thread exiting.
```

As you can see, once started, all three child threads share the CPU. Notice the call to **sleep(10000)** in **main( )**. This causes the main thread to sleep for ten seconds and ensures that it will finish last.

Using isAlive( ) and join( )

As mentioned, often you will want the main thread to finish last. In the preceding examples, this is accomplished by calling **sleep( )** within **main( )**, with a long enough delay to ensure that all child threads terminate prior to the main thread. However, this is hardly a satisfactory solution, and it also raises a larger question: How can one thread know when another thread has ended? Fortunately, **Thread** provides a means by which you can answer this question.

Two ways exist to determine whether a thread has finished. First, you can call **isAlive( )** on the thread. This method is defined by **Thread**, and its general form is shown here:

final boolean isAlive( )

The **isAlive( )** method returns **true** if the thread upon which it is called is still running. It returns **false** otherwise.

While **isAlive( )** is occasionally useful, the method that you will more commonly use to wait for a thread to finish is called **join( )**, shown here:

final void join( ) throws InterruptedException

This method waits until the thread on which it is called terminates. Its name comes from the concept of the calling thread waiting until the specified thread *joins* it. Additional forms of **join( )** allow you to specify a maximum amount of time that you want to wait for the specified thread to terminate.

Here is an improved version of the preceding example that uses **join( )** to ensure that the main thread is the last to stop. It also demonstrates the **isAlive( )** method.

```java
// Using join() to wait for threads to finish.
class NewThread implements Runnable {
  String name; // name of thread
  Thread t;

  NewThread(String threadname) {
    name = threadname;
    t = new Thread(this, name);
    System.out.println("New thread: " + t);
    t.start(); // Start the thread
  }

  // This is the entry point for thread.
  public void run() {
    try {
      for(int i = 5; i > 0; i--) {
        System.out.println(name + ": " + i);
        Thread.sleep(1000);
      }
    } catch (InterruptedException e) {
      System.out.println(name + " interrupted.");
    }
    System.out.println(name + " exiting.");
  }
}

class DemoJoin {
  public static void main(String args[]) {
    NewThread ob1 = new NewThread("One");
    NewThread ob2 = new NewThread("Two");
    NewThread ob3 = new NewThread("Three");

    System.out.println("Thread One is alive: "
                        + ob1.t.isAlive());
    System.out.println("Thread Two is alive: "
                        + ob2.t.isAlive());
    System.out.println("Thread Three is alive: "
                        + ob3.t.isAlive());
    // wait for threads to finish
    try {
      System.out.println("Waiting for threads to finish.");
      ob1.t.join();
```

```
        ob2.t.join();
        ob3.t.join();
    } catch (InterruptedException e) {
      System.out.println("Main thread Interrupted");
    }

    System.out.println("Thread One is alive: "
                        + ob1.t.isAlive());
    System.out.println("Thread Two is alive: "
                        + ob2.t.isAlive());
    System.out.println("Thread Three is alive: "
                        + ob3.t.isAlive());

    System.out.println("Main thread exiting.");
  }
}
```

Sample output from this program is shown here:

```
New thread: Thread[One,5,main]
New thread: Thread[Two,5,main]
New thread: Thread[Three,5,main]
Thread One is alive: true
Thread Two is alive: true
Thread Three is alive: true
Waiting for threads to finish.
One: 5
Two: 5
Three: 5
One: 4
Two: 4
Three: 4
One: 3
Two: 3
Three: 3
One: 2
Two: 2
Three: 2
One: 1
Two: 1
Three: 1
```

```
Two exiting.
Three exiting.
One exiting.
Thread One is alive: false
Thread Two is alive: false
Thread Three is alive: false
Main thread exiting.
```

As you can see, after the calls to **join( )** return, the threads have stopped executing.

Thread Priorities

Thread priorities are used by the thread scheduler to decide when each thread should be allowed to run. In theory, higher-priority threads get more CPU time than lower-priority threads. In practice, the amount of CPU time that a thread gets often depends on several factors besides its priority. (For example, how an operating system implements multitasking can affect the relative availability of CPU time.) A higher-priority thread can also preempt a lower-priority one. For instance, when a lower-priority thread is running and a higher-priority thread resumes (from sleeping or waiting on I/O, for example), it will preempt the lower-priority thread.

In theory, threads of equal priority should get equal access to the CPU. But you need to be careful. Remember, Java is designed to work in a wide range of environments. Some of those environments implement multitasking fundamentally differently than others. For safety, threads that share the same priority should yield control once in a while. This ensures that all threads have a chance to run under a nonpreemptive operating system. In practice, even in nonpreemptive environments, most threads still get a chance to run, because most threads inevitably encounter some blocking situation, such as waiting for I/O. When this happens, the blocked thread is suspended and other threads can run. But, if you want smooth multithreaded execution, you are better off not relying on this. Also, some types of tasks are CPU-intensive. Such threads dominate the CPU. For these types of threads, you want to yield control occasionally, so that other threads can run.

To set a thread's priority, use the **setPriority( )** method, which is a member of **Thread**. This is its general form:

final void setPriority(int *level*)

Here, *level* specifies the new priority setting for the calling thread. The value of *level* must be within the range **MIN_PRIORITY** and **MAX_PRIORITY**. Currently, these values are 1 and 10, respectively. To return a thread to default priority, specify **NORM_PRIORITY**, which is currently 5. These priorities are defined as **final** variables within **Thread**.

You can obtain the current priority setting by calling the **getPriority( )** method of **Thread**, shown here:

final int getPriority( )

Implementations of Java may have radically different behavior when it comes to scheduling. The Windows XP/98/NT/2000 version works, more or less, as you would expect. However, other versions may work quite differently. Most of the inconsistencies arise when you have threads that are relying on preemptive behavior, instead of cooperatively giving up CPU time. The safest way to obtain predictable, cross-platform behavior with Java is to use threads that voluntarily give up control of the CPU.

The following example demonstrates two threads at different priorities, which do not run on a preemptive platform in the same way as they run on a nonpreemptive platform. One thread is set two levels above the normal priority, as defined by **Thread.NORM_PRIORITY**, and the other is set to two levels below it. The threads are started and allowed to run for ten seconds. Each thread executes a loop, counting the number of iterations. After ten seconds, the main thread stops both threads. The number of times that each thread made it through the loop is then displayed.

```java
// Demonstrate thread priorities.
class clicker implements Runnable {
  int click = 0;
  Thread t;
  private volatile boolean running = true;

  public clicker(int p) {
    t = new Thread(this);
    t.setPriority(p);
  }

  public void run() {
    while (running) {
      click++;
    }
  }

  public void stop() {
    running = false;
  }

  public void start() {
    t.start();
  }
}
```

```
class HiLoPri {
  public static void main(String args[]) {
    Thread.currentThread().setPriority(Thread.MAX_PRIORITY);
    clicker hi = new clicker(Thread.NORM_PRIORITY + 2);
    clicker lo = new clicker(Thread.NORM_PRIORITY - 2);

    lo.start();
    hi.start();
    try {
      Thread.sleep(10000);
    } catch (InterruptedException e) {
      System.out.println("Main thread interrupted.");
    }

    lo.stop();
    hi.stop();

    // Wait for child threads to terminate.
    try {
      hi.t.join();
      lo.t.join();
    } catch (InterruptedException e) {
      System.out.println("InterruptedException caught");
    }

    System.out.println("Low-priority thread: " + lo.click);
    System.out.println("High-priority thread: " + hi.click);
  }
}
```

The output of this program, shown as follows when run under Windows 98, indicates that the threads did context switch, even though neither voluntarily yielded the CPU nor blocked for I/O. The higher-priority thread got approximately 90 percent of the CPU time.

```
Low-priority thread: 4408112
High-priority thread: 589626904
```

Of course, the exact output produced by this program depends on the speed of your CPU and the number of other tasks running in the system. When this same program is run under a nonpreemptive system, different results will be obtained.

One other note about the preceding program. Notice that **running** is preceded by the keyword **volatile**. Although **volatile** is examined more carefully in the next chapter, it is used here to ensure that the value of **running** is examined each time the following loop iterates:

```
while (running) {
  click++;
}
```

Without the use of **volatile**, Java is free to optimize the loop in such a way that a local copy of **running** is created. The use of **volatile** prevents this optimization, telling Java that **running** may change in ways not directly apparent in the immediate code.

Synchronization

When two or more threads need access to a shared resource, they need some way to ensure that the resource will be used by only one thread at a time. The process by which this is achieved is called *synchronization*. As you will see, Java provides unique, language-level support for it.

Key to synchronization is the concept of the monitor (also called a *semaphore*). A *monitor* is an object that is used as a mutually exclusive lock, or *mutex*. Only one thread can *own* a monitor at a given time. When a thread acquires a lock, it is said to have *entered* the monitor. All other threads attempting to enter the locked monitor will be suspended until the first thread *exits* the monitor. These other threads are said to be *waiting* for the monitor. A thread that owns a monitor can reenter the same monitor if it so desires.

If you have worked with synchronization when using other languages, such as C or C++, you know that it can be a bit tricky to use. This is because most languages do not, themselves, support synchronization. Instead, to synchronize threads, your programs need to utilize operating system primitives. Fortunately, because Java implements synchronization through language elements, most of the complexity associated with synchronization has been eliminated.

You can synchronize your code in either of two ways. Both involve the use of the **synchronized** keyword, and both are examined here.

Using Synchronized Methods

Synchronization is easy in Java, because all objects have their own implicit monitor associated with them. To enter an object's monitor, just call a method that has been modified with the **synchronized** keyword. While a thread is inside a synchronized method, all other threads that try to call it (or any other synchronized method) on the same instance have to wait. To exit the monitor and relinquish control of the object to the next waiting thread, the owner of the monitor simply returns from the synchronized method.

To understand the need for synchronization, let's begin with a simple example that does not use it—but should. The following program has three simple classes. The first one, **Callme**, has a single method named **call( )**. The **call( )** method takes a **String** parameter called **msg**. This method tries to print the **msg** string inside of square brackets. The interesting thing to notice is that after **call( )** prints the opening bracket and the **msg** string, it calls **Thread.sleep(1000)**, which pauses the current thread for one second.

The constructor of the next class, **Caller**, takes a reference to an instance of the **Callme** class and a **String**, which are stored in **target** and **msg**, respectively. The constructor also creates a new thread that will call this object's **run( )** method. The thread is started immediately. The **run( )** method of **Caller** calls the **call( )** method on the **target** instance of **Callme**, passing in the **msg** string. Finally, the **Synch** class starts by creating a single instance of **Callme**, and three instances of **Caller**, each with a unique message string. The same instance of **Callme** is passed to each **Caller**.

```java
// This program is not synchronized.
class Callme {
  void call(String msg) {
    System.out.print("[" + msg);
    try {
      Thread.sleep(1000);
    } catch(InterruptedException e) {
      System.out.println("Interrupted");
    }
    System.out.println("]");
  }
}

class Caller implements Runnable {
  String msg;
  Callme target;
  Thread t;

  public Caller(Callme targ, String s) {
    target = targ;
    msg = s;
    t = new Thread(this);
    t.start();
  }

  public void run() {
    target.call(msg);
  }
```

```
    }

class Synch {
  public static void main(String args[]) {
    Callme target = new Callme();
    Caller ob1 = new Caller(target, "Hello");
    Caller ob2 = new Caller(target, "Synchronized");
    Caller ob3 = new Caller(target, "World");

    // wait for threads to end
    try {
      ob1.t.join();
      ob2.t.join();
      ob3.t.join();
    } catch(InterruptedException e) {
      System.out.println("Interrupted");
    }
  }
}
```

Here is the output produced by this program:

```
Hello[Synchronized[World]
]
]
```

As you can see, by calling **sleep( )**, the **call( )** method allows execution to switch to another thread. This results in the mixed-up output of the three message strings. In this program, nothing exists to stop all three threads from calling the same method, on the same object, at the same time. This is known as a *race condition*, because the three threads are racing each other to complete the method. This example used **sleep( )** to make the effects repeatable and obvious. In most situations, a race condition is more subtle and less predictable, because you can't be sure when the context switch will occur. This can cause a program to run right one time and wrong the next.

To fix the preceding program, you must *serialize* access to **call( )**. That is, you must restrict its access to only one thread at a time. To do this, you simply need to precede **call( )**'s definition with the keyword **synchronized**, as shown here:

```
class Callme {
    synchronized void call(String msg) {
    ...
```

This prevents other threads from entering **call( )** while another thread is using it. After **synchronized** has been added to **call( )**, the output of the program is as follows:

```
[Hello]
[Synchronized]
[World]
```

Any time that you have a method, or group of methods, that manipulates the internal state of an object in a multithreaded situation, you should use the **synchronized** keyword to guard the state from race conditions. Remember, once a thread enters any synchronized method on an instance, no other thread can enter any other synchronized method on the same instance. However, nonsynchronized methods on that instance will continue to be callable.

The synchronized Statement

While creating **synchronized** methods within classes that you create is an easy and effective means of achieving synchronization, it will not work in all cases. To understand why, consider the following. Imagine that you want to synchronize access to objects of a class that was not designed for multithreaded access. That is, the class does not use **synchronized** methods. Further, this class was not created by you, but by a third party, and you do not have access to the source code. Thus, you can't add **synchronized** to the appropriate methods within the class. How can access to an object of this class be synchronized? Fortunately, the solution to this problem is quite easy: You simply put calls to the methods defined by this class inside a **synchronized** block.

This is the general form of the **synchronized** statement:

```
synchronized(object) {
    // statements to be synchronized
}
```

Here, *object* is a reference to the object being synchronized. A synchronized block ensures that a call to a method that is a member of *object* occurs only after the current thread has successfully entered *object*'s monitor.

Here is an alternative version of the preceding example, using a synchronized block within the **run( )** method:

```
// This program uses a synchronized block.
class Callme {
  void call(String msg) {
    System.out.print("[" + msg);
    try {
```

```
        Thread.sleep(1000);
      } catch (InterruptedException e) {
        System.out.println("Interrupted");
      }
      System.out.println("]");
    }
  }

class Caller implements Runnable {
  String msg;
  Callme target;
  Thread t;

  public Caller(Callme targ, String s) {
    target = targ;
    msg = s;
    t = new Thread(this);
    t.start();
  }

  // synchronize calls to call()
  public void run() {
    synchronized(target) { // synchronized block
      target.call(msg);
    }
  }
}

class Synch1 {
  public static void main(String args[]) {
    Callme target = new Callme();
    Caller ob1 = new Caller(target, "Hello");
    Caller ob2 = new Caller(target, "Synchronized");
    Caller ob3 = new Caller(target, "World");

    // wait for threads to end
    try {
      ob1.t.join();
      ob2.t.join();
      ob3.t.join();
    } catch(InterruptedException e) {
```

```
        System.out.println("Interrupted");
    }
  }
}
```

Here, the **call( )** method is not modified by **synchronized**. Instead, the **synchronized** statement is used inside **Caller**'s **run( )** method. This causes the same correct output as the preceding example, because each thread waits for the prior one to finish before proceeding.

Interthread Communication

The preceding examples unconditionally blocked other threads from asynchronous access to certain methods. This use of the implicit monitors in Java objects is powerful, but you can achieve a more subtle level of control through interprocess communication. As you will see, this is especially easy in Java.

As discussed earlier, multithreading replaces event loop programming by dividing your tasks into discrete and logical units. Threads also provide a secondary benefit: they do away with polling. Polling is usually implemented by a loop that is used to check some condition repeatedly. Once the condition is true, appropriate action is taken. This wastes CPU time. For example, consider the classic queuing problem, where one thread is producing some data and another is consuming it. To make the problem more interesting, suppose that the producer has to wait until the consumer is finished before it generates more data. In a polling system, the consumer would waste many CPU cycles while it waited for the producer to produce. Once the producer was finished, it would start polling, wasting more CPU cycles waiting for the consumer to finish, and so on. Clearly, this situation is undesirable.

To avoid polling, Java includes an elegant interprocess communication mechanism via the **wait( )**, **notify( )**, and **notifyAll( )** methods. These methods are implemented as **final** methods in **Object**, so all classes have them. All three methods can be called only from within a **synchronized** context. Although conceptually advanced from a computer science perspective, the rules for using these methods are actually quite simple:

- **wait( )** tells the calling thread to give up the monitor and go to sleep until some other thread enters the same monitor and calls **notify( )**.

- **notify( )** wakes up the first thread that called **wait( )** on the same object.

- **notifyAll( )** wakes up all the threads that called **wait( )** on the same object. The highest priority thread will run first.

These methods are declared within **Object**, as shown here:

```
final void wait( ) throws InterruptedException
final void notify( )
final void notifyAll( )
```

Additional forms of **wait( )** exist that allow you to specify a period of time to wait.

The following sample program incorrectly implements a simple form of the producer/consumer problem. It consists of four classes: **Q**, the queue that you're trying to synchronize; **Producer**, the threaded object that is producing queue entries; **Consumer**, the threaded object that is consuming queue entries; and **PC**, the tiny class that creates the single **Q**, **Producer**, and **Consumer**.

```
// An incorrect implementation of a producer and consumer.
class Q {
  int n;

  synchronized int get() {
    System.out.println("Got: " + n);
    return n;
  }

  synchronized void put(int n) {
    this.n = n;
    System.out.println("Put: " + n);
  }
}

class Producer implements Runnable {
  Q q;

  Producer(Q q) {
    this.q = q;
    new Thread(this, "Producer").start();
  }

  public void run() {
    int i = 0;

    while(true) {
      q.put(i++);
```

```
      }
    }
}

class Consumer implements Runnable {
  Q q;

  Consumer(Q q) {
    this.q = q;
    new Thread(this, "Consumer").start();
  }

  public void run() {
    while(true) {
      q.get();
    }
  }
}

class PC {
  public static void main(String args[]) {
    Q q = new Q();
    new Producer(q);
    new Consumer(q);

    System.out.println("Press Control-C to stop.");
  }
}
```

Although the **put( )** and **get( )** methods on **Q** are synchronized, nothing stops the producer from overrunning the consumer, nor will anything stop the consumer from consuming the same queue value twice. Thus, you get the erroneous output shown here (the exact output will vary with processor speed and task load):

```
Put: 1
Got: 1
Got: 1
Got: 1
Got: 1
Got: 1
```

```
Put:  2
Put:  3
Put:  4
Put:  5
Put:  6
Put:  7
Got:  7
```

As you can see, after the producer put 1, the consumer started and got the same 1 five times in a row. Then, the producer resumed and produced 2 through 7 without letting the consumer have a chance to consume them.

The proper way to write this program in Java is to use **wait( )** and **notify( )** to signal in both directions, as shown here:

```java
// A correct implementation of a producer and consumer.
class Q {
  int n;
  boolean valueSet = false;

  synchronized int get() {
    if(!valueSet)
      try {
        wait();

      } catch(InterruptedException e) {
        System.out.println("InterruptedException caught");
      }

    System.out.println("Got: " + n);
    valueSet = false;
    notify();
    return n;
  }

  synchronized void put(int n) {
    if(valueSet)
      try {
        wait();
      } catch(InterruptedException e) {
        System.out.println("InterruptedException caught");
      }

    this.n = n;
```

```
      valueSet = true;
      System.out.println("Put: " + n);
      notify();
  }
}

class Producer implements Runnable {
  Q q;

  Producer(Q q) {
    this.q = q;
    new Thread(this, "Producer").start();
  }

  public void run() {
    int i = 0;

    while(true) {
      q.put(i++);
    }
  }
}

class Consumer implements Runnable {
  Q q;

  Consumer(Q q) {
    this.q = q;
    new Thread(this, "Consumer").start();
  }

  public void run() {
    while(true) {
      q.get();
    }
  }
}

class PCFixed {
  public static void main(String args[]) {
    Q q = new Q();
    new Producer(q);
    new Consumer(q);
```

```
        System.out.println("Press Control-C to stop.");
    }
}
```

Inside **get( )**, **wait( )** is called. This causes its execution to suspend until the **Producer** notifies you that some data is ready. When this happens, execution inside **get( )** resumes. After the data has been obtained, **get( )** calls **notify( )**. This tells **Producer** that it is okay to put more data in the queue. Inside **put( )**, **wait( )** suspends execution until the **Consumer** has removed the item from the queue. When execution resumes, the next item of data is put in the queue, and **notify( )** is called. This tells the **Consumer** that it should now remove it.

Here is some output from this program, which shows the clean synchronous behavior:

```
Put: 1
Got: 1
Put: 2
Got: 2
Put: 3
Got: 3
Put: 4
Got: 4
Put: 5
Got: 5
```

Deadlock

A special type of error that you need to avoid that relates specifically to multitasking is *deadlock*, which occurs when two threads have a circular dependency on a pair of synchronized objects. For example, suppose one thread enters the monitor on object X and another thread enters the monitor on object Y. If the thread in X tries to call any synchronized method on Y, it will block as expected. However, if the thread in Y, in turn, tries to call any synchronized method on X, the thread waits forever, because to access X, it would have to release its own lock on Y so that the first thread could complete. Deadlock is a difficult error to debug for two reasons:

- In general, it occurs only rarely, when the two threads time-slice in just the right way.

- It may involve more than two threads and two synchronized objects. (That is, deadlock can occur through a more convoluted sequence of events than just described.)

To understand deadlock fully, it is useful to see it in action. The next example creates two classes, **A** and **B**, with methods **foo( )** and **bar( )**, respectively, which pause briefly before trying to call a method in the other class. The main class, named **Deadlock**, creates an **A** and a **B** instance, and then starts a second thread to set up the deadlock condition. The **foo( )** and **bar( )** methods use **sleep( )** as a way to force the deadlock condition to occur.

```
// An example of deadlock.
class A {
  synchronized void foo(B b) {
    String name = Thread.currentThread().getName();

    System.out.println(name + " entered A.foo");

    try {
      Thread.sleep(1000);
    } catch(Exception e) {
      System.out.println("A Interrupted");
    }

    System.out.println(name + " trying to call B.last()");
    b.last();
  }

  synchronized void last() {
    System.out.println("Inside A.last");
  }
}

class B {
  synchronized void bar(A a) {
    String name = Thread.currentThread().getName();
    System.out.println(name + " entered B.bar");

    try {
      Thread.sleep(1000);
    } catch(Exception e) {
      System.out.println("B Interrupted");
    }

    System.out.println(name + " trying to call A.last()");
    a.last();
```

```
    }

  synchronized void last() {
    System.out.println("Inside A.last");
  }
}

class Deadlock implements Runnable {
  A a = new A();
  B b = new B();

  Deadlock() {
    Thread.currentThread().setName("MainThread");
    Thread t = new Thread(this, "RacingThread");
    t.start();

    a.foo(b); // get lock on a in this thread.
    System.out.println("Back in main thread");
  }

  public void run() {
    b.bar(a); // get lock on b in other thread.
    System.out.println("Back in other thread");
  }

  public static void main(String args[]) {
    new Deadlock();
  }
}
```

When you run this program, you will see the output shown here:

```
MainThread entered A.foo
RacingThread entered B.bar
MainThread trying to call B.last()
RacingThread trying to call A.last()
```

Because the program has deadlocked, you need to press CTRL-C to end the program. You can see a full thread and monitor cache dump by pressing CTRL-BREAK on a PC . You will see that **RacingThread** owns the monitor on **b**, while it is waiting for the monitor on **a**. At the same time, **MainThread** owns **a** and is waiting to get **b**. This program will never complete. As this example illustrates, if your multithreaded program locks up occasionally, deadlock is one of the first conditions that you should check for.

Suspending, Resuming, and Stopping Threads

Sometimes, suspending execution of a thread is useful. For example, a separate thread can be used to display the time of day. If the user doesn't want a clock, then its thread can be suspended. Whatever the case, suspending a thread is a simple matter. Once suspended, restarting the thread is also a simple matter.

The mechanisms to suspend, stop, and resume threads differ between Java 2 and earlier versions. Although you should use the Java 2 approach for all new code, you still need to understand how these operations were accomplished for earlier Java environments. For example, you may need to update or maintain older, legacy code. You also need to understand why a change was made for Java 2. For these reasons, the next section describes the original way that the execution of a thread was controlled, followed by a section that describes the approach required for Java 2.

Suspending, Resuming, and Stopping Threads Using Java 1.1 and Earlier

Prior to Java 2, a program used **suspend( )** and **resume( )**, which are methods defined by **Thread**, to pause and restart the execution of a thread. They have the form shown below:

```
final void suspend( )
final void resume( )
```

The following program demonstrates these methods:

```
// Using suspend() and resume().
class NewThread implements Runnable {
  String name; // name of thread
  Thread t;

  NewThread(String threadname) {
    name = threadname;
    t = new Thread(this, name);
    System.out.println("New thread: " + t);
    t.start(); // Start the thread
  }

  // This is the entry point for thread.
  public void run() {
    try {
      for(int i = 15; i > 0; i--) {
        System.out.println(name + ": " + i);
        Thread.sleep(200);
```

```
    }
  } catch (InterruptedException e) {
    System.out.println(name + " interrupted.");
  }
  System.out.println(name + " exiting.");
  }
}

class SuspendResume {
  public static void main(String args[]) {
    NewThread ob1 = new NewThread("One");
    NewThread ob2 = new NewThread("Two");

    try {
    Thread.sleep(1000);
      ob1.t.suspend();
    System.out.println("Suspending thread One");
    Thread.sleep(1000);
      ob1.t.resume();
    System.out.println("Resuming thread One");
      ob2.t.suspend();
    System.out.println("Suspending thread Two");
    Thread.sleep(1000);
      ob2.t.resume();
    System.out.println("Resuming thread Two");
    } catch (InterruptedException e) {
    System.out.println("Main thread Interrupted");
    }

    // wait for threads to finish
    try {
      System.out.println("Waiting for threads to finish.");
      ob1.t.join();
      ob2.t.join();
    } catch (InterruptedException e) {
      System.out.println("Main thread Interrupted");
    }
    System.out.println("Main thread exiting.");
  }
}
```

Sample output from this program is shown here:

```
New thread: Thread[One,5,main]
One: 15
New thread: Thread[Two,5,main]
Two: 15
One: 14
Two: 14
One: 13
Two: 13
One: 12
Two: 12
One: 11
Two: 11
Suspending thread One
Two: 10
Two: 9
Two: 8
Two: 7
Two: 6
Resuming thread One
Suspending thread Two
One: 10
One: 9
One: 8
One: 7
One: 6
Resuming thread Two
Waiting for threads to finish.
Two: 5
One: 5
Two: 4
One: 4
Two: 3
One: 3
Two: 2
One: 2
Two: 1
One: 1
Two exiting.
One exiting.
Main thread exiting.
```

The **Thread** class also defines a method called **stop( )** that stops a thread. Its signature is shown here:

final void stop( )

Once a thread has been stopped, it cannot be restarted using **resume( )**.

Suspending, Resuming, and Stopping Threads Using Java 2

While the **suspend( )**, **resume( )**, and **stop( )** methods defined by **Thread** seem to be a perfectly reasonable and convenient approach to managing the execution of threads, they must not be used for new Java programs. Here's why. The **suspend( )** method of the **Thread** class is deprecated in Java 2. This was done because **suspend( )** can sometimes cause serious system failures. Assume that a thread has obtained locks on critical data structures. If that thread is suspended at that point, those locks are not relinquished. Other threads that may be waiting for those resources can be deadlocked.

The **resume( )** method is also deprecated. It does not cause problems, but cannot be used without the **suspend( )** method as its counterpart.

The **stop( )** method of the **Thread** class, too, is deprecated in Java 2. This was done because this method can sometimes cause serious system failures. Assume that a thread is writing to a critically important data structure and has completed only part of its changes. If that thread is stopped at that point, that data structure might be left in a corrupted state.

Because you can't use the **suspend( )**, **resume( )**, or **stop( )** methods in Java 2 to control a thread, you might be thinking that no way exists to pause, restart, or terminate a thread. But, fortunately, this is not true. Instead, a thread must be designed so that the **run( )** method periodically checks to determine whether that thread should suspend, resume, or stop its own execution. Typically, this is accomplished by establishing a flag variable that indicates the execution state of the thread. As long as this flag is set to "running," the **run( )** method must continue to let the thread execute. If this variable is set to "suspend," the thread must pause. If it is set to "stop," the thread must terminate. Of course, a variety of ways exist in which to write such code, but the central theme will be the same for all programs.

The following example illustrates how the **wait( )** and **notify( )** methods that are inherited from **Object** can be used to control the execution of a thread. This example is similar to the program in the previous section. However, the deprecated method calls have been removed. Let us consider the operation of this program.

The **NewThread** class contains a **boolean** instance variable named **suspendFlag**, which is used to control the execution of the thread. It is initialized to **false** by the constructor. The **run( )** method contains a **synchronized** statement block that checks **suspendFlag**. If that variable is **true**, the **wait( )** method is invoked to suspend the execution of the thread. The **mysuspend( )** method sets **suspendFlag** to **true**. The

myresume( ) method sets **suspendFlag** to **false** and invokes **notify( )** to wake up the thread. Finally, the **main( )** method has been modified to invoke the **mysuspend( )** and **myresume( )** methods.

```java
// Suspending and resuming a thread for Java 2
class NewThread implements Runnable {
  String name; // name of thread
  Thread t;
  boolean suspendFlag;

  NewThread(String threadname) {
    name = threadname;
    t = new Thread(this, name);
    System.out.println("New thread: " + t);
    suspendFlag = false;
    t.start(); // Start the thread
  }

  // This is the entry point for thread.
  public void run() {
    try {
      for(int i = 15; i > 0; i--) {
        System.out.println(name + ": " + i);
        Thread.sleep(200);
        synchronized(this) {
          while(suspendFlag) {
            wait();
          }
        }
      }
    } catch (InterruptedException e) {
      System.out.println(name + " interrupted.");
    }
    System.out.println(name + " exiting.");
  }

  void mysuspend() {
    suspendFlag = true;
  }

  synchronized void myresume() {
    suspendFlag = false;
```

```
      notify();
    }
  }

class SuspendResume {
  public static void main(String args[]) {
    NewThread ob1 = new NewThread("One");
    NewThread ob2 = new NewThread("Two");

    try {
      Thread.sleep(1000);
      ob1.mysuspend();
      System.out.println("Suspending thread One");
      Thread.sleep(1000);
      ob1.myresume();
      System.out.println("Resuming thread One");
      ob2.mysuspend();
      System.out.println("Suspending thread Two");
      Thread.sleep(1000);
      ob2.myresume();
      System.out.println("Resuming thread Two");
    } catch (InterruptedException e) {
      System.out.println("Main thread Interrupted");
    }

    // wait for threads to finish
    try {
      System.out.println("Waiting for threads to finish.");
      ob1.t.join();
      ob2.t.join();
    } catch (InterruptedException e) {
      System.out.println("Main thread Interrupted");
    }

    System.out.println("Main thread exiting.");
  }
}
```

The output from this program is identical to that shown in the previous section. Later in this book, you will see more examples that use the Java 2 mechanism of thread control. Although this mechanism isn't as "clean" as the old way, nevertheless, it is the way required to ensure that run-time errors don't occur. It is the approach that *must* be used for all new code.

Using Multithreading

If you are like most programmers, having multithreaded support built into the language will be new to you. The key to utilizing this support effectively is to think concurrently rather than serially. For example, when you have two subsystems within a program that can execute concurrently, make them individual threads. With the careful use of multithreading, you can create very efficient programs. A word of caution is in order, however: If you create too many threads, you can actually degrade the performance of your program rather than enhance it. Remember, some overhead is associated with context switching. If you create too many threads, more CPU time will be spent changing contexts than executing your program!

Chapter 12

I/O, Applets, and Other Topics

This chapter introduces two of Java's most important packages: **io** and **applet**. The **io** package supports Java's basic I/O (input/output) system, including file I/O. The **applet** package supports applets. Support for both I/O and applets comes from Java's core API libraries, not from language keywords. For this reason, an in-depth discussion of these topics is found in Part II of this book, which examines Java's API classes. This chapter discusses the foundation of these two subsystems, so that you can see how they are integrated into the Java language and how they fit into the larger context of the Java programming and execution environment. This chapter also examines the last of Java's keywords: **transient**, **volatile**, **instanceof**, **native**, **strictfp**, and **assert**.

I/O Basics

As you may have noticed while reading the preceding 11 chapters, not much use has been made of I/O in the example programs. In fact, aside from **print( )** and **println( )**, none of the I/O methods have been used significantly. The reason is simple: most real applications of Java are not text-based, console programs. Rather, they are graphically oriented applets that rely upon Java's Abstract Window Toolkit (AWT) for interaction with the user. Although text-based programs are excellent as teaching examples, they do not constitute an important use for Java in the real world. Also, Java's support for console I/O is limited and somewhat awkward to use—even in simple example programs. Text-based console I/O is just not very important to Java programming.

The preceding paragraph notwithstanding, Java does provide strong, flexible support for I/O as it relates to files and networks. Java's I/O system is cohesive and consistent. In fact, once you understand its fundamentals, the rest of the I/O system is easy to master.

Streams

Java programs perform I/O through streams. A *stream* is an abstraction that either produces or consumes information. A stream is linked to a physical device by the Java I/O system. All streams behave in the same manner, even if the actual physical devices to which they are linked differ. Thus, the same I/O classes and methods can be applied to any type of device. This means that an input stream can abstract many different kinds of input: from a disk file, a keyboard, or a network socket. Likewise, an output stream may refer to the console, a disk file, or a network connection. Streams are a clean way to deal with input/output without having every part of your code understand the difference between a keyboard and a network, for example. Java implements streams within class hierarchies defined in the **java.io** package.

Note	*If you are familiar with C/C++/C#, then you are already familiar with the concept of the stream. Java's approach to streams is loosely the same.*

Byte Streams and Character Streams

Java 2 defines two types of streams: byte and character. *Byte streams* provide a convenient means for handling input and output of bytes. Byte streams are used, for example, when reading or writing binary data. *Character streams* provide a convenient means for handling input and output of characters. They use Unicode and, therefore, can be internationalized. Also, in some cases, character streams are more efficient than byte streams.

The original version of Java (Java 1.0) did not include character streams and, thus, all I/O was byte-oriented. Character streams were added by Java 1.1, and certain byte-oriented classes and methods were deprecated. This is why older code that doesn't use character streams should be updated to take advantage of them, where appropriate.

One other point: at the lowest level, all I/O is still byte-oriented. The character-based streams simply provide a convenient and efficient means for handling characters.

An overview of both byte-oriented streams and character-oriented streams is presented in the following sections.

The Byte Stream Classes

Byte streams are defined by using two class hierarchies. At the top are two abstract classes: **InputStream** and **OutputStream**. Each of these abstract classes has several concrete subclasses, that handle the differences between various devices, such as disk files, network connections, and even memory buffers. The byte stream classes are shown in Table 12-1. A few of these classes are discussed later in this section. Others are described in Part II. Remember, to use the stream classes, you must import **java.io**.

The abstract classes **InputStream** and **OutputStream** define several key methods that the other stream classes implement. Two of the most important are **read( )** and **write( )**, which, respectively, read and write bytes of data. Both methods are declared as abstract inside **InputStream** and **OutputStream**. They are overridden by derived stream classes.

The Character Stream Classes

Character streams are defined by using two class hierarchies. At the top are two abstract classes, **Reader** and **Writer**. These abstract classes handle Unicode character streams. Java has several concrete subclasses of each of these. The character stream classes are shown in Table 12-2.

The abstract classes **Reader** and **Writer** define several key methods that the other stream classes implement. Two of the most important methods are **read( )** and **write( )**, which read and write characters of data, respectively. These methods are overridden by derived stream classes.

Stream Class	Meaning
BufferedInputStream	Buffered input stream
BufferedOutputStream	Buffered output stream
ByteArrayInputStream	Input stream that reads from a byte array
ByteArrayOutputStream	Output stream that writes to a byte array
DataInputStream	An input stream that contains methods for reading the Java standard data types
DataOutputStream	An output stream that contains methods for writing the Java standard data types
FileInputStream	Input stream that reads from a file
FileOutputStream	Output stream that writes to a file
FilterInputStream	Implements **InputStream**
FilterOutputStream	Implements **OutputStream**
InputStream	Abstract class that describes stream input
OutputStream	Abstract class that describes stream output
PipedInputStream	Input pipe
PipedOutputStream	Output pipe
PrintStream	Output stream that contains **print( )** and **println( )**
PushbackInputStream	Input stream that supports one-byte "unget," which returns a byte to the input stream
RandomAccessFile	Supports random access file I/O
SequenceInputStream	Input stream that is a combination of two or more input streams that will be read sequentially, one after the other

Table 12-1. *The Byte Stream Classes*

Stream Class	Meaning
BufferedReader	Buffered input character stream
BufferedWriter	Buffered output character stream
CharArrayReader	Input stream that reads from a character array
CharArrayWriter	Output stream that writes to a character array
FileReader	Input stream that reads from a file
FileWriter	Output stream that writes to a file
FilterReader	Filtered reader
FilterWriter	Filtered writer
InputStreamReader	Input stream that translates bytes to characters
LineNumberReader	Input stream that counts lines
OutputStreamWriter	Output stream that translates characters to bytes
PipedReader	Input pipe
PipedWriter	Output pipe
PrintWriter	Output stream that contains **print( )** and **println( )**
PushbackReader	Input stream that allows characters to be returned to the input stream
Reader	Abstract class that describes character stream input
StringReader	Input stream that reads from a string
StringWriter	Output stream that writes to a string
Writer	Abstract class that describes character stream output

Table 12-2.   *The Character Stream I/O Classes*

The Predefined Streams

As you know, all Java programs automatically import the **java.lang** package. This package defines a class called **System**, which encapsulates several aspects of the run-time environment. For example, using some of its methods, you can obtain the current time and the settings of various properties associated with the system. **System** also contains three predefined stream variables, **in**, **out**, and **err**. These fields are declared as **public** and **static** within **System**. This means that they can be used by any other part of your program and without reference to a specific **System** object.

System.out refers to the standard output stream. By default, this is the console. **System.in** refers to standard input, which is the keyboard by default. **System.err** refers to the standard error stream, which also is the console by default. However, these streams may be redirected to any compatible I/O device.

System.in is an object of type **InputStream**; **System.out** and **System.err** are objects of type **PrintStream**. These are byte streams, even though they typically are used to read and write characters from and to the console. As you will see, you can wrap these within character-based streams, if desired.

The preceding chapters have been using **System.out** in their examples. You can use **System.err** in much the same way. As explained in the next section, use of **System.in** is a little more complicated.

Reading Console Input

In Java 1.0, the only way to perform console input was to use a byte stream, and older code that uses this approach persists. Today, using a byte stream to read console input is still technically possible, but doing so may require the use of a deprecated method, and this approach is not recommended. The preferred method of reading console input for Java 2 is to use a character-oriented stream, which makes your program easier to internationalize and maintain.

Note *Java does not have a generalized console input method that parallels the standard C function **scanf( )** or C++ input operators.*

In Java, console input is accomplished by reading from **System.in**. To obtain a character-based stream that is attached to the console, you wrap **System.in** in a **BufferedReader** object, to create a character stream. **BuffereredReader** supports a buffered input stream. Its most commonly used constructor is shown here:

BufferedReader(Reader *inputReader*)

Here, *inputReader* is the stream that is linked to the instance of **BufferedReader** that is being created. **Reader** is an abstract class. One of its concrete subclasses is **InputStreamReader**, which converts bytes to characters. To obtain an **InputStreamReader** object that is linked to **System.in**, use the following constructor:

InputStreamReader(InputStream *inputStream*)

Because **System.in** refers to an object of type **InputStream**, it can be used for *inputStream*. Putting it all together, the following line of code creates a **BufferedReader** that is connected to the keyboard:

```
BufferedReader br = new BufferedReader(new
                    InputStreamReader(System.in));
```

After this statement executes, **br** is a character-based stream that is linked to the console through **System.in**.

Reading Characters

To read a character from a **BufferedReader**, use **read( )**. The version of **read( )** that we will be using is

int read( ) throws IOException

Each time that **read( )** is called, it reads a character from the input stream and returns it as an integer value. It returns –1 when the end of the stream is encountered. As you can see, it can throw an **IOException**.

The following program demonstrates **read( )** by reading characters from the console until the user types a "q":

```
// Use a BufferedReader to read characters from the console.
import java.io.*;

class BRRead {
  public static void main(String args[])
    throws IOException
  {
    char c;
    BufferedReader br = new
          BufferedReader(new InputStreamReader(System.in));
    System.out.println("Enter characters, 'q' to quit.");
```

```
  // read characters
  do {
    c = (char) br.read();
    System.out.println(c);
  } while(c != 'q');
  }
}
```

Here is a sample run:

```
Enter characters, 'q' to quit.
123abcq
1
2
3
a
b
c
q
```

This output may look a little different from what you expected, because **System.in** is line buffered, by default. This means that no input is actually passed to the program until you press ENTER. As you can guess, this does not make **read( )** particularly valuable for interactive, console input.

Reading Strings

To read a string from the keyboard, use the version of **readLine( )** that is a member of the **BufferedReader** class. Its general form is shown here:

String readLine( ) throws IOException

As you can see, it returns a **String** object.

The following program demonstrates **BufferedReader** and the **readLine( )** method; the program reads and displays lines of text until you enter the word "stop":

```
// Read a string from console using a BufferedReader.
import java.io.*;

class BRReadLines {
```

```
  public static void main(String args[])
    throws IOException
  {
    // create a BufferedReader using System.in
    BufferedReader br = new BufferedReader(new
                        InputStreamReader(System.in));
    String str;

    System.out.println("Enter lines of text.");
    System.out.println("Enter 'stop' to quit.");
    do {
      str = br.readLine();
      System.out.println(str);
    } while(!str.equals("stop"));
  }
}
```

The next example creates a tiny text editor. It creates an array of **String** objects and then reads in lines of text, storing each line in the array. It will read up to 100 lines or until you enter "stop". It uses a **BufferedReader** to read from the console.

```
// A tiny editor.
import java.io.*;

class TinyEdit {
  public static void main(String args[])
    throws IOException
  {
    // create a BufferedReader using System.in
    BufferedReader br = new BufferedReader(new
                        InputStreamReader(System.in));
    String str[] = new String[100];

    System.out.println("Enter lines of text.");
    System.out.println("Enter 'stop' to quit.");
    for(int i=0; i<100; i++) {
      str[i] = br.readLine();
      if(str[i].equals("stop")) break;
    }

    System.out.println("\nHere is your file:");
```

```
// display the lines
for(int i=0; i<100; i++) {
  if(str[i].equals("stop")) break;
  System.out.println(str[i]);
}
}
}
```

Here is a sample run:

```
Enter lines of text.
Enter 'stop' to quit.
This is line one.
This is line two.
Java makes working with strings easy.
Just create String objects.
stop
Here is your file:
This is line one.
This is line two.
Java makes working with strings easy.
Just create String objects.
```

Writing Console Output

Console output is most easily accomplished with **print( )** and **println( )**, described earlier, which are used in most of the examples in this book. These methods are defined by the class **PrintStream** (which is the type of the object referenced by **System.out**). Even though **System.out** is a byte stream, using it for simple program output is still acceptable. However, a character-based alternative is described in the next section.

Because **PrintStream** is an output stream derived from **OutputStream**, it also implements the low-level method **write( )**. Thus, **write( )** can be used to write to the console. The simplest form of **write( )** defined by **PrintStream** is shown here:

void write(int *byteval*)

This method writes to the stream the byte specified by *byteval*. Although *byteval* is declared as an integer, only the low-order eight bits are written. Here is a short example that uses **write( )** to output the character "A" followed by a newline to the screen:

```
// Demonstrate System.out.write().
class WriteDemo {
  public static void main(String args[]) {
    int b;

    b = 'A';
    System.out.write(b);
    System.out.write('\n');
  }
}
```

You will not often use **write( )** to perform console output (although doing so might be useful in some situations), because **print( )** and **println( )** are substantially easier to use.

The PrintWriter Class

Although using **System.out** to write to the console is still permissible under Java, its use is recommended mostly for debugging purposes or for sample programs, such as those found in this book. For real-world programs, the recommended method of writing to the console when using Java is through a **PrintWriter** stream. **PrintWriter** is one of the character-based classes. Using a character-based class for console output makes it easier to internationalize your program.

PrintWriter defines several constructors. The one we will use is shown here:

PrintWriter(OutputStream *outputStream*, boolean *flushOnNewline*)

Here, *outputStream* is an object of type **OutputStream**, and *flushOnNewline* controls whether Java flushes the output stream every time a **println( )** method is called. If *flushOnNewline* is **true**, flushing automatically takes place. If **false**, flushing is not automatic.

PrintWriter supports the **print( )** and **println( )** methods for all types including **Object**. Thus, you can use these methods in the same way as they have been used with **System.out**. If an argument is not a simple type, the **PrintWriter** methods call the object's **toString( )** method and then print the result.

To write to the console by using a **PrintWriter**, specify **System.out** for the output stream and flush the stream after each newline. For example, this line of code creates a **PrintWriter** that is connected to console output:

```
PrintWriter pw = new PrintWriter(System.out, true);
```

The following application illustrates using a **PrintWriter** to handle console output:

```
// Demonstrate PrintWriter
import java.io.*;

public class PrintWriterDemo {
  public static void main(String args[]) {
    PrintWriter pw = new PrintWriter(System.out, true);
    pw.println("This is a string");
    int i = -7;
    pw.println(i);
    double d = 4.5e-7;
    pw.println(d);
  }
}
```

The output from this program is shown here:

```
This is a string
-7
4.5E-7
```

Remember, there is nothing wrong with using **System.out** to write simple text output to the console when you are learning Java or debugging your programs. However, using a **PrintWriter** will make your real-world applications easier to internationalize. Because no advantage is gained by using a **PrintWriter** in the sample programs shown in this book, we will continue to use **System.out** to write to the console.

Reading and Writing Files

Java provides a number of classes and methods that allow you to read and write files. In Java, all files are byte-oriented, and Java provides methods to read and write bytes from and to a file. However, Java allows you to wrap a byte-oriented file stream within a character-based object. This technique is described in Part II. This chapter examines the basics of file I/O.

Two of the most often-used stream classes are **FileInputStream** and **FileOutputStream**, which create byte streams linked to files. To open a file, you simply create an object of one of these classes, specifying the name of the file as an argument to the constructor. While both classes support additional, overridden constructors, the following are the forms that we will be using:

FileInputStream(String *fileName*) throws FileNotFoundException
FileOutputStream(String *fileName*) throws FileNotFoundException

Here, *fileName* specifies the name of the file that you want to open. When you create an input stream, if the file does not exist, then **FileNotFoundException** is thrown. For output streams, if the file cannot be created, then **FileNotFoundException** is thrown. When an output file is opened, any preexisting file by the same name is destroyed.

Note
*In earlier versions of Java, **FileOutputStream( )** threw an **IOException** when an output file could not be created. This was changed by Java 2.*

When you are done with a file, you should close it by calling **close( )**. It is defined by both **FileInputStream** and **FileOutputStream**, as shown here:

void close( ) throws IOException

To read from a file, you can use a version of **read( )** that is defined within **FileInputStream**. The one that we will use is shown here:

int read( ) throws IOException

Each time that it is called, it reads a single byte from the file and returns the byte as an integer value. **read( )** returns –1 when the end of the file is encountered. It can throw an **IOException**.

The following program uses **read( )** to input and display the contents of a text file, the name of which is specified as a command-line argument. Note the **try/catch** blocks that handle the two errors that might occur when this program is used—the specified file not being found or the user forgetting to include the name of the file. You can use this same approach whenever you use command-line arguments.

```
/* Display a text file.

   To use this program, specify the name
   of the file that you want to see.
   For example, to see a file called TEST.TXT,
   use the following command line.

   java ShowFile TEST.TXT

*/

import java.io.*;
```

```
class ShowFile {
  public static void main(String args[])
    throws IOException
  {
    int i;
    FileInputStream fin;

    try {
      fin = new FileInputStream(args[0]);
    } catch(FileNotFoundException e) {
      System.out.println("File Not Found");
      return;
    } catch(ArrayIndexOutOfBoundsException e) {
      System.out.println("Usage: ShowFile File");
      return;
    }

    // read characters until EOF is encountered
    do {
      i = fin.read();
      if(i != -1) System.out.print((char) i);
    } while(i != -1);

    fin.close();
  }
}
```

To write to a file, you will use the **write( )** method defined by **FileOutputStream**. Its simplest form is shown here:

void write(int *byteval*) throws IOException

This method writes the byte specified by *byteval* to the file. Although *byteval* is declared as an integer, only the low-order eight bits are written to the file. If an error occurs during writing, an **IOException** is thrown. The next example uses **write( )** to copy a text file:

```
/* Copy a text file.

   To use this program, specify the name
   of the source file and the destination file.
```

```
   For example, to copy a file called FIRST.TXT
   to a file called SECOND.TXT, use the following
   command line.

   java CopyFile FIRST.TXT SECOND.TXT
*/

import java.io.*;

class CopyFile {
  public static void main(String args[])
    throws IOException
  {
    int i;
    FileInputStream fin;
    FileOutputStream fout;

    try {
      // open input file
      try {
        fin = new FileInputStream(args[0]);
      } catch(FileNotFoundException e) {
        System.out.println("Input File Not Found");
        return;
      }

      // open output file
      try {
        fout = new FileOutputStream(args[1]);
      } catch(FileNotFoundException e) {
        System.out.println("Error Opening Output File");
        return;
      }
    } catch(ArrayIndexOutOfBoundsException e) {
      System.out.println("Usage: CopyFile From To");
      return;
    }

    // Copy File
    try {
      do {
        i = fin.read();
```

```
        if(i != -1) fout.write(i);
      } while(i != -1);
    } catch(IOException e) {
      System.out.println("File Error");
    }

    fin.close();
    fout.close();
  }
}
```

Notice the way that potential I/O errors are handled in this program and in the preceding **ShowFile** program. Unlike some other computer languages, including C and C++, which use error codes to report file errors, Java uses its exception handling mechanism. Not only does this make file handling cleaner, but it also enables Java to easily differentiate the end-of-file condition from file errors when input is being performed. In C/C++, many input functions return the same value when an error occurs and when the end of the file is reached. (That is, in C/C++, an EOF condition often is mapped to the same value as an input error.) This usually means that the programmer must include extra program statements to determine which event actually occurred. In Java, errors are passed to your program via exceptions, not by values returned by **read( )**. Thus, when **read( )** returns –1, it means only one thing: the end of the file has been encountered.

Applet Fundamentals

All of the preceding examples in this book have been Java applications. However, applications constitute only one class of Java programs. Another type of program is the applet. As mentioned in Chapter 1, *applets* are small applications that are accessed on an Internet server, transported over the Internet, automatically installed, and run as part of a Web document. After an applet arrives on the client, it has limited access to resources, so that it can produce an arbitrary multimedia user interface and run complex computations without introducing the risk of viruses or breaching data integrity.

Many of the issues connected with the creation and use of applets are found in Part II, when the **applet** package is examined. However, the fundamentals connected to the creation of an applet are presented here, because applets are not structured in the same way as the programs that have been used thus far. As you will see, applets differ from applications in several key areas.

Let's begin with the simple applet shown here:

```
import java.awt.*;
import java.applet.*;

public class SimpleApplet extends Applet {
  public void paint(Graphics g) {
    g.drawString("A Simple Applet", 20, 20);
  }
}
```

This applet begins with two **import** statements. The first imports the Abstract Window Toolkit (AWT) classes. Applets interact with the user through the AWT, not through the console-based I/O classes. The AWT contains support for a window-based, graphical interface. As you might expect, the AWT is quite large and sophisticated, and a complete discussion of it consumes several chapters in Part II of this book. Fortunately, this simple applet makes very limited use of the AWT. The second **import** statement imports the **applet** package, which contains the class **Applet**. Every applet that you create must be a subclass of **Applet**.

The next line in the program declares the class **SimpleApplet**. This class must be declared as **public**, because it will be accessed by code that is outside the program.

Inside **SimpleApplet**, **paint( )** is declared. This method is defined by the AWT and must be overridden by the applet. **paint( )** is called each time that the applet must redisplay its output. This situation can occur for several reasons. For example, the window in which the applet is running can be overwritten by another window and then uncovered. Or, the applet window can be minimized and then restored. **paint( )** is also called when the applet begins execution. Whatever the cause, whenever the applet must redraw its output, **paint( )** is called. The **paint( )** method has one parameter of type **Graphics**. This parameter contains the graphics context, which describes the graphics environment in which the applet is running. This context is used whenever output to the applet is required.

Inside **paint( )** is a call to **drawString( )**, which is a member of the **Graphics** class. This method outputs a string beginning at the specified X,Y location. It has the following general form:

void drawString(String *message*, int *x*, int *y*)

Here, *message* is the string to be output beginning at *x,y*. In a Java window, the upper-left corner is location 0,0. The call to **drawString( )** in the applet causes the message "A Simple Applet" to be displayed beginning at location 20,20.

Notice that the applet does not have a **main( )** method. Unlike Java programs, applets do not begin execution at **main( )**. In fact, most applets don't even have a **main( )** method. Instead, an applet begins execution when the name of its class is passed to an applet viewer or to a network browser.

After you enter the source code for **SimpleApplet**, compile in the same way that you have been compiling programs. However, running **SimpleApplet** involves a different process. In fact, there are two ways in which you can run an applet:

■ Executing the applet within a Java-compatible Web browser.

■ Using an applet viewer, such as the standard SDK tool, **appletviewer**. An applet viewer executes your applet in a window. This is generally the fastest and easiest way to test your applet.

Each of these methods is described next.

To execute an applet in a Web browser, you need to write a short HTML text file that contains the appropriate APPLET tag. Here is the HTML file that executes **SimpleApplet**:

```
<applet code="SimpleApplet" width=200 height=60>
</applet>
```

The **width** and **height** statements specify the dimensions of the display area used by the applet. (The APPLET tag contains several other options that are examined more closely in Part II.) After you create this file, you can execute your browser and then load this file, which causes **SimpleApplet** to be executed.

To execute **SimpleApplet** with an applet viewer, you may also execute the HTML file shown earlier. For example, if the preceding HTML file is called **RunApp.html**, then the following command line will run **SimpleApplet**:

```
C:\>appletviewer RunApp.html
```

However, a more convenient method exists that you can use to speed up testing. Simply include a comment at the head of your Java source code file that contains the APPLET tag. By doing so, your code is documented with a prototype of the necessary HTML statements, and you can test your compiled applet merely by starting the applet viewer with your Java source code file. If you use this method, the **SimpleApplet** source file looks like this:

```
import java.awt.*;
import java.applet.*;
/*
<applet code="SimpleApplet" width=200 height=60>
</applet>
*/

public class SimpleApplet extends Applet {
  public void paint(Graphics g) {
```

```
      g.drawString("A Simple Applet", 20, 20);
   }
}
```

In general, you can quickly iterate through applet development by using these three steps:

1. Edit a Java source file.

2. Compile your program.

3. Execute the applet viewer, specifying the name of your applet's source file. The applet viewer will encounter the APPLET tag within the comment and execute your applet.

The window produced by **SimpleApplet**, as displayed by the applet viewer, is shown in the following illustration:

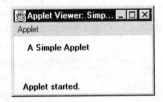

While the subject of applets is more fully discussed later in this book, here are the key points that you should remember now:

■ Applets do not need a **main( )** method.

■ Applets must be run under an applet viewer or a Java-compatible browser.

■ User I/O is not accomplished with Java's stream I/O classes. Instead, applets use the interface provided by the AWT.

The transient and volatile Modifiers

Java defines two interesting type modifiers: **transient** and **volatile**. These modifiers are used to handle somewhat specialized situations.

When an instance variable is declared as **transient**, then its value need not persist when an object is stored. For example:

```
class T {
   transient int a; // will not persist
```

```
      int b; // will persist
}
```

Here, if an object of type **T** is written to a persistent storage area, the contents of **a** would not be saved, but the contents of **b** would.

The **volatile** modifier tells the compiler that the variable modified by **volatile** can be changed unexpectedly by other parts of your program. One of these situations involves multithreaded programs. (You saw an example of this in Chapter 11.) In a multithreaded program, sometimes, two or more threads share the same instance variable. For efficiency considerations, each thread can keep its own, private copy of such a shared variable. The real (or *master*) copy of the variable is updated at various times, such as when a **synchronized** method is entered. While this approach works fine, it may be inefficient at times. In some cases, all that really matters is that the master copy of a variable always reflects its current state. To ensure this, simply specify the variable as **volatile**, which tells the compiler that it must always use the master copy of a **volatile** variable (or, at least, always keep any private copies up to date with the master copy, and vice versa). Also, accesses to the master variable must be executed in the precise order in which they are executed on any private copy.

Note *volatile in Java has, more or less, the same meaning that it has in C/C++/C#.*

Using instanceof

Sometimes, knowing the type of an object during run time is useful. For example, you might have one thread of execution that generates various types of objects, and another thread that processes these objects. In this situation, it might be useful for the processing thread to know the type of each object when it receives it. Another situation in which knowledge of an object's type at run time is important involves casting. In Java, an invalid cast causes a run-time error. Many invalid casts can be caught at compile time. However, casts involving class hierarchies can produce invalid casts that can be detected only at run time. For example, a superclass called A can produce two subclasses, called B and C. Thus, casting a B object into type A or casting a C object into type A is legal, but casting a B object into type C (or vice versa) isn't legal. Because an object of type A can refer to objects of either B or C, how can you know, at run time, what type of object is actually being referred to before attempting the cast to type C? It could be an object of type A, B, or C. If it is an object of type B, a run-time exception will be thrown. Java provides the run-time operator **instanceof** to answer this question.

The **instanceof** operator has this general form:

object instanceof *type*

Here, *object* is an instance of a class, and *type* is a class type. If *object* is of the specified type or can be cast into the specified type, then the **instanceof** operator evaluates to **true**. Otherwise, its result is **false**. Thus, **instanceof** is the means by which your program can obtain run-time type information about an object.

The following program demonstrates **instanceof**:

```
// Demonstrate instanceof operator.
class A {
  int i, j;
}

class B {
  int i, j;
}

class C extends A {
  int k;
}

class D extends A {
  int k;
}

class InstanceOf {
  public static void main(String args[]) {
    A a = new A();
    B b = new B();
    C c = new C();
    D d = new D();

    if(a instanceof A)
      System.out.println("a is instance of A");
    if(b instanceof B)
      System.out.println("b is instance of B");
    if(c instanceof C)
      System.out.println("c is instance of C");
    if(c instanceof A)
      System.out.println("c can be cast to A");

    if(a instanceof C)
      System.out.println("a can be cast to C");
```

```
    System.out.println();

    // compare types of derived types
    A ob;

    ob = d; // A reference to d
    System.out.println("ob now refers to d");
    if(ob instanceof D)
      System.out.println("ob is instance of D");

    System.out.println();

    ob = c; // A reference to c
    System.out.println("ob now refers to c");

    if(ob instanceof D)
      System.out.println("ob can be cast to D");
    else
      System.out.println("ob cannot be cast to D");

    if(ob instanceof A)
      System.out.println("ob can be cast to A");

    System.out.println();

    // all objects can be cast to Object
    if(a instanceof Object)
      System.out.println("a may be cast to Object");
    if(b instanceof Object)
      System.out.println("b may be cast to Object");
    if(c instanceof Object)
      System.out.println("c may be cast to Object");
    if(d instanceof Object)
      System.out.println("d may be cast to Object");
  }
}
```

The output from this program is shown here:

```
a is instance of A
b is instance of B
c is instance of C
c can be cast to A
```

```
ob now refers to d
ob is instance of D

ob now refers to c
ob cannot be cast to D
ob can be cast to A

a may be cast to Object
b may be cast to Object
c may be cast to Object
d may be cast to Object
```

The **instanceof** operator isn't needed by most programs, because, generally, you know the type of object with which you are working. However, it can be very useful when you're writing generalized routines that operate on objects of a complex class hierarchy.

strictfp

Java 2 added a new keyword to the Java language, called **strictfp**. With the creation of Java 2, the floating point computation model was relaxed slightly to make certain floating point computations faster for certain processors, such as the Pentium. Specifically, the new model does not require the truncation of certain intermediate values that occur during a computation. By modifying a class or a method with **strictfp**, you ensure that floating point calculations (and thus all truncations) take place precisely as they did in earlier versions of Java. The truncation affects only the exponent of certain operations. When a class is modified by **strictfp**, all the methods in the class are also modified by **strictfp** automatically.

For example, the following fragment tells Java to use the original floating point model for calculations in all methods defined within **MyClass**:

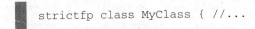

```
strictfp class MyClass { //...
```

Frankly, most programmers never need to use **strictfp**, because it affects only a very small class of problems.

Native Methods

Although it is rare, occasionally, you may want to call a subroutine that is written in a language other than Java. Typically, such a subroutine exists as executable code for the CPU and environment in which you are working—that is, native code. For example, you may want to call a native code subroutine to achieve faster execution time. Or, you may want to use a specialized, third-party library, such as a statistical package.

However, because Java programs are compiled to bytecode, which is then interpreted (or compiled on-the-fly) by the Java run-time system, it would seem impossible to call a native code subroutine from within your Java program. Fortunately, this conclusion is false. Java provides the **native** keyword, which is used to declare native code methods. Once declared, these methods can be called from inside your Java program just as you call any other Java method.

To declare a native method, precede the method with the **native** modifier, but do not define any body for the method. For example:

```
public native int meth() ;
```

After you declare a native method, you must write the native method and follow a rather complex series of steps to link it with your Java code.

Most native methods are written in C. The mechanism used to integrate C code with a Java program is called the *Java Native Interface (JNI)*. This methodology was created by Java 1.1 and then expanded and enhanced by Java 2. (Java 1.0 used a different approach, which is now completely outdated.) A detailed description of the JNI is beyond the scope of this book, but the following description provides sufficient information for most applications.

Note
The precise steps that you need to follow will vary between different Java environments and versions. This also depends on the language that you are using to implement the native method. The following discussion assumes a Windows 95/98/XP/NT/2000 environment. The language used to implement the native method is C.

The easiest way to understand the process is to work through an example. To begin, enter the following short program, which uses a **native** method called **test( )**:

```
// A simple example that uses a native method.
public class NativeDemo {
  int i;
  public static void main(String args[]) {
    NativeDemo ob = new NativeDemo();

    ob.i = 10;
    System.out.println("This is ob.i before the native method:" +
                      ob.i);
    ob.test(); // call a native method
    System.out.println("This is ob.i after the native method:" +
                      ob.i);
  }
```

```
// declare native method
public native void test() ;

// load DLL that contains static method
static {
   System.loadLibrary("NativeDemo");
}
}
```

Notice that the **test( )** method is declared as **native** and has no body. This is the method that we will implement in C shortly. Also notice the **static** block. As explained earlier in this book, a **static** block is executed only once, when your program begins execution (or, more precisely, when its class is first loaded). In this case, it is used to load the dynamic link library that contains the native implementation of **test( )**. (You will see how to create this library soon.)

The library is loaded by the **loadLibrary( )** method, which is part of the **System** class. This is its general form:

static void loadLibrary(String *filename*)

Here, *filename* is a string that specifies the name of the file that holds the library. For the Windows environment, this file is assumed to have the .DLL extension.

After you enter the program, compile it to produce **NativeDemo.class**. Next, you must use **javah.exe** to produce one file: **NativeDemo.h**. (**javah.exe** is included in the SDK.) You will include **NativeDemo.h** in your implementation of **test( )**. To produce **NativeDemo.h**, use the following command:

javah -jni NativeDemo

This command produces a header file called **NativeDemo.h**. This file must be included in the C file that implements **test( )**. The output produced by this command is shown here:

```
/* DO NOT EDIT THIS FILE - it is machine generated */
#include <jni.h>
/* Header for class NativeDemo */

#ifndef _Included_NativeDemo
#define _Included_NativeDemo
#ifdef _ _cplusplus
extern "C" {
#endif
/*
```

```
 * Class:     NativeDemo
 * Method:    test
 * Signature: ()V
 */
JNIEXPORT void JNICALL Java_NativeDemo_test
  (JNIEnv *, jobject);


#ifdef _ _cplusplus
}
#endif
#endif
```

Pay special attention to the following line, which defines the prototype for the
test( ) function that you will create:

```
JNIEXPORT void JNICALL Java_NativeDemo_test(JNIEnv *, jobject);
```

Notice that the name of the function is **Java_NativeDemo_test( )**. You must use this as the
name of the native function that you implement. That is, instead of creating a C function
called **test( )**, you will create one called **Java_NativeDemo_test( )**. The **NativeDemo**
component of the prefix is added because it identifies the **test( )** method as being part of the
NativeDemo class. Remember, another class may define its own native **test( )** method that
is completely different from the one declared by **NativeDemo**. Including the class name in
the prefix provides a way to differentiate between differing versions. As a general rule,
native functions will be given a name whose prefix includes the name of the class in which
they are declared.

After producing the necessary header file, you can write your implementation of
test( ) and store it in a file named **NativeDemo.c**:

```
/* This file contains the C version of the
   test() method.
*/

#include <jni.h>
#include "NativeDemo.h"
#include <stdio.h>

JNIEXPORT void JNICALL Java_NativeDemo_test(JNIEnv *env, jobject obj)
{
  jclass cls;
  jfieldID fid;
  jint i;
```

```
printf("Starting the native method.\n");
cls = (*env)->GetObjectClass(env, obj);
fid = (*env)->GetFieldID(env, cls, "i", "I");

if(fid == 0) {
  printf("Could not get field id.\n");
  return;
}
i = (*env)->GetIntField(env, obj, fid);
printf("i = %d\n", i);
(*env)->SetIntField(env, obj, fid, 2*i);
printf("Ending the native method.\n");
}
```

Notice that this file includes **jni.h**, which contains interfacing information. This file is provided by your Java compiler. The header file **NativeDemo.h** was created by **javah**, earlier.

In this function, the **GetObjectClass( )** method is used to obtain a C structure that has information about the class **NativeDemo**. The **GetFieldID( )** method returns a C structure with information about the field named "i" for the class. **GetIntField( )** retrieves the original value of that field. **SetIntField( )** stores an updated value in that field. (See the file **jni.h** for additional methods that handle other types of data.)

After creating **NativeDemo.c**, you must compile it and create a DLL. To do this by using the Microsoft C/C++ compiler, use the following command line. (You might need to specifiy the path to **jni.h** and its subordinate file **jni_md.h**.)

Cl /LD NativeDemo.c

This produces a file called **NativeDemo.dll**. Once this is done, you can execute the Java program, which will produce the following output:

```
This is ob.i before the native method: 10
Starting the native method.
i = 10
Ending the native method.
This is ob.i after the native method: 20
```

*The specifics surrounding the use of **native** are implementation- and environment-dependent. Furthermore, the specific manner in which you interface to Java code is subject to change. You must consult the documentation that accompanies your Java development system for details on native methods.*

Problems with Native Methods

Native methods seem to offer great promise, because they enable you to gain access to your existing base of library routines, and they offer the possibility of faster run-time execution. But native methods also introduce two significant problems:

- **Potential security risk**   Because a native method executes actual machine code, it can gain access to any part of the host system. That is, native code is not confined to the Java execution environment. This could allow a virus infection, for example. For this reason, applets cannot use native methods. Also, the loading of DLLs can be restricted, and their loading is subject to the approval of the security manager.

- **Loss of portability**   Because the native code is contained in a DLL, it must be present on the machine that is executing the Java program. Further, because each native method is CPU- and operating-system-dependent, each DLL is inherently nonportable. Thus, a Java application that uses native methods will be able to run only on a machine for which a compatible DLL has been installed.

The use of native methods should be restricted, because they render your Java programs nonportable and pose significant security risks.

Using assert

Java 2, version 1.4 added a new keyword to Java: **assert**. It is used during program development to create an *assertion*, which is a condition that should be true during the execution of the program. For example, you might have a method that should always return a positive integer value. You might test this by asserting that the return value is greater than zero using an **assert** statement. At run time, if the condition actually is true, no other action takes place. However, if the condition is false, then an **AssertionError** is thrown. Assertions are often used during testing to verify that some expected condition is actually met. They are not usually used for released code.

The **assert** keyword has two forms. The first is shown here.

assert *condition*;

Here, *condition* is an expression that must evaluate to a Boolean result. If the result is true, then the assertion is true and no other action takes place. If the condition is false, then the assertion fails and a default **AssertionError** object is thrown.

The second form of **assert** is shown here.

assert *condition* : *expr*;

In this version, *expr* is a value that is passed to the **AssertionError** constructor. This value is converted to its string format and displayed if an assertion fails. Typically, you will specify a string for *expr*, but any non-**void** expression is allowed as long as it defines a reasonable string conversion.

Here is an example that uses **assert**. It verifies that the return value of **getnum( )** is positive.

```
// Demonstrate assert.
class AssertDemo {
  static int val = 3;

  // Return an integer.
  static int getnum() {
    return val--;
  }

  public static void main(String args[])
  {
    int n;

    for(int i=0; i < 10; i++) {
      n = getnum();

      assert n > 0; // will fail when n is 0

      System.out.println("n is " + n);
    }
  }
}
```

Programs that use **assert** must be compiled using the **-source 1.4** option. For example, to compile the preceding program, use this line:

```
javac -source 1.4 AssertDemo.java
```

To enable assertion checking at run time, you must specify the **-ea** option. For example, to enable assertions for **AssertDemo**, execute it using this line.

```
java -ea AssertDemo
```

After compiling and running as just described, the program creates the following output.

```
n is 3
n is 2
n is 1
```

```
Exception in thread "main" java.lang.AssertionError
        at AssertDemo.main(AssertDemo.java:17)
```

In **main( )**, repeated calls are made to the method **getnum( )**, which returns an integer value. The return value of **getnum( )** is assigned to **n** and then tested using this **assert** statement.

```
assert n > 0; // will fail when n is 0
```

This statement will fail when **n** equals 0, which it will after the fourth call. When this happens, an exception is thrown.

As explained, you can specify the message displayed when an assertion fails. For example, if you substitute

```
assert n > 0 : "n is negative!";
```

for the assertion in the preceding program, then the following ouptut will be generated.

```
n is 3
n is 2
n is 1
Exception in thread "main" java.lang.AssertionError: n is negative!
        at AssertDemo.main(AssertDemo.java:17)
```

One important point to understand about assertions is that you must not rely on them to perform any action actually required by the program. The reason is that normally, released code will be run with assertions disabled. For example, consider this variation of the preceding program.

```
// A poor way to use assert!!!
class AssertDemo {
  // get a random number generator
  static int val = 3;

  // Return an integer.
  static int getnum() {
    return val--;
  }

  public static void main(String args[])
```

```
   {
     int n = 0;

     for(int i=0; i < 10; i++) {

        assert (n = getnum()) > 0; // This is not a good idea!

        System.out.println("n is " + n);
     }
   }
 }
```

In this version of the program, the call to **getnum( )** is moved inside the **assert** statement. Although this works fine if assertions are enabled, it will cause a malfunction when assertions are disabled because the call to **getnum( )** will never be executed! In fact, **n** must now be initialized, because the compiler will recognize that it might not be assigned a value by the **assert** statement.

Assertions are a good addition to Java because they streamline the type of error checking that is common during development. For example, prior to **assert**, if you wanted to verify that **n** was positive in the preceding program, you had to use a sequence of code similar to this:

```
if(n < 0) {
   System.out.println("n is negative!");
   return; // or throw an exception
}
```

With **assert**, you need only one line of code. Furthermore, you don't have to remove the **assert** statements from your released code.

Assertion Enabling and Disabling Options

When executing code, you can disable assertions by using the **-da** option. You can enable or disable a specific package by specifying its name after the **-ea** or **-da** option. For example, to enable assertions in a package called **MyPack**, use

```
-ea:MyPack
```

To disable assertions in **MyPack** use

```
-da:MyPack
```

To enable or disable all subpackages of a package, follow the package name with three dots. For example,

```
-ea:MyPack...
```

You can also specify a class with the **-ea** or **-da** option. For example, this enables **AssertDemo** individually.

```
-ea:AssertDemo
```

The
Complete
Reference

Part II

The Java Library

The
Complete
Reference

Chapter 13

String Handling

A brief overview of Java's string handling was presented in Chapter 7. In this chapter, it is described in detail. As is the case in most other programming languages, in Java a *string* is a sequence of characters. But, unlike many other languages that implement strings as character arrays, Java implements strings as objects of type **String**.

Implementing strings as built-in objects allows Java to provide a full complement of features that make string handling convenient. For example, Java has methods to compare two strings, search for a substring, concatenate two strings, and change the case of letters within a string. Also, **String** objects can be constructed a number of ways, making it easy to obtain a string when needed.

Somewhat unexpectedly, when you create a **String** object, you are creating a string that cannot be changed. That is, once a **String** object has been created, you cannot change the characters that comprise that string. At first, this may seem to be a serious restriction. However, such is not the case. You can still perform all types of string operations. The difference is that each time you need an altered version of an existing string, a new **String** object is created that contains the modifications. The original string is left unchanged. This approach is used because fixed, immutable strings can be implemented more efficiently than changeable ones. For those cases in which a modifiable string is desired, there is a companion class to **String** called **StringBuffer**, whose objects contain strings that can be modified after they are created.

Both the **String** and **StringBuffer** classes are defined in **java.lang**. Thus, they are available to all programs automatically. Both are declared **final**, which means that neither of these classes may be subclassed. This allows certain optimizations that increase performance to take place on common string operations. Beginning with Java 2, version 1.4, both **String** and **StringBuffer** implement the **CharSequence** interface.

One last point: To say that the strings within objects of type **String** are unchangeable means that the contents of the **String** instance cannot be changed after it has been created. However, a variable declared as a **String** reference can be changed to point at some other **String** object at any time.

The String Constructors

The **String** class supports several constructors. To create an empty **String**, you call the default constructor. For example,

```
String s = new String();
```

will create an instance of **String** with no characters in it.

Frequently, you will want to create strings that have initial values. The **String** class provides a variety of constructors to handle this. To create a **String** initialized by an array of characters, use the constructor shown here:

String(char *chars*[ ])

Here is an example:

```
char chars[] = { 'a', 'b', 'c' };
String s = new String(chars);
```

This constructor initializes **s** with the string "abc".

You can specify a subrange of a character array as an initializer using the following constructor:

String(char *chars*[ ], int *startIndex*, int *numChars*)

Here, *startIndex* specifies the index at which the subrange begins, and *numChars* specifies the number of characters to use. Here is an example:

```
char chars[] = { 'a', 'b', 'c', 'd', 'e', 'f' };
String s = new String(chars, 2, 3);
```

This initializes **s** with the characters **cde**.

You can construct a **String** object that contains the same character sequence as another **String** object using this constructor:

String(String *strObj*)

Here, *strObj* is a **String** object. Consider this example:

```
// Construct one String from another.
class MakeString {
  public static void main(String args[]) {
    char c[] = {'J', 'a', 'v', 'a'};
    String s1 = new String(c);
    String s2 = new String(s1);

    System.out.println(s1);
    System.out.println(s2);
  }
}
```

The output from this program is as follows:

```
Java
Java
```

As you can see, **s1** and **s2** contain the same string.

THE JAVA LIBRARY

Even though Java's **char** type uses 16 bits to represent the Unicode character set, the typical format for strings on the Internet uses arrays of 8-bit bytes constructed from the ASCII character set. Because 8-bit ASCII strings are common, the **String** class provides constructors that initialize a string when given a **byte** array. Their forms are shown here:

String(byte *asciiChars*[ ])
String(byte *asciiChars*[ ], int *startIndex*, int *numChars*)

Here, *asciiChars* specifies the array of bytes. The second form allows you to specify a subrange. In each of these constructors, the byte-to-character conversion is done by using the default character encoding of the platform. The following program illustrates these constructors:

```
// Construct string from subset of char array.
class SubStringCons {
  public static void main(String args[]) {
    byte ascii[] = {65, 66, 67, 68, 69, 70 };

    String s1 = new String(ascii);
    System.out.println(s1);

    String s2 = new String(ascii, 2, 3);
    System.out.println(s2);
  }
}
```

This program generates the following output:

```
ABCDEF
CDE
```

Extended versions of the byte-to-string constructors are also defined in which you can specify the character encoding that determines how bytes are converted to characters. However, most of the time, you will want to use the default encoding provided by the platform.

Note   *The contents of the array are copied whenever you create a **String** object from an array. If you modify the contents of the array after you have created the string, the **String** will be unchanged.*

String Length

The length of a string is the number of characters that it contains. To obtain this value, call the **length( )** method, shown here:

int length( )

The following fragment prints "3", since there are three characters in the string **s**:

```
char chars[] = { 'a', 'b', 'c' };
String s = new String(chars);
System.out.println(s.length());
```

Special String Operations

Because strings are a common and important part of programming, Java has added special support for several string operations within the syntax of the language. These operations include the automatic creation of new **String** instances from string literals, concatenation of multiple **String** objects by use of the **+** operator, and the conversion of other data types to a string representation. There are explicit methods available to perform all of these functions, but Java does them automatically as a convenience for the programmer and to add clarity.

String Literals

The earlier examples showed how to explicitly create a **String** instance from an array of characters by using the **new** operator. However, there is an easier way to do this using a string literal. For each string literal in your program, Java automatically constructs a **String** object. Thus, you can use a string literal to initialize a **String** object. For example, the following code fragment creates two equivalent strings:

```
char chars[] = { 'a', 'b', 'c' };
String s1 = new String(chars);

String s2 = "abc"; // use string literal
```

Because a **String** object is created for every string literal, you can use a string literal any place you can use a **String** object. For example, you can call methods directly on a quoted string as if it were an object reference, as the following statement shows. It calls the **length( )** method on the string "abc". As expected, it prints "3"

```
System.out.println("abc".length());
```

String Concatenation

In general, Java does not allow operators to be applied to **String** objects. The one exception to this rule is the + operator, which concatenates two strings, producing a **String** object as the result. This allows you to chain together a series of + operations. For example, the following fragment concatenates three strings:

```
String age = "9";
String s = "He is " + age + " years old.";
System.out.println(s);
```

This displays the string "He is 9 years old."

One practical use of string concatenation is found when you are creating very long strings. Instead of letting long strings wrap around within your source code, you can break them into smaller pieces, using the + to concatenate them. Here is an example:

```
// Using concatenation to prevent long lines.
class ConCat {
  public static void main(String args[]) {
    String longStr = "This could have been " +
      "a very long line that would have " +
      "wrapped around.  But string concatenation " +
      "prevents this.";

    System.out.println(longStr);
  }
}
```

String Concatenation with Other Data Types

You can concatenate strings with other types of data. For example, consider this slightly different version of the earlier example:

```
int age = 9;
String s = "He is " + age + " years old.";
System.out.println(s);
```

In this case, **age** is an **int** rather than another **String**, but the output produced is the same as before. This is because the **int** value in **age** is automatically converted into its string representation within a **String** object. This string is then concatenated as before. The compiler will convert an operand to its string equivalent whenever the other operand of the + is an instance of **String**.

Be careful when you mix other types of operations with string concatenation expressions, however. You might get surprising results. Consider the following:

```
String s = "four: " + 2 + 2;
System.out.println(s);
```

This fragment displays

```
four: 22
```

rather than the

```
four: 4
```

that you probably expected. Here's why. Operator precedence causes the concatenation of "four" with the string equivalent of 2 to take place first. This result is then concatenated with the string equivalent of 2 a second time. To complete the integer addition first, you must use parentheses, like this:

```
String s = "four: " + (2 + 2);
```

Now **s** contains the string "four: 4".

String Conversion and toString( )

When Java converts data into its string representation during concatenation, it does so by calling one of the overloaded versions of the string conversion method **valueOf( )** defined by **String**. **valueOf( )** is overloaded for all the simple types and for type **Object**. For the simple types, **valueOf( )** returns a string that contains the human-readable equivalent of the value with which it is called. For objects, **valueOf( )** calls the **toString( )** method on the object. We will look more closely at **valueOf( )** later in this chapter. Here, let's examine the **toString( )** method, because it is the means by which you can determine the string representation for objects of classes that you create.

Every class implements **toString( )** because it is defined by **Object**. However, the default implementation of **toString( )** is seldom sufficient. For most important classes that you create, you will want to override **toString( )** and provide your own string representations. Fortunately, this is easy to do. The **toString( )** method has this general form:

String toString( )

To implement **toString( )**, simply return a **String** object that contains the human-readable string that appropriately describes an object of your class.

By overriding **toString( )** for classes that you create, you allow them to be fully integrated into Java's programming environment. For example, they can be used in **print( )** and **println( )** statements and in concatenation expressions. The following program demonstrates this by overriding **toString( )** for the **Box** class:

```
// Override toString() for Box class.
class Box {
  double width;
  double height;
  double depth;

  Box(double w, double h, double d) {
    width = w;
    height = h;
    depth = d;
  }

  public String toString() {
    return "Dimensions are " + width + " by " +
            depth + " by " + height + ".";
  }
}

class toStringDemo {
  public static void main(String args[]) {
    Box b = new Box(10, 12, 14);
    String s = "Box b: " + b; // concatenate Box object

    System.out.println(b); // convert Box to string
    System.out.println(s);
  }
}
```

The output of this program is shown here:

```
Dimensions are 10.0 by 14.0 by 12.0
Box b: Dimensions are 10.0 by 14.0 by 12.0
```

As you can see, **Box**'s **toString( )** method is automatically invoked when a **Box** object is used in a concatenation expression or in a call to **println( )**.

THE JAVA LIBRARY

Character Extraction

The **String** class provides a number of ways in which characters can be extracted from a **String** object. Each is examined here. Although the characters that comprise a string within a **String** object cannot be indexed as if they were a character array, many of the **String** methods employ an index (or offset) into the string for their operation. Like arrays, the string indexes begin at zero.

charAt( )

To extract a single character from a **String**, you can refer directly to an individual character via the **charAt( )** method. It has this general form:

char charAt(int *where*)

Here, *where* is the index of the character that you want to obtain. The value of *where* must be nonnegative and specify a location within the string. **charAt( )** returns the character at the specified location. For example,

```
char ch;
ch = "abc".charAt(1);
```

assigns the value "**b**" to **ch**.

getChars( )

If you need to extract more than one character at a time, you can use the **getChars( )** method. It has this general form:

void getChars(int *sourceStart*, int *sourceEnd*, char *target*[ ], int *targetStart*)

Here, *sourceStart* specifies the index of the beginning of the substring, and *sourceEnd* specifies an index that is one past the end of the desired substring. Thus, the substring contains the characters from *sourceStart* through *sourceEnd*–1. The array that will receive the characters is specified by *target*. The index within *target* at which the substring will be copied is passed in *targetStart*. Care must be taken to assure that the *target* array is large enough to hold the number of characters in the specified substring.

The following program demonstrates **getChars( )**:

```
class getCharsDemo {
  public static void main(String args[]) {
```

```
String s = "This is a demo of the getChars method.";
int start = 10;
int end = 14;
char buf[] = new char[end - start];

s.getChars(start, end, buf, 0);
System.out.println(buf);
  }
}
```

Here is the output of this program:

```
demo
```

getBytes( )

There is an alternative to **getChars( )** that stores the characters in an array of bytes. This method is called **getBytes( )**, and it uses the default character-to-byte conversions provided by the platform. Here is its simplest form:

byte[ ] getBytes( )

Other forms of **getBytes( )** are also available. **getBytes( )** is most useful when you are exporting a **String** value into an environment that does not support 16-bit Unicode characters. For example, most Internet protocols and text file formats use 8-bit ASCII for all text interchange.

toCharArray( )

If you want to convert all the characters in a **String** object into a character array, the easiest way is to call **toCharArray( )**. It returns an array of characters for the entire string. It has this general form:

char[ ] toCharArray( )

This function is provided as a convenience, since it is possible to use **getChars( )** to achieve the same result.

String Comparison

The **String** class includes several methods that compare strings or substrings within strings. Each is examined here.

equals( ) and equalsIgnoreCase( )

To compare two strings for equality, use **equals( )**. It has this general form:

boolean equals(Object *str*)

Here, *str* is the **String** object being compared with the invoking **String** object. It returns **true** if the strings contain the same characters in the same order, and **false** otherwise. The comparison is case-sensitive.

To perform a comparison that ignores case differences, call **equalsIgnoreCase( )**. When it compares two strings, it considers **A-Z** to be the same as **a-z**. It has this general form:

boolean equalsIgnoreCase(String *str*)

Here, *str* is the **String** object being compared with the invoking **String** object. It, too, returns **true** if the strings contain the same characters in the same order, and **false** otherwise.

Here is an example that demonstrates **equals( )** and **equalsIgnoreCase( )**:

```
// Demonstrate equals() and equalsIgnoreCase().
class equalsDemo {
  public static void main(String args[]) {
    String s1 = "Hello";
    String s2 = "Hello";
    String s3 = "Good-bye";
    String s4 = "HELLO";
    System.out.println(s1 + " equals " + s2 + " -> " +
                  s1.equals(s2));
    System.out.println(s1 + " equals " + s3 + " -> " +
                  s1.equals(s3));
    System.out.println(s1 + " equals " + s4 + " -> " +
                  s1.equals(s4));
    System.out.println(s1 + " equalsIgnoreCase " + s4 + " -> " +
                  s1.equalsIgnoreCase(s4));
  }
}
```

The output from the program is shown here:

```
Hello equals Hello -> true
Hello equals Good-bye -> false
Hello equals HELLO -> false
Hello equalsIgnoreCase HELLO -> true
```

regionMatches( )

The **regionMatches( )** method compares a specific region inside a string with another specific region in another string. There is an overloaded form that allows you to ignore case in such comparisons. Here are the general forms for these two methods:

boolean regionMatches(int *startIndex*, String *str2*,
                      int *str2StartIndex*, int *numChars*)

boolean regionMatches(boolean *ignoreCase*,
                      int *startIndex*, String *str2*,
                      int *str2StartIndex*, int *numChars*)

For both versions, *startIndex* specifies the index at which the region begins within the invoking **String** object. The **String** being compared is specified by *str2*. The index at which the comparison will start within *str2* is specified by *str2StartIndex*. The length of the substring being compared is passed in *numChars*. In the second version, if *ignoreCase* is **true**, the case of the characters is ignored. Otherwise, case is significant.

startsWith( ) and endsWith( )

String defines two routines that are, more or less, specialized forms of **regionMatches( )**. The **startsWith( )** method determines whether a given **String** begins with a specified string. Conversely, **endsWith( )** determines whether the **String** in question ends with a specified string. They have the following general forms:

boolean startsWith(String *str*)
boolean endsWith(String *str*)

Here, *str* is the **String** being tested. If the string matches, **true** is returned. Otherwise, **false** is returned. For example,

```
"Foobar".endsWith("bar")
```

and

```
"Foobar".startsWith("Foo")
```

are both **true**.

A second form of **startsWith( )**, shown here, lets you specify a starting point:

boolean startsWith(String *str*, int *startIndex*)

Here, *startIndex* specifies the index into the invoking string at which point the search will begin. For example,

```
"Foobar".startsWith("bar", 3)
```

returns **true**.

equals( ) Versus ==

It is important to understand that the **equals( )** method and the **==** operator perform
two different operations. As just explained, the **equals( )** method compares the
characters inside a **String** object. The **==** operator compares two object references to
see whether they refer to the same instance. The following program shows how two
different **String** objects can contain the same characters, but references to these objects
will not compare as equal:

```
// equals() vs ==
class EqualsNotEqualTo {
  public static void main(String args[]) {
    String s1 = "Hello";
    String s2 = new String(s1);

    System.out.println(s1 + " equals " + s2 + " -> " +
                       s1.equals(s2));
    System.out.println(s1 + " == " + s2 + " -> " + (s1 == s2));
  }
}
```

The variable **s1** refers to the **String** instance created by "Hello". The object
referred to by **s2** is created with **s1** as an initializer. Thus, the contents of the two
String objects are identical, but they are distinct objects. This means that **s1** and **s2**
do not refer to the same objects and are, therefore, not **==**, as is shown here by the
output of the preceding example:

```
Hello equals Hello -> true
Hello == Hello -> false
```

compareTo( )

Often, it is not enough to simply know whether two strings are identical. For sorting
applications, you need to know which is *less than, equal to,* or *greater than* the next. A
string is less than another if it comes before the other in dictionary order. A string is
greater than another if it comes after the other in dictionary order. The **String** method
compareTo( ) serves this purpose. It has this general form:

int compareTo(String *str*)

Here, *str* is the **String** being compared with the invoking **String**. The result of the comparison is returned and is interpreted as shown here:

Value	Meaning
Less than zero	The invoking string is less than *str*.
Greater than zero	The invoking string is greater than *str*.
Zero	The two strings are equal.

Here is a sample program that sorts an array of strings. The program uses **compareTo( )** to determine sort ordering for a bubble sort:

```
// A bubble sort for Strings.
class SortString {
  static String arr[] = {
    "Now", "is", "the", "time", "for", "all", "good", "men",
    "to", "come", "to", "the", "aid", "of", "their", "country"
  };
  public static void main(String args[]) {
    for(int j = 0; j < arr.length; j++) {
      for(int i = j + 1; i < arr.length; i++) {
        if(arr[i].compareTo(arr[j]) < 0) {
          String t = arr[j];
          arr[j] = arr[i];
          arr[i] = t;
        }
      }
      System.out.println(arr[j]);
    }
  }
}
```

The output of this program is the list of words:

```
Now
aid
all
come
country
for
good
is
men
```

```
of
the
the
their
time
to
to
```

As you can see from the output of this example, **compareTo( )** takes into account uppercase and lowercase letters. The word "Now" came out before all the others because it begins with an uppercase letter, which means it has a lower value in the ASCII character set.

If you want to ignore case differences when comparing two strings, use **compareToIgnoreCase( )**, shown here:

int compareToIgnoreCase(String *str*)

This method returns the same results as **compareTo( )**, except that case differences are ignored. This method was added by Java 2. You might want to try substituting it into the previous program. After doing so, "Now" will no longer be first.

Searching Strings

The **String** class provides two methods that allow you to search a string for a specified character or substring:

- **indexOf( )** Searches for the first occurrence of a character or substring.
- **lastIndexOf( )** Searches for the last occurrence of a character or substring.

These two methods are overloaded in several different ways. In all cases, the methods return the index at which the character or substring was found, or –1 on failure.

To search for the first occurrence of a character, use

int indexOf(int *ch*)

To search for the last occurrence of a character, use

int lastIndexOf(int *ch*)

Here, *ch* is the character being sought.

To search for the first or last occurrence of a substring, use

int indexOf(String *str*)
int lastIndexOf(String *str*)

Here, *str* specifies the substring.

You can specify a starting point for the search using these forms:

int indexOf(int *ch*, int *startIndex*)
int lastIndexOf(int *ch*, int *startIndex*)

int indexOf(String *str*, int *startIndex*)
int lastIndexOf(String *str*, int *startIndex*)

Here, *startIndex* specifies the index at which point the search begins. For **indexOf( )**, the search runs from *startIndex* to the end of the string. For **lastIndexOf( )**, the search runs from *startIndex* to zero.

The following example shows how to use the various index methods to search inside of **String**s:

```
// Demonstrate indexOf() and lastIndexOf().
class indexOfDemo {
  public static void main(String args[]) {
    String s = "Now is the time for all good men " +
               "to come to the aid of their country.";

    System.out.println(s);
    System.out.println("indexOf(t) = " +
                       s.indexOf('t'));
    System.out.println("lastIndexOf(t) = " +
                       s.lastIndexOf('t'));
    System.out.println("indexOf(the) = " +
                       s.indexOf("the"));
    System.out.println("lastIndexOf(the) = " +
                       s.lastIndexOf("the"));
    System.out.println("indexOf(t, 10) = " +
                       s.indexOf('t', 10));
    System.out.println("lastIndexOf(t, 60) = " +
                       s.lastIndexOf('t', 60));
    System.out.println("indexOf(the, 10) = " +
                       s.indexOf("the", 10));
    System.out.println("lastIndexOf(the, 60) = " +
                       s.lastIndexOf("the", 60));
  }
}
```

Here is the output of this program:

```
Now is the time for all good men to come to the aid of their country.
indexOf(t) = 7
```

```
lastIndexOf(t) = 65
indexOf(the) = 7
lastIndexOf(the) = 55
indexOf(t, 10) = 11
lastIndexOf(t, 60) = 55
indexOf(the, 10) = 44
lastIndexOf(the, 60) = 55
```

Modifying a String

Because **String** objects are immutable, whenever you want to modify a **String**, you must either copy it into a **StringBuffer** or use one of the following **String** methods, which will construct a new copy of the string with your modifications complete.

substring( )

You can extract a substring using **substring( )**. It has two forms. The first is

String substring(int *startIndex*)

Here, *startIndex* specifies the index at which the substring will begin. This form returns a copy of the substring that begins at *startIndex* and runs to the end of the invoking string.

The second form of **substring( )** allows you to specify both the beginning and ending index of the substring:

String substring(int *startIndex*, int *endIndex*)

Here, *startIndex* specifies the beginning index, and *endIndex* specifies the stopping point. The string returned contains all the characters from the beginning index, up to, but not including, the ending index.

The following program uses **substring( )** to replace all instances of one substring with another within a string:

```
// Substring replacement.
class StringReplace {
  public static void main(String args[]) {
    String org = "This is a test. This is, too.";
    String search = "is";
    String sub = "was";
    String result = "";
    int i;

    do { // replace all matching substrings
      System.out.println(org);
```

```
        i = org.indexOf(search);
        if(i != -1) {
          result = org.substring(0, i);
          result = result + sub;
          result = result + org.substring(i + search.length());
          org = result;
        }
      } while(i != -1);

  }
}
```

The output from this program is shown here:

```
This is a test. This is, too.
Thwas is a test. This is, too.
Thwas was a test. This is, too.
Thwas was a test. Thwas is, too.
Thwas was a test. Thwas was, too.
```

concat( )

You can concatenate two strings using **concat( )**, shown here:

String concat(String *str*)

This method creates a new object that contains the invoking string with the contents of *str* appended to the end. **concat( )** performs the same function as **+**. For example,

```
String s1 = "one";
String s2 = s1.concat("two");
```

puts the string "onetwo" into **s2**. It generates the same result as the following sequence:

```
String s1 = "one";
String s2 = s1 + "two";
```

replace( )

The **replace( )** method replaces all occurrences of one character in the invoking string with another character. It has the following general form:

String replace(char *original*, char *replacement*)

Here, *original* specifies the character to be replaced by the character specified by *replacement*. The resulting string is returned. For example,

```
String s = "Hello".replace('l', 'w');
```

puts the string "Hewwo" into **s**.

trim( )

The **trim( )** method returns a copy of the invoking string from which any leading and trailing whitespace has been removed. It has this general form:

String trim( )

Here is an example:

```
String s = "   Hello World   ".trim();
```

This puts the string "Hello World" into **s**.

The **trim( )** method is quite useful when you process user commands. For example, the following program prompts the user for the name of a state and then displays that state's capital. It uses **trim( )** to remove any leading or trailing whitespace that may have inadvertently been entered by the user.

```
// Using trim() to process commands.
import java.io.*;

class UseTrim {
  public static void main(String args[])
    throws IOException
  {
    // create a BufferedReader using System.in
    BufferedReader br = new
      BufferedReader(new InputStreamReader(System.in));
    String str;

    System.out.println("Enter 'stop' to quit.");
    System.out.println("Enter State: ");
    do {
```

```
        str = br.readLine();
        str = str.trim(); // remove whitespace

        if(str.equals("Illinois"))
          System.out.println("Capital is Springfield.");
        else if(str.equals("Missouri"))
          System.out.println("Capital is Jefferson City.");
        else if(str.equals("California"))
          System.out.println("Capital is Sacramento.");
        else if(str.equals("Washington"))
          System.out.println("Capital is Olympia.");
        // ...
      } while(!str.equals("stop"));
  }
}
```

Data Conversion Using valueOf( )

The **valueOf( )** method converts data from its internal format into a human-readable form. It is a static method that is overloaded within **String** for all of Java's built-in types, so that each type can be converted properly into a string. **valueOf( )** is also overloaded for type **Object**, so an object of any class type you create can also be used as an argument. (Recall that **Object** is a superclass for all classes.) Here are a few of its forms:

> static String valueOf(double *num*)
> static String valueOf(long *num*)
> static String valueOf(Object *ob*)
> static String valueOf(char *chars*[ ])

As we discussed earlier, **valueOf( )** is called when a string representation of some other type of data is needed—for example, during concatenation operations. You can call this method directly with any data type and get a reasonable **String** representation. All of the simple types are converted to their common **String** representation. Any object that you pass to **valueOf( )** will return the result of a call to the object's **toString( )** method. In fact, you could just call **toString( )** directly and get the same result.

For most arrays, **valueOf( )** returns a rather cryptic string, which indicates that it is an array of some type. For arrays of **char**, however, a **String** object is created that contains the characters in the **char** array. There is a special version of **valueOf( )** that allows you to specify a subset of a **char** array. It has this general form:

> static String valueOf(char *chars*[ ], int *startIndex*, int *numChars*)

Here, *chars* is the array that holds the characters, *startIndex* is the index into the array of characters at which the desired substring begins, and *numChars* specifies the length of the substring.

Changing the Case of Characters Within a String

The method **toLowerCase( )** converts all the characters in a string from uppercase to lowercase. The **toUpperCase( )** method converts all the characters in a string from lowercase to uppercase. Nonalphabetical characters, such as digits, are unaffected. Here are the general forms of these methods:

String toLowerCase( )
String toUpperCase( )

Both methods return a **String** object that contains the uppercase or lowercase equivalent of the invoking **String**.

Here is an example that uses **toLowerCase( )** and **toUpperCase( )**:

```
// Demonstrate toUpperCase() and toLowerCase().

class ChangeCase {
  public static void main(String args[])
  {
    String s = "This is a test.";

    System.out.println("Original: " + s);

    String upper = s.toUpperCase();
    String lower = s.toLowerCase();

    System.out.println("Uppercase: " + upper);
    System.out.println("Lowercase: " + lower);
  }
}
```

The output produced by the program is shown here:

```
Original: This is a test.
Uppercase: THIS IS A TEST.
Lowercase: this is a test.
```

String Methods Added by Java 2, Version 1.4

Java 2, version 1.4 adds several methods to the **String** class. These are summarized in the following table.

Method	Description
boolean contentEquals(StringBuffer *str*)	Returns **true** if the invoking string contains the same string as *str*. Otherwise, returns **false**.
CharSequence subSequence(int *startIndex*, int *stopIndex*)	Returns a substring of the invoking string, beginning at *startIndex* and stopping at *stopIndex*. This method is required by the **CharSequence** interface, which is now implemented by **String**.
boolean matches(string *regExp*)	Returns **true** if the invoking string matches the regular expression passed in *regExp*. Otherwise, returns **false**.
String replaceFirst(String *regExp*, String *newStr*)	Returns a string in which the first substring that matches the regular expression specified by *regExp* is replaced by *newStr*.
String replaceAll(String *regExp*, String *newStr*)	Returns a string in which all substrings that match the regular expression specified by *regExp* are replaced by *newStr*.
String[ ] split(String *regExp*)	Decomposes the invoking string into parts and returns an array that contains the result. Each part is delimited by the regular expression passed in *regExp*.
String[ ] split(String *regExp*, int *max*)	Decomposes the invoking string into parts and returns an array that contains the result. Each part is delimited by the regular expression passed in *regExp*. The number of pieces is specified by *max*. If *max* is negative, then the invoking string is fully decomposed. Otherwise, if *max* contains a non-zero value, the last entry in the returned array contains the remainder of the invoking string. If *max* is zero, the invoking string is fully decomposed.

Notice that several of these methods work with regular expressions. Support for regular expression processing was added by Java 2, version 1.4 and is described in Chapter 24.

StringBuffer

StringBuffer is a peer class of **String** that provides much of the functionality of strings. As you know, **String** represents fixed-length, immutable character sequences. In contrast, **StringBuffer** represents growable and writeable character sequences. **StringBuffer** may have characters and substrings inserted in the middle or appended to the end. **StringBuffer** will automatically grow to make room for such additions and often has more characters preallocated than are actually needed, to allow room for growth. Java uses both classes heavily, but many programmers deal only with **String** and let Java manipulate **StringBuffer**s behind the scenes by using the overloaded + operator.

StringBuffer Constructors

StringBuffer defines these three constructors:

StringBuffer( )
StringBuffer(int *size*)
StringBuffer(String *str*)

The default constructor (the one with no parameters) reserves room for 16 characters without reallocation. The second version accepts an integer argument that explicitly sets the size of the buffer. The third version accepts a **String** argument that sets the initial contents of the **StringBuffer** object and reserves room for 16 more characters without reallocation. **StringBuffer** allocates room for 16 additional characters when no specific buffer length is requested, because reallocation is a costly process in terms of time. Also, frequent reallocations can fragment memory. By allocating room for a few extra characters, **StringBuffer** reduces the number of reallocations that take place.

length( ) and capacity( )

The current length of a **StringBuffer** can be found via the **length( )** method, while the total allocated capacity can be found through the **capacity( )** method. They have the following general forms:

int length( )
int capacity( )

Here is an example:

```
// StringBuffer length vs. capacity.
class StringBufferDemo {
  public static void main(String args[]) {
    StringBuffer sb = new StringBuffer("Hello");

    System.out.println("buffer = " + sb);
    System.out.println("length = " + sb.length());
    System.out.println("capacity = " + sb.capacity());
  }
}
```

Here is the output of this program, which shows how **StringBuffer** reserves extra space for additional manipulations:

```
buffer = Hello
length = 5
capacity = 21
```

Since **sb** is initialized with the string "Hello" when it is created, its length is 5. Its capacity is 21 because room for 16 additional characters is automatically added.

ensureCapacity( )

If you want to preallocate room for a certain number of characters after a **StringBuffer** has been constructed, you can use **ensureCapacity( )** to set the size of the buffer. This is useful if you know in advance that you will be appending a large number of small strings to a **StringBuffer**. **ensureCapacity( )** has this general form:

void ensureCapacity(int *capacity*)

Here, *capacity* specifies the size of the buffer.

setLength( )

To set the length of the buffer within a **StringBuffer** object, use **setLength( )**. Its general form is shown here:

void setLength(int *len*)

Here, *len* specifies the length of the buffer. This value must be nonnegative.

When you increase the size of the buffer, null characters are added to the end of the existing buffer. If you call **setLength( )** with a value less than the current value returned by **length( )**, then the characters stored beyond the new length will be lost.

The **setCharAtDemo** sample program in the following section uses **setLength( )** to shorten a **StringBuffer**.

charAt( ) and setCharAt( )

The value of a single character can be obtained from a **StringBuffer** via the **charAt( )** method. You can set the value of a character within a **StringBuffer** using **setCharAt( )**. Their general forms are shown here:

char charAt(int *where*)
void setCharAt(int *where*, char *ch*)

For **charAt( )**, *where* specifies the index of the character being obtained. For **setCharAt( )**, *where* specifies the index of the character being set, and *ch* specifies the new value of that character. For both methods, *where* must be nonnegative and must not specify a location beyond the end of the buffer.

The following example demonstrates **charAt( )** and **setCharAt( )**:

```
// Demonstrate charAt() and setCharAt().
class setCharAtDemo {
  public static void main(String args[]) {
    StringBuffer sb = new StringBuffer("Hello");
    System.out.println("buffer before = " + sb);
    System.out.println("charAt(1) before = " + sb.charAt(1));
    sb.setCharAt(1, 'i');
    sb.setLength(2);
    System.out.println("buffer after = " + sb);
    System.out.println("charAt(1) after = " + sb.charAt(1));
  }
}
```

Here is the output generated by this program:

```
buffer before = Hello
charAt(1) before = e
buffer after = Hi
charAt(1) after = i
```

getChars( )

To copy a substring of a **StringBuffer** into an array, use the **getChars( )** method. It has this general form:

void getChars(int *sourceStart*, int *sourceEnd*, char *target*[ ],
              int *targetStart*)

Here, *sourceStart* specifies the index of the beginning of the substring, and *sourceEnd* specifies an index that is one past the end of the desired substring. This means that the substring contains the characters from *sourceStart* through *sourceEnd*–1. The array that will receive the characters is specified by *target*. The index within *target* at which the substring will be copied is passed in *targetStart*. Care must be taken to assure that the *target* array is large enough to hold the number of characters in the specified substring.

append( )

The **append( )** method concatenates the string representation of any other type of data to the end of the invoking **StringBuffer** object. It has overloaded versions for all the built-in types and for **Object**. Here are a few of its forms:

> StringBuffer append(String *str*)
> StringBuffer append(int *num*)
> StringBuffer append(Object *obj*)

String.valueOf( ) is called for each parameter to obtain its string representation. The result is appended to the current **StringBuffer** object. The buffer itself is returned by each version of **append( )**. This allows subsequent calls to be chained together, as shown in the following example:

```
// Demonstrate append().
class appendDemo {
  public static void main(String args[]) {
    String s;
    int a = 42;
    StringBuffer sb = new StringBuffer(40);

    s = sb.append("a = ").append(a).append("!").toString();
    System.out.println(s);
  }
}
```

The output of this example is shown here:

```
a = 42!
```

The **append( )** method is most often called when the **+** operator is used on **String** objects. Java automatically changes modifications to a **String** instance into similar operations on a **StringBuffer** instance. Thus, a concatenation invokes **append( )** on a **StringBuffer** object. After the concatenation has been performed, the compiler inserts a call to **toString( )** to turn the modifiable **StringBuffer** back into a constant **String**. All of this may seem unreasonably complicated. Why not just have one string class and have it behave more or less like **StringBuffer**? The answer is performance. There are many optimizations that the Java run time can make knowing that **String** objects are immutable. Thankfully, Java hides most of the complexity of conversion between **String**s and **StringBuffer**s. Actually, many programmers will never feel the need to use **StringBuffer** directly and will be able to express most operations in terms of the + operator on **String** variables.

insert( )

The **insert( )** method inserts one string into another. It is overloaded to accept values of all the simple types, plus **String**s and **Object**s. Like **append( )**, it calls **String.valueOf( )** to obtain the string representation of the value it is called with. This string is then inserted into the invoking **StringBuffer** object. These are a few of its forms:

StringBuffer insert(int *index*, String *str*)
StringBuffer insert(int *index*, char *ch*)
StringBuffer insert(int *index*, Object *obj*)

Here, *index* specifies the index at which point the string will be inserted into the invoking **StringBuffer** object.

The following sample program inserts "like" between "I" and "Java":

```
// Demonstrate insert().
class insertDemo {
  public static void main(String args[]) {
    StringBuffer sb = new StringBuffer("I Java!");

    sb.insert(2, "like ");
    System.out.println(sb);
  }
}
```

The output of this example is shown here:

```
I like Java!
```

reverse( )

You can reverse the characters within a **StringBuffer** object using **reverse( )**, shown here:

StringBuffer reverse( )

This method returns the reversed object on which it was called. The following program demonstrates **reverse( )**:

```
// Using reverse() to reverse a StringBuffer.
class ReverseDemo {
```

```
public static void main(String args[]) {
    StringBuffer s = new StringBuffer("abcdef");

    System.out.println(s);
    s.reverse();
    System.out.println(s);
}
}
```

Here is the output produced by the program:

```
abcdef
fedcba
```

delete( ) and deleteCharAt( )

Java 2 added to **StringBuffer** the ability to delete characters using the methods
delete( ) and **deleteCharAt( )**. These methods are shown here:

StringBuffer delete(int *startIndex*, int *endIndex*)
StringBuffer deleteCharAt(int *loc*)

The **delete( )** method deletes a sequence of characters from the invoking object.
Here, *startIndex* specifies the index of the first character to remove, and *endIndex*
specifies an index one past the last character to remove. Thus, the substring deleted
runs from *startIndex* to *endIndex*–1. The resulting **StringBuffer** object is returned.

The **deleteCharAt( )** method deletes the character at the index specified by *loc*.
It returns the resulting **StringBuffer** object.

Here is a program that demonstrates the **delete( )** and **deleteCharAt( )** methods:

```
// Demonstrate delete() and deleteCharAt()
class deleteDemo {
    public static void main(String args[]) {
        StringBuffer sb = new StringBuffer("This is a test.");

        sb.delete(4, 7);
        System.out.println("After delete: " + sb);

        sb.deleteCharAt(0);
        System.out.println("After deleteCharAt: " + sb);
    }
}
```

The following output is produced:

```
After delete: This a test.
After deleteCharAt: his a test.
```

replace( )

Another method added to **StringBuffer** by Java 2 is **replace( )**. It replaces one set of characters with another set inside a **StringBuffer** object. Its signature is shown here:

StringBuffer replace(int *startIndex*, int *endIndex*, String *str*)

The substring being replaced is specified by the indexes *startIndex* and *endIndex*. Thus, the substring at *startIndex* through *endIndex*–1 is replaced. The replacement string is passed in *str*. The resulting **StringBuffer** object is returned.

The following program demonstrates **replace( )**:

```
// Demonstrate replace()
class replaceDemo {
  public static void main(String args[]) {
    StringBuffer sb = new StringBuffer("This is a test.");

    sb.replace(5, 7, "was");
    System.out.println("After replace: " + sb);
  }
}
```

Here is the output:

```
After replace: This was a test.
```

substring( )

Java 2 also added the **substring( )** method, which returns a portion of a **StringBuffer**. It has the following two forms:

String substring(int *startIndex*)
String substring(int *startIndex*, int *endIndex*)

The first form returns the substring that starts at *startIndex* and runs to the end of the invoking **StringBuffer** object. The second form returns the substring that starts at *startIndex* and runs through *endIndex*–1. These methods work just like those defined for **String** that were described earlier.

StringBuffer Methods Added by Java 2, Version 1.4

Java 2, version 1.4 added several new methods to **StringBuffer**. They are summarized in the following table.

Method	Description
CharSequence subSequence(int *startIndex*, int *stopIndex*)	Returns a substring of the invoking string, beginning at *startIndex* and stopping at *stopIndex*. This method is required by the **CharSequence** interface, which is now implemented by **StringBuffer**.
int indexOf(String *str*)	Searches the invoking **StringBuffer** for the first occurrence of *str*. Returns the index of the match, or –1 if no match is found.
int indexOf(String *str*, int *startIndex*)	Searches the invoking **StringBuffer** for the first occurrence of *str*, beginning at *startIndex*. Returns the index of the match, or –1 if no match is found.
int lastIndexOf(String *str*)	Searches the invoking **StringBuffer** for the last occurrence of str. Returns the index of the match, or –1 if no match is found.
int lastIndexOf(String *str*, int *startIndex*)	Searches the invoking **StringBuffer** for the last occurrence of *str*, beginning at *startIndex*. Returns the index of the match, or –1 if no match is found.

Aside from **subSequence( )**, which implements a method required by the **CharSequence** interface, the other methods allow a **StringBuffer** to be searched for an occurrence of a **String**. The following program demonstrates **indexOf( )** and **lastIndexOf( )**.

```
class IndexOfDemo {
  public static void main(String args[]) {
    StringBuffer sb = new StringBuffer("one two one");
    int i;
```

```
    i = sb.indexOf("one");
    System.out.println("First index: " + i);

    i = sb.lastIndexOf("one");
    System.out.println("Last index: " + i);
  }
}
```

The output is shown here.

```
First index: 0
Last index: 8
```

The
Complete
Reference

Chapter 14

Exploring java.lang

This chapter discusses those classes and interfaces defined by **java.lang**. As you know, **java.lang** is automatically imported into all programs. It contains classes and interfaces that are fundamental to virtually all of Java programming. It is Java's most widely used package.

java.lang includes the following classes:

Boolean	Long	StackTraceElement (Java 2,1.4)
Byte	Math	StrictMath (Java 2,1.3)
Character	Number	String
Class	Object	StringBuffer
ClassLoader	Package (Java 2)	System
Compiler	Process	Thread
Double	Runtime	ThreadGroup
Float	RuntimePermission (Java 2)	ThreadLocal (Java 2)
InheritableThreadLocal (Java 2)	SecurityManager	Throwable
Integer	Short	Void

In addition, there are two classes defined by **Character**: **Character.Subset** and **Character.UnicodeBlock**. These were added by Java 2.

java.lang also defines the following interfaces:

- **Cloneable**
- **Comparable**
- **Runnable**
- **CharSequence**

The **Comparable** interface was added by Java 2. **CharSequence** was added by Java 2, version 1.4.

Several of the classes contained in **java.lang** contain deprecated methods, most dating back to Java 1.0. These deprecated methods are still provided by Java 2, to support an ever-shrinking pool of legacy code, and are not recommended for new code. Most of the deprecations took place prior to Java 2 and these deprecated methods are not discussed here. Deprecations that occurred because of Java 2, however, are mentioned.

Java 2 also added several new classes and methods to the **java.lang** package. The new additions are so indicated.

Simple Type Wrappers

As we mentioned in Part I of this book, Java uses simple types, such as **int** and **char**, for performance reasons. These data types are not part of the object hierarchy. They are passed by value to methods and cannot be directly passed by reference. Also, there is no way for two methods to refer to the *same instance* of an **int**. At times, you will need to create an object representation for one of these simple types. For example, there are enumeration classes discussed in Chapter 15 that deal only with objects; to store a simple type in one of these classes, you need to wrap the simple type in a class. To address this need, Java provides classes that correspond to each of the simple types. In essence, these classes encapsulate, or *wrap*, the simple types within a class. Thus, they are commonly referred to as *type wrappers*.

Number

The abstract class **Number** defines a superclass that is implemented by the classes that wrap the numeric types **byte**, **short**, **int**, **long**, **float**, and **double**. **Number** has abstract methods that return the value of the object in each of the different number formats. That is, **doubleValue( )** returns the value as a **double**, **floatValue( )** returns the value as a **float**, and so on. These methods are shown here:

byte byteValue( )
double doubleValue( )
float floatValue( )
int intValue( )
long longValue( )
short shortValue( )

The values returned by these methods can be rounded.

Number has six concrete subclasses that hold explicit values of each numeric type: **Double**, **Float**, **Byte**, **Short**, **Integer**, and **Long**.

Double and Float

Double and **Float** are wrappers for floating-point values of type **double** and **float**, respectively. The constructors for **Float** are shown here:

Float(double *num*)
Float(float *num*)
Float(String *str*) throws NumberFormatException

As you can see, **Float** objects can be constructed with values of type **float** or **double**. They can also be constructed from the string representation of a floating-point number.
The constructors for **Double** are shown here:

Double(double *num*)
Double(String *str*) throws NumberFormatException

Double objects can be constructed with a **double** value or a string containing a floating-point value.

The methods defined by **Float** are shown in Table 14-1. The methods defined by **Double** are shown in Table 14-2. Both **Float** and **Double** define the following constants:

MAX_VALUE	Maximum positive value
MIN_VALUE	Minimum positive value
NaN	Not a number
POSITiVE_INFINITY	Positive infinity
NEGATIVE_INFINITY	Negative infinity
TYPE	The **Class** object for **float** or **double**

Method	Description
byte byteValue( )	Returns the value of the invoking object as a **byte**.
static int compare(float *num1*, float *num2*)	Compares the values of *num1* and *num2*. Returns 0 if the values are equal. Returns a negative value if *num1* is less than *num2*. Returns a positive value if *num1* is greater than *num2*. (Added by Java 2, version 1.4)
int compareTo(Float *f*)	Compares the numerical value of the invoking object with that of *f*. Returns 0 if the values are equal. Returns a negative value if the invoking object has a lower value. Returns a positive value if the invoking object has a greater value. (Added by Java 2)
int compareTo(Object *obj*)	Operates identically to **compareTo(Float)** if *obj* is of class **Float**. Otherwise, throws a **ClassCastException**. (Added by Java 2)
double doubleValue( )	Returns the value of the invoking object as a **double**.
boolean equals(Object *FloatObj*)	Returns **true** if the invoking **Float** object is equivalent to *FloatObj*. Otherwise, it returns **false**.

Table 14-1.   *The Methods Defined by* Float

Method	Description
static int floatToIntBits(float *num*)	Returns the IEEE-compatible, single-precision bit pattern that corresponds to the *num*.
float floatValue( )	Returns the value of the invoking object as a **float**.
int hashCode( )	Returns the hash code for the invoking object.
static float intBitsToFloat(int *num*)	Returns **float** equivalent of the IEEE-compatible, single-precision bit pattern specified by *num*.
int intValue( )	Returns the value of the invoking object as an **int**.
boolean isInfinite( )	Returns **true** if the invoking object contains an infinite value. Otherwise, it returns **false**.
static boolean isInfinite(float *num*)	Returns **true** if *num* specifies an infinite value. Otherwise, it returns **false**.
boolean isNaN( )	Returns **true** if the invoking object contains a value that is not a number. Otherwise, it returns **false**.
static boolean isNaN(float *num*)	Returns **true** if *num* specifies a value that is not a number. Otherwise, it returns **false**.
long longValue( )	Returns the value of the invoking object as a **long**.
static float parseFloat(String *str*) throws NumberFormatException	Returns the **float** equivalent of the number contained in the string specified by *str* using radix 10. (Added by Java 2)
short shortValue( )	Returns the value of the invoking object as a **short**.
String toString( )	Returns the string equivalent of the invoking object.
static String toString(float *num*)	Returns the string equivalent of the value specified by *num*.
static Float valueOf(String *str*) throws NumberFormatException	Returns the **Float** object that contains the value specified by the string in *str*.

Table 14-1. *The Methods Defined by* Float (continued)

Method	Description
byte byteValue( )	Returns the value of the invoking object as a **byte**.
static int compare(double *num1*, double *num2*)	Compares the values of *num1* and *num2*. Returns 0 if the values are equal. Returns a negative value if *num1* is less than *num2*. Returns a positive value if *num1* is greater than *num2*. (Added by Java 2, version 1.4)
int compareTo(Double *d*)	Compares the numerical value of the invoking object with that of *d*. Returns 0 if the values are equal. Returns a negative value if the invoking object has a lower value. Returns a positive value if the invoking object has a greater value. (Added by Java 2)
int compareTo(Object *obj*)	Operates identically to **compareTo(Double)** if *obj* is of class **Double**. Otherwise, throws a **ClassCastException**. (Added by Java 2)
static long doubleToLongBits(double *num*)	Returns the IEEE-compatible, double-precision bit pattern that corresponds to the *num*.
double doubleValue( )	Returns the value of the invoking object as a **double**.
boolean equals(Object *DoubleObj*)	Returns **true** if the invoking **Double** object is equivalent to *DoubleObj*. Otherwise, it returns **false**.
float floatValue( )	Returns the value of the invoking object as a **float**.
int hashcode( )	Returns the hash code for the invoking object.

Table 14-2. *The Methods Defined by* Double

Method	Description
int intValue( )	Returns the value of the invoking object as an **int**.
boolean isInfinite( )	Returns **true** if the invoking object contains an infinite value. Otherwise, it returns **false**.
static boolean isInfinite(double *num*)	Returns **true** if *num* specifies an infinite value. Otherwise, it returns **false**.
boolean isNaN( )	Returns **true** if the invoking object contains a value that is not a number. Otherwise, it returns **false**.
static boolean isNaN(double *num*)	Returns **true** if *num* specifies a value that is not a number. Otherwise, it returns **false**.
static double longBitsToDouble(long *num*)	Returns **double** equivalent of the IEEE-compatible, double-precision bit pattern specified by *num*.
long longValue( )	Returns the value of the invoking object as a **long**.
static double parseDouble(String *str*) throws NumberFormatException	Returns the **double** equivalent of the number contained in the string specified by *str* using radix 10. (Added by Java 2)
short shortValue( )	Returns the value of the invoking object as a **short**.
String toString( )	Returns the string equivalent of the invoking object.
static String toString(double *num*)	Returns the string equivalent of the value specified by *num*.
static Double valueOf(String *str*) throws NumberFormatException	Returns a **Double** object that contains the value specified by the string in *str*.

Table 14-2. *The Methods Defined by* Double (continued)

The following example creates two **Double** objects—one by using a **double** value and the other by passing a string that can be parsed as a **double**:

```
class DoubleDemo {
  public static void main(String args[]) {
    Double d1 = new Double(3.14159);
    Double d2 = new Double("314159E-5");

    System.out.println(d1 + " = " + d2 + " -> " + d1.equals(d2));
  }
}
```

As you can see from the following output, both constructors created identical **Double** instances, as shown by the **equals( )** method returning **true**:

```
3.14159 = 3.14159 -> true
```

Understanding isInfinite( ) and isNaN( )

Float and **Double** provide the methods **isInfinite( )** and **isNaN( )**, which help when manipulating two special **double** and **float** values. These methods test for two unique values defined by the IEEE floating-point specification: infinity and NaN (not a number). **isInfinite( )** returns **true** if the value being tested is infinitely large or small in magnitude. **isNaN( )** returns **true** if the value being tested is not a number.

The following example creates two **Double** objects; one is infinite, and the other is not a number:

```
// Demonstrate isInfinite() and isNaN()
class InfNaN {
  public static void main(String args[]) {
    Double d1 = new Double(1/0.);
    Double d2 = new Double(0/0.);

    System.out.println(d1 + ": " + d1.isInfinite() + ", " + d1.isNaN());
    System.out.println(d2 + ": " + d2.isInfinite() + ", " + d2.isNaN());
  }
}
```

This program generates the following output:

```
Infinity: true, false
NaN: false, true
```

Byte, Short, Integer, and Long

The **Byte**, **Short**, **Integer**, and **Long** classes are wrappers for **byte**, **short**, **int**, and **long** integer types, respectively. Their constructors are shown here:

Byte(byte *num*)
Byte(String *str*) throws NumberFormatException

Short(short *num*)
Short(String *str*) throws NumberFormatException

Integer(int *num*)
Integer(String *str*) throws NumberFormatException

Long(long *num*)
Long(String *str*) throws NumberFormatException

As you can see, these objects can be constructed from numeric values or from strings that contain valid whole number values.

The methods defined by these classes are shown in Tables 14-3 through 14-6. As you can see, they define methods for parsing integers from strings and converting strings back into integers. Variants of these methods allow you to specify the *radix*, or numeric base, for conversion. Common radixes are 2 for binary, 8 for octal, 10 for decimal, and 16 for hexadecimal.

The following constants are defined:

MIN_VALUE	Minimum value
MAX_VALUE	Maximum value
TYPE	The **Class** object for **byte**, **short**, **int**, or **long**

Method	Description
byte byteValue( )	Returns the value of the invoking object as a **byte**.
int compareTo(Byte *b*)	Compares the numerical value of the invoking object with that of *b*. Returns 0 if the values are equal. Returns a negative value if the invoking object has a lower value. Returns a positive value if the invoking object has a greater value. (Added by Java 2)

Table 14-3. *The Methods Defined by* Byte

Method	Description
int compareTo(Object *obj*)	Operates identically to **compareTo(Byte)** if *obj* is of class **Byte**. Otherwise, throws a **ClassCastException**. (Added by Java 2)
static Byte decode(String *str*) throws NumberFormatException	Returns a **Byte** object that contains the value specified by the string in *str*.
double doubleValue( )	Returns the value of the invoking object as a **double**.
boolean equals(Object *ByteObj*)	Returns **true** if the invoking **Byte** object is equivalent to *ByteObj*. Otherwise, it returns **false**.
float floatValue( )	Returns the value of the invoking object as a **float**.
int hashCode( )	Returns the hash code for the invoking object.
int intValue( )	Returns the value of the invoking object as an **int**.
long longValue( )	Returns the value of the invoking object as a **long**.
static byte parseByte(String *str*) throws NumberFormatException	Returns the **byte** equivalent of the number contained in the string specified by *str* using radix 10.
static byte parseByte(String *str*, int *radix*) throws NumberFormatException	Returns the **byte** equivalent of the number contained in the string specified by *str* using the specified radix.
short shortValue( )	Returns the value of the invoking object as a **short**.
String toString( )	Returns a string that contains the decimal equivalent of the invoking object.

Table 14-3.   *The Methods Defined by* Byte *(continued)*

Method	Description
static String toString(byte *num*)	Returns a string that contains the decimal equivalent of *num*.
static Byte valueOf(String *str*) throws NumberFormatException	Returns a **Byte** object that contains the value specified by the string in *str*.
static Byte valueOf(String *str*, int *radix*) throws NumberFormatException	Returns a **Byte** object that contains the value specified by the string in *str* using the specified *radix*.

Table 14-3. *The Methods Defined by* Byte *(continued)*

THE JAVA LIBRARY

Method	Description
byte byteValue( )	Returns the value of the invoking object as a **byte**.
int compareTo(Short *s*)	Compares the numerical value of the invoking object with that of *s*. Returns 0 if the values are equal. Returns a negative value if the invoking object has a lower value. Returns a positive value if the invoking object has a greater value. (Added by Java 2)
int compareTo(Object *obj*)	Operates identically to **compareTo(Short)** if *obj* is of class **Short**. Otherwise, throws a **ClassCastException**. (Added by Java 2)
static Short decode(String *str*) throws NumberFormatException	Returns a **Short** object that contains the value specified by the string in *str*.

Table 14-4. *The Methods Defined by* Short

Method	Description
double doubleValue( )	Returns the value of the invoking object as a **double**.
boolean equals(Object *ShortObj*)	Returns **true** if the invoking **Integer** object is equivalent to *ShortObj*. Otherwise, it returns **false**.
float floatValue( )	Returns the value of the invoking object as a **float**.
int hashCode( )	Returns the hash code for the invoking object.
int intValue( )	Returns the value of the invoking object as an **int**.
long longValue( )	Returns the value of the invoking object as a **long**.
static short parseShort(String *str*) throws NumberFormatException	Returns the **short** equivalent of the number contained in the string specified by *str* using radix 10.
static short parseShort(String *str*, int *radix*) throws NumberFormatException	Returns the **short** equivalent of the number contained in the string specified by *str* using the specified *radix*.
short shortValue( )	Returns the value of the invoking object as a **short**.
String toString( )	Returns a string that contains the decimal equivalent of the invoking object.
static String toString(short *num*)	Returns a string that contains the decimal equivalent of *num*.
static Short valueOf(String *str*) throws NumberFormatException	Returns a **Short** object that contains the value specified by the string in *str* using radix 10.
static Short valueOf(String *str*, int *radix*) throws NumberFormatException	Returns a **Short** object that contains the value specified by the string in *str* using the specified *radix*.

Table 14-4. *The Methods Defined by* Short *(continued)*

Method	Description
byte byteValue( )	Returns the value of the invoking object as a **byte**.
int compareTo(Integer *i*)	Compares the numerical value of the invoking object with that of *i*. Returns 0 if the values are equal. Returns a negative value if the invoking object has a lower value. Returns a positive value if the invoking object has a greater value. (Added by Java 2)
int compareTo(Object *obj*)	Operates identically to **compareTo(Integer)** if *obj* is of class **Integer**. Otherwise, throws a **ClassCastException**. (Added by Java 2)
static Integer decode(String *str*) throws NumberFormatException	Returns an **Integer** object that contains the value specified by the string in *str*.
double doubleValue( )	Returns the value of the invoking object as a **double**.
boolean equals(Object *IntegerObj*)	Returns **true** if the invoking **Integer** object is equivalent to *IntegerObj*. Otherwise, it returns **false**.
float floatValue( )	Returns the value of the invoking object as a **float**.
static Integer getInteger(String *propertyName*)	Returns the value associated with the environmental property specified by *propertyName*. A **null** is returned on failure.
static Integer getInteger(String *propertyName*, int *default*)	Returns the value associated with the environmental property specified by *propertyName*. The value of *default* is returned on failure.

Table 14-5. *The Methods Defined by* Integer

Method	Description
static Integer getInteger(String *propertyName*, Integer *default*)	Returns the value associated with the environmental property specified by *propertyName*. The value of *default* is returned on failure.
int hashCode( )	Returns the hash code for the invoking object.
int intValue( )	Returns the value of the invoking object as an **int**.
long longValue( )	Returns the value of the invoking object as a **long**.
static int parseInt(String *str*) throws NumberFormatException	Returns the integer equivalent of the number contained in the string specified by *str* using radix 10.
static int parseInt(String *str*, int *radix*) throws NumberFormatException	Returns the integer equivalent of the number contained in the string specified by *str* using the specified *radix*.
short shortValue( )	Returns the value of the invoking object as a **short**.
static String toBinaryString(int *num*)	Returns a string that contains the binary equivalent of *num*.
static String toHexString(int *num*)	Returns a string that contains the hexadecimal equivalent of *num*.
static String toOctalString(int *num*)	Returns a string that contains the octal equivalent of *num*.
String toString( )	Returns a string that contains the decimal equivalent of the invoking object.
static String toString(int *num*)	Returns a string that contains the decimal equivalent of *num*.

Table 14-5. *The Methods Defined by* Integer (continued)

Method	Description
static String toString(int *num*, int *radix*)	Returns a string that contains the decimal equivalent of *num* using the specified *radix*.
static Integer valueOf(String *str*) throws NumberFormatException	Returns an **Integer** object that contains the value specified by the string in *str*.
static Integer valueOf(String *str*, int *radix*) throws NumberFormatException	Returns an **Integer** object that contains the value specified by the string in *str* using the specified *radix*.

Table 14-5.   *The Methods Defined by* Integer (continued)

Method	Description
byte byteValue( )	Returns the value of the invoking object as a **byte**.
int compareTo(Long *l*)	Compares the numerical value of the invoking object with that of *l*. Returns 0 if the values are equal. Returns a negative value if the invoking object has a lower value. Returns a positive value if the invoking object has a greater value. (Added by Java 2)
int compareTo(Object *obj*)	Operates identically to **compareTo(Long)** if *obj* is of class **Long**. Otherwise, throws a **ClassCastException**. (Added by Java 2)

Table 14-6.   *The Methods Defined by* Long

Method	Description
static Long decode(String *str*) throws NumberFormatException	Returns a **Long** object that contains the value specified by the string in *str*.
double doubleValue( )	Returns the value of the invoking object as a **double**.
boolean equals(Object *LongObj*)	Returns **true** if the invoking **long** object is equivalent to *LongObj*. Otherwise, it returns **false**.
float floatValue( )	Returns the value of the invoking object as a **float**.
static Long getLong(String *propertyName*)	Returns the value associated with the environmental property specified by *propertyName*. A **null** is returned on failure.
static Long getLong(String *propertyName*, long *default*)	Returns the value associated with the environmental property specified by *propertyName*. The value of *default* is returned on failure.
static Long getLong(String *propertyName*, Long *default*)	Returns the value associated with the environmental property specified by *propertyName*. The value of *default* is returned on failure.
int hashCode( )	Returns the hash code for the invoking object.
int intValue( )	Returns the value of the invoking object as an **int**.
long longValue( )	Returns the value of the invoking object as a **long**.

Table 14-6.   *The Methods Defined by* Long *(continued)*

Method	Description
static long parseLong(String *str*) throws NumberFormatException	Returns the **long** equivalent of the number contained in the string specified by *str* in radix 10.
static long parseLong(String *str*, int *radix*) throws NumberFormatException	Returns the **long** equivalent of the number contained in the string specified by *str* using the specified *radix*.
short shortValue( )	Returns the value of the invoking object as a **short**.
static String toBinaryString(long *num*)	Returns a string that contains the binary equivalent of *num*.
static String toHexString(long *num*)	Returns a string that contains the hexadecimal equivalent of *num*.
static String toOctalString(long *num*)	Returns a string that contains the octal equivalent of *num*.
String toString( )	Returns a string that contains the decimal equivalent of the invoking object.
static String toString(long *num*)	Returns a string that contains the decimal equivalent of *num*.
static String toString(long *num*, int *radix*)	Returns a string that contains the decimal equivalent of *num* using the specified *radix*.
static Long valueOf(String *str*) throws NumberFormatException	Returns a **Long** object that contains the value specified by the string in *str*.
static Long valueOf(String *str*, int *radix*) throws NumberFormatException	Returns a **Long** object that contains the value specified by the string in *str* using the specified *radix*.

Table 14-6. *The Methods Defined by* Long (continued)

Converting Numbers to and from Strings

One of the most common programming chores is converting the string representation of a number into its internal, binary format. Fortunately, Java provides an easy way to accomplish this. The **Byte**, **Short**, **Integer**, and **Long** classes provide the **parseByte( )**, **parseShort( )**, **parseInt( )**, and **parseLong( )** methods, respectively. These methods return the **byte**, **short**, **int**, or **long** equivalent of the numeric string with which they are called. (Similar methods also exist for the **Float** and **Double** classes.)

The following program demonstrates **parseInt( )**. It sums a list of integers entered by the user. It reads the integers using **readLine( )** and uses **parseInt( )** to convert these strings into their **int** equivalents.

```java
/* This program sums a list of numbers entered
   by the user.  It converts the string representation
   of each number into an int using parseInt().
*/

import java.io.*;

class ParseDemo {
  public static void main(String args[])
    throws IOException
  {
    // create a BufferedReader using System.in
    BufferedReader br = new
      BufferedReader(new InputStreamReader(System.in));
    String str;
    int i;
    int sum=0;

    System.out.println("Enter numbers, 0 to quit.");
    do {
      str = br.readLine();
      try {
        i = Integer.parseInt(str);
      } catch(NumberFormatException e) {
        System.out.println("Invalid format");
        i = 0;
      }
      sum += i;
      System.out.println("Current sum is: " + sum);
    } while(i != 0);
  }
}
```

To convert a whole number into a decimal string, use the versions of **toString( )** defined in the **Byte**, **Short**, **Integer**, or **Long** classes. The **Integer** and **Long** classes also provide the methods **toBinaryString( )**, **toHexString( )**, and **toOctalString( )**, which convert a value into a binary, hexadecimal, or octal string, respectively.

The following program demonstrates binary, hexadecimal, and octal conversion:

```
/* Convert an integer into binary, hexadecimal,
   and octal.
*/

class StringConversions {
  public static void main(String args[]) {
    int num = 19648;

    System.out.println(num + " in binary: " +
                       Integer.toBinaryString(num));

    System.out.println(num + " in octal: " +
                       Integer.toOctalString(num));

    System.out.println(num + " in hexadecimal: " +
                       Integer.toHexString(num));

  }
}
```

The output of this program is shown here:

```
19648 in binary: 100110011000000
19648 in octal: 46300
19648 in hexadecimal: 4cc0
```

Character

Character is a simple wrapper around a **char**. The constructor for **Character** is

Character(char *ch*)

Here, *ch* specifies the character that will be wrapped by the **Character** object being created.

To obtain the **char** value contained in a **Character** object, call **charValue( )**, shown here:

char charValue( )

It returns the character.

The **Character** class defines several constants, including the following:

MAX_RADIX	The largest radix
MIN_RADIX	The smallest radix
MAX_VALUE	The largest character value
MIN_VALUE	The smallest character value
TYPE	The **Class** object for **char**

Character includes several static methods that categorize characters and alter their case. They are shown in Table 14-7. The following example demonstrates several of these methods.

```
// Demonstrate several Is... methods.

class IsDemo {
  public static void main(String args[]) {
    char a[] = {'a', 'b', '5', '?', 'A', ' '};

    for(int i=0; i<a.length; i++) {
      if(Character.isDigit(a[i]))
        System.out.println(a[i] + " is a digit.");
      if(Character.isLetter(a[i]))
        System.out.println(a[i] + " is a letter.");
      if(Character.isWhitespace(a[i]))
        System.out.println(a[i] + " is whitespace.");
      if(Character.isUpperCase(a[i]))
        System.out.println(a[i] + " is uppercase.");
      if(Character.isLowerCase(a[i]))
        System.out.println(a[i] + " is lowercase.");
    }
  }
}
```

The output from this program is shown here:

```
a is a letter.
a is lowercase.
b is a letter.
b is lowercase.
5 is a digit.
A is a letter.
A is uppercase.
  is whitespace.
```

Method	Description
static boolean isDefined(char *ch*)	Returns **true** if *ch* is defined by Unicode. Otherwise, it returns **false**.
static boolean isDigit(char *ch*)	Returns **true** if *ch* is a digit. Otherwise, it returns **false**.
static boolean isIdentifierIgnorable(char *ch*)	Returns **true** if *ch* should be ignored in an identifier. Otherwise, it returns **false**.
static boolean isISOControl(char *ch*)	Returns **true** if *ch* is an ISO control character. Otherwise, it returns **false**.
static boolean isJavaIdentifierPart(char *ch*)	Returns **true** if *ch* is allowed as part of a Java identifier (other than the first character). Otherwise, it returns **false**.
static boolean isJavaIdentifierStart(char *ch*)	Returns **true** if *ch* is allowed as the first character of a Java identifier. Otherwise, it returns **false**.
static boolean isLetter(char *ch*)	Returns **true** if *ch* is a letter. Otherwise, it returns **false**.
static boolean isLetterOrDigit(char *ch*)	Returns **true** if *ch* is a letter or a digit. Otherwise, it returns **false**.
static boolean isLowerCase(char *ch*)	Returns **true** if *ch* is a lowercase letter. Otherwise, it returns **false**.
static boolean isMirrored(char *ch*)	Returns **true** if *ch* is a mirrored Unicode character. A mirrored character is one that is reversed for text that is displayed right-to-left. (Added by Java 2, version 1.4)
static boolean isSpaceChar(char *ch*)	Returns **true** if *ch* is a Unicode space character. Otherwise, it returns **false**.

Table 14-7. *Various* Character *Methods*

Method	Description
static boolean isTitleCase(char *ch*)	Returns **true** if *ch* is a Unicode titlecase character. Otherwise, it returns **false**.
static boolean isUnicodeIdentifierPart(char *ch*)	Returns **true** if *ch* is allowed as part of a Unicode identifier (other than the first character). Otherwise, it returns **false**.
static boolean isUnicodeIdentifierStart(char *ch*)	Returns **true** if *ch* is allowed as the first character of a Unicode identifier. Otherwise, it returns **false**.
static boolean isUpperCase(char *ch*)	Returns **true** if *ch* is an uppercase letter. Otherwise, it returns **false**.
static boolean isWhitespace(char *ch*)	Returns **true** if *ch* is whitespace. Otherwise, it returns **false**.
static char toLowerCase(char *ch*)	Returns lowercase equivalent of *ch*.
static char toTitleCase(char *ch*)	Returns titlecase equivalent of *ch*.
static char toUpperCase(char *ch*)	Returns uppercase equivalent of *ch*.

Table 14-7.   *Various* Character *Methods* (continued)

Character defines the **forDigit( )** and **digit( )** methods, shown here:

static char forDigit(int *num,* int *radix*)
static int digit(char *digit*, int *radix*)

forDigit( ) returns the digit character associated with the value of *num.* The radix of the conversion is specified by *radix*. **digit( )** returns the integer value associated with the specified character (which is presumably a digit) according to the specified radix.

Another method defined by **Character** is **compareTo( )**, which has the following two forms:

int compareTo(Character *c*)
int compareTo(Object *obj*)

The first form returns 0 if the invoking object and *c* have the same value. It returns a negative value if the invoking object has a lower value. Otherwise, it returns a positive value. The second form works just like the first if *obj* is a reference to a **Character**. Otherwise, a **ClassCastException** is thrown. These methods were added by Java 2.

Java 2, version 1.4 adds a method called **getDirectionality( )** which can be used to determine the direction of a character. Several new constants have been added which describe directionality. Most programs will not need to use character directionality.

Character also defines the **equals( )** and **hashCode( )** methods.

Two other character-related classes are **Character.Subset**, used to describe a subset of Unicode, and **Character.UnicodeBlock**, which contains Unicode character blocks.

Boolean

Boolean is a very thin wrapper around **boolean** values, which is useful mostly when you want to pass a **boolean** variable by reference. It contains the constants **TRUE** and **FALSE**, which define true and false **Boolean** objects. **Boolean** also defines the **TYPE** field, which is the **Class** object for **boolean**. **Boolean** defines these constructors:

    Boolean(boolean boolValue)
    Boolean(String boolString)

In the first version, boolValue must be either **true** or **false**. In the second version, if boolString contains the string "true" (in uppercase or lowercase), then the new **Boolean** object will be true. Otherwise, it will be false.

Boolean defines the methods shown in Table 14-8.

Method	Description
boolean booleanValue( )	Returns **boolean** equivalent.
boolean equals(Object boolObj)	Returns **true** if the invoking object is equivalent to boolObj. Otherwise, it returns **false**.
static boolean getBoolean(String propertyName)	Returns **true** if the system property specified by propertyName is **true**. Otherwise, it returns **false**.
int hashCode( )	Returns the hash code for the invoking object.
String toString( )	Returns the string equivalent of the invoking object.
static String toString(boolean boolVal)	Returns the string equivalent of boolVal. (Added by Java 2, version 1.4)
static Boolean valueOf(boolean boolVal)	Returns the **Boolean** equivalent of boolVal. (Added by Java 2, version 1.4)
static Boolean valueOf(String boolString)	Returns **true** if boolString contains the string "true" (in uppercase or lowercase). Otherwise, it returns **false**.

Table 14-8. *The Methods Defined by* Boolean

Void

The **Void** class has one field, **TYPE**, which holds a reference to the **Class** object for type **void**. You do not create instances of this class.

Process

The abstract **Process** class encapsulates a *process*—that is, an executing program. It is used primarily as a superclass for the type of objects created by **exec( )** in the **Runtime** class described in the next section. **Process** contains the abstract methods shown in Table 14-9.

Method	Description
void destroy( )	Terminates the process.
int exitValue( )	Returns an exit code obtained from a subprocess.
InputStream getErrorStream( )	Returns an input stream that reads input from the process' **err** output stream.
InputStream getInputStream( )	Returns an input stream that reads input from the process' **out** output stream.
OutputStream getOutputStream( )	Returns an output stream that writes output to the process' **in** input stream.
int waitFor( ) throws InterruptedException	Returns the exit code returned by the process. This method does not return until the process on which it is called terminates.

Table 14-9. *The Abstract Methods Defined by* Process

Runtime

The **Runtime** class encapsulates the run-time environment. You cannot instantiate a **Runtime** object. However, you can get a reference to the current **Runtime** object by calling the static method **Runtime.getRuntime( )**. Once you obtain a reference to the current **Runtime** object, you can call several methods that control the state and behavior of the Java Virtual Machine. Applets and other untrusted code typically cannot call any of the **Runtime** methods without raising a **SecurityException**.

The methods defined by **Runtime** are shown in Table 14-10. Java 2 deprecates the method **runFinalizersOnExit( )**. This method was added by Java 1.1 but was deemed unstable.

Method	Description
void addShutdownHook(Thread *thrd*)	Registers *thrd* as a thread to be run when the Java virtual machine terminates. (Added by Java 2, version 1.3)
Process exec(String *progName*) throws IOException	Executes the program specified by *progName* as a separate process. An object of type **Process** is returned that describes the new process.
Process exec(String *progName*, String *environment*[ ]) throws IOException	Executes the program specified by *progName* as a separate process with the environment specified by *environment*. An object of type **Process** is returned that describes the new process.
Process exec(String *comLineArray*[ ]) throws IOException	Executes the command line specified by the strings in *comLineArray* as a separate process. An object of type **Process** is returned that describes the new process.
Process exec(String *comLineArray*[ ], String *environment*[ ]) throws IOException	Executes the command line specified by the strings in *comLineArray* as a separate process with the environment specified by *environment*. An object of type **Process** is returned that describes the new process.

Table 14-10.   *The Commonly Used Methods Defined by* Runtime

Method	Description
void exit(int *exitCode*)	Halts execution and returns the value of *exitCode* to the parent process. By convention, 0 indicates normal termination. All other values indicate some form of error.
long freeMemory( )	Returns the approximate number of bytes of free memory available to the Java run-time system.
void gc( )	Initiates garbage collection.
static Runtime getRuntime( )	Returns the current **Runtime** object.
void halt(int *code*)	Immediately terminates the Java virtual machine. No termination threads or finalizers are run. The value of *code* is returned to the invoking process. (Added by Java 2, version 1.3)
void load(String *libraryFileName)*	Loads the dynamic library whose file is specified by *libraryFileName*, which must specify its complete path.
void loadLibrary(String *libraryName)*	Loads the dynamic library whose name is associated with *libraryName*.
boolean removeShutdownHook(Thread *thrd*)	Removes *thrd* from the list of threads to run when the Java virtual machine terminates. It returns **true** if successful—that is, if the thread was removed. (Added by Java 2, verison 1.3)
void runFinalization( )	Initiates calls to the **finalize( )** methods of unused but not yet recycled objects.
long totalMemory( )	Returns the total number of bytes of memory available to the program.
void traceInstructions(boolean *traceOn*)	Turns on or off instruction tracing, depending upon the value of *traceOn*. If *traceOn* is **true**, the trace is displayed. If it is **false**, tracing is turned off.
void traceMethodCalls(boolean *traceOn*)	Turns on or off method call tracing, depending upon the value of *traceOn*. If *traceOn* is **true**, the trace is displayed. If it is **false**, tracing is turned off.

Table 14-10. *The Commonly Used Methods Defined by* Runtime (continued)

Let's look at two of the most common uses of the **Runtime** class: memory management and executing additional processes.

Memory Management

Although Java provides automatic garbage collection, sometimes you will want to know how large the object heap is and how much of it is left. You can use this information, for example, to check your code for efficiency or to approximate how many more objects of a certain type can be instantiated. To obtain these values, use the **totalMemory( )** and **freeMemory( )** methods.

As we mentioned in Part I, Java's garbage collector runs periodically to recycle unused objects. However, sometimes you will want to collect discarded objects prior to the collector's next appointed rounds. You can run the garbage collector on demand by calling the **gc( )** method. A good thing to try is to call **gc( )** and then call **freeMemory( )** to get a baseline memory usage. Next, execute your code and call **freeMemory( )** again to see how much memory it is allocating. The following program illustrates this idea:

```java
// Demonstrate totalMemory(), freeMemory() and gc().

class MemoryDemo {
  public static void main(String args[]) {
    Runtime r = Runtime.getRuntime();
    long mem1, mem2;
    Integer someints[] = new Integer[1000];

    System.out.println("Total memory is: " +
                      r.totalMemory());

    mem1 = r.freeMemory();
    System.out.println("Initial free memory: " + mem1);
    r.gc();
    mem1 = r.freeMemory();
    System.out.println("Free memory after garbage collection: "
                      + mem1);

    for(int i=0; i<1000; i++)
      someints[i] = new Integer(i); // allocate integers

    mem2 = r.freeMemory();
    System.out.println("Free memory after allocation: "
                      + mem2);
```

```
       System.out.println("Memory used by allocation: "
                          + (mem1-mem2));

       // discard Integers
       for(int i=0; i<1000; i++) someints[i] = null;

       r.gc(); // request garbage collection

       mem2 = r.freeMemory();
       System.out.println("Free memory after collecting" +
                          " discarded Integers: " + mem2);

    }
  }
```

Sample output from this program is shown here (of course, your actual results may vary):

```
Total memory is: 1048568
Initial free memory: 751392
Free memory after garbage collection: 841424
Free memory after allocation: 824000
Memory used by allocation: 17424
Free memory after collecting discarded Integers: 842640
```

Executing Other Programs

In safe environments, you can use Java to execute other heavyweight processes (that is, programs) on your multitasking operating system. Several forms of the **exec( )** method allow you to name the program you want to run as well as its input parameters. The **exec( )** method returns a **Process** object, which can then be used to control how your Java program interacts with this new running process. Because Java can run on a variety of platforms and under a variety of operating systems, **exec( )** is inherently environment-dependent.

The following example uses **exec( )** to launch **notepad**, Windows' simple text editor. Obviously, this example must be run under the Windows operating system.

```
// Demonstrate exec().
class ExecDemo {
  public static void main(String args[]) {
    Runtime r = Runtime.getRuntime();
    Process p = null;
```

```
    try {
      p = r.exec("notepad");
    } catch (Exception e) {
      System.out.println("Error executing notepad.");
    }
  }
}
```

There are several alternate forms of **exec( )**, but the one shown in the example is the most common. The **Process** object returned by **exec( )** can be manipulated by **Process'** methods after the new program starts running. You can kill the subprocess with the **destroy( )** method. The **waitFor( )** method causes your program to wait until the subprocess finishes. The **exitValue( )** method returns the value returned by the subprocess when it is finished. This is typically 0 if no problems occur. Here is the preceding **exec( )** example modified to wait for the running process to exit:

```
// Wait until notepad is terminated.
class ExecDemoFini {
  public static void main(String args[]) {
    Runtime r = Runtime.getRuntime();
    Process p = null;

    try {
      p = r.exec("notepad");
      p.waitFor();
    } catch (Exception e) {
      System.out.println("Error executing notepad.");
    }
    System.out.println("Notepad returned " + p.exitValue());
  }
}
```

While a subprocess is running, you can write to and read from its standard input and output. The **getOutputStream( )** and **getInputStream( )** methods return the handles to standard **in** and **out** of the subprocess. (I/O is examined in detail in Chapter 17.)

System

The **System** class holds a collection of static methods and variables. The standard input, output, and error output of the Java run time are stored in the **in**, **out**, and **err** variables. The methods defined by **System** are shown in Table 14-11. Many of the methods throw a

SecurityException if the operation is not permitted by the security manager. One other point: Java 2 deprecated the method **runFinalizersOnExit( )**. This method was added by Java 1.1, but was determined to be unstable.

Let's look at some common uses of **System**.

Method	Description

static void arraycopy(Object *source*,
        int *sourceStart*,
        Object *target*,
        int *targetStart*,
        int *size*)
	Copies an array. The array to be copied is passed in *source*, and the index at which point the copy will begin within *source* is passed in *sourceStart*. The array that will receive the copy is passed in *target*, and the index at which point the copy will begin within *target* is passed in *targetStart*. *size* is the number of elements that are copied.

static long currentTimeMillis( )	Returns the current time in terms of milliseconds since midnight, January 1, 1970.
static void exit(int *exitCode*)	Halts execution and returns the value of *exitCode* to the parent process (usually the operating system). By convention, 0 indicates normal termination. All other values indicate some form of error.
static void gc( )	Initiates garbage collection.
static Properties getProperties( )	Returns the properties associated with the Java run-time system. (The **Properties** class is described in Chapter 15.)

Table 14-11. *The Methods Defined by* System

Method	Description
static String getProperty(String *which*)	Returns the property associated with *which*. A **null** object is returned if the desired property is not found.
static String getProperty(String *which*, String *default*)	Returns the property associated with *which*. If the desired property is not found, *default* is returned.
static SecurityManager getSecurityManager( )	Returns the current security manager or a **null** object if no security manager is installed.
static int identityHashCode(Object *obj*)	Returns the identity hash code for *obj*.
static void load(String *libraryFileName*)	Loads the dynamic library whose file is specified by *libraryFileName*, which must specify its complete path.
static void loadLibrary(String *libraryName*)	Loads the dynamic library whose name is associated with *libraryName*.
static String mapLibraryName(String *lib*)	Returns a platform-specific name for the library named *lib*. (Added by Java 2)
static void runFinalization( )	Initiates calls to the **finalize( )** methods of unused but not yet recycled objects.
static void setErr(PrintStream *eStream*)	Sets the standard **err** stream to *eStream*.
static void setIn(InputStream *iStream*)	Sets the standard **in** stream to *iStream*.
static void setOut(PrintStream *oStream*)	Sets the standard **out** stream to *oStream*.

Table 14-11. *The Methods Defined by* System (continued)

Method	Description
static void setProperties(Properties *sysProperties*)	Sets the current system properties as specified by *sysProperties*.
static String setProperty(String *which*, String *v*)	Assigns the value *v* to the property named *which*. (Added by Java 2)
static void setSecurityManager(SecurityManager *secMan*)	Sets the security manager to that specified by *secMan*.

Table 14-11. *The Methods Defined by* System (continued)

Using currentTimeMillis( ) to Time Program Execution

One use of the **System** class that you might find particularly interesting is to use the **currentTimeMillis( )** method to time how long various parts of your program take to execute. The **currentTimeMillis( )** method returns the current time in terms of milliseconds since midnight, January 1, 1970. To time a section of your program, store this value just before beginning the section in question. Immediately upon completion, call **currentTimeMillis( )** again. The elapsed time will be the ending time minus the starting time. The following program demonstrates this:

```java
// Timing program execution.

class Elapsed {
  public static void main(String args[]) {
    long start, end;

    System.out.println("Timing a for loop from 0 to 1,000,000");

    // time a for loop from 0 to 1,000,000
    start = System.currentTimeMillis(); // get starting time
    for(int i=0; i < 1000000; i++) ;
    end = System.currentTimeMillis(); // get ending time

    System.out.println("Elapsed time: " + (end-start));
  }
}
```

Here is a sample run (remember that your results probably will differ):

```
Timing a for loop from 0 to 1,000,000
Elapsed time: 10
```

Using arraycopy( )

The **arraycopy( )** method can be used to copy quickly an array of any type from one place to another. This is much faster than the equivalent loop written out longhand in Java. Here is an example of two arrays being copied by the **arraycopy( )** method. First, **a** is copied to **b**. Next, all of **a**'s elements are shifted *down* by one. Then, **b** is shifted *up* by one.

```java
// Using arraycopy().

class ACDemo {
  static byte a[] = { 65, 66, 67, 68, 69, 70, 71, 72, 73, 74 };
  static byte b[] = { 77, 77, 77, 77, 77, 77, 77, 77, 77, 77 };

  public static void main(String args[]) {
    System.out.println("a = " + new String(a));
    System.out.println("b = " + new String(b));
    System.arraycopy(a, 0, b, 0, a.length);
    System.out.println("a = " + new String(a));
    System.out.println("b = " + new String(b));
    System.arraycopy(a, 0, a, 1, a.length - 1);
    System.arraycopy(b, 1, b, 0, b.length - 1);
    System.out.println("a = " + new String(a));
    System.out.println("b = " + new String(b));
  }
}
```

As you can see from the following output, you can copy using the same source and destination in either direction:

```
a = ABCDEFGHIJ
b = MMMMMMMMMM
a = ABCDEFGHIJ
b = ABCDEFGHIJ
a = AABCDEFGHI
b = BCDEFGHIJJ
```

Environment Properties

The following properties are available in Java 2, version 1.4:

file.separator	java.specification.version	java.vm.version
java.class.path	java.vendor	line.separator
java.class.version	java.vendor.url	os.arch
java.compiler	java.version	os.name
java.ext.dirs	java.vm.name	os.version
java.home	java.vm.specification.name	path.separator
java.io.tmpdir	java.vm.specification.vendor	user.dir
java.library.path	java.vm.specification.version	user.home
java.specification.name	java.vm.vendor	user.name
java.specification.vendor		

You can obtain the values of various environment variables by calling the
System.getProperty( ) method. For example, the following program displays the path
to the current user directory:

```
class ShowUserDir {
  public static void main(String args[]) {
    System.out.println(System.getProperty("user.dir"));
  }
}
```

Object

As we mentioned in Part I, **Object** is a superclass of all other classes. **Object** defines the
methods shown in Table 14-12, which are available to every object.

Using clone( ) and the Cloneable Interface

Most of the methods defined by **Object** are discussed elsewhere in this book. However,
one deserves special attention: **clone( )**. The **clone( )** method generates a duplicate copy
of the object on which it is called. Only classes that implement the **Cloneable** interface
can be cloned.

The **Cloneable** interface defines no members. It is used to indicate that a class
allows a bitwise copy of an object (that is, a *clone*) to be made. If you try to call **clone( )**
on a class that does not implement **Cloneable**, a **CloneNotSupportedException** is

Method	Description
Object clone( ) throws CloneNotSupportedException	Creates a new object that is the same as the invoking object.
boolean equals(Object *object*)	Returns **true** if the invoking object is equivalent to *object*.
void finalize( ) throws Throwable	Default **finalize( )** method. This is usually overridden by subclasses.
final Class getClass( )	Obtains a **Class** object that describes the invoking object.
int hashCode( )	Returns the hash code associated with the invoking object.
final void notify( )	Resumes execution of a thread waiting on the invoking object.
final void notifyAll( )	Resumes execution of all threads waiting on the invoking object.
String toString( )	Returns a string that describes the object.
final void wait( ) throws InterruptedException	Waits on another thread of execution.
final void wait(long *milliseconds*) throws InterruptedException	Waits up to the specified number of *milliseconds* on another thread of execution.
final void wait(long *milliseconds*, int *nanoseconds*) throws InterruptedException	Waits up to the specified number of *milliseconds* plus *nanoseconds* on another thread of execution.

Table 14-12. *The Methods Defined by* Object

thrown. When a clone is made, the constructor for the object being cloned is *not* called. A clone is simply an exact copy of the original.

Cloning is a potentially dangerous action, because it can cause unintended side effects. For example, if the object being cloned contains a reference variable called *obRef*, then when the clone is made, *obRef* in the clone will refer to the same object as does *obRef* in the original. If the clone makes a change to the contents of the object referred to by *obRef*, then it will be changed for the original object, too. Here is another example. If an object opens an I/O stream and is then cloned, two objects will be capable of operating on the same stream. Further, if one of these objects closes the stream, the other object might still attempt to write to it, causing an error.

Because cloning can cause problems, **clone( )** is declared as **protected** inside **Object**. This means that it must either be called from within a method defined by the class that implements **Cloneable**, or it must be explicitly overridden by that class so that it is public. Let's look at an example of each approach.

The following program implements **Cloneable** and defines the method **cloneTest( )**, which calls **clone( )** in **Object**:

```
// Demonstrate the clone() method.

class TestClone implements Cloneable {
  int a;
  double b;

  // This method calls Object's clone().
  TestClone cloneTest() {
    try {
      // call clone in Object.
      return (TestClone) super.clone();
    } catch(CloneNotSupportedException e) {
      System.out.println("Cloning not allowed.");
      return this;
    }
  }
}

class CloneDemo {
  public static void main(String args[]) {
    TestClone x1 = new TestClone();
    TestClone x2;

    x1.a = 10;
    x1.b = 20.98;

    x2 = x1.cloneTest(); // clone x1

    System.out.println("x1: " + x1.a + " " + x1.b);
    System.out.println("x2: " + x2.a + " " + x2.b);
  }
}
```

Here, the method **cloneTest( )** calls **clone( )** in **Object** and returns the result. Notice that the object returned by **clone( )** must be cast into its appropriate type (**TestClone**).

The following example overrides **clone( )** so that it can be called from code outside of its class. To do this, its access specifier must be **public**, as shown here:

```
// Override the clone() method.

class TestClone implements Cloneable {
  int a;
  double b;

  // clone() is now overridden and is public.
  public Object clone() {
    try {
      // call clone in Object.
      return super.clone();
    } catch(CloneNotSupportedException e) {
      System.out.println("Cloning not allowed.");
      return this;
    }
  }
}

class CloneDemo2 {
  public static void main(String args[]) {
    TestClone x1 = new TestClone();
    TestClone x2;

    x1.a = 10;
    x1.b = 20.98;

    // here, clone() is called directly.
    x2 = (TestClone) x1.clone();

    System.out.println("x1: " + x1.a + " " + x1.b);
    System.out.println("x2: " + x2.a + " " + x2.b);
  }
}
```

The side effects caused by cloning are sometimes difficult to see at first. It is easy to think that a class is safe for cloning when it actually is not. In general, you should not implement **Cloneable** for any class without good reason.

THE JAVA LIBRARY

Class

Class encapsulates the run-time state of an object or interface. Objects of type **Class** are created automatically, when classes are loaded. You cannot explicitly declare a **Class** object. Generally, you obtain a **Class** object by calling the **getClass( )** method defined by **Object**. Some of the most commonly used methods defined by **Class** are shown in Table 14-13.

Method	Description
static Class forName(String *name*) throws ClassNotFoundException	Returns a **Class** object given its complete name.

static Class forName(String *name*,
               boolean *how*,
               ClassLoader *ldr*)
    throws ClassNotFoundException
	Returns a **Class** object given its complete name. The object is loaded using the loader specified by *ldr*. If *how* is **true**, the object is initialized; otherwise it is not. (Added by Java 2)

Class[ ] getClasses( )	Returns a **Class** object for each of the public classes and interfaces that are members of the invoking object.
ClassLoader getClassLoader( )	Returns the **ClassLoader** object that loaded the class or interface used to instantiate the invoking object.
Constructor[ ] getConstructors( ) throws SecurityException	Returns a **Constructor** object for all the public constructors of this class.
Constructor[ ] getDeclaredConstructors( ) throws SecurityException	Returns a **Constructor** object for all the constructors that are declared by this class.
Field[ ] getDeclaredFields( ) throws SecurityException	Returns a **Field** object for all the fields that are declared by this class.
Method[ ] getDeclaredMethods( ) throws SecurityException	Returns a **Method** object for all the methods that are declared by this class or interface.

Table 14-13. *Some Methods Defined by* Class

Method	Description
Field[ ] getFields( ) throws SecurityException	Returns a **Field** object for all the public fields of this class.
Class[ ] getInterfaces( )	When invoked on an object, this method returns an array of the interfaces implemented by the class type of the object. When invoked on an interface, this method returns an array of interfaces extended by the interface.
Method[ ] getMethods( ) throws SecurityException	Returns a **Method** object for all the public methods of this class.
String getName( )	Returns the complete name of the class or interface of the invoking object.
ProtectionDomain getProtectionDomain( )	Returns the protection domain associated with the invoking object. (Added by Java 2)
Class getSuperclass( )	Returns the superclass of the invoking object. The return value is **null** if the invoking object is of type **Object**.
boolean isInterface( )	Returns **true** if the invoking object is an interface. Otherwise, it returns **false**.
Object newInstance( ) throws IllegalAccessException, InstantiationException	Creates a new instance (i.e., a new object) that is of the same type as the invoking object. This is equivalent to using **new** with the class' default constructor. The new object is returned.
String toString( )	Returns the string representation of the invoking object or interface.

Table 14-13.   *Some Methods Defined by* Class (continued)

The methods defined by **Class** are often useful in situations where run-time type information about an object is required. As Table 14-13 shows, methods are provided that allow you to determine additional information about a particular class, such as its public constructors, fields, and methods. This is important for the Java Beans functionality, which is discussed later in this book.

The following program demonstrates **getClass( )** (inherited from **Object**) and **getSuperclass( )** (from **Class**):

```
// Demonstrate Run-Time Type Information.

class X {
  int a;
  float b;
}

class Y extends X {
  double c;
}

class RTTI {
  public static void main(String args[]) {
    X x = new X();
    Y y = new Y();
    Class clObj;

    clObj = x.getClass(); // get Class reference
    System.out.println("x is object of type: " +
                  clObj.getName());

    clObj = y.getClass(); // get Class reference
    System.out.println("y is object of type: " +
                  clObj.getName());
    clObj = clObj.getSuperclass();
    System.out.println("y's superclass is " +
                  clObj.getName());
  }
}
```

The output from this program is shown here:

```
x is object of type: X
y is object of type: Y
y's superclass is X
```

ClassLoader

The abstract class **ClassLoader** defines how classes are loaded. Your application can create subclasses that extend **ClassLoader**, implementing its methods. Doing so allows you to load classes in some way other than the way they are normally loaded by the Java run-time system. Some of the methods defined by **ClassLoader** are shown in Table 14-14.

Method	Description

final Class defineClass(String *str*, byte *b*[ ],
                 int *index*,
                 int *numBytes*)
   throws ClassFormatError
	Returns a **Class** object. The name of the class is in *str* and the object is contained in the array of bytes specified by *b*. The object begins within this array at the index specified by *index* and is *numBytes* long. The data in *b* must represent a valid object.

final Class findSystemClass(String *name*) throws ClassNotFoundException	Returns a **Class** object given its name.

Class loadClass(String *name*,
          boolean *callResolveClass*)
   throws ClassNotFoundException
	An implementation of this abstract method must load a class given its name and call **resolveClass( )** if *callResolveClass* is **true**.

final void resolveClass(Class *obj*)	The class referred to by *obj* is resolved (i.e., its name is entered into the class name space).

Table 14-14.   *Some of the Methods Defined by* ClassLoader

Math

The **Math** class contains all the floating-point functions that are used for geometry and trigonometry, as well as several general-purpose methods. **Math** defines two **double** constants: **E** (approximately 2.72) and **PI** (approximately 3.14).

Transcendental Functions

The following three methods accept a **double** parameter for an angle in radians and return the result of their respective transcendental function:

Method	Description
static double sin(double *arg*)	Returns the sine of the angle specified by *arg* in radians.
static double cos(double *arg*)	Returns the cosine of the angle specified by *arg* in radians.
static double tan(double *arg*)	Returns the tangent of the angle specified by *arg* in radians.

The next methods take as a parameter the result of a transcendental function and return, in radians, the angle that would produce that result. They are the inverse of their non-arc companions.

Method	Description
static double asin(double *arg*)	Returns the angle whose sine is specified by *arg*.
static double acos(double *arg*)	Returns the angle whose cosine is specified by *arg*.
static double atan(double *arg*)	Returns the angle whose tangent is specified by *arg*.
static double atan2(double *x*, double *y*)	Returns the angle whose tangent is *x/y*.

Exponential Functions

Math defines the following exponential methods:

Method	Description
static double exp(double *arg*)	Returns e to the *arg*.
static double log(double *arg*)	Returns the natural logarithm of *arg*.

Method	Description
static double pow(double *y*, double *x*)	Returns *y* raised to the *x*; for example, pow(2.0, 3.0) returns 8.0.
static double sqrt(double *arg*)	Returns the square root of *arg*.

Rounding Functions

The **Math** class defines several methods that provide various types of rounding operations. They are shown in Table 14-15.

Method	Description
static int abs(int *arg*)	Returns the absolute value of *arg*.
static long abs(long *arg*)	Returns the absolute value of *arg*.
static float abs(float *arg*)	Returns the absolute value of *arg*.
static double abs(double *arg*)	Returns the absolute value of *arg*.
static double ceil(double *arg*)	Returns the smallest whole number greater than or equal to *arg*.
static double floor(double *arg*)	Returns the largest whole number less than or equal to *arg*.
static int max(int *x*, int *y*)	Returns the maximum of *x* and *y*.
static long max(long *x*, long *y*)	Returns the maximum of *x* and *y*.
static float max(float *x*, float *y*)	Returns the maximum of *x* and *y*.
static double max(double *x*, double *y*)	Returns the maximum of *x* and *y*.
static int min(int *x*, int *y*)	Returns the minimum of *x* and *y*
static long min(long *x*, long *y*)	Returns the minimum of *x* and *y*.
static float min(float *x*, float *y*)	Returns the minimum of *x* and *y*.
static double min(double *x*, double *y*)	Returns the minimum of *x* and *y*.
static double rint(double *arg*)	Returns the integer nearest in value to *arg*.
static int round(float *arg*)	Returns *arg* rounded up to the nearest **int**.
static long round(double *arg*)	Returns *arg* rounded up to the nearest **long**.

Table 14-15. *The Rounding Methods Defined by* Math

THE JAVA LIBRARY

Miscellaneous Math Methods

In addition to the methods just shown, **Math** defines the following methods:

static double IEEEremainder(double *dividend*, double *divisor*)
static double random( )
static double toRadians(double *angle*)
static double toDegrees(double angle)

IEEEremainder( ) returns the remainder of *dividend* / *divisor*. **random( )** returns a pseudorandom number. This value will be between 0 and 1. Most of the time, you will use the **Random** class when you need to generate random numbers. The **toRadians( )** method converts degrees to radians. **toDegrees( )** converts radians to degrees. The last two methods were added by Java 2.

Here is a program that demonstrates **toRadians( )** and **toDegrees( )**:

```
// Demonstrate toDegrees() and toRadians().
class Angles {
  public static void main(String args[]) {
    double theta = 120.0;

    System.out.println(theta + " degrees is " +
                      Math.toRadians(theta) + " radians.");

    theta = 1.312;
    System.out.println(theta + " radians is " +
                      Math.toDegrees(theta) + " degrees.");
  }
}
```

The output is shown here.

```
120.0 degrees is 2.0943951023931953 radians.
1.312 radians is 75.17206272116401 degrees.
```

StrictMath

Java 2, version 1.3 added the **StrictMath** class. This class defines a complete set of mathematical methods that parallel those in **Math**. The difference is that the **StrictMath** version is guaranteed to generate precisely identical results across all Java implementations whereas the methods in **Math** are given more latitude in order to improve performance.

Compiler

The **Compiler** class supports the creation of Java environments in which Java bytecode is compiled into executable code rather than interpreted. It is not for normal programming use.

Thread, ThreadGroup, and Runnable

The **Runnable** interface and the **Thread** and **ThreadGroup** classes support multithreaded programming. Each is examined next.

 *An overview of the techniques used to manage threads, implement the **Runnable** interface, and create multithreaded programs is presented in Chapter 11.*

The Runnable Interface

The **Runnable** interface must be implemented by any class that will initiate a separate thread of execution. **Runnable** only defines one abstract method, called **run( )**, which is the entry point to the thread. It is defined like this:

    abstract void run( )

Threads that you create must implement this method.

Thread

Thread creates a new thread of execution. It defines the following commonly used constructors:

    Thread( )
    Thread(Runnable threadOb)
    Thread(Runnable threadOb, StringthreadName)
    Thread(String threadName)
    Thread(ThreadGroup groupOb, Runnable threadOb)
    Thread(ThreadGroup groupOb, Runnable threadOb, String threadName)
    Thread(ThreadGroup groupOb, String threadName)

threadOb is an instance of a class that implements the **Runnable** interface and defines where execution of the thread will begin. The name of the thread is specified by *threadName*. When a name is not specified, one is created by the Java Virtual Machine. *groupOb* specifies the thread group to which the new thread will belong. When no thread group is specified, the new thread belongs to the same group as the parent thread.

The following constants are defined by **Thread**:

    MAX_PRIORITY
    MIN_PRIORITY
    NORM_PRIORITY

As expected, these constants specify the maximum, minimum, and default thread priorities.

The methods defined by **Thread** are shown in Table 14-16. In versions of Java prior to 2, **Thread** also included the methods **stop( )**, **suspend( )**, and **resume( )**. However, as explained in Chapter 11, these have been deprecated by Java 2 because they were inherently unstable. Also deprecated by Java 2 is **countStackFrames( )**, because it calls **suspend( )**.

Method	Description
static int activeCount( )	Returns the number of threads in the group to which the thread belongs.
void checkAccess( )	Causes the security manager to verify that the current thread can access and/or change the thread on which **checkAccess( )** is called.
static Thread currentThread( )	Returns a **Thread** object that encapsulates the thread that calls this method.
void destroy( )	Terminates the thread.
static void dumpStack( )	Displays the call stack for the thread.
static int enumerate(Thread *threads*[ ])	Puts copies of all **Thread** objects in the current thread's group into *threads*. The number of threads is returned.
ClassLoader getContextClassLoader( )	Returns the class loader that is used to load classes and resources for this thread. (Added by Java 2)
final String getName( )	Returns the thread's name.
final int getPriority( )	Returns the thread's priority setting.
final ThreadGroup getThreadGroup( )	Returns the **ThreadGroup** object of which the invoking thread is a member.
static boolean holdsLock(Object *ob*)	Returns **true** if the invoking thread owns the lock on *ob*. Returns **false** otherwise. (Added by Java 2, version 1.4)

Table 14-16. *The Methods Defined by* Thread

Method	Description
void interrupt( )	Interrupts the thread.
static boolean interrupted( )	Returns **true** if the currently executing thread has been scheduled for interruption. Otherwise, it returns **false**.
final boolean isAlive( )	Returns **true** if the thread is still active. Otherwise, it returns **false**.
final boolean isDaemon( )	Returns **true** if the thread is a daemon thread (one that is part of the Java run-time system). Otherwise, it returns **false**.
boolean isInterrupted( )	Returns **true** if the thread is interrupted. Otherwise, it returns **false**.
final void join( ) throws InterruptedException	Waits until the thread terminates.
final void join(long *milliseconds*) throws InterruptedException	Waits up to the specified number of milliseconds for the thread on which it is called to terminate.
final void join(long *milliseconds*, int *nanoseconds*) throws InterruptedException	Waits up to the specified number of milliseconds plus nanoseconds for the thread on which it is called to terminate.
void run( )	Begins execution of a thread.
void setContextClassLoader(ClassLoader *cl*)	Sets the class loader that will be used by the invoking thread to *cl*. (Added by Java 2)
final void setDaemon(boolean *state*)	Flags the thread as a daemon thread.
final void setName(String *threadName*)	Sets the name of the thread to that specified by *threadName*.
final void setPriority(int *priority*)	Sets the priority of the thread to that specified by *priority*.

Table 14-16.   *The Methods Defined by* Thread *(continued)*

Method	Description
static void sleep(long *milliseconds*) throws InterruptedException	Suspends execution of the thread for the specified number of milliseconds.
static void sleep(long *milliseconds*, int *nanoseconds*) throws InterruptedException	Suspends execution of the thread for the specified number of milliseconds plus nanoseconds.
void start( )	Starts execution of the thread.
String toString( )	Returns the string equivalent of a thread.
static void yield( )	The calling thread yields the CPU to another thread.

Table 14-16. *The Methods Defined by* Thread (continued)

ThreadGroup

ThreadGroup creates a group of threads. It defines these two constructors:

```
ThreadGroup(String groupName)
ThreadGroup(ThreadGroup parentOb, String groupName)
```

For both forms, *groupName* specifies the name of the thread group. The first version creates a new group that has the current thread as its parent. In the second form, the parent is specified by *parentOb*.

The methods defined by **ThreadGroup** are shown in Table 14-17. In versions of Java prior to 2, **ThreadGroup** also included the methods **stop( )**, **suspend( )**, and **resume( )**. These have been deprecated by Java 2 because they were inherently unstable.

Thread groups offer a convenient way to manage groups of threads as a unit. This is particularly valuable in situations in which you want to suspend and resume a number of related threads. For example, imagine a program in which one set of threads is used for printing a document, another set is used to display the document on the screen, and another set saves the document to a disk file. If printing is aborted, you will want an easy way to stop all threads related to printing. Thread groups offer this

Method	Description
int activeCount( )	Returns the number of threads in the group plus any groups for which this thread is a parent.
int activeGroupCount( )	Returns the number of groups for which the invoking thread is a parent.
final void checkAccess( )	Causes the security manager to verify that the invoking thread may access and/or change the group on which **checkAccess( )** is called.
final void destroy( )	Destroys the thread group (and any child groups) on which it is called.
int enumerate(Thread *group*[ ])	The threads that comprise the invoking thread group are put into the *group* array.
int enumerate(Thread *group*[ ], boolean *all*)	The threads that comprise the invoking thread group are put into the *group* array. If *all* is **true**, then threads in all subgroups of the thread are also put into *group*.
int enumerate(ThreadGroup *group*[ ])	The subgroups of the invoking thread group are put into the *group* array.
int enumerate(ThreadGroup *group*[ ], boolean *all*)	The subgroups of the invoking thread group are put into the *group* array. If *all* is **true**, then all subgroups of the subgroups (and so on) are also put into *group*.
final int getMaxPriority( )	Returns the maximum priority setting for the group.

Table 14-17. *The Methods Defined by* ThreadGroup

Method	Description
final String getName( )	Returns the name of the group.
final ThreadGroup getParent( )	Returns **null** if the invoking **ThreadGroup** object has no parent. Otherwise, it returns the parent of the invoking object.
final void interrupt( )	Invokes the **interrupt( )** method of all threads in the group. (Added by Java 2)
final boolean isDaemon( )	Returns **true** if the group is a daemon group. Otherwise, it returns **false**.
boolean isDestroyed( )	Returns **true** if the group has been destroyed. Otherwise, it returns **false**.
void list( )	Displays information about the group.
final boolean parentOf(ThreadGroup *group*)	Returns **true** if the invoking thread is the parent of *group* (or *group*, itself). Otherwise, it returns **false**.
final void setDaemon(boolean *isDaemon*)	If *isDaemon* is **true**, then the invoking group is flagged as a daemon group.
final void setMaxPriority(int *priority*)	Sets the maximum priority of the invoking group to *priority*.
String toString( )	Returns the string equivalent of the group.
void uncaughtException(Thread *thread*, Throwable *e*)	This method is called when an exception goes uncaught.

Table 14-17. *The Methods Defined by* ThreadGroup (continued)

convenience. The following program, which creates two thread groups of two threads each, illustrates this usage:

```java
// Demonstrate thread groups.
class NewThread extends Thread {
  boolean suspendFlag;

  NewThread(String threadname, ThreadGroup tgOb) {
    super(tgOb, threadname);
    System.out.println("New thread: " + this);
    suspendFlag = false;
    start(); // Start the thread
  }

  // This is the entry point for thread.
  public void run() {
    try {
      for(int i = 5; i > 0; i--) {
        System.out.println(getName() + ": " + i);
        Thread.sleep(1000);
        synchronized(this) {
          while(suspendFlag) {
            wait();
          }
        }
      }
    } catch (Exception e) {
      System.out.println("Exception in " + getName());
    }
    System.out.println(getName() + " exiting.");
  }

  void mysuspend() {
    suspendFlag = true;
  }

  synchronized void myresume() {
    suspendFlag = false;
    notify();
```

THE JAVA LIBRARY

```java
    }
}

class ThreadGroupDemo {
  public static void main(String args[]) {
    ThreadGroup groupA = new ThreadGroup("Group A");
    ThreadGroup groupB = new ThreadGroup("Group B");

    NewThread ob1 = new NewThread("One", groupA);
    NewThread ob2 = new NewThread("Two", groupA);
    NewThread ob3 = new NewThread("Three", groupB);
    NewThread ob4 = new NewThread("Four", groupB);

    System.out.println("\nHere is output from list():");
    groupA.list();
    groupB.list();
    System.out.println();

    System.out.println("Suspending Group A");
    Thread tga[] = new Thread[groupA.activeCount()];
    groupA.enumerate(tga); // get threads in group
    for(int i = 0; i < tga.length; i++) {
      ((NewThread)tga[i]).mysuspend(); // suspend each thread
    }

    try {
      Thread.sleep(4000);
    } catch (InterruptedException e) {
      System.out.println("Main thread interrupted.");
    }

    System.out.println("Resuming Group A");
    for(int i = 0; i < tga.length; i++) {
      ((NewThread)tga[i]).myresume(); // resume threads in group
    }

    // wait for threads to finish
    try {
      System.out.println("Waiting for threads to finish.");
      ob1.join();
      ob2.join();
      ob3.join();
```

```
      ob4.join();
    } catch (Exception e) {
      System.out.println("Exception in Main thread");
    }

    System.out.println("Main thread exiting.");
  }
}
```

Sample output from this program is shown here:

```
New thread: Thread[One,5,Group A]
New thread: Thread[Two,5,Group A]
New thread: Thread[Three,5,Group B]
New thread: Thread[Four,5,Group B]
Here is output from list():
java.lang.ThreadGroup[name=Group A,maxpri=10]
  Thread[One,5,Group A]
  Thread[Two,5,Group A]
java.lang.ThreadGroup[name=Group B,maxpri=10]
  Thread[Three,5,Group B]
  Thread[Four,5,Group B]
Suspending Group A
Three: 5
Four: 5
Three: 4
Four: 4
Three: 3
Four: 3
Three: 2
Four: 2
Resuming Group A
Waiting for threads to finish.
One: 5
Two: 5
Three: 1
Four: 1
One: 4
Two: 4
Three exiting.
Four exiting.
One: 3
```

```
Two: 3
One: 2
Two: 2
One: 1
Two: 1
One exiting.
Two exiting.
Main thread exiting.
```

Inside the program, notice that thread group A is suspended for four seconds. As the output confirms, this causes threads One and Two to pause, but threads Three and Four continue running. After the four seconds, threads One and Two are resumed. Notice how thread group A is suspended and resumed. First, the threads in group A are obtained by calling **enumerate( )** on group A. Then, each thread is suspended by iterating through the resulting array. To resume the threads in A, the list is again traversed and each thread is resumed. One last point: this example uses the recommended Java 2 approach to suspending and resuming threads. It does not rely upon the deprecated methods **suspend( )** and **resume( )**.

ThreadLocal and InheritableThreadLocal

Java 2 added two thread-related classes to **java.lang**:

- **ThreadLocal**   Used to create thread local variables. Each thread will have its own copy of a thread local variable.

- **InheritableThreadLocal**   Creates thread local variables that may be inherited.

Package

Java 2 added a class called **Package** that encapsulates version data associated with a package. Package version information is becoming more important because of the proliferation of packages and because a Java program may need to know what version of a package is available. The methods defined by **Package** are shown in Table 14-18. The following program demonstrates **Package**, displaying the packages about which the program currently is aware.

```
// Demonstrate Package
class PkgTest {
  public static void main(String args[]) {
    Package pkgs[];
```

```
    pkgs = Package.getPackages();

    for(int i=0; i < pkgs.length; i++)
      System.out.println(
             pkgs[i].getName() + " " +
             pkgs[i].getImplementationTitle() + " " +
             pkgs[i].getImplementationVendor() + " " +
             pkgs[i].getImplementationVersion()
      );

  }
}
```

Method	Description
String getImplementationTitle( )	Returns the title of the invoking package.
String getImplementationVendor( )	Returns the name of the implementor of the invoking package.
String getImplementationVersion( )	Returns the version number of the invoking package.
String getName( )	Returns the name of the invoking package.
static Package getPackage(String *pkgName*)	Returns a **Package** object with the name specified by *pkgName*.
static Package[ ] getPackages( )	Returns all packages about which the invoking program is currently aware.
String getSpecificationTitle( )	Returns the title of the invoking package's specification.
String getSpecificationVendor( )	Returns the name of the owner of the specification for the invoking package.

Table 14-18.   *The Methods Defined by* Package

Method	Description
String getSpecificationVersion( )	Returns the invoking package's specification version number.
int hashCode( )	Returns the hash code for the invoking package.
boolean isCompatibleWith(String *verNum*) throws NumberFormatException	Returns **true** if *verNum* is less than or equal to the invoking package's version number.
boolean isSealed( )	Returns **true** if the invoking package is sealed. Returns **false** otherwise.
boolean isSealed(URL *url*)	Returns **true** if the invoking package is sealed relative to *url*. Returns **false** otherwise.
String toString( )	Returns the string equivalent of the invoking package.

Table 14-18. *The Methods Defined by* Package (continued)

RuntimePermission

RuntimePermission was added to **java.lang** by Java 2. It relates to Java's security mechanism and is not examined further here.

Throwable

The **Throwable** class supports Java's exception-handling system, and is the class from which all exception classes are derived. It is discussed in Chapter 10.

SecurityManager

SecurityManager is an abstract class that your subclasses can implement to create a security manager. Generally, you don't need to implement your own security manager. If you do, you need to consult the documentation that comes with your Java development system.

StackTraceElement

Java 2, version 1.4 adds the **StackTraceElement** class. This class describes a single *stack frame*, which is an individual element of a stack trace when an exception occurs. Each stack frame represents an *execution point*, which includes such things as the name of the method, the name of the file, and the source-code line number. An array of **StackTraceElement**s is returned by the **getStackTrace( )** method of the **Throwable** class. The methods supported by **StackTraceElement** are shown in Table 14-19. These methods give you programmatical access to a stack trace.

Method	Description
boolean equals(Object *ob*)	Returns **true** if the invoking **StackTraceElement** is the same as the one passed in *ob*. Otherwise, it returns **false**.
String getClassName( )	Returns the class name of the execution point described by the invoking **StackTraceElement**.
String getFileName( )	Returns the file name of the execution point described by the invoking **StackTraceElement**.
int getLineNumber( )	Returns the source-code line number of the execution point described by the invoking **StackTraceElement**. In some situations the line number will not be available, in which case a negative value is returned.
String getMethodName( )	Returns the method name of the execution point described by the invoking **StackTraceElement**.
int hashCode( )	Returns the hash code for the invoking **StackTraceElement**.
boolean isNativeMethod( )	Returns **true** if the invoking **StackTraceElement** describes a native method. Otherwise, returns **false**.
String toString( )	Returns the **String** equivalent of the invoking sequence.

Table 14-19. *The Methods Defined by* StackTraceElement

Method	Description
char charAt(int *idx*)	Returns the character at the index specified by *idx*.
int length( )	Returns the number of characters in the invoking sequence.
CharSequence subSequence(int *startIdx*, int *stopIdx*)	Returns a subset of the invoking sequence beginning at *startIdx* and ending at *stopIdx*–1.
String toString( )	Returns the **String** equivalent of the invoking sequence.

Table 14-20.   *The Methods Defined by* CharSequence

The CharSequence Interface

Java 2, version 1.4 adds the **CharSequence** interface. **CharSequence** defines methods that grant read-only access to a sequence of characters. These methods are shown in Table 14-20. This interface is implemented by **String** and **StringBuffer**. It is also implemented by **CharBuffer**, which is in the new **java.nio** package (described later in this book).

The Comparable Interface

Objects of classes that implement **Comparable** can be ordered. In other words, classes that implement **Comparable** contain objects that can be compared in some meaningful manner. The **Comparable** interface declares one method that is used to determine what Java 2 calls the *natural ordering* of instances of a class. The signature of the method is shown here:

    int compareTo(Object *obj*)

This method compares the invoking object with *obj*. It returns 0 if the values are equal. A negative value is returned if the invoking object has a lower value. Otherwise, a positive value is returned.

This interface is implemented by several of the classes already reviewed in this book. Specifically, the **Byte**, **Character**, **Double**, **Float**, **Long**, **Short**, **String**, and **Integer** classes define a **compareTo( )** method. In addition, as the next chapter explains, objects that implement this interface can be used in various collections. **Comparable** was added by Java 2.

The java.lang.ref and java.lang.reflect Packages

Java defines two subpackages of **java.lang**: **java.lang.ref** and **java.lang.reflect**. Each is briefly described here.

java.lang.ref

You learned earlier that the garbage collection facilities in Java automatically determine when no references exist to an object. The object is then assumed to be no longer needed and its memory is reclaimed. The classes in the **java.lang.ref** package, which was added by Java 2, provide more flexible control over the garbage collection process. For example, assume that your program has created numerous objects that you want to reuse at some later time. You can continue to hold references to these objects, but that may require too much memory.

Instead, you can define "soft" references to these objects. An object that is "softly reachable" can be reclaimed by the garbage collector, if available memory runs low. In that case, the garbage collector sets the "soft" references to that object to **null**. Otherwise, the garbage collector saves the object for possible future use.

A programmer has the ability to determine whether a "softly reachable" object has been reclaimed. If it has been reclaimed, it can be re-created. Otherwise, the object is still available for reuse. You may also create "weak" and "phantom" references to objects. Discussion of these and other features of the **java.lang.ref** package are beyond the scope of this book.

java.lang.reflect

Reflection is the ability of a program to analyze itself. The **java.lang.reflect** package provides the ability to obtain information about the fields, constructors, methods, and modifiers of a class. You need this information to build software tools that enable you to work with Java Beans components. The tools use reflection to determine dynamically the characteristics of a component. This topic is considered in Chapter 25.

In addition, the **java.lang.reflect** package includes a class that enables you to create and access arrays dynamically.

The
Complete
Reference

Java™ 2

Chapter 15

java.util Part 1: The Collections Framework

The **java.util** package contains one of Java's most powerful subsystems: collections. Collections were added by the initial release of Java 2, and enhanced by Java 2, version 1.4. A *collection* is a group of objects. The addition of collections caused fundamental alterations in the structure and architecture of many elements in **java.util**. It also expanded the domain of tasks to which the package can be applied. Collections are a state-of-the-art technology that merits close attention by all Java programmers.

In addition to collections, **java.util** contains a wide assortment of classes and interfaces that support a broad range of functionality. These classes and interfaces are used throughout the core Java packages and, of course, are also available for use in programs that you write. Their applications include generating pseudorandom numbers, manipulating date and time, observing events, manipulating sets of bits, and tokenizing strings. Because of its many features, **java.util** is one of Java's most widely used packages.

The **java.util** classes are listed here.

AbstractCollection (Java 2)	EventObject	PropertyResourceBundle
AbstractList (Java 2)	GregorianCalendar	Random
AbstractMap (Java 2)	HashMap (Java 2)	ResourceBundle
AbstractSequentialList (Java 2)	HashSet (Java 2)	SimpleTimeZone
AbstractSet (Java 2)	Hashtable	Stack
ArrayList (Java 2)	IdentityHashMap (Java 2, v1.4)	StringTokenizer
Arrays (Java 2)	LinkedHashMap (Java 2, v1.4)	Timer (Java 2, v1.3)
BitSet	LinkedHashSet (Java 2, v1.4)	TimerTask (Java 2, v1.3)
Calendar	LinkedList (Java 2)	TimeZone
Collections (Java 2)	ListResourceBundle	TreeMap (Java 2)
Currency (Java 2, v1.4)	Locale	TreeSet (Java 2)
Date	Observable	Vector
Dictionary	Properties	WeakHashMap (Java 2)
EventListenerProxy (Java 2, v1.4)	PropertyPermission (Java 2)	

java.util defines the following interfaces. Notice that most were added by Java 2.

Collection (Java 2)	List (Java 2)	RandomAccess (Java 2, v1.4)
Comparator (Java 2)	ListIterator (Java 2)	Set (Java 2)
Enumeration	Map (Java 2)	SortedMap (Java 2)
EventListener	Map.Entry (Java 2)	SortedSet (Java 2)
Iterator (Java 2)	Observer	

The **ResourceBundle**, **ListResourceBundle**, and **PropertyResourceBundle** classes aid in the internationalization of large programs with many locale-specific resources. These classes are not examined here. **PropertyPermission**, which allows you to grant a read/write permission to a system property, is also beyond the scope of this book. **EventObject**, **EventListener**, and **EventListenerProxy** are described in Chapter 20. The remaining classes and interfaces are examined in detail.

Because **java.util** is quite large, its description is broken into two chapters. This chapter examines those members of **java.util** that relate to collections of objects. Chapter 16 discusses the other classes and interfaces.

Collections Overview

The Java *collections framework* standardizes the way in which groups of objects are handled by your programs. Prior to Java 2, Java provided ad hoc classes such as **Dictionary**, **Vector**, **Stack**, and **Properties** to store and manipulate groups of objects. Although these classes were quite useful, they lacked a central, unifying theme. Thus, the way that you used **Vector** was different from the way that you used **Properties**, for example. Also, the previous, ad hoc approach was not designed to be easily extensible or adaptable. Collections are an answer to these (and other) problems.

The collections framework was designed to meet several goals. First, the framework had to be high-performance. The implementations for the fundamental collections (dynamic arrays, linked lists, trees, and hash tables) are highly efficient. You seldom, if ever, need to code one of these "data engines" manually. Second, the framework had to allow different types of collections to work in a similar manner and with a high degree of interoperability. Third, extending and/or adapting a collection had to be easy. Toward this end, the entire collections framework is designed around a set of standard interfaces. Several standard implementations (such as **LinkedList**, **HashSet**, and **TreeSet**) of these interfaces are provided that you may use as-is. You may also implement your own collection, if you choose. Various special-purpose implementations are created for your convenience, and some partial implementations are provided that make creating your own collection class easier. Finally, mechanisms were added that allow the integration of standard arrays into the collections framework.

Algorithms are another important part of the collection mechanism. Algorithms operate on collections and are defined as static methods within the **Collections** class. Thus, they are available for all collections. Each collection class need not implement its own versions. The algorithms provide a standard means of manipulating collections.

Another item created by the collections framework is the **Iterator** interface. An *iterator* gives you a general-purpose, standardized way of accessing the elements within a collection, one at a time. Thus, an iterator provides a means of *enumerating the contents of a collection*. Because each collection implements **Iterator**, the elements of any collection class can be accessed through the methods defined by **Iterator**. Thus, with only small changes, the code that cycles through a set can also be used to cycle through a list, for example.

In addition to collections, the framework defines several map interfaces and classes. *Maps* store key/value pairs. Although maps are not "collections" in the proper use of the term, they are fully integrated with collections. In the language of the collections framework, you can obtain a *collection-view* of a map. Such a view contains the elements from the map stored in a collection. Thus, you can process the contents of a map as a collection, if you choose.

The collection mechanism was retrofitted to some of the original classes defined by **java.util** so that they too could be integrated into the new system. It is important to understand that although the addition of collections altered the architecture of many of the original utility classes, it did not cause the deprecation of any. Collections simply provide a better way of doing several things.

One last thing: If you are familiar with C++, then you will find it helpful to know that the Java collections technology is similar in spirit to the Standard Template Library (STL) defined by C++. What C++ calls a container, Java calls a collection.

The Collection Interfaces

The collections framework defines several interfaces. This section provides an overview of each interface. Beginning with the collection interfaces is necessary because they determine the fundamental nature of the collection classes. Put differently, the concrete classes simply provide different implementations of the standard interfaces. The interfaces that underpin collections are summarized in the following table:

Interface	Description
Collection	Enables you to work with groups of objects; it is at the top of the collections hierarchy
List	Extends **Collection** to handle sequences (lists of objects)
Set	Extends **Collection** to handle sets, which must contain unique elements
SortedSet	Extends **Set** to handle sorted sets

In addition to the collection interfaces, collections also use the **Comparator**, **Iterator**, **ListIterator** and **RandomAccess** interfaces, which are described in depth later in this chapter. Briefly, **Comparator** defines how two objects are compared; **Iterator** and **ListIterator** enumerate the objects within a collection. By implementing **RandomAccess**, a list indicates that it supports efficient, random access to its elements.

To provide the greatest flexibility in their use, the collection interfaces allow some methods to be optional. The optional methods enable you to modify the contents of a collection. Collections that support these methods are called *modifiable*. Collections that do not allow their contents to be changed are called *unmodifiable*. If an attempt is made to use one of these methods on an unmodifiable collection, an **UnsupportedOperationException** is thrown. All the built-in collections are modifiable. The following sections examine the collection interfaces.

The Collection Interface

The **Collection** interface is the foundation upon which the collections framework is built. It declares the core methods that all collections will have. These methods are summarized in Table 15-1. Because all collections implement **Collection**, familiarity with its methods is necessary for a clear understanding of the framework. Several of these methods can throw an **UnsupportedOperationException**. As explained, this occurs if a collection cannot be modified. A **ClassCastException** is generated when one object is incompatible with another, such as when an attempt is made to add an incompatible object to a collection.

Method	Description
boolean add(Object *obj*)	Adds *obj* to the invoking collection. Returns **true** if *obj* was added to the collection. Returns **false** if *obj* is already a member of the collection, or if the collection does not allow duplicates.
boolean addAll(Collection *c*)	Adds all the elements of *c* to the invoking collection. Returns **true** if the operation succeeded (i.e., the elements were added). Otherwise, returns **false**.
void clear( )	Removes all elements from the invoking collection.
boolean contains(Object *obj*)	Returns **true** if *obj* is an element of the invoking collection. Otherwise, returns **false**.
boolean containsAll(Collection *c*)	Returns **true** if the invoking collection contains all elements of *c*. Otherwise, returns **false**.
boolean equals(Object *obj*)	Returns **true** if the invoking collection and *obj* are equal. Otherwise, returns **false**.
int hashCode( )	Returns the hash code for the invoking collection.

Table 15-1. *The Methods Defined by* Collection

Method	Description
boolean isEmpty( )	Returns **true** if the invoking collection is empty. Otherwise, returns **false**.
Iterator iterator( )	Returns an iterator for the invoking collection.
boolean remove(Object *obj*)	Removes one instance of *obj* from the invoking collection. Returns **true** if the element was removed. Otherwise, returns **false**.
boolean removeAll(Collection *c*)	Removes all elements of *c* from the invoking collection. Returns **true** if the collection changed (i.e., elements were removed). Otherwise, returns **false**.
boolean retainAll(Collection *c*)	Removes all elements from the invoking collection except those in *c*. Returns **true** if the collection changed (i.e., elements were removed). Otherwise, returns **false**.
int size( )	Returns the number of elements held in the invoking collection.
Object[ ] toArray( )	Returns an array that contains all the elements stored in the invoking collection. The array elements are copies of the collection elements.
Object[ ] toArray(Object *array*[ ])	Returns an array containing only those collection elements whose type matches that of *array*. The array elements are copies of the collection elements. If the size of *array* equals the number of matching elements, these are returned in *array*. If the size of *array* is less than the number of matching elements, a new array of the necessary size is allocated and returned. If the size of *array* is greater than the number of matching elements, the array element following the last collection element is set to **null**. An **ArrayStoreException** is thrown if any collection element has a type that is not a subtype of *array*.

Table 15-1. *The Methods Defined by* Collection (continued)

Objects are added to a collection by calling **add( )**. Notice that **add( )** takes an argument of type **Object**. Because **Object** is a superclass of all classes, any type of object may be stored in a collection. However, primitive types may not. For example, a collection cannot directly store values of type **int**, **char**, **double**, and so forth. Of course, if you want to store such objects, you can also use one of the primitive type wrappers described in Chapter 14. You can add the entire contents of one collection to another by calling **addAll( )**.

You can remove an object by using **remove( )**. To remove a group of objects, call **removeAll( )**. You can remove all elements except those of a specified group by calling **retainAll( )**. To empty a collection, call **clear( )**.

You can determine whether a collection contains a specific object by calling **contains( )**. To determine whether one collection contains all the members of another, call **containsAll( )**. You can determine when a collection is empty by calling **isEmpty( )**. The number of elements currently held in a collection can be determined by calling **size( )**.

The **toArray( )** method returns an array that contains the elements stored in the invoking collection. This method is more important than it might at first seem. Often, processing the contents of a collection by using array-like syntax is advantageous. By providing a pathway between collections and arrays, you can have the best of both worlds.

Two collections can be compared for equality by calling **equals( )**. The precise meaning of "equality" may differ from collection to collection. For example, you can implement **equals( )** so that it compares the values of elements stored in the collection Alternatively, **equals( )** can compare references to those elements.

One more very important method is **iterator( )**, which returns an iterator to a collection. As you will see, iterators are crucial to successful programming when using the collections framework.

The List Interface

The **List** interface extends **Collection** and declares the behavior of a collection that stores a sequence of elements. Elements can be inserted or accessed by their position in the list, using a zero-based index. A list may contain duplicate elements.

In addition to the methods defined by **Collection**, **List** defines some of its own, which are summarized in Table 15-2. Note again that several of these methods will throw an **UnsupportedOperationException** if the collection cannot be modified, and a **ClassCastException** is generated when one object is incompatible with another, such as when an attempt is made to add an incompatible object to a collection.

To the versions of **add( )** and **addAll( )** defined by **Collection**, **List** adds the methods **add(int, Object)** and **addAll(int, Collection)**. These methods insert elements at the specified index. Also, the semantics of **add(Object)** and **addAll(Collection)** defined by **Collection** are changed by **List** so that they add elements to the end of the list.

To obtain the object stored at a specific location, call **get( )** with the index of the object. To assign a value to an element in the list, call **set( )**, specifying the index of the object to be changed. To find the index of an object, use **indexOf( )** or **lastIndexOf( )**.

Method	Description
void add(int *index*, Object *obj*)	Inserts *obj* into the invoking list at the index passed in *index*. Any preexisting elements at or beyond the point of insertion are shifted up. Thus, no elements are overwritten.
boolean addAll(int *index*, Collection *c*)	Inserts all elements of *c* into the invoking list at the index passed in *index*. Any preexisting elements at or beyond the point of insertion are shifted up. Thus, no elements are overwritten. Returns **true** if the invoking list changes and returns **false** otherwise.
Object get(int *index*)	Returns the object stored at the specified index within the invoking collection.
int indexOf(Object *obj*)	Returns the index of the first instance of *obj* in the invoking list. If *obj* is not an element of the list, –1 is returned.
int lastIndexOf(Object *obj*)	Returns the index of the last instance of *obj* in the invoking list. If *obj* is not an element of the list, –1 is returned.
ListIterator listIterator( )	Returns an iterator to the start of the invoking list.
ListIterator listIterator(int *index*)	Returns an iterator to the invoking list that begins at the specified index.
Object remove(int *index*)	Removes the element at position *index* from the invoking list and returns the deleted element. The resulting list is compacted. That is, the indexes of subsequent elements are decremented by one.
Object set(int *index*, Object *obj*)	Assigns *obj* to the location specified by *index* within the invoking list.
List subList(int *start*, int *end*)	Returns a list that includes elements from *start* to *end*–1 in the invoking list. Elements in the returned list are also referenced by the invoking object.

Table 15-2. *The Methods Defined by* List

You can obtain a sublist of a list by calling **subList( )**, specifying the beginning and ending indexes of the sublist. As you can imagine, **subList( )** makes list processing quite convenient.

The Set Interface

The **Set** interface defines a set. It extends **Collection** and declares the behavior of a collection that does not allow duplicate elements. Therefore, the **add( )** method returns **false** if an attempt is made to add duplicate elements to a set. It does not define any additional methods of its own.

The SortedSet Interface

The **SortedSet** interface extends **Set** and declares the behavior of a set sorted in ascending order. In addition to those methods defined by **Set**, the **SortedSet** interface declares the methods summarized in Table 15-3. Several methods throw a **NoSuchElementException** when no items are contained in the invoking set. A **ClassCastException** is thrown when an object is incompatible with the elements in a set. A **NullPointerException** is thrown if an attempt is made to use a **null** object and **null** is not allowed in the set.

SortedSet defines several methods that make set processing more convenient. To obtain the first object in the set, call **first( )**. To get the last element, use **last( )**. You can obtain a subset of a sorted set by calling **subSet( )**, specifying the first and last object in the set. If you need the subset that starts with the first element in the set, use **headSet( )**. If you want the subset that ends the set, use **tailSet( )**.

Method	Description
Comparator comparator( )	Returns the invoking sorted set's comparator. If the natural ordering is used for this set, **null** is returned.
Object first( )	Returns the first element in the invoking sorted set.
SortedSet headSet(Object *end*)	Returns a **SortedSet** containing those elements less than *end* that are contained in the invoking sorted set. Elements in the returned sorted set are also referenced by the invoking sorted set.
Object last( )	Returns the last element in the invoking sorted set.

Table 15-3.   *The Methods Defined by* SortedSet

Method	Description
SortedSet subSet(Object *start*, Object *end*)	Returns a **SortedSet** that includes those elements between *start* and *end*–1. Elements in the returned collection are also referenced by the invoking object.
SortedSet tailSet(Object *start*)	Returns a **SortedSet** that contains those elements greater than or equal to *start* that are contained in the sorted set. Elements in the returned set are also referenced by the invoking object.

Table 15-3. *The Methods Defined by* SortedSet (continued)

The Collection Classes

Now that you are familiar with the collection interfaces, you are ready to examine the standard classes that implement them. Some of the classes provide full implementations that can be used as-is. Others are abstract, providing skeletal implementations that are used as starting points for creating concrete collections. None of the collection classes are synchronized, but as you will see later in this chapter, it is possible to obtain synchronized versions.

The standard collection classes are summarized in the following table:

Class	Description
AbstractCollection	Implements most of the **Collection** interface.
AbstractList	Extends **AbstractCollection** and implements most of the **List** interface.
AbstractSequentialList	Extends **AbstractList** for use by a collection that uses sequential rather than random access of its elements.
LinkedList	Implements a linked list by extending **AbstractSequentialList**.
ArrayList	Implements a dynamic array by extending **AbstractList**.

Class	Description
AbstractSet	Extends **AbstractCollection** and implements most of the **Set** interface.
HashSet	Extends **AbstractSet** for use with a hash table.
LinkedHashSet	Extends **HashSet** to allow insertion-order iterations.
TreeSet	Implements a set stored in a tree. Extends **AbstractSet**.

*In addition to the collection classes, several legacy classes, such as **Vector**, **Stack**, and **Hashtable**, have been reengineered to support collections. These are examined later in this chapter.*

The following sections examine the concrete collection classes and illustrate their use.

The ArrayList Class

The **ArrayList** class extends **AbstractList** and implements the **List** interface. **ArrayList** supports dynamic arrays that can grow as needed. In Java, standard arrays are of a fixed length. After arrays are created, they cannot grow or shrink, which means that you must know in advance how many elements an array will hold. But, sometimes, you may not know until run time precisely how large of an array you need. To handle this situation, the collections framework defines **ArrayList**. In essence, an **ArrayList** is a variable-length array of object references. That is, an **ArrayList** can dynamically increase or decrease in size. Array lists are created with an initial size. When this size is exceeded, the collection is automatically enlarged. When objects are removed, the array may be shrunk.

*Dynamic arrays are also supported by the legacy class **Vector**, which is described later in this chapter.*

ArrayList has the constructors shown here:

ArrayList( )
ArrayList(Collection *c*)
ArrayList(int *capacity*)

The first constructor builds an empty array list. The second constructor builds an array list that is initialized with the elements of the collection *c*. The third constructor builds an array list that has the specified initial *capacity*. The capacity is the size of the underlying array that is used to store the elements. The capacity grows automatically as elements are added to an array list.

The following program shows a simple use of **ArrayList**. An array list is created, and then objects of type **String** are added to it. (Recall that a quoted string is translated into a **String** object.) The list is then displayed. Some of the elements are removed and the list is displayed again.

```
// Demonstrate ArrayList.
import java.util.*;

class ArrayListDemo {
  public static void main(String args[]) {
    // create an array list
    ArrayList al = new ArrayList();

    System.out.println("Initial size of al: " +
                       al.size());

    // add elements to the array list
    al.add("C");
    al.add("A");
    al.add("E");
    al.add("B");
    al.add("D");
    al.add("F");
    al.add(1, "A2");

    System.out.println("Size of al after additions: " +
                       al.size());

    // display the array list
    System.out.println("Contents of al: " + al);

    // Remove elements from the array list
    al.remove("F");
    al.remove(2);

    System.out.println("Size of al after deletions: " +
                       al.size());
    System.out.println("Contents of al: " + al);
  }
}
```

The output from this program is shown here:

```
Initial size of al: 0
Size of al after additions: 7
```

```
Contents of al: [C, A2, A, E, B, D, F]
Size of al after deletions: 5
Contents of al: [C, A2, E, B, D]
```

Notice that **a1** starts out empty and grows as elements are added to it. When elements are removed, its size is reduced.

In the preceding example, the contents of a collection are displayed using the default conversion provided by **toString( )**, which was inherited from **AbstractCollection**. Although it is sufficient for short, sample programs, you seldom use this method to display the contents of a real-world collection. Usually, you provide your own output routines. But, for the next few examples, the default output created by **toString( )** will continue to be used.

Although the capacity of an **ArrayList** object increases automatically as objects are stored in it, you can increase the capacity of an **ArrayList** object manually by calling **ensureCapacity( )**. You might want to do this if you know in advance that you will be storing many more items in the collection that it can currently hold. By increasing its capacity once, at the start, you can prevent several reallocations later. Because reallocations are costly in terms of time, preventing unnecessary ones improves performance. The signature for **ensureCapacity( )** is shown here:

void ensureCapacity(int *cap*)

Here, *cap* is the new capacity.

Conversely, if you want to reduce the size of the array that underlies an **ArrayList** object so that it is precisely as large as the number of items that it is currently holding, call **trimToSize( )**, shown here:

void trimToSize( )

Obtaining an Array from an ArrayList

When working with **ArrayList**, you will sometimes want to obtain an actual array that contains the contents of the list. As explained earlier, you can do this by calling **toArray( )**. Several reasons exist why you might want to convert a collection into an array such as:

- To obtain faster processing times for certain operations.

- To pass an array to a method that is not overloaded to accept a collection.

- To integrate your newer, collection-based code with legacy code that does not understand collections.

Whatever the reason, converting an **ArrayList** to an array is a trivial matter, as the following program shows:

```
// Convert an ArrayList into an array.
import java.util.*;
```

```
class ArrayListToArray {
  public static void main(String args[]) {
    // Create an array list
    ArrayList al = new ArrayList();

    // Add elements to the array list
    al.add(new Integer(1));
    al.add(new Integer(2));
    al.add(new Integer(3));
    al.add(new Integer(4));

    System.out.println("Contents of al: " + al);

    // get array
    Object ia[] = al.toArray();
    int sum = 0;

    // sum the array
    for(int i=0; i<ia.length; i++)
      sum += ((Integer) ia[i]).intValue();

    System.out.println("Sum is: " + sum);
  }
}
```

The output from the program is shown here:

```
Contents of al: [1, 2, 3, 4]
Sum is: 10
```

The program begins by creating a collection of integers. As explained, you cannot store primitive types in a collection, so objects of type **Integer** are created and stored. Next, **toArray( )** is called and it obtains an array of **Object**s. The contents of this array are cast to **Integer**, and then the values are summed.

The LinkedList Class

The **LinkedList** class extends **AbstractSequentialList** and implements the **List** interface. It provides a linked-list data structure. It has the two constructors, shown here:

LinkedList( )
LinkedList(Collection c)

The first constructor builds an empty linked list. The second constructor builds a linked list that is initialized with the elements of the collection *c*.

In addition to the methods that it inherits, the **LinkedList** class defines some useful methods of its own for manipulating and accessing lists. To add elements to the start of the list, use **addFirst( )**; to add elements to the end, use **addLast( )**. Their signatures are shown here:

void addFirst(Object *obj*)
void addLast(Object *obj*)

Here, *obj* is the item being added.

To obtain the first element, call **getFirst( )**. To retrieve the last element, call **getLast( )**. Their signatures are shown here:

Object getFirst( )
Object getLast( )

To remove the first element, use **removeFirst( )**; to remove the last element, call **removeLast( )**. They are shown here:

Object removeFirst( )
Object removeLast( )

The following program illustrates several of the methods supported by **LinkedList**:

```java
// Demonstrate LinkedList.
import java.util.*;

class LinkedListDemo {
  public static void main(String args[]) {
    // create a linked list
    LinkedList ll = new LinkedList();

    // add elements to the linked list
    ll.add("F");
    ll.add("B");
    ll.add("D");
    ll.add("E");
    ll.add("C");
    ll.addLast("Z");
    ll.addFirst("A");

    ll.add(1, "A2");
```

```
            System.out.println("Original contents of ll: " + ll);

            // remove elements from the linked list
            ll.remove("F");
            ll.remove(2);

            System.out.println("Contents of ll after deletion: "
                            + ll);

            // remove first and last elements
            ll.removeFirst();
            ll.removeLast();

            System.out.println("ll after deleting first and last: "
                            + ll);

            // get and set a value
            Object val = ll.get(2);
            ll.set(2, (String) val + " Changed");

            System.out.println("ll after change: " + ll);
        }
    }
```

The output from this program is shown here:

```
Original contents of ll: [A, A2, F, B, D, E, C, Z]
Contents of ll after deletion: [A, A2, D, E, C, Z]
ll after deleting first and last: [A2, D, E, C]
ll after change: [A2, D, E Changed, C]
```

Because **LinkedList** implements the **List** interface, calls to **add(Object)** append items to the end of the list, as does **addLast( )**. To insert items at a specific location, use the **add(int, Object)** form of **add( )**, as illustrated by the call to **add(1, "A2")** in the example.

Notice how the third element in **ll** is changed by employing calls to **get( )** and **set( )**. To obtain the current value of an element, pass **get( )** the index at which the element is stored. To assign a new value to that index, pass **set( )** the index and its new value.

The HashSet Class

HashSet extends **AbstractSet** and implements the **Set** interface. It creates a collection that uses a hash table for storage. As most readers likely know, a hash table stores information by using a mechanism called hashing. In *hashing*, the informational content of a key is used to determine a unique value, called its *hash code*. The hash code is then used as the index at which the data associated with the key is stored. The transformation of the key into its hash code is performed automatically—you never see the hash code itself. Also, your code can't directly index the hash table. The advantage of hashing is that it allows the execution time of basic operations, such as **add( )**, **contains( )**, **remove( )**, and **size( )**, to remain constant even for large sets.

The following constructors are defined:

HashSet( )
HashSet(Collection *c*)
HashSet(int *capacity*)
HashSet(int *capacity*, float *fillRatio*)

The first form constructs a default hash set. The second form initializes the hash set by using the elements of *c*. The third form initializes the capacity of the hash set to *capacity*. The fourth form initializes both the capacity and the fill ratio (also called *load capacity*) of the hash set from its arguments. The fill ratio must be between 0.0 and 1.0, and it determines how full the hash set can be before it is resized upward. Specifically, when the number of elements is greater than the capacity of the hash set multiplied by its fill ratio, the hash set is expanded. For constructors that do not take a fill ratio, 0.75 is used.

HashSet does not define any additional methods beyond those provided by its superclasses and interfaces.

Importantly, note that a hash set does not guarantee the order of its elements, because the process of hashing doesn't usually lend itself to the creation of sorted sets. If you need sorted storage, then another collection, such as **TreeSet**, is a better choice.

Here is an example that demonstrates **HashSet**:

```
// Demonstrate HashSet.
import java.util.*;

class HashSetDemo {
  public static void main(String args[]) {
    // create a hash set
    HashSet hs = new HashSet();

    // add elements to the hash set
    hs.add("B");
    hs.add("A");
    hs.add("D");
    hs.add("E");
    hs.add("C");
    hs.add("F");
```

```
    System.out.println(hs);
  }
}
```

The following is the output from this program:

```
[A, F, E, D, C, B]
```

As explained, the elements are not stored in sorted order, and the precise output may vary.

The LinkedHashSet Class

Java 2, version 1.4 adds the **LinkedHashSet** class. This class extends **HashSet**, but adds no members of its own. **LinkedHashSet** maintains a linked list of the entries in the set, in the order in which they were inserted. This allows insertion-order iteration over the set. That is, when cycling through a **LinkedHashSet** using an iterator, the elements will be returned in the order in which they were inserted. This is also the order in which they are contained in the string returned by **toString( )** when called on a **LinkedHashSet** object. To see the effect of **LinkedHashSet**, try substituting **LinkedHashSet** For **HashSet** in the preceding program. The output will be

```
[B, A, D, E, C, F]
```

which is the order in which the elements were inserted.

The TreeSet Class

TreeSet provides an implementation of the **Set** interface that uses a tree for storage. Objects are stored in sorted, ascending order. Access and retrieval times are quite fast, which makes **TreeSet** an excellent choice when storing large amounts of sorted information that must be found quickly.

The following constructors are defined:

TreeSet( )
TreeSet(Collection *c*)
TreeSet(Comparator *comp*)
TreeSet(SortedSet *ss*)

The first form constructs an empty tree set that will be sorted in ascending order according to the natural order of its elements. The second form builds a tree set that contains the elements of *c*. The third form constructs an empty tree set that will be sorted according to the comparator specified by *comp*. (Comparators are described later in this chapter.) The fourth form builds a tree set that contains the elements of *ss*.

Here is an example that demonstrates a **TreeSet**:

```
// Demonstrate TreeSet.
import java.util.*;

class TreeSetDemo {
  public static void main(String args[]) {
    // Create a tree set
    TreeSet ts = new TreeSet();

    // Add elements to the tree set
    ts.add("C");
    ts.add("A");
    ts.add("B");
    ts.add("E");
    ts.add("F");
    ts.add("D");

    System.out.println(ts);
  }
}
```

The output from this program is shown here:

```
[A, B, C, D, E, F]
```

As explained, because **TreeSet** stores its elements in a tree, they are automatically arranged in sorted order, as the output confirms.

Accessing a Collection via an Iterator

Often, you will want to cycle through the elements in a collection. For example, you might want to display each element. By far, the easiest way to do this is to employ an *iterator*, an object that implements either the **Iterator** or the **ListIterator** interface. **Iterator** enables you to cycle through a collection, obtaining or removing elements. **ListIterator** extends **Iterator** to allow bidirectional traversal of a list, and the modification of elements. The **Iterator** interface declares the methods shown in Table 15-4. The methods declared by **ListIterator** are shown in Table 15-5.

Using an Iterator

Before you can access a collection through an iterator, you must obtain one. Each of the collection classes provides an **iterator( )** method that returns an iterator to the start of the collection. By using this iterator object, you can access each element in the

Method	Description
boolean hasNext( )	Returns **true** if there are more elements. Otherwise, returns **false**.
Object next( )	Returns the next element. Throws **NoSuchElementException** if there is not a next element.
void remove( )	Removes the current element. Throws **IllegalStateException** if an attempt is made to call **remove( )** that is not preceded by a call to **next( )**.

Table 15-4. *The Methods Declared by* Iterator

Method	Description
void add(Object *obj*)	Inserts *obj* into the list in front of the element that will be returned by the next call to **next( )**.
boolean hasNext( )	Returns **true** if there is a next element. Otherwise, returns **false**.
boolean hasPrevious( )	Returns **true** if there is a previous element. Otherwise, returns **false**.
Object next( )	Returns the next element. A **NoSuchElementException** is thrown if there is not a next element.
int nextIndex( )	Returns the index of the next element. If there is not a next element, returns the size of the list.
Object previous( )	Returns the previous element. A **NoSuchElementException** is thrown if there is not a previous element.
int previousIndex( )	Returns the index of the previous element. If there is not a previous element, returns –1.
void remove( )	Removes the current element from the list. An **IllegalStateException** is thrown if **remove( )** is called before **next( )** or **previous( )** is invoked.
void set(Object *obj*)	Assigns *obj* to the current element. This is the element last returned by a call to either **next( )** or **previous( )**.

Table 15-5. *The Methods Declared by* ListIterator

collection, one element at a time. In general, to use an iterator to cycle through the contents of a collection, follow these steps:

1. Obtain an iterator to the start of the collection by calling the collection's **iterator( )** method.
2. Set up a loop that makes a call to **hasNext( )**. Have the loop iterate as long as **hasNext( )** returns **true**.
3. Within the loop, obtain each element by calling **next( )**.

For collections that implement **List**, you can also obtain an iterator by calling **ListIterator**. As explained, a list iterator gives you the ability to access the collection in either the forward or backward direction and lets you modify an element. Otherwise, **ListIterator** is used just like **Iterator**.

Here is an example that implements these steps, demonstrating both **Iterator** and **ListIterator**. It uses an **ArrayList** object, but the general principles apply to any type of collection. Of course, **ListIterator** is available only to those collections that implement the **List** interface.

```
// Demonstrate iterators.
import java.util.*;

class IteratorDemo {
  public static void main(String args[]) {
    // create an array list
    ArrayList al = new ArrayList();

    // add elements to the array list
    al.add("C");
    al.add("A");
    al.add("E");
    al.add("B");
    al.add("D");
    al.add("F");

    // use iterator to display contents of al
    System.out.print("Original contents of al: ");
    Iterator itr = al.iterator();
    while(itr.hasNext()) {
      Object element = itr.next();
      System.out.print(element + " ");
    }
    System.out.println();

    // modify objects being iterated
    ListIterator litr = al.listIterator();
    while(litr.hasNext()) {
```

```
      Object element = litr.next();
      litr.set(element + "+");
    }

    System.out.print("Modified contents of al: ");
    itr = al.iterator();
    while(itr.hasNext()) {
      Object element = itr.next();
      System.out.print(element + " ");
    }
    System.out.println();

    // now, display the list backwards
    System.out.print("Modified list backwards: ");
    while(litr.hasPrevious()) {
      Object element = litr.previous();
      System.out.print(element + " ");
    }
    System.out.println();
  }
}
```

The output is shown here:

```
Original contents of al: C A E B D F
Modified contents of al: C+ A+ E+ B+ D+ F+
Modified list backwards: F+ D+ B+ E+ A+ C+
```

Pay special attention to how the list is displayed in reverse. After the list is modified, **litr** points to the end of the list. (Remember, **litr.hasNext( )** returns false when the end of the list has been reached.) To traverse the list in reverse, the program continues to use **litr**, but this time it checks to see whether it has a previous element. As long as it does, that element is obtained and displayed.

Storing User-Defined Classes in Collections

For the sake of simplicity, the foregoing examples have stored built-in objects, such as **String** or **Integer**, in a collection. Of course, collections are not limited to the storage of built-in objects. Quite the contrary. The power of collections is that they can store any type of object, including objects of classes that you create. For example, consider the following example that uses a **LinkedList** to store mailing addresses:

```
// A simple mailing list example.
import java.util.*;
```

```
class Address {
  private String name;
  private String street;
  private String city;
  private String state;
  private String code;

  Address(String n, String s, String c,
          String st, String cd) {
    name = n;
    street = s;
    city = c;
    state = st;
    code = cd;
  }

  public String toString() {
    return name + "\n" + street + "\n" +
           city + " " + state + " " + code;
  }
}

class MailList {
  public static void main(String args[]) {
    LinkedList ml = new LinkedList();

    // add elements to the linked list
    ml.add(new Address("J.W. West", "11 Oak Ave",
                       "Urbana", "IL", "61801"));
    ml.add(new Address("Ralph Baker", "1142 Maple Lane",
                       "Mahomet", "IL", "61853"));
    ml.add(new Address("Tom Carlton", "867 Elm St",
                       "Champaign", "IL", "61820"));

    Iterator itr = ml.iterator();
    while(itr.hasNext()) {
      Object element = itr.next();
      System.out.println(element + "\n");
    }
    System.out.println();
  }
}
```

The output from the program is shown here:

```
J.W. West
11 Oak Ave
Urbana IL 61801

Ralph Baker
1142 Maple Lane
Mahomet IL 61853

Tom Carlton
867 Elm St
Champaign IL 61820
```

Aside from storing a user-defined class in a collection, another important thing to notice about the preceding program is that it is quite short. When you consider that it sets up a linked list that can store, retrieve, and process mailing addresses in about 50 lines of code, the power of the collections framework begins to become apparent. As most readers know, if all of this functionality had to be coded manually, the program would be several times longer. Collections offer off-the-shelf solutions to a wide variety of programming problems. You should use them whenever the situation presents itself.

The RandomAccess Interface

Java 2, version 1.4 adds the **RandomAccess** interface. This interface contains no members. However, by implementing this interface, a collection signals that it supports efficient random access to its elements. Although a collection might support random access, it might not do so efficiently. By checking for the **RandomAccess** interface, client code can determine at run time whether a collection is suitable for certain types of random access operations—especially as they apply to large collections. (You can use **instanceof** to determine if a class implements an interface.) **RandomAccess** is implemented by **ArrayList** and by the legacy **Vector** class.

Working with Maps

A *map* is an object that stores associations between keys and values, or *key/value pairs*. Given a key, you can find its value. Both keys and values are objects. The keys must be unique, but the values may be duplicated. Some maps can accept a **null** key and **null** values, others cannot.

The Map Interfaces

Because the map interfaces define the character and nature of maps, this discussion of maps begins with them. The following interfaces support maps:

Interface	Description
Map	Maps unique keys to values.
Map.Entry	Describes an element (a key/value pair) in a map. This is an inner class of **Map**.
SortedMap	Extends **Map** so that the keys are maintained in ascending order.

Each interface is examined next, in turn.

The Map Interface

The **Map** interface maps unique keys to values. A *key* is an object that you use to retrieve a value at a later date. Given a key and a value, you can store the value in a **Map** object. After the value is stored, you can retrieve it by using its key. The methods declared by **Map** are summarized in Table 15-6. Several methods throw a **NoSuchElementException** when no items exist in the invoking map. A **ClassCastException** is thrown when an object is incompatible with the elements in a map. A **NullPointerException** is thrown if an attempt is made to use a **null** object and **null** is not allowed in the map. An **UnsupportedOperationException** is thrown when an attempt is made to change an unmodifiable map.

Method	Description
void clear( )	Removes all key/value pairs from the invoking map.
boolean containsKey(Object *k*)	Returns **true** if the invoking map contains *k* as a key. Otherwise, returns **false**.
boolean containsValue(Object *v*)	Returns **true** if the map contains *v* as a value. Otherwise, returns **false**.
Set entrySet( )	Returns a **Set** that contains the entries in the map. The set contains objects of type **Map.Entry**. This method provides a set-view of the invoking map.
boolean equals(Object *obj*)	Returns **true** if *obj* is a **Map** and contains the same entries. Otherwise, returns **false**.

Table 15-6. *The Methods Defined by* Map

Method	Description
Object get(Object *k*)	Returns the value associated with the key *k*.
int hashCode( )	Returns the hash code for the invoking map.
boolean isEmpty( )	Returns **true** if the invoking map is empty. Otherwise, returns **false**.
Set keySet( )	Returns a **Set** that contains the keys in the invoking map. This method provides a set-view of the keys in the invoking map.
Object put(Object *k*, Object *v*)	Puts an entry in the invoking map, overwriting any previous value associated with the key. The key and value are *k* and *v*, respectively. Returns **null** if the key did not already exist. Otherwise, the previous value linked to the key is returned.
void putAll(Map *m*)	Puts all the entries from *m* into this map.
Object remove(Object *k*)	Removes the entry whose key equals *k*.
int size( )	Returns the number of key/value pairs in the map.
Collection values( )	Returns a collection containing the values in the map. This method provides a collection-view of the values in the map.

Table 15-6. *The Methods Defined by* Map (continued)

Maps revolve around two basic operations: **get( )** and **put( )**. To put a value into a map, use **put( )**, specifying the key and the value. To obtain a value, call **get( )**, passing the key as an argument. The value is returned.

As mentioned earlier, maps are not collections because they do not implement the **Collection** interface, but you can obtain a collection-view of a map. To do this, you can use the **entrySet( )** method. It returns a **Set** that contains the elements in the map. To obtain a collection-view of the keys, use **keySet( )**. To get a collection-view of the values, use **values( )**. Collection-views are the means by which maps are integrated into the collections framework.

The SortedMap Interface

The **SortedMap** interface extends **Map**. It ensures that the entries are maintained in ascending key order. The methods declared by **SortedMap** are summarized in Table 15-7. Several methods throw a **NoSuchElementException** when no items are in the invoking map. A **ClassCastException** is thrown when an object is incompatible with the elements in a map. A **NullPointerException** is thrown if an attempt is made to use a **null** object when **null** is not allowed in the map.

Sorted maps allow very efficient manipulations of submaps (in other words, a subset of a map). To obtain a submap, use **headMap( )**, **tailMap( )**, or **subMap( )**. To get the first key in the set, call **firstKey( )**. To get the last key, use **lastKey( )**.

Method	Description
Comparator comparator( )	Returns the invoking sorted map's comparator. If the natural ordering is used for the invoking map, **null** is returned.
Object firstKey( )	Returns the first key in the invoking map.
SortedMap headMap(Object *end*)	Returns a sorted map for those map entries with keys that are less than *end*.
Object lastKey( )	Returns the last key in the invoking map.
SortedMap subMap(Object *start*, Object *end*)	Returns a map containing those entries with keys that are greater than or equal to *start* and less than *end*.
SortedMap tailMap(Object *start*)	Returns a map containing those entries with keys that are greater than or equal to *start*.

Table 15-7. *The Methods Defined by* SortedMap

The Map.Entry Interface

The **Map.Entry** interface enables you to work with a map entry. Recall that the **entrySet( )** method declared by the **Map** interface returns a **Set** containing the map entries. Each of these set elements is a **Map.Entry** object. Table 15-8 summarizes the methods declared by this interface.

The Map Classes

Several classes provide implementations of the map interfaces. The classes that can be used for maps are summarized here:

Class	Description
AbstractMap	Implements most of the **Map** interface.
HashMap	Extends **AbstractMap** to use a hash table.
TreeMap	Extends **AbstractMap** to use a tree.
WeakHashMap	Extends **AbstractMap** to use a hash table with weak keys.
LinkedHashMap	Extends **HashMap** to allow insertion-order iterations.
IdentityHashMap	Extends **AbstractMap** and uses reference equality when comparing documents.

Method	Description
boolean equals(Object *obj*)	Returns **true** if *obj* is a **Map.Entry** whose key and value are equal to that of the invoking object.
Object getKey( )	Returns the key for this map entry.
Object getValue( )	Returns the value for this map entry.
int hashCode( )	Returns the hash code for this map entry.
Object setValue(Object *v*)	Sets the value for this map entry to *v*. A **ClassCastException** is thrown if *v* is not the correct type for the map. An **IllegalArgumentException** is thrown if there is a problem with *v*. A **NullPointerException** is thrown if *v* is **null** and the map does not permit **null** keys. An **UnsupportedOperationException** is thrown if the map cannot be changed.

Table 15-8. *The Methods Defined by* Map.Entry

Notice that **AbstractMap** is a superclass for all concrete map implementations. **WeakHashMap** implements a map that uses "weak keys," which allows an element in a map to be garbage-collected when its key is unused. This class is not discussed further here. The others are described next.

The HashMap Class

The **HashMap** class uses a hash table to implement the **Map** interface. This allows the execution time of basic operations, such as **get( )** and **put( )**, to remain constant even for large sets.

The following constructors are defined:

HashMap( )
HashMap(Map *m*)
HashMap(int *capacity*)
HashMap(int *capacity*, float *fillRatio*)

The first form constructs a default hash map. The second form initializes the hash map by using the elements of *m*. The third form initializes the capacity of the hash map to *capacity*. The fourth form initializes both the capacity and fill ratio of the hash map by using its arguments. The meaning of capacity and fill ratio is the same as for **HashSet**, described earlier.

HashMap implements **Map** and extends **AbstractMap**. It does not add any methods of its own.

You should note that a hash map does *not* guarantee the order of its elements. Therefore, the order in which elements are added to a hash map is not necessarily the order in which they are read by an iterator.

The following program illustrates **HashMap**. It maps names to account balances. Notice how a set-view is obtained and used.

```
import java.util.*;

class HashMapDemo {
  public static void main(String args[]) {

    // Create a hash map
    HashMap hm = new HashMap();

    // Put elements to the map
    hm.put("John Doe", new Double(3434.34));
    hm.put("Tom Smith", new Double(123.22));
    hm.put("Jane Baker", new Double(1378.00));
    hm.put("Todd Hall", new Double(99.22));
    hm.put("Ralph Smith", new Double(-19.08));
```

```
    // Get a set of the entries
    Set set = hm.entrySet();

    // Get an iterator
    Iterator i = set.iterator();

    // Display elements
    while(i.hasNext()) {
      Map.Entry me = (Map.Entry)i.next();
      System.out.print(me.getKey() + ": ");
      System.out.println(me.getValue());
    }
    System.out.println();

    // Deposit 1000 into John Doe's account
    double balance = ((Double)hm.get("John Doe")).doubleValue();
    hm.put("John Doe", new Double(balance + 1000));
    System.out.println("John Doe's new balance: " +
      hm.get("John Doe"));
  }
}
```

Output from this program is shown here (the precise order may vary).

```
Todd Hall: 99.22
Ralph Smith: -19.08
John Doe: 3434.34
Jane Baker: 1378.0
Tom Smith: 123.22

John Doe's current balance: 4434.34
```

The program begins by creating a hash map and then adds the mapping of names to balances. Next, the contents of the map are displayed by using a set-view, obtained by calling **entrySet( )**. The keys and values are displayed by calling the **getKey( )** and **getValue( )** methods that are defined by **Map.Entry**. Pay close attention to how the deposit is made into John Doe's account. The **put( )** method automatically replaces any preexisting value that is associated with the specified key with the new value. Thus, after John Doe's account is updated, the hash map will still contain just one "John Doe" account.

The TreeMap Class

The **TreeMap** class implements the **Map** interface by using a tree. A **TreeMap** provides an efficient means of storing key/value pairs in sorted order, and allows rapid retrieval. You should note that, unlike a hash map, a tree map guarantees that its elements will be sorted in ascending key order.

The following **TreeMap** constructors are defined:

```
TreeMap( )
TreeMap(Comparator comp)
TreeMap(Map m)
TreeMap(SortedMap sm)
```

The first form constructs an empty tree map that will be sorted by using the natural order of its keys. The second form constructs an empty tree-based map that will be sorted by using the **Comparator** comp. (Comparators are discussed later in this chapter.) The third form initializes a tree map with the entries from m, which will be sorted by using the natural order of the keys. The fourth form initializes a tree map with the entries from sm, which will be sorted in the same order as sm.

TreeMap implements **SortedMap** and extends **AbstractMap**. It does not define any additional methods of its own.

The following program reworks the preceding example so that it uses **TreeMap**:

```java
import java.util.*;

class TreeMapDemo {
  public static void main(String args[]) {

    // Create a tree map
    TreeMap tm = new TreeMap();

    // Put elements to the map
    tm.put("John Doe", new Double(3434.34));
    tm.put("Tom Smith", new Double(123.22));
    tm.put("Jane Baker", new Double(1378.00));
    tm.put("Todd Hall", new Double(99.22));
    tm.put("Ralph Smith", new Double(-19.08));

    // Get a set of the entries
    Set set = tm.entrySet();

    // Get an iterator
    Iterator i = set.iterator();

    // Display elements
    while(i.hasNext()) {
      Map.Entry me = (Map.Entry)i.next();
```

```
    System.out.print(me.getKey() + ": ");
    System.out.println(me.getValue());
  }
  System.out.println();

  // Deposit 1000 into John Doe's account
  double balance =  ((Double)tm.get("John Doe")).doubleValue();
  tm.put("John Doe", new Double(balance + 1000));
  System.out.println("John Doe's new balance: " +
    tm.get("John Doe"));
  }
}
```

The following is the output from this program:

```
Jane Baker: 1378.0
John Doe: 3434.34
Ralph Smith: -19.08
Todd Hall: 99.22
Tom Smith: 123.22

John Doe's current balance: 4434.34
```

Notice that **TreeMap** sorts the keys. However, in this case, they are sorted by first name instead of last name. You can alter this behavior by specifying a comparator when the map is created, as described shortly.

The LinkedHashMap Class

Java 2, version 1.4 adds the **LinkedHashMap** class. This class extends **HashMap**. **LinkedHashMap** maintains a linked list of the entries in the map, in the order in which they were inserted. This allows insertion-order iteration over the map. That is, when iterating a **LinkedHashMap**, the elements will be returned in the order in which they were inserted. You can also create a **LinkedHashMap** that returns its elements in the order in which they were last accessed.

LinkedHashMap defines the following constructors.

LinkedHashMap( )
LinkedHashMap(Map *m*)
LinkedHashMap(int *capacity*)
LinkedHashMap(int *capacity*, float *fillRatio*)
LinkedHashMap(int *capacity*, float *fillRatio*, boolean *Order*)

The first form constructs a default **LinkedHashMap**. The second form initializes the **LinkedHashMap** with the elements from *m*. The third form initializes the capacity. The fourth form initializes both capacity and fill ratio. The meaning of capacity and fill ratio are the same as for **HashMap**. The last form allows you to specify whether the elements will be stored in the linked list by insertion order, or by order of last access. If *Order* is **true**, then access order is used. If *Order* is **false**, then insertion order is used.

LinkedHashMap adds only one method to those defined by **HashMap**. This method is **removeEldestEntry( )** and it is shown here.

protected boolean removeEldestEntry(Map.Entry *e*)

This method is called by **put( )** and **putAll( )**. The oldest entry is passed in *e*. By default, this method returns **false** and does nothing. However, if you override this method, then you can have the **LinkedHashMap** remove the oldest entry in the map. To do this, have your override return **true**. To keep the oldest entry, return **false**.

The IdentityHashMap Class

Java 2, version 1.4 adds the **IdentityHashMap** class. This class implements **AbstractMap**. It is similar to **HashMap** except that it uses reference equality when comparing elements. The Java 2 documentation explicitly states that **IdentityHashMap** is not for general use.

Comparators

Both **TreeSet** and **TreeMap** store elements in sorted order. However, it is the comparator that defines precisely what "sorted order" means. By default, these classes store their elements by using what Java refers to as "natural ordering," which is usually the ordering that you would expect. (A before B, 1 before 2, and so forth.) If you want to order elements a different way, then specify a **Comparator** object when you construct the set or map. Doing so gives you the ability to govern precisely how elements are stored within sorted collections and maps.

The **Comparator** interface defines two methods: **compare( )** and **equals( )**. The **compare( )** method, shown here, compares two elements for order:

int compare(Object *obj1*, Object *obj2*)

obj1 and *obj2* are the objects to be compared. This method returns zero if the objects are equal. It returns a positive value if *obj1* is greater than *obj2*. Otherwise, a negative value is returned. The method can throw a **ClassCastException** if the types of the objects are not compatible for comparison. By overriding **compare( )**, you can alter the way that objects are ordered. For example, to sort in reverse order, you can create a comparator that reverses the outcome of a comparison.

The **equals( )** method, shown here, tests whether an object equals the invoking comparator:

boolean equals(Object *obj*)

obj is the object to be tested for equality. The method returns **true** if *obj* and the invoking object are both **Comparator** objects and use the same ordering. Otherwise, it returns **false**. Overriding **equals( )** is unnecessary, and most simple comparators will not do so.

Using a Comparator

The following is an example that demonstrates the power of a custom comparator. It implements the **compare( )** method so that it operates in reverse of normal. Thus, it causes a tree set to be stored in reverse order.

```
// Use a custom comparator.
import java.util.*;

// A reverse comparator for strings.
class MyComp implements Comparator {
  public int compare(Object a, Object b) {
    String aStr, bStr;

    aStr = (String) a;
    bStr = (String) b;

    // reverse the comparison
    return bStr.compareTo(aStr);
  }

  // no need to override equals
}

class CompDemo {
  public static void main(String args[]) {
    // Create a tree set
    TreeSet ts = new TreeSet(new MyComp());

    // Add elements to the tree set
    ts.add("C");
    ts.add("A");
```

```
    ts.add("B");
    ts.add("E");
    ts.add("F");
    ts.add("D");

    // Get an iterator
    Iterator i = ts.iterator();

    // Display elements
    while(i.hasNext()) {
      Object element = i.next();
      System.out.print(element + " ");
    }
    System.out.println();
  }
}
```

As the following output shows, the tree is now stored in reverse order:

```
F E D C B A
```

Look closely at the **MyComp** class, which implements **Comparator** and overrides **compare( )**. (As explained earlier, overriding **equals( )** is neither necessary nor common.) Inside **compare( )**, the **String** method **compareTo( )** compares the two strings. However, **bStr**—not **aStr**—invokes **compareTo( )**. This causes the outcome of the comparison to be reversed.

For a more practical example, the following program is an updated version of the **TreeMap** program shown earlier that stores account balances. In the previous version, the accounts were sorted by name, but the sorting began with the first name. The following program sorts the accounts by last name. To do so, it uses a comparator that compares the last name of each account. This results in the map being sorted by last name.

```
// Use a comparator to sort accounts by last name.
import java.util.*;

// Compare last whole words in two strings.
class TComp implements Comparator {
  public int compare(Object a, Object b) {
    int i, j, k;
    String aStr, bStr;
```

```
    aStr = (String) a;
    bStr = (String) b;

    // find index of beginning of last name
    i = aStr.lastIndexOf(' ');
    j = bStr.lastIndexOf(' ');

    k = aStr.substring(i).compareTo(bStr.substring(j));
    if(k==0) // last names match, check entire name
      return aStr.compareTo(bStr);
    else
      return k;
  }

  // no need to override equals
}

class TreeMapDemo2 {
  public static void main(String args[]) {
    // Create a tree map
    TreeMap tm = new TreeMap(new TComp());

    // Put elements to the map
    tm.put("John Doe", new Double(3434.34));
    tm.put("Tom Smith", new Double(123.22));
    tm.put("Jane Baker", new Double(1378.00));
    tm.put("Todd Hall", new Double(99.22));
    tm.put("Ralph Smith", new Double(-19.08));

    // Get a set of the entries
    Set set = tm.entrySet();

    // Get an iterator
    Iterator itr = set.iterator();

    // Display elements
    while(itr.hasNext()) {
      Map.Entry me = (Map.Entry)itr.next();
      System.out.print(me.getKey() + ": ");
      System.out.println(me.getValue());
    }
    System.out.println();
```

```
// Deposit 1000 into John Doe's account
double balance =  ((Double)tm.get("John Doe")).doubleValue();
tm.put("John Doe", new Double(balance + 1000));
System.out.println("John Doe's new balance: " +
   tm.get("John Doe"));
   }
}
```

Here is the output; notice that the accounts are now sorted by last name:

```
Jane Baker: 1378.0
John Doe: 3434.34
Todd Hall: 99.22
Ralph Smith: -19.08
Tom Smith: 123.22

John Doe's new balance: 4434.34
```

The comparator class **TComp** compares two strings that hold first and last names. It does so by first comparing last names. To do this, it finds the index of the last space in each string and then compares the substrings of each element that begin at that point. In cases where last names are equivalent, the first names are then compared. This yields a tree map that is sorted by last name, and within last name by first name. You can see this because Ralph Smith comes before Tom Smith in the output.

The Collection Algorithms

The collections framework defines several algorithms that can be applied to collections and maps. These algorithms are defined as static methods within the **Collections** class. They are summarized in Table 15-9. Several of the methods can throw a **ClassCastException**, which occurs when an attempt is made to compare incompatible types, or an **UnsupportedOperationException**, which occurs when an attempt is made to modify an unmodifiable collection.

Notice that several methods, such as **synchronizedList( )** and **synchronizedSet( )**, are used to obtain synchronized (*thread-safe*) copies of the various collections. As explained, none of the standard collections implementations are synchronized. You must use the synchronization algorithms to provide synchronization. One other point: iterators to synchronized collections must be used within **synchronized** blocks.

The set of methods that begins with **unmodifiable** returns views of the various collections that cannot be modified. These will be useful when you want to grant some process read—but not write—capabilities on a collection.

Method	Description
static int binarySearch(List *list*, Object *value*, Comparator *c*)	Searches for *value* in *list* ordered according to *c*. Returns the position of *value* in *list*, or −1 if *value* is not found.
static int binarySearch(List *list*, Object *value*)	Searches for *value* in *list*. The list must be sorted. Returns the position of *value* in *list*, or −1 if *value* is not found.
static void copy(List *list1*, List *list2*)	Copies the elements of *list2* to *list1*.
static Enumeration enumeration(Collection *c*)	Returns an enumeration over *c*. (See "The Enumeration Interface," later in this chapter.)
static void fill(List *list*, Object *obj*)	Assigns *obj* to each element of *list*.
static int indexOfSubList(List *list*, List *subList*)	Searches *list* for the first occurrence of *subList*. Returns the index of the first match, or −1 if no match is found. (Added by Java 2, v1.4)
static int lastIndexOfSubList(List *list*, List *subList*)	Searches *list* for the last occurrence of *subList*. Returns the index of the last match, or −1 if no match is found. (Added by Java 2, v1.4)
static ArrayList list(Enumeration *enum*)	Returns an **ArrayList** that contains the elements of *enum*. (Added by Java 2, v1.4)
static Object max(Collection *c*, Comparator *comp*)	Returns the maximum element in *c* as determined by *comp*.
static Object max(Collection *c*)	Returns the maximum element in *c* as determined by natural ordering. The collection need not be sorted.

Table 15-9. *The Algorithms Defined by* Collections

Method	Description
static Object min(Collection *c*, Comparator *comp*)	Returns the minimum element in *c* as determined by *comp*. The collection need not be sorted.
static Object min(Collection *c*)	Returns the minimum element in *c* as determined by natural ordering.
static List nCopies(int *num*, Object *obj*)	Returns *num* copies of *obj* contained in an immutable list. *num* must be greater than or equal to zero.
static boolean replaceAll(List *list*, Object *old*, Object *new*)	Replaces all occurrences of *old* with *new* in *list*. Returns **true** if at least one replacement occurred. Returns **false**, otherwise. (Added by Java 2, v1.4)
static void reverse(List *list*)	Reverses the sequence in *list*.
static Comparator reverseOrder( )	Returns a reverse comparator (a comparator that reverses the outcome of a comparison between two elements).
static void rotate(List *list*, int *n*)	Rotates *list* by *n* places to the right. To rotate left, use a negative value for *n*. (Added by Java 2, v1.4)
static void shuffle(List *list*, Random *r*)	Shuffles (i.e., randomizes) the elements in *list* by using *r* as a source of random numbers.
static void shuffle(List *list*)	Shuffles (i.e., randomizes) the elements in *list*.
static Set singleton(Object *obj*)	Returns *obj* as an immutable set. This is an easy way to convert a single object into a set.

Table 15-9.   *The Algorithms Defined by* Collections (continued)

Method	Description
static List singletonList(Object *obj*)	Returns *obj* as an immutable list. This is an easy way to convert a single object into a list. (Added by Java 2, v1.3)
static Map singletonMap(Object *k*, Object *v*)	Returns the key/value pair *k*/*v* as an immutable map. This is an easy way to convert a single key/value pair into a map. (Added by Java 2, v1.3)
static void sort(List *list*, Comparator *comp*)	Sorts the elements of *list* as determined by *comp*.
static void sort(List *list*)	Sorts the elements of *list* as determined by their natural ordering.
static void swap(List *list*, int *idx1*, int *idx2*)	Exchanges the elements in *list* at the indices specified by *idx1* and *idx2*. (Added by Java 2, v1.4)
static Collection synchronizedCollection(Collection *c*)	Returns a thread-safe collection backed by *c*.
static List synchronizedList(List *list*)	Returns a thread-safe list backed by *list*.
static Map synchronizedMap(Map *m*)	Returns a thread-safe map backed by *m*.
static Set synchronizedSet(Set *s*)	Returns a thread-safe set backed by *s*.
static SortedMap synchronizedSortedMap(SortedMap *sm*)	Returns a thread-safe sorted set backed by *sm*.
static SortedSet synchronizedSortedSet(SortedSet *ss*)	Returns a thread-safe set backed by *ss*.
static Collection unmodifiableCollection(Collection *c*)	Returns an unmodifiable collection backed by *c*.
static List unmodifiableList(List *list*)	Returns an unmodifiable list backed by *list*.

Table 15-9. *The Algorithms Defined by* Collections (continued)

Method	Description
static Map unmodifiableMap(Map *m*)	Returns an unmodifiable map backed by *m*.
static Set unmodifiableSet(Set *s*)	Returns an unmodifiable set backed by *s*.
static SortedMap unmodifiableSortedMap(SortedMap *sm*)	Returns an unmodifiable sorted map backed by *sm*.
static SortedSet unmodifiableSortedSet(SortedSet *ss*)	Returns an unmodifiable sorted set backed by *ss*.

Table 15-9. *The Algorithms Defined by* Collections (continued)

Collections defines three static variables: **EMPTY_SET**, **EMPTY_LIST**, and **EMPTY_MAP**. All are immutable. **EMPTY_MAP** was added by Java 2, version 1.3.

The following program demonstrates some of the algorithms. It creates and initializes a linked list. The **reverseOrder( )** method returns a **Comparator** that reverses the comparison of **Integer** objects. The list elements are sorted according to this comparator and then are displayed. Next, the list is randomized by calling **shuffle( )**, and then its minimum and maximum values are displayed.

```
// Demonstrate various algorithms.
import java.util.*;

class AlgorithmsDemo {
  public static void main(String args[]) {

    // Create and initialize linked list
    LinkedList ll = new LinkedList();
    ll.add(new Integer(-8));
    ll.add(new Integer(20));
    ll.add(new Integer(-20));
    ll.add(new Integer(8));

    // Create a reverse order comparator
    Comparator r = Collections.reverseOrder();

    // Sort list by using the comparator
    Collections.sort(ll, r);
```

```
// Get iterator
Iterator li = ll.iterator();

System.out.print("List sorted in reverse: ");
while(li.hasNext())
  System.out.print(li.next() + " ");
System.out.println();

Collections.shuffle(ll);

// display randomized list
li = ll.iterator();
System.out.print("List shuffled: ");
while(li.hasNext())
  System.out.print(li.next() + " ");
System.out.println();

System.out.println("Minimum: " + Collections.min(ll));
System.out.println("Maximum: " + Collections.max(ll));
  }
}
```

Output from this program is shown here:

```
List sorted in reverse: 20 8 -8 -20
List shuffled: 20 -20 8 -8
Minimum: -20
Maximum: 20
```

Notice that **min( )** and **max( )** operate on the list after it has been shuffled. Neither requires a sorted list for its operation.

Arrays

The **Arrays** class provides various methods that are useful when working with arrays. Although these methods technically aren't part of the collections framework, they help bridge the gap between collections and arrays. **Arrays** was added by Java 2. Each method defined by **Arrays** is examined in this section.

The **asList( )** method returns a **List** that is backed by a specified array. In other words, both the list and the array refer to the same location. It has the following signature:

static List asList(Object[ ] *array*)

Here, *array* is the array that contains the data.

The **binarySearch( )** method uses a binary search to find a specified value. This method must be applied to sorted arrays. It has the following forms:

static int binarySearch(byte[ ] *array*, byte *value*)
static int binarySearch(char[ ] *array*, char *value*)
static int binarySearch(double[ ] *array*, double *value*)
static int binarySearch(float[ ] *array*, float *value*)
static int binarySearch(int[ ] *array*, int *value*)
static int binarySearch(long[ ] *array*, long *value*)
static int binarySearch(short[ ] *array*, short *value*)
static int binarySearch(Object[ ] *array*, Object *value*)
static int binarySearch(Object[ ] *array*, Object *value*, Comparator *c*)

Here, *array* is the array to be searched and *value* is the value to be located. The last two forms throw a **ClassCastException** if *array* contains elements that cannot be compared (for example, **Double** and **StringBuffer**) or if *value* is not compatible with the types in *array*. In the last form, the **Comparator** *c* is used to determine the order of the elements in *array*. In all cases, if *value* exists in *array*, the index of the element is returned. Otherwise, a negative value is returned.

The **equals( )** method returns **true** if two arrays are equivalent. Otherwise, it returns **false**. The **equals( )** method has the following forms:

static boolean equals(boolean *array1*[ ], boolean *array2*[ ])
static boolean equals(byte *array1*[ ], byte *array2*[ ])
static boolean equals(char *array1*[ ], char *array2*[ ])
static boolean equals(double *array1*[ ], double *array2*[ ])
static boolean equals(float *array1*[ ], float *array2*[ ])
static boolean equals(int *array1*[ ], int *array2*[ ])
static boolean equals(long *array1*[ ], long *array2*[ ])
static boolean equals(short *array1*[ ], short *array2*[ ])
static boolean equals(Object *array1*[ ], Object *array2*[ ])

Here, *array1* and *array2* are the two arrays that are compared for equality.

The **fill( )** method assigns a value to all elements in an array. In other words, it fills an array with a specified value. The **fill( )** method has two versions. The first version, which has the following forms, fills an entire array:

static void fill(boolean *array*[ ], boolean *value*)
static void fill(byte *array*[ ], byte *value*)
static void fill(char *array*[ ], char *value*)
static void fill(double *array*[ ], double *value*)
static void fill(float *array*[ ], float *value*)
static void fill(int *array*[ ], int *value*)
static void fill(long *array*[ ], long *value*)
static void fill(short *array*[ ], short *value*)
static void fill(Object *array*[ ], Object *value*)

Here, *value* is assigned to all elements in *array*.

The second version of the **fill( )** method assigns a value to a subset of an array. Its forms are shown here:

```
static void fill(boolean array[ ], int start, int end, boolean value)
static void fill(byte array[ ], int start, int end, byte value)
static void fill(char array[ ], int start, int end, char value)
static void fill(double array[ ], int start, int end, double value)
static void fill(float array[ ], int start, int end, float value)
static void fill(int array[ ], int start, int end, int value)
static void fill(long array[ ], int start, int end, long value)
static void fill(short array[ ], int start, int end, short value)
static void fill(Object array[ ], int start, int end, Object value)
```

Here, *value* is assigned to the elements in *array* from position *start* to position *end*–1. These methods may all throw an **IllegalArgumentException** if *start* is greater than *end*, or an **ArrayIndexOutOfBoundsException** if *start* or *end* is out of bounds.

The **sort( )** method sorts an array so that it is arranged in ascending order. The **sort( )** method has two versions. The first version, shown here, sorts the entire array:

```
static void sort(byte array[ ])
static void sort(char array[ ])
static void sort(double array[ ])
static void sort(float array[ ])
static void sort(int array[ ])
static void sort(long array[ ])
static void sort(short array[ ])
static void sort(Object array[ ])
static void sort(Object array[ ], Comparator c)
```

Here, *array* is the array to be sorted. In the last form, *c* is a **Comparator** that is used to order the elements of *array*. The forms that sort arrays of **Object** can also throw a **ClassCastException** if elements of the array being sorted are not comparable.

The second version of **sort( )** enables you to specify a range within an array that you want to sort. Its forms are shown here:

```
static void sort(byte array[ ], int start, int end)
static void sort(char array[ ], int start, int end)
static void sort(double array[ ], int start, int end)
static void sort(float array[ ], int start, int end)
static void sort(int array[ ], int start, int end)
static void sort(long array[ ], int start, int end)
static void sort(short array[ ], int start, int end)
static void sort(Object array[ ], int start, int end)
static void sort(Object array[ ], int start, int end, Comparator c)
```

Here, the range beginning at *start* and running through *end*–1 within *array* will be sorted. In the last form, *c* is a **Comparator** that is used to order the elements of *array*

All of these methods can throw an **IllegalArgumentException** if *start* is greater than *end*, or an **ArrayIndexOutOfBoundsException** if *start* or *end* is out of bounds. The last two forms can also throw a **ClassCastException** if elements of the array being sorted are not comparable.

The following program illustrates how to use some of the methods of the **Arrays** class:

```
// Demonstrate Arrays
import java.util.*;

class ArraysDemo {
  public static void main(String args[]) {

    // allocate and initialize array
    int array[] = new int[10];
    for(int i = 0; i < 10; i++)
      array[i] = -3 * i;

    // display, sort, display
    System.out.print("Original contents: ");
    display(array);
    Arrays.sort(array);
    System.out.print("Sorted: ");
    display(array);

    // fill and display
    Arrays.fill(array, 2, 6, -1);
    System.out.print("After fill(): ");
    display(array);

    // sort and display
    Arrays.sort(array);
    System.out.print("After sorting again: ");
    display(array);

    // binary search for -9
    System.out.print("The value -9 is at location ");
    int index =
      Arrays.binarySearch(array, -9);
    System.out.println(index);
  }

  static void display(int array[]) {
    for(int i = 0; i < array.length; i++)
      System.out.print(array[i] + " ");
```

```
    System.out.println("");
  }
}
```

The following is the output from this program:

```
Original contents: 0 -3 -6 -9 -12 -15 -18 -21 -24 -27
Sorted: -27 -24 -21 -18 -15 -12 -9 -6 -3 0
After fill(): -27 -24 -1 -1 -1 -1 -9 -6 -3 0
After sorting again: -27 -24 -9 -6 -3 -1 -1 -1 -1 0
The value -9 is at location 2
```

The Legacy Classes and Interfaces

As explained at the start of this chapter, the original version of **java.util** did not include the collections framework. Instead, it defined several classes and an interface that provided an ad hoc method of storing objects. With the addition of collections by Java 2, several of the original classes were reengineered to support the collection interfaces. Thus, they are fully compatible with the framework. While no classes have actually been deprecated, one has been rendered obsolete. Of course, where a collection duplicates the functionality of a legacy class, you will usually want to use the collection for new code. In general, the legacy classes are supported because there is still code that uses them.

One other point: None of the collection classes are synchronized, but all the legacy classes are synchronized. This distinction may be important in some situations. Of course, you can easily synchronize collections, too, by using one of the algorithms provided by **Collections**.

The legacy classes defined by **java.util** are shown here:

Dictionary   Hashtable   Properties   Stack   Vector

There is one legacy interface called **Enumeration**. The following sections examine **Enumeration** and each of the legacy classes, in turn.

The Enumeration Interface

The **Enumeration** interface defines the methods by which you can *enumerate* (obtain one at a time) the elements in a collection of objects. This legacy interface has been superceded by **Iterator**. Although not deprecated, **Enumeration** is considered obsolete for new code. However, it is used by several methods defined by the legacy classes (such as **Vector** and **Properties**), is used by several other API classes, and is currently in widespread use in application code.

Enumeration specifies the following two methods:

boolean hasMoreElements( )
Object nextElement( )

When implemented, **hasMoreElements( )** must return **true** while there are still more elements to extract, and **false** when all the elements have been enumerated. **nextElement( )** returns the next object in the enumeration as a generic **Object** reference. That is, each call to **nextElement( )** obtains the next object in the enumeration. The calling routine must cast that object into the object type held in the enumeration.

Vector

Vector implements a dynamic array. It is similar to **ArrayList**, but with two differences: **Vector** is synchronized, and it contains many legacy methods that are not part of the collections framework. With the release of Java 2, **Vector** was reengineered to extend **AbstractList** and implement the **List** interface, so it now is fully compatible with collections.

Here are the **Vector** constructors:

Vector( )
Vector(int *size*)
Vector(int *size*, int *incr*)
Vector(Collection *c*)

The first form creates a default vector, which has an initial size of 10. The second form creates a vector whose initial capacity is specified by *size*. The third form creates a vector whose initial capacity is specified by *size* and whose increment is specified by *incr*. The increment specifies the number of elements to allocate each time that a vector is resized upward. The fourth form creates a vector that contains the elements of collection *c*. This constructor was added by Java 2.

All vectors start with an initial capacity. After this initial capacity is reached, the next time that you attempt to store an object in the vector, the vector automatically allocates space for that object plus extra room for additional objects. By allocating more than just the required memory, the vector reduces the number of allocations that must take place. This reduction is important, because allocations are costly in terms of time. The amount of extra space allocated during each reallocation is determined by the increment that you specify when you create the vector. If you don't specify an increment, the vector's size is doubled by each allocation cycle.

Vector defines these protected data members:

int capacityIncrement;
int elementCount;
Object elementData[ ];

The increment value is stored in **capacityIncrement**. The number of elements currently in the vector is stored in **elementCount**. The array that holds the vector is stored in **elementData**.

In addition to the collections methods defined by **List**, **Vector** defines several legacy methods, which are shown in Table 15-10.

Method	Description
void addElement(Object *element*)	The object specified by *element* is added to the vector.
int capacity( )	Returns the capacity of the vector.
Object clone( )	Returns a duplicate of the invoking vector.
boolean contains(Object *element*)	Returns **true** if *element* is contained by the vector, and returns **false** if it is not.
void copyInto(Object *array*[ ])	The elements contained in the invoking vector are copied into the array specified by *array*.
Object elementAt(int *index*)	Returns the element at the location specified by *index*.
Enumeration elements( )	Returns an enumeration of the elements in the vector.
void ensureCapacity(int *size*)	Sets the minimum capacity of the vector to *size*.
Object firstElement( )	Returns the first element in the vector.
int indexOf(Object *element*)	Returns the index of the first occurrence of *element*. If the object is not in the vector, –1 is returned.
int indexOf(Object *element*, int *start*)	Returns the index of the first occurrence of *element* at or after *start*. If the object is not in that portion of the vector, –1 is returned.

Table 15-10. *The Methods Defined by* Vector

Method	Description
void insertElementAt(Object *element*, int *index*)	Adds *element* to the vector at the location specified by *index*.
boolean isEmpty( )	Returns **true** if the vector is empty and returns **false** if it contains one or more elements.
Object lastElement( )	Returns the last element in the vector.
int lastIndexOf(Object *element*)	Returns the index of the last occurrence of *element*. If the object is not in the vector, −1 is returned.
int lastIndexOf(Object *element*, int *start*)	Returns the index of the last occurrence of *element* before *start*. If the object is not in that portion of the vector, −1 is returned.
void removeAllElements( )	Empties the vector. After this method executes, the size of the vector is zero.
boolean removeElement(Object *element*)	Removes *element* from the vector. If more than one instance of the specified object exists in the vector, then it is the first one that is removed. Returns **true** if successful and **false** if the object is not found.
void removeElementAt(int *index*)	Removes the element at the location specified by *index*.
void setElementAt(Object *element*, int *index*)	The location specified by *index* is assigned *element*.
void setSize(int *size*)	Sets the number of elements in the vector to *size*. If the new size is less than the old size, elements are lost. If the new size is larger than the old size, **null** elements are added.

Table 15-10. *The Methods Defined by* Vector (continued)

Method	Description
int size( )	Returns the number of elements currently in the vector.
String toString( )	Returns the string equivalent of the vector.
void trimToSize( )	Sets the vector's capacity equal to the number of elements that it currently holds.

Table 15-10. *The Methods Defined by* Vector (continued)

Because **Vector** implements **List**, you can use a vector just like you use an **ArrayList** instance. You can also manipulate one using its legacy methods. For example, after you instantiate a **Vector**, you can add an element to it by calling **addElement( )**. To obtain the element at a specific location, call **elementAt( )**. To obtain the first element in the vector, call **firstElement( )**. To retrieve the last element, call **lastElement( )**. You can obtain the index of an element by using **indexOf( )** and **lastIndexOf( )**. To remove an element, call **removeElement( )** or **removeElementAt( )**.

The following program uses a vector to store various types of numeric objects. It demonstrates several of the legacy methods defined by **Vector**. It also demonstrates the **Enumeration** interface.

```
// Demonstrate various Vector operations.
import java.util.*;

class VectorDemo {
  public static void main(String args[]) {

    // initial size is 3, increment is 2
    Vector v = new Vector(3, 2);

    System.out.println("Initial size: " + v.size());
    System.out.println("Initial capacity: " +
                    v.capacity());
```

```
    v.addElement(new Integer(1));
    v.addElement(new Integer(2));
    v.addElement(new Integer(3));
    v.addElement(new Integer(4));

    System.out.println("Capacity after four additions: " +
                    v.capacity());
    v.addElement(new Double(5.45));
    System.out.println("Current capacity: " +
                    v.capacity());
    v.addElement(new Double(6.08));
    v.addElement(new Integer(7));

    System.out.println("Current capacity: " +
                    v.capacity());
    v.addElement(new Float(9.4));
    v.addElement(new Integer(10));

    System.out.println("Current capacity: " +
                    v.capacity());
    v.addElement(new Integer(11));
    v.addElement(new Integer(12));


    System.out.println("First element: " +
                    (Integer)v.firstElement());
    System.out.println("Last element: " +
                    (Integer)v.lastElement());

    if(v.contains(new Integer(3)))
       System.out.println("Vector contains 3.");

    // enumerate the elements in the vector.
    Enumeration vEnum = v.elements();

    System.out.println("\nElements in vector:");
    while(vEnum.hasMoreElements())
       System.out.print(vEnum.nextElement() + " ");
    System.out.println();
  }
}
```

The output from this program is shown here:

```
Initial size: 0
Initial capacity: 3
Capacity after four additions: 5
Current capacity: 5
Current capacity: 7
Current capacity: 9
First element: 1
Last element: 12
Vector contains 3.

Elements in vector:
1 2 3 4 5.45 6.08 7 9.4 10 11 12
```

With the release of Java 2, **Vector** added support for iterators. Instead of relying on an enumeration to cycle through the objects (as the preceding program does), you now can use an iterator. For example, the following iterator-based code can be substituted into the program:

```
// use an iterator to display contents
Iterator vItr = v.iterator();

System.out.println("\nElements in vector:");
while(vItr.hasNext())
  System.out.print(vItr.next() + " ");
System.out.println();
```

Because enumerations are not recommended for new code, you will usually use an iterator to enumerate the contents of a vector. Of course, much legacy code exists that employs enumerations. Fortunately, enumerations and iterators work in nearly the same manner.

Stack

Stack is a subclass of **Vector** that implements a standard last-in, first-out stack. **Stack** only defines the default constructor, which creates an empty stack. **Stack** includes all the methods defined by **Vector**, and adds several of its own, shown in Table 15-11.

To put an object on the top of the stack, call **push( )**. To remove and return the top element, call **pop( )**. An **EmptyStackException** is thrown if you call **pop( )** when the invoking stack is empty. You can use **peek( )** to return, but not remove, the top object. The **empty( )** method returns **true** if nothing is on the stack. The **search( )** method determines whether an object exists on the stack, and returns the number of pops that

Method	Description
boolean empty( )	Returns **true** if the stack is empty, and returns **false** if the stack contains elements.
Object peek( )	Returns the element on the top of the stack, but does not remove it.
Object pop( )	Returns the element on the top of the stack, removing it in the process.
Object push(Object *element*)	Pushes *element* onto the stack. *element* is also returned.
int search(Object *element*)	Searches for *element* in the stack. If found, its offset from the top of the stack is returned. Otherwise, –1 is returned.

Table 15-11.   *The Methods Defined by* Stack

are required to bring it to the top of the stack. Here is an example that creates a stack, pushes several **Integer** objects onto it, and then pops them off again:

```
// Demonstrate the Stack class.
import java.util.*;

class StackDemo {
  static void showpush(Stack st, int a) {
    st.push(new Integer(a));
    System.out.println("push(" + a + ")");
    System.out.println("stack: " + st);
  }

  static void showpop(Stack st) {
    System.out.print("pop -> ");
    Integer a = (Integer) st.pop();
    System.out.println(a);
    System.out.println("stack: " + st);
  }

  public static void main(String args[]) {
```

```
      Stack st = new Stack();

      System.out.println("stack: " + st);
      showpush(st, 42);
      showpush(st, 66);
      showpush(st, 99);
      showpop(st);
      showpop(st);
      showpop(st);
      try {
        showpop(st);
      } catch (EmptyStackException e) {
        System.out.println("empty stack");
      }
    }
}
```

The following is the output produced by the program; notice how the exception handler for **EmptyStackException** is caught so that you can gracefully handle a stack underflow:

```
stack: [ ]
push(42)
stack: [42]
push(66)
stack: [42, 66]
push(99)
stack: [42, 66, 99]
pop -> 99
stack: [42, 66]
pop -> 66
stack: [42]
pop -> 42
stack: [ ]
pop -> empty stack
```

Dictionary

Dictionary is an abstract class that represents a key/value storage repository and operates much like **Map**. Given a key and value, you can store the value in a **Dictionary**

object. Once the value is stored, you can retrieve it by using its key. Thus, like a map, a dictionary can be thought of as a list of key/value pairs. Although not actually deprecated by Java 2, **Dictionary** is classified as obsolete, because it is superceded by **Map**. However, **Dictionary** is still in use and thus is fully discussed here.

The abstract methods defined by **Dictionary** are listed in Table 15-12.

To add a key and a value, use the **put( )** method. Use **get( )** to retrieve the value of a given key. The keys and values can each be returned as an **Enumeration** by the **keys( )** and **elements( )** methods, respectively. The **size( )** method returns the number of key/value pairs stored in a dictionary, and **isEmpty( )** returns **true** when the dictionary is empty. You can use the **remove( )** method to delete a key/value pair.

Method	Purpose
Enumeration elements( )	Returns an enumeration of the values contained in the dictionary.
Object get(Object *key*)	Returns the object that contains the value associated with *key*. If *key* is not in the dictionary, a null object is returned.
boolean isEmpty( )	Returns **true** if the dictionary is empty, and returns **false** if it contains at least one key.
Enumeration keys( )	Returns an enumeration of the keys contained in the dictionary.
Object put(Object *key*, Object *value*)	Inserts a key and its value into the dictionary. Returns **null** if *key* is not already in the dictionary; returns the previous value associated with *key* if *key* is already in the dictionary.
Object remove(Object *key*)	Removes *key* and its value. Returns the value associated with *key*. If *key* is not in the dictionary, a **null** is returned.
int size( )	Returns the number of entries in the dictionary.

Table 15-12. *The Abstract Methods Defined by* Dictionary

*The **Dictionary** class is obsolete. You should implement the **Map** interface to obtain key/value storage functionality.*

Hashtable

Hashtable was part of the original **java.util** and is a concrete implementation of a **Dictionary**. However, Java 2 reengineered **Hashtable** so that it also implements the **Map** interface. Thus, **Hashtable** is now integrated into the collections framework. It is similar to **HashMap**, but is synchronized.

Like **HashMap**, **Hashtable** stores key/value pairs in a hash table. When using a **Hashtable**, you specify an object that is used as a key, and the value that you want linked to that key. The key is then hashed, and the resulting hash code is used as the index at which the value is stored within the table.

A hash table can only store objects that override the **hashCode( )** and **equals( )** methods that are defined by **Object**. The **hashCode( )** method must compute and return the hash code for the object. Of course, **equals( )** compares two objects. Fortunately, many of Java's built-in classes already implement the **hashCode( )** method. For example, the most common type of **Hashtable** uses a **String** object as the key. **String** implements both **hashCode( )** and **equals( )**.

The **Hashtable** constructors are shown here:

Hashtable( )
Hashtable(int *size*)
Hashtable(int *size*, float *fillRatio*)
Hashtable(Map *m*)

The first version is the default constructor. The second version creates a hash table that has an initial size specified by *size*. The third version creates a hash table that has an initial size specified by *size* and a fill ratio specified by *fillRatio*. This ratio must be between 0.0 and 1.0, and it determines how full the hash table can be before it is resized upward. Specifically, when the number of elements is greater than the capacity of the hash table multiplied by its fill ratio, the hash table is expanded. If you do not specify a fill ratio, then 0.75 is used. Finally, the fourth version creates a hash table that is initialized with the elements in *m*. The capacity of the hash table is set to twice the number of elements in *m*. The default load factor of 0.75 is used. The fourth constructor was added by Java 2.

In addition to the methods defined by the **Map** interface, which **Hashtable** now implements, **Hashtable** defines the legacy methods listed in Table 15-13.

Method	Description
void clear( )	Resets and empties the hash table.
Object clone( )	Returns a duplicate of the invoking object.
boolean contains(Object *value*)	Returns **true** if some value equal to *value* exists within the hash table. Returns **false** if the value isn't found.
boolean containsKey(Object *key*)	Returns **true** if some key equal to *key* exists within the hash table. Returns **false** if the key isn't found.
boolean containsValue(Object *value*)	Returns **true** if some value equal to *value* exists within the hash table. Returns **false** if the value isn't found. (A non-**Map** method added by Java 2, for consistency.)
Enumeration elements( )	Returns an enumeration of the values contained in the hash table.
Object get(Object *key*)	Returns the object that contains the value associated with *key*. If *key* is not in the hash table, a null object is returned.
boolean isEmpty( )	Returns **true** if the hash table is empty; returns **false** if it contains at least one key.
Enumeration keys( )	Returns an enumeration of the keys contained in the hash table.
Object put(Object *key*, Object *value*)	Inserts a key and a value into the hash table. Returns **null** if *key* isn't already in the hash table; returns the previous value associated with *key* if *key* is already in the hash table.
void rehash( )	Increases the size of the hash table and rehashes all of its keys.

Table 15-13. *The Legacy Methods Defined by* Hashtable

Method	Description
Object remove(Object *key*)	Removes *key* and its value. Returns the value associated with *key*. If *key* is not in the hash table, a null object is returned.
int size( )	Returns the number of entries in the hash table.
String toString( )	Returns the string equivalent of a hash table.

Table 15-13. *The Legacy Methods Defined by* Hashtable *(continued)*

The following example reworks the bank account program, shown earlier, so that it uses a **Hashtable** to store the names of bank depositors and their current balances:

```java
// Demonstrate a Hashtable
import java.util.*;
class HTDemo {
  public static void main(String args[]) {
    Hashtable balance = new Hashtable();
    Enumeration names;
    String str;
    double bal;

    balance.put("John Doe", new Double(3434.34));
    balance.put("Tom Smith", new Double(123.22));
    balance.put("Jane Baker", new Double(1378.00));
    balance.put("Todd Hall", new Double(99.22));
    balance.put("Ralph Smith", new Double(-19.08));

    // Show all balances in hash table.
    names = balance.keys();
    while(names.hasMoreElements()) {
      str = (String) names.nextElement();
      System.out.println(str + ": " +
                          balance.get(str));
    }

    System.out.println();
```

```
      // Deposit 1,000 into John Doe's account
      bal = ((Double)balance.get("John Doe")).doubleValue();
      balance.put("John Doe", new Double(bal+1000));
      System.out.println("John Doe's new balance: " +
                         balance.get("John Doe"));
    }
  }
```

The output from this program is shown here:

```
Todd Hall: 99.22
Ralph Smith: -19.08
John Doe: 3434.34
Jane Baker: 1378.0
Tom Smith: 123.22

John Doe's new balance: 4434.34
```

One important point: like the map classes, **Hashtable** does not directly support iterators. Thus, the preceding program uses an enumeration to display the contents of **balance**. However, you can obtain set-views of the hash table, which permits the use of iterators. To do so, you simply use one of the collection-view methods defined by **Map**, such as **entrySet( )** or **keySet( )**. For example, you can obtain a set-view of the keys and iterate through them. Here is a reworked version of the program that shows this technique:

```
// Use iterators with a Hashtable.
import java.util.*;

class HTDemo2 {
  public static void main(String args[]) {
    Hashtable balance = new Hashtable();
    String str;
    double bal;

    balance.put("John Doe", new Double(3434.34));
    balance.put("Tom Smith", new Double(123.22));
    balance.put("Jane Baker", new Double(1378.00));
    balance.put("Todd Hall", new Double(99.22));
    balance.put("Ralph Smith", new Double(-19.08));

    // show all balances in hashtable
```

```
Set set = balance.keySet(); // get set-view of keys

// get iterator
Iterator itr = set.iterator();
while(itr.hasNext()) {
  str = (String) itr.next();
  System.out.println(str + ": " +
                        balance.get(str));
}

System.out.println();

// Deposit 1,000 into John Doe's account
bal = ((Double)balance.get("John Doe")).doubleValue();
balance.put("John Doe", new Double(bal+1000));
System.out.println("John Doe's new balance: " +
                      balance.get("John Doe"));
  }
}
```

Properties

Properties is a subclass of **Hashtable**. It is used to maintain lists of values in which the key is a **String** and the value is also a **String**. The **Properties** class is used by many other Java classes. For example, it is the type of object returned by **System.getProperties( )** when obtaining environmental values.

    Properties defines the following instance variable:

Properties defaults;

This variable holds a default property list associated with a **Properties** object. **Properties** defines these constructors:

Properties(.)
Properties(Properties *propDefault*)

The first version creates a **Properties** object that has no default values. The second creates an object that uses *propDefault* for its default values. In both cases, the property list is empty.

    In addition to the methods that **Properties** inherits from **Hashtable**, **Properties** defines the methods listed in Table 15-14. **Properties** also contains one deprecated method: **save( )**. This was replaced by **store( )** because **save( )** did not handle errors correctly.

Method	Description
String getProperty(String *key*)	Returns the value associated with *key*. A **null** object is returned if *key* is neither in the list nor in the default property list.
String getProperty(String *key*, String *defaultProperty*)	Returns the value associated with *key*. *defaultProperty* is returned if *key* is neither in the list nor in the default property list.
void list(PrintStream *streamOut*)	Sends the property list to the output stream linked to *streamOut*.
void list(PrintWriter *streamOut*)	Sends the property list to the output stream linked to *streamOut*.
void load(InputStream *streamIn*) throws IOException	Inputs a property list from the input stream linked to *streamIn*.
Enumeration propertyNames( )	Returns an enumeration of the keys. This includes those keys found in the default property list, too.
Object setProperty(String *key*, String *value*)	Associates *value* with *key*. Returns the previous value associated with *key*, or returns **null** if no such association exists. (Added by Java 2, for consistency.)
void store(OutputStream *streamOut*, String *description*)	After writing the string specified by *description*, the property list is written to the output stream linked to *streamOut*. (Added by Java 2.)

Table 15-14. *The Legacy Methods Defined by* Properties

One useful capability of the **Properties** class is that you can specify a default property that will be returned if no value is associated with a certain key. For example, a default value can be specified along with the key in the **getProperty( )** method—such as **getProperty("name", "default value")**. If the "name" value is not found, then "default value" is returned. When you construct a **Properties** object, you can pass another instance of **Properties** to be used as the default properties for the new instance. In this case, if you call **getProperty("foo")** on a given **Properties** object, and "foo" does not exist, Java looks for "foo" in the default **Properties** object. This allows for arbitrary nesting of levels of default properties.

The following example demonstrates **Properties**. It creates a property list in which the keys are the names of states and the values are the names of their capitals. Notice that the attempt to find the capital for Florida includes a default value.

```java
// Demonstrate a Property list.
import java.util.*;

class PropDemo {
  public static void main(String args[]) {
    Properties capitals = new Properties();
    Set states;
    String str;

    capitals.put("Illinois", "Springfield");
    capitals.put("Missouri", "Jefferson City");
    capitals.put("Washington", "Olympia");
    capitals.put("California", "Sacramento");
    capitals.put("Indiana", "Indianapolis");

    // Show all states and capitals in hashtable.
    states = capitals.keySet(); // get set-view of keys
    Iterator itr = states.iterator();

    while(itr.hasNext()) {
      str = (String) itr.next();
      System.out.println("The capital of " +
                   str + " is " +
                   capitals.getProperty(str)
                   + ".");
    }

    System.out.println();

    // look for state not in list -- specify default
    str = capitals.getProperty("Florida", "Not Found");
    System.out.println("The capital of Florida is "
                   + str + ".");
  }
}
```

The output from this program is shown here:

```
The capital of Missouri is Jefferson City.
The capital of Illinois is Springfield.
The capital of Indiana is Indianapolis.
The capital of California is Sacramento.
The capital of Washington is Olympia.

The capital of Florida is Not Found.
```

Since Florida is not in the list, the default value is used.

Although it is perfectly valid to use a default value when you call **getProperty( )**, as the preceding example shows, there is a better way of handling default values for most applications of property lists. For greater flexibility, specify a default property list when constructing a **Properties** object. The default list will be searched if the desired key is not found in the main list. For example, the following is a slightly reworked version of the preceding program, with a default list of states specified. Now, when Florida is sought, it will be found in the default list:

```java
// Use a default property list.
import java.util.*;

class PropDemoDef {
  public static void main(String args[]) {
    Properties defList = new Properties();
    defList.put("Florida", "Tallahassee");
    defList.put("Wisconsin", "Madison");

    Properties capitals = new Properties(defList);
    Set states;
    String str;

    capitals.put("Illinois", "Springfield");
    capitals.put("Missouri", "Jefferson City");
    capitals.put("Washington", "Olympia");
    capitals.put("California", "Sacramento");
    capitals.put("Indiana", "Indianapolis");

    // Show all states and capitals in hashtable.
    states = capitals.keySet(); // get set-view of keys
    Iterator itr = states.iterator();

    while(itr.hasNext()) {
      str = (String) itr.next();
```

```
      System.out.println("The capital of " +
                         str + " is " +
                         capitals.getProperty(str)
                         + ".");
   }

   System.out.println();

   // Florida will now be found in the default list.
   str = capitals.getProperty("Florida");
   System.out.println("The capital of Florida is "
                      + str + ".");
   }
}
```

Using store( ) and load( )

One of the most useful aspects of **Properties** is that the information contained in a
Properties object can be easily stored to or loaded from disk with the **store( )** and
load( ) methods. At any time, you can write a **Properties** object to a stream or read
it back. This makes property lists especially convenient for implementing simple
databases. For example, the following program uses a property list to create a simple
computerized telephone book that stores names and phone numbers. To find a
person's number, you enter his or her name. The program uses the **store( )** and **load( )**
methods to store and retrieve the list. When the program executes, it first tries to load
the list from a file called **phonebook.dat**. If this file exists, the list is loaded. You can
then add to the list. If you do, the new list is saved when you terminate the program.
Notice how little code is required to implement a small, but functional, computerized
phone book.

```
/* A simple telephone number database that uses
   a property list. */
import java.io.*;
import java.util.*;

class Phonebook {
  public static void main(String args[])
    throws IOException
  {
    Properties ht = new Properties();
    BufferedReader br =
```

```
      new BufferedReader(new InputStreamReader(System.in));
String name, number;
FileInputStream fin = null;
boolean changed = false;

// Try to open phonebook.dat file.
try {
  fin = new FileInputStream("phonebook.dat");
} catch(FileNotFoundException e) {
  // ignore missing file
}

/* If phonebook file already exists,
   load existing telephone numbers. */
try {
  if(fin != null) {
    ht.load(fin);
    fin.close();
  }
} catch(IOException e) {
  System.out.println("Error reading file.");
}

// Let user enter new names and numbers.
do {
  System.out.println("Enter new name" +
                     " ('quit' to stop): ");
  name = br.readLine();
  if(name.equals("quit")) continue;

  System.out.println("Enter number: ");
  number = br.readLine();

  ht.put(name, number);
  changed = true;
} while(!name.equals("quit"));

// If phone book data has changed, save it.
if(changed) {
  FileOutputStream fout = new FileOutputStream("phonebook.dat");

  ht.store(fout, "Telephone Book");
```

```
      fout.close();
   }

   // Look up numbers given a name.
   do {
     System.out.println("Enter name to find" +
                        " ('quit' to quit): ");
     name = br.readLine();
     if(name.equals("quit")) continue;

     number = (String) ht.get(name);
     System.out.println(number);
   } while(!name.equals("quit"));
 }
}
```

Collections Summary

The collections framework gives you, the programmer, a powerful set of well-engineered solutions to some of programming's most common tasks. Consider using a collection the next time that you need to store and retrieve information. Remember, collections need not be reserved for only the "large jobs," such as corporate databases, mailing lists, or inventory systems. They are also effective when applied to smaller jobs. For example, a **TreeMap** would make an excellent collection to hold the directory structure of a set of files. A **TreeSet** could be quite useful for storing project-management information. Frankly, the types of problems that will benefit from a collections-based solution are limited only by your imagination.

The
Complete
Reference

Java™ 2

Chapter 16

java.util Part 2: More Utility Classes

This chapter continues our discussion of **java.util** by examining those classes and interfaces that are not part of the collections framework. These include classes that tokenize strings, work with dates, compute random numbers, and observe events. Also, the **java.util.zip** and **java.util.jar** packages are briefly mentioned at the end of this chapter.

StringTokenizer

The processing of text often consists of parsing a formatted input string. *Parsing* is the division of text into a set of discrete parts, or *tokens*, which in a certain sequence can convey a semantic meaning. The **StringTokenizer** class provides the first step in this parsing process, often called the *lexer* (lexical analyzer) or *scanner*. **StringTokenizer** implements the **Enumeration** interface. Therefore, given an input string, you can enumerate the individual tokens contained in it using **StringTokenizer**.

To use **StringTokenizer**, you specify an input string and a string that contains delimiters. *Delimiters* are characters that separate tokens. Each character in the delimiters string is considered a valid delimiter—for example, "*,;:*" sets the delimiters to a comma, semicolon, and colon. The default set of delimiters consists of the whitespace characters: space, tab, newline, and carriage return.

The **StringTokenizer** constructors are shown here:

StringTokenizer(String *str*)
StringTokenizer(String *str*, String *delimiters*)
StringTokenizer(String *str*, String *delimiters*, boolean *delimAsToken*)

In all versions, *str* is the string that will be tokenized. In the first version, the default delimiters are used. In the second and third versions, *delimiters* is a string that specifies the delimiters. In the third version, if *delimAsToken* is **true**, then the delimiters are also returned as tokens when the string is parsed. Otherwise, the delimiters are not returned. Delimiters are not returned as tokens by the first two forms.

Once you have created a **StringTokenizer** object, the **nextToken( )** method is used to extract consecutive tokens. The **hasMoreTokens( )** method returns **true** while there are more tokens to be extracted. Since **StringTokenizer** implements **Enumeration**, the **hasMoreElements( )** and **nextElement( )** methods are also implemented, and they act the same as **hasMoreTokens( )** and **nextToken( )**, respectively. The **StringTokenizer** methods are shown in Table 16-1.

Here is an example that creates a **StringTokenizer** to parse "key=value" pairs. Consecutive sets of "key=value" pairs are separated by a semicolon.

```
// Demonstrate StringTokenizer.
import java.util.StringTokenizer;
```

```
class STDemo {
  static String in = "title=Java: The Complete Reference;" +
    "author=Schildt;" +
    "publisher=Osborne/McGraw-Hill;" +
    "copyright=2002";

  public static void main(String args[]) {
    StringTokenizer st = new StringTokenizer(in, "=;");

    while(st.hasMoreTokens()) {
      String key = st.nextToken();
      String val = st.nextToken();
      System.out.println(key + "\t" + val);
    }
  }
}
```

Method	Description
int countTokens( )	Using the current set of delimiters, the method determines the number of tokens left to be parsed and returns the result.
boolean hasMoreElements( )	Returns **true** if one or more tokens remain in the string and returns **false** if there are none.
boolean hasMoreTokens( )	Returns **true** if one or more tokens remain in the string and returns **false** if there are none.
Object nextElement( )	Returns the next token as an **Object**.
String nextToken( )	Returns the next token as a **String**.
String nextToken(String *delimiters*)	Returns the next token as a **String** and sets the delimiters string to that specified by *delimiters*.

Table 16-1.   *The Methods Defined by* StringTokenizer

The output from this program is shown here:

```
title  Java: The Complete Reference
author  Schildt
publisher  Osborne/McGraw-Hill
copyright  2002
```

BitSet

A **BitSet** class creates a special type of array that holds bit values. This array can increase in size as needed. This makes it similar to a vector of bits. The **BitSet** constructors are shown here:

BitSet( )
BitSet(int *size*)

The first version creates a default object. The second version allows you to specify its initial size (that is, the number of bits that it can hold). All bits are initialized to zero.

BitSet implements the **Cloneable** interface and defines the methods listed in Table 16-2. Notice that several were added by Java 2, version 1.4.

Method	Description
void and(BitSet *bitSet*)	ANDs the contents of the invoking **BitSet** object with those specified by *bitSet*. The result is placed into the invoking object.
void andNot(BitSet *bitSet*)	For each 1 bit in *bitSet*, the corresponding bit in the invoking **BitSet** is cleared. (Added by Java 2)
int cardinality( )	Returns the number of set bits in the invoking object. (Added by Java 2, version 1.4)
void clear( )	Zeros all bits. (Added by Java 2, version 1.4)
void clear(int *index*)	Zeros the bit specified by *index*.
void clear(int *startIndex*, int *endIndex*)	Zeros the bits from *startIndex* to *endIndex*--1. (Added by Java 2, version 1.4)
Object clone( )	Duplicates the invoking **BitSet** object.
boolean equals(Object *bitSet*)	Returns **true** if the invoking bit set is equivalent to the one passed in *bitSet*. Otherwise, the method returns **false**.

Table 16-2. *The Methods Defined by* BitSet

Method	Description
void flip(int *index*)	Reverses the bit specified by *index*. (Added by Java 2, version 1.4)
void flip(int *startIndex*, int *endIndex*)	Reverses the bits from *startIndex* to *endIndex*–1. (Added by Java 2, version 1.4)
boolean get(int *index*)	Returns the current state of the bit at the specified index.
BitSet get(int *startIndex*, int *endIndex*)	Returns a **BitSet** that consists of the bits from *startIndex* to *endIndex*–1. The invoking object is not changed. (Added by Java 2, version 1.4)
int hashCode( )	Returns the hash code for the invoking object.
boolean intersects(BitSet *bitSet*)	Returns **true** if at least one pair of corresponding bits within the invoking object and *bitSet* are 1. (Added by Java 2, version 1.4)
boolean isEmpty( )	Returns **true** if all bits in the invoking object are zero. (Added by Java 2, version 1.4)
int length( )	Returns the number of bits required to hold the contents of the invoking **BitSet**. This value is determined by the location of the last 1 bit. (Added by Java 2)
int nextClearBit(int *startIndex*)	Returns the index of the next cleared bit, (that is, the next zero bit), starting from the index specified by *startIndex*. (Added by Java 2, version 1.4)
int nextSetBit(int *startIndex*)	Returns the index of the next set bit (that is, the next 1 bit), starting from the index specified by *startIndex*. If no bit is set, –1 is returned. (Added by Java 2, version 1.4)
void or(BitSet *bitSet*)	ORs the contents of the invoking **BitSet** object with that specified by *bitSet*. The result is placed into the invoking object.
void set(int *index*)	Sets the bit specified by *index*.

Table 16-2. *The Methods Defined by* BitSet (continued)

Method	Description
void set(int *index*, boolean *v*)	Sets the bit specified by *index* to the value passed in *v*. **true** sets the bit, **false** clears the bit. (Added by Java 2, version 1.4)
void set(int *startIndex*, int *endIndex*)	Sets the bits from *startIndex* to *endIndex*–1. (Added by Java 2, version 1.4)
void set(int *startIndex*, int *endIndex*, boolean *v*)	Sets the bits from *startIndex* to *endIndex*–1, to the value passed in *v*. **true** sets the bits, **false** clears the bits. (Added by Java 2, version 1.4)
int size( )	Returns the number of bits in the invoking **BitSet** object.
String toString( )	Returns the string equivalent of the invoking **BitSet** object.
void xor(BitSet *bitSet*)	XORs the contents of the invoking **BitSet** object with that specified by *bitSet*. The result is placed into the invoking object.

Table 16-2. *The Methods Defined by* BitSet (continued)

Here is an example that demonstrates **BitSet**:

```
// BitSet Demonstration.
import java.util.BitSet;

class BitSetDemo {
  public static void main(String args[]) {
    BitSet bits1 = new BitSet(16);
    BitSet bits2 = new BitSet(16);

    // set some bits
    for(int i=0; i<16; i++) {
      if((i%2) == 0) bits1.set(i);
      if((i%5) != 0) bits2.set(i);
    }
```

```
    System.out.println("Initial pattern in bits1: ");
    System.out.println(bits1);
    System.out.println("\nInitial pattern in bits2: ");
    System.out.println(bits2);

    // AND bits
    bits2.and(bits1);
    System.out.println("\nbits2 AND bits1: ");
    System.out.println(bits2);

    // OR bits
    bits2.or(bits1);
    System.out.println("\nbits2 OR bits1: ");
    System.out.println(bits2);

    // XOR bits
    bits2.xor(bits1);
    System.out.println("\nbits2 XOR bits1: ");
    System.out.println(bits2);
  }
}
```

The output from this program is shown here. When **toString( )** converts a **BitSet** object to its string equivalent, each set bit is represented by its bit position. Cleared bits are not shown.

```
Initial pattern in bits1:
{0, 2, 4, 6, 8, 10, 12, 14}

Initial pattern in bits2:
{1, 2, 3, 4, 6, 7, 8, 9, 11, 12, 13, 14}

bits2 AND bits1:
{2, 4, 6, 8, 12, 14}

bits2 OR bits1:
{0, 2, 4, 6, 8, 10, 12, 14}

bits2 XOR bits1:
{}
```

Date

The **Date** class encapsulates the current date and time. Before beginning our examination of **Date**, it is important to point out that it has changed substantially from its original version defined by Java 1.0. When Java 1.1 was released, many of the functions carried out by the original **Date** class were moved into the **Calendar** and **DateFormat** classes, and as a result, many of the original 1.0 **Date** methods were deprecated. Java 2 added a few new methods to the time and date classes, but otherwise implemented them in the same form as did 1.1. Since the deprecated 1.0 methods should not be used for new code, they are not described here.

Date supports the following constructors:

Date( )
Date(long *millisec*)

The first constructor initializes the object with the current date and time. The second constructor accepts one argument that equals the number of milliseconds that have elapsed since midnight, January 1, 1970. The nondeprecated methods defined by **Date** are shown in Table 16-3. With the advent of Java 2, **Date** also implements the **Comparable** interface.

Method	Description
boolean after(Date *date*)	Returns **true** if the invoking **Date** object contains a date that is later than the one specified by *date*. Otherwise, it returns **false**.
boolean before(Date *date*)	Returns **true** if the invoking **Date** object contains a date that is earlier than the one specified by *date*. Otherwise, it returns **false**.
Object clone( )	Duplicates the invoking **Date** object.
int compareTo(Date *date*)	Compares the value of the invoking object with that of *date*. Returns 0 if the values are equal. Returns a negative value if the invoking object is earlier than *date*. Returns a positive value if the invoking object is later than *date*. (Added by Java 2)
int compareTo(Object *obj*)	Operates identically to **compareTo(Date)** if *obj* is of class **Date**. Otherwise, it throws a **ClassCastException**. (Added by Java 2)

Table 16-3.   *The Nondeprecated Methods Defined by* Date

Method	Description
boolean equals(Object *datc*)	Returns **true** if the invoking **Date** object contains the same time and date as the one specified by *date*. Otherwise, it returns **false**.
long getTime( )	Returns the number of milliseconds that have elapsed since January 1, 1970.
int hashCode( )	Returns a hash code for the invoking object.
void setTime(long *time*)	Sets the time and date as specified by *time*, which represents an elapsed time in milliseconds from midnight, January 1, 1970.
String toString( )	Converts the invoking **Date** object into a string and returns the result.

Table 16-3. *The Nondeprecated Methods Defined by* Date (continued)

As you can see by examining Table 16-3, the **Date** features do not allow you to obtain the individual components of the date or time. As the following program demonstrates, you can only obtain the date and time in terms of milliseconds or in its default string representation as returned by **toString( )**. To obtain more-detailed information about the date and time, you will use the **Calendar** class.

```
// Show date and time using only Date methods.
import java.util.Date;

class DateDemo {
  public static void main(String args[]) {
    // Instantiate a Date object
    Date date = new Date();

    // display time and date using toString()
    System.out.println(date);

    // Display number of milliseconds since midnight, January 1, 1970 GMT
```

```
        long msec = date.getTime();
        System.out.println("Milliseconds since Jan. 1, 1970 GMT = " + msec);
    }
}
```

Sample output is shown here:

```
Mon Apr 22 09:51:52 CDT 2002
Milliseconds since Jan. 1, 1970 GMT = 1019487112894
```

Date Comparison

There are three ways to compare two **Date** objects. First, you can use **getTime( )** to obtain the number of milliseconds that have elapsed since midnight, January 1, 1970, for both objects and then compare these two values. Second, you can use the methods **before( )**, **after( )**, and **equals( )**. Because the 12th of the month comes before the 18th, for example, **new Date(99, 2, 12).before(new Date (99, 2, 18))** returns **true**. Finally, you can use the **compareTo( )** method, which is defined by the **Comparable** interface and implemented by **Date**.

Calendar

The abstract **Calendar** class provides a set of methods that allows you to convert a time in milliseconds to a number of useful components. Some examples of the type of information that can be provided are: year, month, day, hour, minute, and second. It is intended that subclasses of **Calendar** will provide the specific functionality to interpret time information according to their own rules. This is one aspect of the Java class library that enables you to write programs that can operate in several international environments. An example of such a subclass is **GregorianCalendar**.

Calendar provides no public constructors.

Calendar defines several protected instance variables. **areFieldsSet** is a **boolean** that indicates if the time components have been set. **fields** is an array of **int**s that holds the components of the time. **isSet** is a **boolean** array that indicates if a specific time component has been set. **time** is a **long** that holds the current time for this object. **isTimeSet** is a **boolean** that indicates if the current time has been set.

Some commonly used methods defined by **Calendar** are shown in Table 16-4.

Calendar defines the following **int** constants, which are used when you get or set components of the calendar:

AM	FRIDAY	PM
AM_PM	HOUR	SATURDAY
APRIL	HOUR_OF_DAY	SECOND
AUGUST	JANUARY	SEPTEMBER
DATE	JULY	SUNDAY
DAY_OF_MONTH	JUNE	THURSDAY
DAY_OF_WEEK	MARCH	TUESDAY
DAY_OF_WEEK_IN_MONTH	MAY	UNDECIMBER
DAY_OF_YEAR	MILLISECOND	WEDNESDAY
DECEMBER	MINUTE	WEEK_OF_MONTH
DST_OFFSET	MONDAY	WEEK_OF_YEAR
ERA	MONTH	YEAR
FEBRUARY	NOVEMBER	ZONE_OFFSET
FIELD_COUNT	OCTOBER	

Method	Description
abstract void add(int *which*, int *val*)	Adds *val* to the time or date component specified by *which*. To subtract, add a negative value. *which* must be one of the fields defined by **Calendar**, such as **Calendar.HOUR**.
boolean after(Object *calendarObj*)	Returns **true** if the invoking **Calendar** object contains a date that is later than the one specified by *calendarObj*. Otherwise, it returns **false**.
boolean before(Object *calendarObj*)	Returns **true** if the invoking **Calendar** object contains a date that is earlier than the one specified by *calendarObj*. Otherwise, it returns **false**.

Table 16-4. *Commonly Used Methods Defined by* Calendar

Method	Description
final void clear( )	Zeros all time components in the invoking object.
final void clear(int *which*)	Zeros the time component specified by *which* in the invoking object.
Object clone( )	Returns a duplicate of the invoking object.
boolean equals(Object *calendarObj*)	Returns **true** if the invoking **Calendar** object contains a date that is equal to the one specified by *calendarObj*. Otherwise, it returns **false**.
int get(int *calendarField*)	Returns the value of one component of the invoking object. The component is indicated by *calendarField*. Examples of the components that can be requested are **Calendar.YEAR**, **Calendar.MONTH**, **Calendar.MINUTE**, and so forth.
static Locale[ ] getAvailableLocales( )	Returns an array of **Locale** objects that contains the locales for which calendars are available.
static Calendar getInstance( )	Returns a **Calendar** object for the default locale and time zone.
static Calendar getInstance(TimeZone *tz*)	Returns a **Calendar** object for the time zone specified by *tz*. The default locale is used.
static Calendar getInstance(Locale *locale*)	Returns a **Calendar** object for the locale specified by *locale*. The default time zone is used.
static Calendar getInstance(TimeZone *tz*, Locale *locale*)	Returns a **Calendar** object for the time zone specified by *tz* and the locale specified by *locale*.
final Date getTime( )	Returns a **Date** object equivalent to the time of the invoking object.

Table 16-4. *Commonly Used Methods Defined by* Calendar *(continued)*

Method	Description
TimeZone getTimeZone( )	Returns the time zone for the invoking object.
final boolean isSet(int *which*)	Returns **true** if the specified time component is set. Otherwise, it returns **false**.
void set(int *which*, int *val*)	Sets the date or time component specified by *which* to the value specified by *val* in the invoking object. *which* must be one of the fields defined by **Calendar**, such as **Calendar.HOUR**.
final void set(int *year*, int *month*, int *dayOfMonth*)	Sets various date and time components of the invoking object.
final void set(int *year*, int *month*, int *dayOfMonth*, int *hours*, int *minutes*)	Sets various date and time components of the invoking object.
final void set(int *year*, int *month*, int *dayOfMonth*, int *hours*, int *minutes*, int *seconds*)	Sets various date and time components of the invoking object.
final void setTime(Date *d*)	Sets various date and time components of the invoking object. This information is obtained from the **Date** object *d*.
void setTimeZone(TimeZone *tz*)	Sets the time zone for the invoking object to that specified by *tz*.

Table 16-4.   *Commonly Used Methods Defined by* Calendar (continued)

The following program demonstrates several **Calendar** methods:

```
// Demonstrate Calendar
import java.util.Calendar;
```

```
class CalendarDemo {
  public static void main(String args[]) {
    String months[] = {
            "Jan", "Feb", "Mar", "Apr",
            "May", "Jun", "Jul", "Aug",
            "Sep", "Oct", "Nov", "Dec"};

    // Create a calendar initialized with the
    // current date and time in the default
    // locale and timezone.
    Calendar calendar = Calendar.getInstance();

    // Display current time and date information.
    System.out.print("Date: ");
    System.out.print(months[calendar.get(Calendar.MONTH)]);
    System.out.print(" " + calendar.get(Calendar.DATE) + " ");
    System.out.println(calendar.get(Calendar.YEAR));

    System.out.print("Time: ");
    System.out.print(calendar.get(Calendar.HOUR) + ":");
    System.out.print(calendar.get(Calendar.MINUTE) + ":");
    System.out.println(calendar.get(Calendar.SECOND));

    // Set the time and date information and display it.
    calendar.set(Calendar.HOUR, 10);
    calendar.set(Calendar.MINUTE, 29);
    calendar.set(Calendar.SECOND, 22);

    System.out.print("Updated time: ");
    System.out.print(calendar.get(Calendar.HOUR) + ":");
    System.out.print(calendar.get(Calendar.MINUTE) + ":");
    System.out.println(calendar.get(Calendar.SECOND));
  }
}
```

Sample output is shown here:

```
Date: Apr 22 2002
Time: 11:24:25
Updated time: 10:29:22
```

GregorianCalendar

GregorianCalendar is a concrete implementation of a **Calendar** that implements the normal Gregorian calendar with which you are familiar. The **getInstance( )** method of **Calendar** returns a **GregorianCalendar** initialized with the current date and time in the default locale and time zone.

GregorianCalendar defines two fields: **AD** and **BC**. These represent the two eras defined by the Gregorian calendar.

There are also several constructors for **GregorianCalendar** objects. The default, **GregorianCalendar( )**, initializes the object with the current date and time in the default locale and time zone. Three more constructors offer increasing levels of specificity:

GregorianCalendar(int *year*, int *month*, int *dayOfMonth*)
GregorianCalendar(int *year*, int *month*, int *dayOfMonth*, int *hours*,
        int *minutes*)
GregorianCalendar(int *year*, int *month*, int *dayOfMonth*, int *hours*,
        int *minutes*, int *seconds*)

All three versions set the day, month, and year. Here, *year* specifies the number of years that have elapsed since 1900. The month is specified by *month*, with zero indicating January. The day of the month is specified by *dayOfMonth*. The first version sets the time to midnight. The second version also sets the hours and the minutes. The third version adds seconds.

You can also construct a **GregorianCalendar** object by specifying either the locale and/or time zone. The following constructors create objects initialized with the current date and time using the specified time zone and/or locale:

GregorianCalendar(Locale *locale*)
GregorianCalendar(TimeZone *timeZone*)
GregorianCalendar(TimeZone *timeZone*, Locale *locale*)

GregorianCalendar provides an implementation of all the abstract methods in **Calendar**. It also provides some additional methods. Perhaps the most interesting is **isLeapYear( )**, which tests if the year is a leap year. Its form is

boolean isLeapYear(int *year*)

This method returns **true** if *year* is a leap year and **false** otherwise.

The following program demonstrates **GregorianCalendar**:

```
// Demonstrate GregorianCalendar
import java.util.*;
```

```
class GregorianCalendarDemo {
  public static void main(String args[]) {
    String months[] = {
              "Jan", "Feb", "Mar", "Apr",
              "May", "Jun", "Jul", "Aug",
              "Sep", "Oct", "Nov", "Dec"};
    int year;

    // Create a Gregorian calendar initialized
    // with the current date and time in the
    // default locale and timezone.
    GregorianCalendar gcalendar = new GregorianCalendar();

    // Display current time and date information.
    System.out.print("Date: ");
    System.out.print(months[gcalendar.get(Calendar.MONTH)]);
    System.out.print(" " + gcalendar.get(Calendar.DATE) + " ");
    System.out.println(year = gcalendar.get(Calendar.YEAR));

    System.out.print("Time: ");
    System.out.print(gcalendar.get(Calendar.HOUR) + ":");
    System.out.print(gcalendar.get(Calendar.MINUTE) + ":");
    System.out.println(gcalendar.get(Calendar.SECOND));

    // Test if the current year is a leap year
    if(gcalendar.isLeapYear(year)) {
      System.out.println("The current year is a leap year");
    }
    else {
      System.out.println("The current year is not a leap year");
    }
  }
}
```

Sample output is shown here:

```
Date: Apr 22 2002
Time: 11:25:27
The current year is not a leap year
```

TimeZone

Another time-related class is **TimeZone**. The **TimeZone** class allows you to work with time zone offsets from Greenwich mean time (GMT), also referred to as Coordinated Universal Time (UTC). It also computes daylight saving time. **TimeZone** only supplies the default constructor.

Some methods defined by **TimeZone** are summarized in Table 16-5.

Method	Description
Object clone( )	Returns a **TimeZone**-specific version of **clone( )**.
static String[ ] getAvailableIDs( )	Returns an array of **String** objects representing the names of all time zones.
static String[ ] getAvailableIDs(int *timeDelta*)	Returns an array of **String** objects representing the names of all time zones that are *timeDelta* offset from GMT.
static TimeZone getDefault( )	Returns a **TimeZone** object that represents the default time zone used on the host computer.
String getID( )	Returns the name of the invoking **TimeZone** object.
abstract int getOffset(int *era*, int *year*, int *month*, int *dayOfMonth*, int *dayOfWeek*, int *millisec*)	Returns the offset that should be added to GMT to compute local time. This value is adjusted for daylight saving time. The parameters to the method represent date and time components.
abstract int getRawOffset( )	Returns the raw offset that should be added to GMT to compute local time. This value is not adjusted for daylight saving time.

Table 16-5.   *Some of the Methods Defined by* TimeZone

Method	Description
static TimeZone getTimeZone(String *tzName*)	Returns the **TimeZone** object for the time zone named *tzName*.
abstract boolean inDaylightTime(Date *d*)	Returns **true** if the date represented by *d* is in daylight saving time in the invoking object. Otherwise, it returns **false**.
static void setDefault(TimeZone *tz*)	Sets the default time zone to be used on this host. *tz* is a reference to the **TimeZone** object to be used.
void setID(String *tzName*)	Sets the name of the time zone (that is, its ID) to that specified by *tzName*.
abstract void setRawOffset(int *millis*)	Sets the offset in milliseconds from GMT.
abstract boolean useDaylightTime( )	Returns **true** if the invoking object uses daylight saving time. Otherwise, it returns **false**.

Table 16-5.   *Some of the Methods Defined by* TimeZone (continued)

SimpleTimeZone

The **SimpleTimeZone** class is a convenient subclass of **TimeZone**. It implements **TimeZone**'s abstract methods and allows you to work with time zones for a Gregorian calendar. It also computes daylight saving time.

   SimpleTimeZone defines four constructors. One is

SimpleTimeZone(int *timeDelta*, String *tzName*)

   This constructor creates a **SimpleTimeZone** object. The offset relative to Greenwich mean time (GMT) is *timeDelta*. The time zone is named *tzName*.

   The second **SimpleTimeZone** constructor is

SimpleTimeZone(int *timeDelta*, String *tzId*, int *dstMonth0*,
               int *dstDayInMonth0*, int *dstDay0*, int *time0*,
               int *dstMonth1*, int *dstDayInMonth1*, int *dstDay1*,
               int *time1*)

Here, the offset relative to GMT is specified in *timeDelta*. The time zone name is passed in *tzId*. The start of daylight saving time is indicated by the parameters *dstMonth0*, *dstDayInMonth0*, *dstDay0*, and *time0*. The end of daylight saving time is indicated by the parameters *dstMonth1*, *dstDayInMonth1*, *dstDay1*, and *time1*.

The third **SimpleTimeZone** constructor is

```
SimpleTimeZone(int timeDelta, String tzId, int dstMonth0,
               int dstDayInMonth0, int dstDay0, int time0,
               int dstMonth1, int dstDayInMonth1, int dstDay1,
               int time1, int dstDelta)
```

Here, *dstDelta* is the number of milliseconds saved during daylight saving time.

The fourth **SimpleTimeZone** constructor is:

```
SimpleTimeZone(int timeDelta, String tzId, int dstMonth0,
               int dstDayInMonth0, int dstDay0, int time0,
               int time0mode, int dstMonth1, int dstDayInMonth1,
               int dstDay1, int time1, int time1mode, int dstDelta)
```

Here, *time0mode* specifies the mode of the starting time, and *time1mode* specifies the mode of the ending time. Valid mode values include

STANDARD_TIME   WALL_TIME   UTC_TIME

The time mode indicates how the time values are interpreted. The default mode used by the other constructors is **WALL_TIME**. This constructor and the mode values were added by Java 2, version 1.4.

Locale

The **Locale** class is instantiated to produce objects that each describe a geographical or cultural region. It is one of several classes that provide you with the ability to write programs that can execute in several different international environments. For example, the formats used to display dates, times, and numbers are different in various regions.

Internationalization is a large topic that is beyond the scope of this book. However, most programs will only need to deal with its basics, which include setting the current locale.

The **Locale** class defines the following constants that are useful for dealing with the most common locales:

CANADA	GERMAN	KOREAN
CANADA_FRENCH	GERMANY	PRC
CHINA	ITALIAN	SIMPLIFIED_CHINESE
CHINESE	ITALY	TAIWAN

ENGLISH	JAPAN	TRADITIONAL_CHINESE
FRANCE	JAPANESE	UK
FRENCH	KOREA	US

For example, the expression **Locale.CANADA** represents the **Locale** object for Canada. The constructors for **Locale** are

Locale(String *language*)
Locale(String *language*, String *country*)
Locale(String *language*, String *country*, String *data*)

These constructors build a **Locale** object to represent a specific *language* and in the case of the last two, *country*. These values must contain ISO-standard language and country codes. Auxiliary browser and vendor-specific information can be provided in *data*. The first constructor was added by Java 2, version 1.4.

Locale defines several methods. One of the most important is **setDefault( )**, shown here:

static void setDefault(Locale *localeObj*)

This sets the default locale to that specified by *localeObj*.

Some other interesting methods are the following:

final String getDisplayCountry( )
final String getDisplayLanguage( )
final String getDisplayName( )

These return human-readable strings that can be used to display the name of the country, the name of the language, and the complete description of the locale.

The default locale can be obtained using **getDefault( )**, shown here:

static Locale getDefault( )

Calendar and **GregorianCalendar** are examples of classes that operate in a locale-sensitive manner. **DateFormat** and **SimpleDateFormat** also depend on the locale.

Random

The **Random** class is a generator of pseudorandom numbers. These are called *pseudorandom* numbers because they are simply uniformly distributed sequences. **Random** defines the following constructors:

Random( )
Random(long *seed*)

The first version creates a number generator that uses the current time as the starting, or *seed*, value. The second form allows you to specify a seed value manually.

If you initialize a **Random** object with a seed, you define the starting point for the random sequence. If you use the same seed to initialize another **Random** object, you will

Method	Description
boolean nextBoolean( )	Returns the next **boolean** random number. (Added by Java 2)
void nextBytes(byte *vals*[ ])	Fills *vals* with randomly generated values.
double nextDouble( )	Returns the next **double** random number.
float nextFloat( )	Returns the next **float** random number.
double nextGaussian( )	Returns the next Gaussian random number.
int nextInt( )	Returns the next **int** random number.
int nextInt(int *n*)	Returns the next **int** random number within the range zero to *n*. (Added by Java 2)
long nextLong( )	Returns the next **long** random number.
void setSeed(long *newSeed*)	Sets the seed value (that is, the starting point for the random number generator) to that specified by *newSeed*.

Table 16-6. *The Methods Defined by* Random

extract the same random sequence. If you want to generate different sequences, specify different seed values. The easiest way to do this is to use the current time to seed a **Random** object. This approach reduces the possibility of getting repeated sequences.

The public methods defined by **Random** are shown in Table 16-6.

As you can see, there are seven types of random numbers that you can extract from a **Random** object. Random Boolean values are available from **nextBoolean( )**. Random bytes can be obtained by calling **nextBytes( )**. Integers can be extracted via the **nextInt( )** method. Long integers, uniformly distributed over their range, can be obtained with **nextLong( )**. The **nextFloat( )** and **nextDouble( )** methods return a uniformly distributed **float** and **double**, respectively, between 0.0 and 1.0. Finally, **nextGaussian( )** returns a **double** value centered at 0.0 with a standard deviation of 1.0. This is what is known as a *bell curve*.

Here is an example that demonstrates the sequence produced by **nextGaussian( )**. It obtains 100 random Gaussian values and averages these values. The program also counts the number of values that fall within two standard deviations, plus or minus, using increments of 0.5 for each category. The result is graphically displayed sideways on the screen.

```java
// Demonstrate random Gaussian values.
import java.util.Random;
class RandDemo {
  public static void main(String args[]) {
    Random r = new Random();
    double val;
    double sum = 0;
    int bell[] = new int[10];

    for(int i=0; i<100; i++) {
      val = r.nextGaussian();
      sum += val;
      double t = -2;
      for(int x=0; x<10; x++, t += 0.5)
        if(val < t) {
          bell[x]++;
          break;
        }
    }
    System.out.println("Average of values: " +
                        (sum/100));

    // display bell curve, sideways
    for(int i=0; i<10; i++) {
      for(int x=bell[i]; x>0; x--)
        System.out.print("*");
      System.out.println();
    }
  }
}
```

Here is a sample program run. As you can see, a bell-like distribution of numbers is obtained.

```
Average of values: 0.0702235271133344
**
*******
******
**************
*****************
****************
*************
*********
*******
***
```

Observable

The **Observable** class is used to create subclasses that other parts of your program can observe. When an object of such a subclass undergoes a change, observing classes are notified. Observing classes must implement the **Observer** interface, which defines the **update( )** method. The **update( )** method is called when an observer is notified of a change in an observed object.

Observable defines the methods shown in Table 16-7. An object that is being observed must follow two simple rules. First, if it has changed, it must call **setChanged( )**. Second, when it is ready to notify observers of this change, it must call **notifyObservers( )**. This causes the **update( )** method in the observing object(s) to be called. Be careful—if the object calls **notifyObservers( )** without having previously called **setChanged( )**, no action will take place. The observed object must call both **setChanged( )** and **notifyObservers( )** before **update( )** will be called.

Method	Description
void addObserver(Observer *obj*)	Add *obj* to the list of objects observing the invoking object.
protected void clearChanged( )	Calling this method returns the status of the invoking object to "unchanged."
int countObservers( )	Returns the number of objects observing the invoking object.
void deleteObserver(Observer *obj*)	Removes *obj* from the list of objects observing the invoking object.
void deleteObservers( )	Removes all observers for the invoking object.
boolean hasChanged( )	Returns **true** if the invoking object has been modified and **false** if it has not.
void notifyObservers( )	Notifies all observers of the invoking object that it has changed by calling **update( )**. A **null** is passed as the second argument to **update( )**.
void notifyObservers(Object *obj*)	Notifies all observers of the invoking object that it has changed by calling **update( )**. *obj* is passed as an argument to **update( )**.
protected void setChanged( )	Called when the invoking object has changed.

Table 16-7. *The Methods Defined by* Observable

Notice that **notifyObservers( )** has two forms: one that takes an argument and one that does not. If you call **notifyObservers( )** with an argument, this object is passed to the observer's **update( )** method as its second parameter. Otherwise, **null** is passed to **update( )**. You can use the second parameter for passing any type of object that is appropriate for your application.

The Observer Interface

To observe an observable object, you must implement the **Observer** interface. This interface defines only the one method shown here:

> void update(Observable *observOb*, Object *arg*)

Here, *observOb* is the object being observed, and *arg* is the value passed by **notifyObservers( )**. The **update( )** method is called when a change in the observed object takes place.

An Observer Example

Here is an example that demonstrates an observable object. It creates an observer class, called **Watcher**, that implements the **Observer** interface. The class being monitored is called **BeingWatched**. It extends **Observable**. Inside **BeingWatched** is the method **counter( )**, which simply counts down from a specified value. It uses **sleep( )** to wait a tenth of a second between counts. Each time the count changes, **notifyObservers( )** is called with the current count passed as its argument. This causes the **update( )** method inside **Watcher** to be called, which displays the current count. Inside **main( )**, a **Watcher** and a **BeingWatched** object, called **observing** and **observed**, respectively, are created. Then, **observing** is added to the list of observers for **observed**. This means that **observing.update( )** will be called each time **counter( )** calls **notifyObservers( )**.

```
/* Demonstrate the Observable class and the
   Observer interface.
*/

import java.util.*;

// This is the observing class.
class Watcher implements Observer {
  public void update(Observable obj, Object arg) {
    System.out.println("update() called, count is " +
                      ((Integer)arg).intValue());
  }
}
```

```
/ This is the class being observed.
class BeingWatched extends Observable {
  void counter(int period) {
    for( ; period >=0; period--) {
      setChanged();
      notifyObservers(new Integer(period));
      try {
        Thread.sleep(100);
      } catch(InterruptedException e) {
        System.out.println("Sleep interrupted");
      }
    }
  }
}


class ObserverDemo {
  public static void main(String args[]) {
    BeingWatched observed = new BeingWatched();
    Watcher observing = new Watcher();

    /* Add the observing to the list of observers for
       observed object.  */
    observed.addObserver(observing);

    observed.counter(10);
  }
}
```

The output from this program is shown here:

```
update() called, count is 10
update() called, count is 9
update() called, count is 8
update() called, count is 7
update() called, count is 6
update() called, count is 5
update() called, count is 4
update() called, count is 3
update() called, count is 2
update() called, count is 1
update() called, count is 0
```

More than one object can be an observer. For example, the following program implements two observing classes and adds an object of each class to the **BeingWatched** observer list. The second observer waits until the count reaches zero and then rings the bell.

```java
/* An object may be observed by two or more
   observers.
*/

import java.util.*;

// This is the first observing class.
class Watcher1 implements Observer {
  public void update(Observable obj, Object arg) {
    System.out.println("update() called, count is " +
                        ((Integer)arg).intValue());
  }
}

// This is the second observing class.
class Watcher2 implements Observer {
  public void update(Observable obj, Object arg) {
    // Ring bell when done
    if(((Integer)arg).intValue() == 0)
      System.out.println("Done" + '\7');
  }
}

// This is the class being observed.
class BeingWatched extends Observable {
  void counter(int period) {
    for( ; period >=0; period--) {
      setChanged();
      notifyObservers(new Integer(period));
      try {
        Thread.sleep(100);
      } catch(InterruptedException e) {
        System.out.println("Sleep interrupted");
      }
    }
  }
}
```

```
class TwoObservers {
  public static void main(String args[]) {
    BeingWatched observed = new BeingWatched();
    Watcher1 observing1 = new Watcher1();
    Watcher2 observing2 = new Watcher2();

    // add both observers
    observed.addObserver(observing1);
    observed.addObserver(observing2);

    observed.counter(10);
  }
}
```

The **Observable** class and the **Observer** interface allow you to implement sophisticated program architectures based on the document/view methodology. They are also useful in multithreaded situations.

Timer and TimerTask

Java 2, version 1.3 added an interesting and useful feature to **java.util**: the ability to schedule a task for execution at some future time. The classes that support this are **Timer** and **TimerTask**. Using these classes you can create a thread that runs in the background, waiting for a specific time. When the time arrives, the task linked to that thread is executed. Various options allow you to schedule a task for repeated execution, and to schedule a task to run on a specific date. Although it was always possible to manually create a task that would be executed at a specific time using the **Thread** class, **Timer** and **TimerTask** greatly simplify this process.

Timer and **TimerTask** work together. **Timer** is the class that you will use to schedule a task for execution. The task being scheduled must be an instance of **TimerTask**. Thus, to schedule a task, you will first create a **TimerTask** object and then schedule it for execution using an instance of **Timer**.

TimerTask implements the **Runnable** interface; thus it can be used to create a thread of execution. Its constructor is shown here:

TimerTask( )

TimerTask defines the methods shown in Table 16-8. Notice that **run( )** is abstract, which means that it must be overridden. The **run( )** method, defined by the **Runnable** interface, contains the code that will be executed. Thus, the easiest way to create a timer task is to extend **TimerTask** and override **run( )**.

Method	Description
boolean cancel( )	Terminates the task. It returns **true** if an execution of the task is prevented. Otherwise, **false** is returned.
abstract void run( )	Contains the code for the timer task.
long scheduledExecutionTime( )	Returns the time at which the last execution of the task was scheduled to have occurred.

Table 16-8. *The Methods Defined by* TimerTask

Once a task has been created, it is scheduled for execution by an object of type **Timer**. The constructors for **Timer** are shown here.

Timer( )

Timer(boolean *DThread*)

The first version creates a **Timer** object that runs as a normal thread. The second uses a daemon thread if *DThread* is **true**. A daemon thread will execute only as long as the rest of the program continues to execute. The methods defined by **Timer** are shown in Table 16-9.

Method	Description
void cancel( )	Cancels the timer thread.
void schedule(TimerTask *TTask*, long *wait*)	*TTask* is scheduled for execution after the period passed in *wait* has elapsed. The *wait* parameter is specified in milliseconds.
void schedule(TimerTask *TTask*, long *wait*, long *repeat*)	*TTask* is scheduled for execution after the period passed in *wait* has elapsed. The task is then executed repeatedly at the interval specified by *repeat*. Both *wait* and *repeat* are specified in milliseconds.

Table 16-9. *The Methods Defined by* Timer

THE JAVA LIBRARY

void schedule(TimerTask *TTask*, Date *targetTime*)	*TTask* is scheduled for execution at the time specified by *targetTime*.

void schedule(TimerTask *TTask*,
           Date *targetTime*,
           long *repeat*)
	TTask is scheduled for execution at the time specified by *targetTime*. The task is then executed repeatedly at the interval passed in *repeat*. The *repeat* parameter is specified in milliseconds.

void scheduleAtFixedRate(
           TimerTask *TTask*,
           long *wait*, long *repeat*)
	TTask is scheduled for execution after the period passed in *wait* has elapsed. The task is then executed repeatedly at the interval specified by *repeat*. Both *wait* and *repeat* are specified in milliseconds. The time of each repetition is relative to the first execution, not the preceding execution. Thus, the overall rate of execution is fixed.

void scheduleAtFixedRate(
           TimerTask *TTask*,
           Date *targetTime*,
           long *repeat*)
	TTask is scheduled for execution at the time specified by *targetTime*. The task is then executed repeatedly at the interval passed in *repeat*. The *repeat* parameter is specified in milliseconds. The time of each repetition is relative to the first execution, not the preceding execution. Thus, the overall rate of execution is fixed.

Table 16-9.   *The Methods Defined by* Timer (continued)

Once a **Timer** has been created, you will schedule a task by calling **schedule( )** on the **Timer** that you created. As Table 16-9 shows, there are several forms of **schedule( )** which allow you to schedule tasks in a variety of ways.

If you create a non-daemon task, then you will want to call **cancel( )** to end the task when your program ends. If you don't do this, then your program may "hang" for a period of time.

The following program demonstrates **Timer** and **TimerTask**. It defines a timer task whose **run( )** method displays the message "Timer task executed." This task is scheduled to run once very half second after an intial delay of one second.

```java
// Demonstrate Timer and TimerTask.

import java.util.*;

class MyTimerTask extends TimerTask {
  public void run() {
    System.out.println("Timer task executed.");
  }
}

class TTest {
  public static void main(String args[]) {
    MyTimerTask myTask = new MyTimerTask();
    Timer myTimer = new Timer();

    /* Set an initial delay of 1 second,
       then repeat every half second.
    */
    myTimer.schedule(myTask, 1000, 500);

    try {
      Thread.sleep(5000);
    } catch (InterruptedException exc) {}

    myTimer.cancel();
  }
}
```

Currency

Java 2, version 1.4 adds the **Currency** class. This class encapsulates information about a currency. It defines no constructors. The methods supported by **Currency** are shown in Table 16-10. The following program demonstrates **Currency**.

```java
// Demonstrate Currency.
import java.util.*;

class CurDemo {
  public static void main(String args[]) {
    Currency c;
```

```
    c = Currency.getInstance(Locale.US);

    System.out.println("Symbol: " + c.getSymbol());
    System.out.println("Default fractional digits: " +
                       c.getDefaultFractionDigits());
  }
}
```

The output is shown here.

```
Symbol: $
Default fractional digits: 2
```

Method	Description
String getCurrencyCode( )	Returns the code (as defined by ISO 4217) that describes the invoking currency.
int getDefaultFractionDigits( )	Returns the number of digits after the decimal point that are normally used by the invoking currency. For example, there are 2 fractional digits normally used for dollars.
static Currency getInstance(Locale *localeObj*)	Returns a **Currency** object for the locale specified by *localeObj*.
static Currency getInstance(String *code*)	Returns a **Currency** object associated with the currency code passed in *code*.
String getSymbol( )	Returns the currency symbol (such as $) for the invoking object.
String getSymbol(Locale *localeObj*)	Returns the currency symbol (such as $) for the locale passed in *localeObj*.
String toString( )	Returns the currency code for the invoking object.

Table 16-10.   *The Methods Defined by* Currency

The java.util.zip Package

The **java.util.zip** package provides the ability to read and write files in the popular ZIP and GZIP file formats. Both ZIP and GZIP input and output streams are available. Other classes implement the ZLIB algorithms for compression and decompression.

The java.util.jar Package

The **java.util.jar** package provides the ability to read and write Java Archive (JAR) files. You will see in Chapter 25 that JAR files are used to contain software components known as *Java Beans* and any associated files.

The
Complete
Reference

Java™ 2

Chapter 17

Input/Output:
Exploring java.io

This chapter explores **java.io**, which provides support for I/O operations. In Chapter 12, we presented an overview of Java's I/O system. Here, we will examine the Java I/O system in greater detail.

As all programmers learn early on, most programs cannot accomplish their goals without accessing external data. Data is retrieved from an *input* source. The results of a program are sent to an *output* destination. In Java, these sources or destinations are defined very broadly. For example, a network connection, memory buffer, or disk file can be manipulated by the Java I/O classes. Although physically different, these devices are all handled by the same abstraction: the *stream*. A stream, as explained in Chapter 12, is a logical entity that either produces or consumes information. A stream is linked to a physical device by the Java I/O system. All streams behave in the same manner, even if the actual physical devices they are linked to differ.

 *Java 2, version 1.4 includes some additional I/O capabilities which are contained in the **java.nio** package. These are described in Chapter 24.*

The Java I/O Classes and Interfaces

The I/O classes defined by **java.io** are listed here:

BufferedInputStream	FileWriter	PipedInputStream
BufferedOutputStream	FilterInputStream	PipedOutputStream
BufferedReader	FilterOutputStream	PipedReader
BufferedWriter	FilterReader	PipedWriter
ByteArrayInputStream	FilterWriter	PrintStream
ByteArrayOutputStream	InputStream	PrintWriter
CharArrayReader	InputStreamReader	PushbackInputStream
CharArrayWriter	LineNumberReader	PushbackReader
DataInputStream	ObjectInputStream	RandomAccessFile
DataOutputStream	ObjectInputStream.GetField	Reader
File	ObjectOutputStream	SequenceInputStream
FileDescriptor	ObjectOutputStream.PutField	SerializablePermission
FileInputStream	ObjectStreamClass	StreamTokenizer
FileOutputStream	ObjectStreamField	StringReader
FilePermission	OutputStream	StringWriter
FileReader	OutputStreamWriter	Writer

The **ObjectInputStream.GetField** and **ObjectOutputStream.PutField** inner classes were added by Java 2. The **java.io** package also contains two classes that were deprecated by Java 2 and are not shown in the preceding table: **LineNumberInputStream** and **StringBufferInputStream**. These classes should not be used for new code.

The following interfaces are defined by **java.io**:

DataInput	FilenameFilter	ObjectOutput
DataOutput	ObjectInput	ObjectStreamConstants
Externalizable	ObjectInputValidation	Serializable
FileFilter		

The **FileFilter** interface was added by Java 2.

As you can see, there are many classes and interfaces in the **java.io** package. These include byte and character streams, and object serialization (the storage and retrieval of objects). This chapter examines several of the most commonly used I/O components, beginning with one of the most unique: **File**.

File

Although most of the classes defined by **java.io** operate on streams, the **File** class does not. It deals directly with files and the file system. That is, the **File** class does not specify how information is retrieved from or stored in files; it describes the properties of a file itself. A **File** object is used to obtain or manipulate the information associated with a disk file, such as the permissions, time, date, and directory path, and to navigate subdirectory hierarchies.

Files are a primary source and destination for data within many programs. Although there are severe restrictions on their use within applets for security reasons, files are still a central resource for storing persistent and shared information. A directory in Java is treated simply as a **File** with one additional property—a list of filenames that can be examined by the **list( )** method.

The following constructors can be used to create **File** objects:

File(String *directoryPath*)
File(String *directoryPath*, String *filename*)
File(File *dirObj*, String *filename*)
File(URI *uriObj*)

Here, *directoryPath* is the path name of the file, *filename* is the name of the file, *dirObj* is a **File** object that specifies a directory, and *uriObj* is a **URI** object that describes a file. The fourth constructor was added by Java 2, version 1.4.

The following example creates three files: **f1**, **f2**, and **f3**. The first **File** object is constructed with a directory path as the only argument. The second includes two arguments—the path and the filename. The third includes the file path assigned to **f1** and a filename; **f3** refers to the same file as **f2**.

```
File f1 = new File("/");
File f2 = new File("/","autoexec.bat");
File f3 = new File(f1,"autoexec.bat");
```

Note

Java does the right thing with path separators between UNIX and Windows conventions. If you use a forward slash (/) on a Windows version of Java, the path will still resolve correctly. Remember, if you are using the Windows convention of a backslash character (\), you will need to use its escape sequence (\\) within a string. The Java convention is to use the UNIX- and URL-style forward slash for path separators.

File defines many methods that obtain the standard properties of a **File** object. For example, **getName( )** returns the name of the file, **getParent( )** returns the name of the parent directory, and **exists( )** returns **true** if the file exists, **false** if it does not. The **File** class, however, is not symmetrical. By this, we mean that there are many methods that allow you to *examine* the properties of a simple file object, but no corresponding function exists to change those attributes. The following example demonstrates several of the **File** methods:

```
// Demonstrate File.
import java.io.File;

class FileDemo {
  static void p(String s) {
    System.out.println(s);
  }

  public static void main(String args[]) {
    File f1 = new File("/java/COPYRIGHT");
    p("File Name: " + f1.getName());
    p("Path: " + f1.getPath());
    p("Abs Path: " + f1.getAbsolutePath());
    p("Parent: " + f1.getParent());
    p(f1.exists() ? "exists" : "does not exist");
    p(f1.canWrite() ? "is writeable" : "is not writeable");
    p(f1.canRead() ? "is readable" : "is not readable");
    p("is " + (f1.isDirectory() ? "" : "not" + " a directory"));
    p(f1.isFile() ? "is normal file" : "might be a named pipe");
    p(f1.isAbsolute() ? "is absolute" : "is not absolute");
    p("File last modified: " + f1.lastModified());
    p("File size: " + f1.length() + " Bytes");
  }
}
```

When you run this program, you will see something similar to the following:

```
File Name: COPYRIGHT
Path: /java/COPYRIGHT
Abs Path: /java/COPYRIGHT
Parent: /java
exists
is writeable
is readable
is not a directory
is normal file
is absolute
File last modified: 812465204000
File size: 695 Bytes
```

Most of the **File** methods are self-explanatory. **isFile( )** and **isAbsolute( )** are not. **isFile( )** returns **true** if called on a file and **false** if called on a directory. Also, **isFile( )** returns **false** for some special files, such as device drivers and named pipes, so this method can be used to make sure the file will behave as a file. The **isAbsolute( )** method returns **true** if the file has an absolute path and **false** if its path is relative.

File also includes two useful utility methods. The first is **renameTo( )**, shown here:

boolean renameTo(File *newName*)

Here, the filename specified by *newName* becomes the new name of the invoking **File** object. It will return **true** upon success and **false** if the file cannot be renamed (if you either attempt to rename a file so that it moves from one directory to another or use an existing filename, for example).

The second utility method is **delete( )**, which deletes the disk file represented by the path of the invoking **File** object. It is shown here:

boolean delete( )

You can also use **delete( )** to delete a directory if the directory is empty. **delete( )** returns **true** if it deletes the file and **false** if the file cannot be removed.

Here are some other **File** methods that you will find helpful. (They were added by Java 2.)

Method	Description
void deleteOnExit( )	Removes the file associated with the invoking object when the Java Virtual Machine terminates.
boolean isHidden( )	Returns **true** if the invoking file is hidden. Returns **false** otherwise.

Method	Description
boolean setLastModified(long *millisec*)	Sets the time stamp on the invoking file to that specified by *millisec*, which is the number of milliseconds from January 1, 1970, Coordinated Universal Time (UTC).
boolean setReadOnly( )	Sets the invoking file to read-only.

Also, because **File** supports the **Comparable** interface, the method **compareTo( )** is also supported.

Directories

A directory is a **File** that contains a list of other files and directories. When you create a **File** object and it is a directory, the **isDirectory( )** method will return **true**. In this case, you can call **list( )** on that object to extract the list of other files and directories inside. It has two forms. The first is shown here:

   String[ ] list( )

The list of files is returned in an array of **String** objects.

The program shown here illustrates how to use **list( )** to examine the contents of a directory:

```
// Using directories.
import java.io.File;

class DirList {
  public static void main(String args[]) {
    String dirname = "/java";
    File f1 = new File(dirname);

    if (f1.isDirectory()) {
      System.out.println("Directory of " + dirname);
      String s[] = f1.list();

      for (int i=0; i < s.length; i++) {
        File f = new File(dirname + "/" + s[i]);
        if (f.isDirectory()) {
          System.out.println(s[i] + " is a directory");
        } else {
```

```
            System.out.println(s[i] + " is a file");
        }
    }
} else {
    System.out.println(dirname + " is not a directory");
}
```

Here is sample output from the program. (Of course, the output you see will be different, based on what is in the directory.)

```
Directory of /java
bin is a directory
lib is a directory
demo is a directory
COPYRIGHT is a file
README is a file
index.html is a file
include is a directory
src.zip is a file
.hotjava is a directory
src is a directory
```

Using FilenameFilter

You will often want to limit the number of files returned by the **list( )** method to include only those files that match a certain filename pattern, or *filter*. To do this, you must use a second form of **list( )**, shown here:

String[ ] list(FilenameFilter *FFObj*)

In this form, *FFObj* is an object of a class that implements the **FilenameFilter** interface.

FilenameFilter defines only a single method, **accept( )**, which is called once for each file in a list. Its general form is given here:

boolean accept(File *directory*, String *filename*)

The **accept( )** method returns **true** for files in the directory specified by *directory* that should be included in the list (that is, those that match the *filename* argument), and returns **false** for those files that should be excluded.

The **OnlyExt** class, shown next, implements **FilenameFilter**. It will be used to modify the preceding program so that it restricts the visibility of the filenames returned by **list( )** to files with names that end in the file extension specified when the object is constructed.

```
import java.io.*;

public class OnlyExt implements FilenameFilter {
  String ext;

  public OnlyExt(String ext) {
    this.ext = "." + ext;
  }

  public boolean accept(File dir, String name) {
    return name.endsWith(ext);
  }
}
```

The modified directory listing program is shown here. Now it will only display files that use the **.html** extension.

```
// Directory of .HTML files.
import java.io.*;

class DirListOnly {
  public static void main(String args[]) {
    String dirname = "/java";
    File f1 = new File(dirname);
    FilenameFilter only = new OnlyExt("html");
    String s[] = f1.list(only);

    for (int i=0; i < s.length; i++) {
      System.out.println(s[i]);
    }
  }
}
```

The listFiles( ) Alternative

Java 2 added a variation to the **list( )** method, called **listFiles( )**, which you might find useful. The signatures for **listFiles( )** are shown here:

File[ ] listFiles( )
File[ ] listFiles(FilenameFilter *FFObj*)
File[ ] listFiles(FileFilter *FObj*)

These methods return the file list as an array of **File** objects instead of strings. The first method returns all files, and the second returns those files that satisfy the specified **FilenameFilter**. Aside from returning an array of **File** objects, these two versions of **listFiles( )** work like their equivalent **list( )** methods.

The third version of **listFiles( )** returns those files with path names that satisfy the specified **FileFilter**. **FileFilter** defines only a single method, **accept( )**, which is called once for each file in a list. Its general form is given here:

boolean accept(File *path*)

The **accept( )** method returns **true** for files that should be included in the list (that is, those that match the *path* argument), and **false** for those that should be excluded.

Creating Directories

Another two useful **File** utility methods are **mkdir( )** and **mkdirs( )**. The **mkdir( )** method creates a directory, returning **true** on success and **false** on failure. Failure indicates that the path specified in the **File** object already exists, or that the directory cannot be created because the entire path does not exist yet. To create a directory for which no path exists, use the **mkdirs( )** method. It creates both a directory and all the parents of the directory.

The Stream Classes

Java's stream-based I/O is built upon four abstract classes: **InputStream**, **OutputStream**, **Reader**, and **Writer**. These classes were briefly discussed in Chapter 12. They are used to create several concrete stream subclasses. Although your programs perform their I/O operations through concrete subclasses, the top-level classes define the basic functionality common to all stream classes.

InputStream and **OutputStream** are designed for byte streams. **Reader** and **Writer** are designed for character streams. The byte stream classes and the character stream classes form separate hierarchies. In general, you should use the character stream classes when working with characters or strings, and use the byte stream classes when working with bytes or other binary objects.

In the remainder of this chapter, both the byte- and character-oriented streams are examined.

The Byte Streams

The byte stream classes provide a rich environment for handling byte-oriented I/O. A byte stream can be used with any type of object, including binary data. This versatility makes byte streams important to many types of programs. Since the byte stream classes are topped by **InputStream** and **OutputStream**, our discussion will begin with them.

InputStream

InputStream is an abstract class that defines Java's model of streaming byte input. All of the methods in this class will throw an **IOException** on error conditions. Table 17-1 shows the methods in **InputStream**.

Method	Description
int available( )	Returns the number of bytes of input currently available for reading.
void close( )	Closes the input source. Further read attempts will generate an **IOException**.
void mark(int *numBytes*)	Places a mark at the current point in the input stream that will remain valid until *numBytes* bytes are read.
boolean markSupported( )	Returns **true** if **mark( )/reset( )** are supported by the invoking stream.
int read( )	Returns an integer representation of the next available byte of input. –1 is returned when the end of the file is encountered.
int read(byte *buffer*[ ])	Attempts to read up to *buffer.length* bytes into *buffer* and returns the actual number of bytes that were successfully read. –1 is returned when the end of the file is encountered.
int read(byte *buffer*[ ], int *offset*, int *numBytes*)	Attempts to read up to *numBytes* bytes into *buffer* starting at *buffer*[*offset*], returning the number of bytes successfully read. –1 is returned when the end of the file is encountered.

Table 17-1.   *The Methods Defined by* InputStream

Method	Description
void reset( )	Resets the input pointer to the previously set mark.
long skip(long *numBytes*)	Ignores (that is, skips) *numBytes* bytes of input, returning the number of bytes actually ignored.

Table 17-1. *The Methods Defined by* InputStream (continued)

OutputStream

OutputStream is an abstract class that defines streaming byte output. All of the methods in this class return a **void** value and throw an **IOException** in the case of errors. Table 17-2 shows the methods in **OutputStream**.

Method	Description
void close( )	Closes the output stream. Further write attempts will generate an **IOException**.
void flush( )	Finalizes the output state so that any buffers are cleared. That is, it flushes the output buffers.
void write(int *b*)	Writes a single byte to an output stream. Note that the parameter is an **int**, which allows you to call **write( )** with expressions without having to cast them back to **byte**.
void write(byte *buffer*[ ])	Writes a complete array of bytes to an output stream.
void write(byte *buffer*[ ], int *offset*, int *numBytes*)	Writes a subrange of *numBytes* bytes from the array *buffer*, beginning at *buffer*[*offset*].

Table 17-2. *The Methods Defined by* OutputStream

Note Most of the methods described in Tables 17-1 and 17-2 are implemented by the subclasses of **InputStream** and **OutputStream**. The **mark( )** and **reset( )** methods are exceptions; notice their use or lack thereof by each subclass in the discussions that follow.

FileInputStream

The **FileInputStream** class creates an **InputStream** that you can use to read bytes from a file. Its two most common constructors are shown here:

FileInputStream(String *filepath*)
FileInputStream(File *fileObj*)

Either can throw a **FileNotFoundException**. Here, *filepath* is the full path name of a file, and *fileObj* is a **File** object that describes the file.

The following example creates two **FileInputStream**s that use the same disk file and each of the two constructors:

```
FileInputStream f0 = new FileInputStream("/autoexec.bat")
File f = new File("/autoexec.bat");
FileInputStream f1 = new FileInputStream(f);
```

Although the first constructor is probably more commonly used, the second allows us to closely examine the file using the **File** methods, before we attach it to an input stream. When a **FileInputStream** is created, it is also opened for reading. **FileInputStream** overrides six of the methods in the abstract class **InputStream**. The **mark( )** and **reset( )** methods are not overridden, and any attempt to use **reset( )** on a **FileInputStream** will generate an **IOException**.

The next example shows how to read a single byte, an array of bytes, and a subrange array of bytes. It also illustrates how to use **available( )** to determine the number of bytes remaining, and how to use the **skip( )** method to skip over unwanted bytes. The program reads its own source file, which must be in the current directory.

```
// Demonstrate FileInputStream.
import java.io.*;

class FileInputStreamDemo {
  public static void main(String args[]) throws Exception {
    int size;
    InputStream f =
      new FileInputStream("FileInputStreamDemo.java");
```

```
      System.out.println("Total Available Bytes: " +
                        (size = f.available()));
      int n = size/40;
      System.out.println("First " + n +
                        " bytes of the file one read() at a time");
      for (int i=0; i < n; i++) {
        System.out.print((char) f.read());
      }
      System.out.println("\nStill Available: " + f.available());
      System.out.println("Reading the next " + n +
                        " with one read(b[])");
      byte b[] = new byte[n];
      if (f.read(b) != n) {
        System.err.println("couldn't read " + n + " bytes.");
      }
      System.out.println(new String(b, 0, n));
      System.out.println("\nStill Available: " + (size = f.available()));
      System.out.println("Skipping half of remaining bytes with skip()");
      f.skip(size/2);
      System.out.println("Still Available: " + f.available());
      System.out.println("Reading " + n/2 + " into the end of array");
      if (f.read(b, n/2, n/2) != n/2) {
        System.err.println("couldn't read " + n/2 + " bytes.");
      }
      System.out.println(new String(b, 0, b.length));
      System.out.println("\nStill Available: " + f.available());
      f.close();
    }
  }
```

Here is the output produced by this program:

```
Total Available Bytes: 1433
First 35 bytes of the file one read() at a time
// Demonstrate FileInputStream.
im
Still Available: 1398
```

```
Reading the next 35 with one read(b[])
port java.io.*;

class FileInputS

Still Available: 1363
Skipping half of remaining bytes with skip()
Still Available: 682
Reading 17 into the end of array
port java.io.*;
read(b) != n) {
S


Still Available: 665
```

This somewhat contrived example demonstrates how to read three ways, to skip input, and to inspect the amount of data available on a stream.

Java 2, version 1.4 added the **getChannel( )** method to **FileInputStream**. This method returns a channel connected to the **FileInputStream** object. Channels are used by the new I/O classes contained in **java.nio.** (See Chapter 24.)

FileOutputStream

FileOutputStream creates an **OutputStream** that you can use to write bytes to a file. Its most commonly used constructors are shown here:

FileOutputStream(String *filePath*)
FileOutputStream(File *fileObj*)
FileOutputStream(String *filePath*, boolean *append*)
FileOutputStream(File *fileObj*, boolean *append*)

They can throw a **FileNotFoundException** or a **SecurityException**. Here, *filePath* is the full path name of a file, and *fileObj* is a **File** object that describes the file. If *append* is **true**, the file is opened in append mode. The fourth constructor was added by Java 2, version 1.4.

Creation of a **FileOutputStream** is not dependent on the file already existing. **FileOutputStream** will create the file before opening it for output when you create the object. In the case where you attempt to open a read-only file, an **IOException** will be thrown.

The following example creates a sample buffer of bytes by first making a **String** and then using the **getBytes( )** method to extract the byte array equivalent. It then creates three files. The first, **file1.txt**, will contain every other byte from the sample. The second, **file2.txt**, will contain the entire set of bytes. The third and last, **file3.txt**, will contain only the last quarter. Unlike the **FileInputStream** methods, all of the **FileOutputStream** methods have a return type of **void**. In the case of an error, these methods will throw an **IOException**.

```
// Demonstrate FileOutputStream.
import java.io.*;

class FileOutputStreamDemo {
  public static void main(String args[]) throws Exception {
    String source = "Now is the time for all good men\n"
      + " to come to the aid of their country\n"
      + " and pay their due taxes.";
    byte buf[] = source.getBytes();
    OutputStream f0 = new FileOutputStream("file1.txt");
    for (int i=0; i < buf.length; i += 2) {
      f0.write(buf[i]);
    }
    f0.close();

    OutputStream f1 = new FileOutputStream("file2.txt");
    f1.write(buf);
    f1.close();

    OutputStream f2 = new FileOutputStream("file3.txt");
    f2.write(buf,buf.length-buf.length/4,buf.length/4);
    f2.close();
  }
}
```

Here are the contents of each file after running this program. First, **file1.txt**:

```
Nwi h iefralgo e
t oet h i ftercuty n a hi u ae.
```

Next, **file2.txt**:

```
Now is the time for all good men
 to come to the aid of their country
 and pay their due taxes.
```

Finally, **file3.txt**:

```
nd pay their due taxes.
```

Java 2, version 1.4 added the **getChannel( )** method to **FileOutputStream**. This method returns a channel connected to the **FileOutputStream** object. Channels are used by the new I/O classes contained in **java.nio.** (See Chapter 24.)

ByteArrayInputStream

ByteArrayInputStream is an implementation of an input stream that uses a byte array as the source. This class has two constructors, each of which requires a byte array to provide the data source:

> ByteArrayInputStream(byte *array*[ ])
> ByteArrayInputStream(byte *array*[ ], int *start*, int *numBytes*)

Here, *array* is the input source. The second constructor creates an **InputStream** from a subset of your byte array that begins with the character at the index specified by *start* and is *numBytes* long.

The following example creates a pair of **ByteArrayInputStream**s, initializing them with the byte representation of the alphabet:

```
// Demonstrate ByteArrayInputStream.
import java.io.*;

class ByteArrayInputStreamDemo {
  public static void main(String args[]) throws IOException {
    String tmp = "abcdefghijklmnopqrstuvwxyz";
    byte b[] = tmp.getBytes();
    ByteArrayInputStream input1 = new ByteArrayInputStream(b);
    ByteArrayInputStream input2 = new ByteArrayInputStream(b, 0,3);
  }
}
```

The **input1** object contains the entire lowercase alphabet, while **input2** contains only the first three letters.

A **ByteArrayInputStream** implements both **mark( )** and **reset( )**. However, if **mark( )** has not been called, then **reset( )** sets the stream pointer to the start of the stream—which in this case is the start of the byte array passed to the constructor. The next example shows how to use the **reset( )** method to read the same input twice. In this case, we read and print the letters "abc" once in lowercase and then again in uppercase.

```
import java.io.*;

class ByteArrayInputStreamReset {
  public static void main(String args[]) throws IOException {
    String tmp = "abc";
    byte b[] = tmp.getBytes();
```

```
ByteArrayInputStream in = new ByteArrayInputStream(b);

for (int i=0; i<2; i++) {
  int c;
  while ((c = in.read()) != -1) {
    if (i == 0) {
      System.out.print((char) c);
    } else {
      System.out.print(Character.toUpperCase((char) c));
    }
  }
  System.out.println();
  in.reset();
  }
 }
}
```

This example first reads each character from the stream and prints it as is, in lowercase. It then resets the stream and begins reading again, this time converting each character to uppercase before printing. Here's the output:

```
abc
ABC
```

ByteArrayOutputStream

ByteArrayOutputStream is an implementation of an output stream that uses a byte array as the destination. **ByteArrayOutputStream** has two constructors, shown here:

ByteArrayOutputStream( )
ByteArrayOutputStream(int *numBytes*)

In the first form, a buffer of 32 bytes is created. In the second, a buffer is created with a size equal to that specified by *numBytes*. The buffer is held in the protected **buf** field of **ByteArrayOutputStream**. The buffer size will be increased automatically, if needed. The number of bytes held by the buffer is contained in the protected **count** field of **ByteArrayOutputStream**.

The following example demonstrates **ByteArrayOutputStream**:

```
// Demonstrate ByteArrayOutputStream.
import java.io.*;
```

```
class ByteArrayOutputStreamDemo {
  public static void main(String args[]) throws IOException {
    ByteArrayOutputStream f = new ByteArrayOutputStream();
    String s = "This should end up in the array";
    byte buf[] = s.getBytes();

    f.write(buf);
    System.out.println("Buffer as a string");
    System.out.println(f.toString());
    System.out.println("Into array");
    byte b[] = f.toByteArray();
    for (int i=0; i<b.length; i++) {
      System.out.print((char) b[i]);
    }
    System.out.println("\nTo an OutputStream()");
    OutputStream f2 = new FileOutputStream("test.txt");

    f.writeTo(f2);
    f2.close();
    System.out.println("Doing a reset");
    f.reset();
    for (int i=0; i<3; i++)
      f.write('X');
    System.out.println(f.toString());
  }
}
```

When you run the program, you will create the following output. Notice how after the call to **reset( )**, the three *X*'s end up at the beginning.

```
Buffer as a string
This should end up in the array
Into array
This should end up in the array
To an OutputStream()
Doing a reset
XXX
```

This example uses the **writeTo( )** convenience method to write the contents of **f** to **test.txt**. Examining the contents of the **test.txt** file created in the preceding example shows the result we expected:

```
This should end up in the array
```

Filtered Byte Streams

Filtered streams are simply wrappers around underlying input or output streams that transparently provide some extended level of functionality. These streams are typically accessed by methods that are expecting a generic stream, which is a superclass of the filtered streams. Typical extensions are buffering, character translation, and raw data translation. The filtered byte streams are **FilterInputStream** and **FilterOutputStream**. Their constructors are shown here:

FilterOutputStream(OutputStream *os*)
FilterInputStream(InputStream *is*)

The methods provided in these classes are identical to those in **InputStream** and **OutputStream**.

Buffered Byte Streams

For the byte-oriented streams, a *buffered stream* extends a filtered stream class by attaching a memory buffer to the I/O streams. This buffer allows Java to do I/O operations on more than a byte at a time, hence increasing performance. Because the buffer is available, skipping, marking, and resetting of the stream becomes possible. The buffered byte stream classes are **BufferedInputStream** and **BufferedOutputStream**. **PushbackInputStream** also implements a buffered stream.

BufferedInputStream

Buffering I/O is a very common performance optimization. Java's **BufferedInputStream** class allows you to "wrap" any **InputStream** into a buffered stream and achieve this performance improvement.

BufferedInputStream has two constructors:

BufferedInputStream(InputStream *inputStream*)
BufferedInputStream(InputStream *inputStream*, int *bufSize*)

The first form creates a buffered stream using a default buffer size. In the second, the size of the buffer is passed in *bufSize*. Use of sizes that are multiples of memory page, disk block, and so on can have a significant positive impact on performance. This is, however, implementation-dependent. An optimal buffer size is generally dependent on the host operating system, the amount of memory available, and how the machine is configured. To make good use of buffering doesn't necessarily require quite this degree of sophistication. A good guess for a size is around 8,192 bytes, and attaching even a rather small buffer to an I/O stream is always a good idea. That way, the low-level system can read blocks of data from the disk or network and store the results in your buffer. Thus, even if you are reading the data a byte at a time out of the **InputStream**, you will be manipulating fast memory over 99.9 percent of the time.

Buffering an input stream also provides the foundation required to support moving backward in the stream of the available buffer. Beyond the **read( )** and **skip( )** methods implemented in any **InputStream**, **BufferedInputStream** also supports the **mark( )** and **reset( )** methods. This support is reflected by **BufferedInputStream.markSupported( )** returning **true**.

The following example contrives a situation where we can use **mark( )** to remember where we are in an input stream and later use **reset( )** to get back there. This example is parsing a stream for the HTML entity reference for the copyright symbol. Such a reference begins with an ampersand (&) and ends with a semicolon (;) without any intervening whitespace. The sample input has two ampersands to show the case where the **reset( )** happens and where it does not.

```java
// Use buffered input.
import java.io.*;

class BufferedInputStreamDemo {
  public static void main(String args[]) throws IOException {
    String s = "This is a &copy; copyright symbol " +
      "but this is &copy not.\n";
    byte buf[] = s.getBytes();
    ByteArrayInputStream in = new ByteArrayInputStream(buf);
    BufferedInputStream f = new BufferedInputStream(in);
    int c;
    boolean marked = false;

    while ((c = f.read()) != -1) {
      switch(c) {
      case '&':
        if (!marked) {
          f.mark(32);
          marked = true;
        } else {
          marked = false;
        }
        break;
      case ';':
        if (marked) {
          marked = false;
          System.out.print("(c)");
        } else
          System.out.print((char) c);
        break;
```

```
        case ' ':
          if (marked) {
            marked = false;
            f.reset();
            System.out.print("&");
          } else
            System.out.print((char) c);
          break;
      default:
        if (!marked)
            System.out.print((char) c);
        break;
      }
    }
  }
}
```

Notice that this example uses **mark(32)**, which preserves the mark for the next 32 bytes read (which is enough for all entity references). Here is the output produced by this program:

```
This is a (c) copyright symbol but this is &copy not.
```

 *Use of **mark( )** is restricted to access within the buffer. This means that you can only specify a parameter to **mark( )** that is smaller than the buffer size of the stream.*

BufferedOutputStream

A **BufferedOutputStream** is similar to any **OutputStream** with the exception of an added **flush( )** method that is used to ensure that data buffers are physically written to the actual output device. Since the point of a **BufferedOutputStream** is to improve performance by reducing the number of times the system actually writes data, you may need to call **flush( )** to cause any data that is in the buffer to get written.

Unlike buffered input, buffering output does not provide additional functionality. Buffers for output in Java are there to increase performance. Here are the two available constructors:

BufferedOutputStream(OutputStream *outputStream*)
BufferedOutputStream(OutputStream *outputStream*, int *bufSize*)

The first form creates a buffered stream using a buffer of 512 bytes. In the second form, the size of the buffer is passed in *bufSize*.

PushbackInputStream

One of the novel uses of buffering is the implementation of pushback. *Pushback* is used on an input stream to allow a byte to be read and then returned (that is, "pushed back") to the stream. The **PushbackInputStream** class implements this idea. It provides a mechanism to "peek" at what is coming from an input stream without disrupting it.

PushbackInputStream has the following constructors:

PushbackInputStream(InputStream *inputStream*)
PushbackInputStream(InputStream *inputStream*, int *numBytes*)

The first form creates a stream object that allows one byte to be returned to the input stream. The second form creates a stream that has a pushback buffer that is *numBytes* long. This allows multiple bytes to be returned to the input stream.

Beyond the familiar methods of **InputStream**, **PushbackInputStream** provides **unread( )**, shown here:

void unread(int *ch*)
void unread(byte *buffer*[ ])
void unread(byte *buffer*, int *offset*, int *numChars*)

The first form pushes back the low-order byte of *ch*. This will be the next byte returned by a subsequent call to **read( )**. The second form returns the bytes in *buffer*. The third form pushes back *numChars* bytes beginning at *offset* from *buffer*. An **IOException** will be thrown if there is an attempt to return a byte when the pushback buffer is full.

Java 2 made a small change to **PushbackInputStream**: it added the **skip( )** method.

Here is an example that shows how a programming language parser might use a **PushbackInputStream** and **unread( )** to deal with the difference between the = = operator for comparison and the = operator for assignment:

```
// Demonstrate unread().
import java.io.*;

class PushbackInputStreamDemo {
  public static void main(String args[]) throws IOException {
    String s = "if (a == 4) a = 0;\n";
    byte buf[] = s.getBytes();
    ByteArrayInputStream in = new ByteArrayInputStream(buf);
    PushbackInputStream f = new PushbackInputStream(in);
    int c;

    while ((c = f.read()) != -1) {
      switch(c) {
      case '=':
```

```
        if ((c = f.read()) == '=')
          System.out.print(".eq.");
        else {
          System.out.print("<-");
          f.unread(c);
        }
        break;
    default:
      System.out.print((char) c);
      break;
    }
  }
}
}
```

Here is the output for this example. Notice that = = was replaced by ".eq." and = was replaced by "<-".

```
if (a .eq. 4) a <- 0;
```

 Caution   *PushbackInputStream has the side effect of invalidating the mark( ) or reset( )*
methods of the InputStream used to create it. Use markSupported( ) to check any
stream on which you are going to use mark( )/reset( ).

SequenceInputStream

The **SequenceInputStream** class allows you to concatenate multiple **InputStream**s.
The construction of a **SequenceInputStream** is different from any other **InputStream**.
A **SequenceInputStream** constructor uses either a pair of **InputStream**s or an
Enumeration of **InputStream**s as its argument:

SequenceInputStream(InputStream *first*, InputStream *second*)
SequenceInputStream(Enumeration *streamEnum*)

Operationally, the class fulfills read requests from the first **InputStream** until it runs
out and then switches over to the second one. In the case of an **Enumeration**, it will
continue through all of the **InputStream**s until the end of the last one is reached.
    Here is a simple example that uses a **SequenceInputStream** to output the contents
of two files:

```
// Demonstrate sequenced input.
import java.io.*;
import java.util.*;
```

```
class InputStreamEnumerator implements Enumeration {
  private Enumeration files;
  public InputStreamEnumerator(Vector files) {
    this.files = files.elements();
  }

  public boolean hasMoreElements() {
    return files.hasMoreElements();
  }

  public Object nextElement() {
    try {
      return new FileInputStream(files.nextElement().toString());
    } catch (Exception e) {
      return null;
    }
  }
}

class SequenceInputStreamDemo {
  public static void main(String args[]) throws Exception {
    int c;
    Vector files = new Vector();

    files.addElement("/autoexec.bat");
    files.addElement("/config.sys");
    InputStreamEnumerator e = new InputStreamEnumerator(files);
    InputStream input = new SequenceInputStream(e);

    while ((c = input.read()) != -1) {
      System.out.print((char) c);
    }
    input.close();
  }
}
```

This example creates a **Vector** and then adds two filenames to it. It passes that vector of names to the **InputStreamEnumerator** class, which is designed to provide a wrapper on the vector where the elements returned are not the filenames but rather open **FileInputStream**s on those names. The **SequenceInputStream** opens each file in turn, and this example prints the contents of the two files.

PrintStream

The **PrintStream** class provides all of the formatting capabilities we have been using from the **System** file handle, **System.out**, since the beginning of the book. Here are two of its constructors:

PrintStream(OutputStream *outputStream*)
PrintStream(OutputStream *outputStream*, boolean *flushOnNewline*)

where *flushOnNewline* controls whether Java flushes the output stream every time a newline (\n) character is output. If *flushOnNewline* is **true**, flushing automatically takes place. If it is **false**, flushing is not automatic. The first constructor does not automatically flush.

Java's **PrintStream** objects support the **print( )** and **println( )** methods for all types, including **Object**. If an argument is not a simple type, the **PrintStream** methods will call the object's **toString( )** method and then print the result.

RandomAccessFile

RandomAccessFile encapsulates a random-access file. It is not derived from **InputStream** or **OutputStream**. Instead, it implements the interfaces **DataInput** and **DataOutput**, which define the basic I/O methods. It also supports positioning requests—that is, you can position the *file pointer* within the file. It has these two constructors:

RandomAccessFile(File *fileObj*, String *access*)
    throws FileNotFoundException

RandomAccessFile(String *filename*, String *access*)
    throws FileNotFoundException

In the first form, *fileObj* specifies the name of the file to open as a **File** object. In the second form, the name of the file is passed in *filename*. In both cases, *access* determines what type of file access is permitted. If it is "r", then the file can be read, but not written. If it is "rw", then the file is opened in read-write mode. If it is "rws", the file is opened for read-write operations and every change to the file's data or metadata will be immediately written to the physical device. If it is "rwd", the file is opened for read-write operations and every change to the file's data will be immediately written to the physical device.

The method **seek( )**, shown here, is used to set the current position of the file pointer within the file:

void seek(long *newPos*) throws IOException

Here, *newPos* specifies the new position, in bytes, of the file pointer from the beginning of the file. After a call to **seek( )**, the next read or write operation will occur at the new file position.

RandomAccessFile implements the standard input and output methods, which you can use to read and write to random access files. It also includes some additional methods. One is **setLength( )**. It has this signature:

    void setLength(long *len*) throws IOException

This method sets the length of the invoking file to that specified by *len*. This method can be used to lengthen or shorten a file. If the file is lengthened, the added portion is undefined.

Java 2, version 1.4 added the **getChannel( )** method to **RandomAccessFile**. This method returns a channel connected to the **RandomAccessFile** object. Channels are used by the new I/O classes contained in **java.nio**. (See Chapter 24.)

The Character Streams

While the byte stream classes provide sufficient functionality to handle any type of I/O operation, they cannot work directly with Unicode characters. Since one of the main purposes of Java is to support the "write once, run anywhere" philosophy, it was necessary to include direct I/O support for characters. In this section, several of the character I/O classes are discussed. As explained earlier, at the top of the character stream hierarchies are the **Reader** and **Writer** abstract classes. We will begin with them.

 As discussed in Chapter 12, the character I/O classes were added by the 1.1 release of Java. Because of this, you may still find legacy code that uses byte streams where character streams should be. When working on such code, it is a good idea to update it.

Reader

Reader is an abstract class that defines Java's model of streaming character input. All of the methods in this class will throw an **IOException** on error conditions. Table 17-3 provides a synopsis of the methods in **Reader**.

Writer

Writer is an abstract class that defines streaming character output. All of the methods in this class return a **void** value and throw an **IOException** in the case of errors. Table 17-4 shows a synopsis of the methods in **Writer**.

FileReader

The **FileReader** class creates a **Reader** that you can use to read the contents of a file. Its two most commonly used constructors are shown here:

    FileReader(String *filePath*)
    FileReader(File *fileObj*)

Method	Description
abstract void close( )	Closes the input source. Further read attempts will generate an **IOException**.
void mark(int *numChars*)	Places a mark at the current point in the input stream that will remain valid until *numChars* characters are read.
boolean markSupported( )	Returns **true** if **mark( )**/**reset( )** are supported on this stream.
int read( )	Returns an integer representation of the next available character from the invoking input stream. −1 is returned when the end of the file is encountered.
int read(char *buffer*[ ])	Attempts to read up to *buffer.length* characters into *buffer* and returns the actual number of characters that were successfully read. −1 is returned when the end of the file is encountered.
abstract int read(char *buffer*[ ], int *offset*, int *numChars*)	Attempts to read up to *numChars* characters into *buffer* starting at *buffer*[*offset*], returning the number of characters successfully read. −1 is returned when the end of the file is encountered.
boolean ready( )	Returns **true** if the next input request will not wait. Otherwise, it returns **false**.
void reset( )	Resets the input pointer to the previously set mark.
long skip(long *numChars*)	Skips over *numChars* characters of input, returning the number of characters actually skipped.

Table 17-3.   *The Methods Defined by* Reader

Either can throw a **FileNotFoundException**. Here, *filePath* is the full path name of a file, and *fileObj* is a **File** object that describes the file.

Method	Description
abstract void close( )	Closes the output stream. Further write attempts will generate an **IOException**.
abstract void flush( )	Finalizes the output state so that any buffers are cleared. That is, it flushes the output buffers.
void write(int *ch*)	Writes a single character to the invoking output stream. Note that the parameter is an **int**, which allows you to call **write** with expressions without having to cast them back to **char**.
void write(char *buffer*[ ])	Writes a complete array of characters to the invoking output stream.
abstract void write(char *buffer*[ ], int *offset*, int *numChars*)	Writes a subrange of *numChars* characters from the array *buffer*, beginning at *buffer*[*offset*] to the invoking output stream.
void write(String *str*)	Writes *str* to the invoking output stream.
void write(String *str*, int *offset*, int *numChars*)	Writes a subrange of *numChars* characters from the array *str*, beginning at the specified *offset*.

Table 17-4.   *The Methods Defined by* Writer

The following example shows how to read lines from a file and print these to the standard output stream. It reads its own source file, which must be in the current directory.

```java
// Demonstrate FileReader.
import java.io.*;

class FileReaderDemo {
  public static void main(String args[]) throws Exception {
    FileReader fr = new FileReader("FileReaderDemo.java");
    BufferedReader br = new BufferedReader(fr);
    String s;
```

```
      while((s = br.readLine()) != null) {
        System.out.println(s);
      }

      fr.close();
    }
  }
```

FileWriter

FileWriter creates a **Writer** that you can use to write to a file. Its most commonly used constructors are shown here:

FileWriter(String *filePath*)
FileWriter(String *filePath,* boolean *append)*
FileWriter(File *fileObj)*
FileWriter(File *fileObj,* boolean *append)*

They can throw an **IOException**. Here, *filePath* is the full path name of a file, and *fileObj* is a **File** object that describes the file. If *append* is **true**, then output is appended to the end of the file. The fourth constructor was added by Java 2, version 1.4.

Creation of a **FileWriter** is not dependent on the file already existing. **FileWriter** will create the file before opening it for output when you create the object. In the case where you attempt to open a read-only file, an **IOException** will be thrown.

The following example is a character stream version of an example shown earlier when **FileOutputStream** was discussed. This version creates a sample buffer of characters by first making a **String** and then using the **getChars( )** method to extract the character array equivalent. It then creates three files. The first, **file1.txt**, will contain every other character from the sample. The second, **file2.txt**, will contain the entire set of characters. Finally, the third, **file3.txt**, will contain only the last quarter.

```
// Demonstrate FileWriter.
import java.io.*;

class FileWriterDemo {
  public static void main(String args[]) throws Exception {
    String source = "Now is the time for all good men\n"
      + " to come to the aid of their country\n"
      + " and pay their due taxes.";
    char buffer[] = new char[source.length()];
    source.getChars(0, source.length(), buffer, 0);
```

```
      FileWriter f0 = new FileWriter("file1.txt");
      for (int i=0; i < buffer.length; i += 2) {
        f0.write(buffer[i]);
      }
      f0.close();

      FileWriter f1 = new FileWriter("file2.txt");
      f1.write(buffer);
      f1.close();

      FileWriter f2 = new FileWriter("file3.txt");

      f2.write(buffer,buffer.length-buffer.length/4,buffer.length/4);
      f2.close();
    }
}
```

CharArrayReader

CharArrayReader is an implementation of an input stream that uses a character array as the source. This class has two constructors, each of which requires a character array to provide the data source:

CharArrayReader(char *array*[ ])
CharArrayReader(char *array*[ ], int *start*, int *numChars*)

Here, *array* is the input source. The second constructor creates a **Reader** from a subset of your character array that begins with the character at the index specified by *start* and is *numChars* long.

The following example uses a pair of **CharArrayReader**s:

```
// Demonstrate CharArrayReader.
import java.io.*;

public class CharArrayReaderDemo {
  public static void main(String args[]) throws IOException {
    String tmp = "abcdefghijklmnopqrstuvwxyz";
    int length = tmp.length();
    char c[] = new char[length];
```

```
    tmp.getChars(0, length, c, 0);
    CharArrayReader input1 = new CharArrayReader(c);
    CharArrayReader input2 = new CharArrayReader(c, 0, 5);

    int i;
    System.out.println("input1 is:");
    while((i = input1.read()) != -1) {
      System.out.print((char)i);
    }
    System.out.println();

    System.out.println("input2 is:");
    while((i = input2.read()) != -1) {
      System.out.print((char)i);
    }
    System.out.println();
  }
}
```

The **input1** object is constructed using the entire lowercase alphabet, while **input2** contains only the first five letters. Here is the output:

```
input1 is:
abcdefghijklmnopqrstuvwxyz
input2 is:
abcde
```

CharArrayWriter

CharArrayWriter is an implementation of an output stream that uses an array as the destination. **CharArrayWriter** has two constructors, shown here:

CharArrayWriter( )
CharArrayWriter(int *numChars*)

In the first form, a buffer with a default size is created. In the second, a buffer is created with a size equal to that specified by *numChars*. The buffer is held in the **buf** field of **CharArrayWriter**. The buffer size will be increased automatically, if needed. The

number of characters held by the buffer is contained in the **count** field of
CharArrayWriter. Both **buf** and **count** are protected fields.

The following example demonstrates **CharArrayWriter** by reworking the sample
program shown earlier for **ByteArrayOutputStream**. It produces the same output as
the previous version.

```java
// Demonstrate CharArrayWriter.
import java.io.*;

class CharArrayWriterDemo {
  public static void main(String args[]) throws IOException {
    CharArrayWriter f = new CharArrayWriter();
    String s = "This should end up in the array";
    char buf[] = new char[s.length()];

    s.getChars(0, s.length(), buf  0);
    f.write(buf);
    System.out.println("Buffer as a string");
    System.out.println(f.toString());
    System.out.println("Into array");

    char c[] = f.toCharArray();
    for (int i=0; i<c.length; i++) {
      System.out.print(c[i]);
    }

    System.out.println("\nTo a FileWriter()");
    FileWriter f2 = new FileWriter("test.txt");
    f.writeTo(f2);
    f2.close();
    System.out.println("Doing a reset");
    f.reset();
    for (int i=0; i<3; i++)
      f.write('X');
    System.out.println(f.toString());
  }
}
```

BufferedReader

BufferedReader improves performance by buffering input. It has two constructors:

BufferedReader(Reader *inputStream*)
BufferedReader(Reader *inputStream*, int *bufSize*)

The first form creates a buffered character stream using a default buffer size. In the second, the size of the buffer is passed in *bufSize*.

As is the case with the byte-oriented stream, buffering an input character stream also provides the foundation required to support moving backward in the stream within the available buffer. To support this, **BufferedReader** implements the **mark( )** and **reset( )** methods, and **BufferedReader.markSupported( )** returns **true**.

The following example reworks the **BufferedInputStream** example, shown earlier, so that it uses a **BufferedReader** character stream rather than a buffered byte stream. As before, it uses **mark( )** and **reset( )** methods to parse a stream for the HTML entity reference for the copyright symbol. Such a reference begins with an ampersand (&) and ends with a semicolon (;) without any intervening whitespace. The sample input has two ampersands, to show the case where the **reset( )** happens and where it does not. Output is the same as that shown earlier.

```
// Use buffered input.
import java.io.*;

class BufferedReaderDemo {
  public static void main(String args[]) throws IOException {
    String s = "This is a &copy; copyright symbol " +
      "but this is &copy not.\n";
    char buf[] = new char[s.length()];
    s.getChars(0, s.length(), buf, 0);
    CharArrayReader in = new CharArrayReader(buf);
    BufferedReader f = new BufferedReader(in);
    int c;
    boolean marked = false;

    while ((c = f.read()) != -1) {
      switch(c) {
      case '&':
        if (!marked) {
```

THE JAVA LIBRARY

```
          f.mark(32);
          marked = true;
        } else {
          marked = false;
        }
        break;
      case ';':
        if (marked) {
          marked = false;
          System.out.print("(c)");
        } else
          System.out.print((char) c);
        break;
      case '.':
        if (marked) {
          marked = false;
          f.reset();
          System.out.print("&");
        } else
          System.out.print((char) c);
        break;
      default:
        if (!marked)
          System.out.print((char) c);
        break;
      }
    }
  }
}
```

BufferedWriter

A **BufferedWriter** is a **Writer** that adds a **flush( )** method that can be used to ensure that data buffers are physically written to the actual output stream. Using a **BufferedWriter** can increase performance by reducing the number of times data is actually physically written to the output stream.

A **BufferedWriter** has these two constructors:

BufferedWriter(Writer *outputStream*)
BufferedWriter(Writer *outputStream*, int *bufSize*)

The first form creates a buffered stream using a buffer with a default size. In the second, the size of the buffer is passed in *bufSize*.

PushbackReader

The **PushbackReader** class allows one or more characters to be returned to the input stream. This allows you to look ahead in the input stream. Here are its two constructors:

PushbackReader(Reader *inputStream*)
PushbackReader(Reader *inputStream*, int *bufSize*)

The first form creates a buffered stream that allows one character to be pushed back. In the second, the size of the pushback buffer is passed in *bufSize*.

PushbackReader provides **unread( )**, which returns one or more characters to the invoking input stream. It has the three forms shown here:

void unread(int *ch*)
void unread(char *buffer*[ ])
void unread(char *buffer*[ ], int *offset*, int *numChars*)

The first form pushes back the character passed in *ch*. This will be the next character returned by a subsequent call to **read( )**. The second form returns the characters in *buffer*. The third form pushes back *numChars* characters beginning at *offset* from *buffer*. An **IOException** will be thrown if there is an attempt to return a character when the pushback buffer is full.

The following program reworks the earlier **PushBackInputStream** example by replacing **PushBackInputStream** with a **PushbackReader**. As before, it shows how a programming language parser can use a pushback stream to deal with the difference between the == operator for comparison and the = operator for assignment.

```
// Demonstrate unread().
import java.io.*;

class PushbackReaderDemo {
  public static void main(String args[]) throws IOException {
    String s = "if (a == 4) a = 0;\n";
    char buf[] = new char[s.length()];
    s.getChars(0, s.length(), buf, 0);
    CharArrayReader in = new CharArrayReader(buf);
    PushbackReader f = new PushbackReader(in);
    int c;
```

```
while ((c = f.read()) != -1) {
  switch(c) {
  case '=':
    if ((c = f.read()) == '=')
      System.out.print(".eq.");
    else {
      System.out.print("<-");
      f.unread(c);
    }
    break;
  default:
    System.out.print((char) c);
    break;
  }
}
}
}
```

PrintWriter

PrintWriter is essentially a character-oriented version of **PrintStream**. It provides the formatted output methods **print( )** and **println( )**. **PrintWriter** has four constructors:

> PrintWriter(OutputStream *outputStream*)
> PrintWriter(OutputStream *outputStream*, boolean *flushOnNewline*)
> PrintWriter(Writer *outputStream*)
> PrintWriter(Writer *outputStream*, boolean *flushOnNewline*)

where *flushOnNewline* controls whether Java flushes the output stream every time **println( )** is called. If *flushOnNewline* is **true**, flushing automatically takes place. If **false**, flushing is not automatic. The first and third constructors do not automatically flush.

Java's **PrintWriter** objects support the **print( )** and **println( )** methods for all types, including **Object**. If an argument is not a simple type, the **PrintWriter** methods will call the object's **toString( )** method and then print out the result.

Using Stream I/O

The following example demonstrates several of Java's I/O character stream classes and methods. This program implements the standard **wc** (word count) command. The program has two modes: if no filenames are provided as arguments, the program

operates on the standard input stream. If one or more filenames are specified, the
program operates on each of them.

```java
// A word counting utility.
import java.io.*;

class WordCount {
  public static int words = 0;
  public static int lines = 0;
  public static int chars = 0;

  public static void wc(InputStreamReader isr)
    throws IOException {
    int c = 0;
    boolean lastWhite = true;
    String whiteSpace = " \t\n\r";

    while ((c = isr.read()) != -1) {
      // Count characters
      chars++;
      // Count lines
      if (c == '\n') {
        lines++;
      }
      // Count words by detecting the start of a word
      int index = whiteSpace.indexOf(c);
      if(index == -1) {
        if(lastWhite == true) {
          ++words;
        }
        lastWhite = false;
      }
      else {
        lastWhite = true;
      }
    }
    if(chars != 0) {
      ++lines;
    }
  }

  public static void main(String args[]) {
```

```
        FileReader fr;
        try {
          if (args.length == 0) { // We're working with stdin
            wc(new InputStreamReader(System.in));
          }
          else { // We're working with a list of files
            for (int i = 0; i < args.length; i++) {
              fr = new FileReader(args[i]);
              wc(fr);
            }
          }
        }
        catch (IOException e) {
          return;
        }
        System.out.println(lines + " " + words + " " + chars);
      }
    }
```

The **wc( )** method operates on any input stream and counts the number of characters, lines, and words. It tracks the parity of words and whitespace in the **lastNotWhite** variable.

When executed with no arguments, **WordCount** creates an **InputStreamReader** object using **System.in** as the source for the stream. This stream is then passed to **wc( )**, which does the actual counting. When executed with one or more arguments, **WordCount** assumes that these are filenames and creates **FileReader**s for each of them, passing the resultant **FileReader** objects to the **wc( )** method. In either case, it prints the results before exiting.

Improving wc( ) Using a StreamTokenizer

An even better way to look for patterns in an input stream is to use another of Java's I/O classes: **StreamTokenizer**. Similar to **StringTokenizer** from Chapter 16, **StreamTokenizer** breaks up the **InputStream** into *tokens* that are delimited by sets of characters. It has this constructor:

StreamTokenizer(Reader *inStream*)

Here *inStream* must be some form of **Reader**.

StreamTokenizer defines several methods. In this example, we will use only a few. To reset the default set of delimiters, we will employ the **resetSyntax( )** method. The default set of delimiters is finely tuned for tokenizing Java programs and is thus too specialized for this example. We declare that our tokens, or "words," are any consecutive string of visible characters delimited on both sides by whitespace.

We use the **eolIsSignificant( )** method to ensure that newline characters will be delivered as tokens, so we can count the number of lines as well as words. It has this general form:

    void eolIsSignificant(boolean *eolFlag*)

If *eolFlag* is **true**, the end-of-line characters are returned as tokens. If *eolFlag* is **false**, the end-of-line characters are ignored.

The **wordChars( )** method is used to specify the range of characters that can be used in words. Its general form is shown here:

    void wordChars(int *start*, int *end*)

Here, *start* and *end* specify the range of valid characters. In the program, characters in the range 33 to 255 are valid word characters.

The whitespace characters are specified using **whitespaceChars( )**. It has this general form:

    void whitespaceChars(int *start*, int *end*)

Here, *start* and *end* specify the range of valid whitespace characters.

The next token is obtained from the input stream by calling **nextToken( )**. It returns the type of the token.

StreamTokenizer defines four **int** constants: **TT_EOF**, **TT_EOL**, **TT_NUMBER**, and **TT_WORD**. There are three instance variables. **nval** is a public **double** used to hold the values of numbers as they are recognized. **sval** is a public **String** used to hold the value of any words as they are recognized. **ttype** is a public **int** indicating the type of token that has just been read by the **nextToken( )** method. If the token is a word, **ttype** equals **TT_WORD**. If the token is a number, **ttype** equals **TT_NUMBER**. If the token is a single character, **ttype** contains its value. If an end-of-line condition has been encountered, **ttype** equals **TT_EOL**. (This assumes that **eolIsSignificant( )** was invoked with a **true** argument.) If the end of the stream has been encountered, **ttype** equals **TT_EOF**.

The word count program revised to use a **StreamTokenizer** is shown here:

```
// Enhanced word count program that uses a StreamTokenizer
import java.io.*;

class WordCount {
  public static int words=0;
  public static int lines=0;
  public static int chars=0;
```

```
public static void wc(Reader r) throws IOException {
  StreamTokenizer tok = new StreamTokenizer(r);

  tok.resetSyntax();
  tok.wordChars(33, 255);
  tok.whitespaceChars(0, ' ');
  tok.eolIsSignificant(true);

  while (tok.nextToken() != tok.TT_EOF) {
    switch (tok.ttype) {
      case StreamTokenizer.TT_EOL:
        lines++;
        chars++;
        break;
      case StreamTokenizer.TT_WORD:
        words++;
      default: // FALLSTHROUGH
        chars += tok.sval.length();
        break;
    }
  }
}

public static void main(String args[]) {
  if (args.length == 0) { // We're working with stdin
    try {
      wc(new InputStreamReader(System.in));
      System.out.println(lines + " " + words + " " + chars);
    } catch (IOException e) {};
  } else { // We're working with a list of files
    int twords = 0, tchars = 0, tlines = 0;
    for (int i=0; i<args.length; i++) {
      try {
        words = chars = lines = 0;
        wc(new FileReader(args[i]));
        twords += words;
        tchars += chars;
        tlines += lines;
        System.out.println(args[i] + ": " +
          lines + " " + words + " " + chars);
```

```
    } catch (IOException e) {
      System.out.println(args[i] + ": error.");
    }
  }
  System.out.println("total: " +
  tlines + " " + twords + " " + tchars);
  }
  }
}
```

Serialization

Serialization is the process of writing the state of an object to a byte stream. This is useful when you want to save the state of your program to a persistent storage area, such as a file. At a later time, you may restore these objects by using the process of deserialization.

Serialization is also needed to implement Remote Method Invocation (RMI). RMI allows a Java object on one machine to invoke a method of a Java object on a different machine. An object may be supplied as an argument to that remote method. The sending machine serializes the object and transmits it. The receiving machine deserializes it. (More information about RMI is in Chapter 24.)

Assume that an object to be serialized has references to other objects, which, in turn, have references to still more objects. This set of objects and the relationships among them form a directed graph. There may also be circular references within this object graph. That is, object X may contain a reference to object Y, and object Y may contain a reference back to object X. Objects may also contain references to themselves. The object serialization and deserialization facilities have been designed to work correctly in these scenarios. If you attempt to serialize an object at the top of an object graph, all of the other referenced objects are recursively located and serialized. Similarly, during the process of deserialization, all of these objects and their references are correctly restored.

An overview of the interfaces and classes that support serialization follows.

Serializable

Only an object that implements the **Serializable** interface can be saved and restored by the serialization facilities. The **Serializable** interface defines no members. It is simply used to indicate that a class may be serialized. If a class is serializable, all of its subclasses are also serializable.

Variables that are declared as **transient** are not saved by the serialization facilities. Also, **static** variables are not saved.

Externalizable

The Java facilities for serialization and deserialization have been designed so that much of the work to save and restore the state of an object occurs automatically. However, there are cases in which the programmer may need to have control over these processes. For example, it may be desirable to use compression or encryption techniques. The **Externalizable** interface is designed for these situations.

The **Externalizable** interface defines these two methods:

    void readExternal(ObjectInput *inStream*)
        throws IOException, ClassNotFoundException

    void writeExternal(ObjectOutput *outStream*)
        throws IOException

In these methods, *inStream* is the byte stream from which the object is to be read, and *outStream* is the byte stream to which the object is to be written.

ObjectOutput

The **ObjectOutput** interface extends the **DataOutput** interface and supports object serialization. It defines the methods shown in Table 17-5. Note especially the **writeObject( )** method. This is called to serialize an object. All of these methods will throw an **IOException** on error conditions.

Method	Description
void close( )	Closes the invoking stream. Further write attempts will generate an **IOException**.
void flush( )	Finalizes the output state so that any buffers are cleared. That is, it flushes the output buffers.
void write(byte *buffer*[ ])	Writes an array of bytes to the invoking stream.
void write(byte *buffer*[ ], int *offset*, int *numBytes*)	Writes a subrange of *numBytes* bytes from the array *buffer*, beginning at *buffer*[*offset*].
void write(int *b*)	Writes a single byte to the invoking stream. The byte written is the low-order byte of *b*.
void writeObject(Object *obj*)	Writes object *obj* to the invoking stream.

Table 17-5. *The Methods Defined by* ObjectOutput

ObjectOutputStream

The **ObjectOutputStream** class extends the **OutputStream** class and implements the **ObjectOutput** interface. It is responsible for writing objects to a stream. A constructor of this class is

ObjectOutputStream(OutputStream *outStream*) throws IOException

The argument *outStream* is the output stream to which serialized objects will be written.

The most commonly used methods in this class are shown in Table 17-6. They will throw an **IOException** on error conditions. Java 2 added an inner class to **OojectOuputStream** called **PutField**. It facilitates the writing of persistent fields and its use is beyond the scope of this book.

Method	Description
void close( )	Closes the invoking stream. Further write attempts will generate an **IOException**.
void flush( )	Finalizes the output state so that any buffers are cleared. That is, it flushes the output buffers.
void write(byte *buffer*[ ])	Writes an array of bytes to the invoking stream.
void write(byte *buffer*[ ], int *offset*, int *numBytes*)	Writes a subrange of *numBytes* bytes from the array *buffer*, beginning at *buffer*[*offset*].
void write(int *b*)	Writes a single **byte** to the invoking stream. The byte written is the low-order byte of *b*.
void writeBoolean(boolean *b*)	Writes a **boolean** to the invoking stream.
void writeByte(int *b*)	Writes a **byte** to the invoking stream. The byte written is the low-order byte of *b*.
void writeBytes(String *str*)	Writes the bytes representing *str* to the invoking stream.
void writeChar(int *c*)	Writes a **char** to the invoking stream.
void writeChars(String *str*)	Writes the characters in *str* to the invoking stream.

Table 17-6.   *Commonly Used Methods Defined by* ObjectOutputStream

Method	Description
void writeDouble(double *d*)	Writes a **double** to the invoking stream.
void writeFloat(float *f*)	Writes a **float** to the invoking stream.
void writeInt(int *i*)	Writes an **int** to the invoking stream.
void writeLong(long *l*)	Writes a **long** to the invoking stream.
final void writeObject(Object *obj*)	Writes *obj* to the invoking stream.
void writeShort(int i)	Writes a **short** to the invoking stream.

Table 17-6. *Commonly Used Methods Defined by* ObjectOutputStream (continued)

ObjectInput

The **ObjectInput** interface extends the **DataInput** interface and defines the methods shown in Table 17-7. It supports object serialization. Note especially the **readObject( )** method. This is called to deserialize an object. All of these methods will throw an **IOException** on error conditions.

Method	Description
int available( )	Returns the number of bytes that are now available in the input buffer.
void close( )	Closes the invoking stream. Further read attempts will generate an **IOException**.
int read( )	Returns an integer representation of the next available byte of input. –1 is returned when the end of the file is encountered.
int read(byte *buffer*[ ])	Attempts to read up to *buffer.length* bytes into *buffer*, returning the number of bytes that were successfully read. –1 is returned when the end of the file is encountered.

Table 17-7. *The Methods Defined by* ObjectInput

Method	Description
int read(byte *buffer*[ ], int *offset*, int *numBytes*)	Attempts to read up to *numBytes* bytes into *buffer* starting at *buffer*[*offset*], returning the number of bytes that were successfully read. –1 is returned when the end of the file is encountered.
Object readObject( )	Reads an object from the invoking stream.
long skip(long *numBytes*)	Ignores (that is, skips) *numBytes* bytes in the invoking stream, returning the number of bytes actually ignored.

Table 17-7. *The Methods Defined by* ObjectInput (continued)

ObjectInputStream

The **ObjectInputStream** class extends the **InputStream** class and implements the **ObjectInput** interface. **ObjectInputStream** is responsible for reading objects from a stream. A constructor of this class is

ObjectInputStream(InputStream *inStream*)
    throws IOException, StreamCorruptedException

The argument *inStream* is the input stream from which serialized objects should be read. The most commonly used methods in this class are shown in Table 17-8. They will throw an **IOException** on error conditions. Java 2 added an inner class to **ObjectInputStream** called **GetField**. It facilitates the reading of persistent fields and its use is beyond the scope of this book. Also, the method **readLine( )** was deprecated by Java 2 and should no longer be used.

Method	Description
int available( )	Returns the number of bytes that are now available in the input buffer.
void close( )	Closes the invoking stream. Further read attempts will generate an **IOException**.

Table 17-8. *Commonly Used Methods Defined by* ObjectInputStream

Method	Description
int read( )	Returns an integer representation of the next available byte of input. –1 is returned when the end of the file is encountered.
int read(byte *buffer*[ ], int *offset*, int *numBytes*)	Attempts to read up to *numBytes* bytes into *buffer* starting at *buffer*[*offset*], returning the number of bytes successfully read. –1 is returned when the end of the file is encountered.
boolean readBoolean( )	Reads and returns a **boolean** from the invoking stream.
byte readByte( )	Reads and returns a **byte** from the invoking stream.
char readChar( )	Reads and returns a **char** from the invoking stream.
double readDouble( )	Reads and returns a **double** from the invoking stream.
float readFloat( )	Reads and returns a **float** from the invoking stream.
void readFully(byte *buffer*[ ])	Reads *buffer.length* bytes into *buffer*. Returns only when all bytes have been read.
void readFully(byte *buffer*[ ], int *offset*, int *numBytes*)	Reads *numBytes* bytes into *buffer* starting at *buffer*[*offset*]. Returns only when *numBytes* have been read.
int readInt( )	Reads and returns an **int** from the invoking stream.
long readLong( )	Reads and returns a **long** from the invoking stream.
final Object readObject( )	Reads and returns an object from the invoking stream.

Table 17-8. *Commonly Used Methods Defined by* ObjectInputStream (continued)

Method	Description
short readShort( )	Reads and returns a **short** from the invoking stream.
int readUnsignedByte( )	Reads and returns an unsigned **byte** from the invoking stream.
int readUnsignedShort( )	Reads an unsigned **short** from the invoking stream.

Table 17-8. *Commonly Used Methods Defined by* ObjectInputStream (continued)

A Serialization Example

The following program illustrates how to use object serialization and deserialization. It begins by instantiating an object of class **MyClass**. This object has three instance variables that are of types **String**, **int**, and **double**. This is the information we want to save and restore.

A **FileOutputStream** is created that refers to a file named "serial," and an **ObjectOutputStream** is created for that file stream. The **writeObject( )** method of **ObjectOutputStream** is then used to serialize our object. The object output stream is flushed and closed.

A **FileInputStream** is then created that refers to the file named "serial," and an **ObjectInputStream** is created for that file stream. The **readObject( )** method of **ObjectInputStream** is then used to deserialize our object. The object input stream is then closed.

Note that **MyClass** is defined to implement the **Serializable** interface. If this is not done, a **NotSerializableException** is thrown. Try experimenting with this program by declaring some of the **MyClass** instance variables to be **transient**. That data is then not saved during serialization.

```
import java.io.*;

public class SerializationDemo {
  public static void main(String args[]) {

    // Object serialization
    try {
```

```
      MyClass object1 = new MyClass("Hello", -7, 2.7e10);
      System.out.println("object1: " + object1);
      FileOutputStream fos = new FileOutputStream("serial");
      ObjectOutputStream oos = new ObjectOutputStream(fos);
      oos.writeObject(object1);
      oos.flush();
      oos.close();
    }
    catch(Exception e) {
      System.out.println("Exception during serialization: " + e);
      System.exit(0);
    }

    // Object deserialization
    try {
      MyClass object2;
      FileInputStream fis = new FileInputStream("serial");
      ObjectInputStream ois = new ObjectInputStream(fis);
      object2 = (MyClass)ois.readObject();
      ois.close();
      System.out.println("object2: " + object2);
    }
    catch(Exception e) {
      System.out.println("Exception during deserialization: " + e);
      System.exit(0);
    }
  }
}

class MyClass implements Serializable {
  String s;
  int i;
  double d;
  public MyClass(String s, int i, double d) {
    this.s = s;
    this.i = i;
    this.d = d;
  }
  public String toString() {
    return "s=" + s + "; i=" + i + "; d=" + d;
  }
}
```

This program demonstrates that the instance variables of **object1** and **object2** are identical. The output is shown here:

```
object1: s=Hello; i=-7; d=2.7E10
object2: s=Hello; i=-7; d=2.7E10
```

Stream Benefits

The streaming interface to I/O in Java provides a clean abstraction for a complex and often cumbersome task. The composition of the filtered stream classes allows you to dynamically build the custom streaming interface to suit your data transfer requirements. Java programs written to adhere to the abstract, high-level **InputStream**, **OutputStream**, **Reader**, and **Writer** classes will function properly in the future even when new and improved concrete stream classes are invented. As you will see in the next chapter, this model works very well when we switch from a file system-based set of streams to the network and socket streams. Finally, serialization of objects is expected to play an increasingly important role in Java programming in the future. Java's serialization I/O classes provide a portable solution to this sometimes tricky task.

The
Complete
Reference

Chapter 18

Networking

This chapter explores the **java.net** package, which provides support for networking. Its creators have called Java "programming for the Internet." While true, there is actually very little in Java, the programming language, that makes it any more appropriate for writing networked programs than, say, C++ or FORTRAN. What makes Java a good language for networking are the classes defined in the **java.net** package.

These networking classes encapsulate the "socket" paradigm pioneered in the Berkeley Software Distribution (BSD) from the University of California at Berkeley. No discussion of Internet networking libraries would be complete without a brief recounting of the history of UNIX and BSD sockets.

Networking Basics

Ken Thompson and Dennis Ritchie developed UNIX in concert with the C language at Bell Telephone Laboratories, Murray Hill, New Jersey, in 1969. For many years, the development of UNIX remained in Bell Labs and in a few universities and research facilities that had the DEC PDP machines it was designed to be run on. In 1978, Bill Joy was leading a project at Cal Berkeley to add many new features to UNIX, such as virtual memory and full-screen display capabilities. By early 1984, just as Bill was leaving to found Sun Microsystems, he shipped 4.2BSD, commonly known as *Berkeley UNIX*.

4.2BSD came with a fast file system, reliable signals, interprocess communication, and, most important, networking. The networking support first found in 4.2 eventually became the de facto standard for the Internet. Berkeley's implementation of TCP/IP remains the primary standard for communications within the Internet. The socket paradigm for interprocess and network communication has also been widely adopted outside of Berkeley. Even Windows and the Macintosh started talking "Berkeley sockets" in the late '80s.

Socket Overview

A *network socket* is a lot like an electrical socket. Various plugs around the network have a standard way of delivering their payload. Anything that understands the standard protocol can "plug in" to the socket and communicate. With electrical sockets, it doesn't matter if you plug in a lamp or a toaster; as long as they are expecting 60Hz, 115-volt electricity, the devices will work. Think how your electric bill is created. There is a meter somewhere between your house and the rest of the network. For each kilowatt of power that goes through that meter, you are billed. The bill comes to your "address." So even though the electricity flows freely around the power grid, all of the sockets in your house have a particular address.

The same idea applies to network sockets, except we talk about TCP/IP packets and IP addresses rather than electrons and street addresses. *Internet Protocol (IP)* is a low-level routing protocol that breaks data into small packets and sends them to an address across a network, which does not guarantee to deliver said packets to the destination. *Transmission Control Protocol (TCP)* is a higher-level protocol that manages to robustly string together these packets, sorting and retransmitting them as necessary to reliably transmit your data. A third protocol, *User Datagram Protocol (UDP)*, sits next to TCP and can be used directly to support fast, connectionless, unreliable transport of packets.

Client/Server

You often hear the term *client/server* mentioned in the context of networking. It seems complicated when you read about it in corporate marketing statements, but it is actually quite simple. A *server* is anything that has some resource that can be shared. There are *compute servers*, which provide computing power; *print servers*, which manage a collection of printers; *disk servers*, which provide networked disk space; and *web servers*, which store web pages. A *client* is simply any other entity that wants to gain access to a particular server. The interaction between client and server is just like the interaction between a lamp and an electrical socket. The power grid of the house is the server, and the lamp is a power client. The server is a permanently available resource, while the client is free to "unplug" after it is has been served.

In Berkeley sockets, the notion of a socket allows a single computer to serve many different clients at once, as well as serving many different types of information. This feat is managed by the introduction of a *port*, which is a numbered socket on a particular machine. A server process is said to "listen" to a port until a client connects to it. A server is allowed to accept multiple clients connected to the same port number, although each session is unique. To manage multiple client connections, a server process must be multithreaded or have some other means of multiplexing the simultaneous I/O.

Reserved Sockets

Once connected, a higher-level protocol ensues, which is dependent on which port you are using. TCP/IP reserves the lower 1,024 ports for specific protocols. Many of these will seem familiar to you if you have spent any time surfing the Internet. Port number 21 is for FTP, 23 is for Telnet, 25 is for e-mail, 79 is for finger, 80 is for HTTP, 119 is for netnews—and the list goes on. It is up to each protocol to determine how a client should interact with the port.

For example, HTTP is the protocol that web browsers and servers use to transfer hypertext pages and images. It is quite a simple protocol for a basic page-browsing web server. Here's how it works. When a client requests a file from an HTTP server, an action known as a *hit*, it simply prints the name of the file in a special format to a predefined port and reads back the contents of the file. The server also responds with a status code number to tell the client whether the request can be fulfilled and why.

Here's an example of a client requesting a single file, **/index.html**, and the server replying that it has successfully found the file and is sending it to the client:

Server	Client
Listens to port 80.	Connects to port 80.
Accepts the connection.	Writes "GET /index.html HTTP/1.0\n\n".
Reads up until the second end-of-line (\n).	
Sees that GET is a known command and that HTTP/1.0 is a valid protocol version.	
Reads a local file called /index.html.	
Writes "HTTP/1.0 200 OK\n\n".	"200" means "here comes the file."
Copies the contents of the file into the socket.	Reads the contents of the file and displays it.
Hangs up.	Hangs up.

Obviously, the HTTP protocol is much more complicated than this example shows, but this is an actual transaction that you could have with any web server near you.

Proxy Servers

A *proxy server* speaks the client side of a protocol to another server. This is often required when clients have certain restrictions on which servers they can connect to. Thus, a client would connect to a proxy server, which did not have such restrictions, and the proxy server would in turn communicate for the client. A proxy server has the additional ability to filter certain requests or cache the results of those requests for future use. A caching proxy HTTP server can help reduce the bandwidth demands on a local network's connection to the Internet. When a popular web site is being hit by hundreds of users, a proxy server can get the contents of the web server's popular pages once, saving expensive internetwork transfers while providing faster access to those pages to the clients.

Later in this chapter, we will actually build a complete caching proxy HTTP server. The interesting part about this sample program is that it is both a client and a server. To serve certain pages, it must act as a client to other servers to obtain a copy of the requested content.

Internet Addressing

Every computer on the Internet has an *address*. An Internet address is a number that uniquely identifies each computer on the Net. Originally, all Internet addresses consisted of 32-bit values. This address type was specified by IPv4 (Internet Protocol, version 4). However, a new addressing scheme, called IPv6 (Internet Protocol, version 6) has come into play. IPv6 uses a 128-bit value to represent an address. Although there are several reasons for and advantages to IPv6, the main one is that it supports a much larger address space than does IPv4. Fortunately, IPv6 is downwardly compatible with IPv4. Currently, IPv4 is by far the most widely used scheme, but this situation is likely to change over time.

Because of the emerging importance of IPv6, Java 2, version 1.4 has begun to add support for it. However, at the time of this writing, IPv6 is not supported by all environments. Furthermore, for the next few years, IPv4 will continue to be the dominant form of addressing. For these reasons, the form of Internet addresses discussed here, and used in this chapter, are the IPv4 form. As mentioned, IPv4 is, loosely, a subset of IPv6, and the material contained in this chapter is largely applicable to both forms of addressing.

There are 32 bits in an IPv4 IP address, and we often refer to them as a sequence of four numbers between 0 and 255 separated by dots (.). This makes them easier to remember, because they are not randomly assigned—they are hierarchically assigned. The first few bits define which class of network, lettered A, B, C, D, or E, the address represents. Most Internet users are on a class C network, since there are over two million networks in class C. The first byte of a class C network is between 192 and 224, with the last byte actually identifying an individual computer among the 256 allowed on a single class C network. This scheme allows for half a billion devices to live on class C networks.

Domain Naming Service (DNS)

The Internet wouldn't be a very friendly place to navigate if everyone had to refer to their addresses as numbers. For example, it is difficult to imagine seeing "http://192.9.9.1/" at the bottom of an advertisement. Thankfully, a clearinghouse exists for a parallel hierarchy of names to go with all these numbers. It is called the *Domain Naming Service (DNS)*. Just as the four numbers of an IP address describe a network hierarchy from left to right, the name of an Internet address, called its *domain name*, describes a machine's location in a name space, from right to left. For example, **www.osborne.com** is in the COM domain (reserved for U.S. commercial sites), it is called osborne (after the company name), and www is the name of the specific computer that is Osborne's web server. www corresponds to the rightmost number in the equivalent IP address.

Java and the Net

Now that the stage has been set, let's take a look at how Java relates to all of these network concepts. Java supports TCP/IP both by extending the already established stream I/O interface introduced in Chapter 17 and by adding the features required to build I/O objects across the network. Java supports both the TCP and UDP protocol families. TCP is used for reliable stream-based I/O across the network. UDP supports a simpler, hence faster, point-to-point datagram-oriented model.

The Networking Classes and Interfaces

The classes contained in the **java.net** package are listed here:

Authenticator (Java 2)	InetSocketAddress (Java 2, v1.4)	SocketImpl
ContentHandler	JarURLConnection (Java 2)	SocketPermission
DatagramPacket	MulticastSocket	URI (Java 2, v1.4)
DatagramSocket	NetPermission	URL
DatagramSocketImpl	NetworkInterface (Java 2, v1.4)	URLClassLoader (Java 2)
HttpURLConnection	PasswordAuthentication (Java 2)	URLConnection
InetAddress	ServerSocket	URLDecoder (Java 2)
Inet4Address (Java 2, v1.4)	Socket	URLEncoder
Inet6Address (Java 2, v1.4)	SocketAddress (Java 2, v1.4)	URLStreamHandler

As you can see, several new classes were added by Java 2, version 1.4. Some of these are to support the new IPv6 addressing scheme. Others provide some added flexibility to the original **java.net** package. Java 2, version 1.4 also added functionality, such as support for the new I/O classes, to several of the preexisting networking classes. Most of the additions made by Java 2, version 1.4 are beyond the scope of this chapter, but three new classes, **Inet4Address**, **Inet6Address**, and **URI**, are briefly discussed at the end. The **java.net** package's interfaces are listed here:

ContentHandlerFactory	SocketImplFactory	URLStreamHandlerFactory
FileNameMap	SocketOptions	DatagramSocketImplFactory (added by Java 2, v1.3)

In the sections that follow, we will examine the main networking classes and show several examples that apply them.

InetAddress

Whether you are making a phone call, sending mail, or establishing a connection across the Internet, addresses are fundamental. The **InetAddress** class is used to encapsulate both the numerical IP address we discussed earlier and the domain name for that address. You interact with this class by using the name of an IP host, which is more convenient and understandable than its IP address. The **InetAddress** class hides the number inside. As of Java 2, version 1.4, **InetAddress** can handle both IPv4 and IPv6 addresses. This discussion assumes IPv4.

Factory Methods

The **InetAddress** class has no visible constructors. To create an **InetAddress** object, you have to use one of the available factory methods. *Factory methods* are merely a convention whereby static methods in a class return an instance of that class. This is done in lieu of overloading a constructor with various parameter lists when having unique method names makes the results much clearer. Three commonly used **InetAddress** factory methods are shown here.

> static InetAddress getLocalHost( )
>   throws UnknownHostException
>
> static InetAddress getByName(String *hostName*)
>   throws UnknownHostException
>
> static InetAddress[ ] getAllByName(String *hostName*)
>   throws UnknownHostException

The **getLocalHost( )** method simply returns the **InetAddress** object that represents the local host. The **getByName( )** method returns an **InetAddress** for a host name passed to it. If these methods are unable to resolve the host name, they throw an **UnknownHostException**.

On the Internet, it is common for a single name to be used to represent several machines. In the world of web servers, this is one way to provide some degree of scaling. The **getAllByName( )** factory method returns an array of **InetAddress**es that represent all of the addresses that a particular name resolves to. It will also throw an **UnknownHostException** if it can't resolve the name to at least one address.

Java 2, version 1.4 also includes the factory method **getByAddress( )**, which takes an IP address and returns an **InetAddress** object. Either an IPv4 or an IPv6 address can be used.

The following example prints the addresses and names of the local machine and two well-known Internet web sites:

```
// Demonstrate InetAddress.
import java.net.*;

class InetAddressTest
{
  public static void main(String args[]) throws UnknownHostException {
    InetAddress Address = InetAddress.getLocalHost();
    System.out.println(Address);
    Address = InetAddress.getByName("osborne.com");
    System.out.println(Address);
    InetAddress SW[] = InetAddress.getAllByName("www.nba.com");
    for (int i=0; i<SW.length; i++)
      System.out.println(SW[i]);
  }
}
```

Here is the output produced by this program. (Of course, the output you see will be slightly different.)

```
default/206.148.209.138
osborne.com/198.45.24.162
www.nba.com/64.241.238.153
www.nba.com/64.241.233.142
```

Instance Methods

The **InetAddress** class also has several other methods, which can be used on the objects returned by the methods just discussed. Here are some of the most commonly used.

boolean equals(Object *other*)	Returns **true** if this object has the same Internet address as *other*.
byte[ ] getAddress( )	Returns a byte array that represents the object's Internet address in network byte order.
String getHostAddress( )	Returns a string that represents the host address associated with the **InetAddress** object.
String getHostName( )	Returns a string that represents the host name associated with the **InetAddress** object.
boolean isMulticastAddress( )	Returns **true** if this Internet address is a multicast address. Otherwise, it returns **false**.
String toString( )	Returns a string that lists the host name and the IP address for convenience.

Internet addresses are looked up in a series of hierarchically cached servers. That means that your local computer might know a particular name-to-IP-address mapping automatically, such as for itself and nearby servers. For other names, it may ask a local DNS server for IP address information. If that server doesn't have a particular address, it can go to a remote site and ask for it. This can continue all the way up to the root server, called InterNIC (internic.net). This process might take a long time, so it is wise to structure your code so that you cache IP address information locally rather than look it up repeatedly.

TCP/IP Client Sockets

TCP/IP sockets are used to implement reliable, bidirectional, persistent, point-to-point, stream-based connections between hosts on the Internet. A socket can be used to connect Java's I/O system to other programs that may reside either on the local machine or on any other machine on the Internet.

Note *Applets may only establish socket connections back to the host from which the applet was downloaded. This restriction exists because it would be dangerous for applets loaded through a firewall to have access to any arbitrary machine.*

There are two kinds of TCP sockets in Java. One is for servers, and the other is for clients. The **ServerSocket** class is designed to be a "listener," which waits for clients to connect before doing anything. The **Socket** class is designed to connect to server sockets and initiate protocol exchanges.

The creation of a **Socket** object implicitly establishes a connection between the client and server. There are no methods or constructors that explicitly expose the details of establishing that connection. Here are two constructors used to create client sockets:

Socket(String *hostName*, int *port*)	Creates a socket connecting the local host to the named host and port; can throw an **UnknownHostException** or an **IOException**.
Socket(InetAddress *ipAddress*, int *port*)	Creates a socket using a preexisting **InetAddress** object and a port; can throw an **IOException**.

A socket can be examined at any time for the address and port information associated with it, by use of the following methods:

InetAddress getInetAddress( )	Returns the **InetAddress** associated with the **Socket** object.
int getPort( )	Returns the remote port to which this **Socket** object is connected.
int getLocalPort( )	Returns the local port to which this **Socket** object is connected.

Once the **Socket** object has been created, it can also be examined to gain access to the input and output streams associated with it. Each of these methods can throw an **IOException** if the sockets have been invalidated by a loss of connection on the Net. These streams are used exactly like the I/O streams described in Chapter 17 to send and receive data.

InputStream getInputStream( )	Returns the **InputStream** associated with the invoking socket.
OutputStream getOutputStream( )	Returns the **OutputStream** associated with the invoking socket.

THE JAVA LIBRARY

Java 2, version 1.4 added the **getChannel( )** method to **Socket**. This method returns a channel connected to the **Socket** object. Channels are used by the new I/O classes contained in **java.nio**. (See Chapter 24.)

Whois

The very simple example that follows opens a connection to a "whois" port on the InterNIC server, sends the command-line argument down the socket. and then prints the data that is returned. InterNIC will try to look up the argument as a registered Internet domain name, then send back the IP address and contact information for that site.

```
//Demonstrate Sockets.
import java.net.*;
import java.io.*;

class Whois {
  public static void main(String args[]) throws Exception {
    int c;
    Socket s = new Socket("internic.net", 43);
    InputStream in = s.getInputStream();
    OutputStream out = s.getOutputStream();
    String str = (args.length == 0 ? "osborne.com" : args[0]) + "\n";
    byte buf[] = str.getBytes();
    out.write(buf);
    while ((c = in.read()) != -1) {
      System.out.print((char) c);
    }
    s.close();
  }
}
```

If, for example, you obtained information about **osborne.com**, you'd get something similar to the following:

```
Whois Server Version 1.3

Domain names in the .com, .net, and .org domains can now be registered
with many different competing registrars. Go to http://www.internic.net
for detailed information.

  Domain Name: OSBORNE.COM
  Registrar: NETWORK SOLUTIONS, INC.
  Whois Server: whois.networksolutions.com
  Referral URL: http://www.networksolutions.com
  Name Server: NS1.EPPG.COM
  Name Server: NS2.EPPG.COM
```

```
Updated Date: 16-jan-2002


>> Last update of whois database: Thu, 25 Apr 2002 05:05:52 EDT <<

The Registry database contains ONLY .COM, .NET, .ORG, .EDU domains and
Registrars.
```

URL

That last example was rather obscure, because the modern Internet is not about the older protocols, like whois, finger, and FTP. It is about WWW, the World Wide Web. The Web is a loose collection of higher-level protocols and file formats, all unified in a web browser. One of the most important aspects of the Web is that Tim Berners-Lee devised a scaleable way to locate all of the resources of the Net. Once you can reliably name anything and everything, it becomes a very powerful paradigm. The Uniform Resource Locator (URL) does exactly that.

The *URL* provides a reasonably intelligible form to uniquely identify or address information on the Internet. URLs are ubiquitous; every browser uses them to identify information on the Web. In fact, the Web is really just that same old Internet with all of its resources addressed as URLs plus HTML. Within Java's network class library, the **URL** class provides a simple, concise API to access information across the Internet using URLs.

Format

Two examples of URLs are **http://www.osborne.com/** and **http://www.osborne.com:80/ index.htm**. A URL specification is based on four components. The first is the protocol to use, separated from the rest of the locator by a colon (:). Common protocols are http, ftp, gopher, and file, although these days almost everything is being done via HTTP (in fact, most browsers will proceed correctly if you leave off the "http://" from your URL specification). The second component is the host name or IP address of the host to use; this is delimited on the left by double slashes (//) and on the right by a slash (/) or optionally a colon (:). The third component, the port number, is an optional parameter, delimited on the left from the host name by a colon (:) and on the right by a slash (/). (It defaults to port 80, the predefined HTTP port; thus ":80" is redundant.) The fourth part is the actual file path. Most HTTP servers will append a file named **index.html** or **index.htm** to URLs that refer directly to a directory resource. Thus, **http://www.osborne.com/** is the same as **http://www.osborne.com/index.htm**.

Java's **URL** class has several constructors, and each can throw a **MalformedURLException**. One commonly used form specifies the URL with a string that is identical to what you see displayed in a browser:

URL(String *urlSpecifier*)

The next two forms of the constructor allow you to break up the URL into its component parts:

URL(String *protocolName*, String *hostName*, int *port*, String *path*)
URL(String *protocolName*, String *hostName*, String *path*)

Another frequently used constructor allows you to use an existing URL as a reference context and then create a new URL from that context. Although this sounds a little contorted, it's really quite easy and useful.

URL(URL *urlObj*, String *urlSpecifier*)

In the following example, we create a URL to Osborne's download page and then examine its properties:

```
// Demonstrate URL.
import java.net.*;
class URLDemo {
  public static void main(String args[]) throws MalformedURLException {
    URL hp = new URL("http://www.osborne.com/downloads");

    System.out.println("Protocol: " + hp.getProtocol());
    System.out.println("Port: " + hp.getPort());
    System.out.println("Host: " + hp.getHost());
    System.out.println("File: " + hp.getFile());
    System.out.println("Ext:" + hp.toExternalForm());
  }
}
```

When you run this, you will get the following output:

```
Protocol: http
Port: -1
Host: www.osborne.com
File: /downloads
Ext:http://www.osborne.com/downloads
```

Notice that the port is –1; this means that one was not explicitly set. Now that we have created a **URL** object, we want to retrieve the data associated with it. To access the actual bits or content information of a **URL**, you create a **URLConnection** object from it, using its **openConnection( )** method, like this:

```
url.openConnection()
```

openConnection( ) has the following general form:

URLConnection openConnection( )

It returns a **URLConnection** object associated with the invoking **URL** object. It may throw an **IOException**.

URLConnection

URLConnection is a general-purpose class for accessing the attributes of a remote resource. Once you make a connection to a remote server, you can use **URLConnection** to inspect the properties of the remote object before actually transporting it locally. These attributes are exposed by the HTTP protocol specification and, as such, only make sense for **URL** objects that are using the HTTP protocol. We'll examine the most useful elements of **URLConnection** here.

In the following example, we create a **URLConnection** using the **openConnection( )** method of a **URL** object and then use it to examine the document's properties and content:

```
// Demonstrate URLConnection.
import java.net.*;
import java.io.*;
import java.util.Date;

class UCDemo
{
  public static void main(String args[]) throws Exception {
    int c;
    URL hp = new URL("http://www.internic.net");
    URLConnection hpCon = hp.openConnection();

    // get date
    long d = hpCon.getDate();
    if(d==0)
      System.out.println("No date information.");
    else
      System.out.println("Date: " + new Date(d));

    // get content type
    System.out.println("Content-Type: " + hpCon.getContentType());

    // get expiration date
    d = hpCon.getExpiration();
    if(d==0)
```

```
      System.out.println("No expiration information.");
   else
      System.out.println("Expires: " + new Date(d));

   // get last-modified date
   d = hpCon.getLastModified();
   if(d==0)
      System.out.println("No last-modified information.");
   else
      System.out.println("Last-Modified: " + new Date(d));

   // get content length
   int len = hpCon.getContentLength();
   if(len == -1)
      System.out.println("Content length unavailable.");
   else
      System.out.println("Content-Length: " + len);

   if(len != 0) {
      System.out.println("=== Content ===");
      InputStream input = hpCon.getInputStream();
      int i = len;
      while (((c = input.read()) != -1)) { // && (--i > 0)) {
         System.out.print((char) c);
      }
      input.close();

   } else {
      System.out.println("No content available.");
   }

  }
}
```

The program establishes an HTTP connection to **www.internic.net** over port 80. We then list out the header values and retrieve the content. Here are the first lines of the output (the precise output will vary over time).

```
Date: Sat Apr 27 12:17:32 CDT 2002
Content-Type: text/html
No expiration information.
Last-Modified: Tue Mar 19 17:52:42 CST 2002
Content-Length: 5299
=== Content ===
```

```
<html>

<head>
<title>InterNIC | The Internet's Network Information Center</title>
<meta name="keywords" content="internic,network information, domain registration">
<style type="text/css">
<!--
p, li, td, ul {  font-family: Arial, Helvetica, sans-serif}
-->
</style>
</head>
```

The **URL** and **URLConnection** classes are good enough for simple programs that want to connect to HTTP servers to fetch content. For more complex applications, you'll probably find that you are better off studying the specification of the HTTP protocol and implementing your own wrappers.

TCP/IP Server Sockets

As we mentioned earlier, Java has a different socket class that must be used for creating server applications. The **ServerSocket** class is used to create servers that listen for either local or remote client programs to connect to them on published ports. Since the Web is driving most of the activity on the Internet, this section develops an operational web (http) server.

ServerSockets are quite different from normal **Socket**s. When you create a **ServerSocket**, it will register itself with the system as having an interest in client connections. The constructors for **ServerSocket** reflect the port number that you wish to accept connections on and, optionally, how long you want the queue for said port to be. The queue length tells the system how many client connections it can leave pending before it should simply refuse connections. The default is 50. The constructors might throw an **IOException** under adverse conditions. Here are the constructors:

ServerSocket(int *port*)	Creates server socket on the specified port with a queue length of 50.
ServerSocket(int *port*, int *maxQueue*)	Creates a server socket on the specified port with a maximum queue length of *maxQueue*.
ServerSocket(int *port*, int *maxQueue*, InetAddress *localAddress*)	Creates a server socket on the specified port with a maximum queue length of *maxQueue*. On a multihomed host, *localAddress* specifies the IP address to which this socket binds.

ServerSocket has a method called **accept( )**, which is a blocking call that will wait for a client to initiate communications, and then return with a normal **Socket** that is then used for communication with the client.

Java 2, version 1.4 added the **getChannel( )** method to **ServerSocket**. This method returns a channel connected to the **ServerSocket** object. Channels are used by the new I/O classes contained in **java.nio**. (See Chapter 24.)

A Caching Proxy HTTP Server

In the remainder of this section, we will develop a simple caching proxy HTTP server, called **http**, to demonstrate client and server sockets. **http** supports only GET operations and a very limited range of hard-coded MIME types. (*MIME types* are the type descriptors for multimedia content.) The proxy HTTP server is single threaded, in that each request is handled in turn while all others wait. It has fairly naive strategies for caching—it keeps everything in RAM forever. When it is acting as a proxy server, **http** also copies every file it gets to a local cache for which it has no strategy for refreshing or garbage collecting. All of these caveats aside, **http** represents a productive example of client and server sockets, and it is fun to explore and easy to extend.

Source Code

The implementation of this HTTP server is presented here in five classes and one interface. A more complete implementation would likely split many of the methods out of the main class, **httpd**, in order to abstract more of the components. For space considerations in this book, most of the functionality is in the single class, and the small support classes are only acting as data structures. We will take a close look at each class and method to examine how this server works, starting with the support classes and ending with the main program.

MimeHeader.java

MIME is an Internet standard for communicating multimedia content over e-mail systems. This standard was created by Nat Borenstein in 1992. The HTTP protocol uses and extends the notion of MIME headers to pass general attribute/value pairs between the HTTP client and server.

CONSTRUCTORS   This class is a subclass of **Hashtable** so that it can conveniently store and retrieve the key/value pairs associated with a MIME header. It has two constructors. One creates a blank **MimeHeader** with no keys. The other takes a string formatted as a MIME header and parses it for the initial contents of the object. See **parse( )** next.

parse( )   The **parse( )** method is used to take a raw MIME-formatted string and enter its key/value pairs into a given instance of **MimeHeader**. It uses a **StringTokenizer** to split the input data into individual lines, marked by the CRLF (\r\n) sequence. It then iterates through each line using the canonical **while ... hasMoreTokens( ) ... nextToken( )** sequence.

For each line of the MIME header, the **parse( )** method splits the line into two strings separated by a colon (:). The two variables **key** and **val** are set by the **substring( )** method to extract the characters before the colon, those after the colon, and its following space character. Once these two strings have been extracted, the **put( )** method is used to store this association between the key and value in the **Hashtable**.

toString( )   The **toString( )** method (used by the **String** concatenation operator, **+**) is simply the reverse of **parse( )**. It takes the current key/value pairs stored in the **MimeHeader** and returns a string representation of them in the MIME format, where keys are printed followed by a colon and a space, and then the value followed by a CRLF.

put( ), get( ), AND fix( )   The **put( )** and **get( )** methods in **Hashtable** would work fine for this application if not for one rather odd thing. The MIME specification defined several important keys, such as **Content-Type** and **Content-Length**. Some early implementors of MIME systems, notably web browsers, took liberties with the capitalization of these fields. Some use **Content-type**, others **content-type**. To avoid mishaps, our HTTP server tries to convert all incoming and outgoing **MimeHeader** keys to be in the canonical form, **Content-Type**. Thus, we override **put( )** and **get( )** to convert the values' capitalization, using the method **fix( )**, before entering them into the **Hashtable** and before looking up a given key.

THE CODE   Here is the source code for **MimeHeader**:

```
import java.util.*;

class MimeHeader extends Hashtable {
  void parse(String data) {
    StringTokenizer st = new StringTokenizer(data, "\r\n");

    while (st.hasMoreTokens()) {
      String s = st.nextToken();
      int colon = s.indexOf(':');
      String key = s.substring(0, colon);
      String val = s.substring(colon + 2); // skip ": "
      put(key, val);
    }
  }

  MimeHeader() {}

  MimeHeader(String d) {
```

```
    parse(d);
  }

  public String toString() {
    String ret = "";
    Enumeration e = keys();

    while(e.hasMoreElements()) {
      String key = (String) e.nextElement();
      String val = (String) get(key);
      ret += key + ": " + val + "\r\n";
    }
    return ret;
  }

  // This simple function converts a mime string from
  // any variant of capitalization to a canonical form.
  // For example: CONTENT-TYPE or content-type to Content-Type,
  // or Content-length or CoNTeNT-LENgth to Content-Length.
  private String fix(String ms) {
    char chars[] = ms.toLowerCase().toCharArray();
    boolean upcaseNext = true;

    for (int i = 0; i < chars.length - 1; i++) {
      char ch = chars[i];
      if (upcaseNext && 'a' <= ch && ch <= 'z') {
        chars[i] = (char) (ch - ('a' - 'A'));
      }
      upcaseNext = ch == '-';
    }
    return new String(chars);
  }

  public String get(String key) {
    return (String) super.get(fix(key));
  }

  public void put(String key, String val) {
    super.put(fix(key), val);
  }
}
```

HttpResponse.java

The **HttpResponse** class is a wrapper around everything associated with a reply from an HTTP server. This is used by the proxy part of our **httpd** class. When you send a request to an HTTP server, it responds with an integer status code, which we store in **statusCode**, and a textual equivalent, which we store in **reasonPhrase**. This single-line response is followed by a MIME header, which contains further information about the reply. We use the previously explained **MimeHeader** object to parse this string. The **MimeHeader** object is stored inside the **HttpResponse** class in the **mh** variable. These variables are not made private so that the **httpd** class can use them directly.

CONSTRUCTORS   If you construct an **HttpResponse** with a string argument, this is taken to be a raw response from an HTTP server and is passed to **parse( )**, described next, to initialize the object. Alternatively, you can pass in a precomputed status code, reason phrase, and MIME header.

parse( )   The **parse( )** method takes the raw data that was read from the HTTP server, parses the **statusCode** and **reasonPhrase** from the first line, and then constructs a **MimeHeader** out of the remaining lines.

toString( )   The **toString( )** method is the inverse of **parse( )**. It takes the current values of the **HttpResponse** object and returns a string that an HTTP client would expect to read back from a server.

THE CODE   Here is the source code for **HttpResponse**:

```java
import java.io.*;
/*
 * HttpResponse
 * Parse a return message and MIME header from a server.
 * HTTP/1.0 302 Found  =  redirection, check Location for where.
 * HTTP/1.0 200 OK = file data comes after mime header.
 */

class HttpResponse
{
  int statusCode;      // Status-Code in spec
  String reasonPhrase; // Reason-Phrase in spec
  MimeHeader mh;
  static String CRLF = "\r\n";

  void parse(String request) {
```

```
      int fsp = request.indexOf(' ');
      int nsp = request.indexOf(' ', fsp+1);
      int eol = request.indexOf('\n');
      String protocol = request.substring(0, fsp);
      statusCode = Integer.parseInt(request.substring(fsp+1, nsp));
      reasonPhrase = request.substring(nsp+1, eol);
      String raw_mime_header = request.substring(eol + 1);
      mh = new MimeHeader(raw_mime_header);
    }


    HttpResponse(String request) {
      parse(request);
    }


    HttpResponse(int code, String reason, MimeHeader m) {
      statusCode = code;
      reasonPhrase = reason;
      mh = m;
    }

    public String toString() {
      return "HTTP/1.0 " + statusCode + " " + reasonPhrase + CRLF +
        mh + CRLF;
    }
  }
}
```

UrlCacheEntry.java

To cache the contents of a document on a server, we need to make an association
between the URL that was used to retrieve the document and the description of the
document itself. A document is described by its **MimeHeader** and the raw data. For
example, an image might be described by a **MimeHeader** with **Content-Type:
image/gif**, and the raw image data is just an array of bytes. Similarly, a web page will
likely have a **Content-Type: text/html** key/value pair in its **MimeHeader**, while the
raw data is the contents of the HTML page. Again, the instance variables are not
marked as private so that **httpd** can have free access to them.

CONSTRUCTOR   The constructor for a **UrlCacheEntry** object requires the URL to use
as the key and a **MimeHeader** to associate with it. If the **MimeHeader** has a field in it
called **Content-Length** (most do), the data area is preallocated to be large enough to
hold such content.

append( )   The **append( )** method is used to add data to a **UrlCacheEntry** object. The reason this isn't simply a **setData( )** method is that the data might be streaming in over a network and need to be stored a chunk at a time. The **append( )** method deals with three cases. In the first case, the data buffer has not been allocated at all. In the second, the data buffer is too small to accommodate the incoming data, so it is reallocated. In the last case, the incoming data fits just fine and is inserted into the buffer. At any time, the **length** member variable holds the current valid size of the data buffer.

THE CODE   Here is the source code for **UrlCacheEntry**:

```
class UrlCacheEntry
{
  String url;
  MimeHeader mh;
  byte data[];
  int length = 0;

  public UrlCacheEntry(String u, MimeHeader m) {
    url = u;
    mh = m;
    String cl = mh.get("Content-Length");
    if (cl != null) {
      data = new byte[Integer.parseInt(cl)];
    }
  }

  void append(byte d[], int n) {
    if (data == null) {
      data = new byte[n];
      System.arraycopy(d, 0, data, 0, n);
      length = n;
    } else if (length + n > data.length) {
      byte old[] = data;
      data = new byte[old.length + n];
      System.arraycopy(old, 0, data, 0, old.length);
      System.arraycopy(d, 0, data, old.length, n);
    } else {
      System.arraycopy(d, 0, data, length, n);
      length += n;
    }
  }
}
```

LogMessage.java

LogMessage is a simple interface that declares one method, **log( )**, which takes a single **String** parameter. This is used to abstract the output of messages from the **httpd**. In the application case, this method is implemented to print to the standard output of the console in which the application was started. In the applet case, the data is appended to a windowed text buffer.

THE CODE   Here is the source code for **LogMessage**:

```
interface LogMessage {
  public void log(String msg);
}
```

httpd.java

This is a really big class that does a lot. We will walk through it method by method.

CONSTRUCTOR   There are five main instance variables: **port**, **docRoot**, **log**, **cache**, and **stopFlag**, and all of them are private. Three of these can be set by **httpd**'s lone constructor, shown here:

```
httpd(int p, String dr, LogMessage lm)
```

It initializes the port to listen on, the directory to retrieve files from, and the interface to send messages to.

The fourth instance variable, **cache**, is the **Hashtable** where all of the files are cached in RAM, and is initialized when the object is created. **stopFlag** controls the execution of the program.

STATIC SECTION   There are several important static variables in this class. The version reported in the "Server" field of the MIME header is found in the variable **version**. A few constants are defined next: the MIME type for HTML files, **mime_text_html**; the MIME end-of-line sequence, **CRLF**; the name of the HTML file to return in place of raw directory requests, **indexfile**; and the size of the data buffer used in I/O, **buffer_size**.

Then **mt** defines a list of filename extensions and the corresponding MIME types for those files. The **types Hashtable** is statically initialized in the next block to contain the array **mt** as alternating keys and values. Then the **fnameToMimeType( )** method can be used to return the proper MIME type for each **filename** passed in. If the **filename** does not have one of the extensions from the **mt** table, the method returns the **defaultExt**, or "**text/plain**."

STATISTICAL COUNTERS Next, we declare five more instance variables. These are left without the private modifier so that an external monitor can inspect these values to display them graphically. (We will show this in action later.) These variables represent the usage statistics of our web server. The raw number of hits and bytes served is stored in **hits_served** and **bytes_served**. The number of files and bytes currently stored in the cache is stored in **files_in_cache** and **bytes_in_cache**. Finally, we store the number of hits that were successfully served out of the cache in **hits_to_cache**.

toBytes( ) Next, we have a convenience routine, **toBytes( )**, which converts its string argument to an array of bytes. This is necessary, because Java **String** objects are stored as Unicode characters, while the lingua franca of Internet protocols such as HTTP is good old 8-bit ASCII.

makeMimeHeader( ) The **makeMimeHeader( )** method is another convenience routine that is used to create a **MimeHeader** object with a few key values filled in. The **MimeHeader** that is returned from this method has the current time and date in the Date field, the name and version of our server in the Server field, the **type** parameter in the Content-Type field, and the **length** parameter in the Content-Length field.

error( ) The **error( )** method is used to format an HTML page to send back to web clients who make requests that cannot be completed. The first parameter, **code**, is the error code to return. Typically, this will be between 400 and 499. Our server sends back 404 and 405 errors. It uses the **HttpResponse** class to encapsulate the return code with the appropriate **MimeHeader**. The method returns the string representation of that response concatenated with the HTML page to show the user. The page includes a human-readable version of the error code, **msg**, and the **url** request that caused the error.

getRawRequest( ) The **getRawRequest( )** method is very simple. It reads data from a stream until it gets two consecutive newline characters. It ignores carriage returns and just looks for newlines. Once it has found the second newline, it turns the array of bytes into a **String** object and returns it. It will return **null** if the input stream does not produce two consecutive newlines before it ends. This is how messages from HTTP servers and clients are formatted. They begin with one line of status and then are immediately followed by a MIME header. The end of the MIME header is separated from the rest of the content by two newlines.

logEntry( ) The **logEntry( )** method is used to report on each hit to the HTTP server in a standard format. The format this method produces may seem odd, but it matches the current standard for HTTP log files. This method has several helper variables and methods that are used to format the date stamp on each log entry. The **months** array is used to convert the month to a string representation. The **host** variable is set by the main HTTP loop when it accepts a connection from a given host. The **fmt02d( )** method formats integers between 0 and 9 as two-digit, leading-zero numbers. The resulting string is then passed through the **LogMessage** interface variable **log**.

writeString( )   Another convenience method, **writeString( )**, is used to hide the conversion of a **String** to an array of bytes so that it can be written out to a stream.

writeUCE( )   The **writeUCE( )** method takes an **OutputStream** and a **UrlCacheEntry**. It extracts the information out of the cache entry in order to send a message to a web client containing the appropriate response code, MIME header, and content.

serveFromCache( )   This Boolean method attempts to find a particular URL in the cache. If it is successful, then the contents of that cache entry are written to the client, the **hits_to_cache** variable is incremented, and the caller is returned **true**. Otherwise, it simply returns **false**.

loadFile( )   This method takes an **InputStream**, the **url** that corresponds to it, and the **MimeHeader** for that URL. A new **UrlCacheEntry** is created with the information stored in the **MimeHeader**. The input stream is read in chunks of **buffer_size** bytes and appended to the **UrlCacheEntry**. The resulting **UrlCacheEntry** is stored in the cache. The **files_in_cache** and **bytes_in_cache** variables are updated, and the **UrlCacheEntry** is returned to the caller.

readFile( )   The **readFile( )** method might seem redundant with the **loadFile( )** method. It isn't. This method is strictly for reading files out of a local file system, where **loadFile( )** is used to talk to streams of any sort. If the **File** object, **f**, exists, then an **InputStream** is created for it. The size of the file is determined and the MIME type is derived from the filename. These two variables are used to create the appropriate **MimeHeader**, then **loadFile( )** is called to do the actual reading and caching.

writeDiskCache( )   The **writeDiskCache( )** method takes a **UrlCacheEntry** object and writes it persistently into the local disk. It constructs a directory name out of the URL, making sure to replace the slash (/) characters with the system-dependent **separatorChar**. Then it calls **mkdirs( )** to make sure that the local disk path exists for this URL. Lastly, it opens a **FileOutputStream**, writes all the data into it, and closes it.

handleProxy( )   The **handleProxy( )** routine is one of the two major modes of this server. The basic idea is this: If you set your browser to use this server as a proxy server, then the requests that will be sent to it will include the complete URL, where normal GETs remove the "http://" and host name part. We simply pick apart the complete URL, looking for the "://" sequence, the next slash (/), and optionally another colon (:) for servers using nonstandard port numbers. Once we've found these characters, we know the intended host and port number as well as the URL we need to fetch from there. We can then attempt to load a previously saved version of this document out of our RAM cache. If this fails, we can attempt to load it from the file system into the RAM cache and reattempt loading it from the cache. If that fails, then it gets interesting, because we must read the document from the remote site.

To do this, we open a socket to the remote site and port. We send a GET request, asking for the URL that was passed to us. Whatever response header we get back from the remote site, we send on to the client. If that code was 200, for successful file transfer, we also read the ensuing data stream into a new **UrlCacheEntry** and write it onto the client socket. After that, we call **writeDiskCache( )** to save the results of that transfer to the local disk. We log the transaction, close the sockets, and return.

handleGet( )   The **handleGet( )** method is called when the http daemon is acting like a normal web server. It has a local disk document root out of which it is serving files. The parameters to **handleGet( )** tell it where to write the results, the URL to look up, and the **MimeHeader** from the requesting web browser. This MIME header will include the User-Agent string and other useful attributes. First we attempt to serve the URL out of the RAM cache. If this fails, we look in the file system for the URL. If the file does not exist or is unreadable, we report an error back to the web client. Otherwise, we just use **readFile( )** to get the contents of the file and put them in the cache. Then **writeUCE( )** is used to send the contents of the file down the client socket.

doRequest( )   The **doRequest( )** method is called once per connection to the server. It parses the request string and incoming MIME header. It decides to call either **handleProxy( )** or **handleGet( )**, based on whether there is a "://" in the request string. If any methods are used other than GET, such as HEAD or POST, this routine returns a 405 error to the client. Note that the HTTP request is ignored if **stopFlag** is **true**.

run( )   The **run( )** method is called when the server thread is started. It creates a new **ServerSocket** on the given port, goes into an infinite loop calling **accept( )** on the server socket, and then passes the resulting **Socket** off to **doRequest( )** for inspection.

start( ) AND stop( )   These are two methods used to start and stop the server process. These methods set the value of **stopFlag**.

main( )   You can use the **main( )** method to run this application from a command line. It sets the **LogMessage** parameter to be the server itself, and then provides a simple console output implementation of **log( )**.

THE CODE   Here is the source code for **httpd**:

```
import java.net.*;
import java.io.*;
import java.text.*;
import java.util.*;

class httpd implements Runnable, LogMessage {
  private int port;
```

```
private String docRoot;
private LogMessage log;

private Hashtable cache = new Hashtable();
private boolean stopFlag;

private static String version = "1.0";
private static String mime_text_html = "text/html";
private static String CRLF = "\r\n";
private static String indexfile = "index.html";
private static int buffer_size = 8192;
static String mt[] = {  // mapping from file ext to Mime-Type
  "txt", "text/plain",
  "html", mime_text_html,
  "htm", "text/html",
  "gif", "image/gif",
  "jpg", "image/jpg",
  "jpeg", "image/jpg",
  "class", "application/octet-stream"
};
static String defaultExt = "txt";
static Hashtable types = new Hashtable();
static {
  for (int i=0; i<mt.length;i+=2)
    types.put(mt[i], mt[i+1]);
}

static String fnameToMimeType(String filename) {
  if (filename.endsWith("/"))       // special for index files.
    return mime_text_html;
  int dot = filename.lastIndexOf('.');
  String ext = (dot > 0) ? filename.substring(dot + 1) : defaultExt;
  String ret = (String) types.get(ext);
  return ret != null ? ret : (String)types.get(defaultExt);
}

int hits_served = 0;
int bytes_served = 0;
int files_in_cache = 0;
int bytes_in_cache = 0;
int hits_to_cache = 0;
```

```
private final byte toBytes(String s)[] {
  byte b[] = s.getBytes();
  return b;
}

private MimeHeader makeMimeHeader(String type, int length) {
  MimeHeader mh = new MimeHeader();
  Date curDate = new Date();
  TimeZone gmtTz = TimeZone.getTimeZone("GMT");
  SimpleDateFormat sdf =
    new SimpleDateFormat("dd MMM yyyy hh:mm:ss zzz");
  sdf.setTimeZone(gmtTz);
  mh.put("Date", sdf.format(curDate));
  mh.put("Server", "JavaCompleteReference/" + version);
  mh.put("Content-Type", type);
  if (length >= 0)
    mh.put("Content-Length", String.valueOf(length));
  return mh;
}

private String error(int code, String msg, String url) {
  String html_page = "<body>" + CRLF +
              "<h1>" + code + " " + msg + "</h1>" + CRLF;
  if (url != null)
    html_page += "Error when fetching URL: " + url + CRLF;
  html_page += "</body>" + CRLF;
  MimeHeader mh = makeMimeHeader(mime_text_html, html_page.length());
  HttpResponse hr = new HttpResponse(code, msg, mh);

  logEntry("GET", url, code, 0);
  return hr + html_page;
}

// Read 'in' until you get two \n's in a row.
// Return up to that point as a String.
// Discard all \r's.
private String getRawRequest(InputStream in)
  throws IOException {
  byte buf[] = new byte[buffer_size];
  int pos=0;
  int c;
  while ((c = in.read()) != -1) {
```

```
      switch (c) {
        case '\r':
        break;
        case '\n':
          if (buf[pos-1] == c) {

            return new String(buf,0,pos);
          }
        default:
          buf[pos++] = (byte) c;
      }
    }
  return null;
}

static String months[] = {
  "Jan", "Feb", "Mar", "Apr", "May", "Jun",
  "Jul", "Aug", "Sep", "Oct", "Nov", "Dec"
};
private String host;
// fmt02d is the same as C's printf("%02d", i)
private final String fmt02d(int i) {
  if(i < 0) {
    i = -i;
    return ((i < 9) ? "-0" : "-") + i;
  }
  else {
    return ((i < 9) ? "0" : "") + i;
  }
}
private void logEntry(String cmd, String url, int code, int size) {
  Calendar calendar = Calendar.getInstance();
  int tzmin = calendar.get(Calendar.ZONE_OFFSET)/(60*1000);
  int tzhour = tzmin / 60;
  tzmin -= tzhour * 60;
  log.log(host + " - - [" +
    fmt02d(calendar.get(Calendar.DATE) ) + "/" +
    months[calendar.get(Calendar.MONTH)] + "/" +
    calendar.get(Calendar.YEAR) + ":" +
    fmt02d(calendar.get(Calendar.HOUR) ) + ":" +
    fmt02d(calendar.get(Calendar.MINUTE) ) + ":" +
    fmt02d(calendar.get(Calendar.SECOND)) + " " +
```

```
          fmt02d(tzhour) + fmt02d(tzmin) +
          "] \"" +
          cmd + " " +
          url + " HTTP/1.0\" " +
          code + " " +
          size + "\n");

     hits_served++;
     bytes_served += size;
   }

   private void writeString(OutputStream out, String s)
     throws IOException {
     out.write(toBytes(s));
   }

   private void writeUCE(OutputStream out, UrlCacheEntry uce)
     throws IOException {
        HttpResponse hr = new HttpResponse(200, "OK", uce.mh);
        writeString(out, hr.toString());
        out.write(uce.data, 0, uce.length);
        logEntry("GET", uce.url, 200, uce.length);
   }

   private boolean serveFromCache(OutputStream out, String url)
     throws IOException {
     UrlCacheEntry uce;
     if ((uce = (UrlCacheEntry)cache.get(url)) != null) {
       writeUCE(out, uce);
       hits_to_cache++;
       return true;
     }
     return false;
   }

   private UrlCacheEntry loadFile(InputStream in, String url,
                                  MimeHeader mh)
     throws IOException {

     UrlCacheEntry uce;
     byte file_buf[] = new byte[buffer_size];
     uce = new UrlCacheEntry(url, mh);
```

```
    int size = 0;
    int n;
    while ((n = in.read(file_buf)) >= 0) {
      uce.append(file_buf, n);
      size += n;
    }
    in.close();
    cache.put(url, uce);
    files_in_cache++;
    bytes_in_cache += uce.length;
    return uce;
}

private UrlCacheEntry readFile(File f, String url)
    throws IOException {

    if (!f.exists())
      return null;
    InputStream in = new FileInputStream(f);
    int file_length = in.available();
    String mime_type = fnameToMimeType(url);
    MimeHeader mh = makeMimeHeader(mime_type, file_length);
    UrlCacheEntry uce = loadFile(in, url, mh);
    return uce;
}

private void writeDiskCache(UrlCacheEntry uce)
    throws IOException {

    String path = docRoot + uce.url;
    String dir = path.substring(0, path.lastIndexOf("/"));
    dir.replace('/', File.separatorChar);
    new File(dir).mkdirs();
    FileOutputStream out = new FileOutputStream(path);
    out.write(uce.data, 0, uce.length);
    out.close();
}

// A client asks us for a url that looks like this:
// http://the.internet.site/the/url
// we go get it from the site and return it...
private void handleProxy(OutputStream out, String url,
```

```
                        MimeHeader inmh) {
try {
  int start = url.indexOf("://") + 3;
  int path = url.indexOf('/', start);
  String site = url.substring(start, path).toLowerCase();
  int port = 80;
  String server_url = url.substring(path);
  int colon = site.indexOf(':');
  if (colon > 0) {
    port = Integer.parseInt(site.substring(colon + 1));
    site = site.substring(0, colon);
  }
  url = "/cache/" + site + ((port != 80) ? (":" + port) : "") +
        server_url;
  if (url.endsWith("/"))
    url += indexfile;

  if (!serveFromCache(out, url)) {
    if (readFile(new File(docRoot + url), url) != null) {
      serveFromCache(out, url);
      return;
    }

    // If we haven't already cached this page, open a socket
    // to the site's port and send a GET command to it.
    // We modify the user-agent to add ourselves... "via".

    Socket server = new Socket(site, port);
    InputStream server_in = server.getInputStream();
    OutputStream server_out = server.getOutputStream();
    inmh.put("User-Agent", inmh.get("User-Agent") +
             " via JavaCompleteReferenceProxy/" + version);
    String req = "GET " + server_url + " HTTP/1.0" + CRLF +
                 inmh + CRLF;
    writeString(server_out, req);
    String raw_request = getRawRequest(server_in);
    HttpResponse server_response =
                 new HttpResponse(raw_request);
    writeString(out, server_response.toString());
    if (server_response.statusCode == 200) {
      UrlCacheEntry uce = loadFile(server_in, url,
                                   server_response.mh);
```

```
              out.write(uce.data, 0, uce.length);
              writeDiskCache(uce);
              logEntry("GET", site + server_url, 200, uce.length);
            }
            server_out.close();
            server.close();
          }
        } catch (IOException e) {
          log.log("Exception: " + e);
        }
      }


      private void handleGet(OutputStream out, String url,
                              MimeHeader inmh) {
        byte file_buf[] = new byte[buffer_size];
        String filename = docRoot + url +
                          (url.endsWith("/") ? indexfile : "");
        try {
          if (!serveFromCache(out, url)) {
            File f = new File(filename);
            if (! f.exists()) {
              writeString(out, error(404, "Not Found", filename));
              return;
            }
            if (! f.canRead()) {
              writeString(out, error(404, "Permission Denied", filename));
              return;
            }
            UrlCacheEntry uce = readFile(f, url);
            writeUCE(out, uce);
          }
        } catch (IOException e) {
          log.log("Exception: " + e);
        }
      }


      private void doRequest(Socket s) throws IOException {
        if(stopFlag)
          return;
        InputStream in = s.getInputStream();
        OutputStream out = s.getOutputStream();
        String request = getRawRequest(in);
```

```
    int fsp = request.indexOf(' ');
    int nsp = request.indexOf(' ', fsp+1);
    int eol = request.indexOf('\n');
    String method = request.substring(0, fsp);
    String url = request.substring(fsp+1, nsp);
    String raw_mime_header = request.substring(eol + 1);

    MimeHeader inmh = new MimeHeader(raw_mime_header);

    request = request.substring(0, eol);

    if (method.equalsIgnoreCase("get")) {
      if (url.indexOf("://") >= 0) {
        handleProxy(out, url, inmh);
      } else {
        handleGet(out, url, inmh);
      }
    } else {
      writeString(out, error(405, "Method Not Allowed", method));
    }
    in.close();
    out.close();
}

public void run() {
    try {
      ServerSocket acceptSocket;
      acceptSocket = new ServerSocket(port);
      while (true) {
        Socket s = acceptSocket.accept();
        host = s.getInetAddress().getHostName();
        doRequest(s);
        s.close();
      }
    } catch (IOException e) {
      log.log("accept loop IOException: " + e + "\n");
    } catch (Exception e) {
      log.log("Exception: " + e);
    }
}

private Thread t;
public synchronized void start() {
```

```
      stopFlag = false;
      if (t == null) {
        t = new Thread(this);
        t.start();
      }
    }

    public synchronized void stop() {
      stopFlag = true;
      log.log("Stopped at " + new Date() + "\n");
    }

    public httpd(int p, String dr, LogMessage lm) {
      port = p;
      docRoot = dr;
      log = lm;
    }

    // This main and log method allow httpd to be run from the console.
    public static void main(String args[]) {
      httpd h = new httpd(80, "c:\\www", null);
      h.log = h;
      h.start();
      try {
        Thread.currentThread().join();
      } catch (InterruptedException e) {};
    }

    public void log(String m) {
      System.out.print(m);
    }
  }
```

HTTP.java

As an added bonus, here is an applet class that gives the HTTP server a functional "front panel." This applet has two parameters that can be used to configure the server: **port** and **docroot**. This is a very simple applet. It makes an instance of the **httpd**, passing in itself as the **LogMessage** interface. Then it creates a panel that has a simple label at the top, a **TextArea** in the middle for displaying the **LogMessage**s, and a panel at the bottom that has two buttons and another label in it. The **start( )** and **stop( )** methods of the applet call the corresponding methods on the **httpd**. The buttons labeled "Start" and "Stop" call their corresponding methods in the **httpd**. Any time a message is logged, the bottom-right **Label** object is updated to contain the latest statistics from the **httpd**.

```java
import java.util.*;
import java.applet.*;

import java.awt.*;
import java.awt.event.*;

public class HTTP extends Applet implements LogMessage,
                                             ActionListener
{
  private int m_port = 80;
  private String m_docroot = "c:\\www";
  private httpd m_httpd;
  private TextArea m_log;
  private Label status;

  private final String PARAM_port = "port";
  private final String PARAM_docroot = "docroot";
  public HTTP()  {
  }

  public void init()  {
    setBackground(Color.white);
    String param;

    // port: Port number to listen on
    param = getParameter(PARAM_port);
    if (param != null)
      m_port = Integer.parseInt(param);

    // docroot: web document root
    param = getParameter(PARAM_docroot);
    if (param != null)
      m_docroot = param;

    setLayout(new BorderLayout());

    Label lab = new Label("Java HTTPD");

    lab.setFont(new Font("SansSerif", Font.BOLD, 18));
```

```
    add("North", lab);
    m_log = new TextArea("", 24, 80);
    add("Center", m_log);
    Panel p = new Panel();
    p.setLayout(new FlowLayout(FlowLayout.CENTER,1,1));

    add("South", p);
    Button bstart = new Button("Start");
    bstart.addActionListener(this);
    p.add(bstart);
    Button bstop = new Button("Stop");
    bstop.addActionListener(this);
    p.add(bstop);
    status = new Label("raw");
    status.setForeground(Color.green);
    status.setFont(new Font("SansSerif", Font.BOLD, 10));
    p.add(status);
    m_httpd = new httpd(m_port, m_docroot, this);
}

public void destroy() {
  stop();
}

public void paint(Graphics g) {
}

public void start() {
  m_httpd.start();
  status.setText("Running  ");
  clear_log("Log started on " + new Date() + "\n");
}

public void stop() {
  m_httpd.stop();
  status.setText("Stopped  ");
}

public void actionPerformed(ActionEvent ae) {
  String label = ae.getActionCommand();
  if(label.equals("Start")) {
    start();
```

```
    }
    else {
      stop();
    }
  }

  public void clear_log(String msg) {
    m_log.setText(msg + "\n");
  }

  public void log(String msg) {
    m_log.append(msg);
    status.setText(m_httpd.hits_served + " hits (" +
            (m_httpd.bytes_served / 1024) + "K), " +
            m_httpd.files_in_cache + " cached files (" +
            (m_httpd.bytes_in_cache / 1024) + "K), " +
            m_httpd.hits_to_cache + " cached hits");
    status.setSize(status.getPreferredSize());
  }
}
```

Note   *In the files **httpd.java** and **HTTP.java**, the code is built assuming that the document root is "c:\www". You may need to change this value for your configuration. Because this applet writes to a log file, it can work only if it is trusted. For example, an applet is trusted if it is accessible from the user's class path.*

Datagrams

For most of your internetworking needs, you will be happy with TCP/IP-style networking. It provides a serialized, predictable, reliable stream of packet data. This is not without its cost, however. TCP includes many complicated algorithms for dealing with congestion control on crowded networks, as well as pessimistic expectations about packet loss. This leads to a somewhat inefficient way to transport data. Datagrams provide an alternative.

Datagrams are bundles of information passed between machines. They are somewhat like a hard throw from a well-trained but blindfolded catcher to the third baseman. Once the datagram has been released to its intended target, there is no assurance that it will arrive or even that someone will be there to catch it. Likewise, when the datagram is received, there is no assurance that it hasn't been damaged in transit or that whoever sent it is still there to receive a response.

Java implements datagrams on top of the UDP protocol by using two classes: The **DatagramPacket** object is the data container, while the **DatagramSocket** is the mechanism used to send or receive the **DatagramPacket**s.

DatagramPacket

DatagramPacket defines several constructors. Four are described here. The first constructor specifies a buffer that will receive data, and the size of a packet. It is used for receiving data over a **DatagramSocket**. The second form allows you to specify an offset into the buffer at which data will be stored. The third form specifies a target address and port, which are used by a **DatagramSocket** to determine where the data in the packet will be sent. The fourth form transmits packets beginning at the specified offset into the data. Think of the first two forms as building an "in box," and the second two forms as stuffing and addressing an envelope. Here are the four constructors:

DatagramPacket(byte *data*[ ], int *size*)
DatagramPacket(byte *data*[ ], int *offset*, int *size*)
DatagramPacket(byte *data*[ ], int *size*, InetAddress *ipAddress*, int *port*)
DatagramPacket(byte *data*[ ], int *offset*, int *size*, InetAddress *ipAddress*, int *port*)

There are several methods for accessing the internal state of a **DatagramPacket**. They give complete access to the destination address and port number of a packet, as well as the raw data and its length. Here are some of the most commonly used:

InetAddress getAddress( )	Returns the destination **InetAddress**, typically used for sending.
int getPort( )	Returns the port number.
byte[ ] getData( )	Returns the byte array of data contained in the datagram. Mostly used to retrieve data from the datagram after it has been received.
int getLength( )	Returns the length of the valid data contained in the byte array that would be returned from the **getData( )** method. This typically does not equal the length of the whole byte array.

Datagram Server and Client

The following example implements a very simple networked communications client and server. Messages are typed into the window at the server and written across the network to the client side, where they are displayed.

```
// Demonstrate Datagrams.
import java.net.*;
```

```
class WriteServer {
  public static int serverPort = 998;
  public static int clientPort = 999;
  public static int buffer_size = 1024;
  public static DatagramSocket ds;
  public static byte buffer[] = new byte[buffer_size];

  public static void TheServer() throws Exception {
    int pos=0;
    while (true) {
      int c = System.in.read();
      switch (c) {
        case -1:
          System.out.println("Server Quits.");
          return;
        case '\r':
          break;
        case '\n':
          ds.send(new DatagramPacket(buffer,pos,
            InetAddress.getLocalHost(),clientPort));
          pos=0;
          break;
        default:
          buffer[pos++] = (byte) c;
      }
    }
  }

  public static void TheClient() throws Exception {
    while(true) {
      DatagramPacket p = new DatagramPacket(buffer, buffer.length);
      ds.receive(p);
      System.out.println(new String(p.getData(), 0, p.getLength()));
    }
  }

  public static void main(String args[]) throws Exception {
    if(args.length == 1) {
      ds = new DatagramSocket(serverPort);
      TheServer();
    } else {
```

```
        ds = new DatagramSocket(clientPort);
        TheClient();
      }
    }
  }
```

This sample program is restricted by the **DatagramSocket** constructor to running between two ports on the local machine. To use the program, run

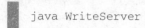

```
java WriteServer
```

in one window; this will be the client. Then run

```
java WriteServer 1
```

This will be the server. Anything that is typed in the server window will be sent to the client window after a newline is received.

Note | *This example requires that your computer be connected to the Internet.*

Inet4Address and Inet6Address

As mentioned at the start of this chapter, Java 2, version 1.4 added support for IPv6 addresses. Because of this, two new subclasses of **InetAddress** were created: **Inet4Address** and **Inet6Address**. **Inet4Address** represents a traditional style, IPv4 address. **Inet6Address** encapsulates a new-style IPv6 address. Because they are subclasses of **InetAddress**, an **InetAddress** reference can refer to either. This is one way that Java was able to add IPv6 functionality without breaking existing code or adding many more classes. For the most part, you can simply use **InetAddress** when working with IP addresses because it can accommodate both styles.

The URI Class

Java 2, version 1.4 added the **URI** class, which encapsulates a *Uniform Resource Identifier*. URIs are similar to URLs. In fact, URLs constitute a subset of URIs. A URI represents a standard way to identify a resource. A URL also describes how to access the resource.

The
Complete
Reference

Chapter 19

The Applet Class

This chapter examines the **Applet** class, which provides the necessary support for applets. In Chapter 12, you were introduced to the general form of an applet and the steps necessary to compile and run one. In this chapter, we will look at applets in detail.

The **Applet** class is contained in the **java.applet** package. **Applet** contains several methods that give you detailed control over the execution of your applet. In addition, **java.applet** also defines three interfaces: **AppletContext**, **AudioClip**, and **AppletStub**.

Let's begin by reviewing the basic elements of an applet and the steps necessary to create and test one.

Applet Basics

All applets are subclasses of **Applet**. Thus, all applets must import **java.applet**. Applets must also import **java.awt**. Recall that AWT stands for the Abstract Window Toolkit. Since all applets run in a window, it is necessary to include support for that window. Applets are not executed by the console-based Java run-time interpreter. Rather, they are executed by either a Web browser or an applet viewer. The figures shown in this chapter were created with the standard applet viewer, called **appletviewer**, provided by the SDK. But you can use any applet viewer or browser you like.

Execution of an applet does not begin at **main( )**. Actually, few applets even have **main( )** methods. Instead, execution of an applet is started and controlled with an entirely different mechanism, which will be explained shortly. Output to your applet's window is not performed by **System.out.println( )**. Rather, it is handled with various AWT methods, such as **drawString( )**, which outputs a string to a specified X,Y location. Input is also handled differently than in an application.

Once an applet has been compiled, it is included in an HTML file using the APPLET tag. The applet will be executed by a Java-enabled web browser when it encounters the APPLET tag within the HTML file. To view and test an applet more conveniently, simply include a comment at the head of your Java source code file that contains the APPLET tag. This way, your code is documented with the necessary HTML statements needed by your applet, and you can test the compiled applet by starting the applet viewer with your Java source code file specified as the target. Here is an example of such a comment:

```
/*
<applet code="MyApplet" width=200 height=60>
</applet>
*/
```

This comment contains an APPLET tag that will run an applet called **MyApplet** in a window that is 200 pixels wide and 60 pixels high. Since the inclusion of an APPLET command makes testing applets easier, all of the applets shown in this book will contain the appropriate APPLET tag embedded in a comment.

The Applet Class

The **Applet** class defines the methods shown in Table 19-1. **Applet** provides all necessary support for applet execution, such as starting and stopping. It also provides methods that load and display images, and methods that load and play audio clips. **Applet** extends the AWT class **Panel**. In turn, **Panel** extends **Container**, which extends **Component**. These classes provide support for Java's window-based, graphical interface. Thus, **Applet** provides all of the necessary support for window-based activities. (The AWT is described in detail in following chapters.)

Method	Description
void destroy( )	Called by the browser just before an applet is terminated. Your applet will override this method if it needs to perform any cleanup prior to its destruction.
AccessibleContext getAccessibleContext( )	Returns the accessibilty context for the invoking object.
AppletContext getAppletContext( )	Returns the context associated with the applet.
String getAppletInfo( )	Returns a string that describes the applet.
AudioClip getAudioClip(URL *url*)	Returns an **AudioClip** object that encapsulates the audio clip found at the location specified by *url*.
AudioClip getAudioClip(URL *url*, String *clipName*)	Returns an **AudioClip** object that encapsulates the audio clip found at the location specified by *url* and having the name specified by *clipName*.
URL getCodeBase( )	Returns the URL associated with the invoking applet.
URL getDocumentBase( )	Returns the URL of the HTML document that invokes the applet.

Table 19-1. *The Methods Defined by* Applet

Method	Description
Image getImage(URL *url*)	Returns an **Image** object that encapsulates the image found at the location specified by *url*.
Image getImage(URL *url*, String *imageName*)	Returns an **Image** object that encapsulates the image found at the location specified by *url* and having the name specified by *imageName*.
Locale getLocale( )	Returns a **Locale** object that is used by various locale-sensitive classes and methods.
String getParameter(String *paramName*)	Returns the parameter associated with *paramName*. **null** is returned if the specified parameter is not found.
String[ ] [ ] getParameterInfo( )	Returns a **String** table that describes the parameters recognized by the applet. Each entry in the table must consist of three strings that contain the name of the parameter, a description of its type and/or range, and an explanation of its purpose.
void init( )	Called when an applet begins execution. It is the first method called for any applet.
boolean isActive( )	Returns **true** if the applet has been started. It returns **false** if the applet has been stopped.
static final AudioClip newAudioClip(URL *url*)	Returns an **AudioClip** object that encapsulates the audio clip found at the location specified by *url*. This method is similar to **getAudioClip( )** except that it is static and can be executed without the need for an **Applet** object. (Added by Java 2)

Table 19-1.   *The Methods Defined by* Applet (continued)

Method	Description
void play(URL *url*)	If an audio clip is found at the location specified by *url*, the clip is played.
void play(URL *url*, String *clipName*)	If an audio clip is found at the location specified by *url* with the name specified by *clipName*, the clip is played.
void resize(Dimension *dim*)	Resizes the applet according to the dimensions specified by *dim*. **Dimension** is a class stored inside **java.awt**. It contains two integer fields: **width** and **height**.
void resize(int *width*, int *height*)	Resizes the applet according to the dimensions specified by *width* and *height*.
final void setStub(AppletStub *stubObj*)	Makes *stubObj* the stub for the applet. This method is used by the run-time system and is not usually called by your applet. A *stub* is a small piece of code that provides the linkage between your applet and the browser.
void showStatus(String *str*)	Displays *str* in the status window of the browser or applet viewer. If the browser does not support a status window, then no action takes place.
void start( )	Called by the browser when an applet should start (or resume) execution. It is automatically called after **init( )** when an applet first begins.
void stop( )	Called by the browser to suspend execution of the applet. Once stopped, an applet is restarted when the browser calls **start( )**.

Table 19-1.   *The Methods Defined by* Applet (continued)

Applet Architecture

An applet is a window-based program. As such, its architecture is different from the so-called normal, console-based programs shown in the first part of this book. If you are familiar with Windows programming, you will be right at home writing applets. If not, then there are a few key concepts you must understand.

First, applets are event driven. Although we won't examine event handling until the following chapter, it is important to understand in a general way how the event-driven architecture impacts the design of an applet. An applet resembles a set of interrupt service routines. Here is how the process works. An applet waits until an event occurs. The AWT notifies the applet about an event by calling an event handler that has been provided by the applet. Once this happens, the applet must take appropriate action and then quickly return control to the AWT. This is a crucial point. For the most part, your applet should not enter a "mode" of operation in which it maintains control for an extended period. Instead, it must perform specific actions in response to events and then return control to the AWT run-time system. In those situations in which your applet needs to perform a repetitive task on its own (for example, displaying a scrolling message across its window), you must start an additional thread of execution. (You will see an example later in this chapter.)

Second, the user initiates interaction with an applet—not the other way around. As you know, in a nonwindowed program, when the program needs input, it will prompt the user and then call some input method, such as **readLine( )**. This is not the way it works in an applet. Instead, the user interacts with the applet as he or she wants, when he or she wants. These interactions are sent to the applet as events to which the applet must respond. For example, when the user clicks a mouse inside the applet's window, a mouse-clicked event is generated. If the user presses a key while the applet's window has input focus, a keypress event is generated. As you will see in later chapters, applets can contain various controls, such as push buttons and check boxes. When the user interacts with one of these controls, an event is generated.

While the architecture of an applet is not as easy to understand as that of a console-based program, Java's AWT makes it as simple as possible. If you have written programs for Windows, you know how intimidating that environment can be. Fortunately, Java's AWT provides a much cleaner approach that is more quickly mastered.

An Applet Skeleton

All but the most trivial applets override a set of methods that provides the basic mechanism by which the browser or applet viewer interfaces to the applet and controls its execution. Four of these methods—**init( )**, **start( )**, **stop( )**, and **destroy( )**—are defined by **Applet**. Another, **paint( )**, is defined by the AWT **Component** class. Default implementations for all of these methods are provided. Applets do not need to override those methods they do not use. However, only very simple applets will not need to define all of them. These five methods can be assembled into the skeleton shown here:

```
// An Applet skeleton.
import java.awt.*;
import java.applet.*;
/*
<applet code="AppletSkel" width=300 height=100>
</applet>
*/

public class AppletSkel extends Applet {
  // Called first.
  public void init() {
    // initialization
  }

  /* Called second, after init().  Also called whenever
     the applet is restarted. */
  public void start() {
    // start or resume execution
  }

  // Called when the applet is stopped.
  public void stop() {
    // suspends execution
  }

  /* Called when applet is terminated.  This is the last
     method executed. */
  public void destroy() {
    // perform shutdown activities
  }

  // Called when an applet's window must be restored.
  public void paint(Graphics g) {
    // redisplay contents of window
  }
}
```

Although this skeleton does not do anything, it can be compiled and run. When run, it generates the following window when viewed with an applet viewer:

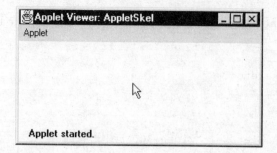

Applet Initialization and Termination

It is important to understand the order in which the various methods shown in the skeleton are called. When an applet begins, the AWT calls the following methods, in this sequence:

1. **init( )**
2. **start( )**
3. **paint( )**

When an applet is terminated, the following sequence of method calls takes place:

1. **stop( )**
2. **destroy( )**

Let's look more closely at these methods.

init( )

The **init( )** method is the first method to be called. This is where you should initialize variables. This method is called only once during the run time of your applet.

start( )

The **start( )** method is called after **init( )**. It is also called to restart an applet after it has been stopped. Whereas **init( )** is called once—the first time an applet is loaded—**start( )** is called each time an applet's HTML document is displayed onscreen. So, if a user leaves a web page and comes back, the applet resumes execution at **start( )**.

paint( )

The **paint( )** method is called each time your applet's output must be redrawn. This situation can occur for several reasons. For example, the window in which the applet is running may be overwritten by another window and then uncovered. Or the applet window may be minimized and then restored. **paint( )** is also called when the applet begins execution. Whatever the cause, whenever the applet must redraw its output, **paint( )** is called. The **paint( )** method has one parameter of type **Graphics**. This parameter will contain the graphics context, which describes the graphics environment in which the applet is running. This context is used whenever output to the applet is required.

stop( )

The **stop( )** method is called when a web browser leaves the HTML document containing the applet—when it goes to another page, for example. When **stop( )** is called, the applet is probably running. You should use **stop( )** to suspend threads that don't need to run when the applet is not visible. You can restart them when **start( )** is called if the user returns to the page.

destroy( )

The **destroy( )** method is called when the environment determines that your applet needs to be removed completely from memory. At this point, you should free up any resources the applet may be using. The **stop( )** method is always called before **destroy( )**.

Overriding update( )

In some situations, your applet may need to override another method defined by the AWT, called **update( )**. This method is called when your applet has requested that a portion of its window be redrawn. The default version of **update( )** first fills an applet with the default background color and then calls **paint( )**. If you fill the background using a different color in **paint( )**, the user will experience a flash of the default background each time **update( )** is called—that is, whenever the window is repainted. One way to avoid this problem is to override the **update( )** method so that it performs all necessary display activities. Then have **paint( )** simply call **update( )**. Thus, for some applications, the applet skeleton will override **paint( )** and **update( )**, as shown here:

```
public void update(Graphics g) {
  // redisplay your window, here.
}

public void paint(Graphics g) {
  update(g);
}
```

For the examples in this book, we will override **update( )** only when needed.

Simple Applet Display Methods

As we've mentioned, applets are displayed in a window and they use the AWT to perform input and output. Although we will examine the methods, procedures, and techniques necessary to fully handle the AWT windowed environment in subsequent chapters, a few are described here, because we will use them to write sample applets.

As we described in Chapter 12, to output a string to an applet, use **drawString( )**, which is a member of the **Graphics** class. Typically, it is called from within either **update( )** or **paint( )**. It has the following general form:

void drawString(String *message*, int *x*, int *y*)

Here, *message* is the string to be output beginning at *x,y*. In a Java window, the upper-left corner is location 0,0. The **drawString( )** method will not recognize newline characters. If you want to start a line of text on another line, you must do so manually, specifying the precise X,Y location where you want the line to begin. (As you will see in later chapters, there are techniques that make this process easy.)

To set the background color of an applet's window, use **setBackground( )**. To set the foreground color (the color in which text is shown, for example), use **setForeground( )**. These methods are defined by **Component**, and they have the following general forms:

void setBackground(Color *newColor*)
void setForeground(Color *newColor*)

Here, *newColor* specifies the new color. The class **Color** defines the constants shown here that can be used to specify colors:

Color.black	Color.magenta
Color.blue	Color.orange
Color.cyan	Color.pink
Color.darkGray	Color.red
Color.gray	Color.white
Color.green	Color.yellow
Color.lightGray	

For example, this sets the background color to green and the text color to red:

```
setBackground(Color.green);
setForeground(Color.red);
```

A good place to set the foreground and background colors is in the **init( )** method. Of course, you can change these colors as often as necessary during the execution of your applet. The default foreground color is black. The default background color is light gray.

You can obtain the current settings for the background and foreground colors by calling **getBackground( )** and **getForeground( )**, respectively. They are also defined by **Component** and are shown here:

Color getBackground( )
Color getForeground( )

Here is a very simple applet that sets the background color to cyan, the foreground color to red, and displays a message that illustrates the order in which the **init( )**, **start( )**, and **paint( )** methods are called when an applet starts up:

```
/* A simple applet that sets the foreground and
   background colors and outputs a string. */
import java.awt.*;
import java.applet.*;
/*
<applet code="Sample" width=300 height=50>
</applet>
*/

public class Sample extends Applet{
  String msg;

  // set the foreground and background colors.
  public void init() {
    setBackground(Color.cyan);
    setForeground(Color.red);
    msg = "Inside init( ) --";
  }

  // Initialize the string to be displayed.
  public void start() {
    msg += " Inside start( ) --";
  }

  // Display msg in applet window.
  public void paint(Graphics g) {
    msg += " Inside paint( ).";
    g.drawString(msg, 10, 30);
  }
}
```

This applet generates the window shown here:

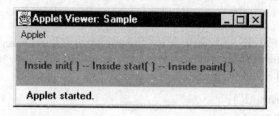

The methods **stop( )** and **destroy( )** are not overridden, because they are not needed by this simple applet.

Requesting Repainting

As a general rule, an applet writes to its window only when its **update( )** or **paint( )** method is called by the AWT. This raises an interesting question: How can the applet itself cause its window to be updated when its information changes? For example, if an applet is displaying a moving banner, what mechanism does the applet use to update the window each time this banner scrolls? Remember, one of the fundamental architectural constraints imposed on an applet is that it must quickly return control to the AWT run-time system. It cannot create a loop inside **paint( )** that repeatedly scrolls the banner, for example. This would prevent control from passing back to the AWT. Given this constraint, it may seem that output to your applet's window will be difficult at best. Fortunately, this is not the case. Whenever your applet needs to update the information displayed in its window, it simply calls **repaint( )**.

The **repaint( )** method is defined by the AWT. It causes the AWT run-time system to execute a call to your applet's **update( )** method, which, in its default implementation, calls **paint( )**. Thus, for another part of your applet to output to its window, simply store the output and then call **repaint( )**. The AWT will then execute a call to **paint( )**, which can display the stored information. For example, if part of your applet needs to output a string, it can store this string in a **String** variable and then call **repaint( )**. Inside **paint( )**, you will output the string using **drawString( )**.

The **repaint( )** method has four forms. Let's look at each one, in turn. The simplest version of **repaint( )** is shown here:

void repaint( )

This version causes the entire window to be repainted. The following version specifies a region that will be repainted:

void repaint(int *left*, int *top*, int *width*, int *height*)

Here, the coordinates of the upper-left corner of the region are specified by *left* and *top*, and the width and height of the region are passed in *width* and *height*. These dimensions are specified in pixels. You save time by specifying a region to repaint. Window updates are costly in terms of time. If you need to update only a small portion of the window, it is more efficient to repaint only that region.

Calling **repaint( )** is essentially a request that your **applet** be repainted sometime soon. However, if your system is slow or busy, **update( )** might not be called immediately. Multiple requests for repainting that occur within a short time can be collapsed by the AWT in a manner such that **update( )** is only called sporadically. This can be a problem in many situations, including animation, in which a consistent update time is necessary. One solution to this problem is to use the following forms of **repaint( )**:

```
void repaint(long maxDelay)
void repaint(long maxDelay, int x, int y, int width, int height)
```

Here, *maxDelay* specifies the maximum number of milliseconds that can elapse before **update( )** is called. Beware, though. If the time elapses before **update( )** can be called, it isn't called. There's no return value or exception thrown, so you must be careful.

> **Note**   *It is possible for a method other than **paint( )** or **update( )** to output to an applet's window. To do so, it must obtain a graphics context by calling **getGraphics( )** (defined by **Component**) and then use this context to output to the window. However, for most applications, it is better and easier to route window output through **paint( )** and to call **repaint( )** when the contents of the window change.*

A Simple Banner Applet

To demonstrate **repaint( )**, a simple banner applet is developed. This applet scrolls a message, from right to left, across the applet's window. Since the scrolling of the message is a repetitive task, it is performed by a separate thread, created by the applet when it is initialized. The banner applet is shown here:

```
/* A simple banner applet.

   This applet creates a thread that scrolls
   the message contained in msg right to left
   across the applet's window.
*/
import java.awt.*;
import java.applet.*;
/*
<applet code="SimpleBanner" width=300 height=50>
</applet>
```

```
*/

public class SimpleBanner extends Applet implements Runnable {
  String msg = " A Simple Moving Banner.";
  Thread t = null;
  int state;
  boolean stopFlag;

  // Set colors and initialize thread.
  public void init() {
    setBackground(Color.cyan);
    setForeground(Color.red);
  }

  // Start thread
  public void start() {
    t = new Thread(this);
    stopFlag = false;
    t.start();
  }

  // Entry point for the thread that runs the banner.
  public void run() {
    char ch;

    // Display banner
    for( ; ; ) {
      try {
        repaint();
        Thread.sleep(250);
        ch = msg.charAt(0);
        msg = msg.substring(1, msg.length());
        msg += ch;
        if(stopFlag)
          break;
      } catch(InterruptedException e) {}
    }
  }

  // Pause the banner.
  public void stop() {
```

```
      stopFlag = true;
      t = null;
   }

   // Display the banner.
   public void paint(Graphics g) {
      g.drawString(msg, 50, 30);
   }
}
```

Following is sample output:

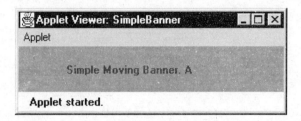

Let's take a close look at how this applet operates. First, notice that **SimpleBanner** extends **Applet**, as expected, but it also implements **Runnable**. This is necessary, since the applet will be creating a second thread of execution that will be used to scroll the banner. Inside **init( )**, the foreground and background colors of the applet are set.

After initialization, the AWT run-time system calls **start( )** to start the applet running. Inside **start( )**, a new thread of execution is created and assigned to the **Thread** variable **t**. Then, the **boolean** variable **stopFlag**, which controls the execution of the applet, is set to **false**. Next, the thread is started by a call to **t.start( )**. Remember that **t.start( )** calls a method defined by **Thread**, which causes **run( )** to begin executing. It does not cause a call to the version of **start( )** defined by **Applet**. These are two separate methods.

Inside **run( )**, the characters in the string contained in **msg** are repeatedly rotated left. Between each rotation, a call to **repaint( )** is made. This eventually causes the **paint( )** method to be called and the current contents of **msg** is displayed. Between each iteration, **run( )** sleeps for a quarter of a second. The net effect of **run( )** is that the contents of **msg** is scrolled right to left in a constantly moving display. The **stopFlag** variable is checked on each iteration. When it is **true**, the **run( )** method terminates.

If a browser is displaying the applet when a new page is viewed, the **stop( )** method is called, which sets **stopFlag** to **true**, causing **run( )** to terminate. This is the mechanism used to stop the thread when its page is no longer in view. When the applet is brought back into view, **start( )** is once again called, which starts a new thread to execute the banner.

Using the Status Window

In addition to displaying information in its window, an applet can also output a message to the status window of the browser or applet viewer on which it is running. To do so, call **showStatus( )** with the string that you want displayed. The status window is a good place to give the user feedback about what is occurring in the applet, suggest options, or possibly report some types of errors. The status window also makes an excellent debugging aid, because it gives you an easy way to output information about your applet.

The following applet demonstrates **showStatus( )**:

```java
// Using the Status Window.
import java.awt.*;
import java.applet.*;
/*
<applet code="StatusWindow" width=300 height=50>
</applet>
*/

public class StatusWindow extends Applet{
  public void init() {
    setBackground(Color.cyan);
  }

  // Display msg in applet window.
  public void paint(Graphics g) {
    g.drawString("This is in the applet window.", 10, 20);
    showStatus("This is shown in the status window.");
  }
}
```

Sample output from this program is shown here:

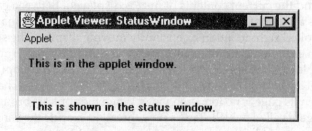

The HTML APPLET Tag

The APPLET tag is used to start an applet from both an HTML document and from an applet viewer. (The newer OBJECT tag also works, but this book will use APPLET.) An applet viewer will execute each APPLET tag that it finds in a separate window, while web browsers like Netscape Navigator, Internet Explorer, and HotJava will allow many applets on a single page. So far, we have been using only a simplified form of the APPLET tag. Now it is time to take a closer look at it.

The syntax for the standard APPLET tag is shown here. Bracketed items are optional.

```
< APPLET
 [CODEBASE = codebaseURL]
 CODE = appletFile
 [ALT = alternateText]
 [NAME = appletInstanceName]
 WIDTH = pixels HEIGHT = pixels
 [ALIGN = alignment]
 [VSPACE = pixels] [HSPACE = pixels]
>
[< PARAM NAME = AttributeName VALUE = AttributeValue>]
[< PARAM NAME = AttributeName2 VALUE = AttributeValue>]
 . . .
[HTML Displayed in the absence of Java]
</APPLET>
```

Let's take a look at each part now.

CODEBASE CODEBASE is an optional attribute that specifies the base URL of the applet code, which is the directory that will be searched for the applet's executable class file (specified by the CODE tag). The HTML document's URL directory is used as the CODEBASE if this attribute is not specified. The CODEBASE does not have to be on the host from which the HTML document was read.

CODE CODE is a required attribute that gives the name of the file containing your applet's compiled **.class** file. This file is relative to the code base URL of the applet, which is the directory that the HTML file was in or the directory indicated by CODEBASE if set.

ALT The ALT tag is an optional attribute used to specify a short text message that should be displayed if the browser understands the APPLET tag but can't currently run Java applets. This is distinct from the alternate HTML you provide for browsers that don't support applets.

NAME   NAME is an optional attribute used to specify a name for the applet instance. Applets must be named in order for other applets on the same page to find them by name and communicate with them. To obtain an applet by name, use **getApplet( )**, which is defined by the **AppletContext** interface.

WIDTH AND HEIGHT   WIDTH and HEIGHT are required attributes that give the size (in pixels) of the applet display area.

ALIGN   ALIGN is an optional attribute that specifies the alignment of the applet. This attribute is treated the same as the HTML IMG tag with these possible values: LEFT, RIGHT, TOP, BOTTOM, MIDDLE, BASELINE, TEXTTOP, ABSMIDDLE, and ABSBOTTOM.

VSPACE AND HSPACE   These attributes are optional. VSPACE specifies the space, in pixels, above and below the applet. HSPACE specifies the space, in pixels, on each side of the applet. They're treated the same as the IMG tag's VSPACE and HSPACE attributes.

PARAM NAME AND VALUE   The PARAM tag allows you to specify applet-specific arguments in an HTML page. Applets access their attributes with the **getParameter( )** method.

HANDLING OLDER BROWSERS   Some very old web browsers can't execute applets and don't recognize the APPLET tag. Although these browsers are now nearly extinct (having been replaced by Java-compatible ones), you may need to deal with them occasionally. The best way to design your HTML page to deal with such browsers is to include HTML text and markup within your <applet></applet> tags. If the applet tags are not recognized by your browser, you will see the alternate markup. If Java is available, it will consume all of the markup between the <applet></applet> tags and disregard the alternate markup.

Here's the HTML to start an applet called **SampleApplet** in Java and to display a message in older browsers:

```
<applet code="SampleApplet" width=200 height=40>
 If you were driving a Java powered browser,
 you'd see &quote;A Sample Applet&quote; here.<p>
</applet>
```

Passing Parameters to Applets

As just discussed, the APPLET tag in HTML allows you to pass parameters to your applet. To retrieve a parameter, use the **getParameter( )** method. It returns the value of the specified parameter in the form of a **String** object. Thus, for numeric and **boolean** values, you will need to convert their string representations into their internal formats. Here is an example that demonstrates passing parameters:

```
// Use Parameters
import java.awt.*;
import java.applet.*;
/*
<applet code="ParamDemo" width=300 height=80>
<param name=fontName value=Courier>
<param name=fontSize value=14>
<param name=leading value=2>
<param name=accountEnabled value=true>
</applet>
*/

public class ParamDemo extends Applet{
  String fontName;
  int fontSize;
  float leading;
  boolean active;

  // Initialize the string to be displayed.
  public void start() {
    String param;

    fontName = getParameter("fontName");
    if(fontName == null)
      fontName = "Not Found";

    param = getParameter("fontSize");
    try {
      if(param != null) // if not found
        fontSize = Integer.parseInt(param);
      else
        fontSize = 0;
    } catch(NumberFormatException e) {
      fontSize = -1;
    }

    param = getParameter("leading");
    try {
```

```
    if(param != null) // if not found
      leading = Float.valueOf(param).floatValue();
    else
      leading = 0;
  } catch(NumberFormatException e) {
    leading = -1;
  }

  param = getParameter("accountEnabled");
  if(param != null)
    active = Boolean.valueOf(param).booleanValue();
}

// Display parameters.
public void paint(Graphics g) {
  g.drawString("Font name: " + fontName, 0, 10);
  g.drawString("Font size: " + fontSize, 0, 26);
  g.drawString("Leading: " + leading, 0, 42);
  g.drawString("Account Active: " + active, 0, 58);
}
}
```

Sample output from this program is shown here:

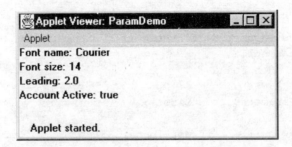

As the program shows, you should test the return values from **getParameter( )**. If a parameter isn't available, **getParameter( )** will return **null**. Also, conversions to numeric types must be attempted in a **try** statement that catches **NumberFormatException**. Uncaught exceptions should never occur within an applet.

Improving the Banner Applet

It is possible to use a parameter to enhance the banner applet shown earlier. In the previous version, the message being scrolled was hard-coded into the applet. However, passing the message as a parameter allows the banner applet to display a different message each time it is executed. This improved version is shown here. Notice that the APPLET tag at the top of the file now specifies a parameter called **message** that is linked to a quoted string.

```
// A parameterized banner
import java.awt.*;
import java.applet.*;
/*
<applet code="ParamBanner" width=300 height=50>
<param name=message value="Java makes the Web move!">
</applet>
*/

public class ParamBanner extends Applet implements Runnable {
  String msg;
  Thread t = null;
  int state;
  boolean stopFlag;

  // Set colors and initialize thread.
  public void init() {
    setBackground(Color.cyan);
    setForeground(Color.red);
  }

  // Start thread
  public void start() {
    msg = getParameter("message");
    if(msg == null) msg = "Message not found.";
    msg = " " + msg;
    t = new Thread(this);
    stopFlag = false;
    t.start();
  }

  // Entry point for the thread that runs the banner.
  public void run() {
```

```
        char ch;

    // Display banner
    for( ; ; ) {
      try {
        repaint();
        Thread.sleep(250);
        ch = msg.charAt(0);
        msg = msg.substring(1, msg.length());
        msg += ch;
        if(stopFlag)
          break;
      } catch(InterruptedException e) {}
    }
  }

  // Pause the banner.
  public void stop() {
    stopFlag = true;
    t = null;
  }

  // Display the banner.
  public void paint(Graphics g) {
    g.drawString(msg, 50, 30);
  }
}
```

getDocumentBase( ) and getCodeBase( )

Often, you will create applets that will need to explicitly load media and text. Java will allow the applet to load data from the directory holding the HTML file that started the applet (the *document base*) and the directory from which the applet's class file was loaded (the *code base*). These directories are returned as **URL** objects (described in Chapter 18) by **getDocumentBase( )** and **getCodeBase( )**. They can be concatenated with a string that names the file you want to load. To actually load another file, you will use the **showDocument( )** method defined by the **AppletContext** interface, discussed in the next section.

The following applet illustrates these methods:

```
// Display code and document bases.
```

```
import java.awt.*;
import java.applet.*;
import java.net.*;
/*
<applet code="Bases" width=300 height=50>
</applet>
*/

public class Bases extends Applet{
  // Display code and document bases.
  public void paint(Graphics g) {
    String msg;

    URL url = getCodeBase(); // get code base
    msg = "Code base: " + url.toString();
    g.drawString(msg, 10, 20);

    url = getDocumentBase(); // get document base
    msg = "Document base: " + url.toString();
    g.drawString(msg, 10, 40);

  }
}
```

Sample output from this program is shown here:

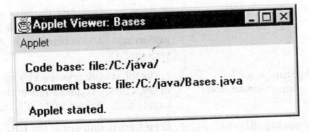

AppletContext and showDocument( )

One application of Java is to use active images and animation to provide a graphical means of navigating the Web that is more interesting than the underlined blue words used by hypertext. To allow your applet to transfer control to another URL, you must use the **showDocument( )** method defined by the **AppletContext** interface.

AppletContext is an interface that lets you get information from the applet's execution environment. The methods defined by **AppletContext** are shown in Table 19-2. The context of the currently executing applet is obtained by a call to the **getAppletContext( )** method defined by **Applet**.

Within an applet, once you have obtained the applet's context, you can bring another document into view by calling **showDocument( )**. This method has no return value and throws no exception if it fails, so use it carefully. There are two **showDocument( )** methods. The method **showDocument(URL)** displays the document

Method	Description
Applet getApplet(String *appletName*)	Returns the applet specified by *appletName* if it is within the current applet context. Otherwise, **null** is returned.
Enumeration getApplets( )	Returns an enumeration that contains all of the applets within the current applet context.
AudioClip getAudioClip(URL *url*)	Returns an **AudioClip** object that encapsulates the audio clip found at the location specified by *url*.
Image getImage(URL *url*)	Returns an **Image** object that encapsulates the image found at the location specified by *url*.
InputStream getStream(String *key*)	Returns the stream linked to *key*. Keys are linked to streams by using the **setStream( )** method. A null reference is returned if no stream is linked to *key*. (Added by Java 2, version 1.4)
Iterator getStreamKeys( )	Returns an iterator for the keys associated with the invoking object. The keys are linked to streams. See **getStream( )** and **setStream( )**. (Added by Java 2, version 1.4)
void setStream(String *key*, InputStream *strm*)	Links the stream specified by *strm* to the key passed in *key*. The *key* is deleted from the invoking object if *strm* is null. (Added by Java 2, version 1.4)
void showDocument(URL *url*)	Brings the document at the **URL** specified by *url* into view. This method may not be supported by applet viewers.
void showDocument(URL *url*, String *where*)	Brings the document at the **URL** specified by *url* into view. This method may not be supported by applet viewers. The placement of the document is specified by *where* as described in the text.
void showStatus(String *str*)	Displays *str* in the status window.

Table 19-2. *The Abstract Methods Defined by the* **AppletContext** *Interface*

at the specified **URL**. The method **showDocument(URL, where)** displays the specified document at the specified location within the browser window. Valid arguments for *where* are "_self" (show in current frame), "_parent" (show in parent frame), "_top" (show in topmost frame), and "_blank" (show in new browser window). You can also specify a name, which causes the document to be shown in a new browser window by that name.

The following applet demonstrates **AppletContext** and **showDocument( )**. Upon execution, it obtains the current applet context and uses that context to transfer control to a file called **Test.html**. This file must be in the same directory as the applet. **Test.html** can contain any valid hypertext that you like.

```
/* Using an applet context, getCodeBase(),
   and showDocument() to display an HTML file.
*/

import java.awt.*;
import java.applet.*;
import java.net.*;
/*
<applet code="ACDemo" width=300 height=50>
</applet>
*/

public class ACDemo extends Applet{
  public void start() {
    AppletContext ac = getAppletContext();
    URL url = getCodeBase(); // get url of this applet

    try {
      ac.showDocument(new URL(url+"Test.html"));
    } catch(MalformedURLException e) {
      showStatus("URL not found");
    }
  }
}
```

The AudioClip Interface

The **AudioClip** interface defines these methods: **play( )** (play a clip from the beginning), **stop( )** (stop playing the clip), and **loop( )** (play the loop continuously). After you have loaded an audio clip using **getAudioClip( )**, you can use these methods to play it.

The AppletStub Interface

The **AppletStub** interface provides the means by which an applet and the browser (or applet viewer) communicate. Your code will not typically implement this interface.

Outputting to the Console

Although output to an applet's window must be accomplished through AWT methods, such as **drawString( )**, it is still possible to use console output in your applet—especially for debugging purposes. In an applet, when you call a method such as **System.out.println( )**, the output is not sent to your applet's window. Instead, it appears either in the console session in which you launched the applet viewer or in the Java console that is available in some browsers. Use of console output for purposes other than debugging is discouraged, since it violates the design principles of the graphical interface most users will expect.

The
Complete
Reference

Java™ 2

Chapter 20

Event Handling

This chapter examines an important aspect of Java that relates to applets: events. As explained in Chapter 19, applets are event-driven programs. Thus, event handling is at the core of successful applet programming. Most events to which your applet will respond are generated by the user. These events are passed to your applet in a variety of ways, with the specific method depending upon the actual event. There are several types of events. The most commonly handled events are those generated by the mouse, the keyboard, and various controls, such as a push button. Events are supported by the **java.awt.event** package.

The chapter begins with an overview of Java's event handling mechanism. It then examines the main event classes and interfaces, and develops several examples that demonstrate the fundamentals of event processing. This chapter also explains how to use adapter classes, inner classes, and anonymous inner classes to streamline event handling code. The examples provided in the remainder of this book make frequent use of these techniques.

Two Event Handling Mechanisms

Before beginning our discussion of event handling, an important point must be made: The way in which events are handled by an applet changed significantly between the original version of Java (1.0) and modern versions of Java, beginning with version 1.1. The 1.0 method of event handling is still supported, but it is not recommended for new programs. Also, many of the methods that support the old 1.0 event model have been deprecated. The modern approach is the way that events should be handled by all new programs, including those written for Java 2, and thus is the method employed by programs in this book.

The Delegation Event Model

The modern approach to handling events is based on the *delegation event model*, which defines standard and consistent mechanisms to generate and process events. Its concept is quite simple: a *source* generates an event and sends it to one or more *listeners*. In this scheme, the listener simply waits until it receives an event. Once received, the listener processes the event and then returns. The advantage of this design is that the application logic that processes events is cleanly separated from the user interface logic that generates those events. A user interface element is able to "delegate" the processing of an event to a separate piece of code.

In the delegation event model, listeners must register with a source in order to receive an event notification. This provides an important benefit: notifications are sent only to listeners that want to receive them. This is a more efficient way to handle events than the design used by the old Java 1.0 approach. Previously, an event was propagated up the containment hierarchy until it was handled by a component. This required components to receive events that they did not process, and it wasted valuable time. The delegation event model eliminates this overhead.

> **Note**
> *Java also allows you to process events without using the delegation event model. This can be done by extending an AWT component. This technique is discussed at the end of Chapter 22. However, the delegation event model is the preferred design for the reasons just cited.*

The following sections define events and describe the roles of sources and listeners.

Events

In the delegation model, an *event* is an object that describes a state change in a source. It can be generated as a consequence of a person interacting with the elements in a graphical user interface. Some of the activities that cause events to be generated are pressing a button, entering a character via the keyboard, selecting an item in a list, and clicking the mouse. Many other user operations could also be cited as examples.

Events may also occur that are not directly caused by interactions with a user interface. For example, an event may be generated when a timer expires, a counter exceeds a value, a software or hardware failure occurs, or an operation is completed. You are free to define events that are appropriate for your application.

Event Sources

A *source* is an object that generates an event. This occurs when the internal state of that object changes in some way. Sources may generate more than one type of event.

A source must register listeners in order for the listeners to receive notifications about a specific type of event. Each type of event has its own registration method. Here is the general form:

public void add*Type*Listener(*Type*Listener *el*)

Here, *Type* is the name of the event and *el* is a reference to the event listener. For example, the method that registers a keyboard event listener is called **addKeyListener( )**. The method that registers a mouse motion listener is called **addMouseMotionListener( )**. When an event occurs, all registered listeners are notified and receive a copy of the event object. This is known as *multicasting* the event. In all cases, notifications are sent only to listeners that register to receive them.

Some sources may allow only one listener to register. The general form of such a method is this:

public void add*Type*Listener(*Type*Listener *el*)
   throws java.util.TooManyListenersException

Here, *Type* is the name of the event and *el* is a reference to the event listener. When such an event occurs, the registered listener is notified. This is known as *unicasting* the event.

A source must also provide a method that allows a listener to unregister an interest in a specific type of event. The general form of such a method is this:

public void remove*Type*Listener(*Type*Listener *el*)

Here, *Type* is the name of the event and *el* is a reference to the event listener. For example, to remove a keyboard listener, you would call **removeKeyListener( )**.

The methods that add or remove listeners are provided by the source that generates events. For example, the **Component** class provides methods to add and remove keyboard and mouse event listeners.

Event Listeners

A *listener* is an object that is notified when an event occurs. It has two major requirements. First, it must have been registered with one or more sources to receive notifications about specific types of events. Second, it must implement methods to receive and process these notifications.

The methods that receive and process events are defined in a set of interfaces found in **java.awt.event**. For example, the **MouseMotionListener** interface defines two methods to receive notifications when the mouse is dragged or moved. Any object may receive and process one or both of these events if it provides an implementation of this interface. Many other listener interfaces are discussed later in this and other chapters.

Event Classes

The classes that represent events are at the core of Java's event handling mechanism. Thus, we begin our study of event handling with a tour of the event classes. As you will see, they provide a consistent, easy-to-use means of encapsulating events.

At the root of the Java event class hierarchy is **EventObject**, which is in **java.util**. It is the superclass for all events. Its one constructor is shown here:

EventObject(Object *src*)

Here, *src* is the object that generates this event.

EventObject contains two methods: **getSource( )** and **toString( )**. The **getSource( )** method returns the source of the event. Its general form is shown here:

Object getSource( )

As expected, **toString( )** returns the string equivalent of the event.

The class **AWTEvent**, defined within the **java.awt** package, is a subclass of **EventObject**. It is the superclass (either directly or indirectly) of all AWT-based events used by the delegation event model. Its **getID( )** method can be used to determine the type of the event. The signature of this method is shown here:

int getID( )

Additional details about **AWTEvent** are provided at the end of Chapter 22. At this point, it is important to know only that all of the other classes discussed in this section are subclasses of **AWTEvent**.

To summarize:

- **EventObject** is a superclass of all events.
- **AWTEvent** is a superclass of all AWT events that are handled by the delegation event model.

The package **java.awt.event** defines several types of events that are generated by various user interface elements. Table 20-1 enumerates the most important of these event classes and provides a brief description of when they are generated. The most commonly used constructors and methods in each class are described in the following sections.

Event Class	Description
ActionEvent	Generated when a button is pressed, a list item is double-clicked, or a menu item is selected.
AdjustmentEvent	Generated when a scroll bar is manipulated.
ComponentEvent	Generated when a component is hidden, moved, resized, or becomes visible.
ContainerEvent	Generated when a component is added to or removed from a container.
FocusEvent	Generated when a component gains or loses keyboard focus.
InputEvent	Abstract super class for all component input event classes.
ItemEvent	Generated when a check box or list item is clicked; also occurs when a choice selection is made or a checkable menu item is selected or deselected.

Table 20-1. *Main Event Classes in* java.awt.event

Event Class	Description
KeyEvent	Generated when input is received from the keyboard.
MouseEvent	Generated when the mouse is dragged, moved, clicked, pressed, or released; also generated when the mouse enters or exits a component.
MouseWheelEvent	Generated when the mouse wheel is moved. (Added by Java 2, version 1.4)
TextEvent	Generated when the value of a text area or text field is changed.
WindowEvent	Generated when a window is activated, closed, deactivated, deiconified, iconified, opened, or quit.

Table 20-1. *Main Event Classes in* java.awt.event (continued)

The ActionEvent Class

An **ActionEvent** is generated when a button is pressed, a list item is double-clicked, or a menu item is selected. The **ActionEvent** class defines four integer constants that can be used to identify any modifiers associated with an action event: **ALT_MASK**, **CTRL_MASK**, **META_MASK**, and **SHIFT_MASK**. In addition, there is an integer constant, **ACTION_PERFORMED**, which can be used to identify action events.

ActionEvent has these three constructors:

ActionEvent(Object *src*, int *type*, String *cmd*)
ActionEvent(Object *src*, int *type*, String *cmd*, int *modifiers*)
ActionEvent(Object *src*, int *type*, String *cmd*, long *when*, int *modifiers*)

Here, *src* is a reference to the object that generated this event. The type of the event is specified by *type*, and its command string is *cmd*. The argument *modifiers* indicates which modifier keys (ALT, CTRL, META, and/or SHIFT) were pressed when the event was generated. The *when* parameter specifies when the event occurred. The third constructor was added by Java 2, version 1.4.

You can obtain the command name for the invoking **ActionEvent** object by using the **getActionCommand( )** method, shown here:

String getActionCommand( )

For example, when a button is pressed, an action event is generated that has a command name equal to the label on that button.

The **getModifiers( )** method returns a value that indicates which modifier keys (ALT, CTRL, META, and/or SHIFT) were pressed when the event was generated. Its form is shown here:

int getModifiers( )

Java 2, version 1.4 added the method **getWhen( )** that returns the time at which the event took place. This is called the event's *timestamp*. The **getWhen( )** method is shown here:

long getWhen( )

Timestamps were added by **ActionEvent** to help support the improved input focus subsystem implemented by Java 2, version 1.4.

The AdjustmentEvent Class

An **AdjustmentEvent** is generated by a scroll bar. There are five types of adjustment events. The **AdjustmentEvent** class defines integer constants that can be used to identify them. The constants and their meanings are shown here:

BLOCK_DECREMENT	The user clicked inside the scroll bar to decrease its value.
BLOCK_INCREMENT	The user clicked inside the scroll bar to increase its value.
TRACK	The slider was dragged.
UNIT_DECREMENT	The button at the end of the scroll bar was clicked to decrease its value.
UNIT_INCREMENT	The button at the end of the scroll bar was clicked to increase its value.

In addition, there is an integer constant, **ADJUSTMENT_VALUE_CHANGED**, that indicates that a change has occurred.

Here is one **AdjustmentEvent** constructor:

AdjustmentEvent(Adjustable *src*, int *id*, int *type*, int *data*)

Here, *src* is a reference to the object that generated this event. The *id* equals **ADJUSTMENT_VALUE_CHANGED**. The type of the event is specified by *type*, and its associated data is *data*.

The **getAdjustable( )** method returns the object that generated the event. Its form is shown here:

Adjustable getAdjustable( )

The type of the adjustment event may be obtained by the **getAdjustmentType( )** method. It returns one of the constants defined by **AdjustmentEvent**. The general form is shown here:

int getAdjustmentType( )

The amount of the adjustment can be obtained from the **getValue( )** method, shown here:

 int getValue( )

For example, when a scroll bar is manipulated, this method returns the value represented by that change.

The ComponentEvent Class

A **ComponentEvent** is generated when the size, position, or visibility of a component is changed. There are four types of component events. The **ComponentEvent** class defines integer constants that can be used to identify them. The constants and their meanings are shown here:

COMPONENT_HIDDEN	The component was hidden.
COMPONENT_MOVED	The component was moved.
COMPONENT_RESIZED	The component was resized.
COMPONENT_SHOWN	The component became visible

ComponentEvent has this constructor:

ComponentEvent(Component *src*, int *type*)

Here, *src* is a reference to the object that generated this event. The type of the event is specified by *type*.

 ComponentEvent is the superclass either directly or indirectly of **ContainerEvent**, **FocusEvent**, **KeyEvent**, **MouseEvent**, and **WindowEvent**.

 The **getComponent( )** method returns the component that generated the event. It is shown here:

 Component getComponent( )

The ContainerEvent Class

A **ContainerEvent** is generated when a component is added to or removed from a container. There are two types of container events. The **ContainerEvent** class defines **int** constants that can be used to identify them: **COMPONENT_ADDED** and **COMPONENT_REMOVED**. They indicate that a component has been added to or removed from the container.

 ContainerEvent is a subclass of **ComponentEvent** and has this constructor:

ContainerEvent(Component *src*, int *type*, Component *comp*)

Here, *src* is a reference to the container that generated this event. The type of the event is specified by *type*, and the component that has been added to or removed from the container is *comp*.

You can obtain a reference to the container that generated this event by using the **getContainer( )** method, shown here:

Container getContainer( )

The **getChild( )** method returns a reference to the component that was added to or removed from the container. Its general form is shown here:

Component getChild( )

The FocusEvent Class

A **FocusEvent** is generated when a component gains or loses input focus. These events are identified by the integer constants **FOCUS_GAINED** and **FOCUS_LOST**.

FocusEvent is a subclass of **ComponentEvent** and has these constructors:

FocusEvent(Component *src*, int *type*)
FocusEvent(Component *src*, int *type*, boolean *temporaryFlag*)
Focus Event(Component *src*, int *type*, boolean *temporaryFlag*, Component *other*)

Here, *src* is a reference to the component that generated this event. The type of the event is specified by *type*. The argument *temporaryFlag* is set to **true** if the focus event is temporary. Otherwise, it is set to **false**. (A temporary focus event occurs as a result of another user interface operation. For example, assume that the focus is in a text field. If the user moves the mouse to adjust a scroll bar, the focus is temporarily lost.)

The other component involved in the focus change, called the *opposite component*, is passed in *other*. Therefore, if a **FOCUS_GAINED** event occurred, *other* will refer to the component that lost focus. Conversely, if a **FOCUS_LOST** event occurred, *other* will refer to the component that gains focus. The third constructor was added by Java 2, version 1.4.

You can determine the other component by calling **getOppositeComponent( )**, shown here.

Component getOppositeComponent( )

The opposite component is returned. This method was added by Java 2, version 1.4.

The **isTemporary( )** method indicates if this focus change is temporary. Its form is shown here:

boolean isTemporary( )

The method returns **true** if the change is temporary. Otherwise, it returns **false**.

The InputEvent Class

The abstract class **InputEvent** is a subclass of **ComponentEvent** and is the superclass for component input events. Its subclasses are **KeyEvent** and **MouseEvent**.

InputEvent defines several integer constants that represent any modifiers, such as the control key being pressed, that might be associated with the event. Originally, the **InputEvent** class defined the following eight values to represent the modifiers.

ALT_MASK	BUTTON2_MASK	META_MASK
ALT_GRAPH_MASK	BUTTON3_MASK	SHIFT_MASK
BUTTON1_MASK	CTRL_MASK	

However, because of possible conflicts between the modifiers used by keyboard events and mouse events, and other issues, Java 2, version 1.4 added the following extended modifier values.

ALT_DOWN_MASK	ALT_GRAPH_DOWN_MASK	BUTTON1_DOWN_MASK
BUTTON2_DOWN_MASK	BUTTON3_DOWN_MASK	CTRL_DOWN_MASK
META_DOWN_MASK	SHIFT_DOWN_MASK	

When writing new code, it is recommended that you use the new, extended modifiers rather than the original modifiers.

To test if a modifier was pressed at the time an event is generated, use the **isAltDown( )**, **isAltGraphDown( )**, **isControlDown( )**, **isMetaDown( )**, and **isShiftDown( )** methods. The forms of these methods are shown here:

```
boolean isAltDown( )
boolean isAltGraphDown( )
boolean isControlDown( )
boolean isMetaDown( )
boolean isShiftDown( )
```

You can obtain a value that contains all of the original modifier flags by calling the **getModifiers( )** method. It is shown here:

```
int getModifiers( )
```

You can obtain the extended modifiers by called **getModifiersEx( )**, which is shown here.

```
int getModifiersEx( )
```

This method was also added by Java 2, version 1.4.

The ItemEvent Class

An **ItemEvent** is generated when a check box or a list item is clicked or when a checkable menu item is selected or deselected. (Check boxes and list boxes are described later in this book.) There are two types of item events, which are identified by the following integer constants:

DESELECTED   The user deselected an item.

SELECTED   The user selected an item.

In addition, **ItemEvent** defines one integer constant, **ITEM_STATE_CHANGED**, that signifies a change of state.

ItemEvent has this constructor:

ItemEvent(ItemSelectable *src*, int *type*, Object *entry*, int *state*)

Here, *src* is a reference to the component that generated this event. For example, this might be a list or choice element. The type of the event is specified by *type*. The specific item that generated the item event is passed in *entry*. The current state of that item is in *state*.

The **getItem( )** method can be used to obtain a reference to the item that generated an event. Its signature is shown here:

Object getItem( )

The **getItemSelectable( )** method can be used to obtain a reference to the **ItemSelectable** object that generated an event. Its general form is shown here:

ItemSelectable getItemSelectable( )

Lists and choices are examples of user interface elements that implement the **ItemSelectable** interface.

The **getStateChange( )** method returns the state change (i.e., **SELECTED** or **DESELECTED**) for the event. It is shown here:

int getStateChange( )

The KeyEvent Class

A **KeyEvent** is generated when keyboard input occurs. There are three types of key events, which are identified by these integer constants: **KEY_PRESSED**, **KEY_RELEASED**, and **KEY_TYPED**. The first two events are generated when any key is pressed or released. The last event occurs only when a character is generated. Remember, not all key presses result in characters. For example, pressing the SHIFT key does not generate a character.

There are many other integer constants that are defined by **KeyEvent**. For example, **VK_0** through **VK_9** and **VK_A** through **VK_Z** define the ASCII equivalents of the numbers and letters. Here are some others:

VK_ENTER	VK_ESCAPE	VK_CANCEL	VK_UP
VK_DOWN	VK_LEFT	VK_RIGHT	VK_PAGE_DOWN
VK_PAGE_UP	VK_SHIFT	VK_ALT	VK_CONTROL

The **VK** constants specify *virtual key codes* and are independent of any modifiers, such as control, shift, or alt.

KeyEvent is a subclass of **InputEvent**. Here are two of its constructors:

KeyEvent(Component *src*, int *type*, long *when*, int *modifiers*, int *code*)
KeyEvent(Component *src*, int *type*, long *when*, int *modifiers*, int *code*, char *ch*)

Here, *src* is a reference to the component that generated the event. The type of the event is specified by *type*. The system time at which the key was pressed is passed in *when*. The *modifiers* argument indicates which modifiers were pressed when this key event occurred. The virtual key code, such as **VK_UP**, **VK_A**, and so forth, is passed in *code*. The character equivalent (if one exists) is passed in *ch*. If no valid character exists, then *ch* contains **CHAR_UNDEFINED**. For **KEY_TYPED** events, *code* will contain **VK_UNDEFINED**.

The **KeyEvent** class defines several methods, but the most commonly used ones are **getKeyChar( )**, which returns the character that was entered, and **getKeyCode( )**, which returns the key code. Their general forms are shown here:

char getKeyChar( )
int getKeyCode( )

If no valid character is available, then **getKeyChar( )** returns **CHAR_UNDEFINED**. When a **KEY_TYPED** event occurs, **getKeyCode( )** returns **VK_UNDEFINED**.

The MouseEvent Class

There are eight types of mouse events. The **MouseEvent** class defines the following integer constants that can be used to identify them:

MOUSE_CLICKED	The user clicked the mouse.
MOUSE_DRAGGED	The user dragged the mouse.
MOUSE_ENTERED	The mouse entered a component.
MOUSE_EXITED	The mouse exited from a component.
MOUSE_MOVED	The mouse moved.
MOUSE_PRESSED	The mouse was pressed.
MOUSE_RELEASED	The mouse was released.
MOUSE_WHEEL	The mouse wheel was moved (Java 2, v1.4).

MouseEvent is a subclass of **InputEvent**. Here is one of its constructors.

MouseEvent(Component *src*, int *type*, long *when*, int *modifiers*,
           int *x*, int *y*, int *clicks*, boolean *triggersPopup*)

Here, *src* is a reference to the component that generated the event. The type of the event is specified by *type*. The system time at which the mouse event occurred is passed in *when.* The *modifiers* argument indicates which modifiers were pressed when a mouse event occurred. The coordinates of the mouse are passed in *x* and *y*. The click count is passed in *clicks*. The *triggersPopup* flag indicates if this event causes a pop-up menu to appear on this platform. Java 2, version 1.4 adds a second constructor which also allows the button that caused the event to be specified.

The most commonly used methods in this class are **getX( )** and **getY( )**. These return the X and Y coordinates of the mouse when the event occurred. Their forms are shown here:

int getX( )
int getY( )

Alternatively, you can use the **getPoint( )** method to obtain the coordinates of the mouse. It is shown here:

Point getPoint( )

It returns a **Point** object that contains the X, Y coordinates in its integer members: **x** and **y**.
The **translatePoint( )** method changes the location of the event. Its form is shown here:

void translatePoint(int *x*, int *y*)

Here, the arguments *x* and *y* are added to the coordinates of the event.
The **getClickCount( )** method obtains the number of mouse clicks for this event. Its signature is shown here:

int getClickCount( )

The **isPopupTrigger( )** method tests if this event causes a pop-up menu to appear on this platform. Its form is shown here:

boolean isPopupTrigger( )

Java 2, version 1.4 added the **getButton( )** method, shown here:

int getButton( )

It returns a value that represents the button that caused the event. The return value will be one of these constants defined by **MouseEvent**.

NOBUTTON   BUTTON1   BUTTON2   BUTTON3

The **NOBUTTON** value indicates that no button was pressed or released.

The MouseWheelEvent Class

The **MouseWheelEvent** class encapsulates a mouse wheel event. It is a subclass of **MouseEvent** and was added by Java 2, version 1.4. Not all mice have wheels.

If a mouse has a wheel, it is located between the left and right buttons. Mouse wheels are used for scrolling. **MouseWheelEvent** defines these two integer constants.

WHEEL_BLOCK_SCROLL   A page-up or page-down scroll event occurred.

WHEEL_UNIT_SCROLL   A line-up or line-down scroll event occurred.

MouseWheelEvent defines the following constructor.

MouseWheelEvent(Component *src*, int *type*, long *when*, int *modifiers*,
                 int *x*, int *y*, int *clicks*, boolean *triggersPopup*,
                 int *scrollHow*, int *amount*, int *count*)

Here, *src* is a reference to the object that generated the event. The type of the event is specified by *type*. The system time at which the mouse event occurred is passed in *when*. The *modifiers* argument indicates which modifiers were pressed when the event occurred. The coordinates of the mouse are passed in *x* and *y*. The number of clicks the wheel has rotated is passed in *clicks*. The *triggersPopup* flag indicates if this event causes a pop-up menu to appear on this platform. The *scrollHow* value must be either **WHEEL_UNIT_SCROLL** or **WHEEL_BLOCK_SCROLL**. The number of units to scroll is passed in *amount*. The *count* parameter indicates the number of rotational units that the wheel moved.

    MouseWheelEvent defines methods that give you access to the wheel event. To obtain the number of rotational units, call **getWheelRotation( )**, shown here.

    int getWheelRotation( )

It returns the number of rotational units. If the value is positive, the wheel moved counterclockwise. If the value is negative, the wheel moved clockwise.

    To obtain the type of scroll, call **getScrollType( )**, shown next.

    int getScrollType( )

It returns either **WHEEL_UNIT_SCROLL** or **WHEEL_BLOCK_SCROLL**.

    If the scroll type is **WHEEL_UNIT_SCROLL**, you can obtain the number of units to scroll by calling **getScrollAmount( )**. It is shown here.

    int getScrollAmount( )

The TextEvent Class

Instances of this class describe text events. These are generated by text fields and text areas when characters are entered by a user or program. **TextEvent** defines the integer constant **TEXT_VALUE_CHANGED**.

The one constructor for this class is shown here:

TextEvent(Object *src*, int *type*)

Here, *src* is a reference to the object that generated this event. The type of the event is specified by *type*.

The **TextEvent** object does not include the characters currently in the text component that generated the event. Instead, your program must use other methods associated with the text component to retrieve that information. This operation differs from other event objects discussed in this section. For this reason, no methods are discussed here for the **TextEvent** class. Think of a text event notification as a signal to a listener that it should retrieve information from a specific text component.

The WindowEvent Class

There are ten types of window events. The **WindowEvent** class defines integer constants that can be used to identify them. The constants and their meanings are shown here:

WINDOW_ACTIVATED	The window was activated.
WINDOW_CLOSED	The window has been closed.
WINDOW_CLOSING	The user requested that the window be closed.
WINDOW_DEACTIVATED	The window was deactivated.
WINDOW_DEICONIFIED	The window was deiconified.
WINDOW_GAINED_FOCUS	The window gained input focus.
WINDOW_ICONIFIED	The window was iconified.
WINDOW_LOST_FOCUS	The window lost input focus.
WINDOW_OPENED	The window was opened.
WINDOW_STATE_CHANGED	The state of the window changed. (Added by Java 2, version 1.4.)

WindowEvent is a subclass of **ComponentEvent**. It defines several constructors. The first is

WindowEvent(Window *src*, int *type*)

Here, *src* is a reference to the object that generated this event. The type of the event is *type*. Java 2, version 1.4 adds the next three constructors.

WindowEvent(Window *src*, int *type*, Window *other*)
WindowEvent(Window *src*, int *type*, int *fromState*, int *toState*)
WindowEvent(Window *src*, int *type*, Window *other*, int *fromState*, int *toState*)

Here, *other* specifies the opposite window when a focus event occurs. The *fromState* specifies the prior state of the window and *toState* specifies the new state that the window will have when a window state change occurs.

The most commonly used method in this class is **getWindow( )**. It returns the **Window** object that generated the event. Its general form is shown here:

Window getWindow( )

Java 2, version 1.4, adds methods that return the opposite window (when a focus event has occurred), the previous window state, and the current window state. These methods are shown here:

Window getOppositeWindow()
int getOldState()
int getNewState()

Sources of Events

Table 20-2 lists some of the user interface components that can generate the events described in the previous section. In addition to these graphical user interface elements, other components, such as an applet, can generate events. For example, you receive key and mouse events from an applet. (You may also build your own components that generate events.) In this chapter we will be handling only mouse and keyboard events, but the following two chapters will be handling events from the sources shown in Table 20-2.

Event Source	Description
Button	Generates action events when the button is pressed.
Checkbox	Generates item events when the check box is selected or deselected.
Choice	Generates item events when the choice is changed.
List	Generates action events when an item is double-clicked; generates item events when an item is selected or deselected.
Menu Item	Generates action events when a menu item is selected; generates item events when a checkable menu item is selected or deselected.
Scrollbar	Generates adjustment events when the scroll bar is manipulated.
Text components	Generates text events when the user enters a character.
Window	Generates window events when a window is activated, closed, deactivated, deiconified, iconified, opened, or quit.

Table 20-2. *Event Source Examples*

Event Listener Interfaces

As explained, the delegation event model has two parts: sources and listeners. Listeners are created by implementing one or more of the interfaces defined by the **java.awt.event** package. When an event occurs, the event source invokes the appropriate method defined by the listener and provides an event object as its argument. Table 20-3 lists commonly used listener interfaces and provides a brief description of the methods that they define. The following sections examine the specific methods that are contained in each interface.

Interface	Description
ActionListener	Defines one method to receive action events.
AdjustmentListener	Defines one method to receive adjustment events.
ComponentListener	Defines four methods to recognize when a component is hidden, moved, resized, or shown.
ContainerListener	Defines two methods to recognize when a component is added to or removed from a container.
FocusListener	Defines two methods to recognize when a component gains or loses keyboard focus.
ItemListener	Defines one method to recognize when the state of an item changes.
KeyListener	Defines three methods to recognize when a key is pressed, released, or typed.
MouseListener	Defines five methods to recognize when the mouse is clicked, enters a component, exits a component, is pressed, or is released.
MouseMotionListener	Defines two methods to recognize when the mouse is dragged or moved.
MouseWheelListener	Defines one method to recognize when the mouse wheel is moved. (Added by Java 2, version 1.4)
TextListener	Defines one method to recognize when a text value changes.
WindowFocusListener	Defines two methods to recognize when a window gains or loses input focus. (Added by Java 2, version 1.4)
WindowListener	Defines seven methods to recognize when a window is activated, closed, deactivated, deiconified, iconified, opened, or quit.

Table 20-3.   *Commonly Used Event Listener Interfaces*

The ActionListener Interface

This interface defines the **actionPerformed( )** method that is invoked when an action event occurs. Its general form is shown here:

void actionPerformed(ActionEvent *ae*)

The AdjustmentListener Interface

This interface defines the **adjustmentValueChanged( )** method that is invoked when an adjustment event occurs. Its general form is shown here:

void adjustmentValueChanged(AdjustmentEvent *ae*)

The ComponentListener Interface

This interface defines four methods that are invoked when a component is resized, moved, shown, or hidden. Their general forms are shown here:

void componentResized(ComponentEvent *ce*)
void componentMoved(ComponentEvent *ce*)
void componentShown(ComponentEvent *ce*)
void componentHidden(ComponentEvent *ce*)

 *The AWT processes the resize and move events. The **componentResized( )** and **componentMoved( )** methods are provided for notification purposes only.*

The ContainerListener Interface

This interface contains two methods. When a component is added to a container, **componentAdded( )** is invoked. When a component is removed from a container, **componentRemoved( )** is invoked. Their general forms are shown here:

void componentAdded(ContainerEvent *ce*)
void componentRemoved(ContainerEvent *ce*)

The FocusListener Interface

This interface defines two methods. When a component obtains keyboard focus, **focusGained( )** is invoked. When a component loses keyboard focus, **focusLost( )** is called. Their general forms are shown here:

void focusGained(FocusEvent *fe*)
void focusLost(FocusEvent *fe*)

The ItemListener Interface

This interface defines the **itemStateChanged( )** method that is invoked when the state of an item changes. Its general form is shown here:

void itemStateChanged(ItemEvent *ie*)

The KeyListener Interface

This interface defines three methods. The **keyPressed( )** and **keyReleased( )** methods are invoked when a key is pressed and released, respectively. The **keyTyped( )** method is invoked when a character has been entered.

For example, if a user presses and releases the A key, three events are generated in sequence: key pressed, typed, and released. If a user presses and releases the HOME key, two key events are generated in sequence: key pressed and released.

The general forms of these methods are shown here:

void keyPressed(KeyEvent *ke*)
void keyReleased(KeyEvent *ke*)
void keyTyped(KeyEvent *ke*)

The MouseListener Interface

This interface defines five methods. If the mouse is pressed and released at the same point, **mouseClicked( )** is invoked. When the mouse enters a component, the **mouseEntered( )** method is called. When it leaves, **mouseExited( )** is called. The **mousePressed( )** and **mouseReleased( )** methods are invoked when the mouse is pressed and released, respectively.

The general forms of these methods are shown here:

void mouseClicked(MouseEvent *me*)
void mouseEntered(MouseEvent *me*)
void mouseExited(MouseEvent *me*)
void mousePressed(MouseEvent *me*)
void mouseReleased(MouseEvent *me*)

The MouseMotionListener Interface

This interface defines two methods. The **mouseDragged( )** method is called multiple times as the mouse is dragged. The **mouseMoved( )** method is called multiple times as the mouse is moved. Their general forms are shown here:

void mouseDragged(MouseEvent *me*)
void mouseMoved(MouseEvent *me*)

The MouseWheelListener Interface

This interface defines the **mouseWheelMoved( )** method that is invoked when the mouse wheel is moved. Its general form is shown here.

    void mouseWheelMoved(MouseWheelEvent *mwe*)

MouseWheelListener was added by Java 2, version 1.4.

The TextListener Interface

This interface defines the **textChanged( )** method that is invoked when a change occurs in a text area or text field. Its general form is shown here:

    void textChanged(TextEvent *te*)

The WindowFocusListener Interface

This interface defines two methods: **windowGainedFocus( )** and **windowLostFocus( )**. These are called when a window gains or losses input focus. Their general forms are shown here.

    void windowGainedFocus(WindowEvent *we*)
    void windowLostFocus(WindowEvent *we*)

WindowFocusListener was added by Java 2, version 1.4.

The WindowListener Interface

This interface defines seven methods. The **windowActivated( )** and **windowDeactivated( )** methods are invoked when a window is activated or deactivated, respectively. If a window is iconified, the **windowIconified( )** method is called. When a window is deiconified, the **windowDeiconified( )** method is called. When a window is opened or closed, the **windowOpened( )** or **windowClosed( )** methods are called, respectively. The **windowClosing( )** method is called when a window is being closed. The general forms of these methods are

    void windowActivated(WindowEvent *we*)
    void windowClosed(WindowEvent *we*)
    void windowClosing(WindowEvent *we*)
    void windowDeactivated(WindowEvent *we*)
    void windowDeiconified(WindowEvent *we*)
    void windowIconified(WindowEvent *we*)
    void windowOpened(WindowEvent *we*)

Using the Delegation Event Model

Now that you have learned the theory behind the delegation event model and have had an overview of its various components, it is time to see it in practice. Applet programming using the delegation event model is actually quite easy. Just follow these two steps:

1. Implement the appropriate interface in the listener so that it will receive the type of event desired.

2. Implement code to register and unregister (if necessary) the listener as a recipient for the event notifications.

Remember that a source may generate several types of events. Each event must be registered separately. Also, an object may register to receive several types of events, but it must implement all of the interfaces that are required to receive these events.

To see how the delegation model works in practice, we will look at examples that handle the two most commonly used event generators: the mouse and keyboard.

Handling Mouse Events

To handle mouse events, you must implement the **MouseListener** and the **MouseMotionListener** interfaces. (You may also want to implement **MouseWheelListener**, but we won't be doing so, here.) The following applet demonstrates the process. It displays the current coordinates of the mouse in the applet's status window. Each time a button is pressed, the word "Down" is displayed at the location of the mouse pointer. Each time the button is released, the word "Up" is shown. If a button is clicked, the message "Mouse clicked" is displayed in the upper-left corner of the applet display area.

As the mouse enters or exits the applet window, a message is displayed in the upper-left corner of the applet display area. When dragging the mouse, a * is shown, which tracks with the mouse pointer as it is dragged. Notice that the two variables, **mouseX** and **mouseY**, store the location of the mouse when a mouse pressed, released, or dragged event occurs. These coordinates are then used by **paint( )** to display output at the point of these occurrences.

```
// Demonstrate the mouse event handlers.
import java.awt.*;
import java.awt.event.*;
import java.applet.*;
/*
  <applet code="MouseEvents" width=300 height=100>
  </applet>
*/
```

```java
public class MouseEvents extends Applet
  implements MouseListener, MouseMotionListener {

  String msg = "";
  int mouseX = 0, mouseY = 0; // coordinates of mouse

  public void init() {
    addMouseListener(this);
    addMouseMotionListener(this);
  }

  // Handle mouse clicked.
  public void mouseClicked(MouseEvent me) {
    // save coordinates
    mouseX = 0;
    mouseY = 10;
    msg = "Mouse clicked.";
    repaint();
  }

  // Handle mouse entered.
  public void mouseEntered(MouseEvent me) {
    // save coordinates
    mouseX = 0;
    mouseY = 10;
    msg = "Mouse entered.";
    repaint();
  }

  // Handle mouse exited.
  public void mouseExited(MouseEvent me) {
    // save coordinates
    mouseX = 0;
    mouseY = 10;
    msg = "Mouse exited.";
    repaint();
  }

  // Handle button pressed.
```

```java
public void mousePressed(MouseEvent me) {
  // save coordinates
  mouseX = me.getX();
  mouseY = me.getY();
  msg = "Down";
  repaint();
}


// Handle button released.
public void mouseReleased(MouseEvent me) {
  // save coordinates
  mouseX = me.getX();
  mouseY = me.getY();
  msg = "Up";
  repaint();
}

// Handle mouse dragged.
public void mouseDragged(MouseEvent me) {
  // save coordinates
  mouseX = me.getX();
  mouseY = me.getY();
  msg = "*";
  showStatus("Dragging mouse at " + mouseX + ", " + mouseY);
  repaint();
}

// Handle mouse moved.
public void mouseMoved(MouseEvent me) {
  // show status
  showStatus("Moving mouse at " + me.getX() + ", " + me.getY());
}

// Display msg in applet window at current X,Y location.
public void paint(Graphics g) {
  g.drawString(msg, mouseX, mouseY);
}
}
```

Sample output from this program is shown here:

Let's look closely at this example. The **MouseEvents** class extends **Applet** and implements both the **MouseListener** and **MouseMotionListener** interfaces. These two interfaces contain methods that receive and process the various types of mouse events. Notice that the applet is both the source and the listener for these events. This works because **Component**, which supplies the **addMouseListener()** and **addMouseMotionListener()** methods, is a superclass of **Applet**. Being both the source and the listener for events is a common situation for applets.

Inside **init()**, the applet registers itself as a listener for mouse events. This is done by using **addMouseListener()** and **addMouseMotionListener()**, which, as mentioned, are members of **Component**. They are shown here:

```
void addMouseListener(MouseListener ml)
void addMouseMotionListener(MouseMotionListener mml)
```

Here, *ml* is a reference to the object receiving mouse events, and *mml* is a reference to the object receiving mouse motion events. In this program, the same object is used for both.

The applet then implements all of the methods defined by the **MouseListener** and **MouseMotionListener** interfaces. These are the event handlers for the various mouse events. Each method handles its event and then returns.

Handling Keyboard Events

To handle keyboard events, you use the same general architecture as that shown in the mouse event example in the preceding section. The difference, of course, is that you will be implementing the **KeyListener** interface.

Before looking at an example, it is useful to review how key events are generated. When a key is pressed, a **KEY_PRESSED** event is generated. This results in a call to the **keyPressed()** event handler. When the key is released, a **KEY_RELEASED** event is generated and the **keyReleased()** handler is executed. If a character is generated by the keystroke, then a **KEY_TYPED** event is sent and the **keyTyped()** handler is invoked. Thus, each time the user presses a key, at least two and often three events are generated. If all you care about are actual characters, then you can ignore the information passed by the key press and release events. However, if your program needs to handle special keys, such as the arrow or function keys, then it must watch for them through the **keyPressed()** handler.

There is one other requirement that your program must meet before it can process keyboard events: it must request input focus. To do this, call **requestFocus( )**, which is defined by **Component**. If you don't, then your program will not receive any keyboard events.

The following program demonstrates keyboard input. It echoes keystrokes to the applet window and shows the pressed/released status of each key in the status window.

```
// Demonstrate the key event handlers.
import java.awt.*;
import java.awt.event.*;
import java.applet.*;
/*
  <applet code="SimpleKey" width=300 height=100>
  </applet>
*/

public class SimpleKey extends Applet
  implements KeyListener {

  String msg = "";
  int X = 10, Y = 20; // output coordinates

  public void init() {
    addKeyListener(this);
    requestFocus(); // request input focus
  }

  public void keyPressed(KeyEvent ke) {
    showStatus("Key Down");
  }

  public void keyReleased(KeyEvent ke) {
    showStatus("Key Up");
  }

  public void keyTyped(KeyEvent ke) {
    msg += ke.getKeyChar();
    repaint();
  }

  // Display keystrokes.
  public void paint(Graphics g) {
    g.drawString(msg, X, Y);
  }
}
```

Sample output is shown here:

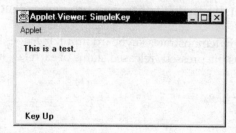

If you want to handle the special keys, such as the arrow or function keys, you need to respond to them within the **keyPressed( )** handler. They are not available through **keyTyped( )**. To identify the keys, you use their virtual key codes. For example, the next applet outputs the name of a few of the special keys:

```java
// Demonstrate some virtual key codes.
import java.awt.*;
import java.awt.event.*;
import java.applet.*;
/*
  <applet code="KeyEvents" width=300 height=100>
  </applet>
*/

public class KeyEvents extends Applet
  implements KeyListener {

  String msg = "";
  int X = 10, Y = 20; // output coordinates

  public void init() {
    addKeyListener(this);
    requestFocus(); // request input focus
  }

  public void keyPressed(KeyEvent ke) {
    showStatus("Key Down");

    int key = ke.getKeyCode();
    switch(key) {
```

```
      case KeyEvent.VK_F1:
        msg += "<F1>";
        break;
      case KeyEvent.VK_F2:
        msg += "<F2>";
        break;
      case KeyEvent.VK_F3:
        msg += "<F3>";
        break;
      case KeyEvent.VK_PAGE_DOWN:
        msg += "<PgDn>";
        break;
      case KeyEvent.VK_PAGE_UP:
        msg += "<PgUp>";
        break;
      case KeyEvent.VK_LEFT:
        msg += "<Left Arrow>";
        break;
      case KeyEvent.VK_RIGHT:
        msg += "<Right Arrow>";
        break;
    }

    repaint();
  }

  public void keyReleased(KeyEvent ke) {
    showStatus("Key Up");
  }

  public void keyTyped(KeyEvent ke) {
    msg += ke.getKeyChar();
    repaint();
  }

  // Display keystrokes.
  public void paint(Graphics g) {
    g.drawString(msg, X, Y);
  }
}
```

Sample output is shown here:

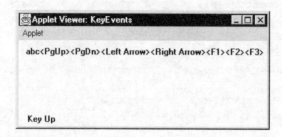

The procedures shown in the preceding keyboard and mouse event examples can be generalized to any type of event handling, including those events generated by controls. In later chapters, you will see many examples that handle other types of events, but they will all follow the same basic structure as the programs just described.

Adapter Classes

Java provides a special feature, called an *adapter class*, that can simplify the creation of event handlers in certain situations. An adapter class provides an empty implementation of all methods in an event listener interface. Adapter classes are useful when you want to receive and process only some of the events that are handled by a particular event listener interface. You can define a new class to act as an event listener by extending one of the adapter classes and implementing only those events in which you are interested.

For example, the **MouseMotionAdapter** class has two methods, **mouseDragged( )** and **mouseMoved( )**. The signatures of these empty methods are exactly as defined in the **MouseMotionListener** interface. If you were interested in only mouse drag events, then you could simply extend **MouseMotionAdapter** and implement **mouseDragged( )**. The empty implementation of **mouseMoved( )** would handle the mouse motion events for you.

Table 20-4 lists the commonly used adapter classes in **java.awt.event** and notes the interface that each implements.

The following example demonstrates an adapter. It displays a message in the status bar of an applet viewer or browser when the mouse is clicked or dragged. However, all other mouse events are silently ignored. The program has three classes. **AdapterDemo** extends **Applet**. Its **init( )** method creates an instance of **MyMouseAdapter** and registers that object to receive notifications of mouse events. It also creates an instance of **MyMouseMotionAdapter** and registers that object to receive notifications of mouse motion events. Both of the constructors take a reference to the applet as an argument.

MyMouseAdapter implements the **mouseClicked( )** method. The other mouse events are silently ignored by code inherited from the **MouseAdapter** class. **MyMouseMotionAdapter** implements the **mouseDragged( )** method. The other mouse motion event is silently ignored by code inherited from the **MouseMotionAdapter** class.

Adapter Class	Listener Interface
ComponentAdapter	ComponentListener
ContainerAdapter	ContainerListener
FocusAdapter	FocusListener
KeyAdapter	KeyListener
MouseAdapter	MouseListener
MouseMotionAdapter	MouseMotionListener
WindowAdapter	WindowListener

Table 20-4.   *Commonly Used Listener Interfaces Implemented by Adapter Classes*

Note that both of our event listener classes save a reference to the applet. This information is provided as an argument to their constructors and is used later to invoke the **showStatus( )** method.

```
// Demonstrate an adapter.
import java.awt.*;
import java.awt.event.*;
import java.applet.*;
/*
  <applet code="AdapterDemo" width=300 height=100>
  </applet>
*/

public class AdapterDemo extends Applet {
  public void init() {
    addMouseListener(new MyMouseAdapter(this));
    addMouseMotionListener(new MyMouseMotionAdapter(this));
  }
}

class MyMouseAdapter extends MouseAdapter {

  AdapterDemo adapterDemo;
  public MyMouseAdapter(AdapterDemo adapterDemo) {
```

```
      this.adapterDemo = adapterDemo;
    }

    // Handle mouse clicked.
    public void mouseClicked(MouseEvent me) {
      adapterDemo.showStatus("Mouse clicked");
    }
  }

  class MyMouseMotionAdapter extends MouseMotionAdapter {
    AdapterDemo adapterDemo;
    public MyMouseMotionAdapter(AdapterDemo adapterDemo) {
      this.adapterDemo = adapterDemo;
    }

    // Handle mouse dragged.
    public void mouseDragged(MouseEvent me) {
      adapterDemo.showStatus("Mouse dragged");
    }
  }
```

As you can see by looking at the program, not having to implement all of the methods defined by the **MouseMotionListener** and **MouseListener** interfaces saves you a considerable amount of effort and prevents your code from becoming cluttered with empty methods. As an exercise, you might want to try rewriting one of the keyboard input examples shown earlier so that it uses a **KeyAdapter**.

Inner Classes

In Chapter 7, the basics of inner classes were explained. Here you will see why they are important. Recall that an *inner class* is a class defined within other class, or even within an expression. This section illustrates how inner classes can be used to simplify the code when using event adapter classes.

To understand the benefit provided by inner classes, consider the applet shown in the following listing. It *does not* use an inner class. Its goal is to display the string "Mouse Pressed" in the status bar of the applet viewer or browser when the mouse is pressed. There are two top-level classes in this program. **MousePressedDemo** extends **Applet**, and **MyMouseAdapter** extends **MouseAdapter**. The **init( )** method of **MousePressedDemo** instantiates **MyMouseAdapter** and provides this object as an argument to the **addMouseListener( )** method.

Notice that a reference to the applet is supplied as an argument to the **MyMouseAdapter** constructor. This reference is stored in an instance variable for later use by the **mousePressed( )** method. When the mouse is pressed, it invokes the **showStatus( )** method of the applet through the stored applet reference. In other words, **showStatus( )** is invoked relative to the applet reference stored by **MyMouseAdapter**.

```
// This applet does NOT use an inner class.
import java.applet.*;
import java.awt.event.*;
/*
  <applet code="MousePressedDemo" width=200 height=100>
  </applet>
*/

public class MousePressedDemo extends Applet {
  public void init() {
    addMouseListener(new MyMouseAdapter(this));
  }
}

class MyMouseAdapter extends MouseAdapter {
  MousePressedDemo mousePressedDemo;
  public MyMouseAdapter(MousePressedDemo mousePressedDemo) {
    this.mousePressedDemo = mousePressedDemo;
  }
  public void mousePressed(MouseEvent me) {
    mousePressedDemo.showStatus("Mouse Pressed.");
  }
}
```

The following listing shows how the preceding program can be improved by using an inner class. Here, **InnerClassDemo** is a top-level class that extends **Applet**. **MyMouseAdapter** is an inner class that extends **MouseAdapter**. Because **MyMouseAdapter** is defined within the scope of **InnerClassDemo**, it has access to all of the variables and methods within the scope of that class. Therefore, the **mousePressed( )** method can call the **showStatus( )** method directly. It no longer needs to do this via a stored reference to the applet. Thus, it is no longer necessary to pass **MyMouseAdapter( )** a reference to the invoking object.

```
// Inner class demo.
import java.applet.*;
import java.awt.event.*;
/*
  <applet code="InnerClassDemo" width=200 height=100>
  </applet>
*/
```

```
public class InnerClassDemo extends Applet {
  public void init() {
    addMouseListener(new MyMouseAdapter());
  }
  class MyMouseAdapter extends MouseAdapter {
    public void mousePressed(MouseEvent me) {
      showStatus("Mouse Pressed");
    }
  }
}
```

Anonymous Inner Classes

An *anonymous* inner class is one that is not assigned a name. This section illustrates how an anonymous inner class can facilitate the writing of event handlers. Consider the applet shown in the following listing. As before, its goal is to display the string "Mouse Pressed" in the status bar of the applet viewer or browser when the mouse is pressed.

```
// Anonymous inner class demo.
import java.applet.*;
import java.awt.event.*;
/*
  <applet code="AnonymousInnerClassDemo" width=200 height=100>
  </applet>
*/

public class AnonymousInnerClassDemo extends Applet {
  public void init() {
    addMouseListener(new MouseAdapter() {
      public void mousePressed(MouseEvent me) {
        showStatus("Mouse Pressed");
      }
    });
  }
}
```

There is one top-level class in this program: **AnonymousInnerClassDemo**. The **init( )** method calls the **addMouseListener( )** method. Its argument is an expression that defines and instantiates an anonymous inner class. Let's analyze this expression carefully.

The syntax **new MouseAdapter( ) { ... }** indicates to the compiler that the code between the braces defines an anonymous inner class. Furthermore, that class extends **MouseAdapter**. This new class is not named, but it is automatically instantiated when this expression is executed.

Because this anonymous inner class is defined within the scope of **AnonymousInnerClassDemo**, it has access to all of the variables and methods within the scope of that class. Therefore, it can call the **showStatus( )** method directly.

As just illustrated, both named and anonymous inner classes solve some annoying problems in a simple yet effective way. They also allow you to create more efficient code.

The
Complete
Reference

Chapter 21

Introducing the AWT: Working with Windows, Graphics, and Text

T he Abstract Window Toolkit (AWT) was introduced in Chapter 19 because it provides support for applets. This chapter begins its in-depth examination. The AWT contains numerous classes and methods that allow you to create and manage windows. A full description of the AWT would easily fill an entire book. Therefore, it is not possible to describe in detail every method, instance variable, or class contained in the AWT. However, this and the following two chapters explain the techniques needed to effectively use the AWT when creating your own applets or stand-alone programs. From there, you will be able to explore other parts of the AWT on your own.

In this chapter, you will learn how to create and manage windows, manage fonts, output text, and utilize graphics. Chapter 22 describes the various controls, such as scroll bars and push buttons, supported by the AWT. It also explains further aspects of Java's event-handling mechanism. Chapter 23 examines the AWT's imaging subsystem and animation.

Although the main purpose of the AWT is to support applet windows, it can also be used to create stand-alone windows that run in a GUI environment, such as Windows. Most of the examples are contained in applets, so to run them, you need to use an applet viewer or a Java-compatible Web browser. A few examples will demonstrate the creation of stand-alone, windowed programs.

If you have not yet read Chapter 20, please do so now. It provides an overview of event handling, which is used by many of the examples in this chapter.

AWT Classes

The AWT classes are contained in the **java.awt** package. It is one of Java's largest packages. Fortunately, because it is logically organized in a top-down, hierarchical fashion, it is easier to understand and use than you might at first believe. Table 21-1 lists some of the many AWT classes.

Class	Description
AWTEvent	Encapsulates AWT events.
AWTEventMulticaster	Dispatches events to multiple listeners.
BorderLayout	The border layout manager. Border layouts use five components: North, South, East, West, and Center.
Button	Creates a push button control.

Table 21-1.   *Some AWT Classes*

Class	Description
Canvas	A blank, semantics-free window.
CardLayout	The card layout manager. Card layouts emulate index cards. Only the one on top is showing.
Checkbox	Creates a check box control.
CheckboxGroup	Creates a group of check box controls.
CheckboxMenuItem	Creates an on/off menu item.
Choice	Creates a pop-up list.
Color	Manages colors in a portable, platform-independent fashion.
Component	An abstract superclass for various AWT components.
Container	A subclass of **Component** that can hold other components.
Cursor	Encapsulates a bitmapped cursor.
Dialog	Creates a dialog window.
Dimension	Specifies the dimensions of an object. The width is stored in **width**, and the height is stored in **height**.
Event	Encapsulates events.
EventQueue	Queues events.
FileDialog	Creates a window from which a file can be selected.
FlowLayout	The flow layout manager. Flow layout positions components left to right, top to bottom.
Font	Encapsulates a type font.
FontMetrics	Encapsulates various information related to a font. This information helps you display text in a window.
Frame	Creates a standard window that has a title bar, resize corners, and a menu bar.
Graphics	Encapsulates the graphics context. This context is used by the various output methods to display output in a window.
GraphicsDevice	Describes a graphics device such as a screen or printer.

Table 21-1. *Some AWT Classes* (continued)

Class	Description
GraphicsEnvironment	Describes the collection of available **Font** and **GraphicsDevice** objects.
GridBagConstraints	Defines various constraints relating to the **GridBagLayout** class.
GridBagLayout	The grid bag layout manager. Grid bag layout displays components subject to the constraints specified by **GridBagConstraints**.
GridLayout	The grid layout manager. Grid layout displays components in a two-dimensional grid.
Image	Encapsulates graphical images.
Insets	Encapsulates the borders of a container.
Label	Creates a label that displays a string.
List	Creates a list from which the user can choose. Similar to the standard Windows list box.
MediaTracker	Manages media objects.
Menu	Creates a pull-down menu.
MenuBar	Creates a menu bar.
MenuComponent	An abstract class implemented by various menu classes.
MenuItem	Creates a menu item.
MenuShortcut	Encapsulates a keyboard shortcut for a menu item.
Panel	The simplest concrete subclass of **Container**.
Point	Encapsulates a Cartesian coordinate pair, stored in x and y.
Polygon	Encapsulates a polygon.
PopupMenu	Encapsulates a pop-up menu.
PrintJob	An abstract class that represents a print job.
Rectangle	Encapsulates a rectangle.
Robot	Supports automated testing of AWT- based applications. (Added by Java 2, vl.3)
Scrollbar	Creates a scroll bar control.

Table 21-1. *Some AWT Classes* (continued)

Class	Description
ScrollPane	A container that provides horizontal and/or vertical scroll bars for another component.
SystemColor	Contains the colors of GUI widgets such as windows, scroll bars, text, and others.
TextArea	Creates a multiline edit control.
TextComponent	A superclass for **TextArea** and **TextField**.
TextField	Creates a single-line edit control.
Toolkit	Abstract class implemented by the AWT.
Window	Creates a window with no frame, no menu bar, and no title.

Table 21-1.   *Some AWT Classes* (continued)

Although the basic structure of the AWT has been the same since Java 1.0, some of the original methods were deprecated and replaced by new ones when Java 1.1 was released. For backward-compatibility, Java 2 still supports all the original 1.0 methods. However, because these methods are not for use with new code, this book does not describe them.

Window Fundamentals

The AWT defines windows according to a class hierarchy that adds functionality and specificity with each level. The two most common windows are those derived from **Panel**, which is used by applets, and those derived from **Frame**, which creates a standard window. Much of the functionality of these windows is derived from their parent classes. Thus, a description of the class hierarchies relating to these two classes is fundamental to their understanding. Figure 21-1 shows the class hierarchy for **Panel** and **Frame**. Let's look at each of these classes now.

Component

At the top of the AWT hierarchy is the **Component** class. **Component** is an abstract class that encapsulates all of the attributes of a visual component. All user interface elements that are displayed on the screen and that interact with the user are subclasses of **Component**. It defines over a hundred public methods that are responsible for managing events, such as mouse and keyboard input, positioning and sizing the window, and repainting. (You already used many of these methods when you created applets in Chapters 19 and 20.) A **Component** object is responsible for remembering the current foreground and background colors and the currently selected text font.

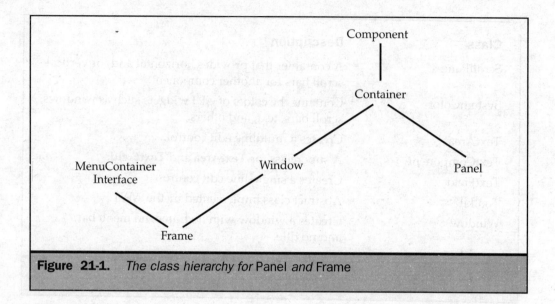

Figure 21-1. *The class hierarchy for* Panel *and* Frame

Container

The **Container** class is a subclass of **Component**. It has additional methods that allow other **Component** objects to be nested within it. Other **Container** objects can be stored inside of a **Container** (since they are themselves instances of **Component**). This makes for a multileveled containment system. A container is responsible for laying out (that is, positioning) any components that it contains. It does this through the use of various layout managers, which you will learn about in Chapter 22.

Panel

The **Panel** class is a concrete subclass of **Container**. It doesn't add any new methods; it simply implements **Container**. A **Panel** may be thought of as a recursively nestable, concrete screen component. **Panel** is the superclass for **Applet**. When screen output is directed to an applet, it is drawn on the surface of a **Panel** object. In essence, a **Panel** is a window that does not contain a title bar, menu bar, or border. This is why you don't see these items when an applet is run inside a browser. When you run an applet using an applet viewer, the applet viewer provides the title and border.

Other components can be added to a **Panel** object by its **add( )** method (inherited from **Container**). Once these components have been added, you can position and resize them manually using the **setLocation( )**, **setSize( )**, or **setBounds( )** methods defined by **Component**.

Window

The **Window** class creates a top-level window. A *top-level window* is not contained within any other object; it sits directly on the desktop. Generally, you won't create **Window** objects directly. Instead, you will use a subclass of **Window** called **Frame**, described next.

Frame

Frame encapsulates what is commonly thought of as a "window." It is a subclass of **Window** and has a title bar, menu bar, borders, and resizing corners. If you create a **Frame** object from within an applet, it will contain a warning message, such as "Java Applet Window," to the user that an applet window has been created. This message warns users that the window they see was started by an applet and not by software running on their computer. (An applet that could masquerade as a host-based application could be used to obtain passwords and other sensitive information without the user's knowledge.) When a **Frame** window is created by a program rather than an applet, a normal window is created.

Canvas

Although it is not part of the hierarchy for applet or frame windows, there is one other type of window that you will find valuable: **Canvas**. **Canvas** encapsulates a blank window upon which you can draw. You will see an example of **Canvas** later in this book.

Working with Frame Windows

After the applet, the type of window you will most often create is derived from **Frame**. You will use it to create child windows within applets, and top-level or child windows for applications. As mentioned, it creates a standard-style window.

Here are two of **Frame**'s constructors:

Frame( )
Frame(String *title*)

The first form creates a standard window that does not contain a title. The second form creates a window with the title specified by *title*. Notice that you cannot specify the dimensions of the window. Instead, you must set the size of the window after it has been created.

There are several methods you will use when working with **Frame** windows. They are examined here.

Setting the Window's Dimensions

The **setSize( )** method is used to set the dimensions of the window. Its signature is shown here:

    void setSize(int *newWidth*, int *newHeight*)
    void setSize(Dimension *newSize*)

The new size of the window is specified by *newWidth* and *newHeight*, or by the **width** and **height** fields of the **Dimension** object passed in *newSize*. The dimensions are specified in terms of pixels.

The **getSize( )** method is used to obtain the current size of a window. Its signature is shown here:

    Dimension getSize( )

This method returns the current size of the window contained within the **width** and **height** fields of a **Dimension** object.

Hiding and Showing a Window

After a frame window has been created, it will not be visible until you call **setVisible( )**. Its signature is shown here:

    void setVisible(boolean *visibleFlag*)

The component is visible if the argument to this method is **true**. Otherwise, it is hidden.

Setting a Window's Title

You can change the title in a frame window using **setTitle( )**, which has this general form:

    void setTitle(String *newTitle*)

Here, *newTitle* is the new title for the window.

Closing a Frame Window

When using a frame window, your program must remove that window from the screen when it is closed, by calling **setVisible(false)**. To intercept a window-close event, you must implement the **windowClosing( )** method of the **WindowListener** interface. Inside **windowClosing( )**, you must remove the window from the screen. The example in the next section illustrates this technique.

Creating a Frame Window in an Applet

While it is possible to simply create a window by creating an instance of **Frame**, you will seldom do so, because you will not be able to do much with it. For example, you will not be able to receive or process events that occur within it or easily output information to it. Most of the time, you will create a subclass of **Frame**. Doing so lets you override **Frame**'s methods and event handling.

Creating a new frame window from within an applet is actually quite easy. First, create a subclass of **Frame**. Next, override any of the standard window methods, such as **init( )**, **start( )**, **stop( )**, and **paint( )**. Finally, implement the **windowClosing( )** method of the **WindowListener** interface, calling **setVisible(false)** when the window is closed.

Once you have defined a **Frame** subclass, you can create an object of that class. This causes a frame window to come into existence, but it will not be initially visible. You make it visible by calling **setVisible( )**. When created, the window is given a default height and width. You can set the size of the window explicitly by calling the **setSize( )** method.

The following applet creates a subclass of **Frame** called **SampleFrame**. A window of this subclass is instantiated within the **init( )** method of **AppletFrame**. Notice that **SampleFrame** calls **Frame**'s constructor. This causes a standard frame window to be created with the title passed in **title**. This example overrides the applet window's **start( )** and **stop( )** methods so that they show and hide the child window, respectively. This causes the window to be removed automatically when you terminate the applet, when you close the window, or, if using a browser, when you move to another page. It also causes the child window to be shown when the browser returns to the applet.

```
// Create a child frame window from within an applet.
import java.awt.*;
import java.awt.event.*;
import java.applet.*;
/*
  <applet code="AppletFrame" width=300 height=50>
  </applet>
*/

// Create a subclass of Frame.
class SampleFrame extends Frame {
  SampleFrame(String title) {
    super(title);
    // create an object to handle window events
    MyWindowAdapter adapter = new MyWindowAdapter(this);
      // register it to receive those events
```

```
      addWindowListener(adapter);
  }
  public void paint(Graphics g) {
    g.drawString("This is in frame window", 10, 40);
  }
}

class MyWindowAdapter extends WindowAdapter {
  SampleFrame sampleFrame;
  public MyWindowAdapter(SampleFrame sampleFrame) {
    this.sampleFrame = sampleFrame;
  }
  public void windowClosing(WindowEvent we) {
    sampleFrame.setVisible(false);
  }
}

// Create frame window.
public class AppletFrame extends Applet {
  Frame f;
  public void init() {
    f = new SampleFrame("A Frame Window");

    f.setSize(250, 250);
    f.setVisible(true);
  }
  public void start() {
    f.setVisible(true);
  }
  public void stop() {
    f.setVisible(false);
  }
  public void paint(Graphics g) {
    g.drawString("This is in applet window", 10, 20);
  }
}
```

Sample output from this program is shown here:

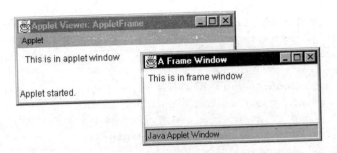

Handling Events in a Frame Window

Since **Frame** is a subclass of **Component**, it inherits all the capabilities defined by **Component**. This means that you can use and manage a frame window that you create just like you manage your applet's main window. For example, you can override **paint( )** to display output, call **repaint( )** when you need to restore the window, and override all event handlers. Whenever an event occurs in a window, the event handlers defined by that window will be called. Each window handles its own events. For example, the following program creates a window that responds to mouse events. The main applet window also responds to mouse events. When you experiment with this program, you will see that mouse events are sent to the window in which the event occurs.

```java
// Handle mouse events in both child and applet windows.
import java.awt.*;
import java.awt.event.*;
import java.applet.*;
/*
  <applet code="WindowEvents" width=300 height=50>
  </applet>
*/

// Create a subclass of Frame.
class SampleFrame extends Frame
  implements MouseListener, MouseMotionListener {

  String msg = "";
  int mouseX=10, mouseY=40;
  int movX=0, movY=0;
```

```
SampleFrame(String title) {
  super(title);
  // register this object to receive its own mouse events
  addMouseListener(this);
  addMouseMotionListener(this);
  // create an object to handle window events
  MyWindowAdapter adapter = new MyWindowAdapter(this);
  // register it to receive those events
  addWindowListener(adapter);
}

// Handle mouse clicked.
public void mouseClicked(MouseEvent me) {
}

// Handle mouse entered.
public void mouseEntered(MouseEvent evtObj) {
  // save coordinates
  mouseX = 10;
  mouseY = 54;
  msg = "Mouse just entered child.";
  repaint();
}

// Handle mouse exited.
public void mouseExited(MouseEvent evtObj) {
  // save coordinates
  mouseX = 10;
  mouseY = 54;
  msg = "Mouse just left child window.";
  repaint();
}

// Handle mouse pressed.
public void mousePressed(MouseEvent me) {
  // save coordinates
  mouseX = me.getX();
  mouseY = me.getY();
  msg = "Down";
  repaint();
}
// Handle mouse released.
```

```java
  public void mouseReleased(MouseEvent me) {
    // save coordinates
    mouseX = me.getX();
    mouseY = me.getY();
    msg = "Up";
    repaint();
  }

  // Handle mouse dragged.
  public void mouseDragged(MouseEvent me) {
    // save coordinates
    mouseX = me.getX();
    mouseY = me.getY();
    movX = me.getX();
    movY = me.getY();
    msg = "*";
    repaint();
  }

  // Handle mouse moved.
  public void mouseMoved(MouseEvent me) {
    // save coordinates
    movX = me.getX();
    movY = me.getY();
    repaint(0, 0, 100, 60);
  }

  public void paint(Graphics g) {
    g.drawString(msg, mouseX, mouseY);
    g.drawString("Mouse at " + movX + ", " + movY, 10, 40);
  }
}

class MyWindowAdapter extends WindowAdapter {
  SampleFrame sampleFrame;
  public MyWindowAdapter(SampleFrame sampleFrame) {
    this.sampleFrame = sampleFrame;
  }
  public void windowClosing(WindowEvent we) {
    sampleFrame.setVisible(false);
  }
}
```

```java
// Applet window.
public class WindowEvents extends Applet
  implements MouseListener, MouseMotionListener {

  SampleFrame f;
  String msg = "";
  int mouseX=0, mouseY=10;
  int movX=0, movY=0;

  // Create a frame window.
  public void init() {
    f = new SampleFrame("Handle Mouse Events");
    f.setSize(300, 200);
    f.setVisible(true);

    // register this object to receive its own mouse events
    addMouseListener(this);
    addMouseMotionListener(this);
  }

  // Remove frame window when stopping applet.
  public void stop() {
    f.setVisible(false);
  }

  // Show frame window when starting applet.
  public void start() {
    f.setVisible(true);
  }

  // Handle mouse clicked.
  public void mouseClicked(MouseEvent me) {
  }

  // Handle mouse entered.
  public void mouseEntered(MouseEvent me) {
    // save coordinates
    mouseX = 0;
    mouseY = 24;
    msg = "Mouse just entered applet window.";
    repaint();
```

```
  }

  // Handle mouse exited.
  public void mouseExited(MouseEvent me) {
    // save coordinates
    mouseX = 0;
    mouseY = 24;
    msg = "Mouse just left applet window.";
    repaint();
  }

  // Handle button pressed.
  public void mousePressed(MouseEvent me) {
    // save coordinates
    mouseX = me.getX();
    mouseY = me.getY();
    msg = "Down";
    repaint();
  }

  // Handle button released.
  public void mouseReleased(MouseEvent me) {
    // save coordinates
    mouseX = me.getX();
    mouseY = me.getY();
    msg = "Up";
    repaint();
  }

  // Handle mouse dragged.
  public void mouseDragged(MouseEvent me) {
    // save coordinates
    mouseX = me.getX();
    mouseY = me.getY();
    movX = me.getX();
    movY = me.getY();
    msg = "*";
    repaint();
  }

  // Handle mouse moved.
  public void mouseMoved(MouseEvent me) {
```

```
    // save coordinates
    movX = me.getX();
    movY = me.getY();
    repaint(0, 0, 100, 20);
}

// Display msg in applet window.
public void paint(Graphics g) {
    g.drawString(msg, mouseX, mouseY);
    g.drawString("Mouse at " + movX + ", " + movY, 0, 10);
}
}
```

Sample output from this program is shown here:

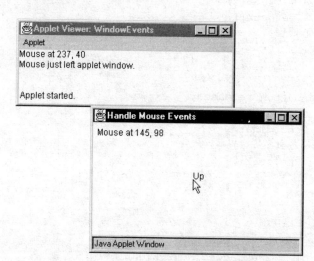

Creating a Windowed Program

Although creating applets is the most common use for Java's AWT, it is possible to create stand-alone AWT-based applications, too. To do this, simply create an instance of the window or windows you need inside **main( )**. For example, the following program creates a frame window that responds to mouse clicks and keystrokes:

```
// Create an AWT-based application.
import java.awt.*;
```

```java
import java.awt.event.*;
import java.applet.*;

// Create a frame window.
public class AppWindow extends Frame {
  String keymsg = "This is a test.";
  String mousemsg = "";
  int mouseX=30, mouseY=30;

  public AppWindow() {
    addKeyListener(new MyKeyAdapter(this));
    addMouseListener(new MyMouseAdapter(this));
    addWindowListener(new MyWindowAdapter());
  }

  public void paint(Graphics g) {
    g.drawString(keymsg, 10, 40);
    g.drawString(mousemsg, mouseX, mouseY);
  }

  // Create the window.
  public static void main(String args[]) {
    AppWindow appwin = new AppWindow();

    appwin.setSize(new Dimension(300, 200));
    appwin.setTitle("An AWT-Based Application");
    appwin.setVisible(true);
  }
}

class MyKeyAdapter extends KeyAdapter {
  AppWindow appWindow;
  public MyKeyAdapter(AppWindow appWindow) {
    this.appWindow = appWindow;
  }
  public void keyTyped(KeyEvent ke) {
    appWindow.keymsg += ke.getKeyChar();
    appWindow.repaint();
  };
}

class MyMouseAdapter extends MouseAdapter {
```

```
    AppWindow appWindow;
    public MyMouseAdapter(AppWindow appWindow) {
      this.appWindow = appWindow;
    }
    public void mousePressed(MouseEvent me) {
      appWindow.mouseX = me.getX();
      appWindow.mouseY = me.getY();
      appWindow.mousemsg = "Mouse Down at " + appWindow.mouseX +
                          ", " + appWindow.mouseY;
      appWindow.repaint();
    }
  }

class MyWindowAdapter extends WindowAdapter {
  public void windowClosing(WindowEvent we) {
    System.exit(0);
  }
}
```

Sample output from this program is shown here:

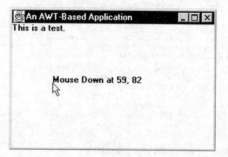

Once created, a frame window takes on a life of its own. Notice that **main( )** ends with the call to **appwin.setVisible(true)**. However, the program keeps running until you close the window. In essence, when creating a windowed application, you will use **main( )** to launch its top-level window. After that, your program will function as a GUI-based application, not like the console-based programs used earlier.

Displaying Information Within a Window

In the most general sense, a window is a container for information. Although we have already output small amounts of text to a window in the preceding examples, we have not begun to take advantage of a window's ability to present high-quality text and graphics. Indeed, much of the power of the AWT comes from its support for these items. For this reason, the remainder of this chapter discusses Java's text-, graphics-, and font-handling capabilities. As you will see, they are both powerful and flexible.

Working with Graphics

The AWT supports a rich assortment of graphics methods. All graphics are drawn relative to a window. This can be the main window of an applet, a child window of an applet, or a stand-alone application window. The origin of each window is at the top-left corner and is 0,0. Coordinates are specified in pixels. All output to a window takes place through a graphics context. A *graphics context* is encapsulated by the **Graphics** class and is obtained in two ways:

- It is passed to an applet when one of its various methods, such as **paint( )** or **update( )**, is called.
- It is returned by the **getGraphics( )** method of **Component**.

For the remainder of the examples in this chapter, we will be demonstrating graphics in the main applet window. However, the same techniques will apply to any other window.

The **Graphics** class defines a number of drawing functions. Each shape can be drawn edge-only or filled. Objects are drawn and filled in the currently selected graphics color, which is black by default. When a graphics object is drawn that exceeds the dimensions of the window, output is automatically clipped. Let's take a look at several of the drawing methods.

Drawing Lines

Lines are drawn by means of the **drawLine( )** method, shown here:

void drawLine(int *startX*, int *startY*, int *endX*, int *endY*)

drawLine( ) displays a line in the current drawing color that begins at *startX,startY* and ends at *endX,endY*.

The following applet draws several lines:

```
// Draw lines
import java.awt.*;
import java.applet.*;
/*
<applet code="Lines" width=300 height=200>
```

```
</applet>
*/
public class Lines extends Applet {
  public void paint(Graphics g) {
    g.drawLine(0, 0, 100, 100);
    g.drawLine(0, 100, 100, 0);
    g.drawLine(40, 25, 250, 180);
    g.drawLine(75, 90, 400, 400);
    g.drawLine(20, 150, 400, 40);
    g.drawLine(5, 290, 80, 19);
  }
}
```

Sample output from this program is shown here:

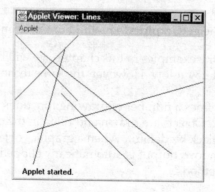

Drawing Rectangles

The **drawRect( )** and **fillRect( )** methods display an outlined and filled rectangle, respectively. They are shown here:

> void drawRect(int *top*, int *left*, int *width*, int *height*)
> void fillRect(int *top*, int *left*, int *width*, int *height*)

The upper-left corner of the rectangle is at *top,left*. The dimensions of the rectangle are specified by *width* and *height*.

To draw a rounded rectangle, use **drawRoundRect( )** or **fillRoundRect( )**, both shown here:

> void drawRoundRect(int *top*, int *left*, int *width*, int *height*,
>   int *xDiam*, int *yDiam*)

void fillRoundRect(int *top*, int *left*, int *width*, int *height*,
int *xDiam*, int *yDiam*)

A rounded rectangle has rounded corners. The upper-left corner of the rectangle
is at *top,left*. The dimensions of the rectangle are specified by *width* and *height*. The
diameter of the rounding arc along the X axis is specified by *xDiam*. The diameter of
the rounding arc along the Y axis is specified by *yDiam*.

The following applet draws several rectangles:

```
// Draw rectangles
import java.awt.*;
import java.applet.*;
/*
<applet code="Rectangles" width=300 height=200>
</applet>
*/

public class Rectangles extends Applet {
  public void paint(Graphics g) {
    g.drawRect(10, 10, 60, 50);
    g.fillRect(100, 10, 60, 50);
    g.drawRoundRect(190, 10, 60, 50, 15, 15);
    g.fillRoundRect(70, 90, 140, 100, 30, 40);
  }
}
```

Sample output from this program is shown here:

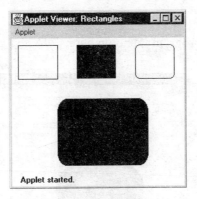

Drawing Ellipses and Circles

To draw an ellipse, use **drawOval( )**. To fill an ellipse, use **fillOval( )**. These methods are shown here:

void drawOval(int *top*, int *left*, int *width*, int *height*)
void fillOval(int *top*, int *left*, int *width*, int *height*)

The ellipse is drawn within a bounding rectangle whose upper-left corner is specified by *top,left* and whose width and height are specified by *width* and *height*.
To draw a circle, specify a square as the bounding rectangle.
The following program draws several ellipses:

```
// Draw Ellipses
import java.awt.*;
import java.applet.*;
/*
<applet code="Ellipses" width=300 height=200>
</applet>
*/

public class Ellipses extends Applet {
  public void paint(Graphics g) {
    g.drawOval(10, 10, 50, 50);
    g.fillOval(100, 10, 75, 50);
    g.drawOval(190, 10, 90, 30);
    g.fillOval(70, 90, 140, 100);
  }
}
```

Sample output from this program is shown here:

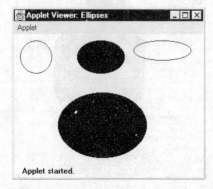

Drawing Arcs

Arcs can be drawn with **drawArc( )** and **fillArc( )**, shown here:

void drawArc(int *top*, int *left*, int *width*, int *height*, int *startAngle*,
              int *sweepAngle*)

void fillArc(int *top*, int *left*, int *width*, int *height*, int *startAngle*,
              int *sweepAngle*)

The arc is bounded by the rectangle whose upper-left corner is specified by *top,left*
and whose width and height are specified by *width* and *height*. The arc is drawn from
startAngle through the angular distance specified by *sweepAngle*. Angles are specified
in degrees. Zero degrees is on the horizontal, at the three o'clock position. The arc is
drawn counterclockwise if *sweepAngle* is positive, and clockwise if *sweepAngle* is
negative. Therefore, to draw an arc from twelve o'clock to six o'clock, the start angle
would be 90 and the sweep angle 180.

The following applet draws several arcs:

```
// Draw Arcs
import java.awt.*;
import java.applet.*;
/*
<applet code="Arcs" width=300 height=200>
</applet>
*/

public class Arcs extends Applet {
  public void paint(Graphics g) {
    g.drawArc(10, 40, 70, 70, 0, 75);
    g.fillArc(100, 40, 70, 70, 0, 75);
    g.drawArc(10, 100, 70, 80, 0, 175);
    g.fillArc(100, 100, 70, 90, 0, 270);
    g.drawArc(200, 80, 80, 80, 0, 180);
  }
}
```

THE JAVA LIBRARY

Sample output from this program is shown here:

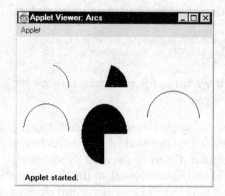

Drawing Polygons

It is possible to draw arbitrarily shaped figures using **drawPolygon( )** and **fillPolygon( )**, shown here:

> void drawPolygon(int *x*[ ], int *y*[ ], int *numPoints*)
> void fillPolygon(int *x*[ ], int *y*[ ], int *numPoints*)

The polygon's endpoints are specified by the coordinate pairs contained within the *x* and *y* arrays. The number of points defined by *x* and *y* is specified by *numPoints*. There are alternative forms of these methods in which the polygon is specified by a **Polygon** object.

The following applet draws an hourglass shape:

```
// Draw Polygon
import java.awt.*;
import java.applet.*;
/*
<applet code="HourGlass" width=230 height=210>
</applet>
*/

public class HourGlass extends Applet {
  public void paint(Graphics g) {
    int xpoints[] = {30, 200, 30, 200, 30};
    int ypoints[] = {30, 30, 200, 200, 30};
    int num = 5;

    g.drawPolygon(xpoints, ypoints, num);
```

```
    }
}
```

Sample output from this program is shown here:

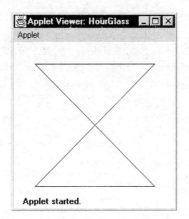

Sizing Graphics

Often, you will want to size a graphics object to fit the current size of the window in which it is drawn. To do so, first obtain the current dimensions of the window by calling **getSize( )** on the window object. It returns the dimensions of the window encapsulated within a **Dimension** object. Once you have the current size of the window, you can scale your graphical output accordingly.

To demonstrate this technique, here is an applet that will start as a 200×200-pixel square and grow by 25 pixels in width and height with each mouse click until the applet gets larger than 500×500. At that point, the next click will return it to 200×200, and the process starts over. Within the window, a rectangle is drawn around the inner border of the window; within that rectangle, an *X* is drawn so that it fills the window. This applet works in **appletviewer**, but it may not work in a browser window.

```
// Resizing output to fit the current size of a window.
import java.applet.*;
import java.awt.*;
import java.awt.event.*;
/*
   <applet code="ResizeMe" width=200 height=200>
   </applet>
*/
```

```
public class ResizeMe extends Applet {
  final int inc = 25;
  int max = 500;
  int min = 200;
  Dimension d;

  public ResizeMe() {
    addMouseListener(new MouseAdapter() {
      public void mouseReleased(MouseEvent me) {
        int w = (d.width + inc) > max?min :(d.width + inc);
        int h = (d.height + inc) > max?min :(d.height + inc);
        setSize(new Dimension(w, h));
      }
    });
  }
  public void paint(Graphics g) {
    d = getSize();

    g.drawLine(0, 0, d.width-1, d.height-1);
    g.drawLine(0, d.height-1, d.width-1, 0);
    g.drawRect(0, 0, d.width-1, d.height-1);
  }
}
```

Working with Color

Java supports color in a portable, device-independent fashion. The AWT color system allows you to specify any color you want. It then finds the best match for that color, given the limits of the display hardware currently executing your program or applet. Thus, your code does not need to be concerned with the differences in the way color is supported by various hardware devices. Color is encapsulated by the **Color** class.

As you saw in Chapter 19, **Color** defines several constants (for example, **Color.black**) to specify a number of common colors. You can also create your own colors, using one of the color constructors. The most commonly used forms are shown here:

Color(int *red*, int *green*, int *blue*)
Color(int *rgbValue*)
Color(float *red*, float *green*, float *blue*)

The first constructor takes three integers that specify the color as a mix of red, green, and blue. These values must be between 0 and 255, as in this example:

```
new Color(255, 100, 100); // light red.
```

The second color constructor takes a single integer that contains the mix of red, green, and blue packed into an integer. The integer is organized with red in bits 16 to 23, green in bits 8 to 15, and blue in bits 0 to 7. Here is an example of this constructor:

```
int newRed = (0xff000000 | (0xc0 << 16) | (0x00 << 8) | 0x00);
Color darkRed = new Color(newRed);
```

The final constructor, **Color(float, float, float)**, takes three float values (between 0.0 and 1.0) that specify the relative mix of red, green, and blue.

Once you have created a color, you can use it to set the foreground and/or background color by using the **setForeground( )** and **setBackground( )** methods described in Chapter 19. You can also select it as the current drawing color.

Color Methods

The **Color** class defines several methods that help manipulate colors. They are examined here.

Using Hue, Saturation, and Brightness

The *hue-saturation-brightness (HSB)* color model is an alternative to red-green-blue (RGB) for specifying particular colors. Figuratively, *hue* is a wheel of color. The hue is specified with a number between 0.0 and 1.0 (the colors are approximately: red, orange, yellow, green, blue, indigo, and violet). *Saturation* is another scale ranging from 0.0 to 1.0, representing light pastels to intense hues. *Brightness* values also range from 0.0 to 1.0, where 1 is bright white and 0 is black. **Color** supplies two methods that let you convert between RGB and HSB. They are shown here:

static int HSBtoRGB(float *hue*, float *saturation*, float *brightness*)
static float[ ] RGBtoHSB(int *red*, int *green*, int *blue*, float *values*[ ])

HSBtoRGB( ) returns a packed RGB value compatible with the **Color(int)** constructor. **RGBtoHSB( )** returns a float array of HSB values corresponding to RGB integers. If *values* is not **null**, then this array is given the HSB values and returned. Otherwise, a new array is created and the HSB values are returned in it. In either case, the array contains the hue at index 0, saturation at index 1, and brightness at index 2.

getRed( ), getGreen( ), getBlue( )

You can obtain the red, green, and blue components of a color independently using **getRed( )**, **getGreen( )**, and **getBlue( )**, shown here:

int getRed( )
int getGreen( )
int getBlue( )

Each of these methods returns the RGB color component found in the invoking **Color** object in the lower 8 bits of an integer.

getRGB( )

To obtain a packed, RGB representation of a color, use **getRGB( )**, shown here:

    int getRGB( )

The return value is organized as described earlier.

Setting the Current Graphics Color

By default, graphics objects are drawn in the current foreground color. You can change this color by calling the **Graphics** method **setColor( )**:

    void setColor(Color newColor)

Here, newColor specifies the new drawing color.
You can obtain the current color by calling **getColor( )**, shown here:

    Color getColor( )

A Color Demonstration Applet

The following applet constructs several colors and draws various objects using these colors:

```
// Demonstrate color.
import java.awt.*;
import java.applet.*;
/*
<applet code="ColorDemo" width=300 height=200>
</applet>
*/

public class ColorDemo extends Applet {
  // draw lines
  public void paint(Graphics g) {
    Color c1 = new Color(255, 100, 100);
    Color c2 = new Color(100, 255, 100);
    Color c3 = new Color(100, 100, 255);

    g.setColor(c1);
    g.drawLine(0, 0, 100, 100);
```

```
    g.drawLine(0, 100, 100, 0);

    g.setColor(c2);
    g.drawLine(40, 25, 250, 180);
    g.drawLine(75, 90, 400, 400);

    g.setColor(c3);
    g.drawLine(20, 150, 400, 40);
    g.drawLine(5, 290, 80, 19);

    g.setColor(Color.red);
    g.drawOval(10, 10, 50, 50);
    g.fillOval(70, 90, 140, 100);

    g.setColor(Color.blue);
    g.drawOval(190, 10, 90, 30);
    g.drawRect(10, 10, 60, 50);

    g.setColor(Color.cyan);
    g.fillRect(100, 10, 60, 50);
    g.drawRoundRect(190, 10, 60, 50, 15, 15);
  }
}
```

Setting the Paint Mode

The *paint mode* determines how objects are drawn in a window. By default, new output to a window overwrites any preexisting contents. However, it is possible to have new objects XORed onto the window by using **setXORMode( )**, as follows:

void setXORMode(Color *xorColor*)

Here, *xorColor* specifies the color that will be XORed to the window when an object is drawn. The advantage of XOR mode is that the new object is always guaranteed to be visible no matter what color the object is drawn over.

To return to overwrite mode, call **setPaintMode( )**, shown here:

void setPaintMode( )

In general, you will want to use overwrite mode for normal output, and XOR mode for special purposes. For example, the following program displays cross hairs that track the mouse pointer. The cross hairs are XORed onto the window and are always visible, no matter what the underlying color is.

```
// Demonstrate XOR mode.
import java.awt.*;
import java.awt.event.*;
import java.applet.*;
/*
  <applet code="XOR" width=400 height=200>
  </applet>
*/

public class XOR extends Applet {
  int chsX=100, chsY=100;

  public XOR() {
    addMouseMotionListener(new MouseMotionAdapter() {
      public void mouseMoved(MouseEvent me) {
        int x = me.getX();
        int y = me.getY();
        chsX = x-10;
        chsY = y-10;
        repaint();
      }
    });
  }

  public void paint(Graphics g) {
    g.drawLine(0, 0, 100, 100);
    g.drawLine(0, 100, 100, 0);
    g.setColor(Color.blue);
    g.drawLine(40, 25, 250, 180);
    g.drawLine(75, 90, 400, 400);
    g.setColor(Color.green);
    g.drawRect(10, 10, 60, 50);
    g.fillRect(100, 10, 60, 50);
    g.setColor(Color.red);
    g.drawRoundRect(190, 10, 60, 50, 15, 15);
    g.fillRoundRect(70, 90, 140, 100, 30, 40);
    g.setColor(Color.cyan);
    g.drawLine(20, 150, 400, 40);
    g.drawLine(5, 290, 80, 19);

    // xor cross hairs
    g.setXORMode(Color.black);
    g.drawLine(chsX-10, chsY, chsX+10, chsY);
```

```
      g.drawLine(chsX, chsY-10, chsX, chsY+10);
      g.setPaintMode();
   }
}
```

Sample output from this program is shown here:

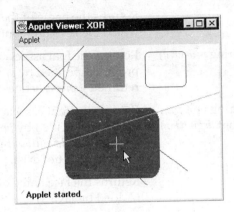

Working with Fonts

The AWT supports multiple type fonts. Fonts have emerged from the domain of traditional typesetting to become an important part of computer-generated documents and displays. The AWT provides flexibility by abstracting font-manipulation operations and allowing for dynamic selection of fonts.

Beginning with Java 2, fonts have a family name, a logical font name, and a face name. The *family name* is the general name of the font, such as Courier. The *logical name* specifies a category of font, such as Monospaced. The *face name* specifies a specific font, such as Courier Italic.

Fonts are encapsulated by the **Font** class. Several of the methods defined by **Font** are listed in Table 21-2.

The **Font** class defines these variables:

Variable	Meaning
String name	Name of the font
float pointSize	Size of the font in points
int size	Size of the font in points
int style	Font style

Method	Description
static Font decode(String *str*)	Returns a font given its name.
boolean equals(Object *FontObj*)	Returns **true** if the invoking object contains the same font as that specified by *FontObj*. Otherwise, it returns **false**.
String getFamily( )	Returns the name of the font family to which the invoking font belongs.
static Font getFont(String *property*)	Returns the font associated with the system property specified by *property*. **null** is returned if *property* does not exist.
static Font getFont(String *property*, Font *defaultFont*)	Returns the font associated with the system property specified by *property*. The font specified by *defaultFont* is returned if *property* does not exist.
String getFontName()	Returns the face name of the invoking font. (Added by Java 2)
String getName( )	Returns the logical name of the invoking font.
int getSize( )	Returns the size, in points, of the invoking font.
int getStyle( )	Returns the style values of the invoking font.
int hashCode( )	Returns the hash code associated with the invoking object.
boolean isBold( )	Returns **true** if the font includes the **BOLD** style value. Otherwise, **false** is returned.
boolean isItalic( )	Returns **true** if the font includes the **ITALIC** style value. Otherwise, **false** is returned.
boolean isPlain( )	Returns **true** if the font includes the **PLAIN** style value. Otherwise, **false** is returned.
String toString( )	Returns the string equivalent of the invoking font.

Table 21-2. *Some Methods Defined by* Font

Determining the Available Fonts

When working with fonts, often you need to know which fonts are available on your machine. To obtain this information, you can use the **getAvailableFontFamilyNames( )** method defined by the **GraphicsEnvironment** class. It is shown here:

String[ ] getAvailableFontFamilyNames( )

This method returns an array of strings that contains the names of the available font families.

In addition, the **getAllFonts( )** method is defined by the **GraphicsEnvironment** class. It is shown here:

Font[ ] getAllFonts( )

This method returns an array of **Font** objects for all of the available fonts.

Since these methods are members of **GraphicsEnvironment**, you need a **GraphicsEnvironment** reference to call them. You can obtain this reference by using the **getLocalGraphicsEnvironment( )** static method, which is defined by **GraphicsEnvironment**. It is shown here:

static GraphicsEnvironment getLocalGraphicsEnvironment( )

Here is an applet that shows how to obtain the names of the available font families:

```
// Display Fonts
/*
<applet code="ShowFonts" width=550 height=60>
</applet>
*/
import java.applet.*;
import java.awt.*;

public class ShowFonts extends Applet {
  public void paint(Graphics g) {
    String msg = "";
    String FontList[];

    GraphicsEnvironment ge =
      GraphicsEnvironment.getLocalGraphicsEnvironment();
    FontList = ge.getAvailableFontFamilyNames();
    for(int i = 0; i < FontList.length; i++)
      msg += FontList[i] + " ";
```

```
        g.drawString(msg, 4, 16);
    }
}
```

Sample output from this program is shown next. However, when you run this program, you may see a different list of fonts than the one shown in this illustration.

> **Note**   Prior to Java 2, you would use the method **getFontList( )** defined by the **Toolkit** class to obtain a list of fonts. This method is now deprecated and should not be used by new programs.

Creating and Selecting a Font

To select a new font, you must first construct a **Font** object that describes that font. One **Font** constructor has this general form:

Font(String *fontName*, int *fontStyle*, int *pointSize*)

Here, *fontName* specifies the name of the desired font. The name can be specified using either the logical or face name. All Java environments will support the following fonts: Dialog, DialogInput, Sans Serif, Serif, Monospaced, and Symbol. Dialog is the font used by your system's dialog boxes. Dialog is also the default if you don't explicitly set a font. You can also use any other fonts supported by your particular environment, but be careful—these other fonts may not be universally available.

The style of the font is specified by *fontStyle*. It may consist of one or more of these three constants: **Font.PLAIN**, **Font.BOLD**, and **Font.ITALIC**. To combine styles, OR them together. For example, **Font.BOLD | Font.ITALIC** specifies a bold, italics style.

The size, in points, of the font is specified by *pointSize*.

To use a font that you have created, you must select it using **setFont( )**, which is defined by **Component**. It has this general form:

void setFont(Font *fontObj*)

Here, *fontObj* is the object that contains the desired font.

The following program outputs a sample of each standard font. Each time you click the mouse within its window, a new font is selected and its name is displayed.

```
// Show fonts.
import java.applet.*;
import java.awt.*;
import java.awt.event.*;
/*
  <applet code="SampleFonts" width=200 height=100>
  </applet>
*/

public class SampleFonts extends Applet {
  int next = 0;
  Font f;
  String msg;
  public void init() {
    f = new Font("Dialog", Font.PLAIN, 12);
    msg = "Dialog";
    setFont(f);
    addMouseListener(new MyMouseAdapter(this));
  }

  public void paint(Graphics g) {
    g.drawString(msg, 4, 20);
  }
}

class MyMouseAdapter extends MouseAdapter {
  SampleFonts sampleFonts;
  public MyMouseAdapter(SampleFonts sampleFonts) {
    this.sampleFonts = sampleFonts;
  }
  public void mousePressed(MouseEvent me) {
    // Switch fonts with each mouse click.
    sampleFonts.next++;
    switch(sampleFonts.next) {
    case 0:
      sampleFonts.f = new Font("Dialog", Font.PLAIN, 12);
      sampleFonts.msg = "Dialog";
      break;
    case 1:
      sampleFonts.f = new Font("DialogInput", Font.PLAIN, 12);
      sampleFonts.msg = "DialogInput";
      break;
    case 2:
```

```
        sampleFonts.f = new Font("SansSerif", Font.PLAIN, 12);
        sampleFonts.msg = "SansSerif";
        break;
    case 3:
        sampleFonts.f = new Font("Serif", Font.PLAIN, 12);
        sampleFonts.msg = "Serif";
        break;
    case 4:
        sampleFonts.f = new Font("Monospaced", Font.PLAIN, 12);
        sampleFonts.msg = "Monospaced";
        break;
    }
    if(sampleFonts.next == 4) sampleFonts.next = -1;
    sampleFonts.setFont(sampleFonts.f);
    sampleFonts.repaint();
  }
}
```

Sample output from this program is shown here:

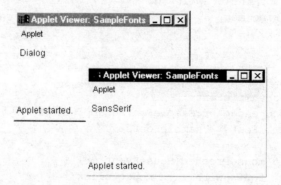

Obtaining Font Information

Suppose you want to obtain information about the currently selected font. To do this, you must first get the current font by calling **getFont( )**. This method is defined by the **Graphics** class, as shown here:

Font getFont( )

Once you have obtained the currently selected font, you can retrieve information about it using various methods defined by **Font**. For example, this applet displays the name, family, size, and style of the currently selected font:

```
// Display font info.
import java.applet.*;
import java.awt.*;
/*
<applet code="FontInfo" width=350 height=60>
</applet>
*/

public class FontInfo extends Applet {
  public void paint(Graphics g) {
    Font f = g.getFont();
    String fontName = f.getName();
    String fontFamily = f.getFamily();
    int fontSize = f.getSize();
    int fontStyle = f.getStyle();

    String msg = "Family: " + fontName;
    msg += ", Font: " + fontFamily;
    msg += ", Size: " + fontSize + ", Style: ";
    if((fontStyle & Font.BOLD) == Font.BOLD)
      msg += "Bold ";
    if((fontStyle & Font.ITALIC) == Font.ITALIC)
      msg += "Italic ";
    if((fontStyle & Font.PLAIN) == Font.PLAIN)
      msg += "Plain ";

    g.drawString(msg, 4, 16);
  }
}
```

Managing Text Output Using FontMetrics

As just explained, Java supports a number of fonts. For most fonts, characters are not all the same dimension—most fonts are proportional. Also, the height of each character, the length of *descenders* (the hanging parts of letters, such as y), and the amount of space between horizontal lines vary from font to font. Further, the point size of a font can be changed. That these (and other) attributes are variable would not be of too much consequence except that Java demands that you, the programmer, manually manage virtually all text output.

Given that the size of each font may differ and that fonts may be changed while your program is executing, there must be some way to determine the dimensions and various other attributes of the currently selected font. For example, to write one line of text after another implies that you have some way of knowing how tall the font is and how many pixels are needed between lines. To fill this need, the AWT includes the **FontMetrics** class, which encapsulates various information about a font. Let's begin by defining the common terminology used when describing fonts:

Height	The top-to-bottom size of the tallest character in the font
Baseline	The line that the bottoms of characters are aligned to (not counting descent)
Ascent	The distance from the baseline to the top of a character
Descent	The distance from the baseline to the bottom of a character
Leading	The distance between the bottom of one line of text and the top of the next

As you know, we have used the **drawString( )** method in many of the previous examples. It paints a string in the current font and color, beginning at a specified location. However, this location is at the left edge of the baseline of the characters, not at the upper-left corner as is usual with other drawing methods. It is a common error to draw a string at the same coordinate that you would draw a box. For example, if you were to draw a rectangle at coordinate 0,0 of your applet, you would see a full rectangle. If you were to draw the string "Typesetting" at 0,0, you would only see the tails (or descenders) of the *y*, *p*, and *g*. As you will see, by using font metrics, you can determine the proper placement of each string that you display.

FontMetrics defines several methods that help you manage text output. The most commonly used are listed in Table 21-3. These methods help you properly display text in a window. Let's look at some examples.

Method	Description
int bytesWidth(byte *b*[ ], int *start*, int *numBytes*)	Returns the width of *numBytes* characters held in array *b*, beginning at *start*.
int charWidth(char *c*[ ], int *start*, int *numChars*)	Returns the width of *numChars* characters held in array *c*, beginning at *start*.
int charWidth(char *c*)	Returns the width of *c*.
int charWidth(int *c*)	Returns the width of *c*.
int getAscent( )	Returns the ascent of the font.

Table 21-3.   *Some Methods Defined by* FontMetrics

Method	Description
int getDescent( )	Returns the descent of the font.
Font getFont( )	Returns the font.
int getHeight( )	Returns the height of a line of text. This value can be used to output multiple lines of text in a window.
int getLeading( )	Returns the space between lines of text.
int getMaxAdvance( )	Returns the width of the widest character. –1 is returned if this value is not available.
int getMaxAscent( )	Returns the maximum ascent.
int getMaxDescent( )	Returns the maximum descent.
int[ ] getWidths( )	Returns the widths of the first 256 characters.
int stringWidth(String *str*)	Returns the width of the string specified by *str*.
String toString( )	Returns the string equivalent of the invoking object.

Table 21-3.   *Some Methods Defined by* FontMetrics (continued)

Displaying Multiple Lines of Text

Perhaps the most common use of **FontMetrics** is to determine the spacing between lines of text. The second most common use is to determine the length of a string that is being displayed. Here, you will see how to accomplish these tasks.

In general, to display multiple lines of text, your program must manually keep track of the current output position. Each time a newline is desired, the Y coordinate must be advanced to the beginning of the next line. Each time a string is displayed, the X coordinate must be set to the point at which the string ends. This allows the next string to be written so that it begins at the end of the preceding one.

To determine the spacing between lines, you can use the value returned by **getLeading( )**. To determine the total height of the font, add the value returned by **getAscent( )** to the value returned by **getDescent( )**. You can then use these values to position each line of text you output. However, in many cases, you will not need to use these individual values. Often, all that you will need to know is the total height of a line, which is the sum of the leading space and the font's ascent and descent values. The easiest way to obtain this value is to call **getHeight( )**. Simply increment the Y coordinate by this value each time you want to advance to the next line when outputting text.

To start output at the end of previous output on the same line, you must know the length, in pixels, of each string that you display. To obtain this value, call **stringWidth( )**. You can use this value to advance the X coordinate each time you display a line.

The following applet shows how to output multiple lines of text in a window. It also displays multiple sentences on the same line. Notice the variables **curX** and **curY**. They keep track of the current text output position.

```java
// Demonstrate multiline output.
import java.applet.*;
import java.awt.*;
/*
<applet code="MultiLine" width=300 height=100>
</applet>
*/

public class MultiLine extends Applet {
  int curX=0, curY=0; // current position

  public void init() {
    Font f = new Font("SansSerif", Font.PLAIN, 12);
    setFont(f);
  }
  public void paint(Graphics g) {
    FontMetrics fm = g.getFontMetrics();

    nextLine("This is on line one.", g);
    nextLine("This is on line two.", g);
    sameLine(" This is on same line.", g);
    sameLine(" This, too.", g);
    nextLine("This is on line three.", g);
  }

  // Advance to next line.
  void nextLine(String s, Graphics g) {
    FontMetrics fm = g.getFontMetrics();

    curY += fm.getHeight(); // advance to next line
    curX = 0;
    g.drawString(s, curX, curY);
```

```
      curX = fm.stringWidth(s); // advance to end of line
    }

    // Display on same line.
    void sameLine(String s, Graphics g) {
      FontMetrics fm = g.getFontMetrics();

      g.drawString(s, curX, curY);
      curX += fm.stringWidth(s); // advance to end of line
    }
  }
```

Sample output from this program is shown here:

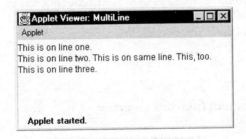

Centering Text

Here is an example that centers text, left to right, top to bottom, in a window. It obtains the ascent, descent, and width of the string and computes the position at which it must be displayed to be centered.

```
// Center text.
import java.applet.*;
import java.awt.*;
/*
  <applet code="CenterText" width=200 height=100>
  </applet>
*/

public class CenterText extends Applet {
  final Font f = new Font("SansSerif", Font.BOLD, 18);

  public void paint(Graphics g) {
```

```
        Dimension d = this.getSize();

        g.setColor(Color.white);
        g.fillRect(0, 0, d.width,d.height);
        g.setColor(Color.black);
        g.setFont(f);
        drawCenteredString("This is centered.", d.width, d.height, g);
        g.drawRect(0, 0, d.width-1, d.height-1);
    }

    public void drawCenteredString(String s, int w, int h,
                                   Graphics g) {
        FontMetrics fm = g.getFontMetrics();
        int x = (w - fm.stringWidth(s)) / 2;
        int y = (fm.getAscent() + (h - (fm.getAscent()
                + fm.getDescent()))/2);
        g.drawString(s, x, y);
    }
}
```

Following is a sample output from this program:

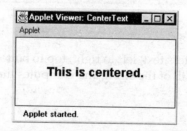

Multiline Text Alignment

If you've used a word processor, you've seen text aligned so that one or more of the edges of the text make a straight line. For example, most word processors can left-justify and/or right-justify text. Most can also center text. In the following program, you will see how to accomplish these actions.

In the program, the string to be justified is broken into individual words. For each word, the program keeps track of its length in the current font and automatically advances to the next line if the word will not fit on the current line. Each completed line is displayed in the window in the currently selected alignment style. Each time you click the mouse in the applet's window, the alignment style is changed. Sample output from this program is shown here:

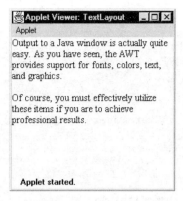 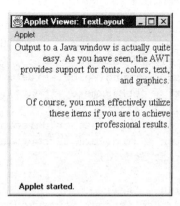

```java
// Demonstrate text alignment.
import java.applet.*;
import java.awt.*;
import java.awt.event.*;
import java.util.*;
/* <title>Text Layout</title>
   <applet code="TextLayout" width=200 height=200>
   <param name="text" value="Output to a Java window is actually
     quite easy.
     As you have seen, the AWT provides support for
     fonts, colors, text, and graphics. <P>  Of course,
     you must effectively utilize these items
     if you are to achieve professional results.">
    <param name="fontname" value="Serif">
    <param name="fontSize" value="14">
   </applet>
*/

public class TextLayout extends Applet {
  final int LEFT = 0;
  final int RIGHT = 1;
  final int CENTER = 2;
  final int LEFTRIGHT =3;
  int align;
  Dimension d;
  Font f;
  FontMetrics fm;
  int fontSize;
  int fh, bl;
  int space;
```

```
String text;

public void init() {
  setBackground(Color.white);
  text = getParameter("text");
  try {
    fontSize = Integer.parseInt(getParameter("fontSize"));}
  catch (NumberFormatException e) {
    fontSize=14;
  }
  align = LEFT;
  addMouseListener(new MyMouseAdapter(this));
}

public void paint(Graphics g) {
  update(g);
}

public void update(Graphics g) {
  d = getSize();
  g.setColor(getBackground());
  g.fillRect(0,0,d.width, d.height);
  if(f==null) f = new Font(getParameter("fontname"),
                           Font.PLAIN, fontSize);
  g.setFont(f);
  if(fm == null) {
      fm = g.getFontMetrics();
      bl = fm.getAscent();
      fh = bl + fm.getDescent();
      space = fm.stringWidth(" ");
  }

  g.setColor(Color.black);
  StringTokenizer st = new StringTokenizer(text);
  int x = 0;
  int nextx;
  int y = 0;
  String word, sp;
  int wordCount = 0;
  String line = "";
  while (st.hasMoreTokens()) {
    word = st.nextToken();
```

```
        if(word.equals("<P>")) {
          drawString(g, line, wordCount,
                      fm.stringWidth(line), y+bl);
          line = "";
          wordCount = 0;
          x = 0;
          y = y + (fh * 2);
        }
        else {
          int w = fm.stringWidth(word);
          if(( nextx = (x+space+w)) > d.width ) {
            drawString(g, line, wordCount,
                        fm.stringWidth(line), y+bl);
            line = "";
            wordCount = 0;
            x = 0;
            y = y + fh;
          }
          if(x!=0) {sp = " ";} else {sp = "";}
          line = line + sp + word;
          x = x + space + w;
          wordCount++;
        }
      }
    drawString(g, line, wordCount, fm.stringWidth(line), y+bl);
  }

public void drawString(Graphics g, String line,
                        int wc, int lineW, int y) {
  switch(align) {
    case LEFT: g.drawString(line, 0, y);
      break;
    case RIGHT: g.drawString(line, d.width-lineW ,y);
      break;
    case CENTER: g.drawString(line, (d.width-lineW)/2, y);
      break;
    case LEFTRIGHT:
      if(lineW < (int)(d.width*.75)) {
        g.drawString(line, 0, y);
      }
      else {
        int toFill = (int)((d.width - lineW)/wc);
```

```
            int nudge = d.width - lineW - (toFill*wc);
            int s = fm.stringWidth(" ");
            StringTokenizer st = new StringTokenizer(line);
            int x = 0;
            while(st.hasMoreTokens()) {
               String word = st.nextToken();
               g.drawString(word, x, y);
               if(nudge>0) {
                  x = x + fm.stringWidth(word) + space + toFill + 1;
                  nudge--;
               } else {
                  x = x + fm.stringWidth(word) + space + toFill;
               }
            }
         }
         break;
      }

   }

}

class MyMouseAdapter extends MouseAdapter {
   TextLayout tl;
   public MyMouseAdapter(TextLayout tl) {
      this.tl = tl;
   }
   public void mouseClicked(MouseEvent me) {
      tl.align = (tl.align + 1) % 4;
      tl.repaint();
   }
}
```

Let's take a closer look at how this applet works. The applet first creates several constants that will be used to determine the alignment style, and then declares several variables. The **init( )** method obtains the text that will be displayed. It then initializes the font size in a **try-catch** block, which will set the font size to 14 if the **fontSize** parameter is missing from the HTML. The **text** parameter is a long string of text, with the HTML tag **<P>** as a paragraph separator.

The **update( )** method is the engine for this example. It sets the font and gets the baseline and font height from a font metrics object. Next, it creates a **StringTokenizer** and uses it to retrieve the next token (a string separated by whitespace) from the string specified by **text**. If the next token is **<P>**, it advances the vertical spacing. Otherwise, **update( )** checks to see if the length of this token in the current font will go beyond the width of the column. If the line is full of text or if there are no more tokens, the line is output by a custom version of **drawString( )**.

The first three cases in **drawString( )** are simple. Each aligns the string that is passed in **line** to the left or right edge or to the center of the column, depending upon the alignment style. The **LEFTRIGHT** case aligns both the left and right sides of the string. This means that we need to calculate the remaining whitespace (the difference between the width of the string and the width of the column) and distribute that space between each of the words. The last method in this class advances the alignment style each time you click the mouse on the applet's window.

Exploring Text and Graphics

Although this chapter covers the most important attributes and common techniques that you will use when displaying text or graphics, it only scratches the surface of Java's capabilities. This is an area in which further refinements and enhancements are expected as Java and the computing environment continue to evolve. For example, Java 2 added a subsystem to the AWT called *Java 2D*. Java 2D supports enhanced control over graphics, including such things as coordinate translations, rotation, and scaling. It also provides advanced imaging features. If advanced graphics handling is of interest to you, then you will definitely want to explore Java 2D in detail.

The

Complete
Reference

Java™ 2

Chapter 22

Using AWT Controls,
Layout Managers,
and Menus

This chapter continues our exploration of the Abstract Window Toolkit (AWT). It examines the standard controls and layout managers defined by Java. It also discusses menus and the menu bar. The chapter includes a discussion of two high-level components: the dialog box and the file dialog box. It concludes with another look at event handling.

Controls are components that allow a user to interact with your application in various ways—for example, a commonly used control is the push button. A *layout manager* automatically positions components within a container. Thus, the appearance of a window is determined by a combination of the controls that it contains and the layout manager used to position them.

In addition to the controls, a frame window can also include a standard-style *menu bar*. Each entry in a menu bar activates a drop-down menu of options from which the user can choose. A menu bar is always positioned at the top of a window. Although different in appearance, menu bars are handled in much the same way as are the other controls.

While it is possible to manually position components within a window, doing so is quite tedious. The layout manager automates this task. For the first part of this chapter, which introduces the various controls, the default layout manager will be used. This displays components in a container using left-to-right, top-to-bottom organization. Once the controls have been covered, the layout managers will be examined. There you will see how to better manage the positioning of your controls.

Control Fundamentals

The AWT supports the following types of controls:

- Labels
- Push buttons
- Check boxes
- Choice lists
- Lists
- Scroll bars
- Text editing

These controls are subclasses of **Component**.

Adding and Removing Controls

To include a control in a window, you must add it to the window. To do this, you must first create an instance of the desired control and then add it to a window by calling **add( )**, which is defined by **Container**. The **add( )** method has several forms. The following form is the one that is used for the first part of this chapter:

Component add(Component *compObj*)

Here, *compObj* is an instance of the control that you want to add. A reference to *compObj* is returned. Once a control has been added, it will automatically be visible whenever its parent window is displayed.

Sometimes you will want to remove a control from a window when the control is no longer needed. To do this, call **remove( )**. This method is also defined by **Container**. It has this general form:

void remove(Component *obj*)

Here, *obj* is a reference to the control you want to remove. You can remove all controls by calling **removeAll( )**.

Responding to Controls

Except for labels, which are passive controls, all controls generate events when they are accessed by the user. For example, when the user clicks on a push button, an event is sent that identifies the push button. In general, your program simply implements the appropriate interface and then registers an event listener for each control that you need to monitor. As explained in Chapter 20, once a listener has been installed, events are automatically sent to it. In the sections that follow, the appropriate interface for each control is specified.

Labels

The easiest control to use is a label. A *label* is an object of type **Label**, and it contains a string, which it displays. Labels are passive controls that do not support any interaction with the user. **Label** defines the following constructors:

Label( )
Label(String *str*)
Label(String *str*, int *how*)

The first version creates a blank label. The second version creates a label that contains the string specified by *str*. This string is left-justified. The third version creates a label that contains the string specified by *str* using the alignment specified by *how*. The value of *how* must be one of these three constants: **Label.LEFT**, **Label.RIGHT**, or **Label.CENTER**.

You can set or change the text in a label by using the **setText( )** method. You can obtain the current label by calling **getText( )**. These methods are shown here:

void setText(String *str*)
String getText( )

For **setText( )**, *str* specifies the new label. For **getText( )**, the current label is returned.
You can set the alignment of the string within the label by calling **setAlignment( )**.
To obtain the current alignment, call **getAlignment( )**. The methods are as follows:

void setAlignment(int *how*)
int getAlignment( )

Here, *how* must be one of the alignment constants shown earlier.

The following example creates three labels and adds them to an applet:

```
// Demonstrate Labels
import java.awt.*;
import java.applet.*;
/*
<applet code="LabelDemo" width=300 height=200>
</applet>
*/

public class LabelDemo extends Applet {
  public void init() {
    Label one = new Label("One");
    Label two = new Label("Two");
    Label three = new Label("Three");

    // add labels to applet window
    add(one);
    add(two);
    add(three);
  }
}
```

Following is the window created by the **LabelDemo** applet. Notice that the labels are organized in the window by the default layout manager. Later, you will see how to control more precisely the placement of the labels.

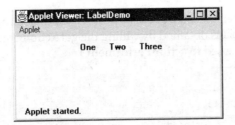

Using Buttons

The most widely used control is the push button. A *push button* is a component that contains a label and that generates an event when it is pressed. Push buttons are objects of type **Button**. **Button** defines these two constructors:

> Button( )
> Button(String *str*)

The first version creates an empty button. The second creates a button that contains *str* as a label.

After a button has been created, you can set its label by calling **setLabel( )**. You can retrieve its label by calling **getLabel( )**. These methods are as follows:

> void setLabel(String *str*)
> String getLabel( )

Here, *str* becomes the new label for the button.

Handling Buttons

Each time a button is pressed, an action event is generated. This is sent to any listeners that previously registered an interest in receiving action event notifications from that component. Each listener implements the **ActionListener** interface. That interface defines the **actionPerformed( )** method, which is called when an event occurs. An **ActionEvent** object is supplied as the argument to this method. It contains both a reference to the button that generated the event and a reference to the string that is the label of the button. Usually, either value may be used to identify the button, as you will see.

Here is an example that creates three buttons labeled "Yes," "No," and "Undecided." Each time one is pressed, a message is displayed that reports which button has been pressed. In this version, the label of the button is used to determine which button has been pressed. The label is obtained by calling the **getActionCommand( )** method on the **ActionEvent** object passed to **actionPerformed( )**.

```java
// Demonstrate Buttons
import java.awt.*;
import java.awt.event.*;
import java.applet.*;
/*
  <applet code="ButtonDemo" width=250 height=150>
  </applet>
*/

public class ButtonDemo extends Applet implements ActionListener {
  String msg = "";
  Button yes, no, maybe;

  public void init() {
    yes = new Button("Yes");
    no = new Button("No");
    maybe = new Button("Undecided");

    add(yes);
    add(no);
    add(maybe);

    yes.addActionListener(this);
    no.addActionListener(this);
    maybe.addActionListener(this);
  }

  public void actionPerformed(ActionEvent ae) {
    String str = ae.getActionCommand();
    if(str.equals("Yes")) {
      msg = "You pressed Yes.";
    }
    else if(str.equals("No")) {
      msg = "You pressed No.";
    }
    else {
      msg = "You pressed Undecided.";
    }
```

```
       repaint();
    }

    public void paint(Graphics g) {
       g.drawString(msg, 6, 100);
    }
}
```

Sample output from the **ButtonDemo** program is shown in Figure 22-1.

As mentioned, in addition to comparing button labels, you can also determine
which button has been pressed, by comparing the object obtained from the **getSource( )**
method to the button objects that you added to the window. To do this, you must keep
a list of the objects when they are added. The following applet shows this approach:

```
// Recognize Button objects.
import java.awt.*;
import java.awt.event.*;
import java.applet.*;
/*
  <applet code="ButtonList" width=250 height=150>
  </applet>
*/
```

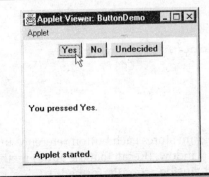

Figure 22-1.   *Sample output from the* ButtonDemo *applet*

```
public class ButtonList extends Applet implements ActionListener {
  String msg = "";
  Button bList[] = new Button[3];

  public void init() {
    Button yes = new Button("Yes");
    Button no = new Button("No");
    Button maybe = new Button("Undecided");

    // store references to buttons as added
    bList[0] = (Button) add(yes);
    bList[1] = (Button) add(no);
    bList[2] = (Button) add(maybe);

    // register to receive action events
    for(int i = 0; i < 3; i++) {
      bList[i].addActionListener(this);
    }
  }

  public void actionPerformed(ActionEvent ae) {
    for(int i = 0; i < 3; i++) {
      if(ae.getSource() == bList[i]) {
        msg = "You pressed " + bList[i].getLabel();
      }
    }
    repaint();
  }

  public void paint(Graphics g) {
    g.drawString(msg, 6, 100);
  }
}
```

In this version, the program stores each button reference in an array when the buttons are added to the applet window. (Recall that the **add( )** method returns a reference to the button when it is added.) Inside **actionPerformed( )**, this array is then used to determine which button has been pressed.

For simple applets, it is usually easier to recognize buttons by their labels. However, in situations in which you will be changing the label inside a button during the execution of your program, or using buttons that have the same label, it may be easier to determine which button has been pushed by using its object reference.

Applying Check Boxes

A *check box* is a control that is used to turn an option on or off. It consists of a small box that can either contain a check mark or not. There is a label associated with each check box that describes what option the box represents. You change the state of a check box by clicking on it. Check boxes can be used individually or as part of a group. Check boxes are objects of the **Checkbox** class.

Checkbox supports these constructors:

Checkbox( )
Checkbox(String *str*)
Checkbox(String *str*, boolean *on*)
Checkbox(String *str*, boolean *on*, CheckboxGroup *cbGroup*)
Checkbox(String *str*, CheckboxGroup *cbGroup*, boolean *on*)

The first form creates a check box whose label is initially blank. The state of the check box is unchecked. The second form creates a check box whose label is specified by *str*. The state of the check box is unchecked. The third form allows you to set the initial state of the check box. If *on* is **true**, the check box is initially checked; otherwise, it is cleared. The fourth and fifth forms create a check box whose label is specified by *str* and whose group is specified by *cbGroup*. If this check box is not part of a group, then *cbGroup* must be **null**. (Check box groups are described in the next section.) The value of *on* determines the initial state of the check box.

To retrieve the current state of a check box, call **getState( )**. To set its state, call **setState( )**. You can obtain the current label associated with a check box by calling **getLabel( )**. To set the label, call **setLabel( )**. These methods are as follows:

boolean getState( )
void setState(boolean *on*)
String getLabel( )
void setLabel(String *str*)

Here, if *on* is **true**, the box is checked. If it is **false**, the box is cleared. The string passed in *str* becomes the new label associated with the invoking check box.

Handling Check Boxes

Each time a check box is selected or deselected, an item event is generated. This is sent to any listeners that previously registered an interest in receiving item event notifications from that component. Each listener implements the **ItemListener** interface. That interface defines the **itemStateChanged( )** method. An **ItemEvent** object is supplied as the argument to this method. It contains information about the event (for example, whether it was a selection or deselection).

The following program creates four check boxes. The initial state of the first box is checked. The status of each check box is displayed. Each time you change the state of a check box, the status display is updated.

```
// Demonstrate check boxes.
import java.awt.*;
import java.awt.event.*;
import java.applet.*;
/*
  <applet code="CheckboxDemo" width=250 height=200>
  </applet>
*/

public class CheckboxDemo extends Applet implements ItemListener {
  String msg = "";
  Checkbox Win98, winNT, solaris, mac;

  public void init() {
    Win98 = new Checkbox("Windows 98/XP", null, true);
    winNT = new Checkbox("Windows NT/2000");
    solaris = new Checkbox("Solaris");
    mac = new Checkbox("MacOS");

    add(Win98);
    add(winNT);
    add(solaris);
    add(mac);

    Win98.addItemListener(this);
    winNT.addItemListener(this);
    solaris.addItemListener(this);
    mac.addItemListener(this);
  }

  public void itemStateChanged(ItemEvent ie) {
    repaint();
  }

  // Display current state of the check boxes.
  public void paint(Graphics g) {
```

```
      msg = "Current state: ";
      g.drawString(msg, 6, 80);
      msg = "  Windows 98/XP: " + Win98.getState();
      g.drawString(msg, 6, 100);
      msg = "  Windows NT/2000: " + winNT.getState();
      g.drawString(msg, 6, 120);
      msg = "  Solaris: " + solaris.getState();
      g.drawString(msg, 6, 140);
      msg = "  MacOS: " + mac.getState();
      g.drawString(msg, 6, 160);
    }
  }
```

Sample output is shown in Figure 22-2.

CheckboxGroup

It is possible to create a set of mutually exclusive check boxes in which one and only one
check box in the group can be checked at any one time. These check boxes are often called
radio buttons, because they act like the station selector on a car radio—only one station can

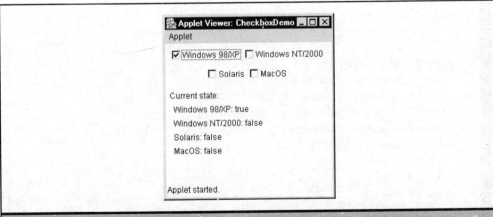

Figure 22-2.   *Sample output from the* CheckboxDemo *applet*

be selected at any one time. To create a set of mutually exclusive check boxes, you must first define the group to which they will belong and then specify that group when you construct the check boxes. Check box groups are objects of type **CheckboxGroup**. Only the default constructor is defined, which creates an empty group.

You can determine which check box in a group is currently selected by calling **getSelectedCheckbox( )**. You can set a check box by calling **setSelectedCheckbox( )**. These methods are as follows:

Checkbox getSelectedCheckbox( )
void setSelectedCheckbox(Checkbox *which*)

Here, *which* is the check box that you want to be selected. The previously selected check box will be turned off.

Here is a program that uses check boxes that are part of a group:

```
// Demonstrate check box group.
import java.awt.*;
import java.awt.event.*;
import java.applet.*;
/*
  <applet code="CBGroup" width=250 height=200>
  </applet>
*/

public class CBGroup extends Applet implements ItemListener {
  String msg = "";
  Checkbox Win98, winNT, solaris, mac;
  CheckboxGroup cbg;

  public void init() {
    cbg = new CheckboxGroup();
    Win98 = new Checkbox("Windows 98/XP", cbg, true);
    winNT = new Checkbox("Windows NT/2000", cbg, false);
    solaris = new Checkbox("Solaris", cbg, false);
    mac = new Checkbox("MacOS", cbg, false);

    add(Win98);
    add(winNT);
    add(solaris);
    add(mac);

    Win98.addItemListener(this);
```

THE JAVA LIBRARY

```
      winNT.addItemListener(this);
      solaris.addItemListener(this);
      mac.addItemListener(this);
   }

   public void itemStateChanged(ItemEvent ie) {
      repaint();
   }

   // Display current state of the check boxes.
   public void paint(Graphics g) {
      msg = "Current selection: ";
      msg += cbg.getSelectedCheckbox().getLabel();
      g.drawString(msg, 6, 100);
   }
}
```

Output generated by the **CBGroup** applet is shown in Figure 22-3. Notice that the check boxes are now circular in shape.

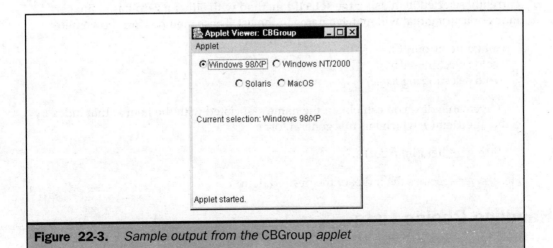

Figure 22-3.   *Sample output from the* CBGroup *applet*

Choice Controls

The **Choice** class is used to create a *pop-up list* of items from which the user may choose. Thus, a **Choice** control is a form of menu. When inactive, a **Choice** component takes up only enough space to show the currently selected item. When the user clicks on it, the whole list of choices pops up, and a new selection can be made. Each item in the list is a string that appears as a left-justified label in the order it is added to the **Choice** object. **Choice** only defines the default constructor, which creates an empty list.

To add a selection to the list, call **add( )**. It has this general form:

void add(String *name*)

Here, *name* is the name of the item being added. Items are added to the list in the order in which calls to **add( )** occur.

To determine which item is currently selected, you may call either **getSelectedItem( )** or **getSelectedIndex( )**. These methods are shown here:

String getSelectedItem( )
int getSelectedIndex( )

The **getSelectedItem( )** method returns a string containing the name of the item. **getSelectedIndex( )** returns the index of the item. The first item is at index 0. By default, the first item added to the list is selected.

To obtain the number of items in the list, call **getItemCount( )**. You can set the currently selected item using the **select( )** method with either a zero-based integer index or a string that will match a name in the list. These methods are shown here:

int getItemCount( )
void select(int *index*)
void select(String *name*)

Given an index, you can obtain the name associated with the item at that index by calling **getItem( )**, which has this general form:

String getItem(int *index*)

Here, *index* specifies the index of the desired item.

Handling Choice Lists

Each time a choice is selected, an item event is generated. This is sent to any listeners that previously registered an interest in receiving item event notifications from that component. Each listener implements the **ItemListener** interface. That interface defines the **itemStateChanged( )** method. An **ItemEvent** object is supplied as the argument to this method.

Here is an example that creates two **Choice** menus. One selects the operating system. The other selects the browser.

```java
// Demonstrate Choice lists.
import java.awt.*;
import java.awt.event.*;
import java.applet.*;
/*
  <applet code="ChoiceDemo" width=300 height=180>
  </applet>
*/

public class ChoiceDemo extends Applet implements ItemListener {
  Choice os, browser;
  String msg = "";

  public void init() {
    os = new Choice();
    browser = new Choice();

    // add items to os list
    os.add("Windows 98/XP");
    os.add("Windows NT/2000");
    os.add("Solaris");
    os.add("MacOS");

    // add items to browser list
    browser.add("Netscape 3.x");
    browser.add("Netscape 4.x");
    browser.add("Netscape 5.x");
    browser.add("Netscape 6.x");

    browser.add("Internet Explorer 4.0");
    browser.add("Internet Explorer 5.0");
    browser.add("Internet Explorer 6.0");

    browser.add("Lynx 2.4");

    browser.select("Netscape 4.x");

    // add choice lists to window
    add(os);
```

```
  add(browser);

  // register to receive item events
  os.addItemListener(this);
  browser.addItemListener(this);
}

public void itemStateChanged(ItemEvent ie) {
  repaint();
}

// Display current selections.
public void paint(Graphics g) {
  msg = "Current OS: ";
  msg += os.getSelectedItem();
  g.drawString(msg, 6, 120);
  msg = "Current Browser: ";
  msg += browser.getSelectedItem();
  g.drawString(msg, 6, 140);
}
}
```

Sample output is shown in Figure 22-4.

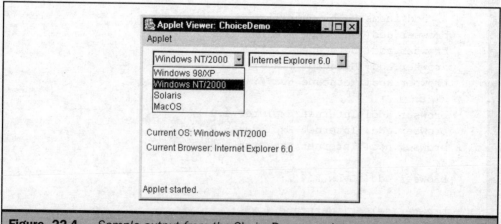

Figure 22-4. *Sample output from the* ChoiceDemo *applet*

Using Lists

The **List** class provides a compact, multiple-choice, scrolling selection list. Unlike the **Choice** object, which shows only the single selected item in the menu, a **List** object can be constructed to show any number of choices in the visible window. It can also be created to allow multiple selections. **List** provides these constructors:

List( )
List(int *numRows*)
List(int *numRows*, boolean *multipleSelect*)

The first version creates a **List** control that allows only one item to be selected at any one time. In the second form, the value of *numRows* specifies the number of entries in the list that will always be visible (others can be scrolled into view as needed). In the third form, if *multipleSelect* is **true**, then the user may select two or more items at a time. If it is **false**, then only one item may be selected.

To add a selection to the list, call **add( )**. It has the following two forms:

void add(String *name*)
void add(String *name*, int *index*)

Here, *name* is the name of the item added to the list. The first form adds items to the end of the list. The second form adds the item at the index specified by *index*. Indexing begins at zero. You can specify –1 to add the item to the end of the list.

For lists that allow only single selection, you can determine which item is currently selected by calling either **getSelectedItem( )** or **getSelectedIndex( )**. These methods are shown here:

String getSelectedItem( )
int getSelectedIndex( )

The **getSelectedItem( )** method returns a string containing the name of the item. If more than one item is selected or if no selection has yet been made, **null** is returned. **getSelectedIndex( )** returns the index of the item. The first item is at index 0. If more than one item is selected, or if no selection has yet been made, –1 is returned.

For lists that allow multiple selection, you must use either **getSelectedItems( )** or **getSelectedIndexes( )**, shown here, to determine the current selections:

String[ ] getSelectedItems( )
int[ ] getSelectedIndexes( )

getSelectedItems( ) returns an array containing the names of the currently selected items. **getSelectedIndexes( )** returns an array containing the indexes of the currently selected items.

To obtain the number of items in the list, call **getItemCount( )**. You can set the currently selected item by using the **select( )** method with a zero-based integer index. These methods are shown here:

int getItemCount( )
void select(int *index*)

Given an index, you can obtain the name associated with the item at that index by calling **getItem( )**, which has this general form:

String getItem(int *index*)

Here, *index* specifies the index of the desired item.

Handling Lists

To process list events, you will need to implement the **ActionListener** interface. Each time a **List** item is double-clicked, an **ActionEvent** object is generated. Its **getActionCommand( )** method can be used to retrieve the name of the newly selected item. Also, each time an item is selected or deselected with a single click, an **ItemEvent** object is generated. Its **getStateChange( )** method can be used to determine whether a selection or deselection triggered this event. **getItemSelectable( )** returns a reference to the object that triggered this event.

Here is an example that converts the **Choice** controls in the preceding section into **List** components, one multiple choice and the other single choice:

```
// Demonstrate Lists.
import java.awt.*;
import java.awt.event.*;
import java.applet.*;
/*
  <applet code="ListDemo" width=300 height=180>
  </applet>
*/

public class ListDemo extends Applet implements ActionListener {
  List os, browser;
  String msg = "";

  public void init() {
    os = new List(4, true);
    browser = new List(4, false);
```

```
// add items to os list
os.add("Windows 98/XP");
os.add("Windows NT/2000");
os.add("Solaris");
os.add("MacOS");

// add items to browser list
browser.add("Netscape 3.x");
browser.add("Netscape 4.x");
browser.add("Netscape 5.x");
browser.add("Netscape 6.x");

browser.add("Internet Explorer 4.0");
browser.add("Internet Explorer 5.0");
browser.add("Internet Explorer 6.0");

browser.add("Lynx 2.4");

browser.select(1);

// add lists to window
add(os);
add(browser);

// register to receive action events
os.addActionListener(this);
browser.addActionListener(this);
}

public void actionPerformed(ActionEvent ae) {
  repaint();
}

// Display current selections.
public void paint(Graphics g) {
  int idx[];

  msg = "Current OS: ";
  idx = os.getSelectedIndexes();
  for(int i=0; i<idx.length; i++)
    msg += os.getItem(idx[i]) + "   ";
```

```
      g.drawString(msg, 6, 120);
      msg = "Current Browser: ";
      msg += browser.getSelectedItem();
      g.drawString(msg, 6, 140);
   }
}
```

Sample output generated by the **ListDemo** applet is shown in Figure 22-5. Notice that the browser list has a scroll bar, since all of the items won't fit in the number of rows specified when it is created.

Managing Scroll Bars

Scroll bars are used to select continuous values between a specified minimum and maximum. Scroll bars may be oriented horizontally or vertically. A scroll bar is actually a composite of several individual parts. Each end has an arrow that you can click to move the current value of the scroll bar one unit in the direction of the arrow. The current value of the scroll bar relative to its minimum and maximum values is indicated by the *slider box* (or *thumb*) for the scroll bar. The slider box can be dragged by the user to a new position. The scroll bar will then reflect this value. In the background space on either side of the

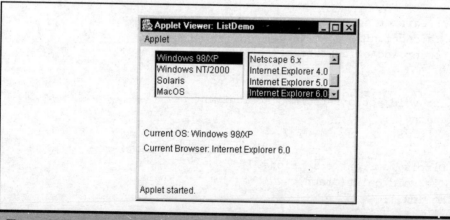

Figure 22-5. *Sample output from the* ListDemo *applet*

thumb, the user can click to cause the thumb to jump in that direction by some increment larger than 1. Typically, this action translates into some form of page up and page down. Scroll bars are encapsulated by the **Scrollbar** class.

Scrollbar defines the following constructors:

```
Scrollbar( )
Scrollbar(int style)
Scrollbar(int style, int initialValue, int thumbSize, int min, int max)
```

The first form creates a vertical scroll bar. The second and third forms allow you to specify the orientation of the scroll bar. If *style* is **Scrollbar.VERTICAL**, a vertical scroll bar is created. If *style* is **Scrollbar.HORIZONTAL**, the scroll bar is horizontal. In the third form of the constructor, the initial value of the scroll bar is passed in *initialValue*. The number of units represented by the height of the thumb is passed in *thumbSize*. The minimum and maximum values for the scroll bar are specified by *min* and *max*.

If you construct a scroll bar by using one of the first two constructors, then you need to set its parameters by using **setValues( )**, shown here, before it can be used:

```
void setValues(int initialValue, int thumbSize, int min, int max)
```

The parameters have the same meaning as they have in the third constructor just described.

To obtain the current value of the scroll bar, call **getValue( )**. It returns the current setting. To set the current value, call **setValue( )**. These methods are as follows:

```
int getValue( )
void setValue(int newValue)
```

Here, *newValue* specifies the new value for the scroll bar. When you set a value, the slider box inside the scroll bar will be positioned to reflect the new value.

You can also retrieve the minimum and maximum values via **getMinimum( )** and **getMaximum( )**, shown here:

```
int getMinimum( )
int getMaximum( )
```

They return the requested quantity.

By default, 1 is the increment added to or subtracted from the scroll bar each time it is scrolled up or down one line. You can change this increment by calling **setUnitIncrement( )**. By default, page-up and page-down increments are 10. You can change this value by calling **setBlockIncrement( )**. These methods are shown here:

```
void setUnitIncrement(int newIncr)
void setBlockIncrement(int newIncr)
```

Handling Scroll Bars

To process scroll bar events, you need to implement the **AdjustmentListener** interface. Each time a user interacts with a scroll bar, an **AdjustmentEvent** object is generated. Its **getAdjustmentType( )** method can be used to determine the type of the adjustment. The types of adjustment events are as follows:

BLOCK_DECREMENT   A page-down event has been generated.

BLOCK_INCREMENT   A page-up event has been generated.

TRACK   An absolute tracking event has been generated.

UNIT_DECREMENT   The line-down button in a scroll bar has been pressed.

UNIT_INCREMENT   The line-up button in a scroll bar has been pressed.

The following example creates both a vertical and a horizontal scroll bar. The current settings of the scroll bars are displayed. If you drag the mouse while inside the window, the coordinates of each drag event are used to update the scroll bars. An asterisk is displayed at the current drag position.

```
// Demonstrate scroll bars.
import java.awt.*;
import java.awt.event.*;
import java.applet.*;
/*
  <applet code="SBDemo" width=300 height=200>
  </applet>
*/

public class SBDemo extends Applet
  implements AdjustmentListener, MouseMotionListener {
  String msg = "";
  Scrollbar vertSB, horzSB;

  public void init() {
    int width = Integer.parseInt(getParameter("width"));
    int height = Integer.parseInt(getParameter("height"));

    vertSB = new Scrollbar(Scrollbar.VERTICAL,
                           0, 1, 0, height);
    horzSB = new Scrollbar(Scrollbar.HORIZONTAL,
                           0, 1, 0, width);
```

```
      add(vertSB);
      add(horzSB);

      // register to receive adjustment events
      vertSB.addAdjustmentListener(this);
      horzSB.addAdjustmentListener(this);

      addMouseMotionListener(this);
    }

  public void adjustmentValueChanged(AdjustmentEvent ae) {
    repaint();
  }

  // Update scroll bars to reflect mouse dragging.
  public void mouseDragged(MouseEvent me) {
    int x = me.getX();
    int y = me.getY();
    vertSB.setValue(y);
    horzSB.setValue(x);
    repaint();
  }

  // Necessary for MouseMotionListener
  public void mouseMoved(MouseEvent me) {
  }

  // Display current value of scroll bars.
  public void paint(Graphics g) {
      msg = "Vertical: " + vertSB.getValue();
      msg += ",  Horizontal: " + horzSB.getValue();
      g.drawString(msg, 6, 160);

      // show current mouse drag position
      g.drawString("*", horzSB.getValue(),
                vertSB.getValue());
  }
}
```

Sample output from the **SBDemo** applet is shown in Figure 22-6.

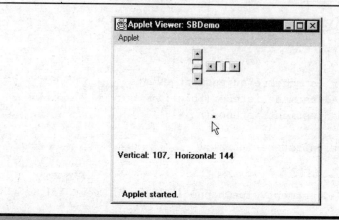

Figure 22-6. *Sample output from the* SBDemo *applet*

Using a TextField

The **TextField** class implements a single-line text-entry area, usually called an *edit control*. Text fields allow the user to enter strings and to edit the text using the arrow keys, cut and paste keys, and mouse selections. **TextField** is a subclass of **TextComponent**. **TextField** defines the following constructors:

```
TextField( )
TextField(int numChars)
TextField(String str)
TextField(String str, int numChars)
```

The first version creates a default text field. The second form creates a text field that is *numChars* characters wide. The third form initializes the text field with the string contained in *str*. The fourth form initializes a text field and sets its width.

    TextField (and its superclass **TextComponent**) provides several methods that allow you to utilize a text field. To obtain the string currently contained in the text field, call **getText( )**. To set the text, call **setText( )**. These methods are as follows:

```
String getText( )
void setText(String str)
```

Here, *str* is the new string.

The user can select a portion of the text in a text field. Also, you can select a portion of text under program control by using **select( )**. Your program can obtain the currently selected text by calling **getSelectedText( )**. These methods are shown here:

String getSelectedText( )
void select(int *startIndex*, int *endIndex*)

getSelectedText( ) returns the selected text. The **select( )** method selects the characters beginning at *startIndex* and ending at *endIndex*–1.

You can control whether the contents of a text field may be modified by the user by calling **setEditable( )**. You can determine editability by calling **isEditable( )**. These methods are shown here:

boolean isEditable( )
void setEditable(boolean *canEdit*)

isEditable( ) returns **true** if the text may be changed and **false** if not. In **setEditable( )**, if *canEdit* is **true**, the text may be changed. If it is **false**, the text cannot be altered.

There may be times when you will want the user to enter text that is not displayed, such as a password. You can disable the echoing of the characters as they are typed by calling **setEchoChar( )**. This method specifies a single character that the **TextField** will display when characters are entered (thus, the actual characters typed will not be shown). You can check a text field to see if it is in this mode with the **echoCharIsSet( )** method. You can retrieve the echo character by calling the **getEchoChar( )** method. These methods are as follows:

void setEchoChar(char *ch*)
boolean echoCharIsSet( )
char getEchoChar( )

Here, *ch* specifies the character to be echoed.

Handling a TextField

Since text fields perform their own editing functions, your program generally will not respond to individual key events that occur within a text field. However, you may want to respond when the user presses ENTER. When this occurs, an action event is generated. Here is an example that creates the classic user name and password screen:

```
// Demonstrate text field.
import java.awt.*;
import java.awt.event.*;
import java.applet.*;
/*
```

```
  <applet code="TextFieldDemo" width=380 height=150>
  </applet>
*/

public class TextFieldDemo extends Applet
  implements ActionListener {

  TextField name, pass;

  public void init() {
    Label namep = new Label("Name: ", Label.RIGHT);
    Label passp = new Label("Password: ", Label.RIGHT);
    name = new TextField(12);
    pass = new TextField(8);
    pass.setEchoChar('?');

    add(namep);
    add(name);
    add(passp);
    add(pass);

    // register to receive action events
    name.addActionListener(this);
    pass.addActionListener(this);
  }

  // User pressed Enter.
  public void actionPerformed(ActionEvent ae) {
    repaint();
  }

  public void paint(Graphics g) {
    g.drawString("Name: " + name.getText(), 6, 60);
    g.drawString("Selected text in name: "
                     + name.getSelectedText(), 6, 80);
    g.drawString("Password: " + pass.getText(), 6, 100);
  }
}
```

Sample output from the **TextFieldDemo** applet is shown in Figure 22-7.

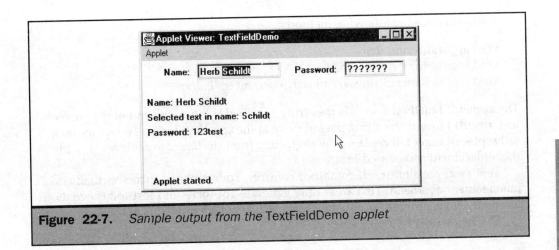

Figure 22-7. *Sample output from the* TextFieldDemo *applet*

Using a TextArea

Sometimes a single line of text input is not enough for a given task. To handle these situations, the AWT includes a simple multiline editor called **TextArea**. Following are the constructors for **TextArea**:

TextArea( )
TextArea(int *numLines*, int *numChars*)
TextArea(String *str*)
TextArea(String *str*, int *numLines*, int *numChars*)
TextArea(String *str*, int *numLines*, int *numChars*, int *sBars*)

Here, *numLines* specifies the height, in lines, of the text area, and *numChars* specifies its width, in characters. Initial text can be specified by *str*. In the fifth form you can specify the scroll bars that you want the control to have. *sBars* must be one of these values:

SCROLLBARS_BOTH   SCROLLBARS_NONE

SCROLLBARS_HORIZONTAL_ONLY   SCROLLBARS_VERTICAL_ONLY

TextArea is a subclass of **TextComponent**. Therefore, it supports the **getText( )**, **setText( )**, **getSelectedText( )**, **select( )**, **isEditable( )**, and **setEditable( )** methods described in the preceding section.

TextArea adds the following methods:

void append(String *str*)
void insert(String *str*, int *index*)
void replaceRange(String *str*, int *startIndex*, int *endIndex*)

The **append( )** method appends the string specified by *str* to the end of the current text. **insert( )** inserts the string passed in *str* at the specified index. To replace text, call **replaceRange( )**. It replaces the characters from *startIndex* to *endIndex*–1, with the replacement text passed in *str*.

Text areas are almost self-contained controls. Your program incurs virtually no management overhead. Text areas only generate got-focus and lost-focus events. Normally, your program simply obtains the current text when it is needed.

The following program creates a **TextArea** control:

```
// Demonstrate TextArea.
import java.awt.*;
import java.applet.*;
/*
<applet code="TextAreaDemo" width=300 height=250>
</applet>
*/

public class TextAreaDemo extends Applet {
  public void init() {
    String val = "There are two ways of constructing " +
      "a software design.\n" +
      "One way is to make it so simple\n" +
      "that there are obviously no deficiencies.\n" +
      "And the other way is to make it so complicated\n" +
      "that there are no obvious deficiencies.\n\n" +
      "          -C.A.R. Hoare\n\n" +
      "There's an old story about the person who wished\n" +
      "his computer were as easy to use as his telephone.\n" +
      "That wish has come true,\n" +
      "since I no longer know how to use my telephone.\n\n" +
      "          -Bjarne Stroustrup, AT&T, (inventor of C++)";

    TextArea text = new TextArea(val, 10, 30);
    add(text);
  }
}
```

Here is sample output from the **TextAreaDemo** applet:

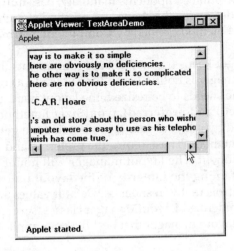

Understanding Layout Managers

All of the components that we have shown so far have been positioned by the default layout manager. As we mentioned at the beginning of this chapter, a layout manager automatically arranges your controls within a window by using some type of algorithm. If you have programmed for other GUI environments, such as Windows, then you are accustomed to laying out your controls by hand. While it is possible to lay out Java controls by hand, too, you generally won't want to, for two main reasons. First, it is very tedious to manually lay out a large number of components. Second, sometimes the width and height information is not yet available when you need to arrange some control, because the native toolkit components haven't been realized. This is a chicken-and-egg situation; it is pretty confusing to figure out when it is okay to use the size of a given component to position it relative to another.

Each **Container** object has a layout manager associated with it. A layout manager is an instance of any class that implements the **LayoutManager** interface. The layout manager is set by the **setLayout( )** method. If no call to **setLayout( )** is made, then the default layout manager is used. Whenever a container is resized (or sized for the first time), the layout manager is used to position each of the components within it.

The **setLayout( )** method has the following general form:

void setLayout(LayoutManager *layoutObj*)

Here, *layoutObj* is a reference to the desired layout manager. If you wish to disable the layout manager and position components manually, pass **null** for *layoutObj*. If you do this, you will need to determine the shape and position of each component manually, using the **setBounds( )** method defined by **Component**. Normally, you will want to use a layout manager.

Each layout manager keeps track of a list of components that are stored by their names. The layout manager is notified each time you add a component to a container. Whenever the container needs to be resized, the layout manager is consulted via its **minimumLayoutSize( )** and **preferredLayoutSize( )** methods. Each component that is being managed by a layout manager contains the **getPreferredSize( )** and **getMinimumSize( )** methods. These return the preferred and minimum size required to display each component. The layout manager will honor these requests if at all possible, while maintaining the integrity of the layout policy. You may override these methods for controls that you subclass. Default values are provided otherwise.

Java has several predefined **LayoutManager** classes, several of which are described next. You can use the layout manager that best fits your application.

FlowLayout

FlowLayout is the default layout manager. This is the layout manager that the preceding examples have used. **FlowLayout** implements a simple layout style, which is similar to how words flow in a text editor. Components are laid out from the upper-left corner, left to right and top to bottom. When no more components fit on a line, the next one appears on the next line. A small space is left between each component, above and below, as well as left and right. Here are the constructors for **FlowLayout**:

```
FlowLayout( )
FlowLayout(int how)
FlowLayout(int how, int horz, int vert)
```

The first form creates the default layout, which centers components and leaves five pixels of space between each component. The second form lets you specify how each line is aligned. Valid values for *how* are as follows:

```
FlowLayout.LEFT
FlowLayout.CENTER
FlowLayout.RIGHT
```

These values specify left, center, and right alignment, respectively. The third form allows you to specify the horizontal and vertical space left between components in *horz* and *vert*, respectively.

Here is a version of the **CheckboxDemo** applet shown earlier in this chapter, modified so that it uses left-aligned flow layout.

```
// Use left-aligned flow layout.
import java.awt.*;
import java.awt.event.*;
import java.applet.*;
/*
  <applet code="FlowLayoutDemo" width=250 height=200>
  </applet>
*/

public class FlowLayoutDemo extends Applet
  implements ItemListener {

  String msg = "";
  Checkbox Win98, winNT, solaris, mac;

  public void init() {
    // set left-aligned flow layout
    setLayout(new FlowLayout(FlowLayout.LEFT));

    Win98 = new Checkbox("Windows 98/XP", null, true);
    winNT = new Checkbox("Windows NT/2000");
    solaris = new Checkbox("Solaris");
    mac = new Checkbox("MacOS");

    add(Win98);
    add(winNT);
    add(solaris);
    add(mac);

    // register to receive item events
    Win98.addItemListener(this);
    winNT.addItemListener(this);
    solaris.addItemListener(this);
    mac.addItemListener(this);
  }

  // Repaint when status of a check box changes.
  public void itemStateChanged(ItemEvent ie) {
    repaint();
  }

  // Display current state of the check boxes.
  public void paint(Graphics g) {
```

```
    msg = "Current state: ";
    g.drawString(msg, 6, 80);
    msg = "  Windows 98/XP: " + Win98.getState();
    g.drawString(msg, 6, 100);
    msg = "  Windows NT/2000: " + winNT.getState();
    g.drawString(msg, 6, 120);
    msg = "  Solaris: " + solaris.getState();
    g.drawString(msg, 6, 140);
    msg = "  Mac: " + mac.getState();
    g.drawString(msg, 6, 160);
  }
}
```

Following is sample output generated by the **FlowLayoutDemo** applet:

Compare this with the output from the **CheckboxDemo** applet, shown earlier in Figure 22-2.

BorderLayout

The **BorderLayout** class implements a common layout style for top-level windows. It has four narrow, fixed-width components at the edges and one large area in the center. The four sides are referred to as north, south, east, and west. The middle area is called the center. Here are the constructors defined by **BorderLayout**:

BorderLayout( )
BorderLayout(int *horz*, int *vert*)

The first form creates a default border layout. The second allows you to specify the horizontal and vertical space left between components in *horz* and *vert*, respectively.

BorderLayout defines the following constants that specify the regions:

BorderLayout.CENTER   BorderLayout.SOUTH

BorderLayout.EAST   BorderLayout.WEST

BorderLayout.NORTH

When adding components, you will use these constants with the following form of **add( )**, which is defined by **Container**:

void add(Component *compObj*, Object *region*);

Here, *compObj* is the component to be added, and *region* specifies where the component will be added.

Here is an example of a **BorderLayout** with a component in each layout area:

```java
// Demonstrate BorderLayout.
import java.awt.*;
import java.applet.*;
import java.util.*;
/*
<applet code="BorderLayoutDemo" width=400 height=200>
</applet>
*/

public class BorderLayoutDemo extends Applet {
  public void init() {
    setLayout(new BorderLayout());

    add(new Button("This is across the top."),
      BorderLayout.NORTH);
    add(new Label("The footer message might go here."),
      BorderLayout.SOUTH);
    add(new Button("Right"), BorderLayout.EAST);
    add(new Button("Left"), BorderLayout.WEST);

    String msg = "The reasonable man adapts " +
      "himself to the world;\n" +
      "the unreasonable one persists in " +
      "trying to adapt the world to himself.\n" +
```

```
          "Therefore all progress depends " +
          "on the unreasonable man.\n\n" +
          "          - George Bernard Shaw\n\n";

      add(new TextArea(msg), BorderLayout.CENTER);
    }
}
```

Sample output from the **BorderLayoutDemo** applet is shown here:

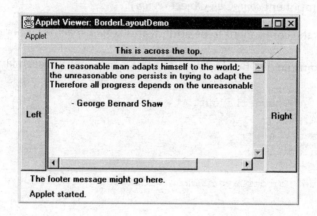

Using Insets

Sometimes you will want to leave a small amount of space between the container
that holds your components and the window that contains it. To do this, override
the **getInsets( )** method that is defined by **Container**. This function returns an **Insets**
object that contains the top, bottom, left, and right inset to be used when the container
is displayed. These values are used by the layout manager to inset the components
when it lays out the window. The constructor for **Insets** is shown here:

Insets(int *top*, int *left*, int *bottom*, int *right*)

The values passed in *top*, *left*, *bottom*, and *right* specify the amount of space between the
container and its enclosing window.

The **getInsets( )** method has this general form:

Insets getInsets( )

When overriding one of these methods, you must return a new **Insets** object that contains the inset spacing you desire.

Here is the preceding **BorderLayout** example modified so that it insets its components ten pixels from each border. The background color has been set to cyan to help make the insets more visible.

```java
// Demonstrate BorderLayout with insets.
import java.awt.*;
import java.applet.*;
import java.util.*;
/*
<applet code="InsetsDemo" width=400 height=200>
</applet>
*/

public class InsetsDemo extends Applet {
  public void init() {
    // set background color so insets can be easily seen
    setBackground(Color.cyan);

    setLayout(new BorderLayout());

    add(new Button("This is across the top."),
        BorderLayout.NORTH);
    add(new Label("The footer message might go here."),
        BorderLayout.SOUTH);
    add(new Button("Right"), BorderLayout.EAST);
    add(new Button("Left"), BorderLayout.WEST);

    String msg = "The reasonable man adapts " +
      "himself to the world;\n" +
      "the unreasonable one persists in " +
      "trying to adapt the world to himself.\n" +
      "Therefore all progress depends " +
      "on the unreasonable man.\n\n" +
      "          - George Bernard Shaw\n\n";

    add(new TextArea(msg), BorderLayout.CENTER);
  }
```

```
// add insets
public Insets getInsets() {
  return new Insets(10, 10, 10, 10);
}
}
```

Output from the **InsetsDemo** applet is shown here:

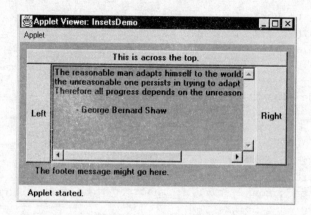

GridLayout

GridLayout lays out components in a two-dimensional grid. When you instantiate a **GridLayout**, you define the number of rows and columns. The constructors supported by **GridLayout** are shown here:

GridLayout( )
GridLayout(int *numRows*, int *numColumns*)
GridLayout(int *numRows*, int *numColumns*, int *horz*, int *vert*)

The first form creates a single-column grid layout. The second form creates a grid layout with the specified number of rows and columns. The third form allows you to specify the horizontal and vertical space left between components in *horz* and *vert*, respectively. Either *numRows* or *numColumns* can be zero. Specifying *numRows* as zero allows for unlimited-length columns. Specifying *numColumns* as zero allows for unlimited-length rows.

Here is a sample program that creates a 4×4 grid and fills it in with 15 buttons, each labeled with its index:

```
// Demonstrate GridLayout
import java.awt.*;
import java.applet.*;
/*
<applet code="GridLayoutDemo" width=300 height=200>
</applet>
*/

public class GridLayoutDemo extends Applet {
  static final int n = 4;
  public void init() {
    setLayout(new GridLayout(n, n));

    setFont(new Font("SansSerif", Font.BOLD, 24));

    for(int i = 0; i < n; i++) {
      for(int j = 0; j < n; j++) {
        int k = i * n + j;
        if(k > 0)
          add(new Button("" + k));
      }
    }
  }
}
```

Following is the output generated by the **GridLayoutDemo** applet:

You might try using this example as the starting point for a 15-square puzzle.

CardLayout

The **CardLayout** class is unique among the other layout managers in that it stores several different layouts. Each layout can be thought of as being on a separate index card in a deck that can be shuffled so that any card is on top at a given time. This can be useful for user interfaces with optional components that can be dynamically enabled and disabled upon user input. You can prepare the other layouts and have them hidden, ready to be activated when needed.

CardLayout provides these two constructors:

CardLayout( )
CardLayout(int *horz*, int *vert*)

The first form creates a default card layout. The second form allows you to specify the horizontal and vertical space left between components in *horz* and *vert*, respectively.

Use of a card layout requires a bit more work than the other layouts. The cards are typically held in an object of type **Panel**. This panel must have **CardLayout** selected as its layout manager. The cards that form the deck are also typically objects of type **Panel**. Thus, you must create a panel that contains the deck and a panel for each card in the deck. Next, you add to the appropriate panel the components that form each card. You then add these panels to the panel for which **CardLayout** is the layout manager. Finally, you add this panel to the main applet panel. Once these steps are complete, you must provide some way for the user to select between cards. One common approach is to include one push button for each card in the deck.

When card panels are added to a panel, they are usually given a name. Thus, most of the time, you will use this form of **add( )** when adding cards to a panel:

void add(Component *panelObj*, Object *name*);

Here, *name* is a string that specifies the name of the card whose panel is specified by *panelObj*.

After you have created a deck, your program activates a card by calling one of the following methods defined by **CardLayout**:

void first(Container *deck*)
void last(Container *deck*)
void next(Container *deck*)
void previous(Container *deck*)
void show(Container *deck*, String *cardName*)

Here, *deck* is a reference to the container (usually a panel) that holds the cards, and *cardName* is the name of a card. Calling **first( )** causes the first card in the deck to be

shown. To show the last card, call **last( )**. To show the next card, call **next( )**. To show
the previous card, call **previous( )**. Both **next( )** and **previous( )** automatically cycle
back to the top or bottom of the deck, respectively. The **show( )** method displays the
card whose name is passed in *cardName*.

The following example creates a two-level card deck that allows the user to select
an operating system. Windows-based operating systems are displayed in one card.
Macintosh and Solaris are displayed in the other card.

```
// Demonstrate CardLayout.
import java.awt.*;
import java.awt.event.*;
import java.applet.*;
/*
   <applet code="CardLayoutDemo" width=300 height=100>
   </applet>
*/

public class CardLayoutDemo extends Applet
   implements ActionListener, MouseListener {

   Checkbox Win98, winNT, solaris, mac;
   Panel osCards;
   CardLayout cardLO;
   Button Win, Other;

   public void init() {
      Win = new Button("Windows");
      Other = new Button("Other");
      add(Win);
      add(Other);

      cardLO = new CardLayout();
      osCards = new Panel();
      osCards.setLayout(cardLO); // set panel layout to card layout

      Win98 = new Checkbox("Windows 98/XP", null, true);
      winNT = new Checkbox("Windows NT/2000");
      solaris = new Checkbox("Solaris");
      mac = new Checkbox("MacOS");

      // add Windows check boxes to a panel
      Panel winPan = new Panel();
```

```
    winPan.add(Win98);
    winPan.add(winNT);

    // Add other OS check boxes to a panel
    Panel otherPan = new Panel();
    otherPan.add(solaris);
    otherPan.add(mac);

    // add panels to card deck panel
    osCards.add(winPan, "Windows");
    osCards.add(otherPan, "Other");

    // add cards to main applet panel
    add(osCards);

    // register to receive action events
    Win.addActionListener(this);
    Other.addActionListener(this);

    // register mouse events
    addMouseListener(this);
  }

  // Cycle through panels.
  public void mousePressed(MouseEvent me) {
    cardLO.next(osCards);
  }

  // Provide empty implementations for the other MouseListener methods.
  public void mouseClicked(MouseEvent me) {
  }
  public void mouseEntered(MouseEvent me) {
  }
  public void mouseExited(MouseEvent me) {
  }
  public void mouseReleased(MouseEvent me) {
  }

  public void actionPerformed(ActionEvent ae) {
    if(ae.getSource() == Win) {
```

```
        cardLO.show(osCards, "Windows");
    }
    else {
        cardLO.show(osCards, "Other");
    }
  }
}
```

Following is the output generated by the **CardLayoutDemo** applet. Each card is activated
by pushing its button. You can also cycle through the cards by clicking the mouse.

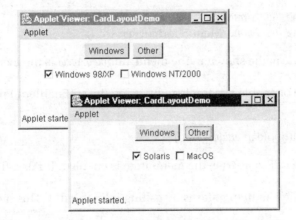

Menu Bars and Menus

A top-level window can have a menu bar associated with it. A menu bar displays
a list of top-level menu choices. Each choice is associated with a drop-down menu.
This concept is implemented in Java by the following classes: **MenuBar**, **Menu**, and
MenuItem. In general, a menu bar contains one or more **Menu** objects. Each **Menu**
object contains a list of **MenuItem** objects. Each **MenuItem** object represents something
that can be selected by the user. Since **Menu** is a subclass of **MenuItem**, a hierarchy of
nested submenus can be created. It is also possible to include checkable menu items.
These are menu options of type **CheckboxMenuItem** and will have a check mark next
to them when they are selected.

To create a menu bar, first create an instance of **MenuBar**. This class only defines the default constructor. Next, create instances of **Menu** that will define the selections displayed on the bar. Following are the constructors for **Menu**:

Menu( )
Menu(String *optionName*)
Menu(String *optionName*, boolean *removable*)

Here, *optionName* specifies the name of the menu selection. If *removable* is **true**, the pop-up menu can be removed and allowed to float free. Otherwise, it will remain attached to the menu bar. (Removable menus are implementation-dependent.) The first form creates an empty menu.

Individual menu items are of type **MenuItem**. It defines these constructors:

MenuItem( )
MenuItem(String *itemName*)
MenuItem(String *itemName*, MenuShortcut *keyAccel*)

Here, *itemName* is the name shown in the menu, and *keyAccel* is the menu shortcut for this item.

You can disable or enable a menu item by using the **setEnabled( )** method. Its form is shown here:

void setEnabled(boolean *enabledFlag*)

If the argument *enabledFlag* is **true**, the menu item is enabled. If **false**, the menu item is disabled.

You can determine an item's status by calling **isEnabled( )**. This method is shown here:

boolean isEnabled( )

isEnabled( ) returns **true** if the menu item on which it is called is enabled. Otherwise, it returns **false**.

You can change the name of a menu item by calling **setLabel( )**. You can retrieve the current name by using **getLabel( )**. These methods are as follows:

void setLabel(String *newName*)
String getLabel( )

Here, *newName* becomes the new name of the invoking menu item. **getLabel( )** returns the current name.

You can create a checkable menu item by using a subclass of **MenuItem** called **CheckboxMenuItem**. It has these constructors:

CheckboxMenuItem( )
CheckboxMenuItem(String *itemName*)
CheckboxMenuItem(String *itemName*, boolean *on*)

Here, *itemName* is the name shown in the menu. Checkable items operate as toggles. Each time one is selected, its state changes. In the first two forms, the checkable entry is unchecked. In the third form, if *on* is **true**, the checkable entry is initially checked. Otherwise, it is cleared.

You can obtain the status of a checkable item by calling **getState( )**. You can set it to a known state by using **setState( )**. These methods are shown here:

boolean getState( )
void setState(boolean *checked*)

If the item is checked, **getState( )** returns **true**. Otherwise, it returns **false**. To check an item, pass **true** to **setState( )**. To clear an item, pass **false**.

Once you have created a menu item, you must add the item to a **Menu** object by using **add( )**, which has the following general form:

MenuItem add(MenuItem *item*)

Here, *item* is the item being added. Items are added to a menu in the order in which the calls to **add( )** take place. The *item* is returned.

Once you have added all items to a **Menu** object, you can add that object to the menu bar by using this version of **add( )** defined by **MenuBar**:

Menu add(Menu *menu*)

Here, *menu* is the menu being added. The *menu* is returned.

Menus only generate events when an item of type **MenuItem** or **CheckboxMenuItem** is selected. They do not generate events when a menu bar is accessed to display a drop-down menu, for example. Each time a menu item is selected, an **ActionEvent** object is generated. Each time a check box menu item is checked or unchecked, an **ItemEvent** object is generated. Thus, you must implement the **ActionListener** and **ItemListener** interfaces in order to handle these menu events.

The **getItem( )** method of **ItemEvent** returns a reference to the item that generated this event. The general form of this method is shown here:

Object getItem( )

Following is an example that adds a series of nested menus to a pop-up window. The item selected is displayed in the window. The state of the two check box menu items is also displayed.

```
// Illustrate menus.
import java.awt.*;
import java.awt.event.*;
import java.applet.*;
/*
  <applet code="MenuDemo" width=250 height=250>
  </applet>
*/

// Create a subclass of Frame
class MenuFrame extends Frame {
  String msg = "";
  CheckboxMenuItem debug, test;

  MenuFrame(String title) {
    super(title);

    // create menu bar and add it to frame
    MenuBar mbar = new MenuBar();
    setMenuBar(mbar);

    // create the menu items
    Menu file = new Menu("File");
    MenuItem item1, item2, item3, item4, item5;
    file.add(item1 = new MenuItem("New..."));
    file.add(item2 = new MenuItem("Open..."));
    file.add(item3 = new MenuItem("Close"));
    file.add(item4 = new MenuItem("-"));
    file.add(item5 = new MenuItem("Quit..."));
    mbar.add(file);

    Menu edit = new Menu("Edit");
    MenuItem item6, item7, item8, item9;
    edit.add(item6 = new MenuItem("Cut"));
    edit.add(item7 = new MenuItem("Copy"));
    edit.add(item8 = new MenuItem("Paste"));
    edit.add(item9 = new MenuItem("-"));
    Menu sub = new Menu("Special");
```

```
MenuItem item10, item11, item12;
sub.add(item10 = new MenuItem("First"));
sub.add(item11 = new MenuItem("Second"));
sub.add(item12 = new MenuItem("Third"));
edit.add(sub);

// these are checkable menu items
debug = new CheckboxMenuItem("Debug");
edit.add(debug);
test = new CheckboxMenuItem("Testing");
edit.add(test);

mbar.add(edit);

// create an object to handle action and item events
MyMenuHandler handler = new MyMenuHandler(this);
// register it to receive those events
item1.addActionListener(handler);
item2.addActionListener(handler);
item3.addActionListener(handler);
item4.addActionListener(handler);
item5.addActionListener(handler);
item6.addActionListener(handler);
item7.addActionListener(handler);
item8.addActionListener(handler);
item9.addActionListener(handler);
item10.addActionListener(handler);
item11.addActionListener(handler);
item12.addActionListener(handler);
debug.addItemListener(handler);
test.addItemListener(handler);

// create an object to handle window events
MyWindowAdapter adapter = new MyWindowAdapter(this);
  // register it to receive those events
addWindowListener(adapter);
}

public void paint(Graphics g) {
  g.drawString(msg, 10, 200);
```

```java
      if(debug.getState())
        g.drawString("Debug is on.", 10, 220);
      else
        g.drawString("Debug is off.", 10, 220);

      if(test.getState())
        g.drawString("Testing is on.", 10, 240);
      else
        g.drawString("Testing is off.", 10, 240);
    }
}

class MyWindowAdapter extends WindowAdapter {
  MenuFrame menuFrame;
  public MyWindowAdapter(MenuFrame menuFrame) {
    this.menuFrame = menuFrame;
  }
  public void windowClosing(WindowEvent we) {
    menuFrame.setVisible(false);
  }
}

class MyMenuHandler implements ActionListener, ItemListener {
  MenuFrame menuFrame;
  public MyMenuHandler(MenuFrame menuFrame) {
    this.menuFrame = menuFrame;
  }
  // Handle action events
  public void actionPerformed(ActionEvent ae) {
      String msg = "You selected ";
      String arg = (String)ae.getActionCommand();
      if(arg.equals("New..."))
        msg += "New.";
      else if(arg.equals("Open..."))
        msg += "Open.";
      else if(arg.equals("Close"))
        msg += "Close.";
      else if(arg.equals("Quit..."))
        msg += "Quit.";
      else if(arg.equals("Edit"))
        msg += "Edit.";
```

```
      else if(arg.equals("Cut"))
        msg += "Cut.";
      else if(arg.equals("Copy"))
        msg += "Copy.";
      else if(arg.equals("Paste"))
        msg += "Paste.";
      else if(arg.equals("First"))
        msg += "First.";
      else if(arg.equals("Second"))
        msg += "Second.";
      else if(arg.equals("Third"))
        msg += "Third.";
      else if(arg.equals("Debug"))
        msg += "Debug.";
      else if(arg.equals("Testing"))
        msg += "Testing.";
      menuFrame.msg = msg;
      menuFrame.repaint();
    }
    // Handle item events
    public void itemStateChanged(ItemEvent ie) {
      menuFrame.repaint();
    }
  }

// Create frame window.
public class MenuDemo extends Applet {
  Frame f;

  public void init() {
    f = new MenuFrame("Menu Demo");
    int width = Integer.parseInt(getParameter("width"));
    int height = Integer.parseInt(getParameter("height"));

    setSize(new Dimension(width, height));

    f.setSize(width, height);
    f.setVisible(true);
  }

  public void start() {
```

```
      f.setVisible(true);
   }

   public void stop() {
      f.setVisible(false);
   }
}
```

Sample output from the **MenuDemo** applet is shown in Figure 22-8.

There is one other menu-related class that you might find interesting: **PopupMenu**. It works just like **Menu** but produces a menu that can be displayed at a specific location. **PopupMenu** provides a flexible, useful alternative for some types of menuing situations.

Dialog Boxes

Often, you will want to use a *dialog box* to hold a set of related controls. Dialog boxes are primarily used to obtain user input. They are similar to frame windows, except that dialog boxes are always child windows of a top-level window. Also, dialog boxes don't have menu bars. In other respects, dialog boxes function like frame windows. (You can add controls to them, for example, in the same way that you add controls to a frame window.) Dialog boxes may be modal or modeless. When a *modal* dialog box is active,

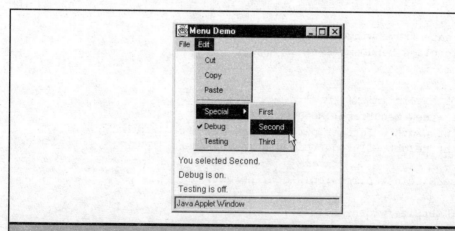

Figure 22-8. *Sample output from the* MenuDemo *applet*

all input is directed to it until it is closed. This means that you cannot access other parts of your program until you have closed the dialog box. When a *modeless* dialog box is active, input focus can be directed to another window in your program. Thus, other parts of your program remain active and accessible. Dialog boxes are of type **Dialog**. Two commonly used constructors are shown here:

Dialog(Frame *parentWindow*, boolean *mode*)
Dialog(Frame *parentWindow*, String *title*, boolean *mode*)

Here, *parentWindow* is the owner of the dialog box. If *mode* is **true**, the dialog box is modal. Otherwise, it is modeless. The title of the dialog box can be passed in *title*. Generally, you will subclass **Dialog**, adding the functionality required by your application.

Following is a modified version of the preceding menu program that displays a modeless dialog box when the New option is chosen. Notice that when the dialog box is closed, **dispose( )** is called. This method is defined by **Window**, and it frees all system resources associated with the dialog box window.

```
// Demonstrate Dialog box.
import java.awt.*;
import java.awt.event.*;
import java.applet.*;
/*
  <applet code="DialogDemo" width=250 height=250>
  </applet>
*/

// Create a subclass of Dialog.
class SampleDialog extends Dialog implements ActionListener {
  SampleDialog(Frame parent, String title) {
    super(parent, title, false);
    setLayout(new FlowLayout());
    setSize(300, 200);

    add(new Label("Press this button:"));
    Button b;
    add(b = new Button("Cancel"));
    b.addActionListener(this);
  }

  public void actionPerformed(ActionEvent ae) {
    dispose();
  }
}
```

```java
  public void paint(Graphics g) {
    g.drawString("This is in the dialog box", 10, 70);
  }
}

// Create a subclass of Frame.
class MenuFrame extends Frame {
  String msg = "";
  CheckboxMenuItem debug, test;

  MenuFrame(String title) {
    super(title);

    // create menu bar and add it to frame
    MenuBar mbar = new MenuBar();
    setMenuBar(mbar);

    // create the menu items
    Menu file = new Menu("File");
    MenuItem item1, item2, item3, item4;
    file.add(item1 = new MenuItem("New..."));
    file.add(item2 = new MenuItem("Open..."));
    file.add(item3 = new MenuItem("Close"));
    file.add(new MenuItem("-"));
    file.add(item4 = new MenuItem("Quit..."));
    mbar.add(file);

    Menu edit = new Menu("Edit");
    MenuItem item5, item6, item7;
    edit.add(item5 = new MenuItem("Cut"));
    edit.add(item6 = new MenuItem("Copy"));
    edit.add(item7 = new MenuItem("Paste"));
    edit.add(new MenuItem("-"));

    Menu sub = new Menu("Special", true);
    MenuItem item8, item9, item10;
    sub.add(item8 = new MenuItem("First"));
    sub.add(item9 = new MenuItem("Second"));
    sub.add(item10 = new MenuItem("Third"));
    edit.add(sub);
```

```java
    // these are checkable menu items
    debug = new CheckboxMenuItem("Debug");
    edit.add(debug);
    test = new CheckboxMenuItem("Testing");
    edit.add(test);

    mbar.add(edit);

    // create an object to handle action and item events
    MyMenuHandler handler = new MyMenuHandler(this);
    // register it to receive those events
    item1.addActionListener(handler);
    item2.addActionListener(handler);
    item3.addActionListener(handler);
    item4.addActionListener(handler);
    item5.addActionListener(handler);
    item6.addActionListener(handler);
    item7.addActionListener(handler);
    item8.addActionListener(handler);
    item9.addActionListener(handler);
    item10.addActionListener(handler);
    debug.addItemListener(handler);
    test.addItemListener(handler);

    // create an object to handle window events
    MyWindowAdapter adapter = new MyWindowAdapter(this);
    // register it to receive those events
    addWindowListener(adapter);
  }
public void paint(Graphics g) {
  g.drawString(msg, 10, 200);

  if(debug.getState())
    g.drawString("Debug is on.", 10, 220);
  else
    g.drawString("Debug is off.", 10, 220);

  if(test.getState())
    g.drawString("Testing is on.", 10, 240);
  else
```

```
      g.drawString("Testing is off.", 10, 240);
  }
}

class MyWindowAdapter extends WindowAdapter {
  MenuFrame menuFrame;
  public MyWindowAdapter(MenuFrame menuFrame) {
    this.menuFrame = menuFrame;
  }
  public void windowClosing(WindowEvent we) {
    menuFrame.dispose();
  }
}

class MyMenuHandler implements ActionListener, ItemListener {
  MenuFrame menuFrame;
  public MyMenuHandler(MenuFrame menuFrame) {
    this.menuFrame = menuFrame;
  }
  // Handle action events
  public void actionPerformed(ActionEvent ae) {
      String msg = "You selected ";
      String arg = (String)ae.getActionCommand();
    // Activate a dialog box when New is selected.
    if(arg.equals("New...")) {
      msg += "New.";
      SampleDialog d = new
        SampleDialog(menuFrame, "New Dialog Box");
      d.setVisible(true);
    }
    // Try defining other dialog boxes for these options.
    else if(arg.equals("Open..."))
      msg += "Open.";
    else if(arg.equals("Close"))
      msg += "Close.";
    else if(arg.equals("Quit..."))
      msg += "Quit.";
    else if(arg.equals("Edit"))
      msg += "Edit.";
    else if(arg.equals("Cut"))
      msg += "Cut.";
```

```
      else if(arg.equals("Copy"))
        msg += "Copy.";
      else if(arg.equals("Paste"))
        msg += "Paste.";
      else if(arg.equals("First"))
        msg += "First.";
      else if(arg.equals("Second"))
        msg += "Second.";
      else if(arg.equals("Third"))
        msg += "Third.";
      else if(arg.equals("Debug"))
        msg += "Debug.";
      else if(arg.equals("Testing"))
        msg += "Testing.";
      menuFrame.msg = msg;
      menuFrame.repaint();
    }
    public void itemStateChanged(ItemEvent ie) {
      menuFrame.repaint();
    }
  }


// Create frame window.
public class DialogDemo extends Applet {
  Frame f;

  public void init() {
    f = new MenuFrame("Menu Demo");
    int width = Integer.parseInt(getParameter("width"));
    int height = Integer.parseInt(getParameter("height"));

    setSize(width, height);

    f.setSize(width, height);
    f.setVisible(true);
  }

  public void start() {
    f.setVisible(true);
  }

  public void stop() {
```

```
        f.setVisible(false);
    }
}
```

Here is sample output from the **DialogDemo** applet:

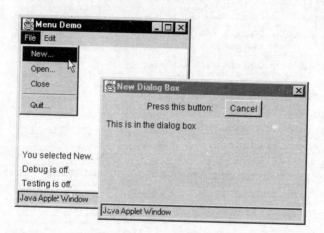

 On your own, try defining dialog boxes for the other options presented by the menus.

FileDialog

Java provides a built-in dialog box that lets the user specify a file. To create a file dialog box, instantiate an object of type **FileDialog**. This causes a file dialog box to be displayed. Usually, this is the standard file dialog box provided by the operating system. **FileDialog** provides these constructors:

FileDialog(Frame *parent*, String *boxName*)
FileDialog(Frame *parent*, String *boxName*, int *how*)
FileDialog(Frame *parent*)

Here, *parent* is the owner of the dialog box, and *boxName* is the name displayed in the box's title bar. If *boxName* is omitted, the title of the dialog box is empty. If *how* is **FileDialog.LOAD**, then the box is selecting a file for reading. If *how* is **FileDialog.SAVE**, the box is selecting a file for writing. The third constructor creates a dialog box for selecting a file for reading.

FileDialog( ) provides methods that allow you to determine the name of the file and its path as selected by the user. Here are two examples:

String getDirectory( )
String getFile( )

These methods return the directory and the filename, respectively.

The following program activates the standard file dialog box:

```
/* Demonstrate File Dialog box.

   This is an application, not an applet.
*/
import java.awt.*;
import java.awt.event.*;

// Create a subclass of Frame
class SampleFrame extends Frame {
  SampleFrame(String title) {
    super(title);
    // create an object to handle window events
    MyWindowAdapter adapter = new MyWindowAdapter(this);
    // register it to receive those events
    addWindowListener(adapter);
  }
}

class MyWindowAdapter extends WindowAdapter {
  SampleFrame sampleFrame;
  public MyWindowAdapter(SampleFrame sampleFrame) {
    this.sampleFrame = sampleFrame;
  }
  public void windowClosing(WindowEvent we) {
    sampleFrame.setVisible(false);
  }
}

// Create frame window.
class FileDialogDemo {
  public static void main(String args[]) {
    Frame f = new SampleFrame("File Dialog Demo");
    f.setVisible(true);
    f.setSize(100, 100);
```

```
        FileDialog fd = new FileDialog(f, "File Dialog");
        fd.setVisible(true);
    }
}
```

The output generated by this program is shown here. (The precise configuration of the dialog box may vary.)

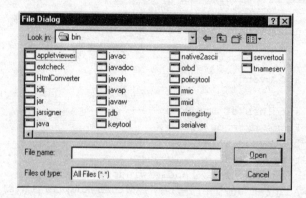

Handling Events by Extending AWT Components

Before concluding our look at the AWT, one more topic needs to be discussed: handling events by extending AWT components. The delegation event model was introduced in Chapter 20, and all of the programs in this book so far have used that design. But Java also allows you to handle events by subclassing AWT components. Doing so allows you to handle events in much the same way as they were handled under the original 1.0 version of Java. Of course, this technique is discouraged, because it has the same disadvantages of the Java 1.0 event model, the main one being inefficiency. Handling events by extending AWT components is described in this section for completeness. However, this technique is not used in any other sections of this book.

To extend an AWT component, you must call the **enableEvents( )** method of **Component**. Its general form is shown here:

protected final void enableEvents(long *eventMask*)

The *eventMask* argument is a bit mask that defines the events to be delivered to this component. The **AWTEvent** class defines **int** constants for making this mask. Several are shown here:

ACTION_EVENT_MASK	KEY_EVENT_MASK
ADJUSTMENT_EVENT_MASK	MOUSE_EVENT_MASK
COMPONENT_EVENT_MASK	MOUSE_MOTION_EVENT_MASK
CONTAINER_EVENT_MASK	MOUSE_WHEEL_EVENT_MASK
FOCUS_EVENT_MASK	TEXT_EVENT_MASK
INPUT_METHOD_EVENT_MASK	WINDOW_EVENT_MASK
ITEM_EVENT_MASK	

You must also override the appropriate method from one of your superclasses in order to process the event. Table 22-1 lists the methods most commonly used and the classes that provide them.

The following sections provide simple programs that show how to extend several AWT components.

Class	Processing Methods
Button	processActionEvent( )
Checkbox	processItemEvent( )
CheckboxMenuItem	processItemEvent( )
Choice	processItemEvent( )
Component	processComponentEvent( ), processFocusEvent( ), processKeyEvent( ), processMouseEvent( ), processMouseMotionEvent( ), processMouseWheelEvent ( )
List	processActionEvent( ), processItemEvent( )
MenuItem	processActionEvent( )
Scrollbar	processAdjustmentEvent( )
TextComponent	processTextEvent( )

Table 22-1.   *Event Processing Methods*

Extending Button

The following program creates an applet that displays a button labeled "Test Button". When the button is pressed, the string "action event: " is displayed on the status line of the applet viewer or browser, followed by a count of the number of button presses.

The program has one top-level class named **ButtonDemo2** that extends **Applet**. A static integer variable named **i** is defined and initialized to zero. This records the number of button pushes. The **init( )** method instantiates **MyButton** and adds it to the applet.

MyButton is an inner class that extends **Button**. Its constructor uses **super** to pass the label of the button to the superclass constructor. It calls **enableEvents( )** so that action events may be received by this object. When an action event is generated, **processActionEvent( )** is called. That method displays a string on the status line and calls **processActionEvent( )** for the superclass. Because **MyButton** is an inner class, it has direct access to the **showStatus( )** method of **ButtonDemo2**.

```
/*
 * <applet code=ButtonDemo2 width=200 height=100>
 * </applet>
 */
import java.awt.*;
import java.awt.event.*;
import java.applet.*;

public class ButtonDemo2 extends Applet {
  MyButton myButton;
  static int i = 0;
  public void init() {
    myButton = new MyButton("Test Button");
    add(myButton);
  }
  class MyButton extends Button {
    public MyButton(String label) {
      super(label);
      enableEvents(AWTEvent.ACTION_EVENT_MASK);
    }
    protected void processActionEvent(ActionEvent ae) {
      showStatus("action event: " + i++);
      super.processActionEvent(ae);
    }
  }
}
```

Extending Checkbox

The following program creates an applet that displays three check boxes labeled "Item 1", "Item 2", and "Item 3". When a check box is selected or deselected, a string containing the name and state of that check box is displayed on the status line of the applet viewer or browser.

The program has one top-level class named **CheckboxDemo2** that extends **Applet**. Its **init( )** method creates three instances of **MyCheckbox** and adds these to the applet. **MyCheckbox** is an inner class that extends **Checkbox**. Its constructor uses **super** to pass the label of the check box to the superclass constructor. It calls **enableEvents( )** so that item events may be received by this object. When an item event is generated, **processItemEvent( )** is called. That method displays a string on the status line and calls **processItemEvent( )** for the superclass.

```
/*
 * <applet code=CheckboxDemo2 width=300 height=100>
 * </applet>
 */
import java.awt.*;
import java.awt.event.*;
import java.applet.*;

public class CheckboxDemo2 extends Applet {
  MyCheckbox myCheckbox1, myCheckbox2, myCheckbox3;
  public void init() {
    myCheckbox1 = new MyCheckbox("Item 1");
    add(myCheckbox1);
    myCheckbox2 = new MyCheckbox("Item 2");
    add(myCheckbox2);
    myCheckbox3 = new MyCheckbox("Item 3");
    add(myCheckbox3);
  }
  class MyCheckbox extends Checkbox {
    public MyCheckbox(String label) {
      super(label);
      enableEvents(AWTEvent.ITEM_EVENT_MASK);
    }
    protected void processItemEvent(ItemEvent ie) {
      showStatus("Checkbox name/state: " + getLabel() +
                 "/" + getState());
      super.processItemEvent(ie);
    }
```

```
    }
  }
```

Extending a Check Box Group

The following program reworks the preceding check box example so that the check boxes form a check box group. Thus, only one of the check boxes may be selected at any time.

```
/*
 * <applet code=CheckboxGroupDemo2 width=300 height=100>
 * </applet>
*/
import java.awt.*;
import java.awt.event.*;
import java.applet.*;

public class CheckboxGroupDemo2 extends Applet {
  CheckboxGroup cbg;
  MyCheckbox myCheckbox1, myCheckbox2, myCheckbox3;
  public void init() {
    cbg = new CheckboxGroup();
    myCheckbox1 = new MyCheckbox("Item 1", cbg, true);
    add(myCheckbox1);
    myCheckbox2 = new MyCheckbox("Item 2", cbg, false);
    add(myCheckbox2);
    myCheckbox3 = new MyCheckbox("Item 3", cbg, false);
    add(myCheckbox3);
  }
  class MyCheckbox extends Checkbox {
    public MyCheckbox(String label, CheckboxGroup cbg,
                      boolean flag) {
      super(label, cbg, flag);
      enableEvents(AWTEvent.ITEM_EVENT_MASK);
    }
    protected void processItemEvent(ItemEvent ie) {
      showStatus("Checkbox name/state: " + getLabel() +
                 "/" + getState());
      super.processItemEvent(ie);
    }
  }
}
```

Extending Choice

The following program creates an applet that displays a choice list with items labeled "Red", "Green", and "Blue". When an entry is selected, a string that contains the name of the color is displayed on the status line of the applet viewer or browser.

There is one top-level class named **ChoiceDemo2** that extends **Applet**. Its **init( )** method creates a choice element and adds it to the applet. **MyChoice** is an inner class that extends **Choice**. It calls **enableEvents( )** so that item events may be received by this object. When an item event is generated, **processItemEvent( )** is called. That method displays a string on the status line and calls **processItemEvent( )** for the superclass.

```
/*
 * <applet code=ChoiceDemo2 width=300 height=100>
 * </applet>
 */
import java.awt.*;
import java.awt.event.*;
import java.applet.*;

public class ChoiceDemo2 extends Applet {
  MyChoice choice;
  public void init() {
    choice = new MyChoice();
    choice.add("Red");
    choice.add("Green");
    choice.add("Blue");
    add(choice);
  }
  class MyChoice extends Choice {
    public MyChoice() {
      enableEvents(AWTEvent.ITEM_EVENT_MASK);
    }
    protected void processItemEvent(ItemEvent ie) {
      showStatus("Choice selection: " + getSelectedItem());
      super.processItemEvent(ie);
    }
  }
}
```

Extending List

The following program modifies the preceding example so that it uses a list instead of a choice menu. There is one top-level class named **ListDemo2** that extends **Applet**. Its **init( )** method creates a list element and adds it to the applet. **MyList** is an inner class that extends **List**. It calls **enableEvents( )** so that both action and item events may be received by this object. When an entry is selected or deselected, **processItemEvent( )** is called. When an entry is double-clicked, **processActionEvent( )** is also called. Both methods display a string and then hand control to the superclass.

```
/*
 * <applet code=ListDemo2 width=300 height=100>
 * </applet>
 */
import java.awt.*;
import java.awt.event.*;
import java.applet.*;

public class ListDemo2 extends Applet {
  MyList list;
  public void init() {
    list = new MyList();
    list.add("Red");
    list.add("Green");
    list.add("Blue");
    add(list);
  }
  class MyList extends List {
    public MyList() {
      enableEvents(AWTEvent.ITEM_EVENT_MASK |
                   AWTEvent.ACTION_EVENT_MASK);
    }
    protected void processActionEvent(ActionEvent ae) {
      showStatus("Action event: " + ae.getActionCommand());
      super.processActionEvent(ae);
    }
    protected void processItemEvent(ItemEvent ie) {
      showStatus("Item event: " + getSelectedItem());
      super.processItemEvent(ie);
    }
  }
}
```

Extending Scrollbar

The following program creates an applet that displays a scroll bar. When this control is manipulated, a string is displayed on the status line of the applet viewer or browser. That string includes the value represented by the scroll bar.

There is one top-level class named **ScrollbarDemo2** that extends **Applet**. Its **init( )** method creates a scroll bar element and adds it to the applet. **MyScrollbar** is an inner class that extends **Scrollbar**. It calls **enableEvents( )** so that adjustment events may be received by this object. When the scroll bar is manipulated, **processAdjustmentEvent( )** is called. When an entry is selected, **processAdjustmentEvent( )** is called. It displays a string and then hands control to the superclass.

```
/*
 * <applet code=ScrollbarDemo2 width=300 height=100>
 * </applet>
 */
import java.awt.*;
import java.awt.event.*;
import java.applet.*;

public class ScrollbarDemo2 extends Applet {
  MyScrollbar myScrollbar;
  public void init() {
    myScrollbar = new MyScrollbar(Scrollbar.HORIZONTAL,
                                  0, 1, 0, 100);

    add(myScrollbar);
  }
  class MyScrollbar extends Scrollbar {
    public MyScrollbar(int style, int initial, int thumb,
                       int min, int max) {
      super(style, initial, thumb, min, max);
      enableEvents(AWTEvent.ADJUSTMENT_EVENT_MASK);
    }
    protected void processAdjustmentEvent(AdjustmentEvent ae) {
      showStatus("Adjustment event: " + ae.getValue());
      setValue(getValue());
      super.processAdjustmentEvent(ae);
    }
  }
}
```

Exploring the Controls, Menus, and Layout Managers

This chapter has discussed the classes that comprise the AWT controls, menus, and layout managers. However, the AWT provides a rich programming environment that you will want to continue exploring on your own. Here are some suggestions:

■ Try nesting a canvas inside an applet panel.

■ Explore the **FileDialog** component.

■ Experiment with manual positioning of components by using **setBounds( )**.

■ Try nesting controls within panels to gain more control over layouts.

■ Create your own layout manager by implementing the **LayoutManager** interface.

■ Explore **PopupMenu**.

The more you know about the AWT components, the more control you will have over the look, feel, and performance of your applets and applications.

In the next chapter, we will examine one more of the AWT's classes: **Image**. This class is used to support imaging and animation.

The
Complete
Reference

Java™ 2

Chapter 23

Images

This chapter examines the AWT's **Image** class and the **java.awt.image** package. Together, they provide support for *imaging* (the display and manipulation of graphical images). An *image* is simply a rectangular graphical object. Images are a key component of web design. In fact, the inclusion of the **<img>** tag in the Mosaic browser at NCSA (National Center for Supercomputer Applications) is what caused the Web to begin to grow explosively in 1993. This tag was used to include an image *inline* with the flow of hypertext. Java expands upon this basic concept, allowing images to be managed under program control. Because of its importance, Java provides extensive support for imaging.

Images are objects of the **Image** class, which is part of the **java.awt** package. Images are manipulated using the classes found in the **java.awt.image** package. There are a large number of imaging classes and interfaces defined by **java.awt.image** and it is not possible to examine them all. Instead, we will focus on those that form the foundation of imaging. Here are the **java.awt.image** classes discussed in this chapter:

CropImageFilter	MemoryImageSource
FilteredImageSource	PixelGrabber
ImageFilter	RGBImageFilter

These are the interfaces that we will use.

ImageConsumer	ImageObserver	ImageProducer

Also examined is the **MediaTracker** class, which is part of **java.awt**.

File Formats

Originally, web images could only be in GIF format. The GIF image format was created by CompuServe in 1987 to make it possible for images to be viewed while online, so it was well suited to the Internet. GIF images can have only up to 256 colors each. This limitation caused the major browser vendors to add support for JPEG images in 1995. The JPEG format was created by a group of photographic experts to store full-color-spectrum, continuous-tone images. These images, when properly created, can be of much higher fidelity as well as more highly compressed than a GIF encoding of the same source image. In almost all cases, you will never care or notice which format is being used in your programs. The Java image classes abstract the differences behind a clean interface.

Image Fundamentals: Creating, Loading, and Displaying

There are three common operations that occur when you work with images: creating an image, loading an image, and displaying an image. In Java, the **Image** class is used to refer to images in memory and to images that must be loaded from external sources. Thus, Java provides ways for you to create a new image object and ways to load one. It also provides a means by which an image can be displayed. Let's look at each.

Creating an Image Object

You might expect that you create a memory image using something like the following:

```
Image test = new Image(200, 100); // Error -- won't work
```

Not so. Because images must eventually be painted on a window to be seen, the **Image** class doesn't have enough information about its environment to create the proper data format for the screen. Therefore, the **Component** class in **java.awt** has a factory method called **createImage( )** that is used to create **Image** objects. (Remember that all of the AWT components are subclasses of **Component**, so all support this method.)

The **createImage( )** method has the following two forms:

Image createImage(ImageProducer *imgProd*)
Image createImage(int *width*, int *height*)

The first form returns an image produced by *imgProd*, which is an object of a class that implements the **ImageProducer** interface. (We will look at image producers later.) The second form returns a blank (that is, empty) image that has the specified width and height. Here is an example:

```
Canvas c = new Canvas();
Image test = c.createImage(200, 100);
```

This creates an instance of **Canvas** and then calls the **createImage( )** method to actually make an **Image** object. At this point, the image is blank. Later you will see how to write data to it.

Loading an Image

The other way to obtain an image is to load one. To do this, use the **getImage( )** method defined by the **Applet** class. It has the following forms:

Image getImage(URL *url*)
Image getImage(URL *url*, String *imageName*)

THE JAVA LIBRARY

The first version returns an **Image** object that encapsulates the image found at the location specified by *url*. The second version returns an **Image** object that encapsulates the image found at the location specified by *url* and having the name specified by *imageName*.

Displaying an Image

Once you have an image, you can display it by using **drawImage( )**, which is a member of the **Graphics** class. It has several forms. The one we will be using is shown here:

boolean drawImage(Image *imgObj*, int *left*, int *top*, ImageObserver *imgOb*)

This displays the image passed in *imgObj* with its upper-left corner specified by *left* and *top*. *imgOb* is a reference to a class that implements the **ImageObserver** interface. This interface is implemented by all AWT components. An *image observer* is an object that can monitor an image while it loads. **ImageObserver** is described in the next section.

With **getImage( )** and **drawImage( )**, it is actually quite easy to load and display an image. Here is a sample applet that loads and displays a single image. The file **seattle.jpg** is loaded, but you can substitute any GIF or JPG file you like (just make sure it is available in the same directory with the HTML file that contains the applet).

```
/*
 * <applet code="SimpleImageLoad" width=248 height=146>
 *   <param name="img" value="seattle.jpg">
 * </applet>
 */
import java.awt.*;
import java.applet.*;

public class SimpleImageLoad extends Applet
{
  Image img;

  public void init() {
    img = getImage(getDocumentBase(), getParameter("img"));
  }

  public void paint(Graphics g) {
    g.drawImage(img, 0, 0, this);
  }
}
```

In the **init( )** method, the **img** variable is assigned to the image returned by **getImage( )**. The **getImage( )** method uses the string returned by **getParameter("img")** as the filename for the image. This image is loaded from a **URL** that is relative to the result of **getDocumentBase( )**, which is the **URL** of the HTML page this applet tag was in. The filename returned by **getParameter("img")** comes from the applet tag **<param name="img" value="seattle.jpg">**. This is the equivalent, if a little slower, of using the HTML tag **<img src="seattle.jpg" width=248 height=146>**. Figure 23-1 shows what it looks like when you run the program.

When this applet runs, it starts loading **img** in the **init( )** method. Onscreen you can see the image as it loads from the network, because **Applet**'s implementation of the **ImageObserver** interface calls **paint( )** every time more image data arrives.

Seeing the image load is somewhat informative, but it might be better if you use the time it takes to load the image to do other things in parallel. That way, the fully formed image can simply appear on the screen in an instant, once it is fully loaded. You can use **ImageObserver**, described next, to monitor loading an image while you paint the screen with other information.

ImageObserver

ImageObserver is an interface used to receive notification as an image is being generated. **ImageObserver** defines only one method: **imageUpdate( )**. Using an image observer allows you to perform other actions, such as show a progress indicator or an attract screen, as you are informed of the progress of the download. This kind of

Figure 23-1.   *Sample output from* SimpleImageLoad

notification is very useful when an image is being loaded over the network, where the content designer rarely appreciates that people are often trying to load applets over a slow modem.

The **imageUpdate( )** method has this general form:

boolean imageUpdate(Image *imgObj*, int *flags*, int *left*, int *top*, int *width*, int *height*)

Here, *imgObj* is the image being loaded, and *flags* is an integer that communicates the status of the update report. The four integers *left*, *top*, *width*, and *height* represent a rectangle that contains different values depending on the values passed in *flags*. **imageUpdate( )** should return **false** if it has completed loading, and **true** if there is more image to process.

The *flags* parameter contains one or more bit flags defined as static variables inside the **ImageObserver** interface. These flags and the information they provide are listed in Table 23-1.

Flag	Meaning
WIDTH	The *width* parameter is valid and contains the width of the image.
HEIGHT	The *height* parameter is valid and contains the height of the image.
PROPERTIES	The properties associated with the image can now be obtained using **imgObj.getProperty( )**.
SOMEBITS	More pixels needed to draw the image have been received. The parameters *left*, *top*, *width*, and *height* define the rectangle containing the new pixels.
FRAMEBITS	A complete frame that is part of a multiframe image, which was previously drawn, has been received. This frame can be displayed. The *left*, *top*, *width*, and *height* parameters are not used.
ALLBITS	The image is now complete. The *left*, *top*, *width*, and *height* parameters are not used.
ERROR	An error has occurred to an image that was being tracked asynchronously. The image is incomplete and cannot be displayed. No further image information will be received. The **ABORT** flag will also be set to indicate that the image production was aborted.
ABORT	An image that was being tracked asynchronously was aborted before it was complete. However, if an error has not occurred, accessing any part of the image's data will restart the production of the image.

Table 23-1.   *Bit Flags of the* imageUpdate( ) *flags Parameter*

The **Applet** class has an implementation of the **imageUpdate( )** method for the **ImageObserver** interface that is used to repaint images as they are loaded. You can override this method in your class to change that behavior.

Here is a simple example of an **imageUpdate( )** method:

```
public boolean imageUpdate(Image img, int flags,
                        int x, int y, int w, int h) {
  if ((flags & ALLBITS) == 0) {
    System.out.println("Still processing the image.");
    return true;
  } else {
    System.out.println("Done processing the image.");
    return false;
  }
}
```

ImageObserver Example

Now let's look at a practical example that overrides **imageUpdate( )** to make a version of the **SimpleImageLoad** applet that doesn't flicker as much. The default implementation of **imageUpdate( )** in **Applet** has several problems. First, it repaints the entire image each time any new data arrives. This causes flashing between the background color and the image. Second, it uses a feature of **Applet.repaint( )** to cause the system to only repaint the image every tenth of a second or so. This causes a jerky, uneven feel as the image is painting. Finally, the default implementation knows nothing about images that may fail to load properly. Many beginning Java programmers are frustrated by the fact that **getImage( )** always succeeds even when the image specified does not exist. You don't find out about missing images until **imageUpdate( )** occurs. If you use the default implementation of **imageUpdate( )**, then you'll never know what happened. Your **paint( )** method will simply do nothing when you call **g.drawImage( )**.

The example that follows fixes all three of these problems in ten lines of code. First, it eliminates the flickering with two small changes. It overrides **update( )** so that it calls **paint( )** without painting the background color first. The background is set via **setBackground( )** in **init( )**, so the initial color is painted just once. Also, it uses a version of **repaint( )** that specifies the rectangle in which to paint. The system will set the clipping area such that nothing outside of this rectangle is painted. This reduces repaint flicker and improves performance.

Second, it eliminates the jerky, uneven display of the incoming image by painting every time it receives an update. These updates occur on a scan line-by-scan line basis, so an image that is 100 pixels tall will be "repainted" 100 times as it loads. Note that this is not the fastest way to display an image, just the smoothest.

Finally, it handles the error caused by the desired file not being found by examining the **flags** parameter for the **ABORT** bit. If it is set, the instance variable **error** is set to **true** and then **repaint( )** is called. The **paint( )** method is modified to print an error message over a bright red background if **error** is **true**.

Here is the code.

```
/*
 * <applet code="ObservedImageLoad" width=248 height=146>
 *   <param name="img" value="seattle.jpg">
 * </applet>
 */
import java.awt.*;
import java.applet.*;

public class ObservedImageLoad extends Applet {
  Image img;
  boolean error = false;
  String imgname;

  public void init() {
    setBackground(Color.blue);
    imgname = getParameter("img");
    img = getImage(getDocumentBase(), imgname);
  }

  public void paint(Graphics g) {
    if (error) {
      Dimension d = getSize();
      g.setColor(Color.red);
      g.fillRect(0, 0, d.width, d.height);
      g.setColor(Color.black);
      g.drawString("Image not found: " + imgname, 10, d.height/2);
    } else {
      g.drawImage(img, 0, 0, this);
    }
  }

  public void update(Graphics g) {
    paint(g);
  }
```

```
public boolean imageUpdate(Image img, int flags,
                          int x, int y, int w, int h) {
  if ((flags & SOMEBITS) != 0) {   // new partial data
    repaint(x, y, w, h);           // paint new pixels
  } else if ((flags & ABORT) != 0) {
    error = true;                  // file not found
    repaint();                     // paint whole applet
  }
  return (flags & (ALLBITS|ABORT)) == 0;
}
}
```

Figure 23-2 shows two separate screens of this applet running. The top screen shows the image half loaded, and the bottom screen displays a filename that has been mistyped in the applet tag.

Here is an interesting variation of **imageUpdate( )** you might want to try. It waits until the image is completely loaded before snapping it onto the screen in a single repaint.

```
public boolean imageUpdate(Image img, int flags,
                          int x, int y, int w, int h) {
  if ((flags & ALLBITS) != 0) {
    repaint();
  } else if ((flags & (ABORT|ERROR)) != 0) {
    error = true; // file not found
    repaint();
  }
  return (flags & (ALLBITS|ABORT|ERROR)) == 0;
}
```

Double Buffering

Not only are images useful for storing pictures, as we've just shown, but you can also use them as offscreen drawing surfaces. This allows you to render any image, including text and graphics, to an offscreen buffer that you can display at a later time. The advantage to doing this is that the image is seen only when it is complete. Drawing a complicated image could take several milliseconds or more, which can be seen by the user as flashing or flickering. This flashing is distracting and causes the user to perceive your rendering as slower than it actually is. Use of an offscreen image to reduce flicker

Figure 23-2. *Sample output from* ObservedImageLoad

is called *double buffering*, because the screen is considered a buffer for pixels, and the offscreen image is the second buffer, where you can prepare pixels for display.

Earlier in this chapter, you saw how to create a blank **Image** object. Now you will see how to draw on that image rather than the screen. As you recall from earlier chapters, you need a **Graphics** object in order to use any of Java's rendering methods. Conveniently, the **Graphics** object that you can use to draw on an **Image** is available via the **getGraphics( )** method. Here is a code fragment that creates a new image, obtains its graphics context, and fills the entire image with red pixels:

```
Canvas c = new Canvas();
Image test = c.createImage(200, 100);
Graphics gc = test.getGraphics();
gc.setColor(Color.red);
gc.fillRect(0, 0, 200, 100);
```

Once you have constructed and filled an offscreen image, it will still not be visible. To actually display the image, call **drawImage( )**. Here is an example that draws a time-consuming image, to demonstrate the difference that double buffering can make in perceived drawing time:

```
/*
 * <applet code=DoubleBuffer width=250 height=250>
 * </applet>
 */
import java.awt.*;
import java.awt.event.*;
import java.applet.*;

public class DoubleBuffer extends Applet {
  int gap = 3;
  int mx, my;
  boolean flicker = true;
  Image buffer = null;
  int w, h;

  public void init() {
    Dimension d = getSize();
    w = d.width;
    h = d.height;
    buffer = createImage(w, h);
    addMouseMotionListener(new MouseMotionAdapter() {
      public void mouseDragged(MouseEvent me) {
        mx = me.getX();
        my = me.getY();
        flicker = false;
        repaint();
      }
      public void mouseMoved(MouseEvent me) {
        mx = me.getX();
        my = me.getY();
        flicker = true;
```

```
            repaint();
        }
    });
}

public void paint(Graphics g) {
    Graphics screengc = null;

    if (!flicker) {
        screengc = g;
        g = buffer.getGraphics();
    }

    g.setColor(Color.blue);
    g.fillRect(0, 0, w, h);

    g.setColor(Color.red);
    for (int i=0; i<w; i+=gap)
        g.drawLine(i, 0, w-i, h);
    for (int i=0; i<h; i+=gap)
        g.drawLine(0, i, w, h-i);

    g.setColor(Color.black);
    g.drawString("Press mouse button to double buffer", 10, h/2);

    g.setColor(Color.yellow);
    g.fillOval(mx - gap, my - gap, gap*2+1, gap*2+1);

    if (!flicker) {
        screengc.drawImage(buffer, 0, 0, null);
    }
}
public void update(Graphics g) {
    paint(g);
}
}
```

This simple applet has a complicated **paint( )** method. It fills the background with blue and then draws a red moiré pattern on top of that. It paints some black text on top of that and then paints a yellow circle centered at the coordinates **mx,my**. The **mouseMoved( )** and **mouseDragged( )** methods are overridden to track the mouse position. These methods are identical, except for the setting of the **flicker** Boolean variable. **mouseMoved( )** sets **flicker** to **true**, and **mouseDragged( )** sets it to **false**. This has the effect of calling **repaint( )** with **flicker** set to **true** when the mouse is moved (but no button is pressed) and set to **false** when the mouse is dragged with any button pressed.

When **paint( )** gets called with **flicker** set to **true**, we see each drawing operation as it is executed on the screen. In the case where a mouse button is pressed and **paint( )** is called with **flicker** set to **false**, we see quite a different picture. The **paint( )** method swaps the **Graphics** reference **g** with the graphics context that refers to the offscreen canvas, **buffer**, which we created in **init( )**. Then all of the drawing operations are invisible. At the end of **paint( )**, we simply call **drawImage( )** to show the results of these drawing methods all at once.

Notice that it is okay to pass in a **null** as the fourth parameter to **drawImage( )**. This is the parameter used to pass an **ImageObserver** object that receives notification of image events. Since this is an image that is not being produced from a network stream, we have no need for notification. The left snapshot in Figure 23-3 is what the applet looks like with the mouse buttons not pressed. As you can see, the image was in the middle of repainting when this snapshot was taken. The right snapshot shows how, when a mouse button is pressed, the image is always complete and clean due to double buffering.

MediaTracker

Many early Java developers found the **ImageObserver** interface far too difficult to understand and manage when there were multiple images to be loaded. The developer community asked for a simpler solution that would allow programmers to load all of their images synchronously, without having to worry about **imageUpdate( )**. In response to this, Sun Microsystems added a class to **java.awt** called **MediaTracker** in a subsequent release of the JDK. A **MediaTracker** is an object that will check the status of an arbitrary number of images in parallel.

To use **MediaTracker**, you create a new instance and use its **addImage( )** method to track the loading status of an image. **addImage( )** has the following general forms:

```
void addImage(Image imgObj, int imgID)
void addImage(Image imgObj, int imgID, int width, int height)
```

Here, *imgObj* is the image being tracked. Its identification number is passed in *imgID*. ID numbers do not need to be unique. You can use the same number with several images as a means of identifying them as part of a group. In the second form, *width* and *height* specify the dimensions of the object when it is displayed.

THE JAVA LIBRARY

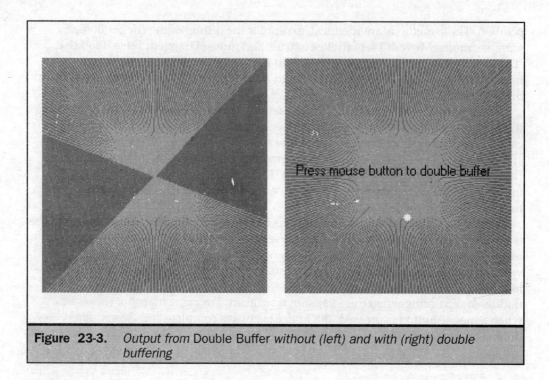

Figure 23-3. *Output from* Double Buffer *without (left) and with (right) double buffering*

Once you've registered an image, you can check whether it's loaded, or you can wait for it to completely load. To check the status of an image, call **checkID( )**. The version used in this chapter is shown here:

boolean checkID(int *imgID*)

Here, *imgID* specifies the ID of the image you want to check. The method returns **true** if all images that have the specified ID have been loaded (or if an error or user- abort has terminated loading). Otherwise, it returns **false**. You can use the **checkAll( )** method to see if all images being tracked have been loaded.

You should use **MediaTracker** when loading a group of images. If all of the images that you're interested in aren't downloaded, you can display something else to entertain the user until they all arrive.

*If you use **MediaTracker** once you've called **addImage( )** on an image, a reference in **MediaTracker** will prevent the system from garbage collecting it. If you want the system to be able to garbage collect images that were being tracked, make sure it can collect the **MediaTracker** instance as well.*

Here's an example that loads a seven-image slide show and displays a nice bar chart of the loading progress:

```java
/*
 * <applet code="TrackedImageLoad" width=300 height=400>
 * <param name="img"
 * value="vincent+leonardo+matisse+picasso+renoir+seurat+vermeer">
 * </applet>
 */
import java.util.*;
import java.applet.*;
import java.awt.*;

public class TrackedImageLoad extends Applet implements Runnable {
  MediaTracker tracker;
  int tracked;
  int frame_rate = 5;
  int current_img = 0;
  Thread motor;
  static final int MAXIMAGES = 10;
  Image img[] = new Image[MAXIMAGES];
  String name[] = new String[MAXIMAGES];
  boolean stopFlag;

  public void init() {
    tracker = new MediaTracker(this);
    StringTokenizer st = new StringTokenizer(getParameter("img"),
                                             "+");

    while(st.hasMoreTokens() && tracked <= MAXIMAGES) {
      name[tracked] = st.nextToken();
      img[tracked] = getImage(getDocumentBase(),
                              name[tracked] + ".jpg");
      tracker.addImage(img[tracked], tracked);
      tracked++;
    }
  }

  public void paint(Graphics g) {
    String loaded = "";
    int donecount = 0;
```

```java
    for(int i=0; i<tracked; i++) {
      if (tracker.checkID(i, true)) {
        donecount++;
        loaded += name[i] + " ";
      }
    }

    Dimension d = getSize();
    int w = d.width;
    int h = d.height;

    if (donecount == tracked) {
      frame_rate = 1;
      Image i = img[current_img++];
      int iw = i.getWidth(null);
      int ih = i.getHeight(null);
      g.drawImage(i, (w - iw)/2, (h - ih)/2, null);
      if (current_img >= tracked)
        current_img = 0;
    } else {
      int x = w * donecount / tracked;
      g.setColor(Color.black);
      g.fillRect(0, h/3, x, 16);
      g.setColor(Color.white);
      g.fillRect(x, h/3, w-x, 16);
      g.setColor(Color.black);
      g.drawString(loaded, 10, h/2);
    }
  }

public void start() {
  motor = new Thread(this);
  stopFlag = false;
  motor.start();
}

public void stop() {
  stopFlag = true;
}

public void run() {
```

```
     motor.setPriority(Thread.MIN_PRIORITY);
     while (true) {
       repaint();
       try {
         Thread.sleep(1000/frame_rate);
       } catch (InterruptedException e) { };
       if(stopFlag)
         return;
     }
   }
 }
```

This example creates a new **MediaTracker** in the **init( )** method, and then adds each of the named images as a tracked image with **addImage( )**. In the **paint( )** method, it calls **checkID( )** on each of the images that we're tracking. If all of the images are loaded, they are displayed. If not, a simple bar chart of the number of images loaded is shown, with the names of the fully loaded images displayed underneath the bar. Figure 23-4 shows two scenes from this applet running. One is the bar chart, displaying that three of the images have been loaded. The other is the Van Gogh self-portrait during the slide show.

ImageProducer

ImageProducer is an interface for objects that want to produce data for images. An object that implements the **ImageProducer** interface will supply integer or byte arrays that represent image data and produce **Image** objects. As you saw earlier, one form of the **createImage( )** method takes an **ImageProducer** object as its argument. There are two image producers contained in **java.awt.image**: **MemoryImageSource** and **FilteredImageSource**. Here, we will examine **MemoryImageSource** and create a new **Image** object from data generated in an applet.

MemoryImageSource

MemoryImageSource is a class that creates a new **Image** from an array of data. It defines several constructors. Here is the one we will be using:

MemoryImageSource(int *width*, int *height*, int *pixel*[ ], int *offset*, int *scanLineWidth*)

The **MemoryImageSource** object is constructed out of the array of integers specified by *pixel*, in the default RGB color model to produce data for an **Image** object. In the default color model, a pixel is an integer with Alpha, Red, Green, and Blue (0xAARRGGBB). The Alpha value represents a degree of transparency for the pixel. Fully transparent is

Figure 23-4.   *Sample output from* TrackedImageLoad

0 and fully opaque is 255. The width and height of the resulting image are passed in *width* and *height*. The starting point in the pixel array to begin reading data is passed in *offset*. The width of a scan line (which is often the same as the width of the image) is passed in *scanLineWidth*.

The following short example generates a **MemoryImageSource** object using a variation on a simple algorithm (a bitwise-exclusive-OR of the x and y address of each pixel) from the book *Beyond Photography, The Digital Darkroom* by Gerard J. Holzmann (Prentice Hall, 1988).

```
/*
 * <applet code="MemoryImageGenerator" width=256 height=256>
 * </applet>
 */
import java.applet.*;
import java.awt.*;
import java.awt.image.*;

public class MemoryImageGenerator extends Applet {
  Image img;
  public void init() {
    Dimension d = getSize();
    int w = d.width;
    int h = d.height;
    int pixels[] = new int[w * h];
    int i = 0;

    for(int y=0; y<h; y++) {
      for(int x=0; x<w; x++) {
        int r = (x^y)&0xff;
        int g = (x*2^y*2)&0xff;
        int b = (x*4^y*4)&0xff;
        pixels[i++] = (255 << 24) | (r << 16) | (g << 8) | b;
      }
    }
    img = createImage(new MemoryImageSource(w, h, pixels, 0, w));
  }
  public void paint(Graphics g) {
    g.drawImage(img, 0, 0, this);
  }
}
```

The data for the new **MemoryImageSource** is created in the **init( )** method. An array of integers is created to hold the pixel values; the data is generated in the nested **for** loops where the **r**, **g**, and **b** values get shifted into a pixel in the **pixels** array. Finally, **createImage( )** is called with a new instance of a **MemoryImageSource** created from the raw pixel data as its parameter. Figure 23-5 shows the image when we run the applet. (It looks much nicer in color.)

ImageConsumer

ImageConsumer is an abstract interface for objects that want to take pixel data from images and supply it as another kind of data. This, obviously, is the opposite of

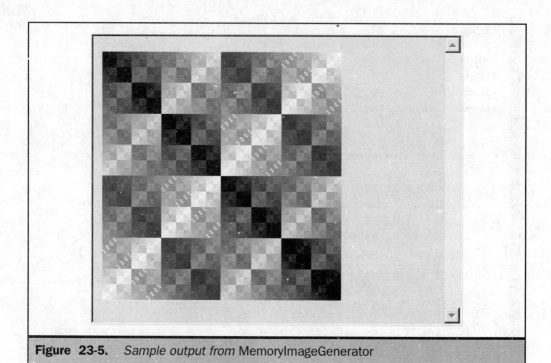

Figure 23-5. *Sample output from* MemoryImageGenerator

ImageProducer, described earlier. An object that implements the **ImageConsumer** interface is going to create **int** or **byte** arrays that represent pixels from an **Image** object. We will examine the **PixelGrabber** class, which is a simple implementation of the **ImageConsumer** interface.

PixelGrabber

The **PixelGrabber** class is defined within **java.lang.image**. It is the inverse of the **MemoryImageSource** class. Rather than constructing an image from an array of pixel values, it takes an existing image and *grabs* the pixel array from it. To use **PixelGrabber**, you first create an array of **int**s big enough to hold the pixel data, and then you create a **PixelGrabber** instance passing in the rectangle that you want to grab. Finally, you call **grabPixels( )** on that instance.

The **PixelGrabber** constructor that is used in this chapter is shown here:

PixelGrabber(Image *imgObj*, int *left*, int *top*, int *width*, int *height*, int *pixel*[ ],
　　　　　int *offset*, int *scanLineWidth*)

Here, *imgObj* is the object whose pixels are being grabbed. The values of *left* and *top* specify the upper-left corner of the rectangle, and *width* and *height* specify the dimensions of the rectangle from which the pixels will be obtained. The pixels will be stored in *pixel* beginning at *offset*. The width of a scan line (which is often the same as the width of the image) is passed in *scanLineWidth*.

grabPixels( ) is defined like this:

boolean grabPixels( )
   throws InterruptedException

boolean grabPixels(long *milliseconds*)
   throws InterruptedException

Both methods return **true** if successful and **false** otherwise. In the second form, *milliseconds* specifies how long the method will wait for the pixels.

Here is an example that grabs the pixels from an image and then creates a histogram of pixel brightness. The *histogram* is simply a count of pixels that are a certain brightness for all brightness settings between 0 and 255. After the applet paints the image, it draws the histogram over the top.

```
/*
 * <applet code=HistoGrab.class width=341 height=400>
 * <param name=img value=vermeer.jpg>
 * </applet> */
import java.applet.*;
import java.awt.* ;
import java.awt.image.* ;

public class HistoGrab extends Applet {
  Dimension d;
  Image img;
  int iw, ih;
  int pixels[];
  int w, h;
  int hist[] = new int[256];
  int max_hist = 0;

  public void init() {
    d = getSize();
    w = d.width;
    h = d.height;

    try {
      img = getImage(getDocumentBase(), getParameter("img"));
      MediaTracker t = new MediaTracker(this);
      t.addImage(img, 0);
```

```
            t.waitForID(0);
            iw = img.getWidth(null);
            ih = img.getHeight(null);
            pixels = new int[iw * ih];
            PixelGrabber pg = new PixelGrabber(img, 0, 0, iw, ih,
                                               pixels, 0, iw);
            pg.grabPixels();
        } catch (InterruptedException e) { };

        for (int i=0; i<iw*ih; i++) {
            int p = pixels[i];
            int r = 0xff & (p >> 16);
            int g = 0xff & (p >> 8);
            int b = 0xff & (p);
            int y = (int) (.33 * r + .56 * g + .11 * b);
            hist[y]++;
        }
        for (int i=0; i<256; i++) {
            if (hist[i] > max_hist)
                max_hist = hist[i];
        }
    }

    public void update() {}

    public void paint(Graphics g) {
        g.drawImage(img, 0, 0, null);
        int x = (w - 256) / 2;
        int lasty = h - h * hist[0] / max_hist;
        for (int i=0; i<256; i++, x++) {
            int y = h - h * hist[i] / max_hist;
            g.setColor(new Color(i, i, i));
            g.fillRect(x, y, 1, h);
            g.setColor(Color.red);
            g.drawLine(x-1,lasty,x,y);
            lasty = y;
        }
    }
}
```

Figure 23-6 shows the image and histogram for a famous Vermeer painting.

Figure 23-6. *Sample output from* HistoGrab

ImageFilter

Given the **ImageProducer** and **ImageConsumer** interface pair—and their concrete classes **MemoryImageSource** and **PixelGrabber**—you can create an arbitrary set of translation filters that takes a source of pixels, modifies them, and passes them on to an arbitrary consumer. This mechanism is analogous to the way concrete classes are created from the abstract I/O classes **InputStream**, **OutputStream**, **Reader**, and **Writer** (described in Chapter 17). This stream model for images is completed by the introduction of the **ImageFilter** class. Some subclasses of **ImageFilter** in the **java.awt.image** package are **AreaAveragingScaleFilter**, **CropImageFilter**, **ReplicateScaleFilter**, and **RGBImageFilter**. There is also an implementation of **ImageProducer** called **FilteredImageSource**, which takes an arbitrary **ImageFilter** and wraps it around an **ImageProducer** to filter the pixels it produces. An instance of **FilteredImageSource** can be used as an **ImageProducer** in calls to **createImage**, in much the same way that **BufferedInputStream**s can be passed off as **InputStream**s.

In this chapter, we examine two filters: **CropImageFilter** and **RGBImageFilter**.

CropImageFilter

CropImageFilter filters an image source to extract a rectangular region. One situation in which this filter is valuable is where you want to use several small images from a single, larger source image. Loading twenty 2K images takes much longer than loading a single 40K image that has many frames of an animation tiled into it. If every subimage is the same size, then you can easily extract these images by using **CropImageFilter** to disassemble the block once your applet starts. Here is an example that creates 16 images taken from a single image. The tiles are then scrambled by swapping a random pair from the 16 images 32 times.

```
/*
 * <applet code=TileImage.class width=288 height=399>
 * <param name=img value=picasso.jpg>
 * </applet>
 */
import java.applet.*;
import java.awt.*;
import java.awt.image.*;

public class TileImage extends Applet {
  Image img;
  Image cell[] = new Image[4*4];
  int iw, ih;
  int tw, th;

  public void init() {
    try {
      img = getImage(getDocumentBase(), getParameter("img"));
      MediaTracker t = new MediaTracker(this);
      t.addImage(img, 0);
      t.waitForID(0);
      iw = img.getWidth(null);
      ih = img.getHeight(null);
      tw = iw / 4;
      th = ih / 4;
      CropImageFilter f;
      FilteredImageSource fis;
      t = new MediaTracker(this);
      for (int y=0; y<4; y++) {
        for (int x=0; x<4; x++) {
          f = new CropImageFilter(tw*x, th*y, tw, th);
          fis = new FilteredImageSource(img.getSource(), f);
          int i = y*4+x;
          cell[i] = createImage(fis);
          t.addImage(cell[i], i);
```

```
        }
      }
    t.waitForAll();
    for (int i=0; i<32; i++) {
      int si = (int)(Math.random() * 16);
      int di = (int)(Math.random() * 16);
      Image tmp = cell[si];
      cell[si] = cell[di];
      cell[di] = tmp;
    }
  } catch (InterruptedException e) { };
}

public void update(Graphics g) {
  paint(g);
}

public void paint(Graphics g) {
  for (int y=0; y<4; y++) {
    for (int x=0; x<4; x++) {
      g.drawImage(cell[y*4+x], x * tw, y * th, null);
    }
  }
}
```

Figure 23-7 shows a famous Picasso painting scrambled by the **TileImage** applet.

RGBImageFilter

The **RGBImageFilter** is used to convert one image to another, pixel by pixel,
transforming the colors along the way. This filter could be used to brighten an
image, to increase its contrast, or even to convert it to grayscale.

To demonstrate **RGBImageFilter**, we have developed a somewhat complicated
example, which employs a dynamic plug-in strategy for image-processing filters.
We've created an interface for generalized image filtering so that our applet can simply
load these filters based on **<param>** tags without having to know about all of the
ImageFilters in advance. This example consists of the main applet class called
ImageFilterDemo, the interface called **PlugInFilter**, and a utility class called
LoadedImage, which encapsulates some of the **MediaTracker** methods we've been
using in this chapter. Also included are three filters—**Grayscale**, **Invert**, and
Contrast—which simply manipulate the color space of the source image using

Figure 23-7. *Sample output from* TileImage

RGBImageFilters, and two more classes—**Blur** and **Sharpen**—which do more complicated "convolution" filters that change pixel data based on the pixels surrounding each pixel of source data. **Blur** and **Sharpen** are subclasses of an abstract helper class called **Convolver**. Let's look at each part of our example.

ImageFilterDemo.java

The **ImageFilterDemo** class is the applet framework for our sample image filters. It employs a simple **BorderLayout**, with a **Panel** at the *South* position to hold the buttons that will represent each filter. A **Label** object occupies the *North* slot for informational messages about filter progress. The *Center* is where the image (which is encapsulated in the **LoadedImage Canvas** subclass, described later) is put. We parse the buttons/filters out of the **filters <param>** tag, separating them with +'s using a **StringTokenizer**.

The **actionPerformed( )** method is interesting because it uses the label from a button as the name of a filter class that it tries to load with **(PlugInFilter) Class.forName(a).newInstance( )**. This method is robust and takes appropriate action if the button does not correspond to a proper class that implements **PlugInFilter**.

```
/*
 * <applet code=ImageFilterDemo width=350 height=450>
 * <param name=img value=vincent.jpg>
 * <param name=filters value="Grayscale+Invert+Contrast+Blur+ Sharpen">
 * </applet>
 */
import java.applet.*;
import java.awt.*;
import java.awt.event.*;
import java.util.*;

public class ImageFilterDemo extends Applet implements ActionListener {
  Image img;
  PlugInFilter pif;
  Image fimg;
  Image curImg;
  LoadedImage lim;
  Label lab;
  Button reset;

  public void init() {
    setLayout(new BorderLayout());
    Panel p = new Panel();
    add(p, BorderLayout.SOUTH);
    reset = new Button("Reset");
    reset.addActionListener(this);
    p.add(reset);
    StringTokenizer st = new StringTokenizer(getParameter("filters"), "+");
    while(st.hasMoreTokens()) {
      Button b = new Button(st.nextToken());
      b.addActionListener(this);
      p.add(b);
    }

    lab = new Label("");
    add(lab, BorderLayout.NORTH);

    img = getImage(getDocumentBase(), getParameter("img"));
    lim = new LoadedImage(img);
```

```
    add(lim, BorderLayout.CENTER);

  }

  public void actionPerformed(ActionEvent ae) {
    String a = "";

    try {
      a = (String)ae.getActionCommand();
      if (a.equals("Reset")) {
        lim.set(img);
        lab.setText("Normal");
      }
      else {
        pif = (PlugInFilter) Class.forName(a).newInstance();
        fimg = pif.filter(this, img);
        lim.set(fimg);
        lab.setText("Filtered: " + a);
      }
      repaint();
    } catch (ClassNotFoundException e) {
      lab.setText(a + " not found");
      lim.set(img);
      repaint();
    } catch (InstantiationException e) {
      lab.setText("could't new " + a);
    } catch (IllegalAccessException e) {
      lab.setText("no access: " + a);
    }
  }
}
```

Figure 23-8 shows what the applet looks like when it is first loaded using the applet tag shown at the top of this source file.

PlugInFilter.java

PlugInFilter is a simple interface used to abstract image filtering. It has only one method, **filter( )**, which takes the applet and the source image and returns a new image that has been filtered in some way.

```
interface PlugInFilter {
  java.awt.Image filter(java.applet.Applet a, java.awt.Image in);
}
```

Figure 23-8.   *Sample normal output from* ImageFilterDemo

LoadedImage.java

LoadedImage is a convenient subclass of **Canvas**, which takes an image at construction time and synchronously loads it using **MediaTracker**. **LoadedImage** then behaves properly inside of **LayoutManager** control, because it overrides the **getPreferredSize( )** and **getMinimumSize( )** methods. Also, it has a method called **set( )** that can be used to set a new **Image** to be displayed in this **Canvas**. That is how the filtered image is displayed after the plug-in is finished.

```
import java.awt.*;

public class LoadedImage extends Canvas {
  Image img;

  public LoadedImage(Image i) {
    set(i);
  }

  void set(Image i) {
```

```
      MediaTracker mt = new MediaTracker(this);
      mt.addImage(i, 0);
      try {
        mt.waitForAll();
      } catch (InterruptedException e) { };
      img = i;
      repaint();
    }

    public void paint(Graphics g) {
      if (img == null) {
        g.drawString("no image", 10, 30);
      } else {
        g.drawImage(img, 0, 0, this);
      }
    }

    public Dimension getPreferredSize()  {
      return new Dimension(img.getWidth(this), img.getHeight(this));
    }

    public Dimension getMinimumSize()  {
      return getPreferredSize();
    }
}
```

Grayscale.java

The **Grayscale** filter is a subclass of **RGBImageFilter**, which means that **Grayscale** can use itself as the **ImageFilter** parameter to **FilteredImageSource**'s constructor. Then all it needs to do is override **filterRGB( )** to change the incoming color values. It takes the red, green, and blue values and computes the brightness of the pixel, using the NTSC (National Television Standards Committee) color-to-brightness conversion factor. It then simply returns a gray pixel that is the same brightness as the color source.

```
import java.applet.*;
import java.awt.*;
import java.awt.image.*;

class Grayscale extends RGBImageFilter implements PlugInFilter {
  public Image filter(Applet a, Image in) {
```

```
        return a.createImage(new FilteredImageSource(in.getSource(), this));
    }

    public int filterRGB(int x, int y, int rgb) {
        int r = (rgb >> 16) & 0xff;
        int g = (rgb >> 8) & 0xff;
        int b = rgb & 0xff;
        int k = (int) (.56 * g + .33 * r + .11 * b);
        return (0xff000000 | k << 16 | k << 8 | k);
    }
}
```

Invert.java

The **Invert** filter is also quite simple. It takes apart the red, green, and blue channels and then inverts them by subtracting them from 255. These inverted values are packed back into a pixel value and returned.

```
import java.applet.*;
import java.awt.*;
import java.awt.image.*;

class Invert extends RGBImageFilter implements PlugInFilter {
    public Image filter(Applet a, Image in) {
        return a.createImage(new FilteredImageSource(in.getSource(), this));
    }

    public int filterRGB(int x, int y, int rgb) {
        int r = 0xff - (rgb >> 16) & 0xff;
        int g = 0xff - (rgb >> 8) & 0xff;
        int b = 0xff - rgb & 0xff;
        return (0xff000000 | r << 16 | g << 8 | b);
    }
}
```

Figure 23-9 shows the image after it has been run through the **Invert** filter.

Contrast.java

The **Contrast** filter is very similar to **Grayscale**, except its override of **filterRGB( )** is slightly more complicated. The algorithm it uses for contrast enhancement takes the red, green, and blue values separately and boosts them by 1.2 times if they are already brighter than 128. If they are below 128, then they are divided by 1.2. The boosted values are properly clamped at 255 by the **multclamp( )** method.

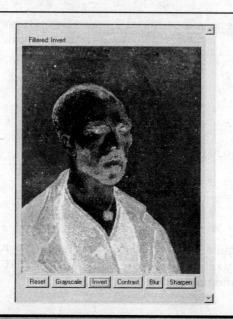

Figure 23-9. *Using the* Invert *filter with* ImageFilterDemo

```
import java.applet.*;
import java.awt.*;
import java.awt.image.*;

public class Contrast extends RGBImageFilter implements PlugInFilter {

  public Image filter(Applet a, Image in) {
    return a.createImage(new FilteredImageSource(in.getSource(), this));
  }

  private int multclamp(int in, double factor) {
    in = (int) (in * factor);
    return in > 255 ? 255 : in;
  }

  double gain = 1.2;
```

```
    private int cont(int in) {
        return (in < 128) ? (int)(in/gain) : multclamp(in, gain);
    }

    public int filterRGB(int x, int y, int rgb) {
        int r = cont((rgb >> 16) & 0xff);
        int g = cont((rgb >> 8) & 0xff);
        int b = cont(rgb & 0xff);
        return (0xff000000 | r << 16 | g << 8 | b);
    }
}
```

Figure 23-10 shows the image after **Contrast** is pressed.

Convolver.java

The abstract class **Convolver** handles the basics of a convolution filter by implementing
the **ImageConsumer** interface to move the source pixels into an array called **imgpixels**.
It also creates a second array called **newimgpixels** for the filtered data. Convolution
filters sample a small rectangle of pixels around each pixel in an image, called the

Figure 23-10.   *Using the* Contrast *filter with* ImageFilterDemo

convolution kernel. This area, 3×3 pixels in this demo, is used to decide how to change the center pixel in the area. The two concrete subclasses, shown in the next section, simply implement the **convolve( )** method, using **imgpixels** for source data and **newimgpixels** to store the result.

> **Note** *The reason that the filter can't modify the **imgpixels** array in place is that the next pixe on a scan line would try to use the original value for the previous pixel, which would have just been filtered away.*

```java
import java.applet.*;
import java.awt.*;
import java.awt.image.*;

abstract class Convolver implements ImageConsumer, PlugInFilter {
  int width, height;
  int imgpixels[], newimgpixels[];

  abstract void convolve();  // filter goes here...

  public Image filter(Applet a, Image in) {
    in.getSource().startProduction(this);
    waitForImage();
    newimgpixels = new int[width*height];

    try {
      convolve();
    } catch (Exception e) {
      System.out.println("Convolver failed: " + e);
      e.printStackTrace();
    }

    return a.createImage(
      new MemoryImageSource(width, height, newimgpixels, 0, width));
  }

  synchronized void waitForImage() {
    try { wait(); } catch (Exception e) { };
  }

  public void setProperties(java.util.Hashtable dummy) { }
  public void setColorModel(ColorModel dummy) { }
```

```
public void setHints(int dummy) { }

public synchronized void imageComplete(int dummy) {
  notifyAll();
}

public void setDimensions(int x, int y) {
  width = x;
  height = y;
  imgpixels = new int[x*y];
}

public void setPixels(int x1, int y1, int w, int h,
  ColorModel model, byte pixels[], int off, int scansize) {
  int pix, x, y, x2, y2, sx, sy;

  x2 = x1+w;
  y2 = y1+h;
  sy = off;
  for(y=y1; y<y2; y++) {
    sx = sy;
    for(x=x1; x<x2; x++) {
      pix = model.getRGB(pixels[sx++]);
      if((pix & 0xff000000) == 0)
          pix = 0x00ffffff;
      imgpixels[y*width+x] = pix;
    }
    sy += scansize;
  }
}

public void setPixels(int x1, int y1, int w, int h,
  ColorModel model, int pixels[], int off, int scansize) {
  int pix, x, y, x2, y2, sx, sy;

  x2 = x1+w;
  y2 = y1+h;
  sy = off;
  for(y=y1; y<y2; y++) {
    sx = sy;
    for(x=x1; x<x2; x++) {
```

```
        pix = model.getRGB(pixels[sx++]);
        if((pix & 0xff000000) == 0)
            pix = 0x00ffffff;
        imgpixels[y*width+x] = pix;
      }
      sy += scansize;
    }
  }
}
```

Blur.java

The **Blur** filter is a subclass of **Convolver** and simply runs through every pixel in the
source image array, **imgpixels**, and computes the average of the 3×3 box surrounding
it. The corresponding output pixel in **newimgpixels** is that average value.

```
public class Blur extends Convolver {
   public void convolve() {
      for(int y=1; y<height-1; y++) {
         for(int x=1; x<width-1; x++) {
            int rs = 0;
            int gs = 0;
            int bs = 0;

            for(int k=-1; k<=1; k++) {
               for(int j=-1; j<=1; j++) {
                  int rgb = imgpixels[(y+k)*width+x+j];
                  int r = (rgb >> 16) & 0xff;
                  int g = (rgb >> 8) & 0xff;
                  int b = rgb & 0xff;
                  rs += r;
                  gs += g;
                  bs += b;
               }
            }

            rs /= 9;
            gs /= 9;
            bs /= 9;

            newimgpixels[y*width+x] = (0xff000000 |
```

```
                                           rs << 16 | gs << 8 | bs);
      }
    }
  }
}
```

Figure 23-11 shows the applet after **Blur**.

Sharpen.java

The **Sharpen** filter is also a subclass of **Convolver** and is (more or less) the inverse of **Blur**. It runs through every pixel in the source image array, **imgpixels**, and computes the average of the 3×3 box surrounding it, not counting the center. The corresponding output pixel in **newimgpixels** has the difference between the center pixel and the surrounding average added to it. This basically says that if a pixel is 30 brighter than its surroundings, make it another 30 brighter. If, however, it is 10 darker, then make it another 10 darker. This tends to accentuate edges while leaving smooth areas unchanged.

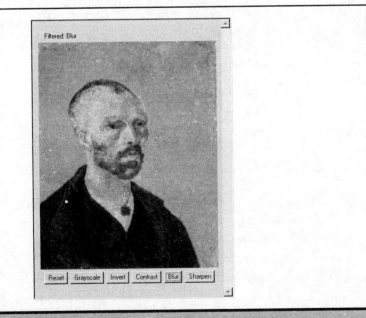

Figure 23-11. *Using the* Blur *filter with* ImageFilterDemo

```
public class Sharpen extends Convolver {

  private final int clamp(int c) {
    return (c > 255 ? 255 : (c < 0 ? 0 : c));
  }

  public void convolve() {
    int r0=0, g0=0, b0=0;
    for(int y=1; y<height-1; y++) {
      for(int x=1; x<width-1; x++) {
        int rs = 0;
        int gs = 0;
        int bs = 0;

        for(int k=-1; k<=1; k++) {
          for(int j=-1; j<=1; j++) {
            int rgb = imgpixels[(y+k)*width+x+j];
            int r = (rgb >> 16) & 0xff;
            int g = (rgb >> 8) & 0xff;
            int b = rgb & 0xff;
            if (j == 0 && k == 0) {
              r0 = r;
              g0 = g;
              b0 = b;
            } else {
              rs += r;
              gs += g;
              bs += b;
            }
          }
        }

        rs >>= 3;
        gs >>= 3;
        bs >>= 3;
        newimgpixels[y*width+x] = (0xff000000 |
                            clamp(r0+r0-rs) << 16 |
                            clamp(g0+g0-gs) << 8 |
                            clamp(b0+b0-bs));
      }
    }
  }
}
```

Figure 23-12 shows the applet after **Sharpen**.

Filtered: Sharpen

Reset | Grayscale | Invert | Contrast | Blur | Sharpen

Applet started

Figure 23-12.   *Using the* Sharpen *filter with* ImageFilterDemo

Cell Animation

Now that we have presented an overview of the image APIs, we can put together
an interesting applet that will display a sequence of animation cells. The animation
cells are taken from a single image that can arrange the cells in a grid specified via
the **rows** and **cols** <param> tags. Each cell in the image is snipped out in a way similar
to that used in the **TileImage** example earlier. We obtain the sequence in which to
display the cells from the **sequence** <param> tag. This is a comma-separated list of
cell numbers that is zero-based and proceeds across the grid from left to right, top
to bottom.

Once the applet has parsed the <param> tags and loaded the source image, it cuts
the image into a number of small subimages. Then, a thread is started that causes the
images to be displayed according to the order described in **sequence**. The thread sleeps
for enough time to maintain the **framerate**. Here is the source code:

```
// Animation example.
import java.applet.*;
import java.awt.*;
```

```java
import java.awt.image.*;
import java.util.*;

public class Animation extends Applet implements Runnable {
  Image cell[];
  final int MAXSEQ = 64;
  int sequence[];
  int nseq;
  int idx;
  int framerate;
  boolean stopFlag;

  private int intDef(String s, int def) {
    int n = def;
    if (s != null)
      try {
        n = Integer.parseInt(s);
      } catch (NumberFormatException e) { };
    return n;
  }


  public void init() {
    framerate = intDef(getParameter("framerate"), 5);
    int tilex = intDef(getParameter("cols"), 1);
    int tiley = intDef(getParameter("rows"), 1);
    cell = new Image[tilex*tiley];

    StringTokenizer st = new
            StringTokenizer(getParameter("sequence"), ",");
    sequence = new int[MAXSEQ];
    nseq = 0;
    while(st.hasMoreTokens() && nseq < MAXSEQ) {
      sequence[nseq] = intDef(st.nextToken(), 0);
      nseq++;
    }

    try {
      Image img = getImage(getDocumentBase(), getParameter("img"));
```

```
      MediaTracker t = new MediaTracker(this);
      t.addImage(img, 0);
      t.waitForID(0);
      int iw = img.getWidth(null);
      int ih = img.getHeight(null);
      int tw = iw / tilex;
      int th = ih / tiley;
      CropImageFilter f;
      FilteredImageSource fis;
      for (int y=0; y<tiley; y++) {
        for (int x=0; x<tilex; x++) {
          f = new CropImageFilter(tw*x, th*y, tw, th);
          fis = new FilteredImageSource(img.getSource(), f);
          int i = y*tilex+x;
          cell[i] = createImage(fis);
          t.addImage(cell[i], i);
        }
      }
      t.waitForAll();
    } catch (InterruptedException e) { };
  }

  public void update(Graphics g) { }

  public void paint(Graphics g) {
      g.drawImage(cell[sequence[idx]], 0, 0, null);
  }

  Thread t;
  public void start() {
    t = new Thread(this);
    stopFlag = false;
    t.start();
  }

  public void stop() {
    stopFlag = true;
```

```
      }

  public void run() {
    idx = 0;
    while (true) {
      paint(getGraphics());
      idx = (idx + 1) % nseq;
      try { Thread.sleep(1000/framerate); } catch (Exception e) { };
      if(stopFlag)
        return;
    }
  }
}
```

The following applet tag shows the famous locomotion study by Eadweard
Muybridge, which proved that horses do, indeed, get all four hooves off the ground at
once. (Of course, you can substitute another image file in your own applet.)

```
<applet code=Animation width=67 height=48>
<param name=img value=horse.gif>
<param name=rows value=3>
<param name=cols value=4>
<param name=sequence value=0,1,2,3,4,5,6,7,8,9,10>
<param name=framerate value=15>
</applet>
```

Figure 23-13 shows the applet running. Notice the source image that has been loaded
below the applet using a normal <**img**> tag.

Additional Imaging Classes

In addition to the imaging classes described in this chapter, **java.awt.image** supplies several
others that offer enhanced control over the imaging process and that support advanced

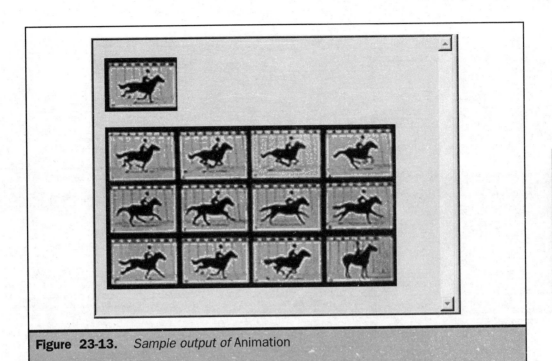

Figure 23-13. *Sampie output of* Animation

imaging techniques. Java 2, version 1.4 also adds a new imaging package called **javax.imageio**. This package supports plug-ins that handle various image formats. If sophisticated graphical output is of special interest to you, then you will want to explore the additional classes found in **java.awt.image** and **javax.imageio.**

Chapter 24

New I/O, Regular Expressions, and Other Packages

W hen Java 1.0 was released, it included a set of eight packages, called the *core API*. These are the packages described in the preceding chapters and are the ones that you will use most often in your day-to-day programming. Each subsequent release added to the core API. Today, the Java API contains a large number of packages. Many of the new packages support areas of specialization that are beyond the scope of this book. However, five packages warrant an examination here: **java.nio**, **java.util.regex**, **java.lang.reflect**, **java.rmi**, and **java.text**. They support the new I/O system, regular expression processing, reflection, Remote Method Invocation (RMI), and text formatting, respectively. Two of these, the new I/O APIs and regular expression processing, were added by Java 2, version 1.4.

The new I/O APIs offer a different way to look at and handle certain types of I/O operations. The regular expression package lets you perform sophisticated pattern matching operations. This chapter provides an in-depth discussion of both of these packages along with extensive examples. Reflection is the ability of software to analyze itself. It is an essential part of the Java Beans technology that is covered in Chapter 25. Examples are provided here to introduce the concept. Remote Method Invocation (RMI) allows you to build Java applications that are distributed among several machines. This chapter provides a simple client/server example that uses RMI. The text formatting capabilities of **java.text** have many uses. The one examined here formats date and time strings.

The Core Java API Packages

Table 24-1 lists all of the Java Core API packages defined by Java 2 and summarizes their functions.

Package	Primary Function
java.applet	Supports construction of applets.
java.awt	Provides capabilities for graphical user interfaces.
java.awt.color	Supports color spaces and profiles.
java.awt.datatransfer	Transfers data to and from the system clipboard.
java.awt.dnd	Supports drag-and-drop operations.

Table 24-1. *The Core Java API Packages*

Package	Primary Function
java.awt.event	Handles events.
java.awt.font	Represents various types of fonts.
java.awt.geom	Allows you to work with geometric shapes.
java.awt.im	Allows input of Japanese, Chinese, and Korean characters to text editing components.
java.awt.im.spi	Supports alternative input devices. (Added by Java 2, v1.3)
java.awt.image	Processes images.
java.awt.image.renderable	Supports rendering-independent images.
java.awt.print	Supports general print capabilities.
java.beans	Allows you to build software components.
java.beans.beancontext	Provides an execution environment for beans.
java.io	Inputs and outputs data.
java.lang	Provides core functionality.
java.lang.ref	Enables some interaction with the garbage collector.
java.lang.reflect	Analyzes code at run time.
java.math	Handles large integers and decimal numbers.
java.net	Supports networking.
java.nio	Top-level package for the new Java I/O classes. Encapsulates buffers. (Added by Java 2, v1.4)
java.nio.channels	Encapsulates channels, which are used by the new I/O system. (Added by Java 2, v1.4)
java.nio.channels.spi	Supports service providers for channels. (Added by Java 2, v1.4)

Table 24-1.   *The Core Java API Packages* (continued)

Package	Primary Function
java.nio.charset	Encapsulates character sets, which are used by the new I/O system. (Added by Java 2, v1.4)
java.nio.charset.spi	Supports service providers for charsets. (Added by Java 2, v1.4)
java.rmi	Provides remote method invocation.
java.rmi.activation	Activates persistent objects.
java.rmi.dgc	Manages distributed garbage collection.
java.rmi.registry	Maps names to remote object references.
java.rmi.server	Supports remote method invocation.
java.security	Handles certificates, keys, digests, signatures, and other security functions.
java.security.acl	Manages access control lists.
java.security.cert	Parses and manages certificates.
java.security.interfaces	Defines interfaces for DSA (Digital Signature Algorithm) keys.
java.security.spec	Specifies keys and algorithm parameters.
java.sql	Communicates with a SQL (Structured Query Language) database.
java.text	Formats, searches, and manipulates text.
java.util	Contains common utilities.
java.util.jar	Creates and reads JAR files.
java.util.logging	Supports logging of information related to a program's execution. (Added by Java 2, v1.4)
java.util.prefs	Encapsulates information relating to user preferences. (Added by Java 2, v1.4)
java.util.regex	Supports regular expression processing. (Added by Java 2, v1.4)
java.util.zip	Reads and writes compressed and uncompressed ZIP files.

Table 24-1. *The Core Java API Packages* (continued)

The New I/O Packages

Java 2, version 1.4 added a new way to handle I/O operations. Called the *new I/O APIs*, it is one of the more interesting additions that Sun included in the 1.4 release because it supports a channel-based approach to I/O operations. The new I/O classes are contained in the five packages shown here.

Package	Purpose
java.nio	Top-level package for the new I/O system. Encapsulates various types of buffers which contain data operated upon by the new I/O system.
java.nio.channels	Supports channels, which are essentially open I/O connections.
java.nio.channels.spi	Supports service providers for channels.
java.nio.charset	Encapsulates character sets. Also supports encoders and decoders that convert characters to bytes and bytes to characters, respectively.
java.nio.charset.spi	Supports service providers for character sets.

Before we begin, it is important to emphasize that the new I/O subsystem (NIO) is not intended to replace the I/O classes found in **java.io**, which are discussed in Chapter 17. Instead, the NIO classes supplement the standard I/O system, giving you an alternative approach, which can be beneficial in some circumstances.

NIO Fundamentals

The new I/O system is built on two foundational items: *buffers* and *channels*. A buffer holds data. A channel represents an open connection to an I/O device, such as a file or a socket. In general, to use the new I/O system, you obtain a channel to an I/O device and a buffer to hold data. You then operate on the buffer, inputting or outputting data as needed. The following sections examine buffers and channels in more detail.

Buffers

Buffers are defined in the **java.nio** package. All buffers are subclasses of the **Buffer** class, which defines the core functionality common to all buffers: current position, limit, and capacity. The *current position* is the index within the buffer at which the next read or write operation will take place. The current position is advanced by most read or write operations. The *limit* is the index of the end of the buffer. The *capacity* is the number of elements that the buffer can hold. **Buffer** also supports mark and reset. **Buffer** defines several methods, which are shown in Table 24-2.

Method	Description
final int capacity( )	Returns the number of elements that the invoking buffer is capable of holding.
final Buffer clear( )	Clears the invoking buffer and returns a reference to the buffer.
final Buffer flip( )	Sets the invoking buffer's limit to the current position and resets the current position to 0. Returns a reference to the buffer.
final boolean hasRemaining( )	Returns **true** if there are elements remaining in the invoking buffer. Returns **false** otherwise.
abstract boolean isReadOnly( )	Returns **true** if the invoking buffer is read-only. Returns **false** otherwise.
final int limit( )	Returns the invoking buffer's limit.
final Buffer limit(int *n*)	Sets the invoking buffer's limit to *n*. Returns a reference to the buffer.
final Buffer mark( )	Sets the mark and returns a reference to the invoking buffer.
final int position( )	Returns the current position.
final Buffer position(int *n*)	Sets the invoking buffer's current position to *n*. Returns a reference to the buffer.
final Buffer reset( )	Resets the current position of the invoking buffer to the previously set mark. Returns a reference to the buffer.
final Buffer rewind( )	Sets the position of the invoking buffer to 0. Returns a reference to the buffer.

Table 24-2. *The methods defined by* Buffer

From **Buffer** are derived the following specific buffer classes, which hold the type of data that their names imply.

ByteBuffer	CharBuffer	DoubleBuffer	FloatBuffer
IntBuffer	LongBuffer	MappedByteBuffer	ShortBuffer

MappedByteBuffer is a subclass of **ByteBuffer** that is used to map a file to a buffer.

All buffers support various **get( )** and **put( )** methods, which allow you to get data from a buffer or put data into a buffer. For example, Table 24-3 shows the **get( )** and

Method	Description
abstract byte get( )	Returns the byte at the current position.
ByteBuffer get(byte *vals*[ ])	Copies the invoking buffer into the array referred to by *vals*. Returns a reference to the buffer.
ByteBuffer get(byte *vals*[ ], int *start*, int *num*)	Copies *num* elements from the invoking buffer into the array referred to by *vals*, beginning at the index specified by *start*. Returns a reference to the buffer. If there are not *num* elements remaining in the buffer, a **BufferUnderflowException** is thrown.
abstract byte get(int *idx*)	Returns the byte at the index specified by *idx* within the invoking buffer.
abstract ByteBuffer put(byte *b*)	Copies *b* into the invoking buffer at the current position. Returns a reference to the buffer.
final ByteBuffer put(byte vals[ ])	Copies all elements of *vals* into the invoking buffer, beginning at the current position. Returns a reference to the buffer.
ByteBuffer put(byte *vals*[ ], int *start*, int *num*)	Copies *num* elements from *vals*, beginning at *start*, into the invoking buffer. Returns a reference to the buffer. If the buffer cannot hold all of the elements, a **BufferOverflowException** is thrown.
ByteBuffer put(ByteBuffer bb)	Copies the elements in *bb* to the invoking buffer, beginning at the current position. If the buffer cannot hold all of the elements, a **BufferOverflowException** is thrown. Returns a reference to the buffer.
abstract ByteBuffer put(int *idx*, byte *b*)	Copies *b* into the invoking buffer at the location specified by *idx*. Returns a reference to the buffer.

Table 24-3.   *The* get( ) *and* put( ) *methods defined for* ByteBuffer

put( ) methods defined by **ByteBuffer**. (The other buffer classes have similar methods.) All buffer classes also support methods that perform various buffer operations. For example, you can allocate a buffer manually using **allocate( )**. You can wrap an array inside a buffer using **wrap( )**. You can create a subsequence of a buffer using **slice( )**.

Channels

Channels are defined in **java.nio.channels**. A channel represents an open connection to an I/O source or destination. You obtain a channel by calling **getChannel( )** on an object that supports channels. Java 2, version 1.4 added **getChannel( )** to the following I/O classes.

FileInputStream	FileOutputStream	RandomAccessFile
Socket	ServerSocket	DatagramSocket

Thus, to obtain a channel, you first obtain an object of one of these classes and then call **getChannel( )** on that object.

The specific type of channel returned depends upon the type of object **getChannel( )** is called on. For example, when called on a **FileInputStream**, **FileOuputStream**, or **RandomAccessFile**, **getChannel( )** returns a channel of type **FileChannel**. When called on a **Socket**, **getChannel( )** returns a **SocketChannel**.

Channels such as **FileChannel** and **SocketChannel** support various **read( )** and **write( )** methods that enable you to perform I/O operations through the channel. For example, here are a few of the **read( )** and **write( )** methods defined for **FileChannel**. All can throw an **IOException**.

Method	Description
abstract int read(ByteBuffer *bb*)	Reads bytes from the invoking channel into *bb* until the buffer is full, or there is no more input. Returns the number of bytes actually read.
abstract int read(ByteBuffer *bb*, long *start*)	Beginning at the file location specified by *start*, reads bytes from the invoking channel into *bb* until the buffer is full, or there is no more input. The current position is unchanged. Returns the number of bytes actually read, or –1 if *start* is beyond the end of the file.
abstract int write(ByteBuffer *bb*)	Writes the contents of *bb* to the invoking channel, starting at the current position. Returns the number of bytes written.
abstract int write(ByteBuffer *bb*, long *start*)	Beginning at the file location specified by *start*, writes the contents of *bb* to the invoking channel. The current position is unchanged. Returns the number of bytes written.

All channels support additional methods that give you access to and control over the channel. For example, **FileChannel** supports methods to get or set the current position, transfer information between file channels, obtain the current size of the channel, and lock the channel, among others. **FileChannel** also provides the **map( )** method, which lets you map a file to a buffer.

Charsets and Selectors

Two other entities used by NIO are charsets and selectors. A *charset* defines the way that bytes are mapped to characters. You can encode a sequence of characters into bytes using an *encoder*. You can decode a sequence of bytes into characters using a *decoder*. Charsets, encoders, and decoders are supported by classes defined in the **java.nio.charset** package. Because default encoders and decoders are provided, you will not often need to work explicitly with charsets.

A *selector* supports key-based, non-blocking, multiplexed I/O. In other words, selectors enable you to perform I/O through multiple channels. Selectors are supported by classes defined in the **java.nio.channels** package. Selectors are most applicable to socket-backed channels.

We will not use charsets or selectors in this chapter, but you might find them useful in your own applications.

Using the New I/O System

Because the most common I/O device is the disk file, the rest of this section examines how to access a disk file using the new I/O system. Because all file channel operations are byte-based, the type of buffers that we will be using are of type **ByteBuffer**.

Reading a File

There are several ways to read data from a file using the new I/O system. We will look at two. The first reads a file by manually allocating a buffer and then performing an explicit read operation. The second uses a mapped file, which automates the process.

To read a file using a channel and a manually allocated buffer, follow this procedure. First open the file for input using **FileInputStream**. Then, obtain a channel to this file by calling **getChannel( )**. It has this general form:

FileChannel getChannel( )

It returns a **FileChannel** object, which encapsulates the channel for file operations. Once a file channel has been opened, obtain the size of the file by calling **size( )**, shown here:

long size( ) throws IOException

It returns the current size, in bytes, of the channel, which reflects the underlying file. Next, call **allocate( )** to allocate a buffer large enough to hold the file's contents. Because file channels operate on byte buffers you will use the **allocate( )** method defined by **ByteBuffer**. It has this general form.

  static ByteBuffer allocate(int *cap*)

Here, *cap* specifies the capacity of the buffer. A reference to the buffer is returned. After you have created the buffer, call **read( )** on the channel, passing a reference to the buffer.

  The following program shows how to read a text file called **test.txt** through a channel using explicit input operations.

```
// Use the new I/O system to read a text file.
import java.io.*;
import java.nio.*;
import java.nio.channels.*;

public class ExplicitChannelRead {
  public static void main(String args[])
    FileInputStream fIn;
    FileChannel fChan;
    long fSize;
    ByteBuffer mBuf;

    try
      // First, open a file for input.
      fIn = new FileInputStream("test.txt");

      // Next, obtain a channel to that file.
      fChan = fIn.getChannel();

      // Now, get the file's size.
      fSize = fChan.size();

      // Allocate a buffer of the necessary size.
      mBuf = ByteBuffer.allocate((int)fSize);

      // Read the file into the buffer.
      fChan.read(mBuf);

      // Rewind the buffer so that it can be read.
      mBuf.rewind();

      // Read bytes from the buffer.
      for(int i=0; i < fSize; i++)
```

```
        System.out.print((char)mBuf.get());

      System.out.println();

      fChan.close(); // close channel
      fIn.close();   // close file
    } catch (IOException exc) {
      System.out.println(exc);
      System.exit(1);
    }
  }
}
```

Here is how the program works. First, a file is opened by using the **FileInputStream** constructor and a reference to that object is assigned to **fIn**. Next, a channel connected to the file is obtained by calling **getChannel( )** on **fIn** and the size of the file is obtained by calling **size( )**. The program then calls the **allocate( )** method of **ByteBuffer** to allocate a buffer that will hold the contents of the file when it is read. A byte buffer is used because **FileChannel** operates on bytes. A reference to this buffer is stored in **mBuf**. The contents of the file are then read into **mBuf** through a call to **read( )**. Next, the buffer is rewound through a call to **rewind( )**. This call is necessary because the current position is at the end of the buffer after the call to **read( )**. It must be reset to the start of the buffer in order for the bytes in **mBuf** to be read by calling **get( )**. Because **mBuf** is a byte buffer, the values returned by **get( )** are bytes. They are cast to **char** so that the file can be displayed as text. (Alternatively, it is possible to create a buffer that encodes the bytes into characters, and then read that buffer.) The program ends by closing the channel and the file.

A second, and often easier way to read a file is to map it to a buffer. The advantage to this approach is that the buffer automatically contains the contents of the file. No explicit read operation is necessary. To map and read the contents of a file, follow this general procedure. First, open the file using **FileInputStream**. Next, obtain a channel to that file by calling **getChannel( )** on the file object. Then, map the channel to a buffer by calling **map( )** on the **FileChannel** object. The **map( )** method is shown here:

MappedByteBuffer map(FileChannel.MapMode *how*,
                  long *pos*, long *size*) throws IOException

The **map( )** method causes the data in the file to be mapped into a buffer in memory. The value in *how* determines what type of operations are allowed. It must be one of these values.

MapMode.READ   MapMode.READ_WRITE   MapMode.PRIVATE

For reading a file, use **MapMode.READ**. To read and write, use **MapeMode.READ_ WRITE**. **MapMode.PRIVATE** causes a private copy of the file to be made and changes to the buffer do not affect the underlying file. The location within the file to begin mapping is specified by *pos* and the number of bytes to map are specified by *size*. A reference to this buffer is returned as a **MappedByteBuffer**, which is a subclass of **ByteBuffer**. Once the file has been mapped to a buffer, you can read the file from that buffer.

The following program reworks the first example so that it uses a mapped file.

```java
// Use a mapped file to read a text file.
import java.io.*;
import java.nio.*;
import java.nio.channels.*;

public class MappedChannelRead {
  public static void main(String args[]) {
    FileInputStream fIn;
    FileChannel fChan;
    long fSize;
    MappedByteBuffer mBuf;

    try {
      // First, open an file for input.
      fIn = new FileInputStream("test.txt");

      // Next, obtain a channel to that file.
      fChan = fIn.getChannel();

      // Get the size of the file.
      fSize = fChan.size();

      // Now, map the file into a buffer.
      mBuf = fChan.map(FileChannel.MapMode.READ_ONLY,
                       0, fSize);

      // Read bytes from the buffer.
      for(int i=0; i < fSize; i++)
        System.out.print((char)mBuf.get());

      fChan.close(); // close channel
      fIn.close();   // close file
    } catch (IOException exc) {
```

```
        System.out.println(exc);
        System.exit(1);
      }
    }
  }
```

As before, the file is opened by using the **FileInputStream** constructor and a reference to that object is assigned to **fIn**. A channel connected to the file is obtained by calling **getChannel( )** on **fIn**, and the size of the file is obtained. Then the entire file is mapped into memory by calling **map( )** and a reference to the buffer is stored in **mBuf**. The bytes in **mBuf** are read by calling **get( )**.

Writing to a File

There are several ways to write to a file through a channel. Again, we will look at two. First, you can write data to an output file through a channel, by using explicit write operations. Second, if the file is opened for read/write operations, you can map the file to a buffer and then write to that buffer. Changes to the buffer will automatically be reflected in the file. Both ways are described here.

To write to a file through a channel using explicit calls to **write( )**, follow these steps. First, open the file for output. Then, allocate a byte buffer, put the data you want to write into that buffer, and then called **write( )** on the channel. The following program demonstrates this procedure. It writes the alphabet to a file called **test.txt**.

```
// Write to a file using the new I/O.
import java.io.*;
import java.nio.*;
import java.nio.channels.*;

public class ExplicitChannelWrite {
  public static void main(String args[]) {
    FileOutputStream fOut;
    FileChannel fChan;
    ByteBuffer mBuf;

    try {
      fOut = new FileOutputStream("test.txt");

      // Get a channel to the output file.
      fChan = fOut.getChannel();

      // Create a buffer.
```

```
        mBuf = ByteBuffer.allocateDirect(26);

        // Write some bytes to the buffer.
        for(int i=0; i<26; i++)
          mBuf.put((byte)('A' + i));

        // Rewind the buffer so that it can written.
        mBuf.rewind();

        // Write the buffer to the output file.
        fChan.write(mBuf);

        // close channel and file.
        fChan.close();
        fOut.close();
      } catch (IOException exc) {
        System.out.println(exc);
        System.exit(1);
      }
    }
  }
```

The call to **rewind( )** on **mBuf** is necessary in order to reset the current position to zero after data has been written to **mBuf**. Remember, each call to **put( )** advances the current position. Therefore, it is necessary for the current position to be reset to the start of the buffer before calling **write( )**. If this is not done, **write( )** will think that there is no data in the buffer.

To write to a file using a mapped file, follow these steps. First, open the file for read/write operations. Next, map that file to a buffer by calling **map( )**. Then, write to the buffer. Because the buffer is mapped to the file, any changes to that buffer are automatically reflected in the file. Thus, no explicit write operations to the channel are necessary. Here is the preceding program reworked so that a mapped file is used. Notice that the file is opened as a **RandomAccessFile**. This is necessary to allow the file to be read and written.

```
// Write to a mapped file.
import java.io.*;
import java.nio.*;
import java.nio.channels.*;

public class MappedChannelWrite {
```

```
public static void main(String args[]) {
  RandomAccessFile fOut;
  FileChannel fChan;
  ByteBuffer mBuf;

  try {
    fOut = new RandomAccessFile("test.txt", "rw");

    // Next, obtain a channel to that file.
    fChan = fOut.getChannel();

    // Then, map the file into a buffer.
    mBuf = fChan.map(FileChannel.MapMode.READ_WRITE,
                     0, 26);

    // Write some bytes to the buffer.
    for(int i=0; i<26; i++)
      mBuf.put((byte)('A' + i));

    // close channel and file.
    fChan.close();
    fOut.close();
  } catch (IOException exc) {
    System.out.println(exc);
    System.exit(1);
  }
}
```

As you can see, there are no explicit write operations to the channel, itself. Because **mBuf** is mapped to the file, changes to **mBuf** are automatically reflected in the underlying file.

Copying a File Using the New I/O

The new I/O system simplifies some types of file operations. For example, the following program copies a file. It does so by opening an input channel to the source file and an output channel to the target file. It then writes the mapped input buffer to the output file in a single operation. You might want to compare this version of the file copy program to the one found in Chapter 12. As you will find, the part of the program that actually copies the file is substantially shorter.

```
// Copy a file using NIO.
```

```java
import java.io.*;
import java.nio.*;
import java.nio.channels.*;

public class NIOCopy {

  public static void main(String args[]) {
    FileInputStream fIn;
    FileOutputStream fOut;
    FileChannel fIChan, fOChan;
    long fSize;
    MappedByteBuffer mBuf;

    try {
      fIn = new FileInputStream(args[0]);
      fOut = new FileOutputStream(args[1]);

      // Get channels to the input and output files.
      fIChan = fIn.getChannel();
      fOChan = fOut.getChannel();

      // Get the size of the file.
      fSize = fIChan.size();

      // Map the input file to a buffer.
      mBuf = fIChan.map(FileChannel.MapMode.READ_ONLY,
                  0, fSize);

      // Write the buffer to the output file.
      fOChan.write(mBuf); // this copies the file

      // Close the channels and files.
      fIChan.close();
      fIn.close();

      fOChan.close();
      fOut.close();
    } catch (IOException exc) {
      System.out.println(exc);
      System.exit(1),
    } catch (ArrayIndexOutOfBoundsException exc) {
      System.out.println("Usage: Copy from to");
```

```
        System.exit(1);
    }
  }
}
```

Because the input file is mapped to **mBuf**, it contains the entire source file. Thus, the call to **write( )** copies all of **mBuf** to the target file. This, of course, means that the target file is an identical copy of the source file.

Is NIO the Future of I/O Handling?

The new I/O APIs offer an exciting new way to think about and handle some types of file operations. Because of this it is natural to ask the question, "Is NIO the future of I/O handling?" Unfortunately, at the time of this writing, this question cannot be answered. Certainly, channels and buffers offer a clean way of thinking about I/O. However, they also add another layer of abstraction. Furthermore, the traditional stream-based approach is both well-understood, and widely used. As explained at the outset, channel-based I/O is currently designed to supplement, not replace the standard I/O mechanisms defined in **java.io**. In this role, the channel/buffer approach used by the NIO APIs succeeds admirably. Whether the new approach will someday supplant the traditional approach, only time and usage patterns will tell.

Regular Expression Processing

Another exciting package added by Java 2, version 1.4 is **java.util.regex**, which supports regular expression processing. As the term is used here, a *regular expression* is a string of characters that describes a character sequence. This general description, called a *pattern*, can then be used to find matches in other character sequences. Regular expressions can specify wildcard characters, sets of characters, and various quantifiers. Thus, you can specify a regular expression that represents a general form that can match several different specific character sequences.

There are two classes that support regular expression processing: **Pattern** and **Matcher**. These classes work together. Use **Pattern** to define a regular expression. Match the pattern against another sequence using **Matcher**.

Pattern

The **Pattern** class defines no constructors. Instead, a pattern is created by calling the **compile( )** factory method. One of its forms is shown here:

static Pattern compile(String *pattern*)

Here, *pattern* is the regular expression that you want to use. The **compile( )** method transforms the string in *pattern* into a pattern that can be used for pattern matching by the **Matcher** class. It returns a **Pattern** object that contains the pattern.

Once you have created a **Pattern** object, you will use it to create a **Matcher**. This is done by calling the **matcher( )** factory method defined by **Pattern**. It is shown here:

Matcher matcher(CharSequence *str*)

Here *str* is the character sequence that the pattern will be matched against. This is called the *input sequence*. **CharSequence** is an interface that was added by Java 2, version 1.4 that defines a read-only set of characters. It is implemented by the **String** class, among others. Thus, you can pass a string to **matcher( )**.

Matcher

The **Matcher** class has no constructors. Instead, you create a **Matcher** by calling the **matcher( )** factory method defined by **Pattern**, as just explained. Once you have created a **Matcher**, you will use its methods to perform various pattern matching operations.

The simplest pattern matching method is **matches( )**, which simply determines whether the character sequence matches the pattern. It is shown here:

boolean matches( )

It returns **true** if the sequence and the pattern match, and **false** otherwise. Understand that the entire sequence must match the pattern, not just a subsequence of it.

To determine if a subsequence of the input sequence matches the pattern, use **find( )**. One version is shown here:

boolean find( )

It returns **true** if there is a matching subsequence and **false** otherwise. This method can be called repeatedly, allowing it to find all matching subsequences. Each call to **find( )** begins where the previous one left off.

You can obtain a string containing the last matching sequence by calling **group( )**. One of its forms is shown here:

String group( )

The matching string is returned. If no match exists, then an **IllegalStateException** is thrown.

You can obtain the index within the input sequence of the current match by calling **start( )**. The index one past the end of the current match is obtained by calling **end( )**. These methods are shown here:

int start( )
int end( )

You can replace all occurrences of a matching sequence with another sequence by calling **replaceAll( )**, shown here:

String replaceAll(String *newStr*)

Here, *newStr* specifies the new character sequence that will replace the ones that match the pattern. The updated input sequence is returned as a string.

Regular Expression Syntax

Before demonstrating **Pattern** and **Matcher** it is necessary to explain how to construct a regular expression. The syntax and rules that define a regular expression are similar to those used by Perl 5. Although no rule is complicated by itself, there are a large number of them, and a complete discussion is beyond the scope of this chapter. However, a few of the more commonly used constructs are described here.

In general, a regular expression is comprised of normal characters, character classes (sets of characters), wildcard characters, and quantifiers. A normal character is matched as-is. Thus, if a pattern consists of "xy", then the only input sequence that will match it is "xy". Characters such as newline and tab are specified using the standard escape sequences, which begin with a \. For example, a newline is specified by **\n**. In the language of regular expressions, a normal character is also called a *literal*.

A character class is a set of characters. A character class is specified by putting the characters in the class between brackets. For example, the class [wxyz] matches w, x, y, or z. To specify an inverted set, precede the characters with a ^. For example, [^wxyz] matches any character except w, x, y, or z. You can specify a range of characters using a hypen. For example, to specify a character class that will match the digits 1 through 9 use [1-9].

The wildcard character is the . (dot) and it matches any character. Thus, a pattern that consists of "." will match these (and other) input seqeunces: "A", "a", "x", and so on.

A quantifier determines how many times an expression is matched. The quantifiers are shown here:

+	Match one or more.
*	Match zero or more.
?	Match zero or one.

For example, the pattern "x+" will match "x", "xx", and "xxx", among others.

Demonstrating Pattern Matching

The best way to understand how regular expression pattern matching operates is to work through some examples. The first, shown here, looks for a match with a literal pattern.

```
// A simple pattern matching demo.
import java.util.regex.*;

class RegExpr {
  public static void main(String args[]) {
    Pattern pat;
    Matcher mat;
    boolean found;

    pat = Pattern.compile("Java");
    mat = pat.matcher("Java");

    found = mat.matches(); // check for a match

    System.out.println("Testing Java against Java.");
    if(found) System.out.println("Matches");
    else System.out.println("No Match");

    System.out.println();

    System.out.println("Testing Java against Java 2.");
    mat = pat.matcher("Java 2"); // create a new matcher

    found = mat.matches(); // check for a match

    if(found) System.out.println("Matches");
    else System.out.println("No Match");
  }
}
```

The output from the program is shown here:

```
Testing Java against Java.
Matches

Testing Java against Java 2.
No Match
```

Let's look closely at this program. The program begins by creating the pattern that contains the sequence "Java". Next, a **Matcher** is created for that pattern that has the input sequence "Java". Then, the **matches( )** method is called to determine if the input sequence matches the pattern. Because, the sequence and the pattern are the same,

matches( ) returns **true**. Next, a new **Matcher** is created with the input sequence "Java 2" and **matches( )** is called again. In this case, the pattern and the input sequence differ, and no match is found. Remember, the **matches( )** function returns true only when the input sequence precisely matches the pattern. It will not return true just because a subsequence matches.

You can use **find( )** to determine if the input sequence contains a subsequence that matches the pattern. Consider the following program.

```
// Use find() to find a subsequence.
import java.util.regex.*;

class RegExpr2 {
  public static void main(String args[]) {
    Pattern pat = Pattern.compile("Java");
    Matcher mat = pat.matcher("Java 2");

    System.out.println("Looking for Java in Java 2.");

    if(mat.find()) System.out.println("subsequence found");
    else System.out.println("No Match");
  }
}
```

The output is shown here:

```
Looking for Java in Java 2.
subsequence found
```

In this case, **find( )** finds the subsequence "Java".

The **find( )** method can be used to search the input sequence for repeated occurrences of the pattern because each call to **find( )** picks up where the previous one left off. For example, the following program finds two occurrences of the pattern "test".

```
// Use find() to find multiple subsequences.
import java.util.regex.*;

class RegExpr3 {
  public static void main(String args[]) {
    Pattern pat = Pattern.compile("test");
    Matcher mat = pat.matcher("test 1 2 3 test");
```

```
    while(mat.find()) {
      System.out.println("test found at index " +
                            mat.start());
    }
  }
}
```

The output is shown here:

```
test found at index 0
test found at index 11
```

As the output shows, two matches were found. The program uses the **start( )** method to obtain the index of each match.

Using Wildcards and Quantifiers

Although the preceding programs show the general technique for using **Pattern** and **Matcher**, they don't show their power. The real benefit of regular expression processing is not seen until wildcards and quantifiers are used. To begin, consider the following example that uses the + quantifier to match any arbitrarily long sequence of Ws.

```
// Use a quantifier.
import java.util.regex.*;

class RegExpr4 {
  public static void main(String args[]) {
    Pattern pat = Pattern.compile("W+");
    Matcher mat = pat.matcher("W WW WWW");

    while(mat.find())
      System.out.println("Match: " + mat.group());
  }
}
```

The output from the program is shown here:

```
Match: W
Match: WW
Match: WWW
```

As the output shows, the regular expression pattern "W+" matches any arbitrarily long sequence of Ws.

The next program uses a wildcard to create a pattern that will match any sequence that begins with e and ends with d. To do this, it uses the dot wildcard character along with the + quantifier.

```
// Use wildcard and quantifier.
import java.util.regex.*;

class RegExpr5 {
  public static void main(String args[]) {
    Pattern pat = Pattern.compile("e.+d");
    Matcher mat = pat.matcher("extend cup end table");

    while(mat.find())
      System.out.println("Match: " + mat.group());
  }
}
```

You might be surprised by the the output produced by the program, which is shown here:

```
Match: extend cup end
```

Only one match is found, and it is the longest sequence that begins with e and ends with d. You might have expected two matches: extend and end. The reason that the longer sequence is found is that by default, **find( )** matches the longest sequence that fits the pattern. This is called *greedy behavior*. You can specify *reluctant behavior* by adding the **?** quantifier to the pattern, as shown in this version of the program. It causes the shortest matching pattern to be obtained.

```
// Use the ? quantifier.
import java.util.regex.*;

class RegExpr6 {
  public static void main(String args[]) {
    // Use reluctant matching behavior.
    Pattern pat = Pattern.compile("e.+?d");
    Matcher mat = pat.matcher("extend cup end table");

    while(mat.find())
```

```
          System.out.println("Match: " + mat.group());
    }
}
```

The output from the program is shown here:

```
Match: extend
Match: end
```

As the output shows, the pattern "e.+?d" will match the shortest sequence that begins with e and ends with d. Thus, two matches are found.

Working with Classes of Characters

Sometimes you will want to match any sequence that contains one or more characters, in any order, that are part of a set of characters. For example, to match whole words, you want to match any sequence of the letters of the alphabet. One of the easiest ways to do this is to use a character class, which defines a set of characters. Recall that a character class is created by putting the characters you want to match between brackets. For example, to match the lowercase characters a through z, use [a-z]. The following program demonstrates this technique.

```
// Use a character class.
import java.util.regex.*;

class RegExpr7 {
  public static void main(String args[]) {
    // Match lowercase words.
    Pattern pat = Pattern.compile("[a-z]+");
    Matcher mat = pat.matcher("this is a test.");

    while(mat.find())
      System.out.println("Match: " + mat.group());
  }
}
```

The output is shown here:

```
Match: this
Match: is
Match: a
Match: test
```

Using replaceAll( )

The **replaceAll( )** method supplied by **Matcher** lets you perform powerful search and replace operations that use regular expressions. For example, the following program replaces all occurrences of sequences that begin with "Jon" with "Eric".

```
// Use replaceAll().
import java.util.regex.*;

class RegExpr8 {
  public static void main(String args[]) {
    String str = "Jon Jonathan Frank Ken Todd";

    Pattern pat = Pattern.compile("Jon.*? ");
    Matcher mat = pat.matcher(str);

    System.out.println("Original sequence: " + str);

    str = mat.replaceAll("Eric ");

    System.out.println("Modified sequence: " + str);

  }
}
```

The output is shown here:

```
Original sequence: Jon Jonathan Frank Ken Todd
Modified sequence: Eric Eric Frank Ken Todd
```

Because the regular expression "Jon.*? " matches any string that begins with Jon followed by zero or more characters, ending in a space, it can be used to match and replace both Jon and Jonathan with the name Eric. Such a substitution is not possible without pattern matching capabilities.

Using split( )

You can reduce an input sequence into its individual tokens by using the **split( )** method defined by **Pattern**. The **split( )** method is shown here:

String[ ] split(CharSequence *str*)

It processes the input sequence passed in *str*, reducing it into tokens based on the delimiters specified by the pattern.

For example, the following program finds tokens that are separated by spaces, commas, periods, and exclamation points.

```
// Use split().
import java.util.regex.*;

class RegExpr9 {
  public static void main(String args[]) {

    // Match lowercase words.
    Pattern pat = Pattern.compile("[ ,.!]");

    String strs[] = pat.split("one two,alpha9 12!done.");

    for(int i=0; i < strs.length; i++)
      System.out.println("Next token: " + strs[i]);

  }
}
```

The output is shown here:

```
Next token: one
Next token: two
Next token: alpha9
Next token: 12
Next token: done
```

As the output shows, the input sequence is reduced to its individual tokens. Notice that the delimiters are not included.

Two Pattern-Matching Options

Although the pattern-matching techniques described in the foregoing offer the greatest flexibility and power, there are two alternatives which you might find useful in some circumstances. If you only need to perform a one-time pattern match, you can use the **matches( )** method defined by **Pattern**. It is shown here:

static boolean matches(String *pattern*, CharSequence *str*)

It returns **true** if *pattern* matches *str* and **false** otherwise. This method automatically compiles *pattern* and then looks for a match. If you will be using the same pattern repeatedly, then using **matches( )** is less·efficient than compiling the pattern and using the pattern-matching methods defined by **Matcher**, as described previously.

You can also perform a pattern match by using the **matches( )** method implemented by **String**. It is shown here:

boolean matches(String *pattern*)

If the invoking string matches the regular expression in *pattern*, then **matches( )** returns **true**. Otherwise, it returns **false**.

Exploring Regular Expressions

The overview of regular expressions presented in this section only hints at their power. Since text parsing, manipulation, and tokenization are a large part of programming, you will likely find Java's regular expression subsystem a powerful tool that you can use to your advantage. It is, therefore, wise to explore the capabilities of regular expressions. Experiment with several different types of patterns and input sequences. Once you understand how regular expression pattern matching works, you will find it useful in many of your programming endeavors.

Reflection

Reflection is the ability of software to analyze itself. This is provided by the **java.lang.reflect** package and elements in **Class**. Reflection is an important capability, needed when using components called Java Beans. It allows you to analyze a software component and describe its capabilities dynamically, at run time rather than at compile time. For example, by using reflection, you can determine what methods, constructors, and fields a class supports.

The package **java.lang.reflect** has an interface, called **Member**, which defines methods that allow you to get information about a field, constructor, or method of a class. There are also eight classes in this package. These are listed in Table 24-4.

The following application illustrates a simple use of the Java reflection capabilities. It prints the constructors, fields, and methods of the class **java.awt.Dimension**. The program begins by using the **forName( )** method of **Class** to get a class object for **java.awt.Dimension**. Once this is obtained, **getConstructors( )**, **getFields( )**, and **getMethods( )** are used to analyze this class object. They return arrays of **Constructor**, **Field**, and **Method** objects that provide the information about the object. The **Constructor**, **Field**, and **Method** classes define several methods that can be used

Class	Primary Function
AccessibleObject	Allows you to bypass the default access control checks. (Added by Java 2)
Array	Allows you to dynamically create and manipulate arrays.
Constructor	Provides information about a constructor.
Field	Provides information about a field.
Method	Provides information about a method.
Modifier	Provides information about class and member access modifiers.
Proxy	Supports dynamic proxy classes. (Added by Java 2, v1.3)
ReflectPermission	Allows reflection of private or protected members of a class. (Added by Java 2)

Table 24-4. *Classes Defined in* java.lang.reflect

to obtain information about an object. You will want to explore these on your own. However, each supports the **toString( )** method. Therefore, using **Constructor**, **Field**, and **Method** objects as arguments to the **println( )** method is straightforward, as shown in the program.

```
// Demonstrate reflection.
import java.lang.reflect.*;
public class ReflectionDemo1 {
  public static void main(String args[]) {
    try {
      Class c = Class.forName("java.awt.Dimension");
      System.out.println("Constructors:");
      Constructor constructors[] = c.getConstructors();
      for(int i = 0; i < constructors.length; i++) {
        System.out.println("  " + constructors[i]);
      }

      System.out.println("Fields:");
      Field fields[] = c.getFields();
      for(int i = 0; i < fields.length; i++) {
        System.out.println("  " + fields[i]);
```

```
      }
      System.out.println("Methods:");
      Method methods[] = c.getMethods();
      for(int i = 0; i < methods.length; i++) {
        System.out.println("  " + methods[i]);
      }
    }
    catch(Exception e) {
      System.out.println("Exception: " + e);
    }
  }
}
```

Here is the output from this program:

```
Constructors:
 public java.awt.Dimension(java.awt.Dimension)
 public java.awt.Dimension(int,int)
 public java.awt.Dimension()
Fields:
 public int java.awt.Dimension.width
 public int java.awt.Dimension.height
Methods:
 public int java.awt.Dimension.hashCode()
 public boolean java.awt.Dimension.equals(java.lang.Object)
 public java.lang.String java.awt.Dimension.toString()
 public void java.awt.Dimension.setSize(java.awt.Dimension)
 public void java.awt.Dimension.setSize(int,int)
 public void java.awt.Dimension.setSize(double,double)
 public java.awt.Dimension java.awt.Dimension.getSize()
 public double java.awt.Dimension.getWidth()
 public double java.awt.Dimension.getHeight()
 public java.lang.Object java.awt.geom.Dimension2D.clone()
 public void java.awt.geom.Dimension2D.
   setSize(java.awt.geom.Dimension2D)
 public final native java.lang.Class java.lang.Object.getClass()
 public final void java.lang.Object.wait(long,int) throws
   java.lang.InterruptedException
 public final void java.lang.Object.wait()
   throws java.lang.InterruptedException
 public final native void java.lang.Object.wait(long) throws
   java.lang.InterruptedException
 public final native void java.lang.Object.notify()
 public final native void java.lang.Object.notifyAll()
```

The next example uses Java's reflection capabilities to obtain the public methods of a class. The program begins by instantiating class **A**. The **getClass( )** method is applied to this object reference and it returns the **Class** object for class **A**. The **getDeclaredMethods( )** method returns an array of **Method** objects that describe only the methods declared by this class. Methods inherited from superclasses such as **Object** are not included.

Each element of the **methods** array is then processed. The **getModifiers( )** method returns an **int** containing flags that describe which access modifiers apply for this element. The **Modifier** class provides a set of methods, shown in Table 24-5, that can be

Method	Description
static boolean isAbstract(int *val*)	Returns **true** if *val* has the **abstract** flag set and **false** otherwise.
static boolean isFinal(int *val*)	Returns **true** if *val* has the **final** flag set and **false** otherwise.
static boolean isInterface(int *val*)	Returns **true** if *val* has the **interface** flag set and **false** otherwise.
static boolean isNative(int *val*)	Returns **true** if *val* has the **native** flag set and **false** otherwise.
static boolean isPrivate(int *val*)	Returns **true** if *val* has the **private** flag set and **false** otherwise.
static boolean isProtected(int *val*)	Returns **true** if *val* has the **protected** flag set and **false** otherwise.
static boolean isPublic(int *val*)	Returns **true** if *val* has the **public** flag set and **false** otherwise.
static boolean isStatic(int *val*)	Returns **true** if *val* has the **static** flag set and **false** otherwise.
static boolean isStrict(int *val*)	Returns **true** if *val* has the **strict** flag set and **false** otherwise.
static boolean isSynchronized(int *val*)	Returns **true** if *val* has the **synchronized** flag set and **false** otherwise.
static boolean isTransient(int *val*)	Returns **true** if *val* has the **transient** flag set and **false** otherwise.
static boolean isVolatile(int *val*)	Returns **true** if *val* has the **volatile** flag set and **false** otherwise.

Table 24-5.   *Methods Defined by* Modifier *That Determine Access Modifiers*

used to examine this value. For example, the static method **isPublic( )** returns **true** if its argument includes the **public** access modifier. Otherwise, it returns **false**. In the following program, if the method supports public access, its name is obtained by the **getName( )** method and is then printed.

```java
// Show public methods.
import java.lang.reflect.*;
public class ReflectionDemo2 {
  public static void main(String args[]) {
    try {
      A a = new A();
      Class c = a.getClass();
      System.out.println("Public Methods:");
      Method methods[] = c.getDeclaredMethods();
      for(int i = 0; i < methods.length; i++) {
        int modifiers = methods[i].getModifiers();
        if(Modifier.isPublic(modifiers)) {
          System.out.println("  " + methods[i].getName());
        }
      }
    }
    catch(Exception e) {
      System.out.println("Exception: " + e);
    }
  }
}

class A {
  public void a1() {
  }
  public void a2() {
  }
  protected void a3() {
  }
  private void a4() {
  }
}
```

Here is the output from this program:

```
Public Methods:
 a1
 a2
```

Remote Method Invocation (RMI)

Remote Method Invocation (RMI) allows a Java object that executes on one machine to invoke a method of a Java object that executes on another machine. This is an important feature, because it allows you to build distributed applications. While a complete discussion of RMI is outside the scope of this book, the following example describes the basic principles involved.

A Simple Client/Server Application Using RMI

This section provides step-by-step directions for building a simple client/server application by using RMI. The server receives a request from a client, processes it, and returns a result. In this example, the request specifies two numbers. The server adds these together and returns the sum.

Step One: Enter and Compile the Source Code

This application uses four source files. The first file, **AddServerIntf.java**, defines the remote interface that is provided by the server. It contains one method that accepts two **double** arguments and returns their sum. All remote interfaces must extend the **Remote** interface, which is part of **java.rmi**. **Remote** defines no members. Its purpose is simply to indicate that an interface uses remote methods. All remote methods can throw a **RemoteException.**

```
import java.rmi.*;
public interface AddServerIntf extends Remote {
  double add(double d1, double d2) throws RemoteException;
}
```

The second source file, **AddServerImpl.java**, implements the remote interface. The implementation of the **add( )** method is straightforward. All remote objects must extend **UnicastRemoteObject**, which provides functionality that is needed to make objects available from remote machines.

```
import java.rmi.*;
import java.rmi.server.*;
public class AddServerImpl extends UnicastRemoteObject
  implements AddServerIntf {

  public AddServerImpl() throws RemoteException {
  }
  public double add(double d1, double d2) throws RemoteException {
    return d1 + d2;
  }
}
```

The third source file, **AddServer.java**, contains the main program for the server machine. Its primary function is to update the RMI registry on that machine. This is done by using the **rebind( )** method of the **Naming** class (found in **java.rmi**). That method associates a name with an object reference. The first argument to the **rebind( )** method is a string that names the server as "AddServer". Its second argument is a reference to an instance of **AddServerImpl**.

```java
import java.net.*;
import java.rmi.*;
public class AddServer {
  public static void main(String args[]) {
    try {
      AddServerImpl addServerImpl = new AddServerImpl();
      Naming.rebind("AddServer", addServerImpl);
    }
    catch(Exception e) {
      System.out.println("Exception: " + e);
    }
  }
}
```

The fourth source file, **AddClient.java**, implements the client side of this distributed application. **AddClient.java** requires three command line arguments. The first is the IP address or name of the server machine. The second and third arguments are the two numbers that are to be summed.

The application begins by forming a string that follows the URL syntax. This URL uses the **rmi** protocol. The string includes the IP address or name of the server and the string "AddServer". The program then invokes the **lookup( )** method of the **Naming** class. This method accepts one argument, the **rmi** URL, and returns a reference to an object of type **AddServerIntf**. All remote method invocations can then be directed to this object.

The program continues by displaying its arguments and then invokes the remote **add( )** method. The sum is returned from this method and is then printed.

```java
import java.rmi.*;
public class AddClient {
  public static void main(String args[]) {
    try {
      String addServerURL = "rmi://" + args[0] + "/AddServer";
      AddServerIntf addServerIntf =
                (AddServerIntf)Naming.lookup(addServerURL);
      System.out.println("The first number is: " + args[1]);
```

```
      double d1 = Double.valueOf(args[1]).doubleValue();
      System.out.println("The second number is: " + args[2]);

      double d2 = Double.valueOf(args[2]).doubleValue();
      System.out.println("The sum is: " + addServerIntf.add(d1, d2));
    }
    catch(Exception e) {
      System.out.println("Exception: " + e);
    }
  }
}
```

After you enter all the code, use **javac** to compile the four source files that you created.

Step Two: Generate Stubs and Skeletons

Before you can use the client and server, you must generate the necessary stub. You may also need to generate a skeleton. In the context of RMI, a *stub* is a Java object that resides on the client machine. Its function is to present the same interfaces as the remote server. Remote method calls initiated by the client are actually directed to the stub. The stub works with the other parts of the RMI system to formulate a request that is sent to the remote machine.

A remote method may accept arguments that are simple types or objects. In the latter case, the object may have references to other objects. All of this information must be sent to the remote machine. That is, an object passed as an argument to a remote method call must be serialized and sent to the remote machine. Recall from Chapter 17 that the serialization facilities also recursively process all referenced objects.

Skeletons are not required by Java 2. However, they are required for the Java 1.1 RMI model. Because of this, skeletons are still required for compatibility between Java 1.1 and Java 2. A *skeleton* is a Java object that resides on the server machine. It works with the other parts of the 1.1 RMI system to receive requests, perform deserialization, and invoke the appropriate code on the server. Again, the skeleton mechanism is not required for Java 2 code that does not require compatibility with 1.1. Because many readers will want to generate the skeleton, one is used by this example.

If a response must be returned to the client, the process works in reverse. Note that the serialization and deserialization facilities are also used if objects are returned to a client.

To generate stubs and skeletons, you use a tool called the *RMI compiler*, which is invoked from the command line, as shown here:

    rmic AddServerImpl

This command generates two new files: **AddServerImpl_Skel.class** (skeleton) and
AddServerImpl_Stub.class (stub). When using **rmic**, be sure that **CLASSPATH** is set
to include the current directory. As you can see, by default, **rmic** generates both a stub
and a skeleton file. If you do not need the skeleton, you have the option to suppress it.

Step Three: Install Files on the Client and Server Machines

Copy **AddClient.class**, **AddServerImpl_Stub.class**, and **AddServerIntf.class** to a
directory on the client machine. Copy **AddServerIntf.class**, **AddServerImpl.class**,
AddServerImpl_Skel.class, **AddServerImpl_Stub.class**, and **AddServer.class** to a
directory on the server machine.

 *RMI has techniques for dynamic class loading, but they are not used by the example at
hand. Instead, all of the files that are used by the client and server applications must be
installed manually on those machines.*

Step Four: Start the RMI Registry on the Server Machine

The Java 2 SDK provides a program called **rmiregistry**, which executes on the server
machine. It maps names to object references. First, check that the **CLASSPATH**
environment variable includes the directory in which your files are located. Then,
start the RMI Registry from the command line, as shown here:

    start rmiregistry

When this command returns, you should see that a new window has been created.
You need to leave this window open until you are done experimenting with the
RMI example.

Step Five: Start the Server

The server code is started from the command line, as shown here:

    java AddServer

Recall that the **AddServer** code instantiates **AddServerImpl** and registers that object
with the name "AddServer".

Step Six: Start the Client

The **AddClient** software requires three arguments: the name or IP address of the server
machine and the two numbers that are to be summed together. You may invoke it from
the command line by using one of the two formats shown here:

    java AddClient server1 8 9
    java AddClient 11.12.13.14 8 9

In the first line, the name of the server is provided. The second line uses its IP address (11.12.13.14).

You can try this example without actually having a remote server. To do so, simply install all of the programs on the same machine, start **rmiregistry**, start **AddSever**, and then execute **AddClient** using this command line:

    java AddClient 127.0.0.1 8 9

Here, the address 127.0.0.1 is the "loop back" address for the local machine. Using this address allows you to exercise the entire RMI mechanism without actually having to install the server on a remote computer.

In either case, sample output from this program is shown here:

    The first number is: 8
    The second number is: 9
    The sum is: 17.0

Text Formatting

The package **java.text** allows you to format, search, and manipulate text. This section takes a brief look at its most commonly used classes: those that format date and time information.

DateFormat Class

DateFormat is an abstract class that provides the ability to format and parse dates and times. The **getDateInstance( )** method returns an instance of **DateFormat** that can format date information. It is available in these forms:

    static final DateFormat getDateInstance( )
    static final DateFormat getDateInstance(int style)
    static final DateFormat getDateInstance(int style, Locale locale)

The argument style is one of the following values: **DEFAULT**, **SHORT**, **MEDIUM**, **LONG**, or **FULL**. These are **int** constants defined by **DateFormat**. They cause different details about the date to be presented. The argument locale is one of the static references defined by **Locale** (refer to Chapter 16 for details). If the style and/or locale is not specified, defaults are used.

One of the most commonly used methods in this class is **format( )**. It has several overloaded forms, one of which is shown here:

    final String format(Date d)

The argument is a **Date** object that is to be displayed. The method returns a string containing the formatted information.

The following listing illustrates how to format date information. It begins by creating a **Date** object. This captures the current date and time information. Then it outputs the date information by using different styles and locales.

```
// Demonstrate date formats.
import java.text.*;
import java.util.*;

public class DateFormatDemo {
  public static void main(String args[]) {
    Date date = new Date();
    DateFormat df;

    df = DateFormat.getDateInstance(DateFormat.SHORT, Locale.JAPAN);
    System.out.println("Japan: " + df.format(date));

    df = DateFormat.getDateInstance(DateFormat.MEDIUM, Locale.KOREA);
    System.out.println("Korea: " + df.format(date));

    df = DateFormat.getDateInstance(DateFormat.LONG, Locale.UK);
    System.out.println("United Kingdom: " + df.format(date));

    df = DateFormat.getDateInstance(DateFormat.FULL, Locale.US);
    System.out.println("United States: " + df.format(date));
  }
}
```

Sample output from this program is shown here:

```
Japan: 02/05/08
Korea: 2002-05-08
United Kingdom: 08 May 2002
United States: Wednesday, May 8, 2002
```

The **getTimeInstance( )** method returns an instance of **DateFormat** that can format time information. It is available in these versions:

static final DateFormat getTimeInstance( )
static final DateFormat getTimeInstance(int *style*)
static final DateFormat getTimeInstance(int *style*, Locale *locale*)

The argument *style* is one of the following values: **DEFAULT**, **SHORT**, **MEDIUM**, **LONG**, or **FULL**. These are **int** constants defined by **DateFormat**. They cause different details about the time to be presented. The argument *locale* is one of the static references defined by **Locale**. If the *style* and/or *locale* is not specified, defaults are used.

The following listing illustrates how to format time information. It begins by creating a **Date** object. This captures the current date and time information and then outputs the time information by using different styles and locales.

```
// Demonstrate time formats.
import java.text.*;
import java.util.*;
public class TimeFormatDemo {
  public static void main(String args[]) {
    Date date = new Date();
    DateFormat df;

    df = DateFormat.getTimeInstance(DateFormat.SHORT, Locale.JAPAN);
    System.out.println("Japan: " + df.format(date));

    df = DateFormat.getTimeInstance(DateFormat.LONG, Locale.UK);
    System.out.println("United Kingdom: " + df.format(date));

    df = DateFormat.getTimeInstance(DateFormat.FULL, Locale.CANADA);
    System.out.println("Canada: " + df.format(date));
  }
}
```

Sample output from this program is shown here:

```
Japan: 20:25
United Kingdom: 20:25:14 CDT
Canada: 8:25:14 o'clock PM CDT
```

The **DateFormat** class also has a **getDateTimeInstance( )** method that can format both date and time information. You may wish to experiment with it on your own.

SimpleDateFormat Class

SimpleDateFormat is a concrete subclass of **DateFormat**. It allows you to define your own formatting patterns that are used to display date and time information.

One of its constructors is shown here:

SimpleDateFormat(String *formatString*)

The argument *formatString* describes how date and time information is displayed. An example of its use is given here:

```
SimpleDateFormat sdf = SimpleDateFormat("dd MMM yyyy hh:mm:ss zzz");
```

The symbols used in the formatting string determine the information that is displayed. Table 24-6 lists these symbols and gives a description of each.

In most cases, the number of times a symbol is repeated determines how that data is presented. Text information is displayed in an abbreviated form if the pattern letter is repeated less than four times. Otherwise, the unabbreviated form is used. For

Symbol	Description
a	AM or PM
d	Day of month (1–31)
h	Hour in AM/PM (1–12)
k	Hour in day (1–24)
m	Minute in hour (0–59)
s	Second in minute (0–59)
w	Week of year (1–52)
y	Year
z	Time zone
D	Day of year (1–366)
E	Day of week (for example, Thursday)
F	Day of week in month
G	Era (that is, AD or BC)
H	Hour in day (0–23)
K	Hour in AM/PM (0–11)
M	Month
S	Millisecond in second
W	Week of month (1–5)
Z	Time zone in RFC822 format

Table 24-6.   *Formatting String Symbols for* SimpleDateFormat

example, a zzzz pattern can display Pacific Daylight Time, and a zzz pattern can display PDT.

For numbers, the number of times a pattern letter is repeated determines how many digits are presented. For example, hh:mm:ss can present 01:51:15, but h:m:s displays the same time value as 1:51:15.

Finally, M or MM causes the month to be displayed as one or two digits. However, three or more repetitions of M cause the month to be displayed as a text string.

The following program shows how this class is used:

```java
// Demonstrate SimpleDateFormat.
import java.text.*;
import java.util.*;

public class SimpleDateFormatDemo {
  public static void main(String args[]) {
    Date date = new Date();
    SimpleDateFormat sdf;
    sdf = new SimpleDateFormat("hh:mm:ss");
    System.out.println(sdf.format(date));
    sdf = new SimpleDateFormat("dd MMM yyyy hh:mm:ss zzz");
    System.out.println(sdf.format(date));
    sdf = new SimpleDateFormat("E MMM dd yyyy");
    System.out.println(sdf.format(date));
  }
}
```

Sample output from this program is shown here:

```
02:18:23
08 May 2002 02:18:23 CDT
Wed May 08 2002
```

The
Complete
Reference

Java™ 2

Part III

Software Development Using Java

Chapter 25

Java Beans

This chapter provides an overview of an exciting technology that is at the forefront of Java programming: Java Beans. Beans are important, because they allow you to build complex systems from software components. These components may be provided by you or supplied by one or more different vendors. Java Beans defines an architecture that specifies how these building blocks can operate together.

To better understand the value of Beans, consider the following. Hardware designers have a wide variety of components that can be integrated together to construct a system. Resistors, capacitors, and inductors are examples of simple building blocks. Integrated circuits provide more advanced functionality. All of these different parts can be reused. It is not necessary or possible to rebuild these capabilities each time a new system is needed. Also, the same pieces can be used in different types of circuits. This is possible because the behavior of these components is understood and documented.

Unfortunately, the software industry has not been as successful in achieving the benefits of reusability and interoperability. Large applications grow in complexity and become very difficult to maintain and enhance. Part of the problem is that, until recently, there has not been a standard, portable way to write a software component. To achieve the benefits of component software, a component architecture is needed that allows programs to be assembled from software building blocks, perhaps provided by different vendors. It must also be possible for a designer to select a component, understand its capabilities, and incorporate it into an application. When a new version of a component becomes available, it should be easy to incorporate this functionality into existing code. Fortunately, Java Beans provides just such an architecture.

What Is a Java Bean?

A *Java Bean* is a software component that has been designed to be reusable in a variety of different environments. There is no restriction on the capability of a Bean. It may perform a simple function, such as checking the spelling of a document, or a complex function, such as forecasting the performance of a stock portfolio. A Bean may be visible to an end user. One example of this is a button on a graphical user interface. A Bean may also be invisible to a user. Software to decode a stream of multimedia information in real time is an example of this type of building block. Finally, a Bean may be designed to work autonomously on a user's workstation or to work in cooperation with a set of other distributed components. Software to generate a pie chart from a set of data points is an example of a Bean that can execute locally. However, a Bean that provides real-time price information from a stock or commodities exchange would need to work in cooperation with other distributed software to obtain its data.

You will see shortly what specific changes a software developer must make to a class so that it is usable as a Java Bean. However, one of the goals of the Java designers was to make it easy to use this technology. Therefore, the code changes are minimal.

Advantages of Java Beans

A software component architecture provides standard mechanisms to deal with software building blocks. The following list enumerates some of the specific benefits that Java technology provides for a component developer:

- A Bean obtains all the benefits of Java's "write-once, run-anywhere" paradigm.

- The properties, events, and methods of a Bean that are exposed to an application builder tool can be controlled.

- A Bean may be designed to operate correctly in different locales, which makes it useful in global markets.

- Auxiliary software can be provided to help a person configure a Bean. This software is only needed when the design-time parameters for that component are being set. It does not need to be included in the run-time environment.

- The configuration settings of a Bean can be saved in persistent storage and restored at a later time.

- A Bean may register to receive events from other objects and can generate events that are sent to other objects.

Application Builder Tools

When working with Java Beans, most developers use an *application builder tool*, a utility that enables you to configure a set of Beans, connect them together, and produce a working application. In general, Bean builder tools have the following capabilities.

- A palette is provided that lists all of the available Beans. As additional Beans are developed or purchased, they can be added to the palette.

- A worksheet is displayed that allows the designer to lay out Beans in a graphical user interface. A designer may drag and drop a Bean from the palette to this worksheet.

- Special editors and customizers allow a Bean to be configured. This is the mechanism by which the behavior of a Bean may be adapted for a particular environment.

- Commands allow a designer to inquire about the state and behavior of a Bean. This information automatically becomes available when a Bean is added to the palette.

- Capabilities exist to interconnect Beans. This means that events generated by one component are mapped to method invocations on other components.

■ When a collection of Beans has been configured and connected, it is possible to save all of this information in a persistent storage area. At a later time, this information can then be used to restore the state of the application.

Sun provides two Bean application builder tools. The first is the BeanBox, which is part of the Bean Developers Kit (BDK). The BDK is the original builder tool provided by Sun. The second is the new Bean Builder. Because Bean Builder is designed to supplant the BeanBox, Sun has stopped development of the BDK and all new Bean applications will be created using Bean Builder.

Although Bean Builder is the future of Bean development, it is not the sole focus of this chapter. Instead, both BeanBox and Bean Builder are discussed. The reason for this is that Bean Builder requires Java 2, version 1.4. It is incompatible with earlier versions of Java 2. This means that readers of this book using Java 2, version 1.2 or version 1.3 will not be able to use Bean Builder. Instead, they must continue to use the BDK. Further, readers using version 1.4 *cannot* use the BDK because it is not compatible with Java 2, version 1.4. So, if you are using version 1.4, then you *must use* Bean Builder. If you are using a version of Java prior to 1.4, you *must use* the BDK. Thus, both approaches are described here, beginning with the BDK. Keep in mind that the information about Beans, Bean architecture, JAR files, and so on, apply to either Bean development tool.

One other point: At the time of this writing, Java 2, version 1.4 is a released product, but Bean Builder is currently in beta testing. This means that the only way for a 1.4 user to create a Bean application is to do so using latest Bean Builder beta. For this reason, we will not examine its features in depth at this time. However, at the end of this chapter, a general overview is presented and a sample application is created.

Using the Bean Developer Kit (BDK)

The Bean Developer Kit (BDK), available from the JavaSoft site, is a simple example of a tool that enables you to create, configure, and connect a set of Beans. There is also a set of sample Beans with their source code. This section provides step-by-step instructions for installing and using this tool. Remember, the BDK is for use with versions of Java 2 prior to 1.4. For Java 2, v1.4 you must use the Bean Builder Tool described at the end of this chapter.

Note *In this chapter, instructions are provided for a Windows environment. The procedures for a UNIX platform are similar, but some of the commands are different.*

Installing the BDK

The Java 2 SDK must be installed on your machine for the BDK to work. Confirm that the SDK tools are accessible from your environment.

The BDK can then be downloaded from the JavaSoft site (**http://java.sun.com**). It is packaged as one file that is a self-extracting archive. Follow the instructions to install it on your machine. The discussion that follows assumes that the BDK is installed in a directory called **bdk**. If this is not the case with your system, substitute the proper directory.

Starting the BDK

To start the BDK, follow these steps:

1. Change to the directory **c:\bdk\beanbox**.

2. Execute the batch file called **run.bat**. This causes the BDK to display the three windows shown in Figure 25-1. ToolBox lists all of the different Beans that have been included with the BDK. BeanBox provides an area to lay out and connect the Beans selected from the ToolBox. Properties provides the ability to configure a selected Bean. You may also see a window called Method Tracer, but we won't be using it.

Using the BDK

This section describes how to create an application by using some of the Beans provided with the BDK. First, the **Molecule** Bean displays a three-dimensional view of a molecule. It may be configured to present one of the following molecules: hyaluronic acid, benzene, buckminsterfullerine, cyclohexane, ethane, or water. This component also has methods that allow the molecule to be rotated in space along its X or Y axis.

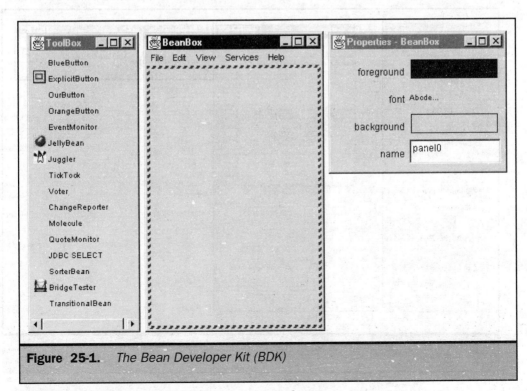

Figure 25-1. *The Bean Developer Kit (BDK)*

Second, the **OurButton** Bean provides a push-button functionality. We will have one button labeled "Rotate X" to rotate the molecule along its X axis and another button labeled "Rotate Y" to rotate the molecule along its Y axis.

Figure 25-2 shows how this application appears.

Create and Configure an Instance of the Molecule Bean

Follow these steps to create and configure an instance of the **Molecule** Bean:

1. Position the cursor on the ToolBox entry labeled **Molecule** and click the left mouse button. You should see the cursor change to a cross.

2. Move the cursor to the BeanBox display area and click the left mouse button in approximately the area where you wish the Bean to be displayed. You should see a rectangular region appear that contains a 3-D display of a molecule. This area is surrounded by a hatched border, indicating that it is currently selected.

3. You can reposition the **Molecule** Bean by positioning the cursor over one of the hatched borders and dragging the Bean.

4. You can change the molecule that is displayed by changing the selection in the Properties window. Notice that the Bean display changes immediately when you change the selected molecule.

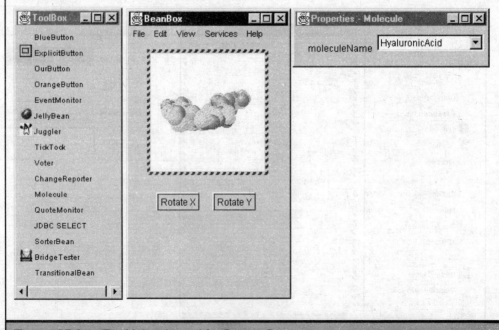

Figure 25-2. *The* Molecule *and* OurButton *Beans*

Create and Configure an Instance of the OurButton Bean

Follow these steps to create and configure an instance of the **OurButton** Bean and connect it to the **Molecule** Bean:

1. Position the cursor on the ToolBox entry labeled **OurButton** and click the left mouse button. You should see the cursor change to a cross.

2. Move the cursor to the BeanBox display area and click the left mouse button in approximately the area where you wish the Bean to be displayed. You should see a rectangular region appear that contains a button. This area is surrounded by a hatched border indicating that it is currently selected.

3. You may reposition the **OurButton** Bean by positioning the cursor over one of the hatched borders and dragging the Bean.

4. Go to the Properties window and change the label of the Bean to "Rotate X". The button appearance changes immediately when this property is changed.

5. Go to the menu bar of the BeanBox and select Edit | Events | action | actionPerformed. You should now see a line extending from the button to the cursor. Notice that one end of the line moves as the cursor moves. However, the other end of the line remains fixed at the button.

6. Move the cursor so that it is inside the **Molecule** Bean display area, and click the left mouse button. You should see the Event Target Dialog dialog box.

7. The dialog box allows you to choose a method that should be invoked when this button is clicked. Select the entry labeled "rotateOnX" and click the OK button. You should see a message box appear very briefly, stating that the tool is "Generating and compiling adaptor class."

Test the application. Each time you press the button, the molecule should move a few degrees around one of its axes.

Now create another instance of the **OurButton** Bean. Label it "Rotate Y" and map its action event to the "rotateY" method of the **Molecule** Bean. The steps to do this are very similar to those just described for the button labeled "Rotate X".

Test the application by clicking these buttons and observing how the molecule moves.

JAR Files

Before developing your own Bean, it is necessary for you to understand JAR (Java Archive) files, because tools such as the BDK expect Beans to be packaged within JAR files. A JAR file allows you to efficiently deploy a set of classes and their associated resources. For example, a developer may build a multimedia application that uses various sound and image files. A set of Beans can control how and when this information is presented. All of these pieces can be placed into one JAR file.

JAR technology makes it much easier to deliver and install software. Also, the elements in a JAR file are compressed, which makes downloading a JAR file much faster than separately downloading several uncompressed files. Digital signatures may also be associated with the individual elements in a JAR file. This allows a consumer to be sure that these elements were produced by a specific organization or individual.

Note *The package **java.util.zip** contains classes that read and write JAR files.*

Manifest Files

A developer must provide a *manifest file* to indicate which of the components in a JAR file are Java Beans. An example of a manifest file is provided in the following listing. It defines a JAR file that contains four **.gif** files and one **.class** file. The last entry is a Bean.

```
Name: sunw/demo/slides/slide0.gif
Name: sunw/demo/slides/slide1.gif
Name: sunw/demo/slides/slide2.gif
Name: sunw/demo/slides/slide3.gif
Name: sunw/demo/slides/Slides.class
Java-Bean: True
```

A manifest file may reference several **.class** files. If a **.class** file is a Java Bean, its entry must be immediately followed by the line "Java-Bean: True".

The JAR Utility

A utility is used to generate a JAR file. Its syntax is shown here:

jar *options files*

Table 25-1 lists the possible options and their meanings. The following examples show how to use this utility.

Creating a JAR File

The following command creates a JAR file named **Xyz.jar** that contains all of the **.class** and **.gif** files in the current directory:

```
jar cf Xyz.jar *.class *.gif
```

If a manifest file such as **Yxz.mf** is available, it can be used with the following command:

```
jar cfm Xyz.jar Yxz.mf *.class *.gif
```

Option	Description
c	A new archive is to be created.
C	Change directories during command execution.
f	The first element in the file list is the name of the archive that is to be created or accessed.
i	Index information should be provided.
m	The second element in the file list is the name of the external manifest file.
M	Manifest file not created.
t	The archive contents should be tabulated.
u	Update existing JAR file.
v	Verbose output should be provided by the utility as it executes.
x	Files are to be extracted from the archive. (If there is only one file, that is the name of the archive, and all files in it are extracted. Otherwise, the first element in the file list is the name of the archive, and the remaining elements in the list are the files that should be extracted from the archive.)
0	Do not use compression.

Table 25-1. *JAR Command Options*

Tabulating the Contents of a JAR File

The following command lists the contents of **Xyz.jar**:

```
jar tf Xyz.jar
```

Extracting Files from a JAR File

The following command extracts the contents of **Xyz.jar** and places those files in the current directory:

```
jar xf Xyz.jar
```

Updating an Existing JAR File

The following command adds the file **file1.class** to **Xyz.jar**:

```
jar -uf Xyz.jar file1.class
```

Recursing Directories

The following command adds all files below **directoryX** to **Xyz.jar**:

```
jar -uf Xyz.jar -C directoryX *
```

Introspection

Introspection is the process of analyzing a Bean to determine its capabilities. This is an essential feature of the Java Beans API, because it allows an application builder tool to present information about a component to a software designer. Without introspection, the Java Beans technology could not operate.

There are two ways in which the developer of a Bean can indicate which of its properties, events, and methods should be exposed by an application builder tool. With the first method, simple naming conventions are used. These allow the introspection mechanisms to infer information about a Bean. In the second way, an additional class is provided that explicitly supplies this information. The first approach is examined here. The second method is described later.

The following sections indicate the design patterns for properties and events that enable the functionality of a Bean to be determined.

Design Patterns for Properties

A *property* is a subset of a Bean's state. The values assigned to the properties determine the behavior and appearance of that component. This section discusses three types of properties: simple, Boolean, and indexed.

Simple Properties

A simple property has a single value. It can be identified by the following design patterns, where N is the name of the property and T is its type.

```
public T getN( );
public void setN(T arg);
```

A read/write property has both of these methods to access its values. A read-only property has only a get method. A write-only property has only a set method.

The following listing shows a class that has three read/write simple properties:

```
public class Box {
  private double depth, height, width;
  public double getDepth( ) {
    return depth;
  }
  public void setDepth(double d) {
    depth = d;
  }
  public double getHeight( ) {
    return height;
  }
  public void setHeight(double h) {
    height = h;
  }
  public double getWidth( ) {
    return width;
  }
  public void setWidth(double w) {
    width = w;
  }
}
```

Boolean Properties

A Boolean property has a value of **true** or **false**. It can be identified by the following design patterns, where N is the name of the property:

public boolean isN( );
public boolean getN( );
public void setN(boolean *value*);

Either the first or second pattern can be used to retrieve the value of a Boolean property. However, if a class has both of these methods, the first pattern is used.

The following listing shows a class that has one Boolean property:

```
public class Line {
  private boolean dotted = false;
  public boolean isDotted( ) {
    return dotted;
  }
  public void setDotted(boolean dotted) {
```

```
      this.dotted = dotted;
  }
}
```

Indexed Properties

An indexed property consists of multiple values. It can be identified by the following design patterns, where N is the name of the property and T is its type:

> public T getN(int *index*);
> public void setN(int *index*, T *value*);
> public T[ ] getN( );
> public void setN(T *values*[ ]);

The following listing shows a class that has one read/write indexed property:

```
public class PieChart {
  private double data[ ];
  public double getData(int index) {
    return data[index];
  }
 public void setData(int index, double value) {
    data[index] = value;
  }
  public double[ ] getData( ) {
    return data;
  }
  public void setData(double[ ] values) {
    data = new double[values.length];
    System.arraycopy(values, 0, data, 0, values.length);
  }
}
```

Design Patterns for Events

Beans use the delegation event model that was discussed earlier in this book. Beans can generate events and send them to other objects. These can be identified by the following design patterns, where T is the type of the event:

> public void addTListener(TListener *eventListener*);
> public void addTListener(TListener *eventListener*) throws TooManyListeners;
> public void removeTListener(TListener *eventListener*);

These methods are used by event listeners to register an interest in events of a specific type. The first pattern indicates that a Bean can multicast an event to multiple listeners. The second pattern indicates that a Bean can unicast an event to only one listener. The third pattern is used by a listener when it no longer wishes to receive a specific type of event notification from a Bean.

The following listing outlines a class that notifies other objects when a temperature value moves outside a specific range. The two methods indicated here allow other objects that implement the **TemperatureListener** interface to receive notifications when this occurs.

```
public class Thermometer {
  public void addTemperatureListener(TemperatureListener tl) {
    ...
  }
  public void removeTemperatureListener(TemperatureListener tl) {
    ...
  }
}
```

Methods

Design patterns are not used for naming nonproperty methods. The introspection mechanism finds all of the public methods of a Bean. Protected and private methods are not presented.

Developing a Simple Bean Using the BDK

This section presents an example that shows how to develop a simple Bean and connect it to other components via the BDK.

Our new component is called the **Colors** Bean. It appears as either a rectangle or ellipse that is filled with a color. A color is chosen at random when the Bean begins execution. A public method can be invoked to change it. Each time the mouse is clicked on the Bean, another random color is chosen. There is one **boolean** read/write property that determines the shape.

The BDK is used to lay out an application with one instance of the **Colors** Bean and one instance of the **OurButton** Bean. The button is labeled "Change." Each time it is pressed, the color changes.

Figure 25-3 shows how this application appears.

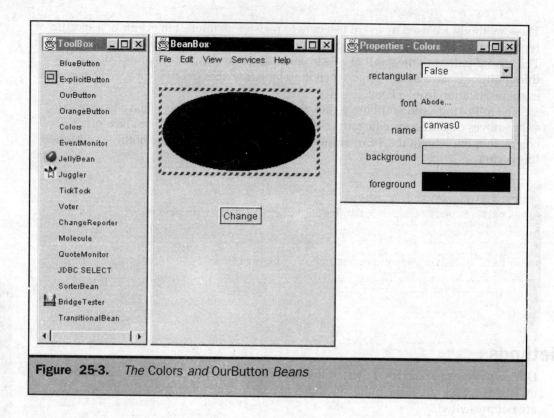

Figure 25-3. *The* Colors *and* OurButton *Beans*

Create a New Bean

Here are the steps that you must follow to create a new Bean:

1. Create a directory for the new Bean.
2. Create the Java source file(s).
3. Compile the source file(s).
4. Create a manifest file.
5. Generate a JAR file.
6. Start the BDK.
7. Test.

The following sections discuss each of these steps in detail.

Create a Directory for the New Bean

You need to make a directory for the Bean. To follow along with this example, create **c:\bdk\demo\sunw\demo\colors**. Then change to that directory.

Create the Source File for the New Bean

The source code for the **Colors** component is shown in the following listing. It is located in the file **Colors.java**.

The **import** statement at the beginning of the file places it in the package named **sunw.demo.colors**. Recall from Chapter 9 that the directory hierarchy corresponds to the package hierarchy. Therefore, this file must be located in a subdirectory named **sunw\demo\colors** relative to the **CLASSPATH** environment variable.

The color of the component is determined by the private **Color** variable **color**, and its shape is determined by the private **boolean** variable **rectangular**.

The constructor defines an anonymous inner class that extends **MouseAdapter** and overrides its **mousePressed( )** method. The **change( )** method is invoked in response to mouse presses. The component is initialized to a rectangular shape of 200 by 100 pixels. The **change( )** method is invoked to select a random color and repaint the component.

The **getRectangular( )** and **setRectangular( )** methods provide access to the one property of this Bean. The **change( )** method calls **randomColor( )** to choose a color and then calls **repaint( )** to make the change visible. Notice that the **paint( )** method uses the **rectangular** and **color** variables to determine how to present the Bean.

```
// A simple Bean.
package sunw.demo.colors;
import java.awt.*;
import java.awt.event.*;
public class Colors extends Canvas {
  transient private Color color;
  private boolean rectangular;
  public Colors() {
    addMouseListener(new MouseAdapter() {
      public void mousePressed(MouseEvent me) {
        change();
      }
    });
    rectangular = false;
    setSize(200, 100);
    change();
  }
  public boolean getRectangular() {
    return rectangular;
  }
  public void setRectangular(boolean flag) {
    this.rectangular = flag;
    repaint();
  }
  public void change() {
```

```
      color = randomColor();
      repaint();
    }
    private Color randomColor() {
      int r = (int)(255*Math.random());
      int g = (int)(255*Math.random());
      int b = (int)(255*Math.random());
      return new Color(r, g, b);
    }
    public void paint(Graphics g) {
      Dimension d = getSize();
      int h = d.height;
      int w = d.width;
      g.setColor(color);
      if(rectangular) {
        g.fillRect(0, 0, w-1, h-1);
      }
      else {
        g.fillOval(0, 0, w-1, h-1);
      }
    }
  }
```

Compile the Source Code for the New Bean

Compile the source code to create a class file. Type the following:

```
javac Colors.java.
```

Create a Manifest File

You must now create a manifest file. First, switch to the **c:\bdk\demo** directory. This is the directory in which the manifest files for the BDK demos are located. Put the source code for your manifest file in the file **colors.mft**. It is shown here:

```
Name: sunw/demo/colors/Colors.class
Java-Bean: True
```

This file indicates that there is one **.class** file in the JAR file and that it is a Java Bean. Notice that the **Colors.class** file is in the package **sunw.demo.colors** and in the subdirectory **sunw\demo\colors** relative to the current directory.

Generate a JAR File

Beans are included in the ToolBox window of the BDK only if they are in JAR files in the directory **c:\bdk\jars**. These files are generated with the jar utility. Enter the following:

```
jar cfm ..\jars\colors.jar colors.mft sunw\demo\colors\*.class
```

This command creates the file **colors.jar** and places it in the directory **c:\bdk\jars**. (You may wish to put this in a batch file for future use.)

Start the BDK

Change to the directory **c:\bdk\beanbox** and type **run**. This causes the BDK to start. You should see three windows, titled ToolBox, BeanBox, and Properties. The ToolBox window should include an entry labeled "Colors" for your new Bean.

Create an Instance of the Colors Bean

After you complete the preceding steps, create an instance of the **Colors** Bean in the BeanBox window. Test your new component by pressing the mouse anywhere within its borders. Its color immediately changes. Use the Properties window to change the **rectanguiar** property from **false** to **true**. Its shape immediately changes.

Create and Configure an Instance of the OurButton Bean

Create an instance of the **OurButton** Bean in the BeanBox window. Then follow these steps:

1. Go to the Properties window and change the label of the Bean to "Change". You should see that the button appearance changes immediately when this property is changed.

2. Go to the menu bar of the BeanBox and select Edit I Events I action I actionPerformed.

3. Move the cursor so that it is inside the **Colors** Bean display area, and click the left mouse button. You should see the Event Target Dialog dialog box.

4. The dialog box allows you to choose a method that should be invoked when this button is clicked. Select the entry labeled "change" and click the OK button. You should see a message box appear very briefly, stating that the tool is "Generating and compiling adaptor class."

5. Click on the button. You should see the color change.

You might want to experiment with the **Colors** Bean a bit before moving on.

Using Bound Properties

A Bean that has a bound property generates an event when the property is changed. The event is of type **PropertyChangeEvent** and is sent to objects that previously registered an interest in receiving such notifications.

The **TickTock** Bean is supplied with the BDK. It generates a property change event every N seconds. N is a property of the Bean that can be changed via the Properties window of the BDK. The next example builds an application that uses the **TickTock** Bean to automatically control the **Colors** Bean. Figure 25-4 shows how this application appears.

Steps

For this example, start the BDK and create an instance of the **Colors** Bean in the BeanBox window.

Create an instance of the **TickTock** Bean. The Properties window should show one property for this component. It is "Interval" and its initial value is 5. This represents the number of seconds that elapse between property change events generated by the **TickTock** Bean. Change the value to 1.

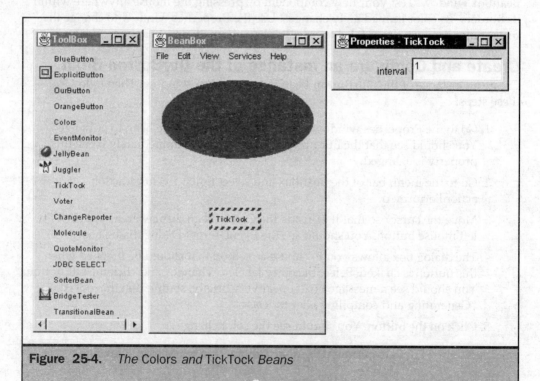

Figure 25-4.   *The* Colors *and* TickTock *Beans*

Now you need to map events generated by the **TickTock** Bean into method calls on the **Colors** Bean. Follow these steps:

1. Go to the menu bar of the BeanBox and select Edit | Events | propertyChange | propertyChange. You should now see a line extending from the button to the cursor.

2. Move the cursor so that it is inside the **Colors** Bean display area, and click the left mouse button. You should see the Event Target Dialog dialog box.

3. The dialog box allows you to choose a method that should be invoked when this event occurs. Select the entry labeled "change" and click the OK button. You should see a message box appear very briefly, stating that the tool is "Generating and compiling adaptor class."

You should now see the color of your component change every second.

Using the BeanInfo Interface

In our previous examples, design patterns were used to determine the information that was provided to a Bean user. This section describes how a developer can use the **BeanInfo** interface to explicitly control this process.

This interface defines several methods, including these:

```
PropertyDescriptor[ ] getPropertyDescriptors( )
EventSetDescriptor[ ] getEventSetDescriptors( )
MethodDescriptor[ ] getMethodDescriptors( )
```

They return arrays of objects that provide information about the properties, events, and methods of a Bean. By implementing these methods, a developer can designate exactly what is presented to a user.

SimpleBeanInfo is a class that provides default implementations of the **BeanInfo** interface, including the three methods just shown. You may extend this class and override one or more of them. The following listing shows how this is done for the **Colors** Bean that was developed earlier. **ColorsBeanInfo** is a subclass of **SimpleBeanInfo**. It overrides **getPropertyDescriptors( )** in order to designate which properties are presented to a Bean user. This method creates a **PropertyDescriptor** object for the **rectangular** property. The **PropertyDescriptor** constructor that is used is shown here:

```
PropertyDescriptor(String property, Class beanCls)
    throws IntrospectionException
```

Here, the first argument is the name of the property, and the second argument is the class of the Bean.

```
// A Bean information class.
package sunw.demo.colors;
import java.beans.*;
public class ColorsBeanInfo extends SimpleBeanInfo {
  public PropertyDescriptor[] getPropertyDescriptors() {
    try {
      PropertyDescriptor rectangular = new
        PropertyDescriptor("rectangular", Colors.class);
      PropertyDescriptor pd[] = {rectangular};
      return pd;
    }
    catch(Exception e) {
    }
    return null;
  }
}
```

You must compile this file from the **BDK\demo** directory or set **CLASSPATH** so that it includes **c:\bdk\demo**. If you don't, the compiler won't find the **Colors.class** file properly. After this file is successfully compiled, the **colors.mft** file can be updated, as shown here:

```
Name: sunw/demo/colors/ColorsBeanInfo.class
Name: sunw/demo/colors/Colors.class
Java-Bean: True
```

Use the JAR tool to create a new **colors.jar** file. Restart the BDK and create an instance of the **Colors** Bean in the BeanBox.

The introspection facilities are designed to look for a **BeanInfo** class. If it exists, its behavior explicitly determines the information that is presented to a Bean user. Otherwise, design patterns are used to infer this information.

Figure 25-5 shows how the Properties window now appears. Compare it with Figure 24-3. You can see that the properties inherited from **Component** are no longer presented for the **Colors** Bean. Only the **rectangular** property appears.

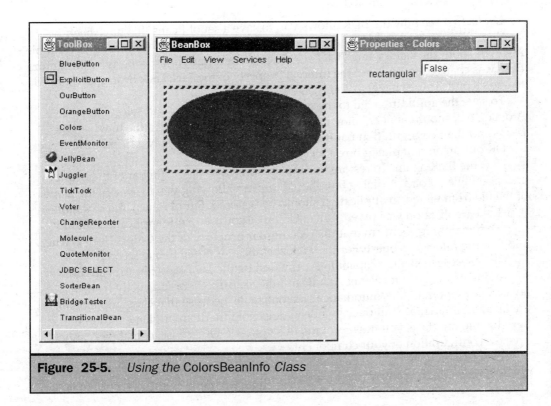

Figure 25-5. *Using the* ColorsBeanInfo *Class*

Constrained Properties

A Bean that has a *constrained* property generates an event when an attempt is made to change its value. The event is of type **PropertyChangeEvent**. It is sent to objects that previously registered an interest in receiving such notifications. Those other objects have the ability to veto the proposed change. This capability allows a Bean to operate differently according to its run-time environment. A full discussion of constrained properties is beyond the scope of this book.

Persistence

Persistence is the ability to save a Bean to nonvolatile storage and retrieve it at a later time. The information that is particularly important are the configuration settings.

Let us first see how the BDK allows you to save a set of Beans that have been configured and connected together to form an application. Recall our previous example involving both the **Colors** and **TickTock** Beans. The **rectangular** property of the **Colors** Bean was changed to **true**, and the **interval** property of the **TickTock** Bean was changed to one second. These changes can be saved.

To save the application, go to the menu bar of the BeanBox and select File | Save. A dialog box should appear, allowing you to specify the name of a file to which the Beans and their configuration parameters should be saved. Supply a filename and click the OK button on that dialog box. Exit from the BDK.

Start the BDK again. To restore the application, go to the menu bar of the BeanBox and select File | Load. A dialog box should appear, allowing you to specify the name of the file from which an application should be restored. Supply the name of the file in which the application was saved, and click the OK button. Your application should now be functioning. Confirm that the **rectangular** property of the **Colors** Bean is **true** and that the **interval** property for the **TickTock** Bean is equal to one second.

The object serialization capabilities provided by the Java class libraries are used to provide persistence for Beans. If a Bean inherits directly or indirectly from **java.awt.Component**, it is automatically serializable, because that class implements the **java.io.Serializable** interface. If a Bean does not inherit an implementation of the Serializable interface, you must provide this yourself. Otherwise, containers cannot save the configuration of your component.

The **transient** keyword can be used to designate data members of a Bean that should not be serialized. The **color** variable of the **Colors** class is an example of such an item.

Customizers

The Properties window of the BDK allows a developer to modify the properties of a Bean. However, this may not be the best user interface for a complex component with many interrelated properties. Therefore, a Bean developer can provide a *customizer* that helps another developer configure this software. A customizer can provide a step-by-step guide through the process that must be followed to use the component in a specific context. Online documentation can also be provided. A Bean developer has great flexibility to develop a customizer that can differentiate his or her product in the marketplace.

The Java Beans API

The Java Beans functionality is provided by a set of classes and interfaces in the **java.beans** package. This section provides a brief overview of its contents. Table 25-2 lists the interfaces in **java.beans** and provides a brief description of their functionality. Table 25-3 lists the classes in **java.beans**.

Interface	Description
AppletInitializer	Methods in this interface are used to initialize Beans that are also applets.
BeanInfo	This interface allows a designer to specify information about the properties, events, and methods of a Bean.
Customizer	This interface allows a designer to provide a graphical user interface through which a Bean may be configured.
DesignMode	Methods in this interface determine if a Bean is executing in design mode.
ExceptionListener	A method in this interface is invoked when an exception has occurred. (Added by Java 2, version 1.4.)
PropertyChangeListener	A method in this interface is invoked when a bound property is changed.
PropertyEditor	Objects that implement this interface allow designers to change and display property values.
VetoableChangeListener	A method in this interface is invoked when a constrained property is changed.
Visibility	Methods in this interface allow a Bean to execute in environments where a graphical user interface is not available.

Table 25-2. *The Interfaces Defined in* java.beans

Class	Description
BeanDescriptor	This class provides information about a Bean. It also allows you to associate a customizer with a Bean.
Beans	This class is used to obtain information about a Bean.

Table 25-3. *The Classes Defined in* java.beans

Class	Description
DefaultPersistenceDelegate	A concrete subclass of **PersistenceDelegate**. (Added by Java 2, version 1.4.)
Encoder	Encodes the state of a set of Beans. Can be used to write this information to a stream. (Added by Java 2, version 1.4.)
EventHandler	Supports dynamic event listener creation. (Added by Java 2, version 1.4.)
EventSetDescriptor	Instances of this class describe an event that can be generated by a Bean.
Expression	Encapsulates a call to a method that returns a result. (Added by Java 2, version 1.4.)
FeatureDescriptor	This is the superclass of the **PropertyDescriptor**, **EventSetDescriptor**, and **MethodDescriptor** classes.
IndexedPropertyDescriptor	Instances of this class describe an indexed property of a Bean.
IntrospectionException	An exception of this type is generated if a problem occurs when analyzing a Bean.
Introspector	This class analyzes a Bean and constructs a **BeanInfo** object that describes the component.
MethodDescriptor	Instances of this class describe a method of a Bean.
ParameterDescriptor	Instances of this class describe a method parameter.
PersistenceDelegate	Handles the state information of an object. (Added by Java 2, version 1.4.)
PropertyChangeEvent	This event is generated when bound or constrained properties are changed. It is sent to objects that registered an interest in these events and implement either the **PropertyChangeListener** or **VetoableChangeListener** interfaces.

Table 25-3. *The Classes Defined in* java.beans *(continued)*

Class	Description
PropertyChangeListenerProxy	Extends **EventListenerProxy** and implements **PropertyChangeListener**. (Added by Java 2, version 1.4.)
PropertyChangeSupport	Beans that support bound properties can use this class to notify **PropertyChangeListener** objects.
PropertyDescriptor	Instances of this class describe a property of a Bean.
PropertyEditorManager	This class locates a **PropertyEditor** object for a given type.
PropertyEditorSupport	This class provides functionality that can be used when writing property editors.
PropertyVetoException	An exception of this type is generated if a change to a constrained property is vetoed.
SimpleBeanInfo	This class provides functionality that can be used when writing **BeanInfo** classes.
Statement	Encapsulates a call to a method. (Added by Java 2, version 1.4.)
VetoableChangeListenerProxy	Extends **EventListenerProxy** and implements **VetoableChangeListener**. (Added by Java 2, version 1.4.)
VetoableChangeSupport	Beans that support constrained properties can use this class to notify **VetoableChangeListener** objects.
XMLDecoder	Used to read a Bean from an XML document. (Added by Java 2, version 1.4.)
XMLEncoder	Used to write a Bean to an XML document. (Added by Java 2, version 1.4.)

Table 25-3.   *The Classes Defined in* java.beans (continued)

A complete discussion of these classes and interfaces is beyond the scope of this book. However, the following program illustrates the **Introspector**, **BeanDescriptor**,

PropertyDescriptor, and **EventSetDescriptor** classes and the **BeanInfo** interface. It lists the properties and events of the **Colors** Bean that was developed earlier in this chapter.

```java
// Show properties and events.
package sunw.demo.colors;
import java.awt.*;
import java.beans.*;
public class IntrospectorDemo {
  public static void main(String args[]) {
    try {
      Class c = Class.forName("sunw.demo.colors.Colors");
      BeanInfo beanInfo = Introspector.getBeanInfo(c);
      BeanDescriptor beanDescriptor = beanInfo.getBeanDescriptor();

      System.out.println("Bean name = " +
                          beanDescriptor.getName());

      System.out.println("Properties:");
      PropertyDescriptor propertyDescriptor[] =
        beanInfo.getPropertyDescriptors();
      for(int i = 0; i < propertyDescriptor.length; i++) {
        System.out.println("\t" + propertyDescriptor[i].getName());
      }

      System.out.println("Events:");
      EventSetDescriptor eventSetDescriptor[] =
        beanInfo.getEventSetDescriptors();
      for(int i = 0; i < eventSetDescriptor.length; i++) {
        System.out.println("\t" + eventSetDescriptor[i].getName());
      }
    }
    catch(Exception e) {
      System.out.println("Exception caught. " + e);
    }
  }
}
```

The output from this program is the following:

```
Bean name = Colors
Properties:
```

```
                    rectangular
Events:
                    propertyChange
                    component
                    mouseMotion
                    mouse
                    hierarchy
                    key
                    focus
                    hierarchyBounds
                    inputMethod
```

Using Bean Builder

As explained at the start of the chapter, the BDK is not compatible with Java 2, version 1.4. Instead, 1.4 users will need to use the new Bean Builder tool for Bean development. At the time of this writing, Bean Builder is available only as a beta release, and its final form and feature set are subject to change. However, because it is the tool that Java 2, version 1.4 users must use to develop Beans, an overview of Bean Builder is presented here. (Subsequent editions of this book will cover Bean Builder in detail after it is a released product.) Keep in mind that the basic Bean information, such as introspection, described earlier, also applies to Beans used by Bean Builder. Bean Builder is available from **http://java.sun.com**.

Bean Builder is similar to the BeanBox offered by the BDK, except that it is more powerful and sophisticated. Its operation is also similar to the BeanBox except that it is easier to use. Perhaps the most striking feature of Bean Builder is that it supports two separate modes of operation: design and test. In *design mode*, you construct a Bean-based application, adding the various components, and wiring them together. In *test mode*, also called *run-time mode*, the application is executed and all of the components are live. Thus, it is extremely easy to construct and then test your application. Futhermore, you switch between these two modes by checking or clearing a single check box.

Bean Builder provides the three windows shown in Figure 25-6. The top (main) window holds the current palette set. This includes a default palette from which you can choose various user-interface objects, such as buttons, scroll bars, lists, and menus. These are Swing rather than AWT objects. (You will find an overview of Swing in Chapter 26, but no knowledge of Swing is required to follow along with the example developed later in this section.) You can also load other palettes and JAR files. Each component has associated with it a set of properties. You can examine and set these using the Property Inspector window provided by Bean Builder. The third window,

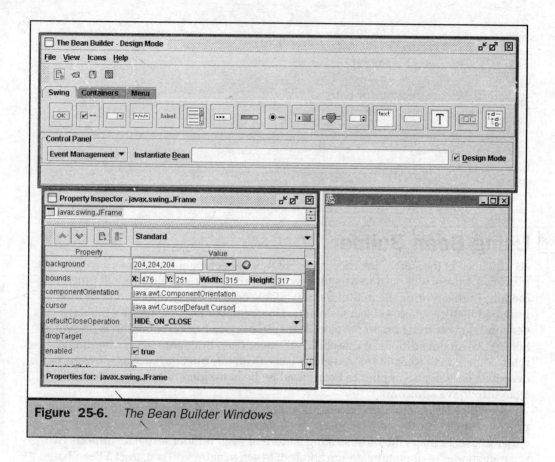

Figure 25-6.   *The Bean Builder Windows*

called the design window (or, *designer* for short), is the window in which you will assemble various components into an application.

In general, to build an application, you will select items from a palette and instantiate them on the designer, setting their properties as necessary by using the Property Inspector window. Once you have assembled the components, you will wire them together by dragging a line from one to another. In the process, you will define the input and output methods that will be called, and what action causes them to be called. For example, you might wire a push button to a text field, specifying that when the push button is pressed, the text field will be cleared.

uilding a Simple Bean Builder Application

It is really quite easy to build an application using Bean Builder. In this section, we will walk through the construction of a very simple one that contains a label, a slider control, and a scroll bar. When the slider control is moved, the scroll bar is also moved by the same amount, and vice versa. Thus, moving one causes the other to move, too. Once you have completed this walk through, you will be able to easily build other applications on your own.

First, create a new project by selecting New from the File menu. Next, select **javax.swing.JFrame** in the list at the top of the Property Inspector window. **JFrame** is the top-level Swing class for the design window. Next, scroll down in the Property Inspector window until you find **title**. Change the title to "A Bean Builder App". Your screen should look like the one shown in Figure 25-7.

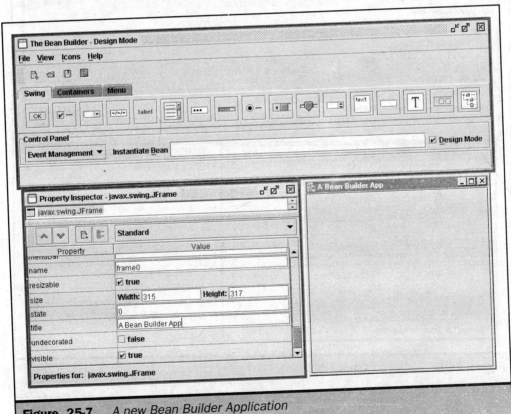

Figure 25-7. *A new Bean Builder Application*

Next, we will add a label to the design. Click on the label button in the Swing palette. This instantiates a **JLabel** object, which is the Swing class for a label. Then, move the mouse to the designer and outline a rectangle near the top of the window. This defines were the text will go. Then, using the Property Inspector window, find the **text** entry. Change it to "Move slider or scroll bar." After you do this, your screen will look like Figure 25-8. Now, find the **horizontalAlignment** field in the Property Inspector and change its value to CENTER. This will center the text within the label.

Next, select a slider from the palette and add it to the designer. Then, add a scroll bar. The slider is an instance of the Swing class **JSlider** and the scroll bar is an instance

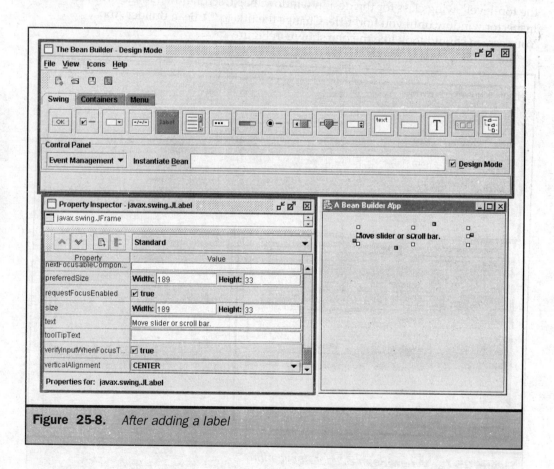

Figure 25-8. *After adding a label*

of the Swing class **JScrollbar**. By default, both the slider and the scroll bar have the same range (0 to 100), so the value of one will translate directly to the value of the other. To make your application look like the one in this book, position them as shown in Figure 25-9.

Now it is time to wire the components together. To do this, you will position the mouse pointer over one of the *connection handles*, then drag a "wire" from the connection handle on one component to a connection handle on another component. The component at which you start is the source of some event and the component at which you end is the recipient of the event. Each component has four connection

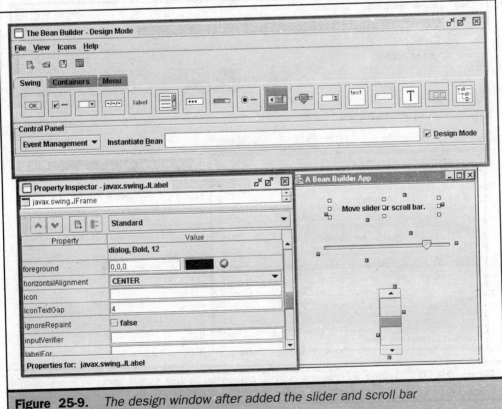

Figure 25-9. *The design window after added the slider and scroll bar*

handles, and it doesn't matter which one you choose. Begin by wiring a connection from the slider to the scroll bar, as shown in Figure 25-10.

After you have completed the connection, the Interaction Wizard will appear. It lets you specify how the two components communicate. In this case, you will define what takes place when the slider is moved. On the first page you will select the event method that will be called when the source object (in this case, the slider) changes position. First, select the Event Adapter radio button (if it is not already selected).

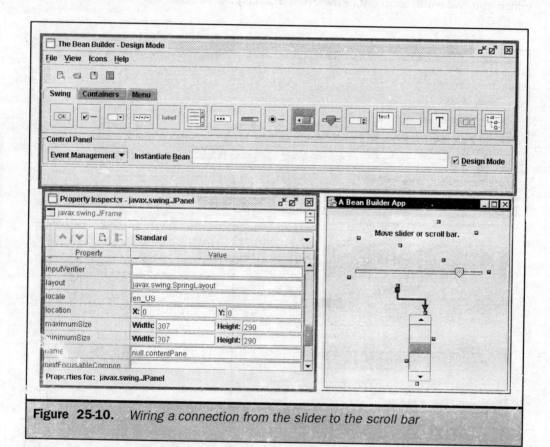

Figure 25-10. Wiring a connection from the slider to the scroll bar

Then, select **change** in the Event Sets list. In Event Methods, **stateChanged(ChangeEvent)** should already be selected. Your screen will look like Figure 25-11.

Press Next. You will now select the method on the target object (in this case, the scroll bar) that you want called when the source object changes. In this case, select the **JScrollbar** method **setValue(int)**. It sets the current position of the scroll bar. Your screen will look like Figure 25-12.

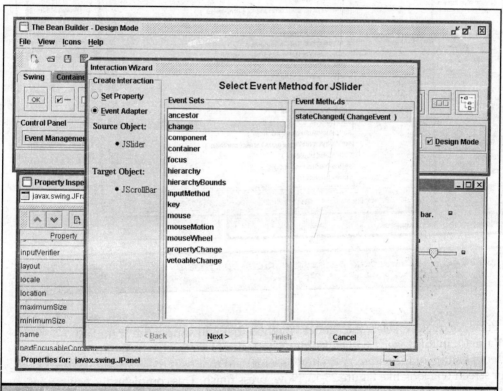

Figure 25-11. *The first page of the Interaction Wizard*

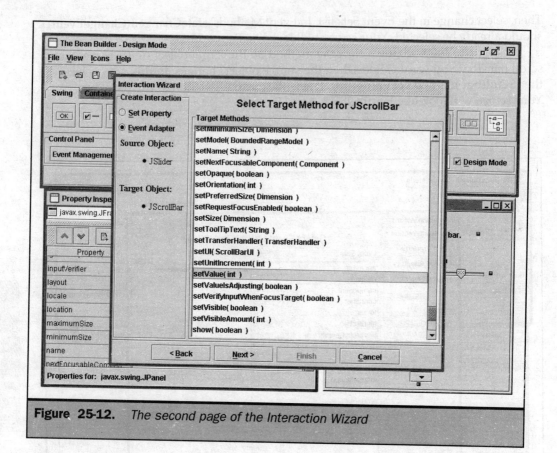

Figure 25-12. The second page of the Interaction Wizard

Press Next. Now, select the "getter" method that will supply the argument to **setValue( )**. In this case, it will be **JSlider**'s **getValue( )** method, which returns the current position of the slider. A "getter" is a method that uses the *get* design pattern. Your screen will look like Figure 25-13. Now, press finish. This completes the connection. Now, each time the slider changes, the **setValue( )** method of the scroll bar is called with an argument supplied by the **getValue( )** method of the slider. Thus, moving the slider also causes the scroll bar to move.

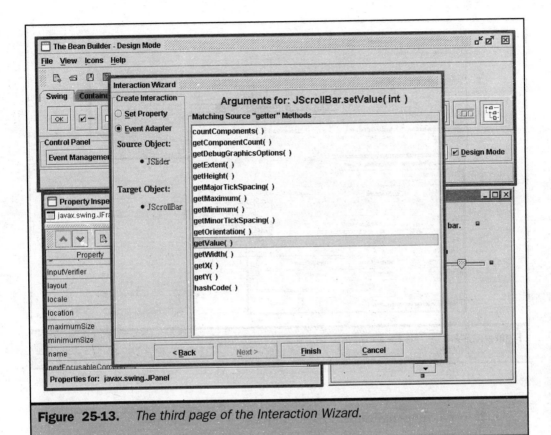

Figure 25-13.   *The third page of the Interaction Wizard.*

Next, repeat this process, except this time, wire the connection from the scroll bar to the slider box.

Finally, test the application. To do this, uncheck the Design Mode check box. This causes the application to execute, as shown in Figure 25-14. Try moving the slider box. When it moves, the scroll bar automatically moves, too. This is because of the connection that we wired from the slider to the scroll bar. Assuming that you also wired the reverse connection, moving the scroll bar will cause the slider to move.

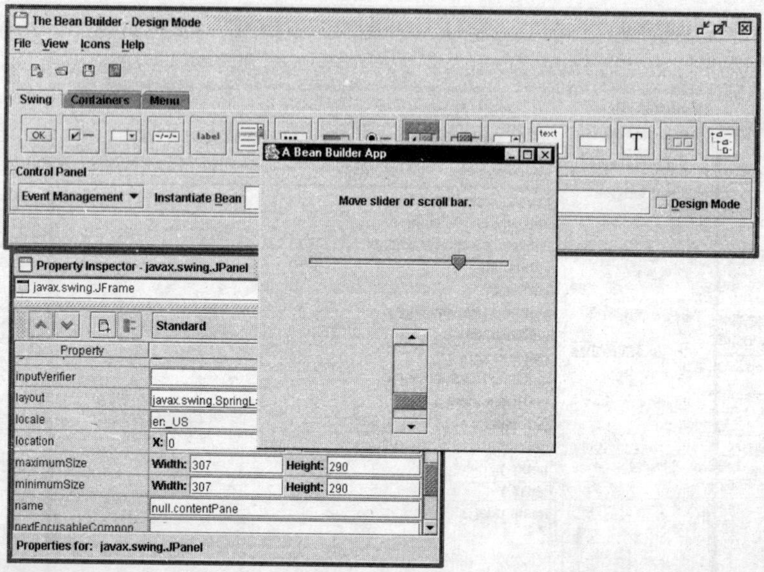

Figure 25-14.   *The Bean Builder application executing*

You can save your application by selecting Save in the file menu.

The Bean Builder is a powerful, yet easy to use development tool. If Bean development is in your future, you will want to master its features. The best way to do this is to create a number of sample Bean applications. Also, try creating your own Beans and loading them into the palette. (To do so, create a JAR file containing your Beans, as described earlier.)

Chapter 26

A Tour of Swing

In Part II, you saw how to build user interfaces with the AWT classes. Here, we will take a tour of a supercharged alternative called *Swing*. Swing is a set of classes that provides more powerful and flexible components than are possible with the AWT. In addition to the familiar components, such as buttons, check boxes, and labels, Swing supplies several exciting additions, including tabbed panes, scroll panes, trees, and tables. Even familiar components such as buttons have more capabilities in Swing. For example, a button may have both an image and a text string associated with it. Also, the image can be changed as the state of the button changes.

Unlike AWT components, Swing components are not implemented by platform-specific code. Instead, they are written entirely in Java and, therefore, are platform-independent. The term *lightweight* is used to describe such elements.

The number of classes and interfaces in the Swing packages is substantial, and this chapter provides an overview of just a few. Swing is an area that you will want to explore further on your own.

The Swing component classes that are used in this book are shown here:

Class	Description
AbstractButton	Abstract superclass for Swing buttons.
ButtonGroup	Encapsulates a mutually exclusive set of buttons.
ImageIcon	Encapsulates an icon.
JApplet	The Swing version of **Applet**.
JButton	The Swing push button class.
JCheckBox	The Swing check box class.
JComboBox	Encapsulates a combo box (an combination of a drop-down list and text field).
JLabel	The Swing version of a label.
JRadioButton	The Swing version of a radio button.
JScrollPane	Encapsulates a scrollable window.
JTabbedPane	Encapsulates a tabbed window.
JTable	Encapsulates a table-based control.
JTextField	The Swing version of a text field.
JTree	Encapsulates a tree-based control.

The Swing-related classes are contained in **javax.swing** and its subpackages, such as **javax.swing.tree**. Many other Swing-related classes and interfaces exist that are not examined in this chapter.

The remainder of this chapter examines various Swing components and illustrates them through sample applets.

JApplet

Fundamental to Swing is the **JApplet** class, which extends **Applet**. Applets that use Swing must be subclasses of **JApplet**. **JApplet** is rich with functionality that is not found in **Applet**. For example, **JApplet** supports various "panes," such as the content pane, the glass pane, and the root pane. For the examples in this chapter, we will not be using most of **JApplet**'s enhanced features. However, one difference between **Applet** and **JApplet** is important to this discussion, because it is used by the sample applets in this chapter. When adding a component to an instance of **JApplet**, do not invoke the **add( )** method of the applet. Instead, call **add( )** for the *content pane* of the **JApplet** object. The content pane can be obtained via the method shown here:

    Container getContentPane( )

The **add( )** method of **Container** can be used to add a component to a content pane. Its form is shown here:

    void add(*comp*)

Here, *comp* is the component to be added to the content pane.

Icons and Labels

In Swing, icons are encapsulated by the **ImageIcon** class, which paints an icon from an image. Two of its constructors are shown here:

    ImageIcon(String *filename*)
    ImageIcon(URL *url*)

The first form uses the image in the file named *filename*. The second form uses the image in the resource identified by *url*.

The **ImageIcon** class implements the **Icon** interface that declares the methods shown here:

Method	Description
int getIconHeight( )	Returns the height of the icon in pixels.
int getIconWidth( )	Returns the width of the icon in pixels.
void paintIcon(Component *comp*, Graphics *g*, int *x*, int *y*)	Paints the icon at position *x*, *y* on the graphics context *g*. Additional information about the paint operation can be provided in *comp*.

Swing labels are instances of the **JLabel** class, which extends **JComponent**. It can display text and/or an icon. Some of its constructors are shown here:

```
JLabel(Icon i)
Label(String s)
JLabel(String s, Icon i, int align)
```

Here, *s* and *i* are the text and icon used for the label. The *align* argument is either **LEFT**, **RIGHT**, **CENTER**, **LEADING**, or **TRAILING**. These constants are defined in the **SwingConstants** interface, along with several others used by the Swing classes.

The icon and text associated with the label can be read and written by the following methods:

```
Icon getIcon( )
String getText( )
void setIcon(Icon i)
void setText(String s)
```

Here, *i* and *s* are the icon and text, respectively.

The following example illustrates how to create and display a label containing both an icon and a string. The applet begins by getting its content pane. Next, an **ImageIcon** object is created for the file **france.gif**. This is used as the second argument to the **JLabel** constructor. The first and last arguments for the **JLabel** constructor are the label text and the alignment. Finally, the label is added to the content pane.

```
import java.awt.*;
import javax.swing.*;
/*
```

```
   <applet code="JLabelDemo" width=250 height=150>
   </applet>
*/

public class JLabelDemo extends JApplet {

  public void init() {
     // Get content pane
     Container contentPane = getContentPane();

     // Create an icon
     ImageIcon ii = new ImageIcon("france.gif");

     // Create a label
     JLabel jl = new JLabel("France", ii, JLabel.CENTER);

     // Add label to the content pane
     contentPane.add(jl);
  }
}
```

Output from this applet is shown here:

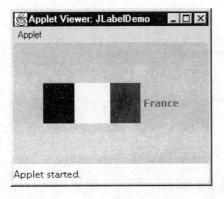

Text Fields

The Swing text field is encapsulated by the **JTextComponent** class, which extends **JComponent**. It provides functionality that is common to Swing text components. One of its subclasses is **JTextField**, which allows you to edit one line of text. Some of its constructors are shown here:

JTextField( )
JTextField(int *cols*)
JTextField(String *s*, int *cols*)
JTextField(String *s*)

Here, *s* is the string to be presented, and *cols* is the number of columns in the text field.

The following example illustrates how to create a text field. The applet begins by getting its content pane, and then a flow layout is assigned as its layout manager. Next, a **JTextField** object is created and is added to the content pane.

```
import java.awt.*;
import javax.swing.*;
/*
  <applet code="JTextFieldDemo" width=300 height=50>
  </applet>
*/

public class JTextFieldDemo extends JApplet {
  JTextField jtf;

  public void init() {

    // Get content pane
    Container contentPane = getContentPane();
    contentPane.setLayout(new FlowLayout());

    // Add text field to content pane
    jtf = new JTextField(15);
    contentPane.add(jtf);
  }
}
```

Output from this applet is shown here:

Buttons

Swing buttons provide features that are not found in the **Button** class defined by the AWT. For example, you can associate an icon with a Swing button. Swing buttons are subclasses of the **AbstractButton** class, which extends **JComponent**. **AbstractButton** contains many methods that allow you to control the behavior of buttons, check boxes, and radio buttons. For example, you can define different icons that are displayed for the component when it is disabled, pressed, or selected. Another icon can be used as a *rollover* icon, which is displayed when the mouse is positioned over that component. The following are the methods that control this behavior:

```
void setDisabledIcon(Icon di)
void setPressedIcon(Icon pi)
void setSelectedIcon(Icon si)
void setRolloverIcon(Icon ri)
```

Here, *di*, *pi*, *si*, and *ri* are the icons to be used for these different conditions. The text associated with a button can be read and written via the following methods:

```
String getText( )
void setText(String s)
```

Here, *s* is the text to be associated with the button.

Concrete subclasses of **AbstractButton** generate action events when they are pressed. Listeners register and unregister for these events via the methods shown here:

```
void addActionListener(ActionListener al)
void removeActionListener(ActionListener al)
```

Here, *al* is the action listener.

AbstractButton is a superclass for push buttons, check boxes, and radio buttons. Each is examined next.

The JButton Class

The **JButton** class provides the functionality of a push button. **JButton** allows an icon, a string, or both to be associated with the push button. Some of its constructors are shown here:

```
JButton(Icon i)
JButton(String s)
JButton(String s, Icon i)
```

Here, *s* and *i* are the string and icon used for the button.

The following example displays four push buttons and a text field. Each button displays an icon that represents the flag of a country. When a button is pressed, the name of that country is displayed in the text field. The applet begins by getting its content pane and setting the layout manager of that pane. Four image buttons are created and added to the content pane. Next, the applet is registered to receive action events that are generated by the buttons. A text field is then created and added to the applet. Finally, a handler for action events displays the command string that is associated with the button. The text field is used to present this string.

```java
import java.awt.*;
import java.awt.event.*;
import javax.swing.*;
/*
  <applet code="JButtonDemo" width=250 height=300>
  </applet>
*/

public class JButtonDemo extends JApplet
implements ActionListener {
  JTextField jtf;

  public void init() {

    // Get content pane
    Container contentPane = getContentPane();
    contentPane.setLayout(new FlowLayout());

    // Add buttons to content pane
    ImageIcon france = new ImageIcon("france.gif");
    JButton jb = new JButton(france);
    jb.setActionCommand("France");
    jb.addActionListener(this);
    contentPane.add(jb);

    ImageIcon germany = new ImageIcon("germany.gif");
    jb = new JButton(germany);
    jb.setActionCommand("Germany");
    jb.addActionListener(this);
    contentPane.add(jb);

    ImageIcon italy = new ImageIcon("italy.gif");
    jb = new JButton(italy);
    jb.setActionCommand("Italy");
```

```
    jb.addActionListener(this);
    contentPane.add(jb);

    ImageIcon japan = new ImageIcon("japan.gif");
    jb = new JButton(japan);
    jb.setActionCommand("Japan");
    jb.addActionListener(this);
    contentPane.add(jb);

    // Add text field to content pane
    jtf = new JTextField(15);
    contentPane.add(jtf);
  }

  public void actionPerformed(ActionEvent ae) {
    jtf.setText(ae.getActionCommand());
  }
}
```

Output from this applet is shown here:

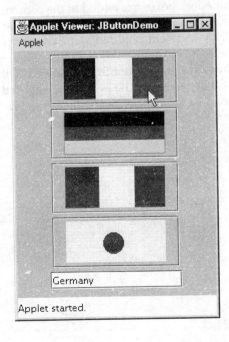

Check Boxes

The **JCheckBox** class, which provides the functionality of a check box, is a concrete implementation of **AbstractButton**. Its immediate superclass is **JToggleButton**, which provides support for two-state buttons. Some of its constructors are shown here:

JCheckBox(Icon *i*)
JCheckBox(Icon *i*, boolean *state*)
JCheckBox(String *s*)
JCheckBox(String *s*, boolean *state*)
JCheckBox(String *s*, Icon *i*)
JCheckBox(String *s*, Icon *i*, boolean *state*)

Here, *i* is the icon for the button. The text is specified by *s*. If *state* is **true**, the check box is initially selected. Otherwise, it is not.

The state of the check box can be changed via the following method:

void setSelected(boolean *state*)

Here, *state* is **true** if the check box should be checked.

The following example illustrates how to create an applet that displays four check boxes and a text field. When a check box is pressed, its text is displayed in the text field. The content pane for the **JApplet** object is obtained, and a flow layout is assigned as its layout manager. Next, four check boxes are added to the content pane, and icons are assigned for the normal, rollover, and selected states. The applet is then registered to receive item events. Finally, a text field is added to the content pane.

When a check box is selected or deselected, an item event is generated. This is handled by **itemStateChanged( )**. Inside **itemStateChanged( )**, the **getItem( )** method gets the **JCheckBox** object that generated the event. The **getText( )** method gets the text for that check box and uses it to set the text inside the text field.

```java
import java.awt.*;
import java.awt.event.*;
import javax.swing.*;
/*
  <applet code="JCheckBoxDemo" width=400 height=50>
  </applet>
*/

public class JCheckBoxDemo extends JApplet
implements ItemListener {
  JTextField jtf;

  public void init() {
```

```java
    // Get content pane
    Container contentPane = getContentPane();
    contentPane.setLayout(new FlowLayout());

    // Create icons
    ImageIcon normal = new ImageIcon("normal.gif");
    ImageIcon rollover = new ImageIcon("rollover.gif");
    ImageIcon selected = new ImageIcon("selected.gif");

    // Add check boxes to the content pane
    JCheckBox cb = new JCheckBox("C", normal);
    cb.setRolloverIcon(rollover);
    cb.setSelectedIcon(selected);
    cb.addItemListener(this);
    contentPane.add(cb);

    cb = new JCheckBox("C++", normal);
    cb.setRolloverIcon(rollover);
    cb.setSelectedIcon(selected);
    cb.addItemListener(this);
    contentPane.add(cb);

    cb = new JCheckBox("Java", normal);
    cb.setRolloverIcon(rollover);
    cb.setSelectedIcon(selected);
    cb.addItemListener(this);
    contentPane.add(cb);

    cb = new JCheckBox("Perl", normal);
    cb.setRolloverIcon(rollover);
    cb.setSelectedIcon(selected);
    cb.addItemListener(this);
    contentPane.add(cb);

    // Add text field to the content pane
    jtf = new JTextField(15);
    contentPane.add(jtf);
  }

  public void itemStateChanged(ItemEvent ie) {
    JCheckBox cb = (JCheckBox)ie.getItem();
    jtf.setText(cb.getText());
  }
}
```

Output from this applet is shown here:

Radio Buttons

Radio buttons are supported by the **JRadioButton** class, which is a concrete implementation of **AbstractButton**. Its immediate superclass is **JToggleButton**, which provides support for two-state buttons. Some of its constructors are shown here:

JRadioButton(Icon *i*)
JRadioButton(Icon *i*, boolean *state*)
JRadioButton(String *s*)
JRadioButton(String *s*, boolean *state*)
JRadioButton(String *s*, Icon *i*)
JRadioButton(String *s*, Icon *i*, boolean *state*)

Here, *i* is the icon for the button. The text is specified by *s*. If *state* is **true**, the button is initially selected. Otherwise, it is not.

Radio buttons must be configured into a group. Only one of the buttons in that group can be selected at any time. For example, if a user presses a radio button that is in a group, any previously selected button in that group is automatically deselected. The **ButtonGroup** class is instantiated to create a button group. Its default constructor is invoked for this purpose. Elements are then added to the button group via the following method:

void add(AbstractButton *ab*)

Here, *ab* is a reference to the button to be added to the group.

The following example illustrates how to use radio buttons. Three radio buttons and one text field are created. When a radio button is pressed, its text is displayed in the text field. First, the content pane for the **JApplet** object is obtained and a flow layout is assigned as its layout manager. Next, three radio buttons are added to the content pane. Then, a button group is defined and the buttons are added to it. Finally, a text field is added to the content pane.

Radio button presses generate action events that are handled by **actionPerformed( )**. The **getActionCommand( )** method gets the text that is associated with a radio button and uses it to set the text field.

```
import java.awt.*;
import java.awt.event.*;
import javax.swing.*;
/*
  <applet code="JRadioButtonDemo" width=300 height=50>
  </applet>
*/

public class JRadioButtonDemo extends JApplet
implements ActionListener {
  JTextField tf;

  public void init() {

    // Get content pane
    Container contentPane = getContentPane();
    contentPane.setLayout(new FlowLayout());

    // Add radio buttons to content pane
    JRadioButton b1 = new JRadioButton("A");
    b1.addActionListener(this);
    contentPane.add(b1);

    JRadioButton b2 = new JRadioButton("B");
    b2.addActionListener(this);
    contentPane.add(b2);

    JRadioButton b3 = new JRadioButton("C");
    b3.addActionListener(this);
    contentPane.add(b3);

    // Define a button group
    ButtonGroup bg = new ButtonGroup();
    bg.add(b1);
    bg.add(b2);
    bg.add(b3);

    // Create a text field and add it
    // to the content pane
    tf = new JTextField(5);
    contentPane.add(tf);
  }
```

```
public void actionPerformed(ActionEvent ae) {
  tf.setText(ae.getActionCommand());
}
}
```

Output from this applet is shown here:

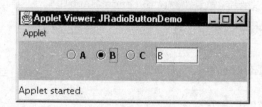

Combo Boxes

Swing provides a *combo box* (a combination of a text field and a drop-down list) through the **JComboBox** class, which extends **JComponent**. A combo box normally displays one entry. However, it can also display a drop-down list that allows a user to select a different entry. You can also type your selection into the text field. Two of **JComboBox**'s constructors are shown here:

JComboBox( )
JComboBox(Vector *v*)

Here, *v* is a vector that initializes the combo box.

Items are added to the list of choices via the **addItem( )** method, whose signature is shown here:

void addItem(Object *obj*)

Here, *obj* is the object to be added to the combo box.

The following example contains a combo box and a label. The label displays an icon. The combo box contains entries for "France", "Germany", "Italy", and "Japan". When a country is selected, the label is updated to display the flag for that country.

```java
import java.awt.*;
import java.awt.event.*;
import javax.swing.*;
/*
  <applet code="JComboBoxDemo" width=300 height=100>
  </applet>
*/

public class JComboBoxDemo extends JApplet
implements ItemListener {
  JLabel jl;
  ImageIcon france, germany, italy, japan;

  public void init() {

    // Get content pane
    Container contentPane = getContentPane();
    contentPane.setLayout(new FlowLayout());

    // Create a combo box and add it
    // to the panel
    JComboBox jc = new JComboBox();
    jc.addItem("France");
    jc.addItem("Germany");
    jc.addItem("Italy");
    jc.addItem("Japan");
    jc.addItemListener(this);
    contentPane.add(jc);

    // Create label
    jl = new JLabel(new ImageIcon("france.gif"));
    contentPane.add(jl);
  }

  public void itemStateChanged(ItemEvent ie) {
    String s = (String)ie.getItem();
    jl.setIcon(new ImageIcon(s + ".gif"));
  }
}
```

Output from this applet is shown here:

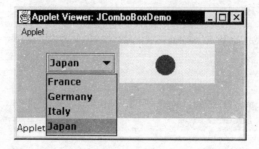

Tabbed Panes

A *tabbed pane* is a component that appears as a group of folders in a file cabinet. Each folder has a title. When a user selects a folder, its contents become visible. Only one of the folders may be selected at a time. Tabbed panes are commonly used for setting configuration options.

Tabbed panes are encapsulated by the **JTabbedPane** class, which extends **JComponent**. We will use its default constructor. Tabs are defined via the following method:

  void addTab(String *str*, Component *comp*)

Here, *str* is the title for the tab, and *comp* is the component that should be added to the tab. Typically, a **JPanel** or a subclass of it is added.

The general procedure to use a tabbed pane in an applet is outlined here:

1. Create a **JTabbedPane** object.
2. Call **addTab( )** to add a tab to the pane. (The arguments to this method define the title of the tab and the component it contains.)
3. Repeat step 2 for each tab.
4. Add the tabbed pane to the content pane of the applet.

The following example illustrates how to create a tabbed pane. The first tab is titled "Cities" and contains four buttons. Each button displays the name of a city. The second tab is titled "Colors" and contains three check boxes. Each check box displays the name of a color. The third tab is titled "Flavors" and contains one combo box. This enables the user to select one of three flavors.

```java
import javax.swing.*;
/*
  <applet code="JTabbedPaneDemo" width=400 height=100>
  </applet>
*/


public class JTabbedPaneDemo extends JApplet {

  public void init() {

    JTabbedPane jtp = new JTabbedPane();
    jtp.addTab("Cities", new CitiesPanel());
    jtp.addTab("Colors", new ColorsPanel());
    jtp.addTab("Flavors", new FlavorsPanel());
    getContentPane().add(jtp);
  }
}

class CitiesPanel extends JPanel {

  public CitiesPanel() {

    JButton b1 = new JButton("New York");
    add(b1);
    JButton b2 = new JButton("London");
    add(b2);
    JButton b3 = new JButton("Hong Kong");
    add(b3);
    JButton b4 = new JButton("Tokyo");
    add(b4);
  }
}

class ColorsPanel extends JPanel {

  public ColorsPanel() {
```

```
      JCheckBox cb1 = new JCheckBox("Red");
      add(cb1);
      JCheckBox cb2 = new JCheckBox("Green");
      add(cb2);
      JCheckBox cb3 = new JCheckBox("Blue");
      add(cb3);
    }
  }

class FlavorsPanel extends JPanel {

  public FlavorsPanel() {

    JComboBox jcb = new JComboBox();
    jcb.addItem("Vanilla");
    jcb.addItem("Chocolate");
    jcb.addItem("Strawberry");
    add(jcb);
  }
}
```

Output from this applet is shown in the following three illustrations:

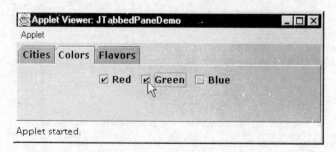

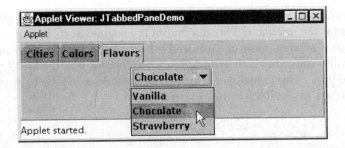

Scroll Panes

A *scroll pane* is a component that presents a rectangular area in which a component may be viewed. Horizontal and/or vertical scroll bars may be provided if necessary. Scroll panes are implemented in Swing by the **JScrollPane** class, which extends **JComponent**. Some of its constructors are shown here:

JScrollPane(Component *comp*)
JScrollPane(int *vsb*, int *hsb*)
JScrollPane(Component *comp*, int *vsb*, int *hsb*)

Here, *comp* is the component to be added to the scroll pane. *vsb* and *hsb* are **int** constants that define when vertical and horizontal scroll bars for this scroll pane are shown. These constants are defined by the **ScrollPaneConstants** interface. Some examples of these constants are described as follows:

Constant	Description
HORIZONTAL_SCROLLBAR_ALWAYS	Always provide horizontal scroll bar
HORIZONTAL_SCROLLBAR_AS_NEEDED	Provide horizontal scroll bar, if needed
VERTICAL_SCROLLBAR_ALWAYS	Always provide vertical scroll bar
VERTICAL_SCROLLBAR_AS_NEEDED	Provide vertical scroll bar, if needed

Here are the steps that you should follow to use a scroll pane in an applet:

1. Create a **JComponent** object.
2. Create a **JScrollPane** object. (The arguments to the constructor specify the component and the policies for vertical and horizontal scroll bars.)
3. Add the scroll pane to the content pane of the applet.

The following example illustrates a scroll pane. First, the content pane of the **JApplet** object is obtained and a border layout is assigned as its layout manager. Next, a **JPanel** object is created and four hundred buttons are added to it, arranged into twenty columns. The panel is then added to a scroll pane, and the scroll pane is added to the content pane. This causes vertical and horizontal scroll bars to appear. You can use the scroll bars to scroll the buttons into view.

```
import java.awt.*;
import javax.swing.*;
/*
  <applet code="JScrollPaneDemo" width=300 height=250>
  </applet>
*/

public class JScrollPaneDemo extends JApplet {

  public void init() {

    // Get content pane
    Container contentPane = getContentPane();
    contentPane.setLayout(new BorderLayout());

    // Add 400 buttons to a panel
    JPanel jp = new JPanel();
    jp.setLayout(new GridLayout(20, 20));
    int b = 0;
    for(int i = 0; i < 20; i++) {
      for(int j = 0; j < 20; j++) {
        jp.add(new JButton("Button " + b));
        ++b;
      }
    }

    // Add panel to a scroll pane
    int v = ScrollPaneConstants.VERTICAL_SCROLLBAR_AS_NEEDED;
    int h = ScrollPaneConstants.HORIZONTAL_SCROLLBAR_AS_NEEDED;
    JScrollPane jsp = new JScrollPane(jp, v, h);

    // Add scroll pane to the content pane
    contentPane.add(jsp, BorderLayout.CENTER);
  }
}
```

Output from this applet is shown here:

Trees

A *tree* is a component that presents a hierarchical view of data. A user has the ability to expand or collapse individual subtrees in this display. Trees are implemented in Swing by the **JTree** class, which extends **JComponent**. Some of its constructors are shown here:

```
JTree(Hashtable ht)
JTree(Object obj[ ])
JTree(TreeNode tn)
JTree(Vector v)
```

The first form creates a tree in which each element of the hash table *ht* is a child node. Each element of the array *obj* is a child node in the second form. The tree node *tn* is the root of the tree in the third form. Finally, the last form uses the elements of vector *v* as child nodes.

A **JTree** object generates events when a node is expanded or collapsed. The **addTreeExpansionListener( )** and **removeTreeExpansionListener( )** methods allow listeners to register and unregister for these notifications. The signatures of these methods are shown here:

```
void addTreeExpansionListener(TreeExpansionListener tel)
void removeTreeExpansionListener(TreeExpansionListener tel)
```

Here, *tel* is the listener object.

The **getPathForLocation( )** method is used to translate a mouse click on a specific point of the tree to a tree path. Its signature is shown here:

TreePath getPathForLocation(int *x*, int *y*)

Here, *x* and *y* are the coordinates at which the mouse is clicked. The return value is a **TreePath** object that encapsulates information about the tree node that was selected by the user.

The **TreePath** class encapsulates information about a path to a particular node in a tree. It provides several constructors and methods. In this book, only the **toString( )** method is used. It returns a string equivalent of the tree path.

The **TreeNode** interface declares methods that obtain information about a tree node. For example, it is possible to obtain a reference to the parent node or an enumeration of the child nodes. The **MutableTreeNode** interface extends **TreeNode**. It declares methods that can insert and remove child nodes or change the parent node.

The **DefaultMutableTreeNode** class implements the **MutableTreeNode** interface. It represents a node in a tree. One of its constructors is shown here:

DefaultMutableTreeNode(Object *obj*)

Here, *obj* is the object to be enclosed in this tree node. The new tree node doesn't have a parent or children.

To create a hierarchy of tree nodes, the **add( )** method of **DefaultMutableTreeNode** can be used. Its signature is shown here:

void add(MutableTreeNode *child*)

Here, *child* is a mutable tree node that is to be added as a child to the current node.

Tree expansion events are described by the class **TreeExpansionEvent** in the **javax.swing.event** package. The **getPath( )** method of this class returns a **TreePath** object that describes the path to the changed node. Its signature is shown here:

TreePath getPath( )

The **TreeExpansionListener** interface provides the following two methods:

void treeCollapsed(TreeExpansionEvent *tee*)
void treeExpanded(TreeExpansionEvent *tee*)

Here, *tee* is the tree expansion event. The first method is called when a subtree is hidden, and the second method is called when a subtree becomes visible.

Here are the steps that you should follow to use a tree in an applet:

1. Create a **JTree** object.

2. Create a **JScrollPane** object. (The arguments to the constructor specify the tree and the policies for vertical and horizontal scroll bars.)

3. Add the tree to the scroll pane.

4. Add the scroll pane to the content pane of the applet.

The following example illustrates how to create a tree and recognize mouse clicks on it. The **init( )** method gets the content pane for the applet. A **DefaultMutableTreeNode** object labeled "Options" is created. This is the top node of the tree hierarchy. Additional tree nodes are then created, and the **add( )** method is called to connect these nodes to the tree. A reference to the top node in the tree is provided as the argument to the **JTree** constructor. The tree is then provided as the argument to the **JScrollPane** constructor. This scroll pane is then added to the applet. Next, a text field is created and added to the applet. Information about mouse click events is presented in this text field. To receive mouse events from the tree, the **addMouseListener( )** method of the **JTree** object is called. The argument to this method is an anonymous inner class that extends **MouseAdapter** and overrides the **mouseClicked( )** method.

The **doMouseClicked( )** method processes mouse clicks. It calls **getPathForLocation( )** to translate the coordinates of the mouse click into a **TreePath** object. If the mouse is clicked at a point that does not cause a node selection, the return value from this method is **null**. Otherwise, the tree path can be converted to a string and presented in the text field.

```
import java.awt.*;
import java.awt.event.*;
import javax.swing.*;
import javax.swing.tree.*;
/*
  <applet code="JTreeEvents" width=400 height=200>
  </applet>
*/


public class JTreeEvents extends JApplet {
  JTree tree;
  JTextField jtf;

  public void init() {
```

```
// Get content pane
Container contentPane = getContentPane();

// Set layout manager
contentPane.setLayout(new BorderLayout());

// Create top node of tree
DefaultMutableTreeNode top = new DefaultMutableTreeNode("Options");

// Create subtree of "A"
DefaultMutableTreeNode a = new DefaultMutableTreeNode("A");
top.add(a);
DefaultMutableTreeNode a1 = new DefaultMutableTreeNode("A1");
a.add(a1);
DefaultMutableTreeNode a2 = new DefaultMutableTreeNode("A2");
a.add(a2);

// Create subtree of "B"
DefaultMutableTreeNode b = new DefaultMutableTreeNode("B");
top.add(b);
DefaultMutableTreeNode b1 = new DefaultMutableTreeNode("B1");
b.add(b1);
DefaultMutableTreeNode b2 = new DefaultMutableTreeNode("B2");
b.add(b2);
DefaultMutableTreeNode b3 = new DefaultMutableTreeNode("B3");
b.add(b3);

// Create tree
tree = new JTree(top);

// Add tree to a scroll pane
int v = ScrollPaneConstants.VERTICAL_SCROLLBAR_AS_NEEDED;
int h = ScrollPaneConstants.HORIZONTAL_SCROLLBAR_AS_NEEDED;
JScrollPane jsp = new JScrollPane(tree, v, h);

// Add scroll pane to the content pane
contentPane.add(jsp, BorderLayout.CENTER);
```

```
    // Add text field to applet
    jtf = new JTextField("", 20);
    contentPane.add(jtf, BorderLayout.SOUTH);

    // Anonymous inner class to handle mouse clicks
    tree.addMouseListener(new MouseAdapter() {
      public void mouseClicked(MouseEvent me) {
        doMouseClicked(me);
      }
    });
  }

  void doMouseClicked(MouseEvent me) {
    TreePath tp = tree.getPathForLocation(me.getX(), me.getY());
    if(tp != null)
      jtf.setText(tp.toString());
    else
      jtf.setText("");
  }
}
```

Output from this applet is shown here:

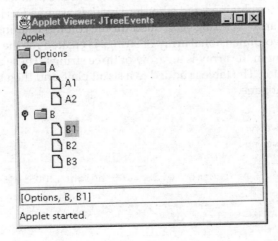

The string presented in the text field describes the path from the top tree node to the selected node.

Tables

A *table* is a component that displays rows and columns of data. You can drag the cursor on column boundaries to resize columns. You can also drag a column to a new position. Tables are implemented by the **JTable** class, which extends **JComponent**. One of its constructors is shown here:

JTable(Object *data*[ ][ ], Object *colHeads*[ ])

Here, *data* is a two-dimensional array of the information to be presented, and *colHeads* is a one-dimensional array with the column headings.

Here are the steps for using a table in an applet:

1. Create a **JTable** object.

2. Create a **JScrollPane** object. (The arguments to the constructor specify the table and the policies for vertical and horizontal scroll bars.)

3. Add the table to the scroll pane.

4. Add the scroll pane to the content pane of the applet.

The following example illustrates how to create and use a table. The content pane of the **JApplet** object is obtained and a border layout is assigned as its layout manager. A one-dimensional array of strings is created for the column headings. This table has three columns. A two-dimensional array of strings is created for the table cells. You can see that each element in the array is an array of three strings. These arrays are passed to the **JTable** constructor. The table is added to a scroll pane and then the scroll pane is added to the content pane.

```
import java.awt.*;
import javax.swing.*;
/*
  <applet code="JTableDemo" width=400 height=200>
  </applet>
*/


public class JTableDemo extends JApplet {
```

```java
public void init() {

  // Get content pane
  Container contentPane = getContentPane();

  // Set layout manager
  contentPane.setLayout(new BorderLayout());

  // Initialize column headings
  final String[] colHeads = { "Name", "Phone", "Fax" };

  // Initialize data
  final Object[][] data = {
    { "Gail", "4567", "8675" },
    { "Ken", "7566", "5555" },
    { "Viviane", "5634", "5887" },
    { "Melanie", "7345", "9222" },
    { "Anne", "1237", "3333" },
    { "John", "5656", "3144" },
    { "Matt", "5672", "2176" },
    { "Claire", "6741", "4244" },
    { "Erwin", "9023", "5159" },
    { "Ellen", "1134", "5332" },
    { "Jennifer", "5689", "1212" },
    { "Ed", "9030", "1313" },
    { "Helen", "6751", "1415" }
  };

  // Create the table
  JTable table = new JTable(data, colHeads);

  // Add table to a scroll pane
  int v = ScrollPaneConstants.VERTICAL_SCROLLBAR_AS_NEEDED;
  int h = ScrollPaneConstants.HORIZONTAL_SCROLLBAR_AS_NEEDED;
  JScrollPane jsp = new JScrollPane(table, v, h);

  // Add scroll pane to the content pane
  contentPane.add(jsp, BorderLayout.CENTER);
  }
}
```

Output from this applet is shown here:

Exploring Swing

As mentioned earlier, Swing is a large system, and it has many features that you will want to explore on your own. For example, Swing provides toolbars, tooltips, and progress bars. Also, Swing components can provide a pluggable look and feel, which means that it is easy to substitute another appearance and behavior for an element. This can be done dynamically. You may even design your own look and feel. Frankly, the Swing approach to GUI components might replace the AWT classes some time in the future, so familiarizing yourself with it now is a good idea.

Swing is just one part of the Java Foundation Classes (JFC). You may want to explore other JFC features. The Accessibility API can be used to build programs that are usable by people with disabilities. The Java 2-D API provides advanced capabilities for working with shapes, text, and images. The Drag-and-Drop API allows information to be exchanged between Java and non-Java programs.

The Complete Reference

Java™ 2

Chapter 27

Servlets

This chapter presents an overview of *servlets*. Servlets are small programs that execute on the server side of a Web connection. Just as applets dynamically extend the functionality of a Web browser, servlets dynamically extend the functionality of a Web server. The topic of servlets is quite large, and it is beyond the scope of this chapter to cover it all. Instead, we will focus on the core concepts, interfaces, and classes, and develop several examples.

Background

In order to understand the advantages of servlets, you must have a basic understanding of how Web browsers and servers cooperate to provide content to a user. Consider a request for a static Web page. A user enters a Uniform Resource Locator (URL) into a browser. The browser generates an HTTP request to the appropriate Web server. The Web server maps this request to a specific file. That file is returned in an HTTP response to the browser. The HTTP header in the response indicates the type of the content. The Multipurpose Internet Mail Extensions (MIME) are used for this purpose. For example, ordinary ASCII text has a MIME type of text/plain. The Hypertext Markup Language (HTML) source code of a Web page has a MIME type of text/html.

Now consider dynamic content. Assume that an online store uses a database to store information about its business. This would include items for sale, prices, availability, orders, and so forth. It wishes to make this information accessible to customers via Web pages. The contents of those Web pages must be dynamically generated in order to reflect the latest information in the database.

In the early days of the Web, a server could dynamically construct a page by creating a separate process to handle each client request. The process would open connections to one or more databases in order to obtain the necessary information. It communicated with the Web server via an interface known as the Common Gateway Interface (CGI). CGI allowed the separate process to read data from the HTTP request and write data to the HTTP response. A variety of different languages were used to build CGI programs. These included C, C++, and Perl.

However, CGI suffered serious performance problems. It was expensive in terms of processor and memory resources to create a separate process for each client request. It was also expensive to open and close database connections for each client request. In addition, the CGI programs were not platform-independent. Therefore, other techniques were introduced. Among these are servlets.

Servlets offer several advantages in comparison with CGI. First, performance is significantly better. Servlets execute within the address space of a Web server. It is not necessary to create a separate process to handle each client request. Second, servlets are platform-independent because they are written in Java. A number of Web servers from different vendors offer the Servlet API. Programs developed for this API can be moved to any of these environments without recompilation. Third, the Java security manager on the server enforces a set of restrictions to protect the resources on a server machine. You will see that some servlets are trusted and others are untrusted. Finally, the full functionality of the Java class libraries is available to a servlet. It can communicate with applets, databases, or other software via the sockets and RMI mechanisms that you have seen already.

The Life Cycle of a Servlet

Three methods are central to the life cycle of a servlet. These are **init( )**, **service( )**, and **destroy( )**. They are implemented by every servlet and are invoked at specific times by the server. Let us consider a typical user scenario to understand when these methods are called.

First, assume that a user enters a Uniform Resource Locator (URL) to a Web browser. The browser then generates an HTTP request for this URL. This request is then sent to the appropriate server.

Second, this HTTP request is received by the Web server. The server maps this request to a particular servlet. The servlet is dynamically retrieved and loaded into the address space of the server.

Third, the server invokes the **init( )** method of the servlet. This method is invoked only when the servlet is first loaded into memory. It is possible to pass initialization parameters to the servlet so it may configure itself.

Fourth, the server invokes the **service( )** method of the servlet. This method is called to process the HTTP request. You will see that it is possible for the servlet to read data that has been provided in the HTTP request. It may also formulate an HTTP response for the client.

The servlet remains in the server's address space and is available to process any other HTTP requests received from clients. The **service( )** method is called for each HTTP request.

Finally, the server may decide to unload the servlet from its memory. The algorithms by which this determination is made are specific to each server. The server calls the **destroy( )** method to relinquish any resources such as file handles that are allocated for the servlet. Important data may be saved to a persistent store. The memory allocated for the servlet and its objects can then be garbage collected.

Using Tomcat For Servlet Development

To create servlets, you will need to download a servlet development environment. The one currently recommended by Sun is Tomcat 4.0, which supports the latest servlet specification, which is 2.3. (The complete servlet specification is available for download through **java.sun.com**.) Tomcat replaces the old JSDK (Java Servlet Development Kit) that was previously provided by Sun. Tomcat is an open-source product maintained by the Jakarta Project of the Apache Software Foundation. It contains the class libraries, documentation, and run-time support that you will need to create and test servlets.

You can download Tomcat through the Sun Microsystems Web site at **java.sun.com**. The current version is 4.0. Follow the instructions to install this toolkit on your machine. The examples in this chapter assume a Windows environment. The default location for Tomcat 4.0 is

```
C:\Program Files\Apache Tomcat 4.0\
```

This is the location assumed by the examples in this book. If you load Tomcat in a different location, you will need to make appropriate changes to the examples. You may need to set the environmental variable **JAVA_HOME** to the top-level directory in which the Java Software Development Kit is installed. For Java 2, version 1.4, the default directory is **C:\j2sdk1.4.0**, but you will need to confirm this for your environment.

To start Tomcat, select Start Tomcat in the Start | Programs menu, or run **startup.bat** from the

```
C:\Program Files\Apache Tomcat 4.0\bin\
```

directory. When you are done testing servlets, you can stop Tomcat by selecting Stop Tomcat in the Start | Programs menu, or run **shutdown.bat**.

The directory

```
C:\Program Files\Apache Tomcat 4.0\common\lib\
```

contains **servlet.jar**. This JAR file contains the classes and interfaces that are needed to build servlets. To make this file accessible, update your **CLASSPATH** environment variable so that it includes

```
C:\Program Files\Apache Tomcat 4.0\common\lib\servlet.jar.
```

Alternatively, you can specify this class file when you compile the servlets. For example, the following command compiles the first servlet example:

```
javac HelloServlet.java -classpath "C:\Program Files\Apache Tomcat
4.0\common\lib\servlet.jar"
```

Once you have compiled a servlet, you must copy the class file into the directory that Tomcat uses for example servlet class files. For the purposes of this chapter, you must put the servlet files into the following directory:

```
C:\Program Files\Apache Tomcat 4.0\webapps\examples\WEB-INF\classes
```

A Simple Servlet

To become familiar with the key servlet concepts, we will begin by building and testing a simple servlet. The basic steps are the following:

1. Create and compile the servlet source code.

2. Start Tomcat.

3. Start a Web browser and request the servlet.

Let us examine each of these steps in detail.

Create and Compile the Servlet Source Code

To begin, create a file named **HelloServlet.java** that contains the following program:

```java
import java.io.*;
import javax.servlet.*;

public class HelloServlet extends GenericServlet {

  public void service(ServletRequest request,
    ServletResponse response)
  throws ServletException, IOException {
    response.setContentType("text/html");
    PrintWriter pw = response.getWriter();
    pw.println("<B>Hello!");
    pw.close();
  }
}
```

Let's look closely at this program. First, note that it imports the **javax.servlet** package. This package contains the classes and interfaces required to build servlets. You will learn more about these later in this chapter. Next, the program defines **HelloServlet** as a subclass of **GenericServlet**. The **GenericServlet** class provides functionality that makes it easy to handle requests and responses.

Inside **HelloServlet**, the **service( )** method (which is inherited from **GenericServlet**) is overridden. This method handles requests from a client. Notice that the first argument is a **ServletRequest** object. This enables the servlet to read data that is provided via the client request. The second argument is a **ServletResponse** object. This enables the servlet to formulate a response for the client.

The call to **setContentType( )** establishes the MIME type of the HTTP response. In this program, the MIME type is text/html. This indicates that the browser should interpret the content as HTML source code.

Next, the **getWriter( )** method obtains a **PrintWriter**. Anything written to this stream is sent to the client as part of the HTTP response. Then **println( )** is used to write some simple HTML source code as the HTTP response.

Compile this source code and place the **HelloServlet.class** file in the Tomcat class files directory as described in the previous section.

Start Tomcat

As explained, to start Tomcat, select Start Tomcat in the Start | Programs menu, or run **startup.bat** from the

```
C:\Program Files\Apache Tomcat 4.0\bin\
```

directory.

Start a Web Browser and Request the Servlet

Start a Web browser and enter the URL shown here:

```
http://localhost:8080/examples/servlet/HelloServlet
```

Alternatively, you may enter the URL shown here:

```
http://127.0.0.1:8080/examples/servlet/HelloServlet
```

This can be done because 127.0.0.1 is defined as the IP address of the local machine.

You will observe the output of the servlet in the browser display area. It will contain the string **Hello!** in bold type.

The Servlet API

Two packages contain the classes and interfaces that are required to build servlets. These are **javax.servlet** and **javax.servlet.http**. They constitute the Servlet API. Keep in mind that these packages are not part of the Java core packages. Instead, they are standard extensions. Therefore, they are not included in the Java Software Development Kit. You must download Tomcat to obtain their functionality.

The Servlet API has been in a process of ongoing development and enhancement. The current servlet specification is version is 2.3 and that is the one used in this book. However, because changes happen fast in the world of Java, you will want to check for any additions or alterations. This chapter discusses the core of the Servlet API, which will be available to most readers.

The Servlet API is supported by most Web servers, such as those from Sun, Microsoft, and others. Check at **http://java.sun.com** for the latest information.

The javax.servlet Package

The **javax.servlet** package contains a number of interfaces and classes that establish the framework in which servlets operate. The following table summarizes the core interfaces that are provided in this package. The most significant of these is **Servlet**. All servlets must implement this interface or extend a class that implements the interface. The **ServletRequest** and **ServletResponse** interfaces are also very important.

Interface	Description
Servlet	Declares life cycle methods for a servlet.
ServletConfig	Allows servlets to get initialization parameters.
ServletContext	Enables servlets to log events and access information about their environment.
ServletRequest	Used to read data from a client request.
ServletResponse	Used to write data to a client response.
SingleThreadModel	Indicates that the servlet is thread safe.

The following table summarizes the core classes that are provided in the **javax.servlet** package.

Class	Description
GenericServlet	Implements the **Servlet** and **ServletConfig** interfaces.
ServletInputStream	Provides an input stream for reading requests from a client.
ServletOutputStream	Provides an output stream for writing responses to a client.
ServletException	Indicates a servlet error occurred.
UnavailableException	Indicates a servlet is unavailable.

Let us examine these interfaces and classes in more detail.

The Servlet Interface

All servlets must implement the **Servlet** interface. It declares the **init( )**, **service( )**, and **destroy( )** methods that are called by the server during the life cycle of a servlet. A method is also provided that allows a servlet to obtain any initialization parameters. The methods defined by **Servlet** are shown in Table 27-1.

Method	Description
void destroy( )	Called when the servlet is unloaded.
ServletConfig getServletConfig( )	Returns a **ServletConfig** object that contains any initialization parameters.
String getServletInfo( )	Returns a string describing the servlet.
void init(ServletConfig *sc*) throws ServletException	Called when the servlet is initialized. Initialization parameters for the servlet can be obtained from *sc*. An **UnavailableException** should be thrown if the servlet cannot be initialized.

void service(ServletRequest *req*,
             ServletResponse *res*)
   throws ServletException,
       IOException
	Called to process a request from a client. The request from the client can be read from *req*. The response to the client can be written to *res*. An exception is generated if a servlet or IO problem occurs.

Table 27-1.   *The Methods Defined by* Servlet

The **init( )**, **service( )**, and **destroy( )** methods are the life cycle methods of the servlet. These are invoked by the server. The **getServletConfig( )** method is called by the servlet to obtain initialization parameters. A servlet developer overrides the **getServletInfo( )** method to provide a string with useful information (for example, author, version, date, copyright). This method is also invoked by the server.

The ServletConfig Interface

The **ServletConfig** interface is implemented by the server. It allows a servlet to obtain configuration data when it is loaded. The methods declared by this interface are summarized here:

Method	Description
ServletContext getServletContext( )	Returns the context for this servlet.
String getInitParameter(String *param*)	Returns the value of the initialization parameter named *param*.
Enumeration getInitParameterNames( )	Returns an enumeration of all initialization parameter names.
String getServletName( )	Returns the name of the invoking servlet.

The ServletContext Interface

The **ServletContext** interface is implemented by the server. It enables servlets to obtain information about their environment. Several of its methods are summarized in Table 27-2.

The ServletRequest Interface

The **ServletRequest** interface is implemented by the server. It enables a servlet to obtain information about a client request. Several of its methods are summarized in Table 27-3.

The ServletResponse Interface

The **ServletResponse** interface is implemented by the server. It enables a servlet to formulate a response for a client. Several of its methods are summarized in Table 27-4.

The SingleThreadModel Interface

This interface is used to indicate that only a single thread will execute the **service( )** method of a servlet at a given time. It defines no constants and declares no methods. If a servlet implements this interface, the server has two options. First, it can create several instances of the servlet. When a client request arrives, it is sent to an available instance of the servlet. Second, it can synchronize access to the servlet.

Method	Description
Object getAttribute(String *attr*)	Returns the value of the server attribute named *attr*.
String getMimeType(String *file*)	Returns the MIME type of *file*.
String getRealPath(String *vpath*)	Returns the real path that corresponds to the virtual path *vpath*.
String getServerInfo( )	Returns information about the server.
void log(String *s*)	Writes *s* to the servlet log.
void log(String *s*, Throwable *e*)	Write *s* and the stack trace for *e* to the servlet log.
void setAttribute(String *attr*, Object *val*)	Sets the attribute specified by *attr* to the value passed in *val*.

Table 27-2. *Various Methods Defined by* ServletContext

Method	Description
Object getAttribute(String *attr*)	Returns the value of the attribute named *attr*.
String getCharacterEncoding( )	Returns the character encoding of the request.
int getContentLength( )	Returns the size of the request. The value –1 is returned if the size is unavailable.
String getContentType( )	Returns the type of the request. A **null** value is returned if the type cannot be determined.
ServletInputStream getInputStream( ) throws IOException	Returns a **ServletInputStream** that can be used to read binary data from the request. An **IllegalStateException** is thrown if **getReader( )** has already been invoked for this request.
String getParameter(String *pname*)	Returns the value of the parameter named *pname*.
Enumeration getParameterNames( )	Returns an enumeration of the parameter names for this request.
String[ ] getParameterValues(String *name*)	Returns an array containing values associated with the parameter specified by *name*.
String getProtocol( )	Returns a description of the protocol.
BufferedReader getReader( ) throws IOException	Returns a buffered reader that can be used to read text from the request. An **IllegalStateException** is thrown if **getInputStream( )** has already been invoked for this request.

Table 27-3. *Various Methods Defined by* ServletRequest

Method	Description
String getRemoteAddr( )	Returns the string equivalent of the client IP address.
String getRemoteHost( )	Returns the string equivalent of the client host name.
String getScheme( )	Returns the transmission scheme of the URL used for the request (for example, "http", "ftp").
String getServerName( )	Returns the name of the server.
int getServerPort( )	Returns the port number.

Table 27-3. *Various Methods Defined by* ServletRequest (continued)

Method	Description
String getCharacterEncoding( )	Returns the character encoding for the response.
ServletOutputStream getOutputStream( ) throws IOException	Returns a **ServletOutputStream** that can be used to write binary data to the response. An **IllegalStateException** is thrown if **getWriter( )** has already been invoked for this request.
PrintWriter getWriter( ) throws IOException	Returns a **PrintWriter** that can be used to write character data to the response. An **IllegalStateException** is thrown if **getOutputStream( )** has already been invoked for this request.
void setContentLength(int *size*)	Sets the content length for the response to *size*.
void setContentType(String *type*)	Sets the content type for the response to *type*.

Table 27-4. *Various Methods Defined by* ServletResponse

The GenericServlet Class

The **GenericServlet** class provides implementations of the basic life cycle methods for a servlet and is typically subclassed by servlet developers. **GenericServlet** implements the **Servlet** and **ServletConfig** interfaces. In addition, a method to append a string to the server log file is available. The signatures of this method are shown here:

```
void log(String s)
void log(String s, Throwable e)
```

Here, *s* is the string to be appended to the log, and *e* is an exception that occurred.

The ServletInputStream Class

The **ServletInputStream** class extends **InputStream**. It is implemented by the server and provides an input stream that a servlet developer can use to read the data from a client request. It defines the default constructor. In addition, a method is provided to read bytes from the stream. Its signature is shown here:

```
int readLine(byte[ ] buffer, int offset, int size) throws IOException
```

Here, *buffer* is the array into which *size* bytes are placed starting at *offset*. The method returns the actual number of bytes read or –1 if an end-of-stream condition is encountered.

The ServletOutputStream Class

The **ServletOutputStream** class extends **OutputStream**. It is implemented by the server and provides an output stream that a servlet developer can use to write data to a client response. A default constructor is defined. It also defines the **print( )** and **println( )** methods, which output data to the stream.

The Servlet Exception Classes

javax.servlet defines two exceptions. The first is **ServletException**, which indicates that a servlet problem has occurred. The second is **UnavailableException**, which extends **ServletException**. It indicates that a servlet is unavailable.

Reading Servlet Parameters

The **ServletRequest** class includes methods that allow you to read the names and values of parameters that are included in a client request. We will develop a servlet that illustrates their use. The example contains two files. A Web page is defined in **PostParameters.htm** and a servlet is defined in **PostParametersServlet.java**.

The HTML source code for **PostParameters.htm** is shown in the following listing. It defines a table that contains two labels and two text fields. One of the labels is Employee and the other is Phone. There is also a submit button. Notice that the action parameter of the form tag specifies a URL. The URL identifies the servlet to process the HTTP POST request.

```html
<html>
<body>
<center>
<form name="Form1"
  method="post"
  action="http://localhost:8080/examples/servlet/PostParametersServlet">
<table>
<tr>
  <td><B>Employee</td>
  <td><input type=textbox name="e" size="25" value=""></td>
</tr>
<tr>
  <td><B>Phone</td>
  <td><input type=textbox name="p" size="25" value=""></td>
</tr>
</table>
<input type=submit value="Submit">
</body>
</html>
```

The source code for **PostParametersServlet.java** is shown in the following listing. The **service( )** method is overridden to process client requests. The **getParameterNames( )** method returns an enumeration of the parameter names. These are processed in a loop. You can see that the parameter name and value are output to the client. The parameter value is obtained via the **getParameter( )** method.

```java
import java.io.*;
import java.util.*;
import javax.servlet.*;

public class PostParametersServlet
extends GenericServlet {

  public void service(ServletRequest request,
    ServletResponse response)
  throws ServletException, IOException {

    // Get print writer.
    PrintWriter pw = response.getWriter();
```

```
  // Get enumeration of parameter names.
  Enumeration e = request.getParameterNames();

  // Display parameter names and values.
  while(e.hasMoreElements()) {
    String pname = (String)e.nextElement();
    pw.print(pname + " = ");
    String pvalue = request.getParameter(pname);
    pw.println(pvalue);
  }
  pw.close();
  }
}
```

Compile the servlet and perform these steps to test this example:

1. Start Tomcat (if it is not already running).
2. Display the Web page in a browser.
3. Enter an employee name and phone number in the text fields.
4. Submit the Web page.

After following these steps, the browser will display a response that is dynamically generated by the servlet.

The javax.servlet.http Package

The **javax.servlet.http** package contains a number of interfaces and classes that are commonly used by servlet developers. You will see that its functionality makes it easy to build servlets that work with HTTP requests and responses.

The following table summarizes the core interfaces that are provided in this package:

Interface	Description
HttpServletRequest	Enables servlets to read data from an HTTP request.
HttpServletResponse	Enables servlets to write data to an HTTP response.
HttpSession	Allows session data to be read and written.
HttpSessionBindingListener	Informs an object that it is bound to or unbound from a session.

The following table summarizes the core classes that are provided in this package. The most important of these is **HttpServlet**. Servlet developers typically extend this class in order to process HTTP requests.

Class	Description
Cookie	Allows state information to be stored on a client machine.
HttpServlet	Provides methods to handle HTTP requests and responses.
HttpSessionEvent	Encapsulates a session-changed event.
HttpSessionBindingEvent	Indicates when a listener is bound to or unbound from a session value, or that a session attribute changed.

The HttpServletRequest Interface

The **HttpServletRequest** interface is implemented by the server. It enables a servlet to obtain information about a client request. Several of its methods are shown in Table 27-5.

Method	Description
String getAuthType( )	Returns authentication scheme.
Cookie[ ] getCookies( )	Returns an array of the cookies in this request.
long getDateHeader(String *field*)	Returns the value of the date header field named *field*.
String getHeader(String *field*)	Returns the value of the header field named *field*.
Enumeration getHeaderNames( )	Returns an enumeration of the header names.
int getIntHeader(String *field*)	Returns the **int** equivalent of the header field named *field*.

Table 27-5. *Various Methods Defined by* HttpServletRequest

Method	Description
String getMethod( )	Returns the HTTP method for this request.
String getPathInfo( )	Returns any path information that is located after the servlet path and before a query string of the URL.
String getPathTranslated( )	Returns any path information that is located after the servlet path and before a query string of the URL after translating it to a real path.
String getQueryString( )	Returns any query string in the URL.
String getRemoteUser( )	Returns the name of the user who issued this request.
String getRequestedSessionId( )	Returns the ID of the session.
String getRequestURI( )	Returns the URI.
StringBuffer getRequestURL( )	Returns the URL.
String getServletPath( )	Returns that part of the URL that identifies the servlet.
HttpSession getSession( )	Returns the session for this request. If a session does not exist, one is created and then returned.
HttpSession getSession(boolean *new*)	If *new* is **true** and no session exists, creates and returns a session for this request. Otherwise, returns the existing session for this request.
boolean isRequestedSessionIdFromCookie( )	Returns **true** if a cookie contains the session ID. Otherwise, returns **false**.
boolean isRequestedSessionIdFromURL( )	Returns **true** if the URL contains the session ID. Otherwise, returns **false**.
boolean isRequestedSessionIdValid( )	Returns **true** if the requested session ID is valid in the current session context.

Table 27-5. *Various Methods Defined by* HttpServletRequest (continued)

The HttpServletResponse Interface

The **HttpServletResponse** interface is implemented by the server. It enables a servlet to formulate an HTTP response to a client. Several constants are defined. These correspond to the different status codes that can be assigned to an HTTP response. For example, **SC_OK** indicates that the HTTP request succeeded and **SC_NOT_FOUND** indicates that the requested resource is not available. Several methods of this interface are summarized in Table 27-6.

Method	Description
void addCookie(Cookie *cookie*)	Adds *cookie* to the HTTP response.
boolean containsHeader(String *field*)	Returns **true** if the HTTP response header contains a field named *field*.
String encodeURL(String *url*)	Determines if the session ID must be encoded in the URL identified as *url*. If so, returns the modified version of *url*. Otherwise, returns *url*. All URLs generated by a servlet should be processed by this method.
String encodeRedirectURL(String *url*)	Determines if the session ID must be encoded in the URL identified as *url*. If so, returns the modified version of *url*. Otherwise, returns *url*. All URLs passed to **sendRedirect( )** should be processed by this method.
void sendError(int *c*) throws IOException	Sends the error code *c* to the client.
void sendError(int *c*, String *s*) throws IOException	Sends the error code *c* and message *s* to the client.
void sendRedirect(String *url*) throws IOException	Redirects the client to *url*.

Table 27-6. *Various Methods Defined by* HttpServletResponse

Method	Description
void setDateHeader(String *field*, long *msec*)	Adds *field* to the header with date value equal to *msec* (milliseconds since midnight, January 1, 1970, GMT).
void setHeader(String *field*, String *value*)	Adds *field* to the header with value equal to *value*.
void setIntHeader(String *field*, int *value*)	Adds *field* to the header with value equal to *value*.
void setStatus(int *code*)	Sets the status code for this response to *code*.

Table 27-6. *Various Methods Defined by* HttpServletResponse (continued)

The HttpSession Interface

The **HttpSession** interface is implemented by the server. It enables a servlet to read and write the state information that is associated with an HTTP session. Several of its methods are summarized in Table 27-7. All of these methods throw an **IllegalStateException** if the session has already been invalidated.

Method	Description
Object getAttribute(String *attr*)	Returns the value associated with the name passed in *attr*. Returns **null** if *attr* is not found.
Enumeration getAttributeNames( )	Returns an enumeration of the attribute names associated with the session.
long getCreationTime( )	Returns the time (in milliseconds since midnight, January 1, 1970, GMT) when this session was created.
String getId( )	Returns the session ID.

Table 27-7. *The Methods Defined by* HttpSession

Method	Description
long getLastAccessedTime( )	Returns the time (in milliseconds since midnight, January 1, 1970, GMT) when the client last made a request for this session.
void invalidate( )	Invalidates this session and removes it from the context.
boolean isNew( )	Returns **true** if the server created the session and it has not yet been accessed by the client.
void removeAttribute(String *attr*)	Removes the attribute specified by *attr* from the session.
void setAttribute(String *attr*, Object *val*)	Associates the value passed in *val* with the attribute name passed in *attr*.

Table 27-7. *The Methods Defined by* HttpSession (continued)

The HttpSessionBindingListener Interface

The **HttpSessionBindingListener** interface is implemented by objects that need to be notified when they are bound to or unbound from an HTTP session. The methods that are invoked when an object is bound or unbound are

> void valueBound(HttpSessionBindingEvent *e*)
> void valueUnbound(HttpSessionBindingEvent *e*)

Here, *e* is the event object that describes the binding.

The Cookie Class

The **Cookie** class encapsulates a cookie. A cookie is stored on a client and contains state information. Cookies are valuable for tracking user activities. For example, assume that a user visits an online store. A cookie can save the user's name, address, and other information. The user does not need to enter this data each time he or she visits the store.

A servlet can write a cookie to a user's machine via the **addCookie( )** method of the **HttpServletResponse** interface. The data for that cookie is then included in the header of the HTTP response that is sent to the browser.

The names and values of cookies are stored on the user's machine. Some of the information that is saved for each cookie includes the following:

- The name of the cookie
- The value of the cookie
- The expiration date of the cookie
- The domain and path of the cookie

The expiration date determines when this cookie is deleted from the user's machine. If an expiration date is not explicitly assigned to a cookie, it is deleted when the current browser session ends. Otherwise, the cookie is saved in a file on the user's machine.

The domain and path of the cookie determine when it is included in the header of an HTTP request. If the user enters a URL whose domain and path match these values, the cookie is then supplied to the Web server. Otherwise, it is not.

There is one constructor for **Cookie**. It has the signature shown here:

Cookie(String *name*, String *value*)

Here, the name and value of the cookie are supplied as arguments to the constructor. The methods of the **Cookie** class are summarized in Table 27-8.

Method	Description
Object clone( )	Returns a copy of this object.
String getComment( )	Returns the comment.
String getDomain( )	Returns the domain.
int getMaxAge( )	Returns the age (in seconds).
String getName( )	Returns the name.
String getPath( )	Returns the path.
boolean getSecure( )	Returns **true** if the cookie must be sent using only a secure protocol. Otherwise, returns **false**.
String getValue( )	Returns the value.
int getVersion( )	Returns the cookie protocol version. (Will be 0 or 1.)

Table 27-8. *The Methods Defined by* Cookie

Method	Description
void setComment(String *c*)	Sets the comment to *c*.
void setDomain(String *d*)	Sets the domain to *d*.
void setMaxAge(int *secs*)	Sets the maximum age of the cookie to *secs*. This is the number of seconds after which the cookie is deleted. Passing –1 causes the cookie to be removed when the browser is terminated.
void setPath(String *p*)	Sets the path to *p*.
void setSecure(boolean *secure*)	Sets the security flag to *secure*, which means that cookies will be sent only when a secure protocol is being used.
void setValue(String *v*)	Sets the value to *v*.
void setVersion(int v)	Sets the cookie protocol version to *v*, which will be 0 or 1.

Table 27-8.   *The Methods Defined by* Cookie (continued)

The HttpServlet Class

The **HttpServlet** class extends **GenericServlet**. It is commonly used when developing servlets that receive and process HTTP requests. The methods of the **HttpServlet** class are summarized in Table 27-9.

Method	Description
void doDelete(HttpServletRequest *req*, HttpServletResponse *res*) throws IOException, ServletException	Performs an HTTP DELETE.
void doGet(HttpServletRequest *req*, HttpServletResponse *res*) throws IOException, ServletException	Performs an HTTP GET.

Table 27-9.   *The Methods Defined by* HttpServlet

Method	Description
void doHead(HttpServletRequest *req*, HttpServletResponse *res*) throws IOException, ServletException	Performs an HTTP HEAD.
void doOptions(HttpServletRequest *req*, HttpServletResponse *res*) throws IOException, ServletException	Performs an HTTP OPTIONS.
void doPost(HttpServletRequest *req*, HttpServletResponse *res*) throws IOException, ServletException	Performs an HTTP POST.
void doPut(HttpServletRequest *req*, HttpServletResponse *res*) throws IOException, ServletException	Performs an HTTP PUT.
void doTrace(HttpServletRequest *req*, HttpServletResponse *res*) throws IOException, ServletException	Performs an HTTP TRACE.
long getLastModified(HttpServletRequest *req*)	Returns the time (in milliseconds since midnight, January 1, 1970, GMT) when the requested resource was last modified.
void service(HttpServletRequest *req*, HttpServletResponse *res*) throws IOException, ServletException	Called by the server when an HTTP request arrives for this servlet. The arguments provide access to the HTTP request and response, respectively.

Table 27-9. *The Methods Defined by* HttpServlet (continued)

The HttpSessionEvent Class

HttpSessionEvent encapsulates session events. It extents **EventObject** and is generated when a change occurs to the session. It defines this constructor:

HttpSessionEvent(HttpSession *session*)

Here, *session* is the source of the event.

HttpSessionEvent defines one method, **getSession( )**, which is shown here:

HttpSession getSession( )

It returns the session in which the event occurred.

The HttpSessionBindingEvent Class

The **HttpSessionBindingEvent** class extends **HttpSessionEvent**. It is generated when a listener is bound to or unbound from a value in an **HttpSession** object. It is also generated when an attribute is bound or unbound. Here are its constructors:

HttpSessionBindingEvent(HttpSession *session*, String *name*)
HttpSessionBindingEvent(HttpSession *session*, String *name*, Object *val*)

Here, *session* is the source of the event and *name* is the name associated with the object that is being bound or unbound. If an attribute is being bound or unbound, its value is passed in *val*.

The **getName( )** method obtains the name that is being bound or unbound. Its is shown here:

String getName( )

The **getSession( )** method, shown next, obtains the session to which the listener is being bound or unbound:

HttpSession getSession( )

The **getValue( )** method obtains the value of the attribute that is being bound or unbound. It is shown here:

Object getValue( )

Handling HTTP Requests and Responses

The **HttpServlet** class provides specialized methods that handle the various types of HTTP requests. A servlet developer typically overrides one of these methods. These methods are **doDelete( )**, **doGet( )**, **doHead( )**, **doOptions( )**, **doPost( )**, **doPut( )**, and **doTrace( )**. A complete description of the different types of HTTP requests is beyond the scope of this book. However, the GET and POST requests are commonly used when handling form input. Therefore, this section presents examples of these cases.

Handling HTTP GET Requests

Here we will develop a servlet that handles an HTTP GET request. The servlet is invoked when a form on a Web page is submitted. The example contains two files. A Web page is defined in **ColorGet.htm** and a servlet is defined in **ColorGetServlet.java**. The HTML source code for **ColorGet.htm** is shown in the following listing. It defines a form that contains a select element and a submit button. Notice that the action parameter of the form tag specifies a URL. The URL identifies a servlet to process the HTTP GET request.

```
<html>
<body>
<center>
<form name="Form1"
  action="http://localhost:8080/examples/servlet/ColorGetServlet">
<B>Color:</B>
<select name="color" size="1">
<option value="Red">Red</option>
<option value="Green">Green</option>
<option value="Blue">Blue</option>
</select>
<br><br>
<input type=submit value="Submit">
</form>
</body>
</html>
```

The source code for **ColorGetServlet.java** is shown in the following listing. The **doGet( )** method is overridden to process any HTTP GET requests that are sent to this servlet. It uses the **getParameter( )** method of **HttpServletRequest** to obtain the selection that was made by the user. A response is then formulated.

```
import java.io.*;
import javax.servlet.*;
import javax.servlet.http.*;

public class ColorGetServlet extends HttpServlet {

  public void doGet(HttpServletRequest request,
    HttpServletResponse response)
  throws ServletException, IOException {

    String color = request.getParameter("color");
    response.setContentType("text/html");
    PrintWriter pw = response.getWriter();
    pw.println("<B>The selected color is:  ");
    pw.println(color);
```

```
    pw.close();
  }
}
```

Compile the servlet and perform these steps to test this example:

1. Start Tomcat, if it is not already running.

2. Display the Web page in a browser.

3. Select a color.

4. Submit the Web page.

After completing these steps, the browser will display the response that is dynamically generated by the servlet.

One other point: Parameters for an HTTP GET request are included as part of the URL that is sent to the Web server. Assume that the user selects the red option and submits the form. The URL sent from the browser to the server is

```
http://localhost:8080/examples/servlet/ColorGetServlet?color=Red
```

The characters to the right of the question mark are known as the *query string*.

Handling HTTP POST Requests

Here we will develop a servlet that handles an HTTP POST request. The servlet is invoked when a form on a Web page is submitted. The example contains two files. A Web page is defined in **ColorPost.htm** and a servlet is defined in **ColorPostServlet.java**.

The HTML source code for **ColorPost.htm** is shown in the following listing. It is identical to **ColorGet.htm** except that the method parameter for the form tag explicitly specifies that the POST method should be used, and the action parameter for the form tag specifies a different servlet.

```
<html>
<body>
<center>
<form name="Form1"
  method="post"
  action="http://localhost:8080/examples/servlet/ColorPostServlet">
<B>Color:</B>
<select name="color" size="1">
<option value="Red">Red</option>
<option value="Green">Green</option>
```

```
<option value="Blue">Blue</option>
</select>                    '
<br><br>
<input type=submit value="Submit">
</form>
</body>
</html>
```

The source code for **ColorPostServlet.java** is shown in the following listing. The **doPost( )** method is overridden to process any HTTP POST requests that are sent to this servlet. It uses the **getParameter( )** method of **HttpServletRequest** to obtain the selection that was made by the user. A response is then formulated.

```
import java.io.*;
import javax.servlet.*;
import javax.servlet.http.*;

public class ColorPostServlet extends HttpServlet {

  public void doPost(HttpServletRequest request,
    HttpServletResponse response)
  throws ServletException, IOException {

    String color = request.getParameter("color");
    response.setContentType("text/html");
    PrintWriter pw = response.getWriter();
    pw.println("<B>The selected color is:  ");
    pw.println(color);
    pw.close();
  }
}
```

Compile the servlet and perform the same steps as described in the previous section to test it.

Note: Parameters for an HTTP POST request are not included as part of the URL that is sent to the Web server. In this example, the URL sent from the browser to the server is:

```
http://localhost:8080/examples/servlet/ColorGetServlet
```

The parameter names and values are sent in the body of the HTTP request.

Using Cookies

Now, let's develop a servlet that illustrates how to use cookies. The servlet is invoked when a form on a Web page is submitted. The example contains three files as summarized here:

File	Description
AddCookie.htm	Allows a user to specify a value for the cookie named **MyCookie**.
AddCookieServlet.java	Processes the submission of **AddCookie.htm**.
GetCookiesServlet.java	Displays cookie values.

The HTML source code for **AddCookie.htm** is shown in the following listing. This page contains a text field in which a value can be entered. There is also a submit button on the page. When this button is pressed, the value in the text field is sent to **AddCookieServlet** via an HTTP POST request.

```
<html>
<body>
<center>
<form name="Form1"
  method="post"
  action="http://localhost:8080/examples/servlet/AddCookieServlet">
<B>Enter a value for MyCookie:</B>
<input type=textbox name="data" size=25 value="">
<input type=submit value="Submit">
</form>
</body>
</html>
```

The source code for **AddCookieServlet.java** is shown in the following listing. It gets the value of the parameter named "data". It then creates a **Cookie** object that has the name "MyCookie" and contains the value of the "data" parameter. The cookie is then added to the header of the HTTP response via the **addCookie( )** method. A feedback message is then written to the browser.

```
import java.io.*;
import javax.servlet.*;
import javax.servlet.http.*;
```

```
public class AddCookieServlet extends HttpServlet {

  public void doPost(HttpServletRequest request,
    HttpServletResponse response)
  throws ServletException, IOException {

    // Get parameter from HTTP request.
    String data = request.getParameter("data");

    // Create cookie.
    Cookie cookie = new Cookie("MyCookie", data);

    // Add cookie to HTTP response.
    response.addCookie(cookie);

    // Write output to browser.
    response.setContentType("text/html");
    PrintWriter pw = response.getWriter();
    pw.println("<B>MyCookie has been set to");
    pw.println(data);
    pw.close();
  }
}
```

The source code for **GetCookiesServlet.java** is shown in the following listing. It invokes the **getCookies( )** method to read any cookies that are included in the HTTP GET request. The names and values of these cookies are then written to the HTTP response. Observe that the **getName( )** and **getValue( )** methods are called to obtain this information.

```
import java.io.*;
import javax.servlet.*;
import javax.servlet.http.*;

public class GetCookiesServlet extends HttpServlet {

  public void doGet(HttpServletRequest request,
    HttpServletResponse response)
  throws ServletException, IOException {

    // Get cookies from header of HTTP request.
```

```
    Cookie[] cookies = request.getCookies();

    // Display these cookies.
    response.setContentType("text/html");
    PrintWriter pw = response.getWriter();
    pw.println("<B>");
    for(int i = 0; i < cookies.length; i++) {
      String name = cookies[i].getName();
      String value = cookies[i].getValue();
      pw.println("name = " + name +
        "; value = " + value);
    }
    pw.close();
  }
}
```

Compile the servlet and perform these steps:

1. Start Tomcat, if it is not already running.
2. Display **AddCookie.htm** in a browser.
3. Enter a value for **MyCookie.**
4. Submit the Web page.

After completing these steps you will observe that a feedback message is displayed by the browser.

Next, request the following URL via the browser:

```
http://localhost:8080/examples/servlet/GetCookiesServlet
```

Observe that the name and value of the cookie are displayed in the browser.

In this example, an expiration date is not explicitly assigned to the cookie via the **setMaxAge( )** method of **Cookie.** Therefore, the cookie expires when the browser session ends. You can experiment by using **setMaxAge( )** and observe that the cookie is then saved to the disk on the client machine.

Session Tracking

HTTP is a stateless protocol. Each request is independent of the previous one. However, in some applications, it is necessary to save state information so that information can be collected from several interactions between a browser and a server. Sessions provide such a mechanism.

A session can be created via the **getSession( )** method of **HttpServletRequest**. An **HttpSession** object is returned. This object can store a set of bindings that associate names with objects. The **setAttribute( )**, **getAttribute( )**, **getAttributeNames( )**, and **removeAttribute( )** methods of **HttpSession** manage these bindings. It is important to note that session state is shared among all the servlets that are associated with a particular client.

The following servlet illustrates how to use session state. The **getSession( )** method gets the current session. A new session is created if one does not already exist. The **getAttribute( )** method is called to obtain the object that is bound to the name "date". That object is a **Date** object that encapsulates the date and time when this page was last accessed. (Of course, there is no such binding when the page is first accessed.) A **Date** object encapsulating the current date and time is then created. The **setAttribute( )** method is called to bind the name "date" to this object.

```java
import java.io.*;
import java.util.*;
import javax.servlet.*;
import javax.servlet.http.*;

public class DateServlet extends HttpServlet {

  public void doGet(HttpServletRequest request,
    HttpServletResponse response)
  throws ServletException, IOException {

    // Get the HttpSession object.
    HttpSession hs = request.getSession(true);

    // Get writer.
    response.setContentType("text/html");
    PrintWriter pw = response.getWriter();
    pw.print("<B>");

    // Display date/time of last access.
    Date date = (Date)hs.getAttribute("date");
    if(date != null) {
      pw.print("Last access: " + date + "<br>");
    }

    // Display current date/time.
    date = new Date();
    hs.setAttribute("date", date);
```

```
      pw.println("Current date: " + date);
   }
}
```

When you first request this servlet, the browser displays one line with the current date and time information. On subsequent invocations, two lines are displayed. The first line shows the date and time when the servlet was last accessed. The second line shows the current date and time.

Security Issues

In earlier chapters of this book, you learned that untrusted applets are constrained to operate in a "sandbox". They cannot perform operations that are potentially dangerous to a user's machine. This includes reading and writing files, opening sockets to arbitrary machines, calling native methods, and creating new processes. Other restrictions also apply.

Similar constraints also exist for untrusted servlets. Code that is loaded from a remote machine is untrusted. However, trusted servlets are not limited in this manner. Trusted servlets are those which are loaded from the local machine.

The
Complete
Reference

Java™ 2

Chapter 28

Migrating from C++ to Java

This chapter discusses several of the issues that arise when you move from C++ to Java. Since many Java programmers come from a C++ background, it is natural to want to carry over the skills, techniques, and code acquired in this language. Although C++ and Java were designed to address the programming needs of two very different environments, many of the same coding techniques, algorithms, and optimizations apply to both. However, as explained in Part One, Java is not "the Internet version of C++." While there are many similarities between the two languages, there are also several differences. This chapter reviews those differences and shows ways to handle some of the more challenging ones.

The Differences Between C++ and Java

Before we look at specific situations, let's review the basic differences between C++ and Java. The differences fall into three categories:

- C++ features not supported by Java
- Features unique to Java
- Shared features which differ between C++ and Java

Each is examined here.

What Java Has Removed from C++

There are a number of C++ features that Java does not support. In some cases, a specific C++ feature simply didn't relate to the Java environment. In other cases, the designers of Java eliminated some of the duplication of features that exists in C++. In still other instances, a feature of C++ is not supported by Java because it was deemed too dangerous for Internet applets.

Perhaps the single biggest difference between Java and C++ is that Java does not support pointers. As a C++ programmer you know that the pointer is one of C++'s most powerful and important language features. It is also one of its most dangerous when used improperly. Pointers don't exist in Java for two reasons:

- Pointers are inherently insecure. For example, using a C++-style pointer, it is possible to gain access to memory addresses outside a program's code and data. A malicious program could make use of this fact to damage the system, perform unauthorized accesses (such as obtaining passwords), or otherwise violate security restrictions.

■ Even if pointers could be restricted to the confines of the Java run-time system (which is theoretically possible), the designers of Java believed that they were inherently troublesome.

 Since pointers don't exist in Java, neither does the -> operator.

Here are a few more of the most important "omissions":

■ Java does not include structures or unions. These were felt to be redundant since the class encompasses them.

■ Java does not support operator overloading. Operator overloading is sometimes a source of ambiguity in a C++ program, and the Java design team felt that it causes more trouble than benefit.

■ Java does not include a preprocessor nor does it support the preprocessor directives. The preprocessor plays a less important role in C++ than it does in C. The designers of Java felt that it was time to eliminate it entirely.

■ Java does not perform any automatic type conversions that result in a loss of precision. For example, a conversion from **long** integer to integer must be explicitly cast.

■ All the code in a Java program is encapsulated within one or more classes. Therefore, Java does not have what you normally think of as global variables or global functions.

■ Java does not allow default arguments. In C++, you may specify a value that a parameter will have when there is no argument corresponding to that parameter when the function is invoked. This is not allowed in Java.

■ Java does not support the inheritance of multiple superclasses by a subclass.

■ Although Java supports constructors, it does not have destructors. It does, however, add the **finalize( )** function.

■ Java does not support **typedef**.

■ It is not possible to declare unsigned integers in Java.

■ Java does not allow the **goto**.

■ Java does not have the **delete** operator.

■ The << and >> in Java are not overloaded for I/O operations.

■ In Java, objects are passed by reference only. In C++, objects may be passed by value or by reference.

New Features Added by Java

There are a number of features in Java that have no equivalent in C++. Perhaps the three most important are multithreading, packages, and interfaces, but there are several others that enrich the Java programming environment as well.

■ As explained earlier, multithreading allows two or more pieces of the same program to execute concurrently. Further, this approach to concurrence is supported at the language level. There is no parallel for this in C++. If you need to multithread a C++ program, you will need to do so manually, using operating system functions. While both methods allow for concurrent execution of two or more threads, Java's approach is cleaner and easier to use.

■ There is no feature in C++ that directly corresponds to a Java package. The closest similarity is a set of library functions that use a common header file. However, constructing and using a library in C++ is completely different from constructing and using a package in Java.

■ The Java **interface** is somewhat similar to a C++ abstract class. (An *abstract class* in C++ is a class that contains at least one pure virtual function.) For example, it is impossible to create an instance of a C++ abstract class or a Java **interface**. Both are used to specify a consistent interface that subclasses will implement. The main difference is that an **interface** more cleanly represents this concept.

■ Java has a streamlined approach to memory allocation. Like C++, it supports the **new** keyword. However, it does not have **delete**. Instead, when the last reference to an object is destroyed, the object, itself, is automatically deleted the next time that garbage collection occurs.

■ Java "removes" the C++ standard library, replacing it with its own set of API classes. While there is substantial functional similarity, there are significant differences in the names and parameters. Also, since all of the Java API library is object-oriented, and only a portion of the C++ library is, there will be differences in the way library routines are invoked.

■ The **break** and **continue** statements have been enhanced in Java to accept labels as targets.

■ The **char** type in Java declares 16-bit-wide Unicode characters. This makes them similar to C++'s **wchar_t** type. The use of Unicode helps ensure portability.

■ Java adds the >>> operator, which performs an unsigned right shift.

■ In addition to supporting single-line and multiline comments, Java adds a third comment form: the *documentation comment*. Documentation comments begin with a /** and end with a */.

■ Java contains a built-in string type called **String**. **String** is somewhat similar to the standard **string** class type provided by C++. Of course, in C++ **string** is only available if you include its class declarations in your program. It is not a built-in type.

Features That Differ

There are some features common to both C++ and Java that each language handles a bit differently:

■ While both C++ and Java support a Boolean data type, Java does not implement true and false in the same way as C++. In C++, true is any nonzero value. False is zero. In Java, **true** and **false** are predefined literals, and these are the only values that a **boolean** expression may have. While C++ also defines **true** and **false**, which may be assigned to a **bool** variable, C++ automatically converts nonzero values into **true** and zero values into **false**. This does not occur in Java.

■ When you create a C++ class, the access specifiers apply to groups of statements. In Java, access specifiers apply only to the declarations that they immediately precede.

■ C++ supports exception handling that is fairly similar to Java's. However, in C++ there is no requirement that a thrown exception be caught.

With these additions, deletions, and differences as a backdrop, the rest of this chapter will look closely at a few of the key issues that you must deal with when converting code from C++ to Java.

Eliminating Pointers

When you convert a C++ program into Java, perhaps the greatest number of changes will be caused by pointers. Most C++ code is heavily dependent upon pointers for its operation. You can't program anything very significant in C++ without using a pointer.

There are four general categories of pointer usage that you will encounter in C++ code:

■ **As parameters to functions.**   Although C++ supports the reference parameter, there is a large base of legacy code that was originally written in C. C does not support reference parameters. In C, if a function needs to change the value of an argument, it is necessary to explicitly pass a pointer to that argument. Therefore, it is still common to find pointer parameters used in C++ code that was originally ported from C. Also, in some cases the same function library will need to be shared by both C and C++ code, which prevents the use of reference parameters.

Additionally, many of the standard library functions supported by C++ are holdovers from C. When one of these C-based functions requires the address of an argument, a pointer to the argument is used. Inside the function, the argument is then accessed through its pointer.

■ **To provide a more efficient means of implementing certain constructs—especially array indexing.**   For example, it is often more efficient to sequentially move through an array using a pointer rather than an array index. While modern compilers implement highly efficient optimizations, pointers can still provide a significant performance boost. Thus, the use of pointers to access arrays is ubiquitous in C++ code.

■ **To support memory allocation.**   In C++, when you allocate memory, an address (that is, a pointer) to that memory is returned. This address must be assigned to a pointer variable. Once this has been done, the pointer can point to any part of the allocated memory—or anywhere else, for that matter—by means of pointer arithmetic. In Java, when an object is allocated by **new**, a reference to the object is returned. This reference must be assigned to a reference variable of a compatible type. While Java reference variables do implicitly point to the object that was allocated by the **new** operator, they cannot be manipulated in the same way as C++ pointers. And they cannot point to memory outside of the Java run-time context.

■ **To provide access to any arbitrary machine address, possibly to call a ROM routine or to read/write directly to memory.**   Since Java purposely disallows such actions, this use of pointers has no direct parallel. If you are writing applications, not applets, you can always use Java's **native** capabilities (described in Part One) to gain access to native code routines that would be allowed access to such system resources.

Let's look at two situations in which pointer-based C++ code is converted to Java.

Converting Pointer Parameters

For the most part, it is quite easy to convert a C++ function that uses pointer parameters into its equivalent Java method. Since Java passes all objects by reference, sometimes the conversion simply requires the removal of C++'s pointer operators. For example, consider this C++ program that reverses the signs of a **Coord** object, which stores a pair of Cartesian coordinates. The function **reverseSign( )** is passed a pointer to the **Coord** object that will be reversed. As you can see, C++'s *, &, and -> pointer operators are used to perform the operation.

```cpp
// Reverse the signs of a coordinate - C++ version.
#include <iostream>
using namespace std;

class Coord {
public:
  int x;
  int y;
};

// Reverse the sign of the coordinates.
void reverseSign(Coord *ob) {
  ob->x = -ob->x;
  ob->y = -ob->y;
}

int main()
{
  Coord ob;

  ob.x = 10;
  ob.y = 20;

  cout << "Original values for ob: ";
  cout << ob.x << ", " << ob.y << "\n";

  reverseSign(&ob);

  cout << "Sign reversed values for ob: ";
  cout << ob.x << ", " << ob.y << "\n";


  return 0;
}
```

This program can be recoded into the following Java version. As you can see, most of the conversion involves the deletion of the C++ pointer operators. Since Java passes objects by reference, changes to the parameter automatically affect the argument.

```java
// Reverse the signs of a coordinate - Java version.
class Coord {
  int x;
  int y;
};

class DropPointers {
  // Reverse the sign of the coordinates.
  static void reverseCoord(Coord ob) {
    ob.x = -ob.x;
    ob.y = -ob.y;
  }
  public static void main(String args[]) {
    Coord ob = new Coord();

    ob.x = 10;
    ob.y = 20;

    System.out.println("Original values for ob: " +
      ob.x + ", " + ob.y);

    reverseCoord(ob);

    System.out.println("Sign reversed values for ob: " +
      ob.x + ", " + ob.y);
  }
}
```

The output from both of these programs is the same and is shown here:

```
Original values for ob: 10, 20
Sign reversed values for ob: -10, -20
```

Converting Pointers that Operate on Arrays

Conceptually, converting C++-style pointer-based array accessing into the equivalent Java-compatible array indexing is straightforward—simply substitute the appropriate array-indexing statements. However, in practice this may require some thought. Pointer-based array accessing can be a bit difficult to follow, because the normal C++ coding style encourages rather dense, complex expressions. For example, this short C++ program copies the contents of one array to another. It uses 0 to mark the end of the arrays. Pay special attention to the pointer expressions. Even in this simple example, if you did not know that this program copied the contents of **nums** to **copy** (and later displayed the arrays), it would require some careful thought before you were completely sure that you knew what the code was doing.

```cpp
// Copy an array in C++ using pointers.
#include <iostream>
using namespace std;

int main()
{
  int nums[] = {10, 12, 24, 45, 23, 19, 44,
                88, 99, 65, 76, 12, 89, 0};
  int copy[20];

  int *p1, *p2; // integer pointers

  // copy array
  p1 = nums; // p1 points to start of nums array
  p2 = copy;
  while(*p1) *p2++ = *p1++;
  *p2 = 0; // terminate copy with zero

  // Display contents of each array.
  cout << "Here is the original array:\n";
  p1 = nums;
  while(*p1) cout << *p1++ << " ";
  cout << endl;

  cout << "Here is the copy:\n";
  p1 = copy;
  while(*p1) cout << *p1++ << " ";
  cout << endl;

  return 0;
}
```

Even though it is quite simple for C++ code, at first glance the line

```
while(*p1) *p2++ = *p1++;
```

still requires a moment of thought to decipher its exact operation. One of the
advantages of Java is that it does not encourage the creation of such expressions
in the first place. Here is the Java version of the program. As you can see, its purpose
and effects are transparent.

```java
// Array copy without pointers using Java.
class CopyArray {
  public static void main(String args[]) {
    int nums[] = {10, 12, 24, 45, 23, 19, 44,
                  88, 99, 65, 76, 12, 89, 0};
    int copy[] = new int[14];
    int i;

    // copy array
    for(i=0; nums[i]!=0; i++)
      copy[i] = nums[i];
    nums[i] = 0; // terminate copy with zero

    // Display contents of each array.
    System.out.println("Here is the original array:");
    for(i=0; nums[i]!=0; i++)
      System.out.print(nums[i] + " ");
    System.out.println();

    System.out.println("Here is the copy:");
    for(i=0; nums[i]!=0; i++)
      System.out.print(copy[i] + " ");
    System.out.println();
  }
}
```

Both versions of the program produce the following results:

```
Here is the original array:
10 12 24 45 23 19 44 88 99 65 76 12 89
Here is the copy:
10 12 24 45 23 19 44 88 99 65 76 12 89
```

Much C++ code is sprinkled with obscure, difficult to understand pointer expressions. While these expressions do tend to increase speed of execution, they are one of the most troubling issues associated with the maintenance of C++ programs. They will also present difficulty when you convert the code to Java. When you are confronted with a complex pointer expression, it is sometimes useful to begin by breaking it into its subexpressions so that its exact operation becomes clear.

C++ Reference Parameters Versus Java Reference Parameters

In the preceding section, you saw an example of a C++ program that used a pointer parameter. In Java, this became a *reference* parameter. Of course, C++ also supports reference parameters. As mentioned, most pointer parameters found in C++ code are simply holdovers from C. Nearly all new C++ code will use reference parameters when a function needs access to the argument, itself. (In essence, pointer parameters, although still common, are actually anachronisms in most C++ code.) Since both Java and C++ support reference parameters, you might think that the conversion of a C++ function that uses reference parameters to a Java method would involve few changes. Unfortunately, this is not always the case. To understand why, let's convert the following C++ program, which swaps the contents of two **Coord** objects using reference parameters:

```
// Swap coordinates -- C++ version.
#include <iostream>
using namespace std;

class Coord {
public:
  int x;
  int y;
};

// Swap contents of two Coord objects.
void swap(Coord &a, Coord &b) {
  Coord temp;

  // swap contents of objects
  temp = a;
  a = b;
  b = temp;
}
```

```
int main()
{
  Coord ob1, ob2;

  ob1.x = 10;
  ob1.y = 20;

  ob2.x = 88;
  ob2.y = 99;

  cout << "Original values:\n";
  cout << "ob1: " << ob1.x << ", " << ob1.y << "\n";
  cout << "ob2: " << ob2.x << ", " << ob2.y << "\n";
  cout << "\n";
  swap(ob1, ob2);

  cout << "Swapped values:\n";
  cout << "ob1: " << ob1.x << ", " << ob1.y << "\n";
  cout << "ob2: " << ob2.x << ", " << ob2.y << "\n";

  return 0;
}
```

Following is the output produced by this program. As you can see, the contents of **ob1** and **ob2** have been exchanged:

```
Original values:
ob1: 10, 20
ob2: 88, 99

Swapped values:
ob1: 88, 99
ob2: 10, 20
```

In Java, all objects are accessed via an object reference variable. Thus, when an object is passed to a method, only its reference is passed. This means that all objects are automatically passed by reference to a Java method. Without thinking any deeper about what is actually occurring, someone might initially try the following (incorrect) conversion of the preceding program:

```
// Swap program incorrectly converted to Java.
class Coord {
  int x;
  int y;
};

class SwapDemo {
  static void swap(Coord a, Coord b) {
    Coord temp = new Coord();

    // this won't swap contents of a and b!
    temp = a;
    a = b;
    b = temp;
  }

  public static void main(String args[]) {
    Coord ob1 = new Coord();
    Coord ob2 = new Coord();

    ob1.x = 10;
    ob1.y = 20;

    ob2.x = 88;
    ob2.y = 99;

    System.out.println("Original values:");
    System.out.println("ob1: " +
            ob1.x + ",  " + ob1.y);
    System.out.println("ob2: " +
            ob2.x + ",  " + ob2.y + "\n");

    swap(ob1, ob2);

    System.out.println("Swapped values:");
    System.out.println("ob1: " +
            ob1.x + ",  " + ob1.y);
    System.out.println("ob2: " +
            ob2.x + ",  " + ob2.y + "\n");
  }
}
```

The output produced by this incorrect program is shown here:

```
Original values:
ob1: 10, 20
ob2: 88, 99

Swapped values:
ob1: 10, 20
ob2: 88, 99
```

As you can see, the values of **ob1** and **ob2** in **main( )** have not been exchanged! Although a bit counterintuitive at first, the reason is actually obvious, once you understand precisely what happens when an object reference is passed to a method. Java passes all arguments to methods using call-by-value. This means that a copy of the argument is made, and what occurs to the copy inside the method has no effect on the argument used to call the method. However, this situation is blurred a bit in the case of object references.

When an object reference is passed to a method, a copy of the reference variable is made, as just explained. This means that the parameter inside the method will refer to the same object as does the reference variable used as an argument outside the method. Therefore, operations on the object through the parameter will affect the object referred to by the argument (since they are one and the same). But operations on the reference parameter, itself, affect only that parameter. Thus, when the preceding program attempts to swap the objects by exchanging the objects pointed to by **a** and **b**, all that is happening is that the parameters (that is, the copies of the arguments) are exchanging what they are referring to, but this does not alter what **ob1** and **ob2** refer to back in **main( )**.

To fix the program, **swap( )** needs to be rewritten so that the contents of the objects are exchanged, not what the parameters refer to. Here is the corrected version of **swap( )**:

```
// Corrected version of swap().
static void swap(Coord a, Coord b) {
  Coord temp = new Coord();

  // swap contents of objects
  temp.x = a.x;
  temp.y = a.y;
  a.x = b.x;
  a.y = b.y;
  b.x = temp.x;
  b.y = temp.y;
}
```

If you substitute this version of **swap( )** into the preceding program, the correct results will be achieved.

Converting C++ Abstract Classes into Java Interfaces

One of the most innovative aspects of Java is the **interface**. As explained earlier in this book, an **interface** specifies the form of its various methods without specifying any implementation details. Each class that implements an **interface** does so by creating the actual methods declared by the **interface**. Thus, in Java an **interface** is the means by which you can define the general form of a class while ensuring that all specific versions of the class conform to the same set of rules. The **interface** is one of the ways that Java provides support for polymorphism.

In C++, there is no direct parallel to the **interface**. Instead, in C++, if you wish to define the form of a class without defining implementation details, you must do so by using an abstract class. Abstract classes in C++ are similar to abstract classes in Java: they do not contain a full set of implementation details. In C++, an abstract class contains at least one pure virtual function. A pure virtual function defines no implementation; it only defines the function prototype. Thus, a pure virtual function in C++ is essentially the same as an **abstract** method in Java. In C++, abstract classes serve a function similar to **interface**s in Java. For this reason, they are one of the items that you will want to watch for when converting code to Java. While not all C++ abstract classes can be converted into Java interfaces, many can. Let's look at two examples.

Here is a short C++ program that uses an abstract class called **IntList** to define the form of an integer list. An implementation of this class is created by **IntArray**, which uses an array to implement a list of integers.

```cpp
// A C++-style abstract class and its implementation.
#include <iostream>
#include <cstdlib>
using namespace std;

// An abstract class that defines the form of an integer list.
class IntList {
public:
  virtual int getNext() = 0; // pure virtual functions
  virtual void putOnList(int i) = 0;
};

// Create an implementation of an integer list.
class IntArray : public IntList {
  int storage[100];
  int putIndex, getIndex;
public:
  IntArray() {
    putIndex = 0;
    getIndex = 0;
```

```
    }

    // Return next integer in list.
    int getNext() {
      if(getIndex >= 100) {
        cout << "List Underflow";
        exit(1);
      }
      getIndex++;
      return storage[getIndex-1];
    }

    // Put an integer on the list.
    void putOnList(int i) {
      if(putIndex < 100) {
        storage[putIndex] = i;
        putIndex++;
      }
      else {
        cout << "List Overflow";
        exit(1);
      }
    }
};

int main()
{
  IntArray nums;
  int i;

  for(i=0; i<10; i++) nums.putOnList(i);

  for(i=0; i<10; i++)
    cout << nums.getNext() << endl;

  return 0;
}
```

In this program, the abstract class **IntList** defines only the form of an integer list. It contains only pure virtual functions and does not declare any data. For these reasons, it can be made into an **interface** when the program is converted into Java, as shown here:

```
// Here, IntList is made into an interface which IntArray implements.

// Define interface for an integer list
interface IntListIF {
  int getNext();
  void putOnList(int i);
}

// Create an implementation of an integer list.
class IntArray implements IntListIF {
  private int storage[];
  private int putIndex, getIndex;

  IntArray() {
    storage = new int[100];
    putIndex = 0;
    getIndex = 0;
  }

  // Create an implementation of an integer list.
  public int getNext() {
    if(getIndex >= 100) {
      System.out.println("List Underflow");
      System.exit(1);
    }
    getIndex++;
    return storage[getIndex-1];
  }

  // Put an integer on the list.
  public void putOnList(int i) {
    if(putIndex < 100) {
      storage[putIndex] = i;
      putIndex++;
    }
    else {
      System.out.println("List Overflow");
```

```
          System.exit(1);
        }
    }
}

class ListDemo {
  public static void main(String args[]) {
    IntArray nums = new IntArray();
    int i;

    for(i=0; i<10; i++) nums.putOnList(i);

    for(i=0; i<10; i++)
      System.out.println(nums.getNext());
  }
}
```

As you can see, there is nearly a one-to-one correspondence between the C++ abstract class **IntList** and the Java interface **IntListIF**. It is possible to convert **IntList** into **IntListIF** because it contained only pure virtual functions. This is the key. If **IntList** had contained any data or function implementations, then it would not have qualified for conversion into an **interface**.

When you convert or adapt C++ code into Java, look for examples of abstract classes that contain only pure virtual functions. These are prime candidates for conversion to Java interfaces. But don't overlook abstract C++ classes that contain a small number of implemented functions or data. It is possible that these items don't really belong in the abstract class to begin with and should be defined by individual implementations. Since C++ does not define an interface construct, there was no reason for C++ programmers to think in terms of one.

Sometimes a concrete member is contained in an otherwise abstract class simply for expedience—not because it is the most logical place for it. For example, consider the following abstract C++ class:

```
// An abstract C++ class.
class SomeClass {
  bool isOK;
public:
  virtual int f1() = 0;
  virtual void f2(int i) = 0;
  virtual double f3() = 0;
  virtual int f4(int a, char ch) = 0;
};
```

The only reason that this class cannot be made into a Java interface is the existence of **isOK**. Presumably, **isOK** is used to indicate some status associated with the class. However, if you think about it, there really is no reason for **isOK** to be defined as a variable. Instead, you could specify a method called **isOK( )** that returns the status. In this approach, **isOK( )** will be defined, along with the other methods, by any implementing class. Thus, you could convert the preceding C++ abstract class into the following Java interface:

```
interface SomeClass {
  int f1();
  void f2(int i);
  double f3();
  int f4(int a, char ch);
  boolean isOK();
}
```

Many abstract classes in C++ can—and should—be converted into interfaces when you move code to Java. In doing so, you will probably find that it clarifies the structure of the class hierarchy.

Converting Default Arguments

One extensively used feature of C++ that Java does not support is default function arguments. For example, the **area( )** function shown in the following C++ program computes the area of a rectangle if called with two arguments, or the area of a square if called with one argument.

```
// C++ program that uses default arguments.
#include <iostream>
using namespace std;

/* Compute area of a rectangle.  For a square,
   pass only one argument.
*/
double area(double l, double w=0) {
  if(w==0)  return l * l;
  else return l * w;
}

int main()
{
  cout << "Area of 2.2 by 3.4 rectangle: ";
  cout << area(2.2, 3.4) << endl;
```

```
cout << "Area of 3.0 by 3.0 square: ";
cout << area(3.0) << endl;
return 0;
}
```

As you can see, when **area( )** is called with only one argument, the second defaults to zero. When this happens, the function simply uses the first argument for both the length and the width of the rectangle.

While convenient, default arguments are not, of course, necessary. In essence, default arguments are actually a shorthand form of function overloading in which one form of the function has a different number of parameters than the other. Thus, to convert a C++ function that contains one or more default arguments into Java, simply create overloaded methods that handle each case. In this example, you need a version of **area( )** that takes two arguments and another that takes only one argument. Using this approach, here is the preceding program rewritten for Java:

```java
// Java version of area program.
class Area {
  // Compute area of a rectangle.
  static double area(double l, double w) {
    if(w==0)  return l * l;
    else return l * w;
  }

  // Overload area( ) for a square.
  static double area(double l) {
    return l * l;
  }

  public static void main(String args[]) {
    System.out.println("Area of 2.2 by 3.4 rectangle: " +
                       area(2.2, 3.4));

    System.out.println("Area of 3.0 by 3.0 square: " +
                       area(3.0));
  }
}
```

Converting C++ Multiple-Inheritance Hierarchies

C++ allows one class to inherit two or more base classes at the same time. Java does not. To understand the difference, consider the two hierarchies depicted here:

Multiple Inheritance   Single Inheritance

In both cases, subclass C inherits classes A and B. However, in the hierarchy on the left, C inherits both A and B at the same time. In the one on the right, B inherits A, and C inherits B. By not allowing the inheritance of multiple base classes by a single subclass, Java greatly simplifies the inheritance model. Multiple inheritance carries with it several special cases that must be handled. This adds overhead to both the compiler and the run-time system, while providing only marginal benefit for the programmer.

Since C++ supports multiple inheritance and Java does not, you may have to deal with this issue when porting C++ applications to Java. While every situation is different, two general pieces of advice can be offered. First, in many cases, multiple inheritance is employed in a C++ program when there is actually no need to do so. When this is the case, just convert the class structure to a single-inheritance hierarchy. For example, consider this C++ class hierarchy that defines a class called **House**:

```
class Foundation {
  // ...
};

class Walls {
  // ...
};

class Rooms {
  // ...
};

class House : public Foundation, Walls, Rooms {
  // ...
};
```

Notice that **House** multiply inherits **Foundation**, **Walls**, and **Rooms**. While there is nothing wrong with structuring a C++ hierarchy like this, it is not necessary. For example, here is the same set of classes structured for Java:

```
class Foundation {
  // ...
}

class Walls extends Foundation {
  // ...
}

class Rooms extends Walls {
  // ...
}

class House extends Rooms {
  // ...
}
```

Here, each class extends the preceding one, with **House** becoming the final extension.

Sometimes a multiple inheritance hierarchy is more readily converted by including objects of the multiply inherited classes in the final object. For example, here is another way that **House** could be constructed in Java:

```
class Foundation {
  // ...
}

class Walls{
  // ...
}

class Rooms {
  // ...
}

/* Now, House includes Foundation, Walls, and Rooms
   as object members.
*/
```

```
class House {
  Foundation f;
  Walls w;
  Rooms r;
  // ...
}
```

Here, **Foundation**, **Walls**, and **Rooms** are objects that are part of **House** rather than inherited by **House**.

One other point: sometimes a C++ program will contain a multiple-inheritance hierarchy simply because of poor initial design. A good time to correct this type of design flaw is when you port to Java.

Destructors Versus Finalization

When you move from C++ to Java, one of the more subtle, yet important issues you will face is the difference between a C++ destructor and a Java **finalize( )** method. Although similar in many respects, their actual operation is distinctively different. Let's begin by reviewing the purpose and effect of a C++ destructor and the Java **finalize( )** method.

In C++, when an object goes out of scope, it is destroyed. Just prior to its destruction, its destructor function is called (if it has one). This is a hard-and-fast rule. There are no exceptions. Let's look more closely at each part of this rule:

■ **Every object is destroyed when it goes out of scope.**   Thus, if you declare a local object inside a function, when that function returns, that local object is automatically destroyed. The same goes for function parameters and for objects returned by functions.

■ **Just before destruction, the object's destructor is called.**   This happens immediately, and before any other program statements will execute. Thus, a C++ destructor will always execute in a deterministic fashion. You can always know when and where a destructor will be executed.

In Java, the tight linkage of the destruction of an object and the calling of its **finalize( )** method does not exist. In Java, objects are not explicitly destroyed when they go out of scope. Rather, an object is marked as unused when there are no longer any references pointing to it. Even then, the **finalize( )** method will not be called until the garbage collector runs. Thus, you cannot know precisely when or where a call to **finalize( )** will occur. Even if you execute a call to **gc( )** (the garbage collector), there is no guarantee that **finalize( )** will immediately be executed.

While the deterministic behavior of a C++ constructor and the somewhat probabilistic aspect of finalization are of little concern in most cases, they will have an impact on others. For example, consider the following C++ program:

```cpp
// This C++ program can call f() indefinitely.
#include <iostream>
#include <cstdlib>
using namespace std;

const int MAX = 5;
int count = 0;

class X {
public:
  // constructor
  X() {
    if(count<MAX) {
      count++;
    }
    else {
      cout << "Error -- can't construct";
      exit(1);
    }
  }

  // destructor
  ~X() {
    count--;
  }
};

void f()
{
  X ob; // allocate an object
  // destruct on way out
}

int main()
{
  int i;

  for(i=0; i < (MAX*2); i++) {
    f();
```

```
      cout << "Current count is: " << count << endl;
  }

  return 0;
}
```

Here is the output generated by this program:

```
Current count is: 0
Current count is: 0
Current count is: 0
Current count is: 0
Current count is: 0
Current count is: 0
Current count is: 0
Current count is: 0
Current count is: 0
Current count is: 0
```

Look carefully at the constructor and destructor for **X**. The constructor increments the value of **count** as long as **count** is less than **MAX**. The destructor decrements **count**. Thus, **count** is incremented when an **X** object is created and decremented when an **X** object is destroyed. But no more than **MAX** objects can exist at any one time. However, in **main( )**, **f( )** is called **MAX***2 times without causing an error! Here is why. Inside **f( )**, an object of type **X** is created, causing **count** to be incremented, and then the function returns. This causes the object to immediately go out of scope and its destructor to be called, which decrements **count**. Thus, calling **f( )** has no net effect on the value of **count**. This means that it can be called indefinitely. However, this is not the case when this program is converted to Java.

Here is the Java version of the preceding program:

```
// This Java program will fail after 5 calls to f().

class X {
  static final int MAX = 5;
  static int count = 0;

  // constructor
  X() {
   if(count<MAX) {
     count++;
```

```
      }
   else  {
      System.out.println("Error -- can't construct");
      System.exit(1);
    }
  }

  // finalization
  protected void finalize() {
    count--;
  }

  static void f()
  {
    X ob = new X(); // allocate an object
    // destruct on way out
  }

  public static void main(String args[]) {
    int i;

    for(i=0; i < (MAX*2); i++) {
      f();
      System.out.println("Current count is: " + count);
    }
  }
}
```

This program will fail after five calls to **f( )**, as this output shows:

```
Current count is: 1
Current count is: 2
Current count is: 3
Current count is: 4
Current count is: 5
Error — can't construct
```

The reason the program fails is that garbage collection does not occur each time **f( )** returns. Thus, **finalize( )** is not invoked, and the value of **count** is not decremented. After five calls to the method, **count** reaches its maximum value and the program fails.

It is important to emphasize that precisely when garbage collection occurs is implementation dependent. It is possible that for some implementation of Java, on some platform, the preceding program will function similarly to its C++ version. However, the point of the example remains: In C++, you know when and where a destructor will be called. In Java, you do not know when or where **finalize( )** will be executed. Therefore, when porting code from C++ to Java, you will need to watch for instances in which the precise timing of the execution of a destructor is relied upon.

The
Complete
Reference

Java™ 2

Part IV

Applying Java

The Complete Reference

Java™ 2

Chapter 29

The DynamicBillboard Applet

obert Temple is a software engineer who has designed several highly used applets. His work includes the ESPNET SportsZone "HitCharts" and "Batter vs. Pitcher" applets. One of his most impressive applets is **DynamicBillboard**, which he wrote while he was at Embry-Riddle Aeronautical University in Florida.

The **DynamicBillboard** applet displays a sequence of images by repeatedly changing the image on the screen to another after a period of time. The transition between one image and the next is done with one of a variety of special effects. One example of a transition is the **SmashTransition**, where the new image drops down from above the old image and appears to smash the old image out of place. The applet links to other pages through a URL associated with each image. When the user presses the mouse button with the cursor over the applet, the browser will go to the new page associated with the current image. The **DynamicBillboard** applet provides web sites with an elegant way to rotate ads, banners, or billboards on a single static page.

Robert has included many interesting optimizations. This applet would not be functional without the careful changes that he crafted. There are enough tips and tricks in this source code to help you make your applets really fly.

The APPLET Tag

The APPLET tag for **DynamicBillboard** is fairly easy to configure. You name the main class in the code parameter and specify the width and height, as with most applets:

```
<applet code=DynamicBillboard width=392 height=72>
```

There are several parameters that must be specified for the applet to function properly. Without them the applet does nothing. Also, you will notice that if you make any mistakes naming files and such, the behavior is a little unfriendly: either nothing happens or some of your billboards will be blank. The following parameters are specified as:

```
<param name=parameter_name value="your value here">
```

- **bgcolor** This parameter is used to set the background color of the applet before the first image loads. You can use this to get rid of the gray applet square quickly.

- **delay** This parameter specifies the number of milliseconds between each billboard. Typically, it's a number like 5000 or 10000, meaning five or ten seconds.

- **billboards**   This parameter specifies the number of billboards you wish to cycle through.

- **bill#**   This is shorthand for **bill0**, **bill1**, **bill2**, and so on, up to one less than the number of billboards you've specified. (Robert is a typical programmer who starts counting at 0.) You will have as many of these as you specified in the **billboards** parameter. The value of each of these **bill#**s will be a pair of strings separated by a comma. The first one is the image name to display for this billboard. The second is the URL of where to go when the user clicks on this billboard. Here is an example:

```
<param name="bill0" value="sample.jpg,http://www.example.com/">
```

- **transitions**   This is a list beginning with the number of items in the list as an integer, followed by the list of **Transition** subclass names. Here is an example:

```
<param name="transitions" value="2,TearTransition,SmashTransition">
```

Here is an example of a complete APPLET tag with all of the transitions discussed in this chapter:

```
<applet code=DynamicBillboard width=392 height=72>
<param name="bgcolor" value="#ffffff">
<param name="delay" value="5000">
<param name="billboards" value="5">
<param name="bill0"
    value="board1.jpg,http://www.someURL">
<param name="bill1"
    value="board2.jpg,http://www.someURL">
<param name="bill2"
    value="board3.jpg,http://www.someURL">
<param name="bill3"
    value="board4.jpg,http://www.someURL">
<param name="bill4"
    value="board5.jpg,http://www.someURL">
<param name="transitions"
    value="5,ColumnTransition,FadeTransition,TearTransition,
                        SmashTransition,UnrollTransition">
</applet>
```

APPLYING JAVA

Source Code Overview

Robert designed the applet with a fast load time in mind. He tries to keep the size of the applet to a minimum so that there is less code to send across the network. He also attempts to delay some of the loading and initializing of the applet until after the first image is displayed. As far as the user is concerned, the applet is running after the first image is fully displayed, even though there is a lot more work to be done.

The applet consists of three main classes and any number of transition classes. The three main classes are **DynamicBillboard**, **BillData**, and **BillTransition**. The **DynamicBillboard** class is a top-level **Applet** subclass that uses all of the other classes. The **BillData** class encapsulates a number of billboard attributes, including the image and the URL associated with the image. The **BillTransition** class is an abstract class that contains methods and attributes common to all transitions. The three main classes are described next, along with five popular transitions.

DynamicBillboard.java

This is the main applet class. It implements **Runnable** to include a thread that controls the continuous process of creation and animation of the transitions. The **transition_classes** array stores the names of the transition classes as strings. It uses strings because it loads these classes dynamically using the method **java.lang.Class.forName(String)**. This allows the applet to put off the loading of these classes until they are first instantiated.

init( )

The **init( )** method is called automatically when the applet is first loaded. Most applets use this method to perform all of their necessary initialization. Robert, however, decided to separate his initialization into two methods: **init( )** and **finishInit( )**. The idea behind splitting up the initialization is to try to display the first image within the applet in the least amount of time, minimizing the time that the applet is showing a blank rectangle while it is loading and initializing. The only processing that is done in this **init( )** method is that which is absolutely necessary to get initial content to the screen, because the browser will not call **paint( )** until after **init( )** returns.

The first thing that Robert does with **init( )** is to change the background color of the applet and the parent frame in which the applet is embedded. In the past, the space that an applet uses on the screen was shown as a solid gray box while the applet was loading and initializing. This box would tend to stand out on pages that use a background color other than gray, which is just about every page created since 1994. Robert discovered a way around this problem. He found that applets always have a parent container in which they are embedded. Under both Netscape Navigator and Internet Explorer, this container is derived from the core Java class: **java.awt.Container**. Robert uses the methods inherited from **java.awt.Component**—setBackground( ) and repaint( )—to change the background color to the value of a **bgcolor** applet parameter. This makes the applet space stand out less than it does when it is gray. All this is done even before the applet begins to load the first image.

Note

With newer browsers, this frame no longer defaults to gray but rather uses the background color of the page. Thus, today applets will not benefit from changing the background color. However, this appoach still illustrates an interesting technique, which you can adapt for other purposes.

After changing background colors, Robert's applet reads in a parameter that tells how many different billboards there will be and then allocates an array of **BillData** objects based on this parameter.

With the help of **Math.random( )**, a random billboard is chosen to start. **parseBillData( )** is called to parse the parameters for this billboard.

parseBillData( )

This method creates and initializes the next billboard (**BillData**) object that the applet will use. It only gets called if the billboard object has not been created yet (the element corresponding to the next billboard object in the billboard array will be **null**).

Normally, **parseBillData( )** calls the **BillData** method **initPixels( )** after creating the new object to initialize a pixel array within the **BillData** object. The first time this method is called, however, the applet is still concentrating on getting the first image to the screen as fast as possible. It knows this because the reference to the image that is used to paint the applet is still **null**. So instead it sets the **image** variable and waits to call the processor-intensive **initPixel( )** method until after the first image is loaded.

finishInit( )

After the first image is displayed on the screen, the applet can finish the rest of its initialization. This includes initializing the names of all the transition classes and initializing the pixels array for the first billboard and reading the target parameter.

finishInit( ) is called from the **run( )** method of the applet. The **run( )** method restarts from the top each time the user leaves and comes back to the page. When this happens, **finishInit( )** will be called again. Since the applet has already finished its initialization, Robert does not want it to reinitialize everything. This is why the applet checks to see if the **delay** variable has already been initialized. If it has, then the applet can skip the rest of the initialization.

start( ) and stop( )

The **start( )** and **stop( )** methods respectively are called when the user comes to or leaves the page. They ensure that the applet thread that runs the transitions is on or off.

If **stop( )** is called while the applet is in the middle of running a transition, some data might be left in an improper state. Some variables are reset in **start( )** to make sure the applet restarts with a new transition.

In **start( )**, the mouse cursor is changed to a hand so that when the mouse cursor is over the applet, it will appear to be a link.

run( )

The **run( )** method starts with a loop that waits for the first image to be fully loaded before proceeding. It then finishes the initialization of the applet by calling **finishInit( )**. From there, it enters the main loop of the program.

This main loop drives the transitions between billboards. Using the delay parameter passed in from the HTML to the applet, the applet calculates when the next transition is supposed to be run. While it is waiting, it prepares for the transition. It starts the preparation by determining which billboard is to be displayed next, parsing the billboard data from HTML parameters if this has not been done yet for this billboard. Then it randomly chooses which transition to run next, being careful not to let the applet run the same transition consecutively.

Once the applet has determined what transition will be run next, it creates a new instance of this transition class by dynamically loading the class using the **String** name and then creating a new instance of the class. The dynamic loading of the transition classes has a big impact on the loading time of the applet as a whole. Instead of every single class having to be downloaded before the applet starts, only three classes are sent initially: **DynamicBillboard**, **BillData**, and **BillTransition**. The other transition classes are only downloaded by the applet the first time they are needed. This reduces the initial download of the applet significantly. Some class files might not even need to be sent if the user leaves the page quickly.

Finally, the applet calls the **init( )** method on the transition object, passing the applet and image pixels for the current and next billboard as parameters. This creates all the cell frames that are used to animate a transition. With the transition ready to go, the applet only need wait for the proper time to start the transition.

The applet performs the transition by using simple frame animation—drawing each cell in order onto the screen, with a short delay between each frame. The applet calls the toolkit method **sync( )** just to be sure that the drawing of one cell does not take place before the previous cell has been shown on the screen. After the last cell is displayed, the applet draws the image from the next billboard onto the screen to complete the transition.

Following this, the **mouse_over_applet** flag is checked to see if the mouse cursor is currently over the applet. If so, the URL of the previous billboard is showing on the status bar and must be updated to reflect the URL of the new billboard. This is done with a call to the applet method **showStatus( )**. The applet has completed this transition and is now ready to begin the next one.

mouseMoved( ) and mouseExited( )

mouseMoved( ) and **mouseExited( )** are used to change the text that appears on the status bar. When the mouse cursor is over the applet, the status bar is supposed to show the URL that the current billboard links to. So when **mouseMoved( )** gets called, the applet shows the URL on the status bar. When **mouseExited( )** is called, the URL text is removed from the status bar. Both methods also set the Boolean **mouse_inside_ applet** to the appropriate value. This variable is used in the **run( )** method after a transition is run. If the mouse is positioned over the applet when the transition completes, then the applet knows to show the URL of the new billboard on the status bar.

mouseReleased( )

When the mouse button is pressed with the cursor over the applet and then released, the **mouseReleased( )** method is called. The applet uses **getAppletContext( ).show--Document( )** to send the browser to the URL that the current billboard points to. As Robert found out, sometimes browsers take a long time to display this new page. To keep the applet from running more transitions while the new page is waiting to load, **stop( )** is called to force the main thread to quit. To let users know that the applet is loading the new page, the applet changes the mouse cursor to the wait cursor.

It is important to remember that users can come back to this page after going to a new page. The wait cursor will still be present on the applet when users come back. The **start( )** method is always called when the user comes back to a page with an applet, so the applet resets the cursor to the hand cursor there.

The Code

Here is the source code for the **DynamicBillboard** class:

```java
import java.awt.*;
import java.awt.event.*;
import java.net.*;
import java.awt.*;
import java.awt.image.*;

public class DynamicBillboard
        extends java.applet.Applet
        implements Runnable {

    BillData[] billboards;
    int current_billboard;
    int next_billboard;

    String[] transition_classes;
    Thread thread = null;
    Image image = null;
    long delay = -1;
    boolean mouse_inside_applet;
```

```java
String link_target_frame;
boolean stopFlag;

public void init() {
  String s = getParameter("bgcolor");
  if(s != null) {
    Color color = new Color(Integer.parseInt(s.substring(1), 16));
    setBackground(color);
    getParent().setBackground(color);
    getParent().repaint();
  }
  billboards = new
    BillData[Integer.parseInt(getParameter("billboards"))];
  current_billboard = next_billboard
                    = (int)(Math.random() *billboards.length);
  parseBillData();
}

void parseBillData() {
  String s = getParameter("bill" + next_billboard);
  int field_end = s.indexOf(",");
  Image new_image = getImage(getDocumentBase(),
                             s.substring(0, field_end));
  URL link;
  try {
    link = new URL(getDocumentBase(),
                   s.substring(field_end + 1));
  }
  catch (java.net.MalformedURLException e) {
    e.printStackTrace();
    link = getDocumentBase();
  }
  billboards[next_billboard] = new BillData(link, new_image);
  if(image == null) {
    image = new_image;
  }
  else {
    prepareImage(new_image, this);
    billboards[next_billboard].initPixels(getSize().width,
                                           getSize().height);
  }
}
```

```
}

void finishInit() {
  if(delay != -1) {
    return;
  }
  delay = Long.parseLong(getParameter("delay"));

  link_target_frame = getParameter("target");
  if(link_target_frame == null) {
    link_target_frame = "_top";
  }

  String s = getParameter("transitions");
  int field_end = s.indexOf(",");

  int trans_count = Integer.parseInt(s.substring(0, field_end));
  transition_classes = new String[trans_count];
  for(--trans_count; trans_count > 0; --trans_count) {
    s = s.substring(field_end + 1);
    field_end = s.indexOf(",");
    transition_classes[trans_count] = s.substring(0, field_end);
  }
  transition_classes[0] = s.substring(field_end + 1);
  billboards[next_billboard].initPixels(getSize().width,
                                        getSize().height);

  mouse_inside_applet = false;
}

public void paint(Graphics g) {
  g.drawImage(image, 0, 0, this);
}

public void update(Graphics g) {
  paint(g);
}

public void start() {
  next_billboard = current_billboard;
  image = billboards[current_billboard].image;
  setCursor(new Cursor(Cursor.HAND_CURSOR));
```

```
    if(thread == null) {
      thread = new Thread(this);
      thread.start();
    }
  }

  public void stop() {
    if(thread != null) {
      stopFlag = true;
    }
  }

  public void run() {
    while((checkImage(image, this) & ImageObserver.ALLBITS) == 0) {
      try { Thread.sleep(600); } catch (InterruptedException e) {}
    }
    finishInit();

    addMouseListener(new MyMouseAdapter());
    addMouseMotionListener(new MyMouseMotionAdapter());

    int last_transition_type = -1;
    BillTransition transition;
    long next_billboard_time;
    while(true) {
      if(stopFlag)
        return;
      next_billboard_time = System.currentTimeMillis() + delay;
      current_billboard = next_billboard;
      if(++next_billboard >= billboards.length) {
        next_billboard = 0;
      }
      if(billboards[next_billboard] == null) {
        parseBillData();
        try { Thread.sleep(120); } catch (InterruptedException e) {}
      }
      int transition_type = (int)(Math.random() *
                            (transition_classes.length - 1));
      if(transition_type >= last_transition_type) {
        ++transition_type;
```

```
    }
    last_transition_type = transition_type;

    try {
      String trans = transition_classes[last_transition_type];
      transition = (BillTransition)Class.forName(trans)
                                   .newInstance();

    }
    catch(Exception e) {
      e.printStackTrace();
      continue;
    }

    transition.init(this,billboards[current_billboard].image_pixels,
      billboards[next_billboard].image_pixels);

    if(System.currentTimeMillis() < next_billboard_time) {
      try {
        Thread.sleep(next_billboard_time -
                    System.currentTimeMillis());
      } catch (InterruptedException e) { };
    }
    Graphics g = getGraphics();
    for(int c = 0; c < transition.cells.length; ++c) {
      image = transition.cells[c];
      g.drawImage(image, 0, 0, null);
      getToolkit().sync();
      try { Thread.sleep(transition.delay); }
      catch(InterruptedException e) { };
    }
    image = billboards[next_billboard].image;
    g.drawImage(image, 0, 0, null);
    getToolkit().sync();
    g.dispose();
    if(mouse_inside_applet == true) {
      showStatus(billboards[next_billboard].link.toExternalForm());
    }
    transition = null;
    try { Thread.sleep(120); } catch (InterruptedException e) {}
  }
}
```

```
public class MyMouseAdapter extends MouseAdapter {
  public void mouseExited(MouseEvent me) {
    mouse_inside_applet = false;
    showStatus("");
  }
  public void mouseReleased(MouseEvent me) {
    stop();
    setCursor(new Cursor(Cursor.WAIT_CURSOR));
    getAppletContext().showDocument(billboards[current_billboard].link,
                                    link_target_frame);
  }
}
public class MyMouseMotionAdapter extends MouseMotionAdapter {
  public void mouseMoved(MouseEvent me) {
    mouse_inside_applet = true;
    showStatus(billboards[current_billboard].link.toExternalForm());
  }
}
}
```

BillData.java

The **BillData** class is mostly just a data structure for encapsulating attributes associated with individual billboards. It contains three variables. The first variable stores the **URL** to which the billboard is a link. The second variable has an **Image** that the applet uses to draw on the screen. The third variable includes a pixel array of the image in RGB format.

The pixel array is used by transitions in combination with another **BillData** pixel array to create the cells for transition animation. The array is only one-dimensional. The pixels in it are arranged in such a way that the first element in this array is the top-left corner of the image. The second element is the pixel just to the right of this corner. Elements that follow are the pixels to the right of this one, and so on, until the rightmost pixel is reached. Then the leftmost pixel on the next line of the image is used. This continues until the last index in the array, which corresponds to the pixel on the bottom-right corner of the image.

You might notice that Robert has made all of the variables in this class public. Normally, it is good programming practice to hide the data members that should be read only by other classes. This is done by making them protected or private and then creating functions to return references to the variables. Unfortunately, in Java this increases the size of the compiled bytecode even when the one line function is made

final and the code is compiled with optimizations. So to make the applet smaller and hence faster to download, Robert made the data members public.

The Constructor
The constructor for a **BillData** object simply initializes the **URL** and **Image** variables with the two parameters passed in. Initializing the pixel array is done in a separate method, because it is very processor-intensive. This gives the applet a chance to initialize the pixel array only when it needs it.

initPixels( )
The **initPixels( )** method creates the pixel array from the image using the Java core class: **java.awt.image.PixelGrabber**.

The Code
Here is the source code for the **BillData** class:

```
import java.net.*;
import java.awt.*;
import java.awt.image.*;

public class BillData {
   public URL link;
   public Image image;
   public int[] image_pixels;

   public BillData(URL link, Image image) {
     this.link = link;
     this.image = image;
   }

   public void initPixels(int image_width, int image_height) {
     image_pixels = new int[image_width * image_height];
     PixelGrabber pixel_grabber = new
     PixelGrabber(image.getSource(), 0, 0,
          image_width, image_height, image_pixels, 0, image_width);
     try {
       pixel_grabber.grabPixels();
     }
     catch (InterruptedException e) {
       image_pixels = null;
     }
```

```
        }
    }
```

BillTransition.java

The **BillTransition** class is used as a base class for other transition classes. These other classes create transition cells between two individual billboard images. This abstract class contains variables and methods that are common to all transitions.

There are no constructors provided in the **BillTransition** class. This is because the applet does not use "new" to create new instances and instead uses the factory method, **java.lang.Class.newInstance( )**. Objects created in this way have no way to directly initialize themselves using parameters in constructors. This factory method indirectly creates objects using a default constructor, one without any parameters. The **BillTransition** class provides a number of overloaded **init( )** methods to initialize instances with parameters.

In previous versions of **DynamicBillboard**, Robert used static variables within different transition classes to store data that only needed to be initialized once. It was discovered, however, that when more than one instance of the applet ran from a web server, the applets would share the static variables. This led to some problems if one applet needed a different static value than the other when the applets were different sizes. An example is the **FadeTransition** class used to create an array whose size depended on the dimensions of the applet. When another **DynamicBillboard** was created with dimensions that were smaller than the previous applet, it would overwrite this array with an array too small for the first applet. This would cause the first applet to crash.

Robert introduced the static hash table called **object_table** in this version of the applet to work around this problem. Now transition classes can store data inside this hash table using the transition name in conjunction with the applet size as a key. When this data needs to be used, the applet can look to see if it exists for the applet's size within the hash table. If it does not, then it can create the data and store it in the hash table for later use. Now if there is more than one applet on a web server and both are the same size, then only one has to initialize the data.

init( )

The **init( )** method is overloaded three times. The first method, which has three parameters, is abstract and must be overridden by classes derived from this class. The other two methods initialize data members within this class. Robert's intention was to have the **init( )** method of classes that are derived from this class call one of these two methods to initialize data members of **BillTransition**.

createCellFromWorkPixels( )

The **createCellFromWorkPixels( )** method is used to perform the common task of converting the **work_pixels** array into an **Image** object. Notice that it uses the **owner** variable to complete this task. This is the only reason the **owner** variable is needed by transition classes. When a transition has completed assembly of a new cell in the **work_pixels** array, it should call this method.

The Code

Here is the source code for the **BillTransition** class:

```java
import java.util.*;
import java.awt.*;
import java.awt.image.*;

public abstract class BillTransition {
  static Hashtable object_table = new Hashtable(20);

  public Image[] cells;
  public int delay;

  Component owner;
  int cell_w;
  int cell_h;
  int pixels_per_cell;
  int[] current_pixels;
  int[] next_pixels;
  int[] work_pixels;

  public abstract void
  init(Component owner, int[] current_pixels, int[] next_pixels);

  final protected void
  init(Component owner, int[] current_pixels, int[] next_pixels,
                        int number_of_cells, int delay) {
    this.delay = delay;
    this.next_pixels = next_pixels;
    this.current_pixels = current_pixels;
    this.owner = owner;

    cells = new Image[number_of_cells];
    cell_w = owner.getSize().width;
    cell_h = owner.getSize().height;
```

```
        pixels_per_cell = cell_w * cell_h;
        work_pixels = new int[pixels_per_cell];
    }

    final protected void
    init(Component owner, int[] current_pixels, int[] next_pixels,
                        int number_of_cells) {
        init(owner, current_pixels, next_pixels, number_of_cells, 120);
    }

    final void createCellFromWorkPixels(int cell) {
        cells[cell] = owner.createImage(
            new MemoryImageSource(cell_w, cell_h,
                                work_pixels, 0, cell_w));
        owner.prepareImage(cells[cell], null);
    }
}
```

ColumnTransition.java

The **ColumnTransition** class changes one image into another by drawing increasingly large columns of the new image onto the old image. The column sizes increase to the left, and the same pixels are always drawn on the left side of each column. This makes the billboard appear to be sliding in from behind the old billboard through vertical slots in the current billboard.

To create the cells for this transition, the billboard space is split up into a number of columns, each column 24 pixels wide. Each of the seven image cells the transition will create will have pixels on the left side of each column from the old image and pixels on the right side from the new image. The first cell that is created starts out with only the three right pixels in each column taken from the new image. With each successive cell, three more pixels are filled in from the new image. The last cell has only the three left pixels in each column from the old image.

Because the width of the image space is most likely not perfectly divisible by 24, there will be some remaining pixels remaining on the right side of the image. These pixels are accounted for in each cell with the **rightmost_columns_max_width** and **rightmost_columns_x_start** variables.

init( )

The **init( )** function starts by calling the base class' **init( )** method to initialize the variables contained within this base class. It goes on to initialize the variables associated with the rightmost column and then copies all of the pixels from the current billboard into the work pixels. The loop that follows creates all of the cell frames.

The **nextCell( )** method changes **work_pixels**, and the method inherited from the **BillTransition** class, **createCellFromWorkPixels( )**, is used to convert these pixels into an image. Because the process of creating the cells can be very demanding on the CPU, Robert tells the thread to sleep occasionally to allow other threads to run.

nextCell( )

The **nextCell( )** method modifies the **work_pixels** array for the next cell. It loops through each line of the image starting from the bottom line and fills part of each column by copying pixels from the next billboard onto the **work_pixels** array. It does not ever need to copy pixels from the old billboard, because these were already copied to the array in the **init( )** method.

It's worth repeating that the pixel arrays used to form the images are only one-dimensional. Every **width** pixel represents one horizontal line of the image.

The Code

Here is the source code for the **ColumnTransition** class:

```java
import java.awt.*;
import java.awt.image.*;

public class ColumnTransition extends BillTransition {
  final static int CELLS = 7;
  final static int WIDTH_INCREMENT = 3;
  final static int MAX_COLUMN_WIDTH = 24;

  int rightmost_columns_max_width;
  int rightmost_columns_x_start;
  int column_width = WIDTH_INCREMENT;

  public void init(Component owner, int[] current, int[] next) {
    init(owner, current, next, CELLS, 200);

    rightmost_columns_max_width = cell_w % MAX_COLUMN_WIDTH;
    rightmost_columns_x_start = cell_w - rightmost_columns_max_ width;

    System.arraycopy(current_pixels, 0,
                     work_pixels, 0, pixels_per_cell);

    for(int c = 0; c < CELLS; ++c) {
      try { Thread.sleep(100); } catch (InterruptedException e) {}
      NextCell();
```

```
    try { Thread.sleep(100); } catch (InterruptedException e) {}
    createCellFromWorkPixels(c);
    column_width += WIDTH_INCREMENT;
  }
  work_pixels = null;
}

void NextCell() {
  int old_column_width = MAX_COLUMN_WIDTH - column_width;
  for(int p = pixels_per_cell - cell_w; p >= 0; p -= cell_w) {
    for (int x = 0; x < rightmost_columns_x_start; x +=
        MAX_COLUMN_WIDTH) {
      System.arraycopy(next_pixels, x + p, work_pixels,
            old_column_width + x + p, column_width);
    }
    if(old_column_width <= rightmost_columns_max_width) {
      System.arraycopy(next_pixels, rightmost_columns_x_start + p,
                     work_pixels, rightmost_columns_x_start +
                                  old_column_width + p - 1,
                                  rightmost_columns_max_width -
                                  old_column_width + 1);
    }
  }
}
```

Here is what the column transition looks like before, during, and after:

FadeTransition.java

The **FadeTransition** class changes one image into another by randomly including a number of new pixels from the next billboard in each successive cell frame. This makes the next billboard appear to fade in over the old billboard.

The heart of this transition is a two-dimensional array of **short** integers called **random**. This array holds an index for every element in the next billboard's image pixel array. These indexes are randomly distributed in the two-dimensional array. The eight elements in the first dimension of this array will be used when cells are created, one for each new cell. The last element is never actually used, because there are only seven cells. It is included when the random array is created to ensure that the indexes are randomly distributed correctly.

The **FadeTransition** uses this array to pick pixels from the next billboard to overwrite pixels of the old billboard. For the first cell, the **work_pixels** array contains nothing but pixels from the old billboard. One-eighth of these pixels get changed to the next billboard's pixels. For the following cell, the same **work_pixels** array is used, and one-eighth more pixels are filled in from the next billboard. For this cell the result has one-fourth of the pixels from the next billboard, while the remainder are from the old billboard. This continues until the last cell, cell number seven, which has seven-eighths of its pixels from the new billboard. Remember, the **DynamicBillboard** applet simply uses the whole image from the next billboard after the last cell to complete the transition.

Because the size of this two-dimensional array is dependent on the size of the applet, it must be unique to each applet. Using a static variable to store this array is unacceptable, because applets of different sizes would share this array. Since it is fairly time-consuming to create this array, it does not make sense to re-create it every time this transition is to be used.

This is where the superclass' static variable, **object_table**, first comes into play. Once this array is created, it can be stored in this hash table with a key that includes the size of the applet. When the array needs to be used, the applet can get the appropriate one out of the hash table. If it does not exist in the hash table, the applet can then create the array and store it in the hash table for future use. New applets of the same size as the current applet will benefit from a usable array already being there. This seems like a lot of effort, but in practice, web sites tend to use this applet on a large number of pages with a standard layout size for each banner advertisement. So, it saves an enormous amount of memory and CPU time to cache these tables.

createRandomArray( )

The **createRandomArray( )** static method creates the two-dimensional random array. It takes two parameters that describe the size of the applet. It is highly optimized, because originally it was too slow. It includes its own random-number generator that is very fast, but with a short cycle. Because of this, it is fairly complicated and beyond the scope of this book. The basic idea is that Java's built-in random-number generator is better at generating truly random distribution, but it is too slow for this application. Plus, the user will not notice exactly how random this transition is, so Robert's home-grown random-number generator is sufficient.

init( )

The **init( )** method for this transition starts like all other transitions, with a call to the base class' **init( )** method. Then, like some other transitions, it copies all of the old billboard's pixels into the **work_pixels** array.

The two-dimensional random array is pulled out of the **object_table** for an applet of this size. If it does not exist yet, it is created and stored in the **object_table**. With the random array in hand, the method just loops through each cell and each index in the random array, copying pixels from the next billboard into the work pixels.

The Code

Here is the source code for the **FadeTransition** class:

```
import java.awt.*;
import java.awt.image.*;

public class FadeTransition extends BillTransition {
  private static final int CELLS = 7;
  private static final int MULTIPLIER = 0x5D1E2F;

  private static short[][] createRandomArray(int number_pixels,
                                             int cell_h) {
    int total_cells = CELLS + 1;
    int new_pixels_per_cell = number_pixels / total_cells;
    short[][] random = new short[total_cells][new_pixels_per_cell];
    int random_count[] = new int[total_cells];
    for(int s = 0; s < total_cells; ++s) {
      random_count[s] = 0;
    }

    int cell;
    int rounded_new_pixels_per_cell =
        new_pixels_per_cell * total_cells;
```

```
int seed = (int)System.currentTimeMillis();

int denominator = 10;
while((new_pixels_per_cell % denominator > 0 ||
  cell_h % denominator == 0) && denominator > 1) {
  --denominator;
}
int new_randoms_per_cell = new_pixels_per_cell / denominator;
int new_randoms = rounded_new_pixels_per_cell / denominator;

for(int p = 0; p < new_randoms_per_cell; ++p) {
  seed *= MULTIPLIER;
  cell = (seed >>> 29);
  random[cell][random_count[cell]++] = (short)p;
}
seed += 0x5050;
try { Thread.sleep(150); } catch (InterruptedException e) {}

for(int p = new_randoms_per_cell; p < new_randoms; ++p) {
  seed *= MULTIPLIER;
  cell = (seed >>> 29);

  while(random_count[cell] >= new_randoms_per_cell) {
    if(++cell >= total_cells) {
      cell = 0;
    }
  }
  random[cell][random_count[cell]++] = (short)p;
}

for(int s = 0; s < CELLS; ++s) {

  for(int ps = new_randoms_per_cell; ps < new_pixels_per_cell;
      ps += new_randoms_per_cell) {

    int offset = ps * total_cells;

    for(int p = 0; p < new_randoms_per_cell; ++p) {
      random[s][ps + p] = (short)(random[s][p] + offset);
    }
  }
}
```

```
      try { Thread.sleep(50); } catch (InterruptedException e) {}
    }
    random[CELLS] = null;
    return random;
  }

  public void init(Component owner, int[] current, int[] next) {
    init(owner, current, next, CELLS);
    System.arraycopy(current_pixels, 0, work_pixels,
                     0, pixels_per_cell);

    short random[][] = (short[][])object_table.get(
           getClass().getName() + pixels_per_cell);

    if(random == null) {
      random = createRandomArray(pixels_per_cell, cell_h);
      object_table.put(getClass().getName() + pixels_per_cell,
                       random);
    }

    for(int c = 0; c < CELLS; ++c) {
      try { Thread.sleep(100); } catch (InterruptedException e) {}
      int limit = random[c].length;
      for(int p = 0; p < limit; ++p) {
        int pixel_index = random[c][p];
        work_pixels[pixel_index] = next_pixels[pixel_index];
      }
      try { Thread.sleep(50); } catch (InterruptedException e) {}
      createCellFromWorkPixels(c);
    }
    work_pixels = null;
  }
}
```

Here is what the fade transition looks like before, during, and after:

SmashTransition.java

The **SmashTransition** class changes one image into another by dropping the new image onto the old one. The old image appears to crumble under the weight of the new image.

Two instance variables, **drop_amount** and **location**, are used to create the frames. The **location** variable keeps track of the pixel that the smashed image starts on. The **drop_amount** variable stores the number of pixels of the new image to drop onto the smashed image every frame. In other words, it is the number to add to the **location** variable each frame. A static array called **fill_pixels** is used to color a whole line of the **work_pixels** array white.

The smash effect is done by drawing the old image in an accordion-like fashion. It starts out by drawing the first lines of the old image offset to the right. Each progressive line is offset a little bit more to the right. This continues until some maximum left offset is reached. At this point, the offset is reduced every line until an offset of zero is reached. This continues until all of the lines of the smashed image are drawn.

It does not draw the lines from the old image in their entirety. It uses a length that is a bit shorter than the actual length.

The number of lines to draw for the smashed image decreases each frame as the old billboard becomes more and more compacted. This transition uses lines that are evenly distributed across the old image. This ensures that the smashed image does not appear to be falling off the bottom of the applet or sliding under the new image.

setupFillPixels( )

The **setupFillPixels( )** static method is used to ensure that the **fill_pixels** array is initialized and is at least as long as one whole line for this applet. If this array has not been initialized yet or is not long enough for this applet, then this method respectively re-creates or creates and fills in the array. If there is more than one instance of this applet running, both can share this **fill_pixels** array, but it must be at least as long as the widest applet.

init( )

The **init( )** method for this transition starts like all other transitions, with a call to the base class' **init( )** method. It follows this with a call to the method described earlier, **setupFillPixels( )**. The initial values of the **drop_amount** and **location** variables are then calculated. After this, the **init( )** method goes into a loop to create each frame. It actually does this in reverse, creating the last frame first. It does not have to be done in reverse. However, running loops in reverse saves one byte of code in the resulting class file. After each cell is created, the **location** variable is incremented to the next proper location.

Smash( )

The **Smash( )** method modifies the **work_pixels** array for the next cell. It creates the smashed image of the old billboard in the **work_pixels** array and draws in the pixels for the new image. This method takes one parameter, **max_fold**, which is used as the maximum right offset that the lines in the fold will have. It is also used by subtracting this from the line width to determine the length of the lines to draw for the folds.

The method begins by copying the pixels from the new image onto **work_ pixels**. It then initializes a number of variables that it uses to draw the smashed image. The drawing of this smashed image is done line by line, in a loop. Within the loop, it first makes the current line totally white. It then copies a portion of the correct line from the old billboard over this line. To get the accordion effect, it does not start drawing onto the same pixel location as it did for drawing the white line. It instead offsets the destination pixels to the right by a few pixels. After drawing in the line, it adds a number to the offset counter. It follows this with a bounds check to see if the offset has gone beyond the minimum or maximum offset. If it has, it flips the sign of the number it adds to the offset counter each line. The effect of this is that the direction of the offset is reversed.

The Code

Here is the source code for the **SmashTransition** class:

```
import java.awt.*;
import java.awt.image.*;

public class SmashTransition extends BillTransition {
   final static int CELLS = 8;
   final static float FOLDS = 8.0f;
   static int[] fill_pixels;

   static void setupFillPixels(int width) {
      if(fill_pixels != null && fill_pixels.length <= width) {
         return;
```

```
    }
    fill_pixels = new int[width];
    for(int f = 0; f < width; ++f) {
      fill_pixels[f] = 0xFFFFFFFF;
    }
  }

  int drop_amount;
  int location;

  public void init(Component owner, int[] current, int[] next) {
    init(owner, current, next, CELLS, 160);
    setupFillPixels(cell_w);
    drop_amount =  (cell_h / CELLS) * cell_w;
    location = pixels_per_cell - ((cell_h / CELLS) / 2) * cell_w;
    for(int c = CELLS - 1; c >= 0; --c) {
      try { Thread.sleep(100); } catch (InterruptedException e) {}
      Smash(c + 1);
      try { Thread.sleep(150); } catch (InterruptedException e) {}
      createCellFromWorkPixels(c);
      location -= drop_amount;
    }
    work_pixels = null;
  }

  void Smash(int max_fold) {
    System.arraycopy(next_pixels, pixels_per_cell - location,
                     work_pixels, 0, location);
    int height = cell_h - location / cell_w;
    float fold_offset_adder = (float)max_fold * FOLDS / (float)height;
    float fold_offset = 0.0f;
    int fold_width = cell_w - max_fold;
    float src_y_adder = (float)cell_h / (float)height;
    float src_y_offset = cell_h - src_y_adder / 2;
    for(int p = pixels_per_cell - cell_w; p >= location; p -=
        cell_w) {
      System.arraycopy(fill_pixels, 0, work_pixels, p, cell_w);
      System.arraycopy(current_pixels, (int)src_y_offset * cell_w,
                       work_pixels, p + (int)fold_offset, fold_width);
      src_y_offset -= src_y_adder;
      fold_offset += fold_offset_adder;
```

```
        if(fold_offset < 0.0 || fold_offset >= max_fold) {
          fold_offset_adder *= -1.0f;
        }
      }
    }
  }
```

Here is what the smash transition looks like before, during, and after:

TearTransition.java

The **TearTransition** creates the illusion of the current billboard getting torn off the applet like a piece of paper. It gets ripped upwards and toward the left to reveal the next billboard image underneath.

There is only one member variable used in this transition, **x_cross**. It is used as a multiplier to create the tear effect. The larger the value of this variable, the smaller the tear effect will appear to be.

The code for this transition has many optimizations. One optimization of significance is to create the cell frames in reverse order, building the last cell frame first and the first, last. In their normal order, each subsequent cell frame reveals a little bit more of the new image underneath. If the frames were to be created in the normal order, the tear effect would have to be drawn, along with the new image pixels revealed in the current frame, which had been covered by the tearing effect in the previous frame. Doing it in reverse only requires redrawing the tearing effect each cell frame. For example, the last frame, created first, starts out with the tearing effect using only a small portion of the upper-left corner of the image, while the rest of the pixels are taken from the new billboard image. In the second to the last frame, which is created second, the new tear effect draws over a little bit more of the upper-left corner of the image, while the rest of the image remains the same. The cell frames that follow draw the new tear effect over more and more of the image, but always covering up the old tear effect from the last frame.

init( )

The **init( )** method for this transition starts like all other transitions, with a call to the base class' **init( )** method. It then copies all of the new billboard's pixels into the **work_pixels** array and copies the first line of the old billboard's pixels onto the first line of the **work_pixels** array. After the **x_cross** variable is initialized, the **init( )** method loops through each cell frame in reverse order. Inside the loop, it creates each cell frame and decreases the value of the **x_cross** variable.

Tear( )

The **Tear( )** method modifies the **work_pixels** array for the next cell. It draws the tear effect onto the work pixels. It draws the tear effect line by line. To draw one line, the method copies pixels from the old image pixels into the **work_pixels** array. It uses two counters, one that is an index into the **work_pixels** array, the *destination*, and one that references an index into the array of pixels for the old billboard, the *source*. Both counters are started at zero. The destination counter is always incremented by one. The source counter, however, is incremented by a floating-point number that is always greater than one. When the loop is run until the destination index is larger than the width of the line, the result is the source index growing faster than the destination index. The overall effect is that in the destination, only a number of pixels on the left side of the image will be copied from the source. The pixels taken from the source will skip some pixels, resulting in pixels taken from the source being evenly distributed across the line.

Each line of the cell frame will use a larger value for the floating-point number on the line above. This makes lines toward the bottom draw on fewer pixels for the tear effect than lines toward the top.

This method has one big optimization that it uses to get around the slow array indexing in Java. Whenever a element in an array is used, bounds checking is done to ensure that the index is within the bounds of the array. There is a performance hit involved in this bounds checking. The standard Java class, **System**, provides a method that allows you to copy sections of arrays from one array to another almost as fast or as fast as copying one array element into another. This method is used to speed up the creation lines within the cell frames. It only uses this method when the applet knows some of the source pixels will be adjacent to one another. If the applet skips at least every other pixel from the source image, then it will use the standard loop method. An **x_increment** value less than 0.5 indicates that less than 1.5 will be added to the source index counter each time, and there will be a speed benefit from using the array copy method for a particular line.

The Code

Here is the source code for the **TearTransition** class:

```java
import java.awt.*;
import java.awt.image.*;
public class TearTransition extends BillTransition {
  static final int CELLS = 7;
  static final float INITIAL_X_CROSS = 1.6f;
  static final float X_CROSS_DIVISOR = 3.5f;
  float x_cross;

  public void init(Component owner, int[] current, int[] next) {
    init(owner, current, next, CELLS);
    System.arraycopy(next_pixels, 0, work_pixels, 0,
                     pixels_per_cell);
    System.arraycopy(current_pixels, 0, work_pixels, 0, cell_w);

    x_cross = INITIAL_X_CROSS;

    for(int c = CELLS - 1; c >= 0; --c) {
      try { Thread.sleep(100); } catch (InterruptedException e) {}
      Tear();
      try { Thread.sleep(150); } catch (InterruptedException e) {}
      createCellFromWorkPixels(c);
      x_cross /= X_CROSS_DIVISOR;
    }
    work_pixels = null;
  }

  final void Tear() {
    float x_increment;
    int p, height_adder;

    p = height_adder = cell_w;
    for (int y = 1; y < cell_h; ++y) {
      x_increment = x_cross * y;
      if(x_increment >= 0.50f) {
        float fx = 0.0f;
```

```
      x_increment += 1.0f;
      int x = 0;
      do {
        work_pixels[p++] = current_pixels[height_adder + x];
        x = (int)(fx += x_increment);
      } while(x < cell_w);
  }
  else {
    float overflow = 1.0f / x_increment;
    float dst_end = overflow / 2.0f + 1.49999999f;
    int dst_start = 0, src_offset = 0, length = (int)dst_end;
    while(dst_start + src_offset + length < cell_w) {
      System.arraycopy(current_pixels, p + src_offset,
                        work_pixels, p, length);
      ++src_offset;
      dst_end += overflow;
      p += length;
      dst_start += length;
      length = (int)dst_end - dst_start;
    }
    length = cell_w - src_offset - dst_start;
    System.arraycopy(current_pixels, p + src_offset,
                      work_pixels, p, length);
  }
  p = height_adder += cell_w;
  }
 }
}
```

Here is what the tear transition looks like before, during, and after:

UnrollTransition.java

UnrollTransition makes it appear as if a rolled-up poster is placed on the bottom of the applet and then unrolled upward, gradually revealing the next image and covering the old image. To enhance the unroll illusion, the roll gradually decreases in size as it makes its way upward on the billboard.

Two instance variables are used during the creation of unroll transitions. The **location** variable references pixels within the pixel arrays. It stores the current pixel that the roll first appears on. The **unroll_amount** array variable tells the class how many vertical pixels the roll should move upward each frame.

The most difficult part of creating each cell frame is drawing the roll. The only other task that needs to be completed each frame is to draw the pixels from the new image onto the space vacated by the roll from the previous frame.

The roll is drawn with scan lines from the new image. The first line of the roll is drawn with the scan line located at the Y coordinate above the roll's Y coordinate on the applet. For example, if the roll is located on line ten for a particular cell frame, then line nine of the new image will be used to draw the first line of the roll. Each subsequent line of the roll is drawn using a line from the image located above the previous line of the new image. So, continuing the example, the second line of the roll will be drawn using line eight of the new image.

The roll is painted with its 3-D appearance by drawing each line of the roll with a slight offset to the left. Lines closer to the center of the roll are drawn with a larger offset than lines close to the top and bottom. The top and bottom lines of the rolls are then shaded to make it look as if a light were above the applet. This results in the top line being a bit brighter than the rest of the roll and the bottom line being a bit darker.

createUnrollAmountArray( )

Each consecutive cell frame in this transition unrolls the roll onto the applet a little bit less than the previous cell frame. The **createUnrollAmountArray( )** static method is used to calculate an array that indicates how much each cell frame should unroll the roll.

init( )

The **init( )** method for this transition starts like all other transitions, with a call to the base class' **init( )** method. Then the **location** variable is initialized to an index past the last pixel in a pixel array. This is followed by copying all of the old billboard's pixels into the **work_pixels** array.

An array that stores the number of pixels to unroll each frame is pulled out of the object_table for an applet of this height. If it does not exist in the hash table, it is created and stored in the **object_table**.

Then the **init( )** method loops through each cell, moving the roll upward by subtracting from the **location** variable and drawing each cell frame. It makes the current thread take a break before and after the processor-intensive cell frame creation, to allow other threads in Java's multitasking environment to execute. After the cell frame is created from the **work_pixels** array with the call to the **createCellFromWorkPixels( )** method, the area the roll was on is drawn over with pixels from the new image. This prepares the **work_pixels** array for the next cell frame.

Unroll( )

The **Unroll( )** method modifies the **work_pixels** array for the next cell. It draws the roll onto the work pixels. This method first calculates the offset that it needs to use for drawing each line of the roll. It then loops through each line of the roll, copying scan lines from the new image onto the **work_pixels** array. The pixels that are exposed due to the left offset of each line are filled in with pixels from the static **fill_pixels** array.

Another loop then increments though each pixel on the top and the bottom lines of the roll, brightening pixels on the top line and darkening pixels on the bottom line.

The Code

Here is the source code for the **UnrollTransition** class:

```
import java.awt.*;
import java.awt.image.*;

public class UnrollTransition extends BillTransition {
  final static int CELLS = 9;
  static int fill_pixels[] = { 0xFFFFFFFF, 0xFF000000,
                               0xFF000000, 0xFFFFFFFF };

  private static int[] createUnrollAmountArray(int cell_h) {
    float unroll_increment =
      ((float)cell_h / (float)(CELLS + 1)) /
      ((float)(CELLS + 2) / 2.0f);

    int total = 0;
    int unroll_amount[] = new int[CELLS + 1];
    for(int u = 0; u <= CELLS; ++u) {
      unroll_amount[u] = (int)(unroll_increment * (CELLS - u + 1));
      total += unroll_amount[u];
    }
```

```
    if(total < 0) {
      unroll_amount[0] -= 1;
    }
    return unroll_amount;
}

int location;
int[] unroll_amount;
public void init(Component owner, int[] current, int[] next) {
  init(owner, current, next, CELLS, 220);
  location = pixels_per_cell;
  System.arraycopy(current_pixels, 0,
                   work_pixels, 0, pixels_per_cell);
  unroll_amount = (int[])object_table.get(getClass().getName() +
                   cell_h);
  if(unroll_amount == null) {
    unroll_amount = createUnrollAmountArray(cell_h);
    object_table.put(getClass().getName() + cell_h, unroll_amount);
  }

  for(int c = 0; c < CELLS; ++c) {
    location -= unroll_amount[c] * cell_w;
    try { Thread.sleep(150); } catch (InterruptedException e) {}
    Unroll(c);
    try { Thread.sleep(100); } catch (InterruptedException e) {}
    createCellFromWorkPixels(c);
    System.arraycopy(next_pixels, location,
                     work_pixels, location,
                     unroll_amount[c] * cell_w);
  }
  work_pixels = null;
}

void Unroll(int c) {
  int y_flip = cell_w;
  int offset[] = new int[unroll_amount[c]];
  for(int o = 0; o < unroll_amount[c]; ++o) {
    offset[o] = 4;
  }
  offset[0] = 2;
```

```
if(unroll_amount[c] > 1) {
  offset[1] = 3;
}
if(unroll_amount[c] > 2) {
  offset[unroll_amount[c] - 1] = 2;
}
if(unroll_amount[c] > 3) {
  offset[unroll_amount[c] - 2] = 3;
}

int offset_index = 0;
int end_location = location + unroll_amount[c] * cell_w;
for(int p = location; p < end_location; p += cell_w) {

  System.arraycopy(next_pixels,
                   p - y_flip + offset[offset_index],
                   work_pixels,
                   p, cell_w - offset[offset_index]);

  System.arraycopy(fill_pixels, 0,
                   work_pixels,
                   p + cell_w - offset[offset_index],
                   offset[offset_index]);

  ++offset_index;
  y_flip += cell_w + cell_w;
}

for(int x = location + cell_w - 1; x > location; --x) {
  work_pixels[x] |= 0xFFAAAAAA;
  work_pixels[x + unroll_amount[c]] &= 0xFF555555;
}
}
}
```

APPLYING JAVA

Here is what the unroll transition looks like before, during, and after:

Dynamic Code

Robert has shown us how to create interactive high-performance graphics by working around many of the apparent limitations in Java. He shows how to use **System.arraycopy( )** to effectively shuffle pixel data around. He shows how to properly use cooperative multithreading to do computation and network transfers in the background while the user isn't waiting. Robert proves that high-performance direct pixel manipulation algorithms can be efficiently written in Java if you are careful.

In addition to containing interesting code, **DynamicBillboard** is a very compelling applet for nonprogrammers and users alike. It is easily configured by HTML editors, extensible by Java programmers, and entertaining to web users. In this age of advertising rates being driven by "click-through," where advertisers only want to pay for transfers from a content site to their site, Robert's applet can be used to increase traffic and ultimately increase revenue.

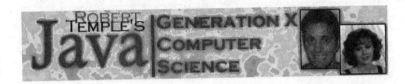

The
Complete
Reference

Java™ 2

Chapter 30

ImageMenu: An Image-Based Web Menu

The **ImageMenu** applet is a simple program that presents an image-based menu with an arbitrary number of choices in a vertical list. When the user moves the mouse cursor over these choices, the one under the cursor changes appearance, indicating that it can be clicked on. When the user clicks on a choice, the web browser changes to a new document specified for that choice. **ImageMenu** was created by David LaVallée, the creator of several interesting applets. Figure 30-1 shows an instance of **ImageMenu**.

ImageMenu uses the **showDocument( )** function in **AppletContext** to make the hypertext leap to the new pages. The novelty of **ImageMenu** is that it uses different portions of a single source image to draw the menu on the screen. Basing a menu on an image rather than on text frees you to design menus that use any font or image you desire. You can also provide various types of selection feedback. You no longer need to rely on the AWT's limited rendering functions.

Figure 30-1.   *An example of* ImageMenu

The **ImageMenu** applet was inspired by an applet called **Navigation**, created by top-notch Java programmer Sean Welch. The difference between **Navigation** and **ImageMenu** is efficiency in bandwidth and applet tag specification. The **Navigation** applet uses a source image that is the applet's width times the number of possible selections wide to display all of its states. Both applets download a single image, which is much more efficient over the Internet than loading multiple files. A menu of seven choices for the **Navigation** applet (100×140 pixels) would require a source image of 700×140. The applet described here, **ImageMenu**, uses a source image that is two times the applet width, or 200×140. Most web designers hate typing when they don't have to, which leads to the second significant difference between **Navigation** and **ImageMenu**: abbreviated applet parameters.

While **ImageMenu** is many times more efficient, using a smaller source image and fewer bytes of parameters, Welch's **Navigation** has one inimitable trait—it can display individually selected "states" that bleed over into the space of the next menu item. The **ImageMenu** applet requires that each menu item be self-contained in a rectangular area that cannot overlap with adjacent items. This would prohibit, for example, ascending letters (like *h*) from overlapping descending letters (such as *j*) in the line above.

The Source Image

While you won't see the code for **Navigation** here, looking at its GIF image shows clearly what it does. The source image for **Navigation** in Figure 30-2 shows seven columns, each of which provides a visual representation of a possible selection. However, each selectable item only has two states, so each row has five redundant copies of the unselected state.

The source image for **ImageMenu** is shown in Figure 30-3. Given this image, it is simple to render any of the seven possible states of a six-choice menu. First, **drawImage( )** displays the left half of the source image. This is the state where no items are selected. If any of the items is selected, then the clipping rectangle is simply set to the bounds of the selected item, and **drawImage( )** is used to display the right-hand side. This will paint just the selected cell through the clipping rectangle.

Figure 30-2. *The source image for the* Navigation *applet*

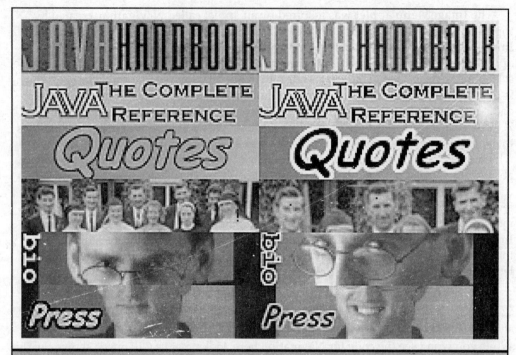

Figure 30-3.   *The source image for* ImageMenu

The APPLET Tag

The APPLET tag for **ImageMenu** contains many pieces of information. We will
use **java.util.StringTokenizer** to read the **urlList** and the frame **targetList** parameters
whose values are plus sign–delimited lists of values. We'll also infer the coordinates of
each menu item by dividing the height of the applet by the number of URLs parsed in
urlList. For readability in the APPLET tag, we also allow a prefix and suffix, which will
be concatenated with a URL when it's time to move to a new page.

```
<applet code="ImageMenu" width=140 height=180 hspace=0 vspace=0>
<param name="img" value="menu.jpg">
<param name="urlPrefix"
          value="http://www.osborne.com/">
<param name="urlList"
          value="pressroom/pressroom.shtml+aboutus/aboutus.shtml+
```

```
                        downloads/downloads.shtml+errata/errata.shtml">
<param name="targetList"
          value="_self+_self+_self+_self+_self+_self">
<param name="urlSuffix" value="">
</applet>
```

The Methods

This is a small applet—about 100 lines of Java source. We will walk through all eight methods here and then show all the source together at the end of the chapter.

init( )

When the applet is being initialized, **init( )** saves the size in the **Dimension** variable **d** and parses the applet **param** tags. It then uses a **StringTokenizer** to parse strings delimited by the plus sign to create the string arrays **url** and **target**. The number of URLs that are parsed is the number that is used to divide the vertical space into menu cells. From this calculation, **init( )** saves the number and height of the cells in **cells** and **cellH**, respectively.

update( )

We nullify the **update( )** method of **Applet** to avoid flashing. As mentioned in Chapter 23, the **update( )** method in the **Applet** superclass fills a rectangle with the background color before calling **paint( )**. Since we're not going to use **repaint( )**, we can just eliminate update completely.

lateInit( )

The **lateInit( )** private method creates the offscreen **Image** object that will be used for double buffering the display of the menu. This method also employs a **MediaTracker** object to synchronously get the source image.

paint( )

The **paint( )** method is quite simple. First, it checks to see if the offscreen buffer has been created yet. If it hasn't, **lateInit( )** is called to create the buffer and load the menu image.

After that, it draws the left half of the image on the offscreen buffer. This requires, of course, that the menu image be twice the width of the applet. That way, the applet will simply clip away the right half of the menu image when **drawImage(img, 0, 0, null)** is called. Then, if any cell is selected (**selectedCell >= 0**), it sets the clip rectangle to the bounds of that menu item. You'll notice that **paint( )** gets the graphics context of the offscreen image every time. This has the effect of resetting the clipping rectangle to the bounds of the image. AWT's lack of a **resetClip( )** method requires some strange coding style.

Next, the entire image is painted again, but this time, it is offset by the width of the applet to the left, via **drawImage(img, -d.width, 0, null)**. This has the effect of placing just the right highlighted menu item in the clip rectangle. Lastly, the offscreen buffer is copied to the applet window.

<table>
<tr><td>**Note**</td><td>*The speed of most graphic displays is largely throttled by the speed of the CPU's access directly to the screen. Additionally, many modern display cards are optimized for copying rectangular areas from memory to the display in support of windowing systems. Therefore, you are much better off doing all your drawing on an offscreen buffer rather than copying the bits to the screen. On similar PC systems, we have seen between 10 and 400 buffer changes a second, depending on pixel depth and display card architecture.*</td></tr>
</table>

mouseExited( )

Special handling is needed for **mouseExited( )**, because it causes all of the menu items to be unselected. All we have to do is set **selectedCell** and **oldCell** to –1, which makes the subsequent **paint( )** call show all the items as unselected. Having **oldCell** set to –1 means that the next time the mouse enters the applet and causes a **mouseMoved( )** call, the first item will paint properly.

mouseDragged( )

The **mouseDragged( )** method is called when the mouse moves with any of its buttons pressed. In this applet, we want to do the same thing on drag or move, so we just call **mouseMoved( )** directly, passing in the same parameters we received.

mouseMoved( )

Whenever the mouse moves, **mouseMoved( )** checks the **y** coordinate to see which of the cells was selected. If the **selectedCell** is different from **oldCell**, meaning the user moved from one cell to another, the menu is repainted. This is an optimization that avoids the constant repainting of identical screen bits every time the mouse moves. You will notice that **repaint( )** is not called here. We are taking a shortcut through the normal applet protocol by calling **paint( )** directly after fetching the **Graphics** context from getGraphics( ). This makes for a much snappier response. After the menu is painted, the status line is set to reflect the newly selected item, which is also saved in **oldCell**.

mouseReleased( )

mouseReleased( ) sends the browser to the URL that corresponds to the currently selected menu item. The desired URL is then constructed. If the URL was improperly formatted in the APPLET tag, the exception is displayed on the status line and returned without attempting to switch documents. The **showDocument( )** method puts the document described in the URL into the frame listed in the **target** array. As a final feature, the state of this SHIFT key is checked by calling the **isShiftDown( )** method of **MouseEvent**. If SHIFT was pressed, the URL is opened into a new blank browser window instead of the one specified in **target**.

The Code

The source code for **ImageMenu** is shown here:

```
import java.awt.* ;
import java.awt.event.*;
import java.applet.*;
import java.util.*;
import java.net.*;

public class ImageMenu extends Applet {
  Dimension d;

  Image img, off;
  Graphics offg;
  int MAXITEMS = 64;
  String url[] = new String[MAXITEMS];
  String target[] = new String[MAXITEMS];
  String urlPrefix, urlSuffix;
  int selectedCell = -1;
  int oldCell = -1;
  int cellH;
  int cells;

  public void init() {
    d = getSize();
    urlPrefix = getParameter("urlPrefix");
```

```
      urlSuffix = getParameter("urlSuffix");
      StringTokenizer st;
      st = new StringTokenizer(getParameter("urlList"), "+");
      int i=0;
      while(st.hasMoreTokens() && i < MAXITEMS)
          url[i++] = st.nextToken();
      cells = i;
      cellH = d.height/cells;
      st = new StringTokenizer(getParameter("targetList"), "+");
      i=0;
      while(st.hasMoreTokens() && i < MAXITEMS)
        target[i++] = st.nextToken();
      addMouseListener(new MyMouseAdapter());
      addMouseMotionListener(new MyMouseMotionAdapter());
    }

    private void lateInit() {
      off = createImage(d.width, d.height);
      try {
        img = getImage(getDocumentBase(), getParameter("img"));
        MediaTracker t = new MediaTracker(this);
        t.addImage(img, 0);
        t.waitForID(0);
      } catch(Exception e) {
        showStatus("error: " + e);
      }
    }

    public void update(Graphics g) {}
    public void paint(Graphics g) {
      if(off == null)
        lateInit();

      offg = off.getGraphics();
      offg.drawImage(img, 0, 0, this);
      if (selectedCell >= 0) {
        offg.clipRect(0, selectedCell * cellH, d.width, cellH)
        offg.drawImage(img, -d.width, 0, this);
      }
```

```
      g.drawImage(off, 0, 0, this);
  }

class MyMouseMotionAdapter extends MouseMotionAdapter {
  public void mouseDragged(MouseEvent me) {
    mouseMoved(me);
  }
  public void mouseMoved(MouseEvent me) {
    int y = me.getY();
    selectedCell = (int)(y/(double)d.height*cells);
    if (selectedCell != oldCell) {
      paint(getGraphics());
      showStatus(urlPrefix + url[selectedCell] + urlSuffix);
      oldCell = selectedCell;
    }
  }
}

class MyMouseAdapter extends MouseAdapter {
  public void mouseExited(MouseEvent me) {
    selectedCell = oldCell = -1;
    paint(getGraphics());
    showStatus("");
  }

  public void mouseReleased(MouseEvent me) {
    URL u = null;
    try {
      u = new URL(urlPrefix + url[selectedCell] + urlSuffix);
    } catch(Exception e) {
      showStatus("error: " + e);
    }

    if (me.isShiftDown())
      getAppletContext().showDocument(u, "_blank");
    else
      getAppletContext().showDocument(u, target[selectedCell]);
  }
}
}
```

Summary

In use, the **ImageMenu** applet can look great and it provides a lot of leverage for a very small program. Use of the **showDocument(URL u, String target)** in this applet allows for a subtle optimization in web page design. If you put an **ImageMenu** applet in a frame in an HTML frameset and use it to send documents to a second frame, the applet never has to be reloaded, which makes the user's experience better.

The
Complete
Reference

Java™ 2

Chapter 31

The Lavatron Applet:
A Sports Arena Display

avatron is a sports arena lightbulb display. Normally, an applet doesn't have much of a history, but this one does. David LaVallée, the author of the ImageMenu applet from Chapter 30, wanted to achieve this kind of effect for a long time. The history of **Lavatron** begins way back in 1974, when LaVallée was the stick boy for the California Golden Seals of the NHL. David recalls, "Our scoreboard just displayed, well, the score. The game was the thing; there wasn't much to distract hockey fans other than the dah-dah-dah-dat-dah-dah of the organ player."

In 1979, LaVallée became fascinated with the idea of a graphical programmable scoreboard when he was the repair guy for the Digital Equipment Corporation PDP 11/34 that ran the scoreboard at the Canadian National Exhibition Stadium (where the Toronto Blue Jays used to play). That scoreboard was based on plain old 100-watt lightbulbs like you use at home. In 1991, Toronto was treated to the Sony Jumbotron HDTV scoreboard at the Skydome: true color, images, video, and three times the height of the Hard Rock Cafe. In 1992, LaVallée wrote the first version of **Lavatron** in Objective-C and PostScript. Finally, in 1995, **Lavatron** was written again from scratch to run under Java, and it has undergone several performance tweaks and iterations since. The version shown here has been updated for Java 2.

There are many possible enhancements to **Lavatron** (see Figure 31-1) that you might want to try, such as drawing the source image dynamically in memory rather than downloading it, or scrolling an animated sequence. But it's an interesting animated display applet that you may find useful as is.

Figure 31-1. *The* Lavatron *applet in action. The source image contains a bitmap of the title* Java 2: The Complete Reference *on a white background.*

How Lavatron Works

Lavatron is able to present an interesting image onscreen because of a small trick that it employs, and its side effect allows the applet to load very quickly. The reason it loads so quickly is that there isn't much data transmitted over the Net. The source image is a JPEG image that is 64 times smaller than the displayed image. Each pixel in the source image is scaled up to an 8×8-pixel square. Here is the trick that **Lavatron** uses to produce the lightbulb effect. An 8×8-pixel image of a transparent circle surrounded by a black bezel, with a white highlight for a dash of style, is painted over the scaled-up color pixel. As an optimization, the bulbs are preassembled into an image that can be painted once for each column. Figure 31-2 shows what the bulb mask looks like blown up. The two white pixels are the highlight. The black pixels in the corner are opaque. Finally, all of the gray pixels in the middle are transparent, to allow the lightbulb color to show through.

Lavatron paints so fast because it doesn't have to repaint what it has already drawn. The technique of *copying* the area of the screen that's good and *painting* just the portion that's new is used in many common operations involving scrolling. The **awt.Graphics** function **copyArea( )** takes a portion of an image defined by a rectangle and moves it by an **x,y** offset from its starting location. As a graphics speed optimization, **copyArea( )** is hard to beat. It consistently outperforms any other technique of image rendering, such as the use of **drawImage( )**, or **drawImage( )** through a **clipRect( )**. Building an

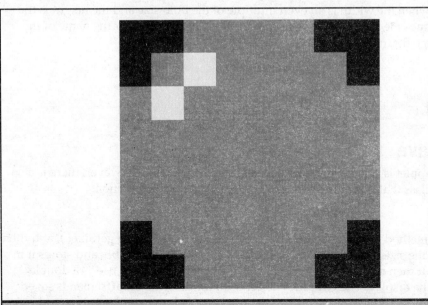

Figure 31-2. *A blown-up light bulb image*

image much larger than your applet, which has several source images concatenated into a single image, and then using **copyArea** to move them into place and clipping the result onscreen is a very fast Java rendering technique.

The Source Code

Lavatron starts by initializing data, which includes loading the source image and creating the column of bulb images. The last stage of the initialization is painting the offscreen (double buffer) image full of dimmed (black) lightbulbs to start the display with a clean image. Subsequent painting of the offscreen image begins by using **copyArea( )** to move the existing portion of the image to the left by the width of the column of bulbs about to be added on the right edge. Then the pixel values for the next column are read and used as the color to fill a column of 8×8 rectangles at the right edge of the applet. The transparent column of bulbs is painted, and then the whole backing image is drawn to the screen. Since this applet doesn't have to do much except scroll the image, it avoids the normal **repaint( )** loop by forking a thread that repeatedly calls **paint( )**, pausing only to call **yield( )** to allow other threads to run.

The APPLET Tag

The source code starts with the APPLET tag for **Lavatron**, shown here. This applet looks best when the width is an even multiple of the bulb size and the height is the bulb size times the source image height. The only parameter is for the name of the source image file, named in **img**.

```
<applet code=Lavatron.class width=560 height=128>
<param name="img" value="swsm.jpg">
</applet>
```

Lavatron.java

The main applet is small, about 100 lines of Java source code. However, there is also a support class that is required, which is described in the next section.

init( )

The **init( )** method first determines the size of the applet by using **getSize( )**, and then rounds up the size to a multiple of the bulb size, specified by **bulbS**, and stores it in **offw,offh**. It then creates an image that size, called **offscreen**, for use as a double buffer for the display. The **Graphics** object used for drawing on **offscreen** is saved in **offGraphics**. The size of the applet, in bulb units rather than pixels, is stored in **bulbsW,bulbsH**.

Next, the image of a column of bulbs is created by calling **createBulbs( )**, passing in the size of the image to create. Then the image named in the **img** applet parameter is loaded. This is done by passing the result of **getImage( )** to **MediaTracker**'s **addImage( )** method, and then calling **waitForID( )**, which waits until the image is fully loaded before returning.

To draw the blown-up version of this image, **init( )** needs to retrieve the color information for each pixel in the image. First, it obtains the size of the image, using **getWidth( )** and **getHeight( )**, saving the width in **pixscan**. It then assigns **pixels** to a new array of **pixscan * h** integers. Then a **PixelGrabber** is created. When **grabPixels( )** is called, the array is filled in with the color values.

The final step of **init( )** is to paint black bulbs on the **offscreen** image, which makes the effect more dramatic as the image scrolls from the right side revealing lighted bulbs.

createBulbs( )

The **createBulbs( )** method is a helper to **init( )**. It returns an **Image** of a stack of bulb images that can be used to mask out a column of colored squares to make them look like lit lightbulbs. It is a little tricky, but quite elegant.

First, it allocates the right number of **int**s in an array to store the pixels. Then, it declares another array, which is a picture of a single bulb, represented by the numbers 0, 1, and 2. The 0s represent black, the 1s transparent pixels, and the 2s represent the white highlight. Next, a short array is declared—**bulbCLUT** (bulb Color Look Up Table). This maps the 0, 1, and 2 just mentioned into full 32-bit pixel values. The 0xff000000 is opaque black. The high-order byte is alpha, or transparency. The 0x00c0c0c0 is a fully transparent light gray, and the 0xffffffff is opaque white.

The **for** loop runs through each pixel, loading the appropriate 0, 1, or 2 from **bulbBits** based on the position in the column. This is achieved by use of the mod (%) operator. This value is then used to look up the color from **bulbCLUT**. Given this array of pixels, **createBulbs( )** returns the output of **createImage( )**, passing in a **MemoryImageSource** object prepared with the pixels we just constructed.

color( )

The **color( )** method returns the color of the pixel at the **x,y** position in the source image as a **Color** object. Since this applet runs continuously, we decided not to simply create a new **Color** object each time a single bulb was painted. This would be abusive of the garbage-collected heap. Instead, unique **Color** objects are stored in a hash table. The maximum number of **Color** objects in the hash table can be as much as the width times the height of the source image, but in practice, it is usually much less.

update( )

Lavatron overrides **update( )** to do nothing, because we don't want AWT's implementation to cause flicker.

paint( )

The **paint( )** method is quite simple. The first step calls **copyArea( )** to move all of the columns to the left by one column's width. Then a **for** loop is used to fill the rightmost column with rectangles in the **Color** of the appropriate pixel, using **color( )**. The **bulb** image strip is then painted over the new column. Then the current scrolled position, **scrollX**, is updated to be one more to the right, modulo the width, **pixscan**.

start( ), stop( ), and run( )

When the applet starts, it creates and starts a new **Thread** called **t**. This thread will call **run( )**, which will keep calling **paint( )** as fast as possible, while maintaining the courtesy of calling **yield( )** so that other threads can run. When the applet **stop( )** method is called, **stopFlag** is set to **true**. This variable is checked by the infinite loop in the **run( )** method. Program control breaks from the loop when **stopFlag** is **true**.

A useful enhancement would be to introduce a threshold frame rate, say 30 fps (frames per second), and change the call to the **yield( )** into an appropriate call to **sleep( )** if the rendering is too fast.

The Code

Here is the source code for the **Lavatron** class:

```
import java.applet.*;
import java.awt.* ;
import java.awt.image.* ;

public class Lavatron extends Applet implements Runnable {
  int scrollX;
  int bulbsW, bulbsH;
  int bulbS = 8;
  Dimension d;
  Image offscreen, bulb, img;
  Graphics offgraphics;
  int pixels[];
  int pixscan;
  IntHash clut = new IntHash();
  boolean stopFlag;

  public void init() {
    d = getSize();
    int offw = (int) Math.ceil(d.width/bulbS) * bulbS;
    int offh = (int) Math.ceil(d.height/bulbS) * bulbS;
    offscreen = createImage(offw, offh);
    offgraphics = offscreen.getGraphics();
    bulbsW = offw/bulbS;
    bulbsH = offh/bulbS;
```

```
    bulb = createBulbs(bulbS, bulbsH*bulbS);
    try {
      img = getImage(getDocumentBase(), getParameter("img"));
      MediaTracker t = new MediaTracker(this);
      t.addImage(img, 0);
      t.waitForID(0);
      pixscan = img.getWidth(null);
      int h = img.getHeight(null);
      pixels = new int[pixscan * h];
      PixelGrabber pg = new PixelGrabber(img, 0, 0, pixscan, h,
                                    pixels, 0, pixscan);
      pg.grabPixels();
    } catch (InterruptedException e) { };
    scrollX = 0;
    // paint black bulbs on the offscreen image
    offgraphics.setColor(Color.black);
    offgraphics.fillRect(0, 0, d.width, d.height);
    for (int x=0; x<bulbsW; x++)
      offgraphics.drawImage(bulb, x*bulbS, 0, null);
  }

  Image createBulbs(int w, int h) {
    int pixels[] = new int[w*h];
    int bulbBits[] = {
      0,0,1,1,1,1,0,0,
      0,1,2,1,1,1,1,0,
      1,2,1,1,1,1,1,1,
      1,1,1,1,1,1,1,1,
      1,1,1,1,1,1,1,1,
      1,1,1,1,1,1,1,1,
      0,1,1,1,1,1,1,0,
      0,0,1,1,1,1,0,0
    };
    int bulbCLUT[] = { 0xff000000, 0x00c0c0c0, 0xffffffff };
    for (int i=0; i<w*h; i++)
      pixels[i] = bulbCLUT[bulbBits[i%bulbBits.length]];
    return createImage(new MemoryImageSource(w, h, pixels, 0, w));
  }

  public final Color color(int x, int y) {
    int p = pixels[y*pixscan+x];
    Color c;
```

```java
      if ((c=(Color)clut.get(p)) == null)
        clut.put(p, c = new Color(p));
      return c;
  }

  public void update() {}

  public void paint(Graphics g) {
    offgraphics.copyArea(bulbS, 0, bulbsW*bulbS-bulbS, d.height,
                         -bulbS, 0);
    for (int y=0; y<bulbsH; y++) {
      offgraphics.setColor(color(scrollX, y));
      offgraphics.fillRect(d.width-bulbS, y*bulbS, bulbS, bulbS);
    }
    offgraphics.drawImage(bulb, d.width-bulbS, 0, null);
    g.drawImage(offscreen, 0, 0, null);
    scrollX = (scrollX + 1) % pixscan;
  }

  Thread t;
  public void run() {
    while (true) {
      paint(getGraphics());
      try{t.yield();} catch(Exception e) { };
      if(stopFlag)
        break;
    }
  }

  public void start() {
    t = new Thread(this);
    t.setPriority(Thread.MIN_PRIORITY);
    stopFlag = false;
    t.start();
  }

  public void stop() {
    stopFlag = true;
  }
}
```

IntHash( )

As mentioned in the preceding section, **Color** objects are stored in a hash table rather than creating the same ones over and over. As a further optimization, we created our own version of Java's **Hashtable** class, which uses normal **ints** as keys rather than requiring an **Object** handle.

Integer data needs much less room to store in the pixel array than **Color** objects, so we use a hash table as a mechanism to look up **Color** objects from the integer value of any individual pixel. Creating **Color** objects on the fly from the integer value of each pixel is very expensive, because it creates a lot of memory garbage that must be collected. One possible solution would be to use a Java **Hashtable**, except that doing so would create just as much garbage, since only objects can be used as keys in a standard Java hash table. Thus, to store an **int** in Java's hash table, you would have to create a new **Integer** object as a key to be matched. In a high duty cycle applet like **Lavatron**, garbage **Integer** objects would be created by the thousands per second. This is not a good solution.

The proper solution was to build our own hash table, **IntHash**, which uses the integer data type values rather than the **Integer** object for its keys. **IntHash** is about 60 lines of code. The **IntHash** class duplicates the interface of the **java.util.Hashtable** class with the exception that the type of the argument to **put( )** and **get( )** is an **int** data type rather than an **Object**. There's no need to explain how a hash table works in this chapter, but suffice it to say that **put(42, "Hello") == get(42)**.

The Code

Here is the source code for the **IntHash** class:

```
class IntHash {
  private int capacity;
  private int size;
  private float load = 0.7F;
  private int keys[];
  private Object vals[];

  public IntHash(int n) {
    capacity = n;
    size = 0;
    keys = new int[n];
    vals = new Object[n];
  }

  public IntHash() {
    this(101);
```

```
    }

    private void rehash() {
      int newcapacity = capacity * 2 + 1;
      Object newvals[] = new Object[newcapacity];
      int newkeys[] = new int[newcapacity];
      for (int i = 0; i < capacity; i++) {
        Object o = vals[i];
        if (o != null) {
          int k = keys[i];
          int newi = (k & 0x7fffffff) % newcapacity;
          while (newvals[newi] != null)
            newi = (newi + 1) % newcapacity;
          newkeys[newi] = k;
          newvals[newi] = o;
        }
      }
      capacity = newcapacity;
      keys = newkeys;
      vals = newvals;
    }

    public void put(int k, Object o) {
      int i = (k & 0x7fffffff) % capacity;
      while (vals[i] != null && k != keys[i]) // hash collision.
        i = (i + 1) % capacity;
      if (vals[i] == null)
        size++;
      keys[i] = k;
      vals[i] = o;
      if (size > (int)(capacity * load))
        rehash();
    }

    public final Object get(int k) {
      int i = (k & 0x7fffffff) % capacity;
      while (vals[i] != null && k != keys[i]) // hash miss
        i = (i + 1) % capacity;
      return vals[i];
    }
```

```
public final boolean contains(int k) {
  return get(k)!=null;
}

public int size() {
  return size;
}

public int capacity() {
  return capacity;
}
```

Hot Lava

This applet is another small example of the kind of amazing performance you can squeeze out of Java if you are careful and diligent. David LaVallée uses many tricks to avoid excessive memory allocation and unnecessary calls to AWT drawing functions. Creating the lightbulb mask image from a small array of integers rather than a loaded GIF image saves download time and increases flexibility. The use of **paint(getGraphics( ))** rather than **repaint( )** increases frame rate significantly. The performance gains from using **copyArea( )** over rerendering the image or calling **drawImage( )** are profound. Finally, the creation and use of **IntHash** makes for that last performance boost by not forcing the system to garbage-collect as often.

Chapter 32

Scrabblet: A Multiplayer Word Game

Scrabblet is a complete multiplayer, networked, client/server game. It is the most complicated applet in this book, and it handles some of the thorniest issues in Java programming. **Scrabblet** consists of more than 1,400 lines of code in 11 classes. Two of these classes are part of the server side of the applet. The other nine are downloaded to a web browser and act as the simulation of the game. All of the code elements used in the game have been described in detail in this book. In this chapter, we will dissect each class and show how easy it is to build a multiplayer game.

Network Security Concerns

Most applets on the Net today don't do much with the network after they have been downloaded. One of the reasons is that networking has been made more difficult in Java out of security concerns. Most Java applet environments, such as Netscape Navigator and Microsoft Internet Explorer, severely restrict an applet's use of the network. This situation is created by TCP/IP's lack of authentication in its most basic protocols. This inherent limitation of the Internet is managed carefully by corporations that want to protect their proprietary data through the use of firewalls. A *firewall* is a computer that sits between a private network and the rest of the Internet. All Internet connections flow through it, and it is able to filter and reject connections and packets, both incoming and outgoing. This way, if a program on the outside of the firewall attempts to attach to an internal network port, the firewall can block it. If it weren't for the firewall, system administrators would have to audit the security of each machine on their internal network. In the case of a firewall-protected network, only the firewall needs to be secure, and every machine inside is considered "friendly" and left unprotected from every other machine inside.

This is where Java could have posed a security threat. If Java-enabled browsers allowed applets to connect to arbitrary Internet addresses, then an applet could act as a proxy to some malicious program on the outside of the firewall. Once an applet had been downloaded and automatically run by the web browser, it could then connect to the neighboring computers and servers. These computers would not expect anything hostile to come from an internal computer, so they would accept the connections. The applet would then be free to steal sensitive data and transmit it back through the firewall to the malicious Internet host.

Because of this scenario, applets are only allowed to make network connections to exactly one host: the one they were loaded from. This restricts the applet from snooping around the internal network. One of the many well-publicized "Java security attacks" from researchers at Princeton University was a way of tricking a Java run-time system into allowing an applet to open network sockets on otherwise forbidden machines. Thankfully, this problem was very difficult to reproduce and has subsequently been addressed.

What does security have to do with a multiplayer game? Plenty. The easiest way to program a multiplayer game would be to have the players communicate directly with each other, in a "peer-to-peer" network. This way, playing the game would not rely on having any particular server software running. Unfortunately, the applet is only able to connect back to the server that it was loaded from. This means that two players have to communicate all of their messages to each other via the server.

In this chapter, you will see the source code to a simple server, which manages a list of connected clients and passes messages between those clients. For the most part, this server knows nothing about the game being played. It just passes the messages blithely from point A to point B. This function is handled by two classes, **Server** and **ClientConnection**. They will be described at the end of this chapter.

The Game

Before users can play a multiplayer game, they must choose somebody to play against. Rather than forcing a phone call to arrange a game, this applet takes a different approach. When it is first run, it prompts the user to enter his or her name (see Figure 32-1). This name is passed to the server, which broadcasts the player's name to all other potential competitors. The user then sees a list of all available players (see Figure 32-2), selects one, and clicks on the Challenge button. Currently, there is no way to confirm or deny a challenge; they are automatically accepted. Once a challenge is made, both players see the game board appear, and all other competitors simply see both players' names disappear from the available list.

It is quite an easy game to play, but it is very difficult to win against a skilled opponent. Players are presented with a 15×15 grid of squares and given a set of seven square tiles with letters of the alphabet engraved on them (see Figure 32-3). These tiles are selected at random from a bag of 100 tiles. The tiles can be clicked on with the mouse and dragged to a destination square on the grid. If the spot is already occupied, the tile is returned to its original position. Tiles may be adjusted on the board during a turn, but not when the turn is over.

The first player starts by placing several tiles in a line on the board to form a word in the English language. The first word must cover the center square. Subsequent words must touch at least one tile already played on the board. The player clicks on the Done button to end the turn. If a player can't find a valid word, the player can pass by clicking on Done twice in a row without having any tiles on the board. The two players take turns placing words until all of the tiles are used.

The board shown in Figure 32-3 is for smaller displays, and thus the multiplier squares are marked with simple characters. 2L doubles the value of the letter on that square. 3L triples the letter's value. 2W means the whole word gets double the points; 3W means triple the word score. If you make the applet big enough, it will use more descriptive labels for these squares, as shown in Figure 32-4.

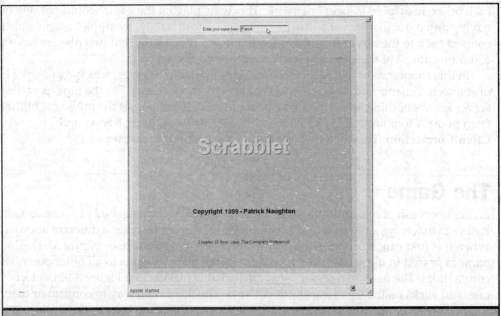

Figure 32-1. *The user must type in his or her name to begin*

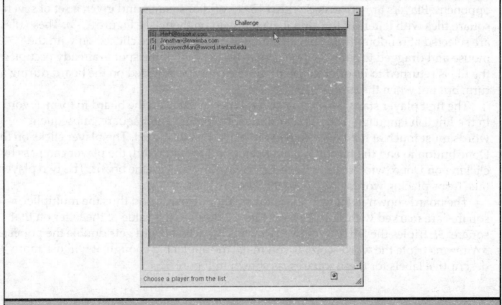

Figure 32-2. *The list of competitors*

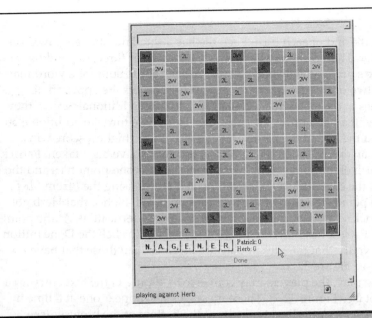

Figure 32-3. *Patrick and Herb are ready to play against each other*

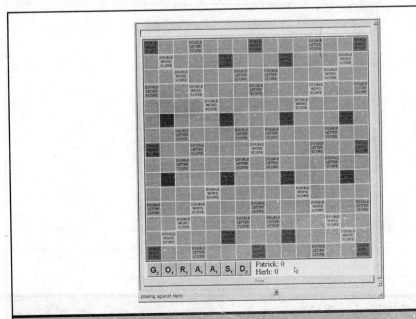

Figure 32-4. *Everything is clearer with a larger applet (650x700)*

Scoring

Scores are assessed at the end of each turn. Each tile has a small number engraved on its face next to the letter. This score may be multiplied by two or three, depending on the value (color) of the square on which it was placed. The entire sum for a word may also be multiplied by two or three if any letter in the word covers the appropriate square. If a word comes in contact with any other tiles to form additional words, they are counted separately. If a player uses all seven tiles in a single turn, an additional 50 points are awarded. At the end of the game, the player with the highest score wins.

Figure 32-5 shows an example of a board after a few turns have been taken. Patrick started with *SIRE*, worth eight points. That came from the four one-point tiles and the double-word score on the center tile. Next, Herb played *HIRE*, using the *I* from *SIRE*. This was worth seven points, the sum of the four tiles involved. Notice that Herb got credit for reusing Patrick's *I* but not the double-word score underneath it. At the point shown in Figure 32-5, Patrick has played *GREAT* and is about to click the Done button to complete his turn. Notice that the tiles in play are brighter than those that have already been played (see Figure 32-6).

At any time during play, the players may converse by typing in the text entry area at the top of the applet (see Figure 32-7). These messages will appear one at a time in the other player's browser's status line, typically at the bottom of the browser (see Figure 32-8).

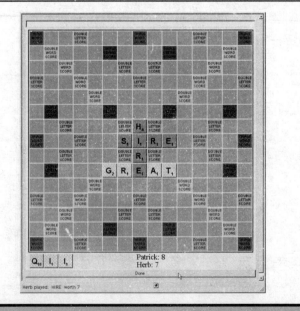

Figure 32-5.   *Scrabblet early in a game*

Figure 32-6.   *Herb is about to place the D to make HEATED*

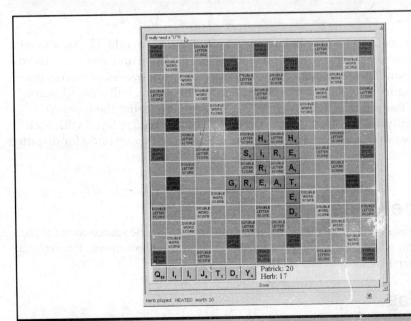

Figure 32-7.   *Patrick is complaining about being stuck with the Q without the U*

APPLYING JAVA

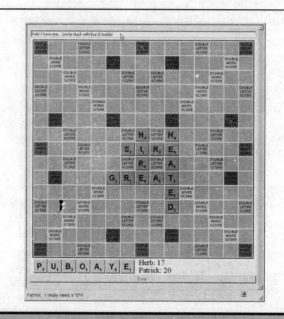

Figure 32-8. *Herb replies. Notice Patrick's last message at the bottom*

One last word about game play before we get into the source code. The way to win at this game is to come up with words that score in one direction and also make words in the other direction. These secondary words tend to be short, two-letter words, but they add up. In Figure 32-9, Patrick places the *Y* in *DEITY*, which will score 21 points because he gets a face value of 9 doubled to 18, plus he gets to count the word *AD*, which runs vertically, for 3 points. Remember that all of the words played with each turn need to be real words. Eventually, this game will need either an undo for disputed words or an automatic dictionary checker to resolve conflicts.

The Source Code

Now that you know how to play the game, it is time to examine the source code for the game. Since several of the classes are quite long, we will sprinkle comments throughout the code rather than leaving the code till the end.

The APPLET Tag

The APPLET tag for this game is simple. Just name the main class and set the size. That's it. There aren't any <param> tags for **Scrabblet**. Remember, the bigger you

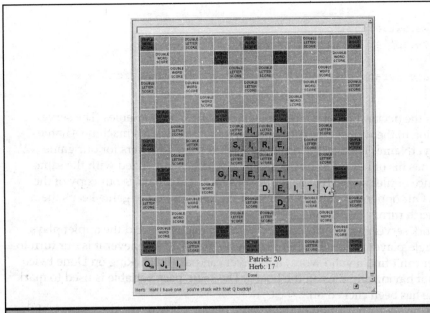

Figure 32-9.   *Patrick scores in two directions!*

make the applet, the nicer the board looks. The aspect ratio should be a little taller than it is wide.

```
<applet code=Scrabblet.class width=400 height=450>
</applet>
```

Scrabblet.java

The main applet class is found in **Scrabblet.java**. At almost 300 lines, this is a fairly complicated applet class, even though most of the game logic is left to the **Board** class, found later in this chapter.

We start with the usual collection of import statements, loading almost every standard Java package. Then we declare **Scrabblet** to be a subclass of **Applet** that implements **ActionListener**.

```
import java.io.*;
import java.net.*;
import java.awt.*;
```

```
import java.awt.event.*;
import java.applet.*;

public class Scrabblet extends Applet implements ActionListener {
```

Next comes the declaration of a large collection of instance variables. The **server** is our connection to the web server running our game server. This machine's name is stored in **serverName**. The **bag** represents the shared bag of letters for our game. Our opponent has his or her own copy of the bag, which is initialized with the same random sequence of tiles so the two bags stay in synch. The **board** is our copy of the playing board. Our opponent also has a copy of the board, and the game keeps them in synch after each turn.

If the network server can't be accessed, the **single** flag is set, and the applet plays the game in single-player mode. The **boolean ourturn** is **true** whenever it is our turn to play. If a player can't find a valid word, the player can pass by clicking on Done twice in a row without having any tiles on the board. The **seen_pass** variable is used to mark if the first Done has been clicked on.

To manage the synchronization of the remote player's board, we keep a copy of the tiles selected in **theirs**. Seeing what the other person has in his or her tray is cheating, so no hacking this applet to display the contents of **theirs**! The two strings, **name** and **others_name**, hold our name and our opponent's name, respectively.

```
private ServerConnection server;
private String serverName;
private Bag bag;
private Board board;
private boolean single = false;
private boolean ourturn;
private boolean seen_pass = false;
private Letter theirs[] = new Letter[7];
private String name;
private String others_name;
```

Next, we declare eight variables used to manage the user interface. These are all AWT components that must be manipulated by the applet in some way. **topPanel** holds the **prompt** and the **namefield** for getting the user's name at start-up. The **done** button is used to signify that you are done with your turn. The **chat TextField** is used to enter chat messages. **idList** is used to display available opponents. The **challenge** button is used to attach us to our opponent. The **ican Canvas** holds the name and copyright notice at start-up.

```
private Panel topPanel;
private Label prompt;
private TextField namefield;
private Button done;
private TextField chat;

private List idList;
private Button challenge;
private Canvas ican;
```

init( )

The **init( )** method is called once and simply sets up the **BorderLayout**, figures out what Internet host the applet came from, and creates the splash screen canvas.

```
public void init() {
  setLayout(new BorderLayout());
  serverName = getCodeBase().getHost();
  if (serverName.equals(""))
    serverName = "localhost";
  ican = new IntroCanvas();
}
```

start( )

The **start( )** method is called whenever the browser redisplays the page in which the applet is found. The large **try** block at the beginning is used to catch the case where the network connection fails. If we succeed in making a new **ServerConnection** and we've never run **start( )** before, we then set up the screen to prompt for the user's name. While we are there, we put the splash screen, **ican**, in the center of the window. In the case where **name** is not **null**, that means the user left the page and has now returned. We presume we've already got the user's name and jump right to **nameEntered( )**, the method that is called when the user types **return** in the name entry field. The **validate( )** at the end makes sure all of the AWT components are updated properly.

If an exception was thrown, we presume that the net connection failed and go into single-player mode. The call to **start_game( )** gets things rolling.

```
public void start() {
  try {
    showStatus("Connecting to " + serverName);
    server = new ServerConnection(this, serverName);
```

```
        server.start();
        showStatus("Connected: " + serverName);

        if (name == null) {
          prompt = new Label("Enter your name here:");
          namefield = new TextField(20);
          namefield.addActionListener(this);
          topPanel = new Panel();
          topPanel.setBackground(new Color(255, 255, 200));
          topPanel.add(prompt);
          topPanel.add(namefield);
          add("North", topPanel);
          add("Center", ican);
        } else {
          if (chat != null) {
            remove(chat);
            remove(board);
            remove(done);
          }
          nameEntered(name);
        }
        validate();
      } catch (Exception e) {
        single = true;
        start_Game((int)(0x7fffffff * Math.random()));
      }
    }
```

stop( )

The **stop( )** method is called whenever the user leaves the page with the applet. Here, we just tell the server that we've left. We re-create the network connection in **start( )** if the user returns to the page later.

```
    public void stop() {
      if (!single)
        server.quit();
```

add( )

The **add( )** method is called by the **ServerConnection** whenever a new player enters the game. We add the player's name to our **List** object. Pay special attention to the formatting of the string in **add( )**. We use that later to extract certain IDs from the list.

```
void add(String id, String hostname, String name) {
   delete(id); // in case it is already there.
   idList.add("(" + id + ")  " + name + "@" + hostname);
   showStatus("Choose a player from the list");
}
```

delete( )

The **delete( )** method is called when a player no longer wants to be identified as available for play. This happens when a player quits or decides to play with someone else. Here, we hunt down the **id** string in our list by extracting the values inside parentheses. If there are no more names on the list (and we aren't playing the game already: **bag == null**), then we display a special message telling the user to hang out until someone comes to make a challenge.

```
void delete(String id) {
   for (int i = 0; i < idList.getItemCount(); i++) {
      String s = idList.getItem(i);
      s = s.substring(s.indexOf("(") + 1, s.indexOf(")"));
      if (s.equals(id)) {
         idList.remove(i);
         break;
      }
   }
   if (idList.getItemCount() == 0 && bag == null)
      showStatus("Wait for other players to arrive.");
}
```

getName( )

The **getName( )** method is very similar to **delete( )**, except it simply extracts the name part of the item and returns it. If the **id** is not found, then **null** is returned.

```
private String getName(String id) {
  for (int i = 0; i < idList.getItemCount(); i++) {
    String s = idList.getItem(i);
    String idl = s.substring(s.indexOf("(") + 1, s.indexOf(")"));
    if (idl.equals(id)) {
      return s.substring(s.indexOf(" ") + 3, s.indexOf("@"));
    }
  }
  return null;
}
```

challenge( )

The **challenge( )** method is called by the **ServerConnection** whenever another player challenges us to a game. We could have made this method more complicated, so that it would prompt the user to accept or refuse the challenge, but instead the challenge is automatically accepted. Notice that the random seed we use to start the game is passed back to the other player in the **accept( )** method. This is used by both sides to initialize the random state of the **tile** bag to ensure a synchronous game. We call **server.delete( )** to ensure that we are no longer solicited by other players wanting to play against us. Notice also that we cede the starting turn to the challenger by setting **ourturn** to false.

```
// we've been challenged to a game by "id".
void challenge(String id) {
  ourturn = false;
  int seed = (int)(0x7fffffff * Math.random());
  others_name = getName(id);   // who was it?
  showStatus("challenged by " + others_name);

  // put some confirmation here...

  server.accept(id, seed);
  server.delete();
  start_Game(seed);
}
```

accept( )

accept( ) is the method called on the remote side in response to the **server.accept( )** call just mentioned. Just as the other player deleted himself or herself from the list of

available players, so must we call **server.delete( )**. We take the first turn by setting
ourturn to true.

```
// our challenge was accepted.
void accept(String id, int seed) {
  ourturn = true;
  others_name = getName(id);
  server.delete();
  start_Game(seed);
}
```

chat( )

The **chat( )** method is called by the server whenever the opponent types in his or her
chat window. In this implementation, the method simply shows the chat message in
the browser's status message. In the future, it might be nice to log these into a
TextArea.

```
void chat(String id, String s) {
  showStatus(others_name + ": " + s);
}
```

move( )

The **move( )** method is called once for each tile your opponent plays. It looks through
the letters saved in **theirs** to find the one used. If the square is already occupied, the tile
is returned to the player's tray. Otherwise, the opponent's letter is moved onto the
board permanently. Next, the tile is replaced in **theirs** by **bag.takeOut( )**. If the **bag** is
empty, a status message appears. The board is repainted to show the new tiles on it.
Note that no scoring is done based on the placement of these tiles. The applet waits
until **turn( )** is called to give the score.

```
// the other guy moved, and placed 'letter' at (x, y).
void move(String letter, int x, int y) {
  for (int i = 0; i < 7; i++) {
    if (theirs[i] != null && theirs[i].getSymbol().equals(letter)) {
      Letter already = board.getLetter(x, y);
      if (already != null) {
        board.moveLetter(already, 15, 15); // on the tray.
      }
      board.moveLetter(theirs[i], x, y);
```

```
        board.commitLetter(theirs[i]);
        theirs[i] = bag.takeOut();
        if (theirs[i] == null)
          showStatus("No more letters");
        break;
      }
    }
    board.repaint();
}
```

turn( )

The **turn( )** method is called after all of the opponent's tiles are moved. The remote instance of **Scrabblet** computes the score and sends it to us, so our copy doesn't have to redo it. Then the score is reported in the status line, and the **setEnabled** method allows us to take a turn. **othersTurn( )** tells the **board** about the score. The **board** will reflect the new score at this point.

```
    void turn(int score, String words) {
      showStatus(others_name + " played: " + words + " worth " +
                 score);
      done.setEnabled(true);
      board.othersTurn(score);
    }
```

quit( )

When the other side quits cleanly, **quit( )** is called. It removes the AWT components of the game and jumps right back into **nameEntered( )**, described next, to get connected back into the player list.

```
    void quit(String id) {
      showStatus(others_name + " just quit.");
      remove(chat);
      remove(board);
      remove(done);
      nameEntered(name);
    }
```

nameEntered( )

The **nameEntered( )** method is called from **actionPerformed( )** whenever ENTER is pressed in the original prompt for the user's name. Any AWT components that might be in the way are removed, and then a new **List** object, **idList**, is created to store the names of the other players. The method also adds a button at the top named **challenge**, then notifies the server that we are here by calling **setName( )**.

```
private void nameEntered(String s) {
  if (s.equals(""))
    return;
  name = s;
  if (ican != null)
    remove(ican);
  if (idList != null)
    remove(idList);
  if (challenge != null)
    remove(challenge);
  idList = new List(10, false);
  add("Center", idList);
  challenge = new Button("Challenge");
  challenge.addActionListener(this);
  add("North", challenge);
  validate();
  server.setName(name);
  showStatus("Wait for other players to arrive.");
  if (topPanel != null)
    remove(topPanel);
}
```

wepick( ) and theypick( )

The methods **wepick( )** and **theypick( )** are simply used to start off the game by picking the seven tiles for each player. It is important that the caller do these in the right order on each side of the challenge, depending on who goes first. The call to **bag.takeOut( )** gets a single letter permanently out of the shared bag. The call to **board.addLetter( )** places the tile on our tray. For the other side, **theypick( )** simply saves the letters in **theirs**.

```
private void wepick() {
  for (int i = 0; i < 7; i++) {
```

```
      Letter l = bag.takeOut();
      board.addLetter(l);
    }
  }

  private void theypick() {
    for (int i = 0; i < 7; i++) {
    Letter l = bag.takeOut();
    theirs[i] = l;
    }
  }
```

start_Game( )

In single-player mode, **start_Game( )** pops up the splash screen in a **Frame** window.
It then creates a playing **board**, passing in no parameters to the constructor, which
indicates single-player mode.

In head-to-head mode, we remove the selection list components and add the **chat**
window to the applet. We then add the **board** and Done button to the applet. Next, we
create the bag, and if it is **ourturn**, **wepick( )** is first, then **theypick( )**. In the case where
we don't have the first turn, we disable the **board** and the Done button, and **theypick( )**
is first. We then force the **board** to repaint, which initializes it.

```
    private void start_Game(int seed) {
      if (single) {
      Frame popup = new Frame("Scrabblet");
      popup.setSize(400, 300);
      popup.add("Center", ican);
      popup.setResizable(false);
      popup.show();
      board = new Board();
      showStatus("no server found, playing solo");
      ourturn = true;
      } else {
      remove(idList);
      remove(challenge);
      board = new Board(name, others_name);
      chat = new TextField();
      chat.addActionListener(this);
      add("North", chat);
```

```
        showStatus("playing against " + others_name);
    }

    add("Center", board);
    done = new Button("Done");
    done.addActionListener(this);
    add("South", done);
    validate();

    bag = new Bag(seed);
    if (ourturn) {
        wepick();
        if (!single)
            theypick();
    } else {
        done.setEnabled(false);
        theypick();
        wepick();
    }
    board.repaint();
}
```

challenge_them( )

The **challenge_them( )** method is called when the **challenge** button is clicked. It simply takes the player you had selected in the **idList** and sends him or her a **challenge( )** message. It removes the list and button to be ready for the game to start.

```
    private void challenge_them() {
        String s = idList.getSelectedItem();
        if (s == null) {
            showStatus("Choose a player from the list then press Challenge");
        } else {
            remove(challenge);
            remove(idList);
            String destid = s.substring(s.indexOf('(')+1,
                                        s.indexOf(')'));
            showStatus("challenging: " + destid);
            server.challenge(destid);  // accept will get called if
```

```
                                            // they accept.
      validate();
    }
  }
```

our_turn( )

When the Done button is clicked, **our_turn( )** is called. First, it checks to see if we've placed tiles in valid locations by calling **board.findwords( )** and storing the result in **word**. If **word** is **null**, then something is amiss with the tiles, and the method shows that in the status line. If **word** is "", then it knows that there were no tiles in play at the time. In single-player mode, this is ignored. In competition mode, if we click Done twice in a row without any tiles in play, we will pass our turn to our opponent.

If you have played tiles and they are in legal positions, you have finished your turn, so **ourturn( )** commits the letters to the board. Notice that **commit( )** takes the **server** as a parameter. It will use this to tell the remote side about the position of each new letter. Then the method replaces the letters you used. In multiplayer mode, we disable ourselves and call **server.turn( )** to tell the other player it is his or her turn.

```
    private void our_turn() {
      String word = board.findwords();
      if (word == null) {
        showStatus("Illegal letter positions");
      } else {
        if ("".equals(word)) {
          if (single)
            return;
          if (seen_pass) {
            done.setEnabled(false);
            server.turn("pass", 0);
            showStatus("You passed");
            seen_pass = false;
          } else {
            showStatus("Press done again to pass");
            seen_pass = true;
            return;
          }
        } else {
          seen_pass = false;
        }
        showStatus(word);
```

```
      board.commit(server);
      for (int i = 0; i < 7; i++) {
        if (board.getTray(i) == null) {
          Letter l = bag.takeOut();
          if (l == null)
            showStatus("No more letters");
          else
            board.addLetter(l);
        }
      }
      if (!single) {
        done.setEnabled(false);
        server.turn(word, board.getTurnScore());
      }
      board.repaint();
    }
  }
```

actionPerformed( )

The **actionPerformed( )** method is used to grab input from the various components the applet uses. It handles the Challenge and Done buttons, as well as the name entry field and the chat entry field.

```
  public void actionPerformed(ActionEvent ae) {
    Object source = ae.getSource();
    if(source == chat) {
      server.chat(chat.getText());
      chat.setText("");
    }
    else if(source == challenge) {
      challenge_them();
    }
    else if(source == done) {
      our_turn();
    }
    else if(source == namefield) {
      TextComponent tc = (TextComponent)source;
      nameEntered(tc.getText());
    }
  }
```

IntroCanvas.java

The **IntroCanvas** subclass of **Canvas** is very simple. It just overrides **paint( )** to draw the name of the applet and a brief copyright notice. It creates some custom colors and fonts. The display strings are held in static variables simply for clarity.

```java
import java.awt.*;
import java.awt.event.*;

class IntroCanvas extends Canvas {
  private Color pink = new Color(255, 200, 200);
  private Color blue = new Color(150, 200, 255);
  private Color yellow = new Color(250, 220, 100);

  private int w, h;
  private int edge = 16;
  private static final String title = "Scrabblet";
  private static final String name =
          "Copyright 1999 - Patrick Naughton";
  private static final String book =
          "Chapter 32 from 'Java: The Complete Reference'";
  private Font namefont, titlefont, bookfont;

IntroCanvas() {
    setBackground(yellow);
    titlefont = new Font("SansSerif", Font.BOLD, 58);
    namefont = new Font("SansSerif", Font.BOLD, 18);
    bookfont = new Font("SansSerif", Font.PLAIN, 12);
    addMouseListener(new MyMouseAdapter());
  }
```

d( )

The private method **d( )** is a convenience method that paints centered text with an optional isometric offset. This is used to give the main title a highlight/shadow effect by drawing a white string up and to the left by 1, a black string down and to the right by 1, and then drawing the string one last time in **pink**, not offset at all.

```java
private void d(Graphics g, String s, Color c, Font f, int y,
               int off) {
    g.setFont(f);
    FontMetrics fm = g.getFontMetrics();
    g.setColor(c);
```

```
      g.drawString(s, (w - fm.stringWidth(s)) / 2 + off, y + off);
  }

  public void paint(Graphics g) {
    Dimension d = getSize();
    w = d.width;
    h = d.height;
    g.setColor(blue);
    g.fill3DRect(edge, edge, w - 2 * edge, h - 2 * edge, true);
    d(g, title, Color.black, titlefont, h / 2, 1);
    d(g, title, Color.white, titlefont, h / 2, -1);
    d(g, title, pink, titlefont, h / 2, 0);
    d(g, name, Color.black, namefont, h * 3 / 4, 0);
    d(g, book, Color.black, bookfont, h * 7 / 8, 0);
  }
```

mousePressed( )

In the following code fragment, notice that **MyMouseAdapter** is an inner class that
extends **MouseAdapter**. It overrides the **mousePressed( )** method to cause this canvas'
parent to **hide( )** if it is clicked on. This is only useful in single-player mode to dismiss
the pop-up frame.

```
  class MyMouseAdapter extends MouseAdapter {
    public void mousePressed(MouseEvent me) {
      ((Frame)getParent()).setVisible(false);
    }
  }
}
```

Board.java

The **Board** class encapsulates most of the game logic as well as the look and feel of the
board. It is the biggest class in the game, weighing in at over 500 lines of code. There
are several private variables that store the game state. The 15×15 array of **Letter**s
named **board** is used to store the tiles on each square of the board. The **tray** array holds
the **Letter**s that are currently on our tray. Remember that the **Scrabblet** applet class
holds the seven **Letter**s from our opponent. The **Point** objects **orig** and **here** are used to
remember letter positions. The **name** and **others_name** variables are used simply to
display names for the scoreboard. In single-player mode, both will be **null**. The two
players' scores are stored in **total_score** and **others_score**, while our last turn's result is

stored in **turn_score**. The two constructors set up the names of the players, or leave them blank in single-player mode.

```java
import java.awt.*;
import java.awt.event.*;

class Board extends Canvas {
  private Letter board[][] = new Letter[15][15];
  private Letter tray[] = new Letter[7];
  private Point orig = new Point(0,0);
  private Point here = new Point(0,0);
  private String name;
  private int total_score = 0;
  private int turn_score = 0;
  private int others_score = 0;
  private String others_name = null;

  Board(String our_name, String other_name) {
    name = our_name;
    others_name = other_name;
    addMouseListener(new MyMouseAdapter());
    addMouseMotionListener(new MyMouseMotionAdapter());
  }

  Board() {
    addMouseListener(new MyMouseAdapter());
    addMouseMotionListener(new MyMouseMotionAdapter());
  }
```

othersTurn( ), getTurnScore( ), and getTray( )

These three methods are used to control the access to several private variables. First, **othersTurn( )** is called by the applet when the other player finishes a turn. It increments the player's score and repaints that area of the board to reflect the change. The **getTurnScore( )** method simply returns the saved last turn's score, after making sure the scoreboard is painted with the correct value. The applet uses this method to pass the score to our opponent, where it will eventually call **othersTurn( )** on the remote machine. The **getTray( )** method simply provides a read-only access to the private **tray** array.

```
void othersTurn(int score) {
  others_score += score;
  paintScore();
  repaint();
}

int getTurnScore() {
  paintScore();
  return turn_score;
}

Letter getTray(int i) {
  return tray[i];
}
```

addLetter( )

The **addLetter( )** method is used to place a letter on the tray. The letter is placed in the first slot that is empty. If the method can't find an empty slot, it returns **false**.

```
synchronized boolean addLetter(Letter l) {
  for (int i = 0; i < 7; i++) {
    if (tray[i] == null) {
      tray[i] = l;
      moveLetter(l, i, 15);
      return true;
    }
  }
  return false;
}
```

existingLetterAt( )

The private method **existingLetterAt( )** is used to check a board position to see if it has a letter in it that is not currently in play. This is used by **findwords( )** next to make sure that at least one letter in a turn is touching an already existing letter.

```
private boolean existingLetterAt(int x, int y) {
  Letter l = null;
  return (x >= 0 && x <= 14 && y >= 0 && y <= 14
    && (l = board[y][x]) != null && l.recall() == null);
}
```

findwords( )

findwords( ) is a very large method used to examine the state of the board for a legal turn. If the rules for letter placement are broken, then **null** is returned. If no tiles were in play, then "" is returned. If all of the tiles played in this turn are legal, then the list of words they formed is returned as a string containing the space-separated words. The instance variables **turn_score** and **total_score** are updated to reflect the value of the words that were just played.

First **findwords( )** counts the tiles at play, **ntiles**, storing them in a separate array called **atplay**. Next, it looks at the first two tiles (if more than one was played) to determine if they are vertically or horizontally oriented. Then it inspects all of the other tiles at play, to make sure they are along the same line. If any of the tiles is out of that row or column, the method returns **null**.

```
synchronized String findwords() {
  String res = "";
  turn_score = 0;

  int ntiles = 0;
  Letter atplay[] = new Letter[7];
  for (int i = 0; i < 7; i++) {
    if (tray[i] != null && tray[i].recall() != null) {
      atplay[ntiles++] = tray[i];
    }
  }
  if (ntiles == 0)
    return res;

  boolean horizontal = true; // if there's one tile,
                             // call it horizontal
  boolean vertical = false;
  if (ntiles > 1) {
    int x = atplay[0].x;
    int y = atplay[0].y;
    horizontal = atplay[1].y == y;
```

```
    vertical = atplay[1].x == x;
    if (!horizontal && !vertical) // diagonal...
      return null;
    for (int i = 2; i < ntiles; i++) {
      if (horizontal && atplay[i].y != y
        || vertical && atplay[i].x != x)
        return null;
    }
  }
```

Next, it looks at each tile to be sure that at least one of them is touching an existing tile on one of its four sides. A special case is made for the beginning of the game: if the center tile is covered and more than one tile is played, it is legal.

```
    // make sure that at least one played tile is
    // touching at least one existing tile.
    boolean attached = false;
    for (int i = 0; i < ntiles; i++) {
      Point p = atplay[i].recall();
      int x = p.x;
      int y = p.y;
      if ((x == 7 && y == 7 && ntiles > 1) ||
          existingLetterAt(x-1, y) || existingLetterAt(x+1, y) ||
          existingLetterAt(x, y-1) || existingLetterAt(x, y+1)) {
        attached = true;
        break;
      }
    }
    if (!attached) {
      return null;
    }
```

This next loop iterates over every letter in the main word, (**i == −1**), then comes back again for each letter (**i == 0..ntiles**), which might also create a word orthogonal to the main direction, which is managed via **horizontal**.

```
    // we use -1 to mean check the major direction first
    // then 0..ntiles checks for words orthogonal to it.
    for (int i = -1; i < ntiles; i++) {
      Point p = atplay[i==-1?0:i].recall(); // where is it?
```

```
int x = p.x;
int y = p.y;

int xinc, yinc;
if (horizontal) {
  xinc = 1;
  yinc = 0;
} else {
  xinc = 0;
  yinc = 1;
}
int mult = 1;

String word = "";
int word_score = 0;
```

The method then picks each tile and moves left or up from it to find the first tile in each word. Once at the beginning of the word, it moves right or down from it, inspecting every letter. It counts the letters in **letters_seen**. For each letter, it determines the point contribution based on the bonus multiplier beneath it. If the square is played for the first time, the multiplier value is applied; otherwise the tile is counted at face value. This score is accumulated in **word_score**.

```
// here we back up to the top/left-most letter
while (x >= xinc && y >= yinc &&
       board[y-yinc][x-xinc] != null) {
  x -= xinc;
  y -= yinc;
}

int n = 0;
int letters_seen = 0; // letters we've just played.
Letter l;
while (x < 15 && y < 15 && (l = board[y][x]) != null) {
  word += l.getSymbol();
  int lscore = l.getPoints();
  if (l.recall() != null) {  // one we just played...
    Color t = tiles[y < 8 ? y : 14 - y][x < 8 ? x : 14 - x];
    if (t == w3)
      mult *= 3;
    else if (t == w2)
```

```
        mult *= 2;
      else if (t == 13)
        lscore *= 3;
      else if (t == 12)
        lscore *= 2;
      if (i == -1) {
        letters_seen++;
      }
    }
    word_score += lscore;
    n++;
    x += xinc;
    y += yinc;
  }
  word_score *= mult;
```

One last error check is done on the main word only. Since the loop ends whenever it hits a blank square or the edge of the board, it should cover all of the freshly played tiles, as well as some previously played ones. If it sees fewer tiles, then there must have been a gap in them, which is an illegal position, so it returns **null**. If that test is passed, it checks to see if all seven tiles were played, awarding a 50-point bonus if they were. After inspecting the main word, **findwords( )** inverts the sense of **horizontal** and looks for orthogonal words on the subsequent passes.

```
if (i == -1) {        // first pass...

  // if we didn't see all the letters, then there was a gap,
  // which is an illegal tile position.
  if (letters_seen != ntiles) {
    return null;
  }

  if (ntiles == 7) {
    turn_score += 50;
  }

  // after the first pass, switch to looking the other way.
  horizontal = !horizontal;
}
```

As **findwords( )** walks across the word, it needs to make sure that it only scores letters that form at least two-letter words. In this case, it adds the **word_score** to the **turn_score** and appends this word to the result string. Once all of the letters have been inspected, it totals the score and returns.

```
    if (n < 2)  // don't count single letters twice.
       continue;

    turn_score += word_score;
    res += word + " ";
  }
  total_score += turn_score;
  return res;
}
```

commit( ) and commitLetter( )

The **commit( )** and **commitLetter( )** methods commit the letters that were tentatively placed on the board. These letters are removed from the tray and painted in a darker color on the board. As each letter is committed, **commit( )** notifies the server of the position of each letter by calling **move( )** so that the opponent's board can be updated.

```
synchronized void commit(ServerConnection s) {
  for (int i = 0 ; i < 7 ; i++) {
    Point p;
    if (tray[i] != null && (p = tray[i].recall()) != null) {
      if (s != null)  // there's a server connection
        s.move(tray[i].getSymbol(), p.x, p.y);
      commitLetter(tray[i]);  // marks this as not in play.
      tray[i] = null;
    }
  }
}

void commitLetter(Letter l) {
  if (l != null && l.recall() != null) {
    l.paint(offGraphics, Letter.DIM);
    l.remember(null);   // marks this as not in play.
  }
}
```

update( ) and paint( )

Many private variables are declared here to provide easy access to the dimensions of the board. This code also declares two offscreen buffers, one to be used as the image of the board and all of the permanently set tiles and another to use as a double buffer for the display. The **update( )** method simply calls **paint( )** to avoid flicker. The **paint( )** method makes a quick call to **checksize( )** to make sure all of the buffers have been created, then checks to see if we are dragging a letter around by means of **pick != null**. If so, then **paint( )** makes a copy of the offscreen graphics context and clips it to the bounds of the letter it is painting, **x0, y0, w0, h0**. Next, it clips the onscreen graphics context to the same rectangle. This will minimize the number of pixels it will have to move for each move of the mouse.

To paint, we copy the background image, **offscreen**, then call paint on each letter in the tray with the setting of **NORMAL**. We paint the letter we are dragging around in the **BRIGHT** mode. Finally, we copy the double buffer image, **offscreen2**, to the screen.

```
   private Letter pick;    // the letter being dragged around.
   private int dx, dy;     // offset to topleft corner of pick.
   private int lw, lh;     // letter width and height.
   private int tm, lm;     // top and left margin.
   private int lt;         // line thickness (between tiles).
   private int aw, ah;     // letter area size.

   private Dimension offscreensize;
   private Image offscreen;
   private Graphics offGraphics;
   private Image offscreen2;
   private Graphics offGraphics2;

   public void update(Graphics g) {
     paint(g);
   }

   public synchronized void paint(Graphics g) {
     Dimension d = checksize();
     Graphics gc = offGraphics2;
     if (pick != null) {
       gc = gc.create();
       gc.clipRect(x0, y0, w0, h0);
       g.clipRect(x0, y0, w0, h0);
     }
```

```
gc.drawImage(offscreen, 0, 0, null);

for (int i = 0 ; i < 7 ; i++) {
  Letter l = tray[i];
  if (l != null && l != pick)
    l.paint(gc, Letter.NORMAL);
}
if (pick != null)
  pick.paint(gc, Letter.BRIGHT);

g.drawImage(offscreen2, 0, 0, null);
}
```

LetterHit( )

LetterHit( ) returns the letter that is under the point **x,y** and returns **null** if no letter
is there.

```
Letter LetterHit(int x, int y) {
  for (int i = 0; i < 7; i++) {
    if (tray[i] != null && tray[i].hit(x, y)) {
      return tray[i];
    }
  }
  return null;
}
```

unplay( )

This simple method removes a letter from play that was placed on the board but was
not yet committed.

```
private void unplay(Letter let) {
  Point p = let.recall();
  if (p != null) {
    board[p.y][p.x] = null;
    let.remember(null);
  }
}
```

moveToTray( )

The **moveToTray( )** method is just a simple convenience to compute the screen position of a letter in a given tray slot.

```
private void moveToTray(Letter l, int i) {
  int x = lm + (lw + lt) * i;
  int y = tm + ah - 2 * lt;
  l.move(x, y);
}
```

dropOnTray( )

The **dropOnTray( )** method is used whenever we drop a letter over the tray area or off the board anywhere. This allows us to shuffle the contents of the tray as well as simply return tiles from the board.

```
private void dropOnTray(Letter l, int x) {
  unplay(l); // unhook where we were.

  // find out what slot this letter WAS in.
  int oldx = 0;
  for (int i = 0 ; i < 7 ; i++) {
    if (tray[i] == l) {
      oldx = i;
      break;
    }
  }

  // if the slot we dropped on was empty,
  // find the rightmost occupied slot.
  if (tray[x] == null) {
    for (int i = 6 ; i >= 0 ; i--) {
      if (tray[i] != null) {
        x = i;
        break;
      }
    }
  }
  // if the slot we dropped on was from a tile already
  // played on the board, just swap slots with it.
  if (tray[x].recall() != null) {
    tray[oldx] = tray[x];
```

```
      } else {
        // we are just rearranging a tile already on the tray.
        if (oldx < x) {    // shuffle left.
          for (int i = oldx ; i < x ; i++) {
            tray[i] = tray[i+1];
            if (tray[i].recall() == null)
              moveToTray(tray[i], i);
          }
        } else {             // shuffle right.
          for (int i = oldx ; i > x ; i--) {
            tray[i] = tray[i-1];
            if (tray[i].recall() == null)
              moveToTray(tray[i], i);
          }
        }
      }
      tray[x] = l;
      moveToTray(l, x);
    }
```

getLetter( )

getLetter( ) is a simple read-only wrapper on the board array.

```
    Letter getLetter(int x, int y) {
      return board[y][x];
    }
```

moveLetter( )

The **moveLetter( )** method handles the cases where we want to move tiles to board positions or set them on the tray. If the **x,y** position is out of range for the board, then the tray is used. When a letter is moved to the board, it must be a blank slot, otherwise the letter is sent back to the value stored in **orig**.

```
    void moveLetter(Letter l, int x, int y) {
      if (y > 14 || x > 14 || y < 0 || x < 0) {
        // if we are off the board.
        if (x > 6)
          x = 6;
        if (x < 0)
```

```
      x = 0;
    dropOnTray(l, x);
  } else {
    if (board[y][x] != null) {
      x = orig.x;
      y = orig.y;
    } else {
      here.x = x;
      here.y = y;
      unplay(l);
      board[y][x] = l;
      l.remember(here);

      // turn it back into pixels
      x = lm + (lw + lt) * x;
      y = tm + (lh + lt) * y;
    }
    l.move(x, y);
  }
}
```

checksize( )

This method has a misleading name. **checksize( )** does a lot more than verify the size of the applet, but it is convenient to do this kind of initialization once, when we confirm the size of the applet. This method contains the drawing code for the main board pattern. It paints all of the squares, including the colors and the bonus score text.

```
private Color bg = new Color(175, 185, 175);
private Color w3 = new Color(255, 50, 100);
private Color w2 = new Color(255, 200, 200);
private Color l3 = new Color(75, 75, 255);
private Color l2 = new Color(150, 200, 255);
private Color tiles[][] = {
  {w3, bg, bg, l2, bg, bg, bg, w3},
  {bg, w2, bg, bg, bg, l3, bg, bg},
  {bg, bg, w2, bg, bg, bg, l2, bg},
  {l2, bg, bg, w2, bg, bg, bg, l2},
  {bg, bg, bg, bg, w2, bg, bg, bg},
  {bg, l3, bg, bg, bg, l3, bg, bg},
  {bg, bg, l2, bg, bg, bg, l2, bg},
```

APPLYING JAVA

```
    {w3, bg, bg, 12, bg, bg, bg, w2}
};

private Dimension checksize() {
  Dimension d = getSize();
  int w = d.width;
  int h = d.height;

  if (w < 1 || h < 1)
    return d;
  if ((offscreen == null) ||
    (w != offscreensize.width) ||
    (h != offscreensize.height)) {
    System.out.println("updating board: " + w + " x " + h + "\r");

    offscreen = createImage(w, h);
    offscreensize = d;
    offGraphics = offscreen.getGraphics();
    offscreen2 = createImage(w, h);
    offGraphics2 = offscreen2.getGraphics();

    offGraphics.setColor(Color.white);
    offGraphics.fillRect(0,0,w,h);

    // lt is the thickness of the white lines between tiles.
    // gaps is the sum of all the whitespace.
    // lw, lh are the dimensions of the tiles.
    // aw, ah are the dimensions of the entire board
    // lm, tm are the left and top margin to center aw, ah in the applet.

    lt = 1 + w / 400;
    int gaps = lt * 20;

    lw = (w - gaps) / 15;
    lh = (h - gaps - lt * 2) / 16; // compensating for tray height;
    aw = lw * 15 + gaps;
    ah = lh * 15 + gaps;
    lm = (w - aw) / 2 + lt;
    tm = (h - ah - (lt * 2 + lh)) / 2 + lt;
```

```
offGraphics.setColor(Color.black);
offGraphics.fillRect(lm,tm,aw-2*lt,ah-2*lt);
lm += lt;
tm += lt;
offGraphics.setColor(Color.white);
offGraphics.fillRect(lm,tm,aw-4*lt,ah-4*lt);
lm += lt;
tm += lt;
int sfh = (lh > 30) ? lh / 4 : lh / 2;
Font font = new Font("SansSerif", Font.PLAIN, sfh);
offGraphics.setFont(font);
for (int j = 0, y = tm; j < 15; j++, y += lh + lt) {
  for (int i = 0, x = lm; i < 15; i++, x += lw + lt) {
    Color c = tiles[j < 8 ? j : 14 - j][i < 8 ? i : 14 - i];
    offGraphics.setColor(c);
    offGraphics.fillRect(x, y, lw, lh);
    offGraphics.setColor(Color.black);
    if (lh > 30) {
      String td = (c == w2 || c == 12) ? "DOUBLE" :
                  (c == w3 || c == 13) ? "TRIPLE" : null;
      String wl = (c == 12 || c == 13) ? "LETTER" :
                  (c == w2 || c == w3) ? "WORD" : null;
      if (td != null) {
        center(offGraphics, td, x, y + 2 + sfh, lw);
        center(offGraphics, wl, x, y + 2 * (2 + sfh), lw);
        center(offGraphics, "SCORE", x, y + 3 * (2 + sfh), lw);
      }
    } else {
      String td = (c == w2 || c == 12) ? "2" :
                  (c == w3 || c == 13) ? "3" : null;
      String wl = (c == 12 || c == 13) ? "L" :
                  (c == w2 || c == w3) ? "W" : null;
      if (td != null) {
        center(offGraphics, td + wl, x,
          y + (lh - sfh) * 4 / 10 + sfh, lw);
      }
    }
  }
}
Color c = new Color(255, 255, 200);
offGraphics.setColor(c);
```

```
        offGraphics.fillRect(lm, tm + ah - 3 * lt, 7 * (lw + lt), lh +
                             2 * lt);

        Letter.resize(lw, lh);

        // if we already have some letters, place them.
        for (int i = 0; i < 7; i++) {
          if (tray[i] != null) {
            moveToTray(tray[i], i);
          }
        }
        paintScore();
      }
      return d;
    }
```

center( )

center( ) is a convenience routine that **checksize( )** uses to center the "Double Letter
Score" text.

```
    private void center(Graphics g, String s, int x, int y, int w) {
      x += (w - g.getFontMetrics().stringWidth(s)) / 2;
      g.drawString(s, x, y);
    }
```

paintScore( )

The **paintScore( )** method paints the two players' scores or just the one score in
single-player mode.

```
    private void paintScore() {
      int x = lm + (lw + lt) * 7 + lm;
      int y = tm + ah - 3 * lt;
      int h = lh + 2 * lt;
      Font font = new Font("TimesRoman", Font.PLAIN, h/2);
      offGraphics.setFont(font);
      FontMetrics fm = offGraphics.getFontMetrics();

      offGraphics.setColor(Color.white);
      offGraphics.fillRect(x, y, aw, h);
      offGraphics.setColor(Color.black);
```

```
      if (others_name == null) {
        int y0 = (h - fm.getHeight()) / 2 + fm.getAscent();
        offGraphics.drawString("Score: " + total_score, x, y + y0);
      } else {
        h/=2;
        int y0 = (h - fm.getHeight()) / 2 + fm.getAscent();
        offGraphics.drawString(name + ": " + total_score, x, y + y0);
        offGraphics.drawString(others_name + ": " + others_score,
                               x, y + h + y0);

      }
    }

    private int x0, y0, w0, h0;
```

selectLetter( )

The **selectLetter( )** method checks the mouse position to see if the cursor is over a letter. If so, it stores that in **pick** and computes how far the mouse was from the upper-left corner of the letter, which is stored in **dx, dy**. It also remembers the original position of this letter in **orig**.

```
    private void selectLetter(int x, int y) {
      pick = LetterHit(x, y);
      if(pick != null) {
        dx = pick.x - x;
        dy = pick.y - y;
        orig.x = pick.x;
        orig.y = pick.y;
      }
      repaint();
    }
```

dropLetter( )

In **dropLetter( )**, the user has dropped the letter if he or she was carrying one. It determines which square on the board the letter was over when it was dropped. It then calls **moveLetter( )** to attempt to move the letter to that square.

```
    private void dropLetter(int x, int y) {
      if(pick != null) {
```

```
            // find the center of the tile
            x += dx + lw / 2;
            y += dy + lh / 2;
            // find the tile index
            x = (x - lm) / (lw + lt);
            y = (y - tm) / (lh + lt);

            moveLetter(pick, x, y);

            pick = null;
            repaint();
        }
    }
```

dragLetter( )

The **dragLetter( )** method is handled differently than the other mouse-related events. This is mainly due to performance considerations. The goal is to have as smooth an interaction with the user as possible. **dragLetter( )** goes to some length to compute the bounding box of where the tile was before this drag plus where it is now. It then directly calls **paint(getGraphics( ))**. This is nonstandard Java applet programming, but it performs much more reliably.

```
    private void dragLetter(int x, int y) {
        if (pick != null) {
            int ox = pick.x;
            int oy = pick.y;
            pick.move(x + dx, y + dy);
            x0 = Math.min(ox, pick.x);
            y0 = Math.min(oy, pick.y);
            w0 = pick.w + Math.abs(ox - pick.x);
            h0 = pick.h + Math.abs(oy - pick.y);
            paint(getGraphics());
        }
    }
```

mousePressed( )

In the following code fragment, notice that **MyMouseAdapter** is an inner class that extends **MouseAdapter**. It overrides the **mousePressed( )** and **mouseReleased( )** methods.

The **mousePressed( )** method invokes the **selectLetter( )** method to do the necessary processing. The x and y coordinates of the current mouse position are obtained from the argument supplied to the **mousePressed( )** method.

```
class MyMouseAdapter extends MouseAdapter {
    public void mousePressed(MouseEvent me) {
        selectLetter(me.getX(), me.getY());
    }
```

mouseReleased( )

The **mouseReleased( )** method invokes the **dropLetter( )** method to do the necessary processing. The x and y coordinates of the current mouse position are obtained from the argument supplied to the **mouseReleased( )** method.

```
    public void mouseReleased(MouseEvent me) {
        dropLetter(me.getX(), me.getY());
    }
}
```

mouseDragged( )

In the following code fragment, notice that **MyMouseMotionAdapter** is an inner class that extends **MouseMotionAdapter**. It overrides the **mouseDragged( )** method.

The **mouseDragged( )** method invokes the **dragLetter( )** method to do the necessary processing. The x and y coordinates of the current mouse position are obtained from the argument supplied to the **mouseDragged( )** method.

```
class MyMouseMotionAdapter extends MouseMotionAdapter {
    public synchronized void mouseDragged(MouseEvent me) {
        dragLetter(me.getX(), me.getY());
    }
  }
}
```

Bag.java

The **Bag** class is very clean compared with **Board**. It is a simple abstraction for the bag of letters. When you create a **Bag**, you pass in a random seed, which allows you to create two bags that are random but the same by passing in the same random seed. The random number generator is stored in **rand**. There are two somewhat strange arrays of integers, named **letter_counts** and **letter_points**. Both arrays are 27 slots long. They represent the blank tile in slot 0, and *A* through *Z* in 1 through 26. The **letter_counts** array says how many of each letter are in a full bag. For example, **letter_counts[1]** is 9, which says there are nine *A* tiles in the bag. Similarly, the **letter_points** array maps each letter to its point value. The *A* tiles are worth only 1 point, and the lone *Z* is worth 10. There are 100 letters stored in the array called **letters**. The number of letters actually left in the bag during game play is stored in **n**.

```java
import java.util.Random;

class Bag {
  private Random rand;
  private int letter_counts[] = {
    2, 9, 2, 2, 4, 12, 2, 3, 2, 9, 1, 1, 4, 2,
    6, 8, 2, 1, 6, 4, 6, 4, 2, 2, 1, 2, 1
  };
  private int letter_points[] = {
    0, 1, 3, 3, 2, 1, 4, 2, 4, 1, 8, 5, 1, 3,
    1, 1, 3, 10, 1, 1, 1, 1, 4, 4, 8, 4, 10
  };
  private Letter letters[] = new Letter[100];
  private int n = 0;
```

Bag( )

The **Bag** constructor takes the seed and makes a **Random** object out of it. It then scans through the **letter_counts** array, making the right number of new **Letter** objects, being careful to replace the blank tile with an asterisk. It then calls **putBack( )** for each letter, to put them in the bag.

```java
  Bag(int seed) {
    rand = new Random(seed);
    for (int i = 0; i < letter_counts.length; i++) {
      for (int j = 0; j < letter_counts[i]; j++) {
        Letter l = new Letter(i == 0 ? '*' : (char)('A' + i - 1),
                              letter_points[i]);
        putBack(l);
      }
    }
  }
```

takeOut( )

This next method is slightly clever and a little inefficient, but in a noncritical way. **takeOut( )** picks a random number between 0 and **n** –1. It then extracts the letter at that offset from the **letters** array. It closes the hole over that slot in **letters** using **System.arraycopy( )**. Then it decrements **n** and returns the letter.

```
synchronized Letter takeOut() {
  if (n == 0)
    return null;
  int i = (int)(rand.nextDouble() * n);
  Letter l = letters[i];
  if (i != n - 1)
    System.arraycopy(letters, i + 1, letters, i, n - i - 1);
  n--;
  return l;
}
```

putBack( )

The **putBack( )** method is used by the constructor to put the tiles in the bag originally. It could also be used by a future game enhancement that would let players trade in tiles they were unhappy with in exchange for losing a turn. It simply puts the letter back at the end of the array.

```
synchronized void putBack(Letter l) {
  letters[n++] = l;
}
}
```

Letter.java

The **Letter** class is fairly clean in that it doesn't know anything about the game or the board. It merely encapsulates the position and visual rendering of a single letter. It uses several static variables to hold information about fonts and sizes. This is done so that the applet doesn't end up with 100 fonts in memory at once. This has the side effect that a browser page cannot contain two instances of the **Scrabblet** applet if they each have different sizes. The second one to initialize will overwrite the values in these static variables.

The **w** and **h** variables hold the constant width and height of every letter. The **font** and **smfont** variables are the AWT font objects for the big letter and the smaller point value. The **int**s **y0** and **ys0** store the offset of the baseline of the letter and the points, respectively. A few constants are provided to be passed back into **paint( )** to describe which color state to paint in: **NORMAL**, **DIM**, and **BRIGHT** mode.

```
import java.awt.*;

class Letter {
  static int w, h;
  private static Font font, smfont;
  private static int y0, ys0;
  private static int lasth = -1;
  static final int NORMAL = 0;
  static final int DIM = 1;
  static final int BRIGHT = 2;
```

colors[ ], mix( ), gain( ), and clamp( )

The **colors** array is initialized statically with nine color objects—three sets of three colors. The **mix( )** method is used to take a set of RGB values like 250, 220, 100 and turn them into three colors, which can be used to provide 3-D–like highlights and lowlights. The **mix( )** method calls on **gain( )** to boost or decimate the brightness of a given color and calls on **clamp( )** to make sure it remains in the legal range.

```
private static Color colors[][] = {
  mix(250, 220, 100),    // normal
  mix(200, 150, 80),     // dim
  mix(255, 230, 150)     // bright
};

private static Color mix(int r, int g, int b)[] {
  Color arr[] = new Color[3];

  arr[NORMAL] = new Color(r, g, b);
  arr[DIM] = gain(arr[0], .71);
  arr[BRIGHT] = gain(arr[0], 1.31);
  return arr;
}
private static int clamp(double d) {
  return (d < 0) ? 0 : ((d > 255) ? 255 : (int) d);
}
```

```
private static Color gain(Color c, double f) {
  return new Color(
    clamp(c.getRed() * f),
    clamp(c.getGreen() * f),
    clamp(c.getBlue() * f));
}
```

Instance Variables

The **valid** flag is used to make sure that all of the sizing variables are set up exactly once, the first time this **Letter** is painted. There are several variables cached here to keep from having to do lots of computation each time the applet paints—such as, **x0**, **w0**, **xs0**, **ws0**, and **gap**—which are all explained in the following comments. The **tile Point** object is used to remember which square on the 15×15 board this **Letter** is on. If this variable is **null**, then the **Letter** is not on the board. The **x,y** pair is used to exactly locate the **Letter**.

```
private boolean valid = false;

// quantized tile position of Letter. (just stored here).
private Point tile = null;
int x, y;                  // position of Letter.
private int x0;            // offset of symbol on tile.
private int w0;            // width in pixels of symbol.
private int xs0;           // offset of points on tile.
private int ws0;           // width in pixels of points.
private int gap = 1;       // pixels between symbol and points.
```

Letter( ), getSymbol( ), and getPoints( )

The **symbol** is a string that holds the letter displayed, and **points** is the point value of this letter. These are both initialized by the only constructor and returned by the wrapper methods **getSymbol( )** and **getPoints( )**, respectively.

```
private String symbol;
private int points;

Letter(char s, int p) {
  symbol = "" + s;
  points = p;
}
```

```
String getSymbol() {
  return symbol;
}

int getPoints() {
  return points;
}
```

move( ), remember( ), and recall( )

The **move( )** method is used to tell this tile where to draw. The **remember( )** method, however, is more complicated. It can be called with a **null**, which means that this tile should "forget" where it was. This indicates that the letter is not in play. Otherwise, it tells which coordinate on the board this letter is occupying. This state is inspected by a call to **recall( )**.

```
void move(int x, int y) {
  this.x = x;
  this.y = y;
}

void remember(Point t) {
  if (t == null) {
    tile = t;
  } else {
    tile = new Point(t.x, t.y);
  }
}

Point recall() {
  return tile;
}
```

resize( )

The **resize( )** method is called once by the board in order to tell every letter how big to be. Remember, **w** and **h** are static, so this affects all **Letter** instances at once.

```
static void resize(int w0, int h0) {
  w = w0;
  h = h0;
}
```

hit( )

The **hit( )** method returns **true** if the **xp,yp** pair passed in falls inside the bounds of this **Letter**.

```
boolean hit(int xp, int yp) {
  return (xp >= x && xp < x + w && yp >= y && yp < y + h);
}
```

validate( )

The **validate( )** method is used to load the fonts to find out how big the letters are, to decide where to paint them. This information is cached in the private variables discussed earlier. The results of these calculations are used next in **paint( )**.

```
private int font_ascent;
void validate(Graphics g) {
  FontMetrics fm;
  if (h != lasth) {
    font = new Font("SansSerif", Font.BOLD, (int)(h * .6));
    g.setFont(font);
    fm = g.getFontMetrics();
    font_ascent = fm.getAscent();

    y0 = (h - font_ascent) * 4 / 10 + font_ascent;

    smfont = new Font("SansSerif", Font.BOLD, (int)(h * .3));
    g.setFont(smfont);
    fm = g.getFontMetrics();
    ys0 = y0 + fm.getAscent() / 2;
    lasth = h;
  }
  if (!valid) {
    valid = true;
    g.setFont(font);
    fm = g.getFontMetrics();
    w0 = fm.stringWidth(symbol);
    g.setFont(smfont);
    fm = g.getFontMetrics();
    ws0 = fm.stringWidth("" + points);
    int slop = w - (w0 + gap + ws0);
    x0 = slop / 2;
    if (x0 < 1)
```

```
      x0 = 1;
    xs0 = x0 + w0 + gap;
    if (points > 9)
      xs0--;
  }
}
```

paint( )

The **paint( )** method is called by the board. It passes in an integer, **i**, which is one of **NORMAL**, **BRIGHT**, or **DIM** from this class. That is used as an index into the **colors** array to select the base color. A sequence of rectangles is filled to create the appearance of a 3-D highlighted and shadowed button. If **points** is greater than zero, indicating a nonblank letter, then the main letter is drawn, and its point value is drawn next to it.

```
void paint(Graphics g, int i) {
  Color c[] = colors[i];
  validate(g);
  g.setColor(c[NORMAL]);
  g.fillRect(x, y, w, h);
  g.setColor(c[BRIGHT]);
  g.fillRect(x, y, w - 1, 1);
  g.fillRect(x, y + 1, 1, h - 2);
  g.setColor(Color.black);
  g.fillRect(x, y + h - 1, w, 1);
  g.fillRect(x + w - 1, y, 1, h - 1);
  g.setColor(c[DIM]);
  g.fillRect(x + 1, y + h - 2, w - 2, 1);
  g.fillRect(x + w - 2, y + 1, 1, h - 3);
  g.setColor(Color.black);
  if (points > 0) {
    g.setFont(font);
    g.drawString(symbol, x + x0, y + y0);
    g.setFont(smfont);
    g.drawString("" + points, x + xs0, y + ys0);
  }
 }
}
```

ServerConnection.java

The last class in the client side of this applet is **ServerConnection**, which encapsulates the communication with the server and our opponent. There are several variables declared at the beginning of the class. The socket **port** number to attach to on the server is 6564. **CRLF** is the Internet constant string representing end-of-line. The I/O streams from and to the server are **in** and **out**, respectively. The unique ID by which this connection is known on the server is stored in **id**. The ID that we are connected to as an opponent is stored in **toid**. The **Scrabblet** applet we are connecting for is **scrabblet**.

```
import java.io.*;
import java.net.*;
import java.util.*;

class ServerConnection implements Runnable {
   private static final int port = 6564;
   private static final String CRLF = "\r\n";
   private BufferedReader in;
   private PrintWriter out;
   private String id, toid = null;
   private Scrabblet scrabblet;
```

ServerConnection( )

The **ServerConnection** constructor takes the name of an Internet site to attach to and attempts to open a socket to the right port on that host. If that succeeds, it wraps an **InputStreamReader** and a **BufferedReader** around the input and a **PrintWriter** around the output. If the connection fails, an exception is thrown to the caller.

```
public ServerConnection(Scrabblet sc, String site) throws
   IOException {
   scrabblet = sc;
   Socket server = new Socket(site, port);
   in = new BufferedReader(new
           InputStreamReader(server.getInputStream()));
   out = new PrintWriter(server.getOutputStream(), true);
}
```

readline( )

The **readline( )** method is merely a convenience function that converts the **IOException** from a **readLine( )** into a simple **null** return.

```
private String readline() {
  try {
    return in.readLine();
  } catch (IOException e) {
    return null;
  }
}
```

setName( ) and delete( )

The **setName( )** method tells the server to associate this name with us, and the **delete( )** method is used to remove us from any lists the server is keeping.

```
void setName(String s) {
  out.println("name " + s);
}

void delete() {
  out.println("delete " + id);
}
```

setTo( ) and send( )

The **setTo( )** method binds the ID of the opponent. Future **send( )** calls will go to this player.

```
void setTo(String to) {
  toid = to;
}

void send(String s) {
  if (toid != null)
    out.println("to " + toid + " " + s);
}
```

challenge( ), accept( ), chat( ), move( ), turn( ), and quit( )

The following short methods send one-line messages from this client to the server, which will in turn send those messages on to our opponent. The **challenge** message is used to initiate starting a game, and **accept** is sent in response to a challenge. For each letter that moves, the **move** message is sent, and then the **turn** message is sent at the end of each turn. If the client quits or leaves the page with the applet on it, it sends the **quit** message.

```java
void challenge(String destid) {
  setTo(destid);
  send("challenge " + id);
}

void accept(String destid, int seed) {
  setTo(destid);
  send("accept " + id + " " + seed);
}

void chat(String s) {
  send("chat " + id + " " + s);
}

void move(String letter, int x, int y) {
  send("move " + letter + " " + x + " " + y);
}

void turn(String words, int score) {
  send("turn " + score + " " + words);
}

void quit() {
  send("quit " + id);  // tell other player
  out.println("quit"); // unhook

}
```

start( )

The next method simply starts the thread that manages the client side of the network.

```
// reading from server...

private Thread t;

void start() {
  t = new Thread(this);
  t.start();
}
```

Keywords

The static variables and static block shown here are used to initialize the **keys Hashtable** with a mapping between the strings in **keystrings** and their position in the array—for example, **keys.get("move") == MOVE**. The **lookup( )** method takes care of unpacking the **Integer** objects into the right **int**, with −1 meaning the keyword was not found.

```
private static final int ID = 1;
private static final int ADD = 2;
private static final int DELETE = 3;
private static final int MOVE = 4;
private static final int CHAT = 5;
private static final int QUIT = 6;
private static final int TURN = 7;
private static final int ACCEPT = 8;
private static final int CHALLENGE = 9;
private static Hashtable keys = new Hashtable();
private static String keystrings[] = {
    "", "id", "add", "delete", "move", "chat",
    "quit", "turn", "accept", "challenge"
};
static {
```

```
 for (int i = 0; i < keystrings.length; i++)
    keys.put(keystrings[i], new Integer(i));
}

private int lookup(String s) {
  Integer i = (Integer) keys.get(s);
  return i == null ? -1 : i.intValue();
}
```

run( )

run( ) is the main loop of the game's connection to the server. It goes into a blocking call to **readline( )** that will return with a **String** whenever a line of text comes from the server. It uses a **StringTokenizer** to break the line into words. The **switch** statement dispatches us to the right code, based on the first word in the input line. Each of the keywords in the protocol parses the input line differently, and most of them make method calls back into the **Scrabblet** class to do their work.

```
public void run() {
   String s;
   StringTokenizer st;
   while ((s = readline()) != null) {
     st = new StringTokenizer(s);
     String keyword = st.nextToken();
     switch (lookup(keyword)) {
     default:
       System.out.println("bogus keyword: " + keyword + "\r");
       break;
     case ID:
       id = st.nextToken();
       break;
     case ADD: {
         String id = st.nextToken();
         String hostname = st.nextToken();
         String name = st.nextToken(CRLF);
         scrabblet.add(id, hostname, name);
       }
       break;
     case DELETE:
```

```java
            scrabblet.delete(st.nextToken());
            break;
        case MOVE: {
            String ch = st.nextToken();
            int x = Integer.parseInt(st.nextToken());
            int y = Integer.parseInt(st.nextToken());
            scrabblet.move(ch, x, y);
        }
            break;
        case CHAT: {
            String from = st.nextToken();
            scrabblet.chat(from, st.nextToken(CRLF));
        }
            break;
        case QUIT: {
            String from = st.nextToken();
            scrabblet.quit(from);
        }
            break;
        case TURN: {
            int score = Integer.parseInt(st.nextToken());
            scrabblet.turn(score, st.nextToken(CRLF));
        }
            break;
        case ACCEPT: {
            String from = st.nextToken();
            int seed = Integer.parseInt(st.nextToken());
            scrabblet.accept(from, seed);
        }
            break;
        case CHALLENGE: {
            String from = st.nextToken();
            scrabblet.challenge(from);
        }
            break;
        }
    }
  }
}
```

The Server Code

These last two classes are not part of this applet. Rather, they must be installed and run separately on the web server that the applet classes are to be loaded from. This will require the security rights to install and run so-called daemon processes on the web site, which not many people have. Fortunately, most users of this game will not be setting up their own servers; more likely, they will just play games connected to existing ones.

Server.java

Server is the main class for the server side of **Scrabblet**. Once this is installed on the web server, you have to run it using the command-line Java interpreter for that system, as shown here:

```
C:\java\Scrabblet> java Server
```

Once running, **Server** will respond with the following message:

Server listening on port 6564

The **Server** class starts out by declaring a few variables. The port has to be the same number, **6564**, as we saw in **ServerConnection**. The **idcon Hashtable** is used to store all of the connections to all of the clients. We use a hash table rather than an array to manage frequent insertion and deletion, which require lots of array copying. The **id** is incremented for each new connection. This corresponds to the **id** instance variable we saw earlier in the client.

```java
import java.net.*;
import java.io.*;
import java.util.*;

public class Server implements Runnable {
   private int port = 6564;
   private Hashtable idcon = new Hashtable();
   private int id = 0;
   static final String CRLF = "\r\n";
```

addConnection( )

The **addConnection( )** method is called every time a new client connects to our applet. This method creates a new instance of **ClientConnection**, described next, to manage the client. It passes in a reference to this **Server**, the socket the client connected with, and the current value of **id**. Finally, it increments the **id** to have it ready for the next connection.

```
synchronized void addConnection(Socket s) {
  ClientConnection con = new ClientConnection(this, s, id);
  // we will wait for the ClientConnection to do a clean
  // handshake setting up its "name" before calling
  // set() below, which makes this connection "live."
  id++;
}
```

set( )

The **set( )** method is called from **ClientConnection** in response to the client telling us its "name." **set( )** tracks all of the connections in the **idcon** hash table, and first it removes this **id** from the table so that it won't get duplicates if the client sends its name twice. The method calls **setBusy(false)** to signify that this connection is available to play a game. Then it walks through all of the other connections by enumeratir.g the keys of the **idcon** hash table. For all nonbusy connections (those players waiting for an opponent), **set( )** sends an "**add**" protocol message so they will all know about this connection.

```
synchronized void set(String the_id, ClientConnection con) {
  idcon.remove(the_id) ;   // make sure we're not in there twice.
  con.setBusy(false);
  // tell this one about the other clients.
  Enumeration e = idcon.keys();
  while (e.hasMoreElements()) {
    String id = (String)e.nextElement();
    ClientConnection other = (ClientConnection) idcon.get(id);
    if (!other.isBusy())
      con.write("add " + other + CRLF);
  }
  idcon.put(the_id, con);
  broadcast(the_id, "add " + con);
}
```

sendto( )

sendto( ) is called in response to a "**to**" protocol message. It writes whatever is in the **body** string directly to the connection identified by **dest**.

```
synchronized void sendto(String dest, String body) {
  ClientConnection con = (ClientConnection)idcon.get(dest);
  if (con != null) {
    con.write(body + CRLF);
  }
}
```

broadcast( )

The **broadcast( )** method is used to send a single message, in **body**, to every single connection except the one identified in **exclude** (typically, the sender).

```
synchronized void broadcast(String exclude, String body) {
  Enumeration e = idcon.keys();
  while (e.hasMoreElements()) {
    String id = (String)e.nextElement();
    if (!exclude.equals(id)) {
      ClientConnection con = (ClientConnection) idcon.get(id);
      con.write(body + CRLF);
    }
  }
}
```

delete( )

The **delete( )** method is used to tell all of the connected clients to forget they ever heard of **the_id**. This is used by clients that are engaged in a game to remove themselves from other players' eligibility lists.

```
synchronized void delete(String the_id) {
  broadcast(the_id, "delete " + the_id);
}
```

kill( )

The **kill( )** method is called whenever a client explicitly quits, sending the "**quit**" message, or when a client simply dies if the browser quits.

```
    synchronized void kill(ClientConnection c) {
      if (idcon.remove(c.getId()) == c) {
        delete(c.getId());
      }
    }
}
```

run( )

The **run( )** method is the main loop of the server. It creates a new socket on port 6564 and goes into an infinite loop accepting socket connections from clients. It calls **addConnection( )** with each socket that it accepts.

```
    public void run() {
      try {
        ServerSocket acceptSocket = new ServerSocket(port);
        System.out.println("Server listening on port " + port);
        while (true) {
          Socket s = acceptSocket.accept();
          addConnection(s);
        }
      } catch (IOException e) {
        System.out.println("accept loop IOException: " + e);
      }
    }
```

main( )

main( ) is, of course, the method run by the Java command-line interpreter. It creates a new instance of **Server** and launches a new **Thread** to run it.

```
    public static void main(String args[]) {
      new Thread(new Server()).start();
      try {
        Thread.currentThread().join();
      } catch (InterruptedException e) { }
    }
}
```

ClientConnection.java

This class is the mirror image of **ServerConnection** in the applet. One of these is created for each client. Its job is to manage all of the I/O to and from a client. The private instance variables hold all of the states about this client. The **Socket** is stored in **sock**. The buffered reader and output streams are stored in **in** and **out**. The host name of the client machine is kept in **host**. A reference to the **Server** instance that created this client is held in **server**. The name of the player on this client is stored in **name**, while the player's automatically assigned ID number is held in **id**. The **busy** Boolean variable stores whether or not this client is actively engaged in a game.

```java
import java.net.*;
import java.io.*;
import java.util.*;

class ClientConnection implements Runnable {
  private Socket sock;
  private BufferedReader in;
  private OutputStream out;
  private String host;
  private Server server;
  private static final String CRLF = "\r\n";
  private String name = null;    // for humans
  private String id;
  private boolean busy = false;
```

ClientConnection( )

The constructor saves the reference to the server and socket and remembers the unique ID. We wrap an **InputStreamReader** and a **BufferedReader** around the input so that it can call **readLine( )** on it. Then it writes the **id** back to the client to let it know what number it is. Finally, it creates and starts a new **Thread** to handle this connection.

```java
public ClientConnection(Server srv, Socket s, int i) {
  try {
    server = srv;
    sock = s;
    in = new BufferedReader(new
                InputStreamReader(s.getInputStream()));
```

```
        out = s.getOutputStream();
        host = s.getInetAddress().getHostName();
        id = "" + i;

        // tell the new one who it is...
        write("id " + id + CRLF);

        new Thread(this).start();
    } catch (IOException e) {
        System.out.println("failed ClientConnection " + e);
    }
}
```

toString( )

We override **toString( )** so that we can have a clean representation of this connection for logging.

```
public String toString() {
    return id + " " + host + " " + name;
}
```

getHost( ), getId( ), isBusy( ), and setBusy( )

We wrap **host**, **id**, and **busy** in public methods to allow read-only access.

```
public String getHost() {
    return host;
}

public String getId() {
    return id;
}

public boolean isBusy() {
    return busy;
}

public void setBusy(boolean b) {
    busy = b;
}
```

close( )

The **close( )** method is called if the client explicitly quits or if we get an exception reading from the socket. We call **kill( )** in the server, which removes us from any lists. Then we close the socket, which also closes both the input and output streams.

```
public void close() {
  server.kill(this);
  try {
    sock.close();    // closes in and out too.
  } catch (IOException e) { }
}
```

write( )

To write a string to a stream, we have to convert it to an array of bytes, using **getBytes( )**.

```
public void write(String s) {
  byte buf[];
  buf = s.getBytes();
  try {
    out.write(buf, 0, buf.length);
  } catch (IOException e) {
    close();
  }
}
```

readline( )

The **readline( )** method merely converts the **IOException** from **readLine( )** into a **null** return value.

```
private String readline() {
  try {
    return in.readLine();
  } catch (IOException e) {
    return null;
  }
}
```

Keywords

This section is very similar to the same part of the **ServerConnection** class, which represents the other end of the wire. The static variables and static block shown here are used to initialize the **keys Hashtable** with a mapping between the strings in **keystrings** and their position in the array—for example, **keys.get("quit") == QUIT**. The **lookup( )** method takes care of unpacking the **Integer** objects into the right **int**, with –1 meaning the keyword was not found.

```java
static private final int NAME = 1;
static private final int QUIT = 2;
static private final int TO = 3;
static private final int DELETE = 4;

static private Hashtable keys = new Hashtable();
static private String keystrings[] = {
  "", "name", "quit", "to", "delete"
};
static {
  for (int i = 0; i < keystrings.length; i++)
    keys.put(keystrings[i], new Integer(i));
}

private int lookup(String s) {
  Integer i = (Integer) keys.get(s);
  return i == null ? -1 : i.intValue();
}
```

run( )

run( ) has the loop that manages all of the communication with this client. It uses a **StringTokenizer** to parse the input lines, keying off of the first word in each line. The **lookup( )** method just shown is used to look up these first words in the **keys** hash table. We then switch, based on the integer value of the keyword. The **NAME** message comes from clients when they first gain a human identity. We call **set( )** in the server to get this connection set up. The **QUIT** message is sent when the client wants to end its server session. The **TO** message contains a destination ID and a message body to be sent to that client. We call **sendto( )** in the server to pass the message along. The last message is **DELETE**, which is sent by clients that want to continue being connected but no longer want to have their names listed as available to play. **run( )** sets the busy flag and calls **delete( )** in the server, which notifies the clients that we don't want to be called.

```java
public void run() {
  String s;
  StringTokenizer st;
  while ((s = readline()) != null) {
    st = new StringTokenizer(s);
    String keyword = st.nextToken();
    switch (lookup(keyword)) {
    default:
      System.out.println("bogus keyword: " + keyword + "\r");
      break;
    case NAME:
      name = st.nextToken() +
        (st.hasMoreTokens() ? " " + st.nextToken(CRLF) : "");
      System.out.println("[" + new Date() + "] " + this + "\r");
      server.set(id, this);
      break;
    case QUIT:
     close();
     return;
    case TO:
      String dest = st.nextToken();
      String body = st.nextToken(CRLF);
      server.sendto(dest, body);
      break;
    case DELETE:
      busy = true;
      server.delete(id);
      break;
    }
  }
  close();
}
}
```

Enhancing Scrabblet

This applet represents a complete client/server, multiplayer board game. In the future, the code in **Server** and **ServerConnection** could be extended in many ways. It could be used to support other turn-based games. It could track and maintain a high-score list for each game. It could be dynamically extensible to understand new protocol verbs.

One such example for the game described in this chapter would be to have a lookup function that checked a series of submitted words against a dictionary stored on the server. The server could then be the arbiter for such disputes as whether *xyzy* is a valid word. You could also construct a word robot, which would reside on the server but act like another player and use the dictionary to generate the best word placement from its current set of seven letters. It could even use a list of pithy quotes to throw into the chat window after each move. You might want to try making some of these enhancements yourself.

This applet is intended for entertainment and educational purposes. Any similarity to any and all commercial products is merely coincidental.

Appendix A

Using Java's
Documentation
Comments

A s explained in Part I, Java supports three types of comments. The first two are the // and the /* */. The third type is called a *documentation comment*. It begins with the character sequence /**. It ends with */. Documentation comments allow you to embed information about your program into the program itself. You can then use the **javadoc** utility program to extract the information and put it into an HTML file. Documentation comments make it convenient to document your programs. You have almost certainly seen documentation generated with **javadoc**, because that is the way the Java API library was documented by Sun.

The javadoc Tags

The **javadoc** utility recognizes the following tags:

Tag	Meaning
@author	Identifies the author of a class.
@deprecated	Specifies that a class or member is deprecated.
{@docRoot}	Specifies the path to the root directory of the current documentation (added by Java 2, version 1.3).
@exception	Identifies an exception thrown by a method.
{@inheritDoc}	Inherits a comment from the immediate superclass. (Added by Java 2, version 1.4, but not currently implemented.)
{@link}	Inserts an in-line link to another topic.
{@linkplain}	Inserts an in-line link to another topic, but the link is displayed in a plain-text font. (Added by Java 2, version 1.4.)
@param	Documents a method's parameter.
@return	Documents a method's return value.
@see	Specifies a link to another topic.
@serial	Documents a default serializable field.
@serialData	Documents the data written by the **writeObject( )** or **writeExternal( )** methods.
@serialField	Documents an **ObjectStreamField** component.
@since	States the release when a specific change was introduced.
@throws	Same as @exception.
{@value}	Displays the value of a constant, which must be a **static** field. (Added by Java 2, version 1.4.)
@version	Specifies the version of a class.

As you can see, all document tags begin with an at sign (@). You may also use other, standard HTML tags in a documentation comment. However, some tags, such as headings, should not be used, because they disrupt the look of the HTML file produced by **javadoc**.

You can use documentation comments to document classes, interfaces, fields, constructors, and methods. In all cases, the documentation comment must immediately precede the item being documented. When you are documenting a variable, the documentation tags you can use are **@see**, **@since**, **@serial**, **@serialField**, {**@value**}, and **@deprecated**. For classes, you can use **@see**, **@author**, **@since**, **@deprecated**, and **@version**. Methods can be documented with **@see**, **@return**, **@param**, **@since**, **@deprecated**, **@throws**, **@serialData**, {**@inheritDoc**}, and **@exception**. A {**@link**}, {**@docRoot**}, or {**@linkplain**} tag can be used anywhere. Each tag is examined next.

@author

The **@author** tag documents the author of a class. It has the following syntax:

@author *description*

Here, *description* will usually be the name of the person who wrote the class. The **@author** tag can be used only in documentation for a class. You may need to specify the **-author** option when executing **javadoc** in order for the **@author** field to be included in the HTML documentation.

@deprecated

The **@deprecated** tag specifies that a class or a member is deprecated. It is recommended that you include **@see** or {**@link**} tags to inform the programmer about available alternatives. The syntax is the following:

@deprecated *description*

Here, *description* is the message that describes the deprecation. Information specified by the **@deprecated** tag is recognized by the compiler and is included in the **.class** file that is generated. Therefore, the programmer can be given this information when compiling Java source files. The **@deprecated** tag can be used in documentation for variables, methods, and classes.

{@docRoot}

{**@docRoot**} specifies the path to the root directory of the current documentation.

@exception

The **@exception** tag describes an exception to a method. It has the following syntax:

@exception *exception-name explanation*

Here, the fully qualified name of the exception is specified by *exception-name*; *explanation* is a string that describes how the exception can occur. The **@exception** tag can only be used in documentation for a method.

{@inheritDoc}

Inherits a comment from the immediate surperclass. (Not currently implemented by Java 2, version 1.4)

{@link}

The **{@link}** tag provides an in-line link to additional information. It has the following syntax:

   {@link *name text*}

Here, *name* is the name of a class or method to which a link is added, and *text* is the string that is displayed.

{@linkplain}

Inserts an in-line link to another topic. The link is displayed in plain-text font. Otherwise, it is similar to **{@link}**.

@param

The **@param** tag documents a parameter to a method. It has the following syntax:

   @param *parameter-name explanation*

Here, *parameter-name* specifies the name of a parameter to a method. The meaning of that parameter is described by *explanation*. The **@param** tag can be used only in documentation for a method.

@return

The **@return** tag describes the return value of a method. It has the following syntax:

   @return *explanation*

Here, *explanation* describes the type and meaning of the value returned by a method. The **@return** tag can be used only in documentation for a method.

@see

The **@see** tag provides a reference to additional information. Its most commonly used forms are shown here.

@see *anchor*
@see *pkg.class#member text*

In the first form, *anchor* is a link to an absolute or relative URL. In the second form, *pkg.class#member* specifies the name of the item, and *text* is the text displayed for that item. The text parameter is optional, and if not used, then the item specified by *pkg.class#member* is displayed. The member name, too, is optional. Thus, you can specify a reference to a package, class, or interface in addition to a reference to a specific method or field. The name can be fully qualified or partially qualified. However, the dot that precedes the member name (if it exists) must be replaced by a hash character.

@serial

The **@serial** tag defines the comment for a default serializable field. It has the following syntax:

@serial *description*

Here, *description* is the comment for that field.

@serialData

The **@serialData** tag documents the data written by the **writeObject( )** and **writeExternal( )** methods. It has the following syntax:

@serialData *description*

Here, *description* is the comment for that data.

@serialField

The **@serialField** tag provides comments for an **ObjectStreamField** component. It has the following syntax:

@serialField *name type description*

Here, *name* is the name of the field, *type* is its type, and *description* is the comment for that field.

@since

The **@since** tag states that a class or member was introduced in a specific release. It has the following syntax:

@since *release*

Here, *release* is a string that designates the release or version in which this feature became available. The **@since** tag can be used in documentation for variables, methods, and classes.

@throws

The **@throws** tag has the same meaning as the **@exception** tag.

{@value}

Displays the value of a constant, which must be a **static** field.

@version

The **@version** tag specifies the version of a class. It has the following syntax:

> @version *info*

Here, *info* is a string that contains version information, typically a version number, such as 2.2. The **@version** tag can be used only in documentation for a class. You may need to specify the **-version** option when executing **javadoc** in order for the **@version** field to be included in the HTML documentation.

The General Form of a Documentation Comment

After the beginning **/****, the first line or lines become the main description of your class, variable, or method. After that, you can include one or more of the various @ tags. Each @ tag must start at the beginning of a new line or follow an asterisk (*) that is at the start of a line. Multiple tags of the same type should be grouped together. For example, if you have three **@see** tags, put them one after the other.

Here is an example of a documentation comment for a class:

```
/**
 * This class draws a bar chart.
 * @author Herbert Schildt
 * @version 3.2
 */
```

What javadoc Outputs

The **javadoc** program takes as input your Java program's source file and outputs several HTML files that contain the program's documentation. Information about each class will be in its own HTML file. **javadoc** will also output an index and a hierarchy tree. Other HTML files can be generated. Since different implementations of **javadoc** may work differently, you will need to check the instructions that accompany your Java development system for details specific to your version.

An Example that Uses Documentation Comments

Following is a sample program that uses documentation comments. Notice the way each comment immediately precedes the item that it describes. After being processed by **javadoc**, the documentation about the **SquareNum** class will be found in **SquareNum.html**.

```java
import java.io.*;

/**
 * This class demonstrates documentation comments.
 * @author Herbert Schildt
 * @version 1.2
 */
public class SquareNum {
  /**
   * This method returns the square of num.
   * This is a multiline description.  You can use
   * as many lines as you like.
   * @param num The value to be squared.
   * @return num squared.
   */
  public double square(double num) {
    return num * num;
  }

  /**
   * This method inputs a number from the user.
   * @return The value input as a double.
   * @exception IOException On input error.
   * @see IOException
   */
  public double getNumber() throws IOException {
    // create a BufferedReader using System.in
    InputStreamReader isr = new InputStreamReader(System.in);
```

```
    BufferedReader inData = new BufferedReader(isr);
    String str;

    str = inData.readLine();
    return (new Double(str)).doubleValue();
  }
/**
 * This method demonstrates square().
 * @param args Unused.
 * @return Nothing.
 * @exception IOException On input error.
 * @see IOException
 */

public static void main(String args[])
  throws IOException
{

  SquareNum ob = new SquareNum();
  double val;

  System.out.println("Enter value to be squared: ");
  val = ob.getNumber();
  val = ob.square(val);

  System.out.println("Squared value is " + val);
  }
}
```

Index

Complete References

C# : The Complete Reference **Herbert Schildt**
0-07-048675-1 Rs.495/-

Learn everything you need to know about Microsoft's new programming language for the .NET platform. Programming guru and best-selling author Herb Schildt presents not only code but valuable insight into best programming practices, so you can implement C# effectively.

Visual Basic.NET: The Complete Reference **Jeffery R. Shapiro**
0-07-049511-4 Rs.395/-

Master this massive programming language upgrade that raises Visual Basic functionality to the level of the .NET platform. Coverage includes all core topics—plus security, debugging, and helpful information on migrating existing Visual Basic projects to Visual Basic.NET.

DB2: The Complete Reference **Paul Zikopoulos**
0-07-049569-6 Rs.495/- (t)

Design and manage well-organized DB2 databases and applications using this comprehensive resource. Includes details on the new features of version 7.2 this guide covers commands, SQL keywords, administration, data replication, performance tuning and much more. Also covered are IBM's business intelligence features including data warehousing and OLAP.

INTERNET : The Complete Reference, 2/e **Margaret Levine Young**
0-07-048699-9 Rs.395/-

Make the most of all the Internet has to offer with help from this comprehensive guide. Learn how to get connected, choose an Internet service provider (ISP) and Web browser, send e-mail, chat, use plug-ins, purchase goods safely, find tons of helpful and fun information online -- even create your own Web page.

VISUAL C++.NET: The Complete Reference **Pappas & William, Murray III**
0-07-049532-7 Rs.450/-

Learn to create large, highly stable e-commerce Web sites with help from this premier resource. Youll find comprehensive coverage on all aspects of Visual C++ .NET, including important topics such as debugging, Web support, attributed programming, and much more.

HTML: The Complete Reference **Thomas Powell**
0-07-048652-2 Rs.450/-

A comprehensive, all-in-one reference for all levels of HTML developers. This bestselling book combines theory and practice, and includes extensive examples.

Complete References

Herbert Schildt
0-07-213485-2

Jeffery R. Shapiro
0-07-213381-3

Chris H. Pappas & William
H. Murray, III
0-07-212958-1

Herbert Schildt
0-07-213084-9

Ron Ben-Natan & Ori Sasson
0-07-222394-4

Arthur Griffith
0-07-222405-3

For the answers to everything related to your technology, drill as deeply as you please into our Complete Reference series. Written by topical authorities, these comprehensive resources offer a full range of knowledge, including extensive product information, theory, step-by-step tutorials, sample projects, and helpful appendixes.

Tata McGraw-Hill Publishing Company Limited
NEW DELHI

13-digit ISBN	Sub-discipline	AUTHOR	TITLE	Edition	Price (Rs.)	Pub Year
			BUSINESS INTELLIGENCE			
9780070265042	CRYSTAL REPORTS	PECK	Crystal Reports 2008: The Complete Reference	1	750.00	2008
9780070264823	IBM COGNOS	VOLITICH	Cognos 8 Business Intelligence: The Official Guide	1	650.00	2008
9780070636415	BUSINESS OBJECTS	HOWSON	Business Objects XI: The Complete Reference	2	595.00	2006
9780070223660		HOWSON	Successful Business Intelligence: Making BI The Killer Applications	1	425.00	2007
9780070248472		UTLEY	Business Intelligence with Microsoft Office Performance Point Server 2007	1	475.00	2008
9780070223653		HARTS	Microsoft ® Office 2007 Business Intelligence	1	525.00	2007
9780070657014		HALARI	IT Portfolio Rationalization	1	495.00	2008
			CAREER			
9780070077928		GANESH	Cracking the C, C++ and Java Interview	1	250.00	2009
9780070599314		SUTARWAALA	Good Programming Skills and Practices	1	265.00	2005
9780070600522		BALASUBRAMANIAM	Cracking the IT Interview	1	340.00	2005
9780070077898		BANERJEE	Cracking The Oracle Apps DBA Interview: 325 Frequently Asked Questions	1	250.00	2008
9780070635456		BABU	Offshoring IT Services	1	395.00	2005
9780070656703		GANESH	60 Tips to Object-Oriented Programming	1	295.00	2007
			CERTIFICATION			
9780070677456	CBAP	PHILLIPS	CBAP Certified Business Analysis Professional All-in-One Exam Guide with CDROM	1	695.00	2009
9780070264816	CCNA	DEAL	CCNA Cisco Certified Network Associate Study Guide (Exam 640-802)	4	525.00	2008
9780070682641	CCNA Security	DEAL	CCNA Cisco Certified Network Associate Security Study Guide with CDROM (Exam 640-553)	1	625.00	2009
9780070700550	CISA	GREGORY	CISA Certified information Systems Auditor All-in-One Exam Guide	1	850.00	2009
9780070701458	CISSP	HARRIS	CISSP All-in-One Certification Exam Guide	5	795.00	2010
9780070702332	CompTIA A+	MEYERS	CompTIA A+ Certification All-in-One Exam Guide, Seventh Edition (Exams 220-701 & 220-702)	7	795.00	2010
9780070670877	CompTIA Network+	CLARKE	CompTIA Network+ Certification Study Guide, Fourth Edition (with CD)	4	695.00	2009
9780070677272	CompTIA Network+	MFYERS	Mike Meyers' CompTIA Network+ Guide to Managing and Troubleshooting Networks, Second Edition	2	725.00	2009
9780070677289	CompTIA Network+	MEYERS	CompTIA Network+ All-in-One Exam Guide, Fourth Edition	4	725.00	2009
9780070701199	CWTS	CARPENTER	CWTS Certified Wireless Technology Specialist Study Guide (Exam PW0-070)	1	695.00	2010
9780070682597	PMI	PHILLIPS	PMP Project Management Professional Study Guide with CDROM, Third Edition	3	650.00	2009
9780070659674	RED HAT CERTIFICATION	JANG	RHCE Red Hat Certified Engineer Linux Study Guide (Exam RH302)	5	595.00	2007
9780070682696	SCJA	LIGUORI	SCJA Sun Certified Java Associate Study Guide (Exam CX-310-019)	1	450.00	2009
9780070264984	SCJP	SIERRA & BATES	SCJP Sun Certified Programmer for Java 6 Study Guide (Exam 310-065)	1	550.00	2008
9780070142756	SECURITY+	WHITE	Security+ Certification All-in-One Exam Guide	2	695.00	2009
9780070249134	CCENT	WALKER	CCENT Cisco Certified Enterprise Technician Study Guide (Exam 640-822)	1	495.00	2008
9780070659650	CompTIA A+	HOLCOMBE	A+ Certification Study Guide, with CD	6	650.00	2007
9780070221987	CompTIA A+	MEYERS	Mike Meyers' A+ Guide: PC Technician (Exams 220-602, 220-603, & 220-604)	2	650.00	2007
9780070222823	COMPTIA LINUX+	TRACY	Linux+ Certification Study Guide	1	695.00	2007
9780070222014	CWNA	CARPENTER	CWNA Certified Wireless Network Administrator Official Study Guide (Exam PW0-100)	4	525.00	2007
9780070636507	CWSP	MOERSCHEL	CWSP Certified Wireless Security Professional: Official Study Guide (Exam PW-200)	2	565.00	2006
9780070142701	MCITP	GIBSON	MCITP Windows Vista Support Technician All-in-One Exam Guide (Exam 70-620, 70-622, & 70-623) w/CD	1	725.00	2009
9780070248700	MCITP	GIBSON	MCITP SQL Server 2005 Database Developer All-in-One Exam Guide (Exams 70-431, 70-441 & 70-442)	1	825.00	2008
9780070142732	MCTS	SUHANOVS	MCTS Windows Server 2008 Active Directory Services Study Guide (Exam 70-640)	1	695.00	2009

ISBN	Category	Author	Title	Qty	Price	Year
9780070139671	PMI	PHILLIPS	Program Management Professional (PgMP) All-in-One Exam Guide with CD	1	525.00	2008
9780070659070	PMI	PHILLIPS	CAPM/PMP Project Management Certification All-In-One Exam Guide with CD	1	495.00	2007
9780074637371	SAP	MILLER	SAP R/3 Certification Exam Guide (With CD)	1	625.00	1999
9780070077881	SCMAD	NAING et al	SCMAD Sun Certified Mobile Application Developer Exam Guide (Exam CX-310-110)	1	625.00	2008
9780070249103	SCWCD	JAGGI	SCWCD Exam Guide with JEE5	1	595.00	2008
9780070265134	UBUNTU	JANG	Ubuntu Certified Professional Study Guide (Exam LPI 199)	1	625.00	2008
9780070619616	WIRELESS#	CARPENTER	Wireless# Certification Official Study Guide (Exam PW0-050)	1	525.00	2006
CISCO NETWORKS						
9780070677241		DEAL	Cisco ASA Configuration	1	695.00	2009
9780070528895		HILL	CISCO: The Complete Reference	1	715.00	2002
9780070659698		VELTE	CISCO: A Beginner's Guide	4	550.00	2007
COMPUTER ARCHITECTURE & ORGANIZATION						
9780070532366		GOVINDARAJALU	Computer Architecture and Organization: Design Principles and Applications	1	450.00	2003
COMPUTER SCIENCE - GENERAL						
9780070472778		HAIGH	Object Oriented Analysis & Design	1	495.00	2001
CUSTOMER RELATIONSHIP MANAGEMENT (CRM)						
9780070590571		GREENBERG	CRM at the Speed of Light	3	550.00	2004
9780070402737		BERSON	Building Data Mining Applications for CRM	1	450.00	2000
DATA PROCESSING						
9780070659377		PARKER	Visualizing Information with Microsoft® Visio 2007	1	495.00	2007
DATA WAREHOUSING/KNOWLEDGE MANAGEMENT						
9780074637401		MATTISON	Web Warehousing and Knowledge Management	1	450.00	1999
9780070635449		MOHANTY	Data Warehousing: Design, Development and Best Practices	1	425.00	2005
DATABASE MANAGEMENT SYSTEMS (DBMS)						
9780070700567	MYSQL	VASWANI	MySQL Database Usage & Administration	1	475.00	2009
9780070586840	MYSQL	VASWANI	MYSQL: The Complete Reference	1	525.00	2004
9780070702349		OPPEL	Data Modeling, A Beginner's Guide	1	395.00	2010
9780070147171		OPPEL	Databases: A Beginner's Guide	1	495.00	2009
9780070677524		GOLFARELLI	Data Warehouse Design: Modern Principles and Methodologies	1	495.00	2009
9780070532830	ADO.NET	OTEY	ADO.NET: The Complete Reference	1	725.00	2003
9780070659537		BERSON	Master Data Management and Customer Data Integration for a Global Enterprise	1	525.00	2007
9780070222847		STERLING	Microsoft® Office SharePoint® Server 2007: The Complete Reference	1	650.00	2007
9780070618442		KAPLAN	Citrix Access Suite 4 Advance Concepts: The Official Guide	2	550.00	2006
DICTIONARIES/ENCYCLOPEDIAS						
9780070447424		SHELDON	Encyclopedia of Networking and Telecommunications (With CD)	1	895.00	2001
9780070597921		McGRAW-HILL	McGraw-Hill Dictionary of Computing & Communications	1	350.00	2004
DISTRIBUTED COMPUTING						
9780070683518		VELTE	Cloud Computing: A Practical Approach	1	450.00	2009
9780070600966	ORACLE 10g & GRID	JANAKIRAM	Grid Computing Models: A Research Monograph (Book + CD)	1	650.00	2005
EMBEDDED SYSTEMS						
9780070482845		IYER & GUPTA	Embedded Realtime Systems Programming	1	350.00	2003
ENTERPRISE RESOURCE PLANNING (SAP R/3, J D EDWARDS etc.)						
9780070264847	SAP	WILLIAMS	Implementing SAP ERP Sales and Distribution	1	475.00	2008
9780070144460	SAP	SHUKLA	SAP Materials Management with CD	1	495.00	2009
9780070142978	SAP	NARAYANAN	Implementing SAP ERP Financials: A Configuration Guide	1	895.00	2009
9780070139701	ENTERPRISE 2.0	NEWMAN	Enterprise 2.0 Implementation	1	495.00	2008
9780070140707	J D EDWARDS	JACOT	J.D. Edwards EnterpriseOne: The Complete Reference	1	595.00	2008
9780070420502	J D EDWARDS	HESTER	J.D. Edwards OneWorld: A Developer's Guide	1	695.00	2000
9780070142107	PEOPLESOFT	DOOLITTLE	PeopleSoft Developer's Guide for PeopleTools & PeopleCode, 1/ed.	1	595.00	2008
9780070656727	SAP	FAUJDAR	SAP Sales & Distribution Certification Guide	1	395.00	2008
9780070634800	SAP	HERNANDEZ	SAP R/3 HANDBOOK, 3/e	3	625.00	2005
9780070421301	SAP	GHOSH	SAP Project Management (With CD)	1	675.00	2000
9780070248571	SAP	DOWLING	SAP Project System Handbook	1	425.00	2008
9780070223998	SAP	JONES	SAP Business Information Warehouse Reporting	1	550.00	2008
9780070264953	SAP	JAY	SAP NetWeaver Portal Technology: The Complete Reference, 1/ed.	1	550.00	2008
9780070587502	SAP	KASTURI	SAP R/3 ALE & EDI Technologies (With CD)	1	450.00	2004
9780074631690	SAP	HOFFMAN	Writing SAP ABAP/4 Programs (Book Only)	1	375.00	1998
HARDWARE MAINTENANCE						
9780070482869		GOVINDARAJALU	IBM PC and Clones: Hardware, Troubleshooting and Maintenance (Book Only)	2	575.00	2002
9780070483118		GOVINDARAJALU	IBM PC and Clones: Hardware, Troubleshooting and Maintenance (Book + CD)	2	725.00	2002
9780070436060		ZACKER	PC Hardware: The Complete Reference (With CD)	1	550.00	2001

ISBN		Author	Title	Qty	Price	Year
9780070473676		BIGELOW	Troubleshooting, Maintaining & Repairing PCs (With CD)	5	825.00	2001
9780070595064		MEYERS	Mike Meyers' A+ Guide to Managing & Troubleshooting PCs	1	695.00	2004
9780070659643		MEYERS	Mike Meyers A+ Guide Essentials (Exam 220-601) with CD	1	750.00	2007
9780070447363		GILSTER	PC Hardware: A Beginner's Guide	1	475.00	2001
			HTML & WEB DESIGNING			
9780070499218		JAMSA	HTML & Web Design: Tips & Techniques	1	495.00	2002
9780070582521		POWELL	Web Design: The Complete Reference	2	550.00	2003
9780070701946		POWELL	HTML & CSS: The Complete Reference, Fifth Edition	5	495.00	2010
9780070677234		WILLARD	HTML: A Beginner's Guide	4	495.00	2009
			INFORMATION TECHNOLOGY			
9780070683495		CHANDY	Event Processing: Designing IT Systems for Agile Companies	1	375.00	2009
			INTERNET AND WEB DIRECTORIES			
9780074631621		HAHN	The Internet Complete Reference	1	495.00	1996
9780070486997		YOUNG	Internet: The Complete Reference	2	475.00	2002
9780070683570		HORN	Microsoft Silverlight 3: A Beginner's Guide	1	375.00	2009
9780074639818		YOUNG	Internet: The Complete Reference: Millenium Edition	1	495.00	1999
			IT PROJECT MANAGEMENT			
9780070598973		RAMESH	Managing Global Software Projects (Softcover)	1	395.00	2005
9780070588035		RAMESH	CBT on Managing Global Software Projects	1	1990.00	2004
9780070593886		PHILLIPS	IT Project Management: On Track from Start to Finish (With CD)	2	595.00	2004
9780070621480		RAO	Steering Project Success	1	475.00	2007
			JAVA PROGRAMMING			
9780070077652		KUMAR	Spring and Hibernate	1	450.00	2009
			MAINFRAME COMPUTING			
9780070601109	CICS	LE BERT	CICS Essentials for Application Developers and Programmers	1	425.00	2005
9780070486362	CICS	KAGEYAMA	CICS Handbook	1	450.00	2002
9780070658493	IBM DB2	ZIKOPOLOUS	IBM DB2 Version 9 New Features	1	525.00	2007
9780070495692	IBM DB2	MELNYK	DB2: The Complete Reference	1	650.00	2002
9780070659131	MVS JCL	ZAMIR	The MVS JCL Primer	1	475.00	2007
			MICROPROCESSORS AND MICROCOMPUTERS			
9780070606272		HINTZ	Microcontrollers	1	375.00	2005
			MICROSOFT .NET FRAMEWORK			
9730070142190	LINQ	MAYO	LINQ PROGRAMMING	1	495.00	2008
			MICROSOFT OFFICE & OTHER SOFTWARE PACKAGES			
9780070222854	ACCESS	ANDERSEN	Microsoft Office Access 2007: The Complete Reference	1	695.00	2007
9780070647671	EXCEL	HART-DAVIS	How to Do Everything with Microsoft Office Excel 2007	1	495.00	2007
9780070447073	EXCEL	IVENS	Excel 2002: The Complete Reference	1	625.00	2001
9780070264618	EXCHANGE SERVER	LUCKETT	Microsoft Exchange Server 2007: The Complete Reference	1	595.00	2008
9780070582996	OFFICE	KETTELL	Microsoft Office 2003: The Complete Reference	1	625.00	2003
9780070447233	OFFICE	NELSON	Office XP: The Complete Reference (With CD)	1	695.00	2001
9780074632673	OFFICE	MANSFIELD	Working in Microsoft Office	1	495.00	2001
9780070658486	PROJECT	MARMEL	How To Do Everything with Microsoft Office Project 2007	1	495.00	2007
9780070230286	PROJECT SERVER	STEWART	Microsoft Office Project Server 2007: The Complete Reference	1	595.00	2008
			MOBILE COMPUTING			
9780070588073		TALUKDER	Mobile Computing: Technology, Application & Service Creation	1	495.00	2005
9780070701922		DWIVEDI	Mobile Application Security	1	495.00	2010
9780070603646		ADELSTEIN	Fundamentals of Mobile & Pervasive Computing	1	395.00	2005
			MULTIMEDIA & ANIMATION			
9780070636811		VAUGHAN	Multimedia: Making it Work (With CD)	7	450.00	2006
9780070248779	CORELDRAW X4	BOUTON	CorelDRAW® X4: The Official Guide	1	650.00	2008
			NANO COMPUTING			
9780070248922		SAHNI	Nano Computing	1	595.00	2008
			NETWORKING & DATA COMMUNICATIONS			
9780070474161		ZACKER	Networking: The Complete Reference	1	695.00	2001
9780070223615		KASIM	Delivering Carrier Ethernet	1	550.00	2007
9780070248502		SCHNEYDERMAN	Fixed Mobile Convergence	1	425.00	2008
9780070700413		HALLBERG	Networking: A Beginner's Guide, Fifth Edition	5	495.00	2009
9780070636927		SMITH	3G Wireless Networks	2	550.00	2006

9780070412675		ZACKER	Upgrading & Troubleshooting Networks: The Complete Reference	1	675.00	2000
9780070530416		SPOHN	Data Network Design	3	550.00	2003
9780070439498		MULLER	Bluetooth Demystified	1	425.00	2001
9780070647664		BATES	Voice & Data Communication Handbook	5	625.00	2007
9780070534544		McMAHON	Introduction to Networking	1	395.00	2003
9780070532922		SPALDING	Storage Networks: The Complete Reference	1	575.00	2003
9780070265035		RUSSELL	Session Initiation Protocol (SIP): Controlling Convergent Networks	1	425.00	2008
9780070223684		RUSSELL	The IP Multimedia Subsystem	1	425.00	2007
9780070472396		GORALSKI	Optical Networking & WDM	1	495.00	2001
OPERATING SYSTEMS MANUALS						
9780070656758	LINUX	HARNAL	Linux Applications and Administration	1	595.00	2009
9780070222946	LINUX	PETERSEN	LINUX: The Complete Reference (With CD)	6	550.00	2007
9780070142503	UBUNTU	JANG	Ubuntu Server Administration	1	550.00	2009
9780070658363	UNIX	ROSEN	UNIX: The Complete Reference	2	625.00	2007
9780070142602	LINUX	SOYINKA/SHAH	Linux Administration: A Beginner's Guide, Fifth Edition	5	550.00	2009
9780070659766	RED HAT LINUX	PETERSEN	Red Hat Fedora Core 7 & Red Hat Enterprise Linux: The Complete Reference	4	695.00	2007
9780070599666	SOLARIS	WATTERS	Solaris 10: The Complete Reference	1	625.00	2005
9780070139770	UBUNTU	ORLOFF	How to Do Everything: Ubuntu	1	495.00	2008
9780070252844	UBUNTU	PETERSEN	Ubuntu: The Complete Reference	1	550.00	2008
9780070658509	WINDOWS	SIMMONS	How To Do Everything with Windows Vista	1	495.00	2007
9780070248588	WINDOWS	RUEST	Microsoft Windows Server 2008: The Complete Reference	1	595.00	2008
9780070540811	WINDOWS	IVENS	Windows Server 2003: The Complete Reference	1	725.00	2003
9780070659001	WINDOWS	LEVINE-YOUNG	Windows Vista: The Complete Reference	1	575.00	2007
9780070540682	WINDOWS	MATTHEWS	Windows Server 2003: A Beginner's Guide	1	475.00	2003
ORACLE PRESS						
9780070601130	ORACLE 10g & GRID COMPUTING	LONEY	Oracle Database 10g DBA Handbook	1	525.00	2005
9780070683501	ORACLE 11i/ORACLE E-BUSINESS SUITE	PASSI	Oracle E-Business Suite Development & Extensibility Handbook	1	595.00	2009
9780070142749	ORACLE DATABASE 10g	MACMILLAN	Transforming Infoglut! A Pragmatic Strategy for Oracle Enterprise Content Management	1	395.00	2009
9780070142695	ORACLE DATABASE 10g	NEW	Oracle Enterprise Manager 10g Grid Control Implementation Guide	1	595.00	2009
9780070142725	ORACLE DATABASE 11g	BRYLA	OCP Oracle Database 11g: Administration II Exam Guide (Exam 1Z0-053)	1	650.00	2009
9780070683556	ORACLE DATABASE 11g	KNOX	Applied Oracle Security: Developing Secure Database and Middleware Environments	1	675.00	2009
9780070683563	ORACLE DATABASE 11g	MILLS	Oracle JDeveloper 11g Handbook	1	750.00	2009
9780070701182	ORACLE DATABASE 11g	DESBIENS	Oracle WebCenter 11g Handbook	1	625.00	2010
9780070682689	ORACLE DATABASE 11g	WATSON	OCA/OCP Oracle Database 11g All-in-One Exam Guide with CD-ROM (Exams 1Z0-051, 1Z0-052, 1Z0-053)	1	750.00	2009
9780070140790	ORACLE DATABASE 11g	LONEY	Oracle Database 11g: The Complete Reference	1	725.00	2008
9780070677463	ORACLE DATABASE 11g	CARPENTER	Oracle Database 11g Data Guard Handbook	1	595.00	2009
9780070702264	ORACLE DATABASE 11g	MCLAUGHLIN	Oracle 11g PL/SQL Programming Workbook, 1/ed.	1	525.00	2010
9780070683587	ORACLE DATABASE 11g	SCHRADER	Oracle Essbase & Oracle OLAP	1	575.00	2009
9780070701410	ORACLE DATABASE 11g	O'HEARN	OCA Oracle Database SQL Certified Expert Exam Guide (Exam 1Z0-047)	1	695.00	2010
9780070701939	ORACLE DATABASE 11g	NIMPHIUS	Oracle Fusion Developer Guide: Building Rich Internet Applications with Oracle ADF Business Components & ADF Faces	1	650.00	2010
9780074637784	ORACLE (8i & PRIOR VERSIONS)	KOLETZKE	Oracle Developer Advanced Forms & Reports	1	625.00	2000
9780070597907	ORACLE 10g & GRID COMPUTING	ROY-FADERMAN	Oracle JDeveloper 10g Handbook	1	650.00	2004
9780070618961	ORACLE 10g & GRID COMPUTING	GOYAL	Grid Revolution: An Introduction to Enterprise Grid Computing	1	165.00	2006
9780070636040	ORACLE 10g & GRID COMPUTING	GOYAL	Enterprise Grid Computing with Oracle	1	425.00	2006
9780070659773	ORACLE 10g & GRID COMPUTING	OSTROWSKI	Oracle Application Server Portal Handbook	1	550.00	2007
9780070598942	ORACLE 10g & GRID COMPUTING	OSTROWSKI	Oracle Application Server 10g Web Development	1	575.00	2005
9780070593879	ORACLE 10g & GRID COMPUTING	ALLEN	Oracle Database 10g PL/SQL 101	1	425.00	2004
9780070636569	ORACLE 10g & GRID COMPUTING	HOTKA	Oracle SQL Developer Handbook	1	395.00	2006
9780070589728	ORACLE 10g & GRID COMPUTING	KNOX	Effective Oracle Database 10g Security by Design	1	475.00	2004

ISBN	Category	Author	Title	Qty	Price	Year
9780070607927	ORACLE 10g & GRID COMPUTING	WHALEN	Oracle Database 10g Linux Administration Handbook	1	525.00	2005
9780070587557	ORACLE 10g & GRID COMPUTING	PRICE	Oracle Database 10g SQL	1	525.00	2004
9780070636057	ORACLE 10g & GRID COMPUTING	ABEL	Oracle E-Business Suite Security	1	450.00	2006
9780070587762	ORACLE 10g & GRID COMPUTING	GARMANY	Oracle Application Server 10g Administration Handbook	1	460.00	2004
9780070637191	ORACLE 10g & GRID COMPUTING	GOPALAKRISHNAN	Oracle Database 10g Real Application Clusters Handbook	1	495.00	2007
9780070594258	ORACLE 10g & GRID COMPUTING	LONEY	Oracle Database 10g: The Complete Reference (With CD)	1	650.00	2004
9780070587939	ORACLE 10g & GRID COMPUTING	ABRAMSON	Oracle Database 10g: A Beginner's Guide	1	425.00	2004
9780070618381	ORACLE 10g & GRID COMPUTING	LINNEMEYER	Oracle HTML DB Handbook	1	475.00	2006
9780070636910	ORACLE 10g & GRID COMPUTING	HART	Oracle Database 10g RMAN Backup & Recovery	1	550.00	2006
9780070588622	ORACLE 10g & GRID COMPUTING	HART	Oracle Database 10g High Availability with RAC, Flashback & Data Guard	1	495.00	2004
9780070618404	ORACLE 10g & GRID COMPUTING	ARMSTRONG-SMITH	Oracle Discoverer 10g Handbook	1	675.00	2006
9780070636644	ORACLE 10g & GRID COMPUTING	McLAUGHLIN	Oracle Database 10g Express Edition PHP Web Programming	1	650.00	2006
9780070222885	ORACLE 10g & GRID COMPUTING	VENGURLEKAR	Oracle Automatic Storage Management, 1/ed.	1	450.00	2007
9780070659667	ORACLE 10g & GRID COMPUTING	NIEMIEC	Oracle Database 10g Performance Tuning Tips & Techniques	1	650.00	2007
9780070590281	ORACLE 10g & GRID COMPUTING	SHEE	Oracle Wait Interface: A Practical Guide to Performance Diagnostics and Tuning	1	525.00	2004
9780070607699	ORACLE 10g & GRID COMPUTING	HARDMAN	Expert Oracle PL/SQL	1	525.00	2005
9780070658516	ORACLE 10g & GRID COMPUTING	ZAPAR	Oracle Collaboration Suite Handbook	1	550.00	2007
9780070597792	ORACLE 10g & GRID COMPUTING	URMAN	Oracle Database 10G PL/SQL Programming	1	495.00	2004
9780070495319	ORACLE 11i/ORACLE E-BUSINESS SUITE	GERALD	Oracle: E-Business Suite Manufacturing & Supply Chain Management	1	550.00	2002
9780070586604	ORACLE 11i/ORACLE E-BUSINESS SUITE	JAMES	Oracle E-Business Suite Financials Handbook	1	650.00	2003
9780070621121	ORACLE 11i/ORACLE E-BUSINESS SUITE	BANERJEE	Oracle Applications DBA	1	525.00	2007
9780070586598	ORACLE 11i/ORACLE E-BUSINESS SUITE	IYER	Oracle E-Business Suite Financials Administration	1	495.00	2003
9780070411692	ORACLE 9i	ALLEN/THOMAS	Oracle Certified Professional Financial Applications Consultant Exam Guide	1	825.00	2000
9780070593930	ORACLE 9i	BURLESON	Oracle 9i High-Performance Tuning with Statspack	1	575.00	2004
9780070495722	ORACLE 9i	BURLESON	Oracle 9i: UNIX Administration Handbook	1	495.00	2002
9780070486829	ORACLE 9i	COUCHMAN	OCP Oracle 9i Database: Fundamental I Exam Guide	1	475.00	2002
9780070499027	ORACLE 9i	LONEY	Oracle 9i: The Complete Reference (With CD)	1	595.00	2002
9780070486744	ORACLE 9i	LONEY	Oracle 9i: DBA Handbook	1	575.00	2002
9780070486935	ORACLE 9i	ABBEY	Oracle 9i: A Beginner's Guide	1	525.00	2002
9780070540651	ORACLE 9i	NIEMIEC	Oracle 9i Performance Tuning: Tips & Techniques	1	575.00	2003
9780070530874	ORACLE 9i	FREEMAN	Oracle 9i: RMAN Backup & Recovery	1	495.00	2002
9780070486805	ORACLE 9i	URMAN	Oracle 9i PL/SQL Programming (With CD)	1	475.00	2002
9780070582804	ORACLE 9i	KYTE	Effective Oracle by Design	1	550.00	2003
9780070495357	ORACLE CERTIFICATION	PACK	Oracle: OCP Oracle 9i Database: Performance Tuning Exam Guide	1	475.00	2002
9780070474178	ORACLE CERTIFICATION	ALLEN	Oracle: OCP Building Internet Applications I & II Exam Guide (With CD)	1	525.00	2001
9780070474208	ORACLE CERTIFICATION	COUCHMAN	Oracle OCP Introduction to Oracle 9i: SQL Exam Guide 1ZO-007	1	475.00	2002
9780070498938	ORACLE CERTIFICATION	COUCHMAN	Oracle: OCA Oracle 9i Associate DBA Certification Exam Guide (With CD)	1	625.00	2002

ISBN	Category	Author	Title	Qty	Price	Year
9780070607682	ORACLE CERTIFICATION	WATSON	Oracle Database 10g OCP Certification All-In-One Exam Guide (With CD)	1	650.00	2005
9780070495067	ORACLE CERTIFICATION	VELPURI	Oracle OCP Oracle 9i Database: Fundamentals II Exam Guide (With CD)	1	525.00	2002
9780070486980	ORACLE CERTIFICATION	O'HEARN	Oracle OCP Developer PL/SQL Program Units Exam Guide (With CD)	1	495.00	2002
9780070139688	ORACLE CRM	LAIRSON	Oracle Siebel CRM On Demand Reporting	1	495.00	2008
9780070598676	ORACLE DATABASE 10g	ALAPATI	OCP Oracle Database 10g: New Features for Administrators Exam Guide (With CD)	1	595.00	2004
9780070618398	ORACLE DATABASE 10g	ALAPATI	OCA Oracle Application Server 10g Administrator Study Guide (Exam 1Z0-311)	1	525.00	2006
9780070223646	ORACLE DATABASE 11g	BRYLA/LONEY	Oracle Database 11g DBA Handbook	1	550.00	2007
9780070142398	ORACLE DATABASE 11g	ABRAMSON	Oracle Database 11g: A Beginner's Guide	1	495.00	2009
9780070222915	ORACLE DATABASE 11g	PRICE	Oracle Database 11g SQL	1	525.00	2007
9780070264793	ORACLE DATABASE 11g	WATSON	OCA Oracle Database 11g: Administration I Exam Guide (Exam 1Z0-052)	1	695.00	2008
9780070264991	ORACLE DATABASE 11g	WATSON	OCA Oracle Database 11g: SQL Fundamentals Exam Guide (Exam 1Z0-051)	1	575.00	2008
9780070248595	ORACLE DATABASE 11g	BARNEY	Oracle Database AJAX & PHP Web Application Development	1	525.00	2008
9780070671010	ORACLE DATABASE 11g	CAMERON	Oracle General Ledger Guide	1	495.00	2009
9780070671027	ORACLE DATABASE 11g	CAMERON	Oracle Procure-to-Pay	1	495.00	2009
9780070248694	ORACLE DATABASE 11g	MCLAUGHLIN	Oracle Database 11g PL/SQL Programming	1	595.00	2008
9780070222892	ORACLE DATABASE 11g	FREEMAN	Oracle Database 11g New Features	1	450.00	2007
9780070264809	ORACLE DATABASE 11g	ALAPATI	OCP Oracle Database 11g: New Features for Administrators Exam Guide (Exam 1Z0-050)	1	650.00	2008
ORACLE SIEBEL CRM						
9780070144583		KALE	A Guide to Implementing Oracle Siebel CRM 8.X	1	695.00	2009
PROGRAMMING						
9780070682665		MANSFIELD	Programming: A Beginner's Guide	1	495.00	2009
PROGRAMMING LANGUAGES						
9780070140806	C, C++ & C#	SCHILDT	C# 3.0: The Complete Reference, 1/ed.	1	595.00	2008
9780070532465	C, C++ & C#	SCHILDT	C++: The Complete Reference	4	495.00	2003
9780070411838	C, C++ & C#	SCHILDT	C: The Complete Reference	4	465.00	2000
9780070264786	C, C++ & C#	SCHILDT	Schildt's C++ Programming Cookbook	1	475.00	2008
9780070611399	C, C++ & C#	SCHILDT	C# 2.0: The Complete Reference	1	575.00	2005
9780070248946	C, C++ & C#	SCHILDT	C# 3.0: A Beginner's Guide, 1/ed.	1	525.00	2008
9780074638705	C, C++ & C#	SCHILDT	Teach Yourself C++	1	450.00	1998
9780074639924	MFC	SCHILDT	MFC Programming from the Ground Up	2	495.00	2000
9780070474475	PERL	BAL	Perl Programming for Bioinformatics	1	625.00	2002
9780070444805	PERL	BROWN	PERL: The Complete Reference	2	750.00	2001
9780070598416		TURLEY	Advanced 80386 Programming Techniques	1	375.00	2005
PROTOCOLS						
9780070264960		FEIT	TCP/IP: Architecture, Protocols, and Implementation with IPv6 and IP Security	2	495.00	2008
QUANTUM COMPUTING						
9780070657007		SAHNI	Quantum Computing	1	595.00	2007
SECURITY						
9780070702356		WHITE	Principles of Computer Security, CompTIA Security+ and Beyond with CD-ROM, Second Edition	2	625.00	2010
9780070586710		BRAGG	Network Security: The Complete Reference	1	595.00	2004
9780070147188		McCLURE	Hacking Exposed 6	6	625.00	2009
9780070616066		ENDORF	Intrusion Detection and Prevention	1	550.00	2006
9780070647688		DAVIS	IT Auditing: Using Controls to Protect Information Assets	1	525.00	2007
9780070223691		SCAMBRAY	Hacking Exposed Windows	3	525.00	2007
9780070647657		ENDLER	Hacking Exposed VoIP: Voice Over IP Security Secrets & Solutions	1	550.00	2007
9780070635326		VLADIMOROV	Hacking Exposed Cisco Networks	1	625.00	2005

9780070187726		ISECOM	Hacking Exposed™ Linux, Third Edition:Linux Security Secrets & Solutions	1	525.00	2008
9780070619807		SCAMBRAY	Hacking Exposed Web Applications	2	495.00	2006
9780070599178		MALLERY	Hardening Network Security	1	550.00	2005
9780070659063		CACHE	Hacking Exposed™ Wireless : Wireless Security Secrets & Solutions	1	495.00	2007
9780070583115		STRASSBERG	Firewalls: The Complete Reference	1	699.00	2003
9780070618466		MANDIA	Incident Response & Computer Forensics	2	525.00	2006
9780070618848		NICHOLS	Wireless Security: Models, Threats and Solutions	1	550.00	2006
9780070248489		CANNINGS	Hacking Exposed Web 2.0: Web 2.0 Security Secrets and Solutions	1	395.00	2008
9780070603592		SLADE	Software Forensics	1	350.00	2005
9780070248649		HARRIS	Gray Hat Hacking: The Ethical Hacker's Handbook	2	550.00	2008
9780070607903		McCLURE & SCAMBRAY	Hacking Exposed: Network Security Secrets and Solutions (With DVD)	5	550.00	2005
			SERVICE-ORIENTED ARCHITECTURE			
9780070677265		ROSHEN	SOA-based Enterprise Integration: A Step-by-Step Guide to Services-based Application	1	525.00	2009
			SOFTWARE ENGINEERING			
9780070147256		BERENBACH	Software Systems Requirements Engineering: In Practice	1	450.00	2009
9780070683594		JONES	Software Engineering Best Practices	1	595.00	2009
9780070403123		KISHORE & NAIK	Software Requirements and Estimation	1	450.00	2001
9780070148819		SANKAR	QuickTest Professional	1	475.00	2009
9780070264649		JONES	Applied Software Measurement, 3/ed.	3	525.00	2008
9780070659490		JONES	Estimating Software Costs	2	525.00	2007
9780070483453		RAMESH	Software Maintenance	1	595.00	2005
9780070603196		MUSA	Software Reliability Engineering: More Reliable Software Faster and Cheaper	2	450.00	2005
9780070248731		MALIK & CHOUDHARY	Software Quality	1	525.00	2008
9780070633780		NANDYAL	Making Sense of Software Quality Assurance	1	725.00	2007
9780070583528		RAJNI & OAK	Software Testing: Methodologies, Tools and Processes	1	450.00	2004
9780070601147		KISHORE & NAIK	ISO 9001: 2000 for Software Organizations (Softcover)	1	395.00	2005
			SQL			
9780070528505		GROFF	SQL: The Complete Reference (With CD)	2	595.00	2003
9780074637081		LEON	SQL: A Complete Reference (With Diskette)	1	475.00	1999
9780070251724		OPPEL / SHELDON	SQL: A Beginner's Guide, 3/ed.	3	525.00	2008
9780070611115		OPPEL	SQL Demystified	1	350.00	2005
9780074621844		KISHORE & NAIK	SQL for Professionals	1	295.00	2002
			SQL SERVERS			
9780070142596	MS SQL SERVER 2008	LARSON	Delivering Business Intelligence with Microsoft SQL Server™ 2008	1	595.00	2009
9780070701847	MS SQL SERVER 2008	OTEY	Microsoft® SQL Server™ 2008 High Availability with Clustering & Database Mirroring	1	450.00	2010
9780070635258	MS SQL SERVER 2005	PETKOVIC	Microsoft SQL Server 2005: A Beginners Guide	1	625.00	2005
9780070636781	MS SQL SERVER 2005	SHAPIRO	Microsoft SQL Server 2005: The Complete Reference	1	550.00	2006
9780070635241	MS SQL SERVER 2005	OTEY	Microsoft SQL Server 2005 Developer's Guide	1	550.00	2005
9730070252196	MS SQL SERVER 2008	LARSON	Microsoft® SQL Server™ 2008 Reporting Services	3	595.00	2008
9780070187696	MS SQL SERVER 2008	PETKOVIC	Microsoft® SQL Server™ 2008: A Beginner's Guide	1	575.00	2008
9780070142404	MS SQL SERVER 2008	OTEY	Microsoft® SQL Server ™ 2008 New Features	1	425.00	2009
			TELECOMMUNICATIONS			
9780070445239		LONG	IP Network Design	1	350.00	2001
9780070603233		COLLINS	Carrier Grade Voice Over IP	2	525.00	2005
9780070636934		DAWSON	IP Location	1	525.00	2006
9780070248687		DAVIS-PHILLIPS	Flex 3: A Beginner's Guide	1	425.00	2008
9780070607156		SHEPARD	Voice Over IP Crash Course	1	350.00	2005
			UML			
9780070531406		ROFF	UML: A Beginner's Guide	1	350.00	2003
			VIRTUALIZATION			
9780070682672		KAPPEL	Microsoft Virtualization with Hyper-V	1	550.00	2009

9780070147195		RUEST	Virtualization: A Beginner's Guide	1	550.00	2009
			VISUAL BASIC MANUALS			
9780074635216	VISUAL BASIC	BRADLEY	Programming in Visual Basic 6.0 (With CD)	1	525.00	2000
9780074636664	VISUAL BASIC	JERKE	Visual Basic 6: The Complete Reference (With CD)	1	495.00	1999
9780074635575	VISUAL BASIC	CORNELL	Visual Basic 6: From the Ground Up	1	465.00	1999
9780070635005	VISUAL BASIC	KENT	Visual Basic 2005 Demystified	1	350.00	2005
9780070529090	VISUAL BASIC	BRADLEY	Programming in Visual Basic.Net (With CD)	4	550.00	2002
			VISUAL PROGRAMMING			
9780070495111	VISUAL BASIC	SHAPIRO	Visual Basic.Net: The Complete Reference	1	550.00	2002
9780074638101	VISUAL C++	PAPPAS	Visual C++6: The Complete Reference	1	575.00	1999
9780070147249	VISUAL STUDIO 2008	PLENDERLEITH	Microsoft Visual Studio 2008 Programming	1	495.00	2009
9780070619869	VISUAL BASIC	PETRUSHA	Visual Basic 2005: The Complete Reference	1	550.00	2006
9780070635036	VISUAL C#	KENT	Visual C# 2005 Demystified	1	375.00	2005
9780074637296	VISUAL C++	MUELLER	Visual C++ 6 From the Ground Up	2	450.00	1999
9780070495326	VISUAL C++.NET	PAPPAS	Visual C++.Net: The Complete Reference	1	650.00	2002
			WEB DEVELOPMENT			
9780070700475	ASP/ASP.NET	KANJILAL	ASP.NET 4.0 Programming	1	450.00	2009
9780070495364	ASP/ASP.NET	MACDONALD	ASP.NET: The Complete Reference	1	595.00	2002
9780070529120	J2EE	KEOGH	J2EE: The Complete Reference	1	575.00	2002
9780070534155	J2ME	KEOGH	J2ME: The Complete Reference	1	525.00	2003
9780070636774	JAVA	SCHILDT	Java: The Complete Reference	7	485.00	2006
9780070590274	JAVASCRIPT	POWELL	Java Script: The Complete Reference	2	625.00	2004
9780070531413	JSP	HANNA	JSP 2.0: The Complete Reference	1	550.00	2003
9780070144521	PHP	HARWANI	Developing Web Applications in PHP and AJAX	1	425.00	2010
9780070223622	PHP	HOLZNER	PHP: The Complete Reference	1	525.00	2007
9780070658455	STRUTS	HOLMES	Struts: The Complete Reference	2	575.00	2007
9780070593787		KUMAR & SUBRAMANYA	An Introduction to Web Services (Softcover)	1	625.00	2004
9780070656734	AJAX	RAO	AJAX	1	425.00	2008
9780070139695	AJAX	HOLZNER	Ajax: A Beginner's Guide	1	450.00	2008
9780070248496	AJAX	POWELL	Ajax: The Complete Reference	1	450.00	2008
9780070495340	ASP/ASP.NET	MERCER	ASP.NET: A Beginner's Guide	1	450.00	2002
9780070436237	ASP/ASP.NET	MERCER	ASP 3.0: A Beginner's Guide	1	395.00	2001
9780070499171	ASP/ASP.NET	BUCZEK	ASP.NET: Developer's Guide	1	575.00	2002
9780070140684	ASP/ASP.NET	SANDERS	ASP-NET 3.5: A Beginner's Guide, 1/ed.	1	450.00	2008
9780070621633	J2EE	KUMAR	J2EE Architecture (with a companion CD)	1	525.00	2006
9780074639757	JAVA	VENNERS	Inside the JAVA 2 Virtual Machine	1	675.00	2000
9780070222878	JAVA	SCHILDT	Schildt's Java Programming Cookbook	1	475.00	2007
9780070659681	JAVA	SCHILDT	Java: A Beginner's Guide	4	525.00	2007
9780070598782	JAVA	SCHILDT	JAVA: The Complete Reference, J2SE 5 Edition (For Sale in AP and KA only)	6	485.00	2004
9780070495432	JAVA	SCHILDT	JAVA 2: The Complete Reference	5	485.00	2002
9780070683488	JAVA	POLLOCK	JavaScript: A Beginner's Guide, Third Edition	3	495.00	2009
9780074632901	JAVA	NAUGHTON	JAVA Handbook	1	395.00	1996
9780074637890	JAVA	O'NEIL	Teach Yourself Java	1	450.00	1999
9780070636422	JAVASERVER FACES	SCHALK	JavaServer Faces: The Complete Reference	1	575.00	2006
9780070140691	PHP	VASWANI	PHP 6: A Beginner's Guide, 1/ed.	1	450.00	2008
9780070659780	PHP	VASWANI	PHP Programming Solutions	1	475.00	2007
9780070636484	SWING	SCHILDT	Swing: A Beginner's Guide	1	525.00	2006
			XML			
9780070447257		WILLIAMSON	XML: The Complete Reference	1	625.00	2001
9780070146990		HOLZNER	XML: A Beginner's Guide	1	450.00	2009